£5.99

VOLTAIRE

1 Voltaire at the age of 41, *from the pastel by Maurice Quentin de La Tour in the Nationalmuseum, Stockholm*

VOLTAIRE

Theodore Besterman

a theme
For reason, much too strong for fantasie.
Donne, *The Dreame*

BASIL BLACKWELL
OXFORD

© *Theodore Besterman 1969, 1976*

First published 1969
Second edition (revised reprint) 1970
Third edition (revised and enlarged throughout) 1976

ISBN 0 631 17060 X

Printed in England by
Cheney & Sons Ltd Banbury Oxfordshire

to
Marie-Louise

Contents

Contents

Illustrations

(All the originals are at the Délices, unless another source is indicated)

9

Illustrations

Map

Pile assumptions on assumptions; accumulate wars on wars; make interminable disturbances succeed to interminable disturbances; let the universe be inundated by a general spirit of confusion; and it will take a hundred thousand years for the works and the name of Voltaire to be lost.

DIDEROT
(letter to E. M. Falconet, c. 15 February 1766)

The handsomest monument of Voltaire is that which he has himself erected, his works, which will last longer than the basilica of Saint Peter, the Louvre, and all those buildings which human vanity consecrates to eternity. When French is no longer spoken, Voltaire will be translated into the language that will have succeeded it.

FREDERICK II
(letter to Alembert, 28 July 1770; Best.D16552)

Profundity, genius, intuition, greatness, spontaneity, talent, merit, nobility, imagination, wit, understanding, feeling, sensibility, taste, good taste, rightness, propriety, tone, good tone, courtliness, variety, abundance, wealth, fecundity, warmth, magic, charm, grace, urbanity, facility, vivacity, fineness, brilliance, boldness, sparkle, mordancy, delicacy, ingenuity, style, versification, harmony, purity, correctness, elegance, perfection.

GOETHE
(on Voltaire, in his notes on the *Neveu de Rameau*)

I devoured them all, volume after volume. Morning, and night, and noon, a volume was ever my companion. I ran to it after my meals, it reposed under my pillow. As I read I roared, I laughed, I shouted with wonder and admiration; I trembled with indignation at the fortunes of my race; my bitter smile sympathised with the searching ridicule and withering mockery.

Pedants, and priests, and tyrants; the folios of dunces, the fires of inquisitors, and the dungeons of kings; and the long, dull system of imposture and misrule that had sat like a gloating incubus on the fair neck of Nature; and all our ignorance, and all our weakness, and all our folly, and all our infinite imperfection. . . .

BENJAMIN DISRAELI
(on Voltaire's works, *Contarini Fleming*, II.ii)

Go to the end of your Rue de Beaune and look for the house at the corner, on the Quai where Voltaire died, at the age of eighty-four, having conquered both the Rulers of this world, and of the next. . . . Consider that life and take courage.

LYTTON STRACHEY
(Michael Holroyd, *Lytton Strachey* [1968], ii.235)

Preface

VOLTAIRE WAS BORN IN 1694 (a generation before the death of Louis XIV) and died in 1778 (two years after the Declaration of Independence); he acquired some reputation when still in his teens, and soon became the most celebrated man in Europe; he touched human activity at almost every point; for over sixty years he knew everybody who was anybody; his friends and acquaintances, who ranged from peasants to popes, have never been counted, but over 1800 of them were also his correspondents; he lived for long periods in the Netherlands, England, Prussia, and what is now Switzerland; he wrote, without a dull page, many hundreds of separate pieces on a great range of subjects and in almost every kind of form, from epigrams to diplomatic reports, and from comedies to a vast universal history, as well as twenty thousand[1] surviving letters—and what letters! He was indeed the most varied and voluminous of the world's great writers; his works have gone into thousands of editions in many languages; unnumbered books and articles were written about him during his lifetime, and even more have been published since.

In short, the mere extent and complexity of Voltaire's life and work are terrifying, and it is not surprising that no full-dress biography has yet been attempted. This is just as well, for by far the most important source, his correspondence, has hitherto been known only in fragmentary and highly defective editions. The earliest biographies are works of advocacy (like that of Condorcet) or of hatred (like that of Harel), or they are unreliable simply because of the ignorance or incapacity of the authors (like Luchet and Duvernet), or they are the products of generally well-meaning

---

1 This is not so great a number, relatively, as is commonly imagined; in only thirty-six years Lewis Carroll wrote and received 98,721 letters, according to Stuart Dodgson Collingwood, *The Life and letters of Lewis Carroll* (London 1899), pp. 265-6.

13

men with unreliable memories (like the secretaries Longchamps, Collini, and even Wagnière).

In this wholesale condemnation of Voltaire's biographers there is one major exception: for I must address a respectful salute to the memory of Gustave Desnoiresterres (1817-92), a novelist and biographer of great talent, to whom the oblivion of time has been too harsh. His eight long volumes on *Voltaire et la société française au XVIIIe siècle* deal with him, it is true, chiefly as a man of the world. Moreover, a century old and based exclusively on French sources, they are now hopelessly narrow and out of date. Again, Desnoiresterres wrote at a time when prudery and intellectual timidity were in the ascendant, and when anecdotes were *de rigueur*. Thus on the one hand he suppressed much that was valuable, and on the other printed many pages of gossip, much of which he himself described as nonsense. Yet all in all his vast book still commands admiration as the surest guide through the Voltairean labyrinth.

Generally speaking, whenever possible I have preferred reliable firsthand accounts, and Voltaire's own works and letters, always checked against the known facts. His autobiographical fragments present a difficult problem. Voltaire was often imprecise in writing about himself, sometimes for reasons of prudence or propaganda, sometimes because of failing memory, but most often from sheer lack of interest in personal details ('nothing is more insipid than the details of infancy and the time spent at school'[2], said he even in old age). Yet whatever he wrote has great value for us, whether as a statement of fact or of his attitude to a fact. An almost unknown autobiographical sketch has therefore been printed at the end of this volume, and has been used as a touchstone throughout.

In general, it has been necessary to examine every detail on its merits. That is, indeed, the main purpose of this book: to present the essential facts and meaning of Voltaire's life and work, stripped of gossip and invention. The stripping has been done silently. It

---

2 See the autobiography, p. 623, below; the reader is invited to note once and for all that all quotations from the autobiography are from the old translation, corrected only when it contains definite misunderstandings of the original.

would have been singularly absurd, though no doubt amusing, to repeat apocryphal anecdotes in order to refute them. Many hundreds of factual mistakes have also been corrected, still silently, or very nearly so. Far too many writers pepper their pages with 'X says so and so, but he is wrong': this kind of showing-off is insufferable. There is no great art in being more accurate than one's predecessors when more facts are available.

Even reduced to plain facts and a minimum of indispensable interpretation a complete biography of Voltaire would be much longer even than that by Desnoiresterres. In a book of modest size and intended for the general reader, much is indispensable, but much more has to be left out, since a mere one-line enumeration of the exactly datable events of Voltaire's life runs to hundreds of pages.

In order to achieve accuracy in the presentation of facts and in the re-creation of the intellectual and physical environment, I have nearly always gone to the original manuscripts. In general, I cannot do better than repeat Voltaire's own words at the beginning of his autobiography: 'I . . . make it my care to advance nothing, except on the authority of original papers. No use will be made of the almost innumerable satires and panegyrics which have been published, unless they are found to be supported by facts properly authenticated.' Photocopies are available to scholars at Les Délices of nearly all the thousands of letters and documents quoted or cited in these pages. Most of the printed sources are available in the Voltaire room of the Taylor institution, Oxford.

Voltaire is one of the greatest of French writers, arguably the very greatest, and his dimensions are also worldwide. Many readers in many countries are interested in him for many reasons, and unfortunately fewer and fewer of them know literary French. Rather reluctantly I have therefore dealt with quotations thus: nearly all the prose extracts are given only in translation, but all the verse passages in the original French, with prose translations below them on the same page. In these renderings from verse the structure and meaning of the original have been followed as closely and as literally as possible. As for the prose, the reader must remember that Voltaire's style is unique in its grace and lucidity: no translation can hope to match it, especially when it aspires to precise accuracy.

Preface

References to Voltaire's works are made to the volumes and pages of the complete critical edition so far as it has been published (thus Voltaire 55, p. 797). Voltaire's correspondence is quoted from my 'definitive' edition; it is cited e. g. Best.D1234. In order to keep footnotes to a minimum, a reference to a Best.D letter often implies also a reference to the notes on that letter. There can be no question of citing all the books and articles consulted (a list of these fills half a volume in my edition of the *Correspondence*), but further guides to the essential printed sources are mentioned in the bibliographical note. The abbreviation Th. B. refers to the collections I have given to Les Délices, and Th.D.N.B. to those presented to the Taylor institution. See also the bibliographical note at the end of this volume.

A few sections of this book have been adapted as lectures and articles. I owe cordial thanks to many organisations for their hospitality, in particular the International congress on the Enlightenment and Les Délices; Columbia, Cornell, Exeter, Geneva, Harvard, London, Princeton, Rutgers, Toronto, Yale universities; the Collège de France, the Folger library, the Pierpont Morgan library, the Académie des sciences morales et politiques, the Academies of Dijon, Lyons, and Marseilles (of these four I have the honour to be a Corresponding Member), the British humanist association, the Institut français du Royaume Uni, the Maison française of Columbia university, the Taylor institution (Zaharoff lecture). I am also grateful to the Oxford university press for permission to use part of my introduction to *Candide and other stories* in the World's classics. I must also thank all those archives, libraries, museums and private collections which have allowed me to use manuscripts, books, pictures, etc. in their possession; but as they number over 400 I hope they will forgive this comprehensive, anonymous but deeply grateful acknowledgement. And not the least cordial of my thanks must go to Barbara Bray, who most generously read the proofs of the first edition; to my admirable secretary for many years Juliane Dubuis; and to Andrew Brown, who read the proofs and compiled the index.

Voltaire was involved in many controversies, some of them no less acute today than they were two hundred years ago. He has always had fervent disciples, and even more fervent detractors. I have been his lifelong admirer this side idolatry, I have spent many years in close and critical study of his life and works, for over a decade I lived in his house, worked in his library, slept in his bedroom. It would be absurd for me to pretend to cold impartiality. Yet I have tried to stick most scrupulously to the facts.

Th. B.

London 1969
Voltaire Room, Oxford 1976

2 Voltaire at the age of 24, *from the painting by Nicolas Largillière*

1. Ancestry?

GENIUS TRANSCENDS HEREDITY, whatever Havelock Ellis and others may say. Yet we never tire of the search for clues and auguries, and nothing would be more natural than to begin this account of one of the world's greatest geniuses with a sketch of his genealogy. Unfortunately this life filled with paradoxes begins with a question mark: we do not know who was Voltaire's father. The works of reference have no qualms: they tell us that it was François Arouet, born in Paris in or about 1650 (he died in 1722) successively notary, *conseiller du roi*[1] and high official in a tax-collecting department. This François was the son of another, an armigerous cloth and silk merchant; grandson of Helenus, a merchant tanner at Saint-Loup, in Poitou; great-grandson of Pierre, of whom little is known beyond his marriage round about 1525 with a member of the higher local bourgeoisie. It is at least true that Voltaire's 'father' married on 7 June 1683, at Saint-Germain-L'Auxerrois, Marie Marguerite Daumart, whose father was also an official of the *parlement*[2], and belonged to the petty provincial nobility; and that mme François Arouet gave

1 *conseiller.* This word is almost undefinable, for it was used, in general without qualification, for a number of very different offices; a *conseiller d'état* was a member of the king's inner cabinet; *conseiller du roi* was an honorific title given to practically all those who held responsible office under the crown; most often a *conseiller* was a member of a *parlement*, in theory holding judicial office but in practice being something very like an advocate; several departments of government were called *conseils*, and its members *conseillers*.

2 *parlement.* The composition and powers of the *parlement* varied considerably during the eighteenth century, but the institution is not in any case to be confused with a parliament in the English sense. The *parlement* was primarily a multi-chambered court of law, but it also had the duty of registering the king's edicts in order to give them the force of law; the *parlement* was not always willing to do so, expressing its objections in so-called remonstrances, which led to frequent tugs of war with the king and his council. When the *parlement* is mentioned without qualification the Paris *parlement* is meant; its jurisdiction extended over half of France, but there were also more local *parlements*, such as those of Toulouse, Grenoble, Bordeaux, Dijon, and others. This led to further difficulties, for the local *parlements* were jealous of their prerogatives, while Paris considered itself supreme.

birth (waiving three other children who died young) successively to Armand (23 March 1685-17 February 1745) who was to become a fervent Jansenist, and everything that Voltaire was not; Marie Marguerite (?1691-1726), who was to marry Pierre François Mignot, another civil servant, and become the mother of Voltaire's nieces, whom the reader is not likely to forget; and finally François Marie, not unknown to posterity under the name of Voltaire (1694-1778)[3].

Voltaire himself was convinced that his mother's husband was not his father.[4] He first said so in 1729, when he wrote that his parents were 'unhealthy and died young'[5]—whereas François Arouet lived out a full span. Again, in some lines Voltaire wrote in 1737 he says 'Je te jure sur ma foy/Qu'une Vierge n'est pas ma mère.'[6] Taken by itself this remark has no particular significance: it could, for instance, be no more than a variation on the preceding lines: 'Ne comparés point au Messie/Un pauvre Bigre comme moy.'[7] It could merely be an allusion to mme Arouet's six children. Writing in 1774 to the duc de Richelieu (who was himself not his father's son[8]) Voltaire calls himself 'the bastard of Rochebrune'[9]; this also could be interpreted innocuously as an exercise in mock modesty, for Rochebrune, a member of an ancient family of the Auvergne, was a minuscule poet and song-writer, known only, and barely at that, as the librettist of Clérambault's cantata *Orphée*. More pre-

---

3 For further details see Jacques Renaud, *Les Ancêtres poitevins de Voltaire* (Niort 1960), which does not entirely supersede Guy Chardonchamp, *La Famille de Voltaire: les Arouet* (Paris 1911). I have found in the Archives de la Seine various documents relating to some nineteenth-century Voltaires. One Louis André Voltaire married Marie Madeleine Cariat, and had five children in 1829-35. There was also an Antoinette Voltaire and an Eugénie Voltaire, each of whom had an illegitimate child, in 1854 and 1859 respectively. None of these people could have had any connection with our man: it was the custom under the revolution to pay homage to its heroes by giving their names to foundling children.

4 I once said the contrary, but I was wrong; later evidence leaves no doubt on that score.

5 Best.D344 (*c.* February 1729).

6 Best.D1455 (16 February 1738); 'I swear on my faith that a virgin was not my mother.'

7 'Don't compare a poor beggar like me with the messiah.'

8 At any rate, this was the current opinion; in 1769 Voltaire assured Richelieu that the duke was his father's son 'whatever you may say' (Best. D15947; 10 October); and 'whatever they say' (Best.D16019; 3 December); however, in writing to his own niece mme de Fontaine Voltaire referred to the marshal's 'putative father' (Best. D6681; 8 January 1756).

9 Best.D2989 (8 June 1744).

cisely, in 1753 Voltaire told his niece Denis that he had symptoms of dropsy, and added: 'You know that Rochebrune is dead, and that I have some reason to claim the same constitution.'[10] During his last illness Voltaire asked his doctor whether his symptoms did not indicate dropsy, which he regarded as a 'family ailment'[11]. The cumulative evidence is now impressive. And finally we have a report which, though thirdhand and from a gossipy source at that, clinches the matter in the light of Voltaire's own references. In 1756 Alembert, who was known to be illegitimate, and who resembled Fontenelle in appearance, visited Voltaire at Les Délices; and Dupan, a Genevese official, was told that Voltaire had exclaimed: 'I believe it is certain that Alembert is the son of Fontenelle[12], as it is sure that I am the son of Roquebrune'; and that when his niece defended their grandmother's good name, Voltaire 'claimed that what was to his mother's honour was that she had preferred an intelligent man like Roquebrune, musketeer, officer, writer, to his [Voltaire's] father, who was by nature a very commonplace man, and said that he had always flattered himself that he owed his birth to Roquebrune'[13].

Voltaire's only other allusion to Rochebrune, so far as I know, is in a suppressed passage of the *Cadenas* he wrote in his youth. This poem, addressed to a lady whose husband had endowed her with a chastity-belt, originally began:

> Jeune beauté qui ne savez que plaire,
> A vos genoux, comme bien vous savez,
> En qualité de prêtre de Cythère,
> J'ai débité, non morale sévère,
> Mais bien sermons par Vénus approuvés,

---

10 Best.D5475 (11 August 1753); cp. Best.D5451 (25 July 1753).

11 Best.D21083 (27 February 1778). It is only fair to mention that in an unpublished letter of 28 August 1753 (cited by Desnoiresterres, i.199) Philippe Néricault Destouches apparently says that Arouet *père* also died of the dropsy; but Destouches was writing thirty years after the event (he was moreover in England at the time of Arouet's death) and his statement can have no value as evidence; it could hardly be more unlikely in view of

Voltaire's remarks, which would be utterly pointless if his supposed father had suffered from the same malady as Rochebrune.

12 But he was wrong; Jean Le Rond d'Alembert was the son of the blue-stocking Claudine Alexandrine Guérin de Tencin by, almost certainly, Louis Camus, chevalier Des Touches.

13 Best.D6968 (15 August 1756). The reader is invited to note once and for all that the spelling of names was very casual at this time; Voltaire himself was even more casual than most.

Gentils propos, et toutes les sornettes
Dont Rochebrune orne ses chansonettes. . . .[14]

The reader must be left to judge whether it is significant that this reference occurs in a poem on such a subject as this, and that it was later omitted.

One other detail may possibly be relevant. In August-November 1730 Voltaire and his neighbours in the rue de Vaugirard had some trouble with a tripe-seller named Travers. This lady got drunk, used bad language, displaying 'what modesty forbids to name', and threatening to set fire to the neighbouring houses. Voltaire pressed his complaints vigorously, but what is interesting is that among the neighbours who, with him, signed a petition to the chief of the police, is a 'de Rocquebrune'.[15] Nothing more is known of him.

As for his putative father, Voltaire does not mention him more often: once to illustrate his bad temper[16], once to say that in his youth the lawyer knew many men of letters[17], once to repeat his father's opinion that Corneille was a bore[18]; and that is all.

If Voltaire had harped on the theme of his illegitimacy it would not have been difficult to find psychological explanations, though less easy to find convincing ones. However, the need does not arise, for he accepted the fact quite placidly. I have quoted all the references he ever made to his illegitimacy, and it is impossible to doubt that he really believed in it. Yet one can only too easily be sure and still mistaken. Why was he so certain? A deathbed confession by his mother? Hardly, since Voltaire was only seven when she died. A man-to-man revelation by Rochebrune? This is possible, but not likely. I am inclined to believe in an explosion of bad temper by François Arouet, who strongly disapproved of his younger son, and whom one can easily imagine exclaiming one day: 'Like mother, like son', followed by a revelatory tirade.

Be this as it may, it is clearly pointless to indulge in triangular

14 'Young beauty who cannot but please, at your knees, as you well know, in my capacity as priest of Cythera, I have preached, not a severe morality, but many a sermon approved by Venus, tender discourses, and all the idle thoughts with which Rochebrune adorns his little songs. . . .'

15 Best.D376; cp. Best.D377-9.

16 Best.D17573 (*c.* 25 January 1772); see also p. 29, below.

17 Best.D9981 (31 August 1761).

18 Best.D9999 (*c.* 10 September 1761).

studies in heredity. In any case we know little about the Arouets, less about the Daumards, and practically nothing about Rochebrune and his family, so the loss is not great.[19]

The fact is that Voltaire took very little interest in his ancestry. 'The author of the *Henriade* need care little what his grandfather was.'[20] No doubt, but had his ancestry been interesting he would perhaps have felt less aloof. 'A Philosopher may reasonably despise the pride of ancestry; and if the philosopher himself be a plebeian, his own pride will be gratified by the indulgence of such contempt.'[21] Anyway, our philosopher's indifference was entire. When at the end of Voltaire's life Dumoustier de La Fond wrote to announce his discovery of a fifteenth-century poet named Arouet (but he had simply misread Adouet), the great man received the news with the calm of a millionaire who inherits a dilapidated dovecot.[22]

Very seldom did Voltaire refer to any but the closest members of his family. Writing of the massacre of St Bartholomew he said that 'one of our relatives' was a victim[23]; we do not know who this could have been, though the early Arouets were indeed Protestants. Nevertheless Voltaire's remark was probably no more than a literary device, like his statement on another occasion that 'one of my relatives named Beauregard'[24] took part in the defence of Bangkok; no trace of him can be found. More precisely, writing on Charles XII Voltaire mentions as one of his sources letters written by his relative m. Bru, first dragoman at the Turkish Porte[25]; he also is otherwise unknown to me.

19 But investigation of Rochebrune's family might be rewarding; the most obvious archival sources have yielded nothing; however, papers in Arouet's inventory show that in 1692-93 and again in 1698 he was in business relations with a Guerin de Rochebrune (Archives nationales: Minutier central, LVII.309, cote 34).

20 *Mémoire sur la satire* (1739).

21 Edward Gibbon, *Memoirs of my life*, ed. Georges A. Bonnard (London 1966), p. 5.

22 Best.D21140 (*c.* 1 April 1778), D21144 (7 April 1778); Desnoiresterres, i.6.

23 *Fragment sur l'histoire générale* (1773).

24 Best.D5049 (28 October 1752).

25 *Histoire de Charles XII* (1731), v.

2. Childhood, 1694-1704

I T WAS NOT UNTIL the middle of the eighteenth century that children came to be regarded as something other than small adults: little indeed has been recorded of their sayings and doings before that period. And as Voltaire was the least self-analytical of men, so little given to autobiography or to public introspection, we know even less than usual of his early years. The very place and date of his birth have been hotly debated[1]: no argument could be more pointless. It is true that both copies of the registers were destroyed by the revolutionary fires of May 1871, but in France to this day documentary evidence of one's *état civil* has to be produced at every turn: dozens of identical copies of Voltaire's baptismal entry and numerous *certificats de vie*[2] have survived; here is a typical abstract:

Le Lundy vingt deux^e jour de novembre mil six Cent quatre vingt quatorze fut baptizé dans l'Eglize de s^t André des arcs par Mre Bonelio pre vicaire de lad. Eglize soussigné François Marie né le jour précédent fils de Me Arroüet Coner du roy ancien no^{re} au Chlet de Paris Et de D^{me} Marie Marguerite Dreunart[3] sa femme. Le parain Mre François de Castagne abbé Commandataire de Varenne, Et La maraine D^e Marie Parent Epouze de Me de Simphorien Daumart Ecuyer Controlleur de la gendarmerie du roy qui ont signé La minutte. Collationné par moy second vicaire de la susd. psse soussigné à Paris Le 8 Juillet 1746. [signed:] Martin.[4]

---

1 Even recently by René Pomeau in his edition of Gustave Lanson, *Voltaire* (Paris [1960]), pp. 224-5.

2. A *certificat de vie* is a document signed and sealed by an authorised official, who certifies that the person named has appeared before him, producing authentic particulars of his birth and identity.

3 This of course is a misreading of Daumart, and shows that the copy was in fact made from the original, and not from another copy, for other transcripts are correct.

4 Archives nationales: Minutier central, CVIII.471; 'On Monday twenty-second day of November 1694, was baptised in the church of St André des arcs, by master Bonelio, principal vicar of the said church, undersigned, François Marie, born the previous day, son of maître François Arroüet, royal councillor, formerly notary at the Châtelet of Paris, and of mrs Marie Marguerite Dreunart, his wife. The godfather, master François de Castagne, associate abbot of Varenne, and the godmother, mrs Marie Parent, wife of

It is also true that Voltaire composed many variations on the theme of his age. No one who has soaked himself in the Voltairean idiom can be led astray by these *jeux d'esprit*. And no special perspicacity is needed to see that Voltaire is joking when he writes, in the third person, in his autobiography: 'Some fix the birth of FRANCIS DE VOLTAIRE to the 20th of February, others to the 20th of November 1694, and there are extant medals of him bearing each of these dates.'[5] This is obviously Voltaire having fun, and we need take no more seriously the words that follow: 'He has several times told me, that at his birth it was thought that he could not live, and that having been privately baptised by the midwife, the ceremony of baptism was put off for several months.'[6]

Whatever may have been the purpose of this little comedy, the fact that it was a comedy is given away once and for all in Voltaire's letter of 1 January 1777 to Argental: 'I beg you not to say that I am only eighty-two: it is a cruel calumny. Even if it be true, according to an accursed baptismal record, that I was born in November 1694, you must always agree with me that I am in my 83rd year.[7] In other words, Voltaire thought it useful or amusing to pretend that he was more than his true age. Of course it was not

maître Simphorien Daumart, esquire, controller of the royal constabulary, who have signed the original. Collated by me, second vicar of the said parish, in Paris, 8 July 1746. [signed:] Martin.'

5 See the autobiography, p. 623, below.

6 [Jean] Clogenson, *Lettre à m. le rédacteur du Nouvelliste de Rouen, sur la naissance de Voltaire* (Rouen 1860), fell into the trap, and persisted in thinking that Voltaire was born at Châtenay in February 1694. Anyone who agrees with this view is invited to produce examples of similar deliberate and concerted falsifications of the registers—I say 'deliberate and concerted' for the vicar could hardly have mistaken a child of nine months, however puny, for a newborn baby. Armand Arouet was born 22 March 1685, but not baptised until 5 April 'because he was found to be in peril of death'; these facts are recorded in the registers (Archives de la Seine, Registres des

baptêmes de la paroisse de Saint-Germain-le-vieil). Voltaire's friend Richelieu, born prematurely and frail, was not baptised until nearly three years after his birth; in the baptismal registers the date of birth was left blank (see A[uguste] Jal, *Dictionnaire critique de biographie et d'histoire* [second edn., Paris 1872], p. 1062).

7 Best.D20493; cp. Best.D16075 (5 January 1770), where Voltaire complains of Argental's stinginess in saying that he was seventy-five, when in fact he was seventy-six. 'You must say that I am 78' because he was being persecuted. Many of Voltaire's professional enemies have said and still say that Voltaire's object was to improve the terms on which he could buy annuities; if the reader will indulge me for once, I must point out that this is very silly indeed, since a *certificat de vie* had to be produced when each annuity was bought and before the receipt of every payment.

very sensible of him to imagine that if the authorities were willing to persecute him at fifty-two or eighty-two, they would hesitate at fifty-three or eighty-three. That was one of Voltaire's amiable weaknesses, that was his notion of being prudent, but nobody was deceived. As mme Denis once told him, it was useless for him to pretend to be older than he really was, since everybody had seen his baptismal extract.[8]

In short, the facts are perfectly clear: Voltaire was born on Sunday, 21 November 1694, in the parish of Saint-André-des-Arts (originally des-Arcs), on the left bank of the Seine, below the pont Saint-Michel. The exact place is unknown, which is a pity, for it is more than likely that the house is still standing. When François was seven his father moved across an arm of the river to the Ile de la Cité, where by virtue of his office he was given quarters in the rue Jérusalem[9], in the great complex of buildings now known as the Palais de justice, but which has remained substantially unchanged[10]. Here Arouet occupied a house of about ten rooms, with cellar, attic, stables and the usual offices. He also owned a country house of about fourteen rooms at Châtenay, near Sceaux, six miles or so from Paris. We can see from the inventory made after Arouet's death that both houses were richly furnished, but without much taste: mediocre tapestries and marble tables abounded, but there were practically no books, and the pictures were few and of little value[11]. Two small details indicate the standard of life to which Voltaire was accustomed in his parental houses: his father possessed 800 ounces of table-silver and forty dozen napkins[12]. No wonder he concluded that the middle classes possessed five hundred times as much silver in Paris as in London.[13]

In the Palais Arouet became the neighbour of Boileau, whom mme Arouet described not unjustly as 'a good book and a silly

8 Best.D15905 (18 September 1769).

9 E[ugène] Labat, *Hôtel de la présidence* (Paris 1844), p. 25; the site of the presentday Préfecture de police was then an open space.

10 As can be seen from the maps by Bernard Jaillot (1713) and Jean de La Caille (1714).

11 By comparing the inventories of valued works of art in other houses, it may reasonably be inferred that Arouet's were also of little merit; the only identifiable picture (other than prints) was a portrait of the duchesse de Sully.

12 Archives nationales; Minutier central, lvii.309.

13 Best.D3927 (16 May 1749); this letter is also known as the *Lettre à l'occasion de l'impôt du vingtième*.

man'[14]. But she cannot have had much time to judge, for she died soon after the move. A friendship, however, must have been struck up between the families, for many years later, in apostrophing the satirist, Voltaire wrote:

> Je vis le jardinier de ta maison d'Auteuil,
> Qui chez toi, pour rimer, planta le chèvre-feuil.[15]

This might have been regarded as poetic licence were it not that Voltaire added prosaically, in a note, 'The house was very ugly, and the garden also'. He goes on, 'I passed my childhood with your nephew Dongois', and in fact Boileau, who died a few months before Voltaire left school, shared with this nephew his apartment in the cour du Palais. Incidentally, François Arouet helped to draft Boileau's will.[16]

Another neighbour was Nicolas Gédoyn, who had lived in the Palais since his appointment in 1701 as canon of the Sainte-Chapelle (which stood and stands in the courtyard): 'The canonry he was to inhabit', says his biographer, 'was close to the house of m. Arouet, a very estimable man, father of the illustrious m. de Voltaire. This occasioned a close friendship.[17] The abbé Gédoyn saw the first efforts of the young writer; he detected the great man in these products of a newborn muse, and from that moment he foretold the dazzling reputation which m. de Voltaire so justly deserves and which new successes confirm every day.'[18]

There is some reason to believe that Gédoyn was liberal in his religious opinions. Not that there is any trace of this in his academic discourse[19], but we find a valuable hint in Voltaire's catalogue of seventeenth-century authors[20], in which he tells us that Gédoyn was so devoted to the writers of antiquity that he wished 'their religion could have been forgiven because of their writings and their mythology: he found a natural and admirable philosophy

14 Best.D9878 (6 July 1761).

15 *Epître à Boileau* (1769); 'I saw the gardener of your house at Auteuil, who there, to make up the rhyme, planted honeysuckle.'

16 [Pierre Tiffin] Saint-Surin, in his edition of Boileau's *Œuvres* (Paris 1821), vol. i, p. xciv.

17 Voltaire said that Gédoyn 'had no home but ours'; *La Défense de mon oncle* (1767).

18 *Œuvres diverses de m. l'abbé Gédoyn* (Paris 1745), p. xii.

19 *Discours prononcez dans l'Académie françoise . . . à la réception de monsieur l'abbé Gédoyn* (Paris 1719).

20 In the *Siècle de Louis XIV*.

in their fables, as well as striking symbols of all the works of God'. The term 'philosophie naturelle' is significant as applied to the beliefs of a canon of the Sainte-Chapelle. This conclusion is to some extent confirmed by the essay on education in Gédoyn's posthumous works, where he contemplates with equanimity the loss of religion so long as the moral virtues are conserved.[21]. Another passage in Voltaire's catalogue gives a further possible hint of Gédoyn's influence: the canon is said to have regarded *Paradise lost* as 'a barbarous and disgustingly fanatical poem'[22], sentiments Voltaire was frequently to echo.

Gédoyn sometimes took François with him to call on Ninon de L'Enclos[23], the last of the famous (as distinct from the notorious) Aspasias, who was one of Arouet's clients. So did his spiritual father François Maurice de Castagnéry, better known as the abbé[24] de Châteauneuf, modest cleric and diplomat, lesser libertine, and minor writer[25]. This rather ambiguous personage assured the little boy ('to form my mind and heart') that it was he, and not Gédoyn, who had enjoyed Ninon's last favours.[26] Beyond this we know nothing of the lucky lover's influence on Voltaire.[27]

We can guess from Voltaire's rare references to him that the boy did not get on too well with his father (we may as well call

21 *Œuvres diverses,* pp. 48-9.

22 Voltaire tells us that Gédoyn had written four dissertations on this subject; they have not been published.

23 In Best.D4456 (*c.* 1 May 1751) Voltaire gives a rather inaccurate account of his visits to Ninon.

24 *abbé.* 'This undefinable being, who is neither an ecclesiastic nor a layman' (*Lettres philosophiques,*v). This word is often translated *abbot,* and it does indeed bear this meaning (see, for instance, note 4, above); but usually, at this time, it meant something very different: it was applied to all those who wore or were entitled to wear ecclesiastical dress by virtue of having made more or less serious theological studies. They did not necessarily belong to the clergy. Broadly speaking, during most of Voltaire's life none but those who had some claim to be regarded as gentry could hope for higher education unless they went to theological schools; hence the enormous number of abbés in eighteenth-century France, nearly all of whom lived exactly like everybody else, except that they did not usually marry; their conduct therefore tended to be even more irregular than that of laymen.

25 He was the author of posthumous *Dialogues sur la musique des anciens* (Paris 1725).

26 *La Défense de mon oncle* (1767).

27 The oft-quoted story that Châteauneuf had the boy learn by heart the *Moïsade,* a long anti-religious poem (probably by one Lourdet), is intrinsically so unlikely that it must be regarded as mythical hindsight; but few biographers have been able to resist so tempting a titbit.

him that); but we know nothing whatever of their relations at this time, unless the fact (if indeed it is a fact) that the little boy was called Zozo[28] by his family be regarded as significant. We do, however, get a fascinating domestic glimpse. Many years later a country priest begged Voltaire to help a mlle Jonquet, who had apparently been a friend of the Arouet family. In his letter of thanks he reminded the great man of a childhood incident, in a passage which also, in the original, serves to illustrate priestly standards of education: 'One day your father and mother noticed that he [Armand] had bad teeth. They could not persuade him to let them be drawn, so they appealed to the tenderness of mlle Jonquet. She got round him with a louis[29], and after having encouraged him with three or four drinks of champagne, led him to the tooth-drawer, who put his mouth right without hurting him.'[30] As Voltaire's brother was no doubt drunk we can well believe it.

However, a story Voltaire told more than half a century after the event leaves a rather more agreeable impression of the relations between father and son. Voltaire said that his father was as great a grumbler as Grichard (the *Grondeur* in the play of that name by Brueys and Palaprat). One day, having horribly and unjustly bawled out the gardener, and having almost beaten him, he said to him: 'Clear off, you wretch, I hope you will find as patient a master as me.' Voltaire persuaded the actor to add these words to his part, took his father to see the *Grondeur*, with some beneficial results.[31] Even a moderately irritable man might have taken such a practical joke amiss, and Arouet *père* evidently did not.[32]

The boy's relations with his sister must have been more normal.

28 Best.D1 (29 December 1704).

29 The nominal and real value of French money varied considerably in the eighteenth century: commodity prices more than doubled in France between the death of Louis XIV and the revolution, while wages increased by only about 20 per cent on the average. Broadly speaking, during the middle of the century the *livre* was about equal in value to the United States dollar of today. The essential details are: 12 deniers = 1 sou (or sol); 20 sous (sols) = 1 livre tournois or franc; 3 livres = 1 écu; 10 livres = 1 pistole; 24 livres = 1 louis. See, in general, C. E. Labrousse, *Esquisse du mouvement des prix et des revenus en France au XVIIIᵉ siècle* (Paris 1932).

30 Best.D2925 (30 January 1744).

31 Best.D17573 (*c.* 25 January 1772).

32 See also p. 22, above.

'My heart was always drawn to her.'[33] And when she died his letters betray more than perfunctory sorrow. He was in England at the time, and wrote to Thieriot, echoing Hamlet: 'J have wept for her death, and j would be with her. Life is but a dream full of starts of folly, and of fancied, and true miseries. Death awakes us from this painful dream, and gives us, either a better existence or no existence at all.'[34] Unfortunately nothing else is known of this sister. It seems probable that it was for her sake, at first, that Voltaire took so much interest in her children.

We have just one trace of a playmate. When Voltaire was in England he wrote to Edward Harley, 2nd earl of Oxford, telling him (also in English), in a letter written from the 'White Wigg' in Maiden lane, that he had been 'in some measure educated in the house of the late Achilles de Harlay, the oracle and first president of our parliament'[35]. This was Achille III de Harley, who had only one child, Louise, afterwards princesse de Tingry. She was just about François's age, and the little boy no doubt crossed the rue Jérusalem to play with her in the hôtel de la Présidence, the official residence of the *premier président*.

33 Best.D141 (*c.* 25 December 1722).   35 Best.D325 (*c.* 1 January 1728).
34 Best.D303 (26 October 1726).

3. Louis-le-grand, 1704-1711

ARMAND AROUET'S GODPARENTS were the duchesse de Saint-Simon[1] (mother of the diarist) and the duc de Richelieu (whose son, the marshal, became one of Voltaire's closest friends), and the boy was sent to the Oratorian seminary of Saint-Magloire. François's godparents were Marie Daumart, his mother's sister-in-law, and François de Châteauneuf (why was he chosen?); and he was sent to the Jesuit college of Louis-le-grand, a far better and more fashionable school than Saint-Magloire. It would be dangerous to read too much significance into these contrasts. Armand was the elder surviving son, and this may sufficiently explain the noble hands into which his spiritual welfare was entrusted. As for the choice of the younger boy's school, François Arouet's social ambitions had certainly not diminished during the nine years between the birth of his sons; and moreover he had had time to observe the effect on Armand of his Oratorian education: his elder son had already become a fanatical devotee of Jansenism in its decadent eighteenth-century form. He had become one of those arid predestinarians who had conflated the worst aspects of Calvinism and Roman Catholicism, and whose exclusive belief in salvation by grace led them to condemn every sort of amusement, and to seek greedily for all apparent manifestations of divine favour, not excluding self-mutilation and graveyard epilepsy.

These speculations are inconclusive. The explanation may simply be that the younger son was seen to be better able to take advantage of a good education. And certainly, whatever its defects, it was the best to be had. When François went to Louis-le-grand in his tenth year he came under the influence of teachers whose beliefs were at least masked by their classical humanism. It

---

1 She borrowed 150 francs from Arouet *père* in 1689; on his death in 1722 this was given up as a bad debt; see Archives nationales: Minutier central, LVII.309, cote 52.

33

was the function of this Jesuit Eton to train men disciplined by the church, but who were also given a sufficient tincture of letters and of manners to enable them to take their place in the world as leaders.[2] This purpose failed utterly, for many of the best men turned out by the school became freethinkers or at least 'liberals'. Diderot and Helvétius, Malesherbes and Choiseul come to mind in addition to those to be mentioned presently. And what did Louis-le-grand have to show on the side of respectable orthodoxy? At worst the absurd Lefranc de Pompignan, at best such a secondrate critic as Fréron: both among Voltaire's favourite butts. How did it come about that the Jesuits, who were intelligent, learned, devoted, and, in general, worthy men, achieved the opposite of what they intended, and indeed wrought their own ruin? This forms a curious chapter, yet to be written, in the history of education and of ideas. In brief, humanism and religion mix about as well as oil and water. It is difficult to induce an intelligent boy to examine modern history with his reason, but ancient history on the basis of faith and authority[3]. The thing *can* be done, able men *can* be found who believe in both *Genesis* and evolution, but it takes diminished vitality and a lot of practice to achieve this mental dichotomy[4]. The whole theory of Jesuit education in eighteenth-century France was false from the point of view of the church. There was no humanistic nonsense in the Jansenist schools. So they did not breed freethinkers or even deists, but only nonentities[5]. Instead of producing Voltaire and Diderot they nurtured the trained gadflies who fed on these great men.

Among Voltaire's teachers and superiors were men like fathers Porée, Tournemine, Thoulier, who were no mere Jesuit mouthpieces; the last of these left the Society, and became a distinguished classical scholar and grammarian under the anagrammatic name of Olivet. Half a century later he wrote to Voltaire: 'You were

2 Much has been written about Jesuit education; a useful but little known paper is by Marcel Bouchard, 'L'Enseignement des Jésuites sous l'ancien régime', *Information historique* (Paris 1954), xvi.127-134.

3 Such lines as 'Tantum religio potuit suadere malorum' ('So potent was religion in persuading to evil deeds') (Lucretius, i.101) were fixed in Voltaire's memory.

4 By a quirk of fate the most fashionable modern example of this dichotomy is Teilhard de Chardin, Voltaire's collateral descendant.

5 Alembert, it is true, was a product of the Jansenist Mazarin college, but he was in every way an exceptional case.

then my disciple, and today I am yours.'[6] Tournemine, who for some time edited the so-called *Mémoires de Trévoux*, to which he contributed a large number of papers on a wide range of subjects, was a learned and skilful controversialist. It was to him that the young Voltaire turned when in trouble with his father because of his Dutch escapade[7]; it was to him that he afterwards wrote, when sending him one of his plays: 'Have you recognised in it some of those generous feelings with which you inspired me in my childhood? *Si placet tuum est*[8]; that is what I always say when speaking of you and of father Porée.'[9]

Porée[10] was a humanist whose good taste helped to form Voltaire's appreciation of the classics. His published dramas and orations reveal a good man rather than a profound thinker. And this is reflected in the terms of Voltaire's message accompanying a copy of the *Henriade*: 'If you still remember a man who will remember you all his life with the most tender gratitude and the highest possible esteem, receive this work with some indulgence, and regard me as a son who, after many years, comes to present to his father the fruit of his labours in an art which he learned from him.'[11]

Thus Voltaire kept in touch with all these men. What he said to them may have been dictated in part by special considerations, but it was clearly sincere: these are not merely the terms of wordly courtesy, nor is this the Voltairean tone of prudential deference.

Of course all the teachers were not of this quality: it is sufficient to name the egregious father Le Jay, who ground out a large number of machine-made Latin plays and ballets for the school-boys, and whose ineptitude is cruelly revealed by what was his first publication, or very nearly so, the so-called *Triomphe de la*

6 Best.D13798 (3 January 1767).

7 Best.D18 (19 December 1713).

8 'If you like it is yours.'

9 Best.D1729(*c.*31 December 1738); of course Voltaire, who made fun of everything, did not spare Tournemine, quoting a schoolboy couplet (Best. D10495; 7 June 1762):

C'est notre père Tournemine
Qui croit tout ce qu'il imagine.

'It is our father Tournemine who believes all that he imagines.' It is rather odd that Montesquieu, who was so colourless in his human relations, detested this Jesuit; see Robert Shackleton, *Montesquieu* (Oxford 1961), p. 63.

10 See J[oseph] de La Servière, *Un professeur d'ancien régime: le p. Charles Porée* (Paris 1899).

11 Best.D381 (*c.* November 1730).

religion sous Louis le grand (1687), in which he makes coarse fun of the Protestants.[12] The education at Louis-le-grand was above all religious—an endless round of prayers and retreats, pious exercises and theological essays—but none of this was done in what the Jansenists would have regarded as a truly religious spirit, that is, sanctimoniously. The pill was sugar-coated and even gilded for the benefit of the favoured youths who came to the school or lived there in the style to which they were accustomed at home. It was not until the end of Arouet's schooldays that cardinal de Noailles forbade the teachers at Louis-le-grand to administer the sacraments to their pupils[13]. Their hold remained strong enough, but by no means what it had been when they still possessed this terrible weapon. Martin Pallu appears to have been the boy's confessor[14], and if so the fact is important, for Pallu later revealed his strictly moral and narrow spirituality in such works as *Des fins dernières de l'homme* and *Du saint et fréquent usage des sacrements de pénitence et d'eucharistie*[15]. However, the only precise evidence we possess is that offered by the catechism in use at Louis-le-grand, the enormously popular one by Peter Canisius. This work, which was first published before the Council of Trent, and whose Jesuit author has been beatified, has undergone very extensive changes. It is probable, however, that the text in use at Louis-le-grand was one based on the edition prepared for schools[16].

Nothing illustrates better the diversity of Christianity, and even the flexibility of Roman doctrine, so often and so falsely thought to be as rigid as revealed truth, than the enormous mass of catechisms produced for the instruction of the young and the

---

12 For what immediately follows I have leaned heavily on Gustave Dupont-Ferrier, *Du collège de Clermont au lycée Louis-le-grand* (Paris 1921-1925); for the religious details see also René Pomeau, *La Religion de Voltaire* (nouvelle édition, Paris 1969), pp. 38 ff.

13 La Servière, pp. 56, 136-7.

14 [T. I. Duvernet], *La Vie de Voltaire* (Genève 1786), p. 15; Dupont-Ferrier, i.270; there are several Genève

1786 editions of Duvernet: the one quoted here is that in 355 pages with the design of a vase on the titlepage.

15 Both books were first published Paris 1739, and went into several editions.

16 Petrus Canisius, *Catechismus graecolatinus, nunc primum in gratiam studiosae juventutis opera cujusdam ex eadem Societate editus* (Ingolstadii 1595); the editor was Georg Mayr.

ignorant.[17] It was clearly impossible for Rome to impose one universal catechism, since even the *Bible* had to be adapted for the use of missionaries in order to avoid dreadful misunderstandings so far as possible. Hence each bishop was free to issue his own catechism, and the resulting instructions vary to a startling degree. In Voltaire's time there were catechisms of Jansenist and Jesuit tendencies, mystic catechisms, gallican catechisms, and many others, among which those of Bellarmino (1603) and Bossuet (1687) were most popular—the latter was first published under the title of *Catéchisme du diocèse de Meaux*, but still, like those of Canisius and Bellarmino, went into very numerous editions.

The relevant editions of Canisius are resolutely anti-Jansenist and antipietistic, which is simply another way of saying that they are emphatically Jesuit. The catechism to which Voltaire was subjected is essentially a practical guide for the man of the world. The subtleties as well as the worst excesses of doctrine are glossed over, with consequences as startling as they were inevitable. Thus the eucharist is deprived of the sacrifice on the cross which is its only basis. Hell is to all intents and purposes passed over in silence. On the contrary, while man's sins are displayed in detail, salvation through repentance is everywhere underlined. The trinity is mentioned, but only just. Broadly speaking, the third person is almost overlooked, the second very nearly so, and even the first becomes merely a celestial and eternal creator, who governs with goodness and wisdom. About the vengeful god, the problem of evil, original sin, and similar awkward problems, there is hardly a word. As Pomeau has implied (p.50), deism is attained by the simple process of forgetting those elements of Christian doctrine pushed into the background by the Jesuit catechism.

On the other hand, the teaching of the classics was comprehensive, at least on paper. If the standard work[18] could be believed a substantial proportion of the boy's time was devoted to Greek. This was probably true in the seventeenth century, but not by

17 This subject has never been adequately explored; see my *World bibliography of bibliographies* (fourth edition, 1965), i.1179-80, in particular Julius Richter, *Die Pädagogische Lite-ratur in Frankreich während des 16. Jahrhunderts* (Leipzig 1904).

18 The Jesuit Joseph de Jouvancy's *Ratio discendi et docendi* (Parisiis 1725).

Voltaire's time: his knowledge of Greek, like that of his non-specialist contemporaries, was very limited. By 1750, says Dupont-Ferrier (i.129), 'the decadence of Hellenic studies seemed consummated': he should have fixed his terminus half a century earlier.

Even Latin was beginning to lose its prestige[19], though among the teachers at Louis-le-grand were several fathers whose works display their love of the language. The rule enjoining Latin as the sole means of communication in the classroom was a dead letter. Yet at the beginning of the eighteenth century Latin still dominated the teaching. The grammar and vocabulary were taught in a well-nigh exhaustive manner. Cicero and the famous historians, Virgil, Horace, Ovid, Phaedrus among the poets, were taught in depth, by reading, translation, retranslation, so that the works studied became rooted in the memories of the pupils. It would, indeed, be almost possible to reconstruct Voltaire's school-books by analysing the quotations that constantly fall from his pen. For instance, he frequently quotes the *Odes*, *Epistles*, *Satires* and *Ars poetica* of Horace, hardly ever the *Epodes*.[20]

French had of course to be taught, but both the language and the literature were instilled less systematically than Latin, and with infinite precautions to protect the boys against unorthodox works. The average graduate of Louis-le-grand wrote and spelled French less accurately than Latin.

For the rest the boys learned much Roman theology but next to no philosophy; much biblical history but not the *Bible* (it was not at school that Voltaire acquired his intimate knowledge of holy writ); much classical and French history of a kind, but almost nothing of the rest of the world; little geography, some elementary mathematics and physics[21], some scraps of Hebrew and philology, no science beyond the most obvious, the most superficial, and the most harmless. Like most great men Voltaire was self-taught—all he really learned at school was Latin, habits of work, and ambition. Perhaps a love for the stage should be added, for the Jesuit

---

19 In part because Descartes had published his *Discours de la méthode* (1637) in French.

20 See in general the 'Index of quo-

tations' in Voltaire 135.

21 *Enseignement et diffusion des sciences en France au XVIII° siècle* (Paris 1964), pp. 27-65.

tradition of school plays in Latin, and even ballets, was kept up at Louis-le-grand on an ambitious scale.

Sixty years later Voltaire made one of his personages, who for once can be confidently identified with the writer himself, complain to an ex-Jesuit about his education. When he first went into the world he was laughed at when he tried to speak. 'It was all very well for me to quote the odes [of Horace] to Ligurinus and the *Pédagogue chrétien*[22], I neither knew whether Francis I had been taken prisoner at Pavia, nor where Pavia is; even the country in which I was born was unknown to me; I knew neither the principal laws nor the interests of my fatherland; not a word of mathematics, not a word of sound philosophy; I knew Latin and nonsense.'[23]

It can hardly have been from his masters, however, that François acquired the ironic humour, the light-hearted attitude to religion, and the graceful style prefigured in this letter[24] written in his seventeenth year to a school-friend:

Monsieur

J'ay différé deux ou trois iours à vous ecrire afin de pouuoir vous dire Des nouuelles de la tragedie[25] que le pere leiay vient de faire représenter;

22 By Philippe d'Outreman, first published about 1630.

23 'Education', *Dictionnaire philosophique*.

24 Best.D6 (*c.* 7 August 1711); this is the earliest Voltaire letter of which I have been able to find the manuscript; it has therefore been reproduced *literatim*; Voltaire never changed some of the habits here visible; erratic punctuation, capitalisation, accentuation, all more or less standard contemporary practice: I have made no attempt to imitate all this in translation.

Sir,

I delayed for two or three days in writing to you in order to be able to give you news of the tragedy which father Lejay has just had performed. Heavy rain made it necessary to divide the spectacle in two after dinner, which pleased the pupils as much as it distressed father Lejay. Two monks broke their necks one after the other, so adroitly that they seemed to fall only to amuse us. His holiness's nuncio gave us a week's holiday, monsieur Thevenart sang, father Lejay shouted himself hoarse. Father Porée prayed for good weather, and the heavens were not unmoved, for at the height of his prayer they sent down rain in torrents. This is pretty well all that has happened here. In order to enjoy the holidays it only remains for me to have the pleasure of having you in Paris, but far from seeing you, I cannot even have the satisfaction of satisfying my friendship by writing you a longer letter. The post, which is about to leave, obliges me to declare myself in haste
    your very humble and very obedient
    servant and friend   Arouet

25 The play performed on this occasion was Le Jay's *Croesus*, together with his *Apollon législateur*, a 'ballet meslé de chant et de déclamation'.

une grosse pluye a fait partager le spectacle en Deux apres dinées ce qui a fait autant de plaisir aux ecoliers que de chagrin au pere leiay; Deux moines se sont cassez le col l'un aprez l'autre si adroitement qu'ils n'ont semblé tomber que pour servir à notre Diuertissement, le nonce[26] de Sa sainteté nous a donnez 8 jours De Congez, monsieur Theuenart a chanté, le pere leiay s'est enroüe; le père Porée a prié Dieu pour obtenir un Bautemps; le ciel n'a pas été D'airan pour luy, au plus fort de sa priere le ciel adonné une pluye abondante, uoylà à peu prez ce qui s'est passé icy; il ne me reste plus pour iouir Des uacances que D'auoir le plaisir De uous uoir a paris, mais bien loing De pouuoir vous posseder; ie ne puis mesme avoir le Bonheur De contenter mon amitié par une plus longue lettre, la poste qui ua partir me force de uous dire à la hate

votre très humble et très obeissant serviteur et amy

Arouët

The boy to whom François wrote this letter, Claude Philippe Fyot de La Marche (1694-1768), became the *premier président*[27] of the Dijon *parlement*, and remained Voltaire's lifelong friend. So did several other of his contemporaries at Louis-le-grand: Argental, Cideville, the brothers d'Argenson, the duc de Fronsac (later de Richelieu), and several more.

Charles Augustin Feriol, comte d'Argental (1700-88), is very nearly the only one of Voltaire's friends who never let him down. During seventy years their friendship was never clouded. Modest, retiring, Argental, without being a prig, was thoroughly sensible, steady, tactful. No yes-man, he never hesitated to question, to criticise; he often disagreed with his ebullient friend, not seldom disapproved of his actions; but he never failed him. He was the great man's 'dear angel', and deserved the epithet. He and his wife formed one of the very rare united couples in Parisian society. A lawyer, he was also the minister plenipotentiary of Parma at the French court.[28]

Pierre Robert Le Cornier de Cideville (1695-1776), later a *conseiller* at Rouen and a minor poet of considerable talent[29], re-

26 Agostino Cusani.

27 *président*. When this term is used without qualification it refers to a judge of a *parlement*; a *président à mortier*, who had the right to wear the judicial cap or mortar-board, was a senior judge; a *premier président* was a chief justice of a *parlement* or court.

28 Some account of Voltaire's

'angel' has at last been given by Maija B. May, 'Comte d'Argental: a magistrate in the literary world', *Studies on Voltaire* (1970), lxxvi.55-114.

29 This was revealed when his letters in prose and verse were published for the first time in the earlier volumes of Best.

mained one of Voltaire's warmest and most appreciative friends until he became devout in old age. He was for long in love with Voltaire's elder niece mme Denis, and would have liked to marry her.

René Louis de Voyer de Paulmy, marquis d'Argenson (1694-1757), who became minister for foreign affairs, was known as 'Argenson la bête', not because he was really stupid but because he thought for himself. He had the gravest of defects for a man in place under the *ancien régime*[30], he was a liberal; and so his stimulating *Considérations sur le gouvernement de la France* circulated in manuscript for thirty years before they could be published (1764). His voluminous memoirs, never completely printed, are invaluable, and even from time to time remind one of Montaigne. He was a notable book-collector. His younger brother, who was also at Louis-le-grand, Marc Pierre, comte d'Argenson (1696-1764), minister for war, was also thoughtful and instructed beyond his rank, as can be inferred from the fact that the *Encyclopédie* was dedicated to him.

Louis François Armand Du Plessis, then duc de Fronsac (1696-1788), grand-nephew of the cardinal, better known as the maréchal-duc de Richelieu, became a famous soldier only because better than he were conspicuously lacking. He was as notorious for his undiscriminatingly numerous sexual affairs as for his lack of scruple in public and private conduct, being not unjustly known as 'père la maraude' ('king of the pirates'). He had a sincere affection and admiration for Voltaire, but his ingrained disloyalty, snobbish susceptibility and inferiority complex usually had the upper hand. Voltaire's steadfast affection for him was often and sorely tried.[31]

Of course not all Voltaire's schoolfellows had equal opportunities, not all were destined to cut grand figures in the world. More than one appealed to the great man for help in later life, none went

30 *ancien régime.* The system of government in pre-revolutionary France, with special reference to the reigns of Louis xiv and Louis xv.

31 By 1722 Voltaire wrote of him: 'I esteem him too much to believe that he could have said with displeasure that I had failed him in respect. I owe him nothing but friendship, certainly not subservience, and if he expected that I would no longer owe him anything' (Best.D121; 11-18 September 1722). The reader may find it surprising that a Richelieu should suffer from feelings of inferiority; if so, see chapter 15, below.

empty away. 'Good heavens, my dear friend', wrote Voltaire to Cideville from Brussels in 1741, 'what wretched people there are in this world! Do you remember your fellow-countryman and old friend Lecoq? I recently saw someone arrive here in dirty linen, with a crooked jaw and a four-inch beard. It was Lecoq, who drags his misery from town to town. It makes one's heart bleed.'[32]

Among Voltaire's contemporaries were also a number of pupils (more than one in ten[33]) from abroad, even as far afield as China[34]. Apart from a certain number of converted Armenians, Greeks, Syrians and the like, most of them were Catholics from Protestant countries, and the children of French Catholic families established overseas. Yet it is not impossible that the missionary ardour of the Jesuits brought a few genuine 'natives' to their principal school. Maurice Pilavoine wrote to Voltaire from Pondicherry, after forty-nine years of silence, that he had told Baudoin de Soupir 'that I was educated at the Collège de Louis le Grand . . . and that I had had the honour of accompanying you, sir, from the seventh form to the highest'[35]. He signed 'l'indien né à Suratte', but this may have been a nickname.

The outside world made itself heard in less agreeable ways, for the years Voltaire spent at school saw one of the blackest periods of French history. In his first year came the defeat at Blenheim, followed by Ramillies in 1706 and Malplaquet in 1709. In this last year (1708-9) there was also a famine in France, and intense cold, teachers and boys alike huddling with empty stomachs round tepid stoves.[36] Sixty years later Voltaire told his younger niece that in this terrible year he was given brown bread only when his father paid a supplementary fee of 100 fr. for his board.[37]

Like everything else at Louis-le-grand discipline was in principle strict, including occasional corporal punishment, in practice easy-going. There was a constant coming and going, since some of the students, like our François, were boarders, while others were day-boys; and, especially when plays were performed, women were freely admitted. There was much drinking and jollification,

32 Best.D2558 (28 October 1741).
33 Dupont-Ferrier iii.224.
34 See Best.D15004 (6 May 1768)
35 Best.D7635 (15 February 1758).
36 Best.D13798 (3 January 1767).

See also the *Siècle de Louis XIV*, xxi; Winston Churchill has entitled a chapter in his *Marlborough* (1938), iv, 'The great frost'.

37 Best.D15494 (1 March 1769).

a great deal of rather rough horseplay, but, it would seem, little sex, and no more than the inevitable minimum of homosexuality. The most emphatic aspect of the moral education was emulation: there was a continuous and relentless system of competition to spur ambition. Every student had his place in order of merit, numerous prizes were given for all sorts of essays and other efforts, and the distribution of prizes was made the excuse for social occasions, graced by the *tout-Paris* and the *tout-Versailles*.[38] A boy's name could thus become known, as was Voltaire's, at court and in the salons while he was still a pupil.

Needless to say, François started to write at school, and of course he composed a tragedy. Only fragments of *Amulius et Numitor* have survived. They serve to show that the boy had acquired considerable skill in handling rhyme, even if he had not mastered the awkward alexandrine[39] to which French tragedy was committed. Indeed, Voltaire never fully mastered it except in short bursts: no metre could have been more unsuited to his impetuous temperament.

One day a teacher confiscated the snuff-box with which the boy was playing in class: he was made to appeal in verse for its return. In a quarter of an hour (but I dare say that the time-keeping was not too accurate) François produced the reasonably graceful lines:

> Adieu, ma pauvre tabatière;
> Adieu, je ne te verrai plus;
> Ni soins, ni larmes, ni prière,
> Ne te rendront à moi; mes efforts sont perdus.
> Adieu, ma pauvre tabatière;
> Adieu, doux fruit de mes écus!
> S'il faut a prix d'argent te racheter encore,
> J'irai plutôt vider les trésors de Plutus.
> Mais ce n'est pas ce dieu que l'on veut que j'implore:
> Pour te revoir, hélas! il faut prier Phébus. . . .
> Qu'on oppose entre nous une forte barrière!
> Me demander des vers, hélas! je n'en puis plus.

38 Dupont-Ferrier devotes an entire chapter to 'Le Stimulant moral des Etudes: l'émulation' (i.240-52); see also André Schimberg, *L'Education morale dans les collèges de la compagnie de Jésus en France sous l'ancien régime* (Paris 1903).

39 The line of twelve syllables, with a pause after the sixth, 'that like a wounded snake, drags its slow length along' (Pope, *Essay on criticism*, 350).

Adieu ma pauvre tabatière;
Adieu, je ne te verrai plus.[40]

Another day an old soldier came to see father Porée. He was in need, wanted to petition the *dauphin*[41], and asked the Jesuit for a few lines of verse that he could use. Porée passed the request to the young Arouet, who produced the set of lines beginning 'Noble sang du plus grand des rois'[42]. The petition was successful, and was naturally talked about in Paris and Versailles. Voltaire's public career had begun.

A different kind of celebrity came to him even earlier. As we have seen, the boy was taken to see Ninon de L'Enclos. He was ten and she ninety; and so impressed was the old lady, she who had known as intimately as one can some of the wittiest and most intelligent men of two generations, that she left him a thousand francs in her will to buy books[43]. Perhaps after all Jean Baptiste Rousseau was mistaken when he said that the boy, though looking lively and wide-awake, had a disagreeable cast of features[44]. In general physique Voltaire described himself in 1716 as 'Thin, tall,

40 *Sur une tabatière confisquée*; 'Farewell, my poor snuff-box; farewell, I shall not see you again; neither care, nor tears, nor prayers will give you back to me; my efforts are in vain. Farewell, my poor snuff-box; farewell, delightful fruit of my crowns! If I had to buy you back I would willingly ransack the treasures of Plutus. But he is not the god I am asked to implore: in order to see you again I must, alas, pray to Phoebus. . . . What an awful barrier is set between us! I am asked for verses, alas! I am undone. Farewell, my poor snuff-box: farewell, I shall not see you again.'

41 *dauphin*. The heir to the French throne; at this time the longevity of the kings and the high mortality rate of their sons, sometimes make these heirs difficult to identify; Louis XVI was the grandson of Louis XV, who was Louis XIV's great-grandson; from 1661 to 14 April 1711 the *dauphin* was Louis, called *monseigneur*, son of Louis XIV; he was succeeded by his son Louis, duc

de Bourgogne, who died 18 February 1712; *his* son Louis, duc d'Anjou, then became the *dauphin*, and ascended the throne as Louis XV on 1 September 1715; his son Louis automatically became the *dauphin* on his birth in 1729, but died 20 December 1765; the next *dauphin* was his son Louis Auguste, duc de Berri, who became Louis XVI on 10 May 1774.

42 *Epitre à monseigneur*; it is quoted and translated in the autobiography, pp. 623-624, below.

43 The will has been reproduced by Marius Barroux, ed. *Soixante facsimilés de documents de 1112 à 1871* (Archives du département de la Seine et de la ville de Paris: [Paris] 1938), no. 13.

44 Best.D1078 (22 May 1736). Voltaire commented on this remark by the notoriously ugly Rousseau: 'I don't know why he says that my appearance displeased him, it is apparently because my hair is brown and because my mouth is not crooked' (Best.D1150; 20 September 1736).

dried-up and bony'[45] and so he remained throughout his life. Height is of course relative; in the museum of Les Délices can be seen an articulated figure of Voltaire made to fit his clothes; these suggest that in his prime he measured about 5 feet 3 inches. For the rest, he was always ailing: he devoured his own vitality, always capable of an effort when needed, but never feeling really well though seldom really ill. It may be doubted whether his mother's alleged fall had much to do with it: this type of self-consuming intellectual is no stranger to us, nor is he a modern invention.

Voltaire's school-days ended in August 1711. At Louis-le-grand he had probably learned as much and come to as little harm as could reasonably be expected. Let him speak for himself in a letter addressed to a later principal of the college, Simon de La Tour (it will be seen that even here he cannot abstain from a little dig at the commercial activities of the Jesuits):

I was brought up for seven years by men who take immense and inde-fatigable pains to form the minds and the morals of youth. Can it be sup-posed that I am without gratitude to these masters? Since it is natural for a man to feel pleasure when he sees the house in which he was born, the village in which he was suckled, how could it not be in his heart to love those who took generous care of his earliest years? If Jesuits go to law with a Capuchin in Malabar for motives of which I have no knowledge, what care I? Is that a reason for me to be ungrateful to those who inspired me with the taste for literature and with feelings which will be my consolation until the end of my life? Nothing will blot out in my heart the memory of father Porée, who is equally dear to all who studied under him. No man ever made study and virtue more agreeable. The hours of his lessons were to us delightful hours; and I could have wished that in Paris, as in Athens, it were possible to attend such lessons whatever one's age. I have had the happiness of being formed by more than one Jesuit of father Porée's character, and I know that he has successors worthy of him. In short, what did I see during the seven years I spent in their house? The most laborious of lives, the most frugal, the most orderly. All their time was divided between the care they lavished on us and the practice of their austere profession. I declare that among the thousands of men educated by them like me, not one will contradict me. This is why I never cease to be astonished that they can be accused of teaching a corrupting morality. Like all religious bodies in the dark ages they have had casuists who argued the pros and cons of propositions now elucidated or

45 Best.D37 (summer 1716).

forgotten. But in truth can their morality be judged by the satirical *Lettres provinciales*?[46]

46 Best.D3348 (*c.* 1 April 1746); the *Lettres provinciales* were Pascal's attack on the Jesuits on behalf of the Jansenists. In this chapter, following Voltaire himself, I have taken an amiable view of Jesuit education; but very different opinions can be justified; thus, Condorcet, looking back on his own years at Louis-le-grand, concluded that its education was fit to make debauchees, atheists and bigoted imbeciles; quoted by Keith Michael Baker, *Condorcet* (Chicago &c. 1975), pp. 3-4.

4. First exile and calf-love, 1711-1713

THAT VOLTAIRE was a brilliant student is certain. Apart from the evidence already produced we know that he won prizes, and that he was presented to Jean Baptiste Rousseau as having 'astonishing aptitude for poetry'[1] and Voltaire's future enemy told a friend that the youth's poems were 'all sparkling with genius'[2]. Legend has it that he was also a little turbulent, and it is quite likely that he was, though the evidence is worthless. Indeed the only incident that has any semblance of authenticity[3] is father Le Jay's angry exclamation: 'Wretch, you will one day be the standard-bearer of deism in France'—a judgment, in his mouth, tantamount to saying: 'You are headed straight for hell.' Even this seems too good to be true—but let it stand. The same legends have it that his turbulence continued after he left Louis-le-grand. Again, very likely, for while at school the boy had got into the hands of a money-lender to the extent of 500 francs[4]. Nor was this the last of such mishaps, for a later adventure of this kind was turned, as he transformed all his financial reverses, into an amusing anecdote.

I remember that needing once to borrow money from a usurer, I saw two crucifixes on his table. I asked him whether they were pledges from his debtors; he answered that they were not, but that he never struck a bargain unless the crucifixes were there. I told him that in that case one would be enough, and that I advised him to place it between two thieves. He accused me of being an unbeliever and declared that he would not lend me any money. I took my leave; he ran down the stairs after me and said, making the sign of the cross, that if I could assure him that I had no evil intentions in speaking those words, he could in conscience conclude our business. I replied that I had had only very good intentions. He therefore resolved to make me the loan for six months, at ten per cent, against security, deducted the interest, and after

---

1 Best.D1078 (22 May 1736).
2 Best.D27 (8 April 1715).
3 For the evidence see Pomeau, *La Religion de Voltaire*, p. 72.

4 See 'Acte notarié passé à Sully par Voltaire', *Bulletin de la Société archéologique de l'Orléanais* (Orléans 1855), [ii].198.

six months decamped with my pledges, which were worth four or five times the money he had lent me.[5]

Yet we also learn from Arouet's will[6] that the debts he paid for his younger son amounted to a relatively modest 4000 francs, so Voltaire's prodigality cannot have been excessive. However, all we know as a clear fact is that he wanted to write, whereupon his father sent him to law school, with a view to buying him a public office—for nearly all government posts had by that time become hereditary, and were consequently for sale. The law was still, far more even than now, an unsavoury mixture of jargon and pedantry; and the youth was driven to an even firmer resolution to devote himself to writing. Voltaire tells us himself that his literary successes at school may well have led him to become a poet; but that 'he was principally, and indeed solely, engaged to addict himself entirely to the cultivation of the Belles-lettres, by the disgust he conceived against the method of teaching Jurisprudence in the law schools'[7]. And elsewhere he added: 'I devoted myself to study from my youth, I refused the office of royal advocate which my family . . . wanted to buy me.'[8] He might perhaps have agreed to become a *conseiller* if he could have done so by merit, but this was impossible. 'One becomes a *maître des requêtes*[9] by dint of money, but money does not enable one to compose an epic poem; and I composed one', said he later with justified arrogance[10].

The epic poem was to come; for the moment Voltaire contented himself with an ode[11] for a prize offered by the Académie française. It was commonplace, and neither won nor deserved to win, but it was at any rate superior to the poem that did win it, though its author, the abbé Du Jarry, described his own lines as 'harmonious, sublime, Christian'[12]. Unfortunately for him his

---

5 Preface of *Le Dépositaire* (1769).

6 Which, with the related documents, is Th. B.

7 See the autobiography, p. 624, below.

8 *Mémoire sur la satire* (1739).

9 *maître des requêtes*. These members of the *parlement* formed in part a court of first instance for petitions addressed to the king, in part a court of appeal, and even in part a sovereign court; roughly speaking, they were a sort of legal *élite* from whose ranks many high offices were filled; it cost 100,000-200,000 francs to purchase the title of *maître des requêtes*.

10 Best.D2035 (21 June 1739).

11 *Sur le vœu de Louis XIII* (1712).

12 In the preface of his *Poésies* (Paris 1715).

poem contained, in addition to these lofty qualities, a line in which, carried away by rhetoric, he referred to burning poles and icy poles. This blunder was immortalised by Voltaire in his first surviving prose composition[13], in which, at the age of twenty, he displays his power of irony and invective in fine flower. He took the lesson to heart, and also the for once sensible advice given by J. B. Rousseau: 'Neither the Corneilles, nor the Racines, nor the Despréaux ever competed for prizes ... they knew too well that only the worst writings have the right to aspire to academic laurels.'[14] Voltaire never again competed for a literary prize.

Instead he composed another ode, *Sur les malheurs du temps*, written spontaneously this time, but still of mediocre interest as poetry, and conventional in content. The ode *Le Vrai dieu* probably followed it closely, but it is very different: the writing is much more skilful and musical, the ideas begin to take shape, and the irony becomes a sharp and skilfully used weapon. The nine ten-line octosyllabic stanzas turn on the difficulties presented by the idea of a god who immolates himself by 'the sacrifice of God to God's own wrath'[15].

> Vous semblez, de vos maux complice,
> Oublier que vous êtes Dieu.[16]

As for man, for whom the sacrifice was accomplished, does he deserve it, and does it not reward evil?

> L'Homme est heureux d'être perfide,
> Et, coupables d'un déicide,
> Tu nous fais devenir des dieux.[17]

The same remarks apply to the ode *La Chambre de justice*, though this time the content throws a bright light, very nearly for the first time, on Voltaire's social thinking. The government,

13 *Lettre à m. D**** (1714).

14 Best.D25 (?1714); Despréaux is now better known as Boileau.

15 Shelley, *The Revolt of Islam*, 4094-5.

16 'You appear to forget, accomplice of the evil you do, that you are god.'

17 'Man does well to be false: we are deicides, and you reward us by making us gods.' Many years later Voltaire disowned this ode; see a note on the *Dialogue de Pégase et du vieillard* and the *Lettre de m. de La Visclède*, but it is certainly his work; it was first published in 1715, over his name, and he did not then protest.

on the brink of bankruptcy as usual, had set up a new court to punish profiteers and tax-evaders, but its methods were less just than indiscriminately severe and unscrupulous. This ode expresses Voltaire's indignation, and, after some very plain speaking, concludes in terms the tone of which reminds one of much later revolutionary songs:

> Vieille erreur, respect chimérique,
> Sortez de nos cœurs mutinés;
> Chassons le sommeil léthargique
> Qui nous a tenus enchaînés.
> Peuple! que la flamme s'apprête;
> J'ai déjà, semblable au prophète,
> Percé le mur d'iniquité:
> Volez, détruisez l'Injustice;
> Saisissez au bout de la lice
> La désirable liberté.[18]

While still at school François had been introduced to the free-thinking group which met at the Temple, so called because it had been the headquarters in France of the knights Templar. It was now the home of the renamed knights of St John of Jerusalem, and when Philippe de Vendôme became its grand prior, it was also the meeting-place of the last of the *libertins*. The *libertins*, though not necessarily libertines, were as free in their behaviour as in their ideas: they were a living demonstration of the fact that freethought is not necessarily as dull as many of its twentieth-century devotees, and that the life of reason does not exclude a passion for beauty and poetry, and the love of women, good food and good wine. Chaulieu, a charming poet and an absentee abbot, who had managed to line his pockets in every one of his posts, sacred and secular, was the leading spirit of the group. He was one of the most complete hedonists of all time, sought every pleasure he could enjoy without too much exertion, and accepted the consequences with the utmost good humour. He ended his lines on an attack of the gout:

18 'Ancient error, vain respect, leave our mutinous hearts; we must expel the lethargic sleep which has kept us in chains. People! let the torch be prepared; I have already, like the prophet, pierced the wall of iniquity: hasten, destroy injustice; seize longed-for liberty at the end of the combat.' This poem also was never included by Voltaire in his works, but I agree with Desnoiresterres i.165-7 that it is his work.

Mais quoi! ma goutte est passée;
Mes chagrins sont écartés:
Pourquoi noircir ma pensée
De ces tristes vérités?
Laissons revenir en foule
Mensonges, erreurs, passions:
Sur ce peu de temps qui coule,
Faut-il des réflexions?
Que sage est qui s'en défie!
J'en connois la vanité:
Bonne et mauvaise santé
Fait notre philosophie.[19]

Though he believed only in his own pleasure, he thought it unseemly to disbelieve emphatically, and so, said Voltaire,

L'autre jour, à son agonie,
Son curé vint de grand matin
Lui donner en cérémonie,
Avec son huile et son latin,
Un passe-port pour l'autre vie.[20]

And this Pococurante *avant la lettre* would have been delighted by his own funeral: for the Benedictine who accompanied his body got drunk, with unseemly consequences[21].

Chaulieu was seventy-two when Voltaire began to frequent his circle at the age of seventeen. There he was treated as an equal by this 'Anacreon of the Temple'[22] and by such epicurean poets as La Fare, whom Voltaire knew by heart[23], and of whose light verse critics have expressed too general a condemnation[24]. The epigram quoted by Voltaire is as good as anything of its kind:

19 *Œuvres de Chaulieu* (La Haye &c. 1774), i.29. 'Never mind! my gout is better; my sorrows are set aside. Why should I make myself gloomy with such sad truths? Let lies, errors and passions come crowding back. What need is there to philosophise about our brief span? The wise man sets such thoughts at naught, and I know their vanity: a man's philosophy depends on his health.'

20 *Epître à monsieur le duc de Sully* (1720); 'The other day, when he was dying, his priest came early in the morning to give him solemnly, with his oil and his Latin, a passport to the other life.' In 1746 these lines were sent to pope Benedict XIV to convince him that Voltaire was a deist (Best. D3464).

21 [Raymond Ismidon Marie, marquis de Bérenger] in the *Lettres inédites de l'abbé de Chaulieu* (Paris 1850), pp. 15-16.

22 Best.D32 (11 July 1716).

23 See the *Notebooks* i.263, and my note thereon; for the *Notebooks* see below, p. 124, note 32.

24 e. g. Gustave Desnoiresterres, *Les Cours galantes* (Paris 1865), i.143.

Quand je goûte avec toy la volupté suprême,
Ouy, je te jure Iris, qu'attaché à tes yeux,
Occupé de toy seule, et m'oubliant moi même
Ton plaisir est celuy que je ressens le mieux.[25]

For the rest the marquis appears to have been more ardent as a lover than as a soldier, and finally died of the pleasures of the table.

The 'fat, heavy, round, short'[26] and 'amiable glutton'[27] abbé Courtin became a close friend, writing and receiving letters jointly with Voltaire. Another of the companions was the abbé Servien, Sully's uncle, who died, says Saint-Simon[28] bashfully, 'surprised in the company of a male dancer of the Opera'. It was he who replied: 'Sir, I have not the honour to be a priest', when a young man whom he had accosted exclaimed, 'What does this bugger of a priest want of me?'[29] When he was imprisoned in 1715 Voltaire apostrophised him:

Aimable abbé, dans Paris autrefois
La Volupté de toi reçut des lois;
Les Ris badins, les Grâces enjouées,
A te servir dès longtemps dévouées,
Et dès longtemps fuyant les yeux du roi,
Marchaient souvent entre Philippe et toi,
Te prodiguaient leurs faveurs libérales,
Et de leurs mains marquaient dans leurs annales,
En lettres d'or, mots et contes joyeux,
Don ton esprit enfants capricieux. . . .[30]

---

25 *Notebooks* i.271. 'When I enjoy with you the supreme delight, yes, I swear, Iris, that, gazing with your eyes, thinking only of you, and forgetting myself, it is your pleasure that I feel the most.'

26 Best.D37 (summer 1716).

27 Best.D38 (summer 1716).

28 *Mémoires*, ed. A. de Boislisle (Paris [1879]-1928), xxx.216

29 [Charles Pinot] Duclos, *Mémoires secrets sur les règnes de Louis XIV et de Louis XV* (Paris 1791), ii.81.

30 *Epître à monsieur l'abbé Servien*; 'Amiable abbé, in other days voluptuousness in Paris received its laws from you; playful Mirth, the sprightly Graces, long devoted to your service, and long fleeing the eyes of the king, often walked between Philip and you, lavished on you their liberal favours, and with their hands noted in their annals, in golden letters, the joyous sayings and stories which were the capricious children of your wit. . . .' This epistle has always been dated 1714, but the references to Servien's imprisonment and to Philippe of Orléans require a later date, perhaps even just before Servien's death in 1716.

There was also the abbé de Bussy, who, when he became bishop of Luçon, was not in the least embarrassed by the verses Voltaire is said to have written to console him for the death of his mistress:

> Tu fuis un repas qui t'attend!
> Tu jeûnes comme un pénitent;
> Pour un chanoine quelle honte!
> Quels maux si rigoureux peuvent donc t'accabler?
> Ta maîtresse n'est plus; et, de ses yeux éprise,
> Ton âme avec la sienne est prête à s'envoler!
> Que l'amour est constant dans un homme d'église![31]

By such men as these the boy's mind was impregnated with a passion for freedom of thought and speech, and incidentally with a profound knowledge of the French seventeenth-century *libertin* poets, from whom he learned the secret

> Pour chanter toujours sur la lyre,
> Ces vers aisés, ces vers coulants,
> De la nature heureux enfants,
> Où l'art ne trouve rien à dire.[32]

Voltaire also planned and wrote at this time, when he was eighteen, a first draft of *Œdipe* and the good taste of the Templars contributed not a little to this first tragedy and to the other productions of his nonage. 'I well remember the criticisms', he told Chaulieu, 'which the grand prior and yourself addressed to me at a certain supper with the abbé de Bussy. This supper much benefited my tragedy, and I think that in order to compose a good one it will suffice to drink with you four or five times. Socrates gave his lessons in bed, and you give them at table.'[33]

I have said that the boy was treated as an equal by these brilliant relics of the century of Louis xiv: but there are two sides to this, and Voltaire behaved to them with equal ease. In his letters he

31 *Epître à monsieur l'abbé de [Bussy]*; 'You flee a meal that awaits you! You fast like a penitent; how shameful for a canon! What grievous ills can afflict you? Your mistress is no more; and, smitten with her eyes, your soul is ready to fly away with hers! How constant is love in a churchman!' It is not certain that these lines were addressed to Bussy.

32 Best.D32 (11 July 1716); 'Always to sing on the lyre these easy verses, these flowing verses, the happy offspring of nature, in which art plays no part.'

33 Best.D35 (20 July 1716); Voltaire read his play in a good many drawing-rooms, including those of the duchesse Du Maine and the prince de Conti.

writes to them with inimitable grace, and with respect, but with no subservience. He gave their advice all the weight it deserved, but did not necessarily accept it. And if the boon companions

> Par quelque gentile vaudeville,
> Nous avons réprimé les fats,
> Qui sans nous inondaient la ville[34],

they directed their shafts also at each other, and even the youngest of them did not deny himself, and them, a good laugh at their own expense. Half a century later Voltaire wrote to La Harpe:

As old men love to tell stories and even to repeat themselves, I will remind you that one day the wits of the kingdom—they were the prince de Vendôme, the chevalier de Bouillon, the abbé de Bussy, who was more intelligent than his father[35], several of Bachaumont's pupils, Chapelle and the famous Ninon —were running down La Motte-Houdart for all they were worth. The fables of La Motte had recently been published. They were dismissed with the greatest disdain, everybody swore that they came nowhere near the most mediocre fables of La Fontaine. I mentioned a new edition of this same La Fontaine, and several fables by this author which had been discovered. I recited one; they were in ecstasy; they cried that La Motte could never have written like that. What subtlety! What grace! One recognises La Fontaine in every word! The fable was by La Motte.[36]

This was regarded by Voltaire's father as a life of dissipation, and in 1713 he packed the youth off to Caen. Why there and for exactly how long we do not know. 'Voltaire was sent to Caen by his father, who feared that he would be completely spoiled in Paris. . . . His father, a decent man much angered by his conduct. . . . At Caen Voltaire visited a lady named Dozeville, who wrote pleasant verse, and who at first received him well because of his nice wit, and sometimes showed him some of her poetry; but this lady, having heard that elsewhere he declaimed verse[37] which was

34 Best.D39 (summer 1716); 'With a polite satirical song we have quelled the fops who but for us would have swamped the town.'

35 Roger de Bussy-Rabutin, author of the *Histoire amoureuse des Gaules* (1665).

36 Best.D17809 (*c.* 1 July 1772).

37 Perhaps the satirical *J'ai vu*, wrongly attributed to Voltaire, who tells us in Best.D16267 that it was in fact by Antoine Louis Lebrun, father of the poet who later introduced the little Marie Corneille to Ferney. It was of the *J'ai vu* that Voltaire wrote a few years later, in a passage afterwards suppressed: 'I remember that at this time, passing through a small provincial place, the wits of the town asked me to recite this composition'; *Lettres sur Œdipe* (1719).

free-thinking in matters of morality and religion, properly forbade him her house. . . . Father Couvrigny, Jesuit, being at Caen, also saw Voltaire and was charmed by his genius.'[38]

These lines are the sole and unique source of everything that has been said about Voltaire at Caen. They were clearly written some years, perhaps even a number of years after the event; the writer obtained his information from père André, who in turn had it from his collegues of the Collège de Caen, who were probably retailing gossip. However, the story is quite plausible, for Françoise d'Osseville (*née* Scelles) and Couvrigny were in fact at Caen at that time, and were the kind of people to whom the youth would have been attracted. Mme d'Osseville does not appear to have been physically attractive: she says herself that 'la Maigreur de tout point'

> a fait un cruel ravage
> Sur mon corps et sur mon visage. . . .

> Ayant trouvé ma seureté
> Dans peu d'attraits et de beauté,
> Je me trouve dédommagée
> D'en estre si mal partagée.[39]

But she was a poet of sorts, and if any other lived then at Caen (unless it was Verrières), his fame has not come down to us. As for father Couvrigny, he was a Jesuit schoolmaster, and something of a debauchee[40]: the combination was clearly ready made to attract the young exile.

Voltaire may have been sent to Caen to get him out of Paris while waiting to go to The Hague; or his father may have decided to exile him to the Netherlands on receiving a report of his life at

38 These passages are from a manuscript by Charles de Quens (Caen MS. 4° 154, pp. 212, 297); they were published by [Antoine] Charma and G[eorges] Mancel, *Le Père André, jésuite* (Caen 1844), i.145n, and more completely by Armand Gasté, 'Voltaire à Caen en 1713', *Mémoires de l'Académie nationale des sciences, arts et belles-lettres de Caen* (Caen 1901), p. 251.

39 Gasté, pp. 259-60. 'Emaciation has cruelly ravaged all my body and face. . . . Realising that I owe my safety to my lack of beauty and attractions, I consider myself sufficiently compensated for my meagre endowments.'

40 [Pierre Joseph] Odolant-Desnos, *Mémoires historiques sur la ville d'Alençon* (Alençon 1787), ii.523; his presence at Caen in 1713 is confirmed by the *Journal d'un bourgeois de Caen, 1652-1733*, edited by G. Mancel (Caen 1848).

Caen. The former hypothesis fits the dates, for Voltaire reached the Dutch capital in October or November, a few weeks only after the new ambassador made his entry. The young man's godfather (who died in 1708) had a brother[41] in the foreign service, Pierre Antoine de Castagnéry, marquis de Châteauneuf, ambassador successively at Constantinople and at Lisbon, and appointed since September 1713 to The Hague, after the treaty of Utrecht (April 1713) had saved France from a final disaster. It was he who agreed to take charge of the young poet. Like many a father of a brilliant son the dusty Arouet thought that he could smother François's literary tastes by sending him away from home. The idea was foolish, and its execution even more so, for at this time the Netherlands were overrun by Frenchmen who had escaped from religious and other persecutions at home. The young attaché naturally gravitated to these people, with unexpected consequences: Voltaire was already one of those over-life-size personages who seem perpetually to attract equally extraordinary events. Even his first love affair conformed to this rule.

Among the refugees whom Voltaire frequented was a mme Du Noyer, who, having ruined her husband, fled to England and then to the Netherlands, where she scraped a living by methods more adventurous than respectable. Her chief activity was the kind of journalism that mingles insinuations and lies with measured doses of the more libellous kind of truth. This lady also had an expendable stock-in-trade: two daughters. She held that a girl should marry first with an eye to the main chance, and a second time for pleasure. In accordance with this elegant principle she had married one daughter to an elderly and wealthy officer on active service: a match the attractions of which are obvious. Another daughter, Catherine Olympe, remained in stock. Olympe had already been engaged to the Camisard hero Jean Cavalier, who left her; after the Voltaire episode her mother married her (after she had passed through the hands of the writer Guyot de Merville) to a 'count' or 'baron' de Winterfeldt—but she was hoist by her own petard, for this nobleman turned out to be an adventurer like herself, named Borillet.

41 Arouet had acted for both brothers in business affairs; see Ar- chives nationales: Minutier central, lvii.309, cote 48.

Olympe (she seems to have been called Pimpette, romantically transformed in her mother's fiction to Annoucha) was barely literate, and no intellectual giant, but she was kind and pretty; when she met the exiled poet at the French embassy she won him and became his mistress. François had the generous instincts of nineteen, and wanted to marry her. But he also had the poverty of nineteen, and was known to be in disgrace at home. Such a match clearly did not suit mme Du Noyer's book and she complained to the ambassador, who was certainly even more anxious to prevent the marriage. He decided to send the young prodigal back to Paris, and in the meanwhile confined him to the house. A clandestine correspondence followed. 'Read your letter downstairs and have confidence in the bearer. I believe, my dear madame, that you love me; so be ready to use all the strength of your mind on this occasion. . . . I must absolutely leave, and leave without seeing you. You can imagine my sorrow. . . . Farewell once again my dear mistress; think a little of your unhappy lover, but do not think of him to be sad.'[42] Three days later followed:

I am a prisoner here in the name of the king, but they have the power only to take my life, not my love for you. Yes, my adorable beloved, I will see you this evening, even if this puts my head on the block. For god's sake don't talk to me in such mournful terms as those of your letter; live, and be discreet: beware of your mother, for she is your cruellest enemy. What do I say! Beware of everybody, trust nobody, be ready as soon as the moon appears, I will leave the hotel incognito, I will take a coach or chaise, we will go like the wind to Schevelin [Scheveningen], I will bring ink and paper, we will write our letters. But if you love me, console yourself; gather all your virtue and presence of mind, control yourself when you are with your mother, try to bring your portrait, and be sure that not even the greatest sufferings will prevent me from serving you. No, nothing is capable of detaching me from you: our love is based on virtue, it will last as long as our life. Order the cobbler to go for a chaise: but no, I don't want you to trust him. Be ready at four o'clock, I will wait for you near your street. Farewell, there is nothing I will not risk for you, you deserve much more. Farewell, my dear heart.[43]

The girl was by no means unwilling, as testifies this charming letter, the spelling and grammar of which I have tried to imitate; it is not much worse than that of most educated eighteenth-century women:

42 Best.D7 (*c.* 25 November 1713).   43 Best.D8 (*c.* 28 November 1713).

In the unsertainty in which i am whether i shall have the pleasure of seeing you this evening I warn you that it wassnt la Vruijere who wass yesterday at our place, twas a misunderstanding by the cobler's wife who a larmed us for nothing at all. My mother does not suspec at all that I have spoken to you and tank heaven she thinks that you have alredy left. I wont speak to you of my health, its what worries me least and I tink too much about you to ave the tim to tink of myself. I asure you my dear heart that if i douted your tanderness my troubles would regoice me. Yes, my dear chile, life would be too great a burden if i did not have the tender ope of being loved by what is dearest to me in all the world. Do what you can so that i can see you this evening, you need only dessend innto the kitchen of the cobler and i asure you that you have nothing to fear for our maker of quintessances[44] thinks that you are already half-wey to Paris, sothat if you want to i shall have the pleasure of seeing you thisevening and ifit cannot be alew me to go to morow to mass at the house. I will big m^r de la Bruyere to showe me the chapel, curiausities is permitted to wimman and then *as if nothing were the mater* i will ask him if they yet had any news of you and sin se wen you were gone. Don't refusse me tis favvour, my dear Arouet, i ask it of you in the nam of what is most tender, that is, in the name of the love i have for you. Fare well my amiable chile, i adore you and i swear to you that my love will last aslon as my life.

Dunoyer

At least i i have not the pleasure of seeing you do not refuse me the satisfaction of reseiving you dere news.[45]

44 Her mother, who contributed to (and possibly edited) *La Quintessence des nouvelles historiques, critiques, politiques, morales et galantes,* an anti-French sheet published at The Hague.

45 Best.D14 (6 December 1713). 'Dans l'insertitude où ie suis si i'aurais le plaisir de te voir se soir ie t'averti que se n'esstes pas la Vruijere qui estet hyer chés nous, s'et une méprise de la cordonière qui nous a larma for mal à propos. Ma mère ne se doute poin que ie t'aye parllée et grasse au Ciel elle te croi dégat parti. Ie ne te parllerai poin de ma santée, s'et se qui me touche le moin et ie panse trop à toy pour à voir le tans de panser à moi mesmes. Ie t'asure mon cher coeur que si ie doutatit de ta tandraisse ie me régouirai de mon mal. Ouy mon cher anfan la vie me serait trop à charge si ie n'avais la douse espairance d'estre haimée de se que i'ai de plus cher au monde. Fait se que tu poura pour que ie te voye se soir, tu n'aura qu'uà dessandre deans la cuisine du cordonier et ie te répon que tu n'a rien à creindre car notre faiseuse de quintessance te crois dégat à moitiés chemein de Paris eins si tu le veu i'aurai le plaisir de te voir sesoir et si sella ne se peut permait moÿ d'aller de mein à la messe à l'hôtel. Ie prirai m^r de la Bruyere de me montrai la chapelle, la curiausités est permise au famme et puis san *faire semblan de rien* ie lui demanderai si l'on n'a pas an corre de tes nouvelle et de puis q'uan tu es parti. Ne me refusse pas sete grasse mon cher Arouet, ie te la demande au non de se qu'il y a de plus tandre, s'est à dire au non de l'amour que i'ai pour toy. A dieu mon haimable anfan, ie t'adore et ie te jurre que mon àmour durera auteans que ma vie.

Dunoyer

Au moins ie ie n'ais pas le plaisir de te voir ne me refuse pas la satisfaction de reservoir de tes cherre nouvelle'.

An assignation was made, and Olympe came to Voltaire dressed as a man; but the plot was discovered, the elopement prevented, and the youth was duly shipped back to France. The correspondence between the lovers continued for a while, and then separation and pressure on both sides did their work. Yet three years later, when Voltaire was arrested, the letter I have just quoted was found on him. In later years, when Olympe was criticised, he defended her warmly[46], at least once he sent her a present[47], when she was in need he helped her[48], and in 1754 he was still writing to her[49]. At the time of her affair with Voltaire she seems to have been a simple, affectionate girl, with strong maternal instincts. This perhaps explains the rather rapid transfer of her affections to Guyot de Merville[50], who addressed her, among more normal epithets, as his 'chère maman'[51]. Much later this became Voltaire's nickname for mme Denis[52]. The term takes its place alongside Olympe's 'mon cher enfant' to Voltaire.

46 *Supplément au Siècle de Louis XIV* (1753).
47 Best.D1115 (16 July 1736), D1118 (30 July 1736).
48 Best.D4397 (22 February 1751).
49 Best.D5652 (5 February 1754).

50 Best.D1531 (23 June 1738).
51 Best.D14n.
52 The case is by no means unique; cp. Robert Blake, *Disraeli* (London 1966), p. 99.

5. *Love, satire and second exile,*
1713-1716

VOLTAIRE EMBARKED at Rotterdam for Ghent, and reached Paris on Christmas eve 1713[1]. He went first to see Tournemine, from whom he learned that his father was in a high tantrum. It was still possible at this time, and indeed until the revolution, for a father to obtain an order for the imprisonment of his children without any process of law. Arouet had secured such a *lettre de cachet*[2], threatened his son with it and with exile to the West Indies. So the young man went into hiding, and only a pathetically submissive letter saved him, for the moment, from jail or exile, though not from being disinherited. 'I agree, my dear father, to go to America, and even to live there on bread and water, on condition that before I leave you allow me to embrace your knees.'[3] The youth also had to agree to be articled to a lawyer, and in mid-January he entered 'en pension'[4] the office of maître Alain, rue Pavée-Saint-Bernard, near the steps of the place Maubert.

There he absorbed some of the higher and lower mysteries of legal chicane: they were not unprofitable to him in later years. It was also in maître Alain's office that Voltaire met a young man whose tastes were then very similar to his own, who had a genuine love for literature and a prodigious memory for verse, whose affection and admiration for his friend were surpassed only by his solicitude for his own comfort and interest. He neglected nearly all the openings Voltaire made for him, and was content to spend

---

1 Best.D20 (28 December 1713).
2 *lettre de cachet.* This was technically any order signed and sealed by the king, but in general parlance the term was applied to an order of imprisonment or exile issued without trial or hearing, and usually without any specified charge.

3 Best.D19 (*c.* 25 December 1713); only this fragment has survived, and I do not swear that it is authentic, since it derives ultimately from Duvernet; but something very like this was certainly written.
4 Best.D22 (20 January 1714).

his life as a professional guest in comfortable homes, living as his 'trumpet' on his friend's fame and generosity, and doing such little jobs as Voltaire forced on him: doing them not very conscientiously, with indifferent loyalty, and even on occasion dishonestly. All these things will emerge in due course, as will Voltaire's unshakeable love (no other word will do) for his shiftless friend, who did not even have any redeeming vice. It would be difficult to find another example of so great a man loving so mean a one for so long. But all this is in the future. For the moment Voltaire had found a kindred soul in Nicolas Claude Thieriot, and with him talked and laughed away the stuffy days of legal drudgery.

Voltaire once said that 'nearly all those who have made a name in the arts cultivated them in spite of their parents . . . in them nature has always been stronger than education'[5]. He was refering to Molière, but could hardly have helped thinking of himself, for his legal studies by no means prevented him from doing a very different kind of writing. First he dashed off his vitriolic criticism of the abbé Du Jarry, then, while in the mood, a bitter verse satire against Antoine Houdard de La Motte, who had voted for the abbé. This *Bourbier*, though written in a sort of fake archaic style, sealed Voltaire's mastery of poetic technique; as for its tone, Voltaire afterwards regretted it, no doubt because Houdard, a better man than he was a poet (though he is no mean versifier), took it with the same good humour that he showed a young man who had smacked his face. 'Sir,' said he to the agressor, 'you are going to be very upset, for I am blind.' He became one of Voltaire's warmest admirers, and Voltaire, with one exception, did not write another verse satire for over forty years. The world of letters is not always a cockpit.

At about the same time (1714) Voltaire wrote the *Anti-Giton*, an allegorical satire on a nobleman well known for his sexual inversion. It was light-hearted, but this did not prevent Voltaire from slipping in a sceptical allusion to Sodom and Gomorrah. The chief interest of the poem for us lies in the fact that it was originally dedicated to mlle Duclos, the actress, whose name was afterwards

5 *Vie de Molière* (1739).

replaced by that of the celebrated and admirable Lecouvreur, after she had 'buried the Duclos'[6]. This she did in more senses than one, for while Voltaire became mlle Lecouvreur's lover, he seems to have been less lucky with mlle Duclos. By the middle of June 1751 he was complaining to the marquise de Mimeure that he had wasted his time in addressing poetry to the actress, for 'she takes every morning a few pinches of senna and cloves, and in the evening several helpings of the comte d'Uzès'[7]. And at about the same time he told a woman friend:

> Mon cœur de la Duclos fut quelque temps charmé;
> L'amour en sa faveur avait monté ma lyre:
> Je chantais la Duclos; d'Uzès en fut aimé:
> C'était bien la peine d'écrire![8]

Happy days, when love was sometimes taken lightly, and a poet could mention one mistress to another! We have no definite information about mme de Montbrun, but with the sprightly marquise Voltaire had a warm and fairly prolonged love-affair. It was ended, indeed, only by Voltaire's exile, and a few charming letters to her have survived[9]. They remained friends, as he nearly always did with the women he had loved, and when a few years later she was attacked by cancer and had to have a breast removed, Voltaire visited her, assuring mme de Bernières (it would not do to claim that jealousy was entirely unknown!) that even Eteocles would have visited Polynices if he had been operated upon for cancer.[10]

Back in Paris Voltaire returned to the Temple like a homing pigeon; the old circle had been augmented by Vendôme[11] (returned from exile at Lyons) and Caumartin and Arenberg, Hénault (of whom we shall see more), Aydie and Froulay (whom he called 'the two parfait gentle knights'[12])—they all became his friends. To Caumartin, in particular, he owed much. Louis Urbain Lefèvre

---

6 Best.D254 (18 October 1725).

7 Best.D27 (*c.* 25 June 1715).

8 *Epître à madame de Montbrun-Villefranche*; 'For a while my heart was bewitched by the Duclos; for her sake love had strung my lyre; I sang the Duclos; she loved Uzès: I need not have troubled to write.'

9 Best.D28, D40, D82, D85-6 (1715-19).

10 Best.D220 (*c.* 25 October 1725). Eteocles and Polynices were the sons of Oedipus by his mother Jocasta; they killed each other in single combat.

11 His brother the duc de Vendôme had died in the meanwhile.

12 Best.D987 (13 January 1736).

de Caumartin, marquis de Saint-Ange, invited the young Arouet to his seat near Fontainebleau. The old gentleman had held high office under Louis XIV, being famous for his rare integrity. Proud of the past, with a prodigious memory for its doings, he gossiped at will about the reign of the late king. Saint-Simon pays tribute to his wonderful memory, his honesty, and his respectability, even though he deplored his insolence in wearing velvet and silk although he belonged only to the minor nobility. Caumartin inspired the impressionable young man with his own veneration for Henri IV. The *Henriade* was the result, for it was begun at Saint-Ange, and possibly the *Siècle de Louis XIV* might not have been undertaken without the innumerable anecdotes learned at the feet of the old man who

> porte en son cerveau
> De son temps l'histoire vivante;
> Caumartin est toujours nouveau
> A mon oreille qu'il enchante;
> Car dans sa tête sont écrits
> Et tous les faits et tous les dits
> Des grands hommes, des beaux esprits;
> Mille charmantes bagatelles,
> Des chansons vieilles et nouvelles,
> Et les annales immortelles
> Des ridicules de Paris.[13]

Of course the freedoms the *libertins* permitted themselves were dangerous. Vendôme had been exiled, Servien exiled and imprisoned. All this was changed when the death of Louis XIV (1 September 1715) and the setting aside of his will brought to the head of affairs that same Philippe of Orléans whom the old king, his uncle, had called a 'flaunter of vice', but whose liberality of character and open intelligence went far beyond mere indulgence. The regent was indeed in many ways the child of the *libertins*, whose principles of sceptical hedonism now spread rapidly through the tight upper structure of the *ancien régime*, in a manner and

13 *Epître à monsieur le prince de Vendôme* (1717); 'carries in his memory the living story of his time; Caumartin is always fresh to my ear, which he delights; for in his head are written all the doings and all the sayings of the great men, of the wits; a thousand charming trifles, old and new songs, and the immortal annals of Parisian absurdities.'

with a speed closely paralleled in modern times by the successive reigns of Victoria and Edward VII.

Voltaire was now at his ease, in the highest of spirits, and relishing to the full the freer intellectual climate. Yet, though always ready for every sort of mental libertinism, Voltaire never shared the Templars' view that wit could flow only in alcohol. He advised one of his friends to drink

> parmi les douceurs d'une agréable vie,
> Un peu plus d'hypocras, un peu moins d'eau-de-vie[14].

Voltaire himself preferred hippocrene even to hippocras, but then he always suffered from a weak stomach.

Obviously the young man was no headlong debauchee, but still, he was young, and was often carried away by his own exuberant brilliance. In a society in which it was hardly possible to go too far he managed to do it, and succeeded in offending even the regent. When Voltaire encouraged the duc d'Arenberg to make love to the girls of Flanders, and to fill with bastards the country-side decimated by war[15]; when he told a distinguished soldier that his victory against the Turks would be hollow unless he also cuckolded the Grand Turk[16]; when he implored the duchesse de Béthune to be kinder and less devout:

> La nuit s'avance avec vitesse;
> Profite de l'éclat du jour:
> Les plaisirs ont leur temps, la sagesse a son tour.
> Dans ta jeunesse fait l'amour,
> Et ton salut dans ta vieillesse[17];

when he reproached another lady in even more precise terms:

> Vous m'avez donc quitté pour votre directeur. . . .
> D'un triste préjugé victime déplorable,
> Vous croyez servir Dieu; mais vous servez le diable,
> Et c'est lui seul que vous craignez. . . .
> Allez, s'il est un Dieu, sa tranquille puissance

14 *Epître à monsieur le duc d'Arenberg* (c. 1716); 'amidst the pleasures of an agreeable life, a little more hippocras, a little less brandy.'

15 same *Epître*.

16 *Epître à monsieur le prince Eugène* (1716).

17 *Epître à une dame un peu mondaine et trop dévote* (1715); 'The night advances speedily; profit from the brightness of the day: there is a time for pleasure, wisdom takes its turn. Make love in your youth, and seek salvation in your old age.'

65

Ne s'abaissera point à troubler nos amours:
Vos baisers pourraient-ils déplaire à sa clémence?
La loi de la nature est sa première loi;
Elle seule autrefois conduisit nos ancêtres;
Elle parle plus haut que la voix de vos prêtres,
Pour vous, pour vos plaisirs, pour l'amour, et pour moi[18];

when the young man indulged in such bold flights as these, the regent and his boon companions applauded; a prince of the blood did not flinch, was even flattered when Arouet exclaimed at his table 'Are we all princes or all poets?'[19] But the indulgence even of the most liberal of princes had and has its limits, and the whole art of the courtier consists in sensing the invisible and variable line which surrounds his master, even if that master is also his friend. This art Voltaire never acquired, and we shall see him again and again stepping over the magic circle. This first time, it must be admitted, he did not so much step over the line as trample on the regent's most sensitive corns—not that he approached the virulence of the *Philippiques* by his senior Lagrange-Chancel, who lacked Voltaire's graceful posture.

Among the offences of which public rumour accused Orléans perhaps the most unconventional was incest with his daughter Marie Louise, duchesse de Berry, an accusation the more deeply resented by them because it was almost certainly true. Voltaire found the subject irresistible, and nothing conveys the atmosphere of the time better than the lines he wrote on this theme, and those in which he disavowed them. This is the epigram he addressed to the regent's daughter:

Enfin votre esprit est guéri
Des craintes du vulgaire;
Belle duchesse de Berry,
Achevez le mystère.

18 *Epître à madame de G**** (1716); 'So you have left me for your confessor. . . . Deplorable victim of a wretched prejudice, you think to serve god; but you are serving the devil, and it is only him whom you fear. . . . Consider, if there is a god, his calm power would not lower itself to trouble our love: could your kisses displease his clemency? The law of nature is his first law; it alone formerly guided our ancestors; it speaks more loudly than the voice of our priests for you, for you pleasures, for love, and for me.' In the same epistle occurs the even more dangerous line 'D'un double Testament la chimérique histoire', 'The chimerical history of a twofold Testament'.

19 See pp. 87, 625-626 below.

Un nouveau Lot vous sert d'époux,
　　Mère des Moabites:
Puisse bientôt naître de vous
　　Un peuple d'Ammonites![20]

As for his disavowal, Voltaire took the line that he could not have written this epigram because

Un rimeur sorti des jésuites
Des peuples de l'ancienne loi
Ne connaît que les Sodomites[21].

A biography of Voltaire is also the history of a social transformation. Louis XIV would undoubtedly have punished this kind of humour very severely, and, as evolution never proceeds smoothly (*natura non facit saltum* is one of the falsest of apophthegms), so in due course did Louis XV. When this monarch arrested the young pretender, one Desforges[22] expressed the popular indignation in this couplet:

Peuple jadis si fier, aujourd'hui si servile,
Des princes malheureux vous n'êtes plus l'asile.[23]

For this fairly mild criticism of the king's action Desforges was kept for three years in an iron cage in the fortress of Mont-Saint-Michel[24]. This was in 1749, and we shall presently encounter even later examples of morbid royal sensibility.

The regent, confronted by Voltaire's far graver satire, laughed, and merely exiled the youth to Tulle, and that so half-heartedly that a fortnight later he was still in Paris, the place of exile being then changed to Sully-sur-Loire[24]. This means that the exile was no punishment at all, for at Sully was the great house of the same name, and there Voltaire was soon installed as the guest of the bachelor duc de Sully, his fellow-disciple of the Temple, and his

20 *A madame la duchesse de Berry* (1716); 'At last your mind is cured of the fears of the vulgar; lovely duchesse de Berry, complete the mystery. Mother of the Moabites, a new Lot serves as your husband: may you soon give birth to a race of Ammonites.'
21 *Au régent* (1716); 'A rhymer educated by the Jesuits among the peoples of the ancient law knows only the Sodomites.'
22 Desforges had some connection with Voltaire, for he was the author of a *Lettre critique sur la tragédie de Sémi-ramis* [1748].
23 'People once so proud, today so servile, you are no longer the refuge of unhappy princes.'
24 Best.D29-31 (4-21 May 1716).

friend—of a kind, as we shall see. In this most agreeable of all sojourns he lacked nothing but the freedom to leave[25]. Sully, he told mme de Mimeure, 'est dans la plus belle situation du monde. Il y a un bois magnifique dont tous les arbres sont découpés par des polissons ou des amants qui se sont amusés à écrire leurs noms sur l'écorce.

> A voir tant de chiffres tracés
> Et tant de noms entrelacés,
> Il n'est pas mal aisé de croire
> Qu'autrefois le beau Céladon
> A quitté les bords du Lignon
> Pour aller à Sully sur Loire. . . .

Vous seriez peut-être étonnée si je vous disais que dans ce beau bois . . . nous avons des nuits blanches comme à Sceaux.'[26] He did not, like most visitors, spend these fine days in murdering partridges. He was on good terms with Apollo, but not with Diana.[27]

It was at Sully that Voltaire began that wonderful series of letters in prose and verse written during the next few years in the country houses of his friends, Maisons, Sceaux, Bélébat, La Source, Bruel, Richelieu, and others. There for the first time Voltaire tasted the pleasures of civilised life in the countryside, away from the tiring if amusing distractions of the capital.

Chaulieu told[28] Voltaire that there was only one road back to favour, and he took it:

> Malgré le penchant de mon cœur
> A vos conseils je m'abandonne.
> Quoy, je vais devenir flatteur?
> Et c'est Chaulieu qui me l'ordonne![29]

25 Best.D32 (11 July 1716), 41 (summer 1716).

26 Best.D41 (summer 1716); 'is in the loveliest setting in the world. There is a magnificent forest in which all the trees have been cut by rascals or lovers who have amused themselves by writing their names on the bark. On seeing written so many monograms, and so many intertwined names, it is not difficult to believe that once upon a time the handsome Celadon left the banks of the Lignon to go to Sully on the Loire. . . . You would perhaps be surprised if I told you that in this beautiful forest . . . we have white nights like those of Sceaux.'

27 Best.D42 (September 1716).

28 Best.D33 (16 July 1716).

29 Best.D35 (20 July 1716). 'For all the inclination of my heart I yield to your advice. What! I am to become a flatterer? And it is Chaulieu who orders me to do it!'

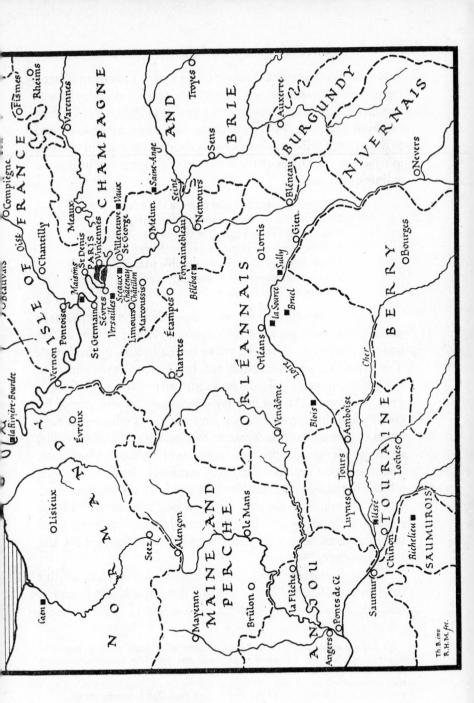

Map of the country houses visited by Voltaire in his youth.

And Chaulieu was right. Nobody could wish a Voltaire to flatter a mere tyrant, a petty prince, or even the great monarchs he was later to know, but such magnanimity as that of Philippe of Orléans deserved a sacrifice. Voltaire must have seen this, for he addressed to the regent a full-dress epistle heavy-laden with graceful unction, in which he went through the formality of denying that he was the author of the satire.

> J'implore ta justice, et non point ta clémence.
> Lis seulement ces vers, et juge de leur prix;
> Vois ce que l'on m'impute, et vois ce que j'écris.
> La libre vérité qui règne en mon ouvrage
> D'une âme sans reproche est le noble partage;
> Et de tes grands talents le sage estimateur
> N'est point de ces couplets l'infâme et vil auteur.[30]

In the eighteenth century, as under Edward VII, appearance was all; one could get away with almost anything so long as one was not caught, or, if caught, swore solemnly that 'it wasn't me'. The expedient was successful, and in October 1716, after five months of enjoyable exile, the poet returned to Paris, to his father's great annoyance. Arouet *père* regarded a poet as one 'cursed by God'[31], and disapproved of his son's release. 'Perhaps you have heard, monseigneur', he wrote to the marquis de Goussainville, an eminent judge who became the trustee of Voltaire's inheritance, 'that the regent has been pleased to recall my son from his exile, which I found less of an affliction than this far too precipitate recall, which will complete the ruin of this young man drunk with the success of his poetry and the praises and the reception he received from the great, who, with all the respect I owe them, are for him sheer poisoners.'[32]

The arid attorney was utterly mistaken, and anyway by this time his son's fate had been dared and determined: his reputation was established well beyond the open circle of his friends. As

---

30 *Epître à monsieur le duc d'Orléans, régent* (1716), 112-18; 'I implore your justice and not your clemency. Only read these lines and judge of their worth; see what is imputed to me, and see what I write. The frank truth which reigns in my work is the noble quality of a soul without reproach; and the judicious esteemer of your great talents is not the infamous and vile author of these couplets.'

31 Best.D38 (summer 1716).

32 Best.D37 (summer 1716).

early as October 1718, when printing one of Voltaire's letters in verse and prose[33], the editor of the *Nouveau mercure galant* was able to remark that the author's reputation was a sufficient guarantee of the merits of his writings. This was the first Voltaire letter to see print: twenty thousand more were to follow.

33 Best.D43 (20 October 1716).

6. The Bastille and third exile, 1717-1718

IT IS NO WONDER that the youth did not return to his father's house, or soon left it if he did. He kept very quiet for a few months, spending much of his time at Saint-Ange. Indeed, no letter by him has been found between his release in October 1716 and May 1717, when a police spy called Beauregard found him living at the inn of the Panier vert, in the rue de la Calandre, near his birthplace. The *agent provocateur* (if he is to be believed) trapped Voltaire into admitting that he was the author of another satire, this time in Latin, on the same subject, lines known from the opening words as the *Puero regnante*[1]. However, I think that the spy is not to be believed, for it is really most unlikely that even the impetuous young Voltaire, in conversation at an inn with a stranger, should have exclaimed, as quoted by Beauregard: 'What! you don't know what that bugger [the regent] did to me? He exiled me because I told the public that his Messalina of a daughter is a whore.'[2] This and more of the same kind Beauregard reported[3] to his superiors, with the result thus described by Voltaire with the utmost good humour:

> Or ce fut donc par un matin, sans faute,
> En beau printemps, un jour de Pentecôte,
> Qu'un bruit étrange en sursaut m'éveilla.
> Un mien valet, qui du soir était ivre:
> 'Maître', dit-il, 'le Saint-Esprit est là;
> C'est lui sans doute, et j'ai lu dans mon livre
> Qu'avec vacarme il entre chez les gens.'

1 See Best.D45, note 3; as this mock inscription, which created a vast scandal, has been published only in Latin, here is a translation: 'A boy [Louis xv] reigning, a man [the regent Philippe of Orléans] notorious for poisoning and incest ruling, with ignorant and unstable councils and more unstable religion, an exhausted treasury, public confidence violated, in peril of an imminent general revolt, the fatherland sacrificed to an iniquitous and premature hope of the crown, France about to perish.' This kind of thing was being said and sung all over Paris.

2 Best.D45 (c. 10 May 1717).

3 Best.D45, D52 (c. 19 May 1717).

Et moi de dire alors entre mes dents:
'Gentil puîné de l'essence suprême,
Beau Paraclet, soyez le bienvenu;
N'êtes-vous pas celui qui fait qu'on aime?'

En achevant ce discours ingénu
Je vois paraître au bout de ma ruelle,
Non un pigeon, non une colombelle,
De l'Esprit saint oiseau tendre et fidèle,
Mais vingt corbeaux de rapine affamés,
Monstres crochus que l'enfer a formés. . . .[4]

In plain prose, the young man was arrested and imprisoned in the Bastille during the night of 16/17 May 1717. His papers were examined, even hunted in the nauseous cesspool that passed for a drain[5], all this by *lettre de cachet*, without any process of law[6]. When arrested Voltaire bantered the officers, sympathised with them for having to work on a holiday, hoped that he would not be deprived of his milk, expressed delight at this opportunity to see again a place he knew so well from his visits to the duc de Richelieu (who had also met with this fashionable fate), and hoped that he would not be freed too soon[7]. A few days later he wrote to the governor, at whose table he dined[8], for the Bastille was all things to all men, to ask for a few comforts:

deux livre d'Homer latin grec
deux mouchoirs d'indienne, deux
un petit bonnet

---

4 *La Bastille* (1717); 'And so it was one morning, to be precise a day of Pentecost, in a fine spring, that a strange noise awakened me with a start. My servant, who had been drunk that evening, "Master", said he, "the Holy Ghost is here; it is certainly he, and I have read in my book that it is with much noise that he comes to one." And I then said between clenched teeth: "Noble cadet of the supreme essence, splendid Paraclete, welcome; are you not he who makes people love?" As I ended this ingenuous discourse I saw coming into sight at the end of my alley, not a pigeon, not a young dove, tender and faithful bird of the holy Ghost, but twenty famished crows of rapine, crooked monsters shaped in hell. . . .'

5 Best.D54 (21 May 1717).

6 Best.D46-51 (15-17 May 1717); a perfunctory interrogation followed the imprisonment; I have printed the text as Best.app.D5.

7 Best.D48 (16 May 1717).

8 On one occasion at least in company with Louis Bénigne de Bauffremont, marquis de Listenois, who was briefly imprisoned because he had subscribed himself with insufficient ceremony, when writing to marshals of France, 'parfaitement à vous' and 'tout à vous'; see *Les Correspondants de la marquise de Balleroy* (Paris 1883), i.187.

Deux Cravattes
une Coeffe de nuit
Une petite bouteille d'essence de geroufle.

Aroüet

ce jeudy 21ᵉ may 1717[9]

In short, Voltaire certainly did not suffer too much in the Bastille. At the moment the worst thing that happened to him took place outside: for he was betrayed by the girl he loved, mlle Livry. The lucky man was Voltaire's close friend Génonville; but the strongest thing that he found to say (three years later it is true) was:

> Je sais que par déloyauté
> Le fripon naguère a tâté
> De la maîtresse tant jolie
> Dont j'étais si fort entêté.
> Un autre eût pu s'en courroucer;
> Mais je sais qu'il faut se passer
> Des bagatelles dans la vie.[10]

And after another three years he had so completely forgotten his friend's offence that he was able to address to his memory the moving *Epître aux mânes de m. de Génonville,* in which he displays feelings his enemies have always denied to him. As for the girl, Voltaire never forgot her, and his reproaches even to her were sympathetic:

> Un cœur tendre, un esprit volage,
> Un sein d'albâtre, et de beaux yeux.
> Avec tant d'attraits précieux,
> Hélas! qui n'eût été friponne?[11]

Now and presently she merely crosses our stage. Legend has it that Voltaire called on her (she was now marquise de Gouvernet) just before his death, and found the old lady seated below Largillière's portrait of him.

9 Best.D53 (21 May 1717). 'Two volumes of Homer, Latin-Greek; two linen handkerchiefs, two; a little bonnet; two cravats; a night-cap; a little bottle of essence of cloves.'

10 Best.D91 (18 August 1720). 'I know that the rascal at that time disloyally tasted the lovely mistress by whom I was obsessed. Another might have taken this very ill; but I know that in this life we must do without trifles.'

11 *Epître des vous et des tu* (c. 1730); 'A tender heart, a fickle mind, an alabaster bosom, and lovely eyes. With so many precious attractions, who, alas, would not be naughty?'

While in prison Arouet composed part of the *Henriade*, and changed his name. Hundreds of pages have been rather unprofitably blackened on this subject. How he changed it leaves little doubt, the new name being an anagram of the old. Why he changed it is even more obvious: for the same reason that Poquelin became Molière. Had the name of the world's greatest poet been Wigglestick, who could have blamed him for changing it to Shakespeare? If anything more need be said on this subject let Casanova have the last word: 'Voltaire could not have become immortal under the name of Arouet. The doors of the temple would have been closed in his face, and he would have been forbidden access to it. He would have felt himself degraded by hearing himself always named *à rouer* [to be beaten].'[12]

Among the treasures of the Pierpont Morgan library is the first letter written over the new name, addressed to the earl of Ashburnham:

à Chatenay ce 12 juin [1718]

Milord,

Vous êtes une divinité à qui j'ay recours ordinairement dans mes tribulations. Souvenez vous qu'autrefois vous m'avez prêté deux chevaux? Je vous demande àprésent la moitié de cette grâce. Ayez la charité de confier un de vos coursiers au porteur. J'aurai l'honneur de vous le renvoyer dans quelque jours; si vous ne pouvez point me prêter de cheval, pardonez moy du moins la liberté que je prends de vous le demander.

Je suis toujours avec bien du respect et de la reconnaissance
   Milord
      Votre très humble et obéissant serviteur

Arouet de Voltaire[13]

In the meanwhile, after just on eleven months, Voltaire was released and exiled[14] from Paris, this time to Châtenay[15], where, it will be remembered, his father had a house. He made the usual

12 *Histoire de ma vie,* ii.x (édition intégrale, Wiesbaden &c. 1960, ii.268).
13 Best.D62; 'You are a divinity to whom I usually appeal in my tribulations. Do you remember that you once lent me two horses? I now ask you for half of that favour. Have the charity to confide one of your coursers to the bearer. I shall have the honour of sending it back to you in a few days. If you cannot lend me a horse, at least forgive me for the liberty I take in asking you for it.'
14 Imprisonment for offences against the state was always followed by exile, the distance from the court being proportionate, broadly speaking, to the gravity of the offence.
15 Best.D56-7 (both 10 April 1718).

declaration of innocence[16], this time true, and Voltaire tells us himself that the regent came to believe him[17]. Soon he was given permission to come to Paris, for a day, for a week, for a month[18], and in October 1718 this not very painful six months' exile was ended, just in time for the production of *Œdipe*.

The germ of the *Henriade* was not the only thing Voltaire brought out of the Bastille, nor the most important. *That* was invisible. He described it himself with an accuracy not often found in such introspective reflections:

> D'une injuste prison je subis la rigueur:
> Mais au moins de mon malheur
> Je sus tirer quelque avantage:
> J'appris à m'endurcir contre l'adversité,
> Et je me vis un courage
> Que je n'attendais pas de la légèreté
> Et des erreurs de mon jeune âge.[19]

The thoughts and studies of the young Huron, when in the Bastille, were certainly not too far removed from those of his creator.[20]

---

16 Best.D58-60 (15-19 April 1718).
17 *Lettres sur Œdipe*, i.
18 Best.D61-7 (May-October 1718).
19 *Epître à monsieur de La Faluère de Génonville*; 'I suffered the rigours of an unjust imprisonment, but at least I was able to draw some advantage from my misfortune: I learned to harden myself against adversity, and I found in myself a courage I had not expected from the flightiness and the errors of my youth.'
20 *L'Ingénu*, ix ff.

7. Œdipe *triumphs*, *1718*

FOR HIS FIRST MAJOR WORK Voltaire measured himself
against a long list of predecessors, of whom the greatest
were Sophocles and Corneille[1]—here was noble emulation
indeed! He started his tragedy when he was eighteen or nineteen,
and finished the first draft the following year; but then he encountered the conservatism of the Comédie française. 'Though I
was young when I wrote *Œdipe*', he said to Porée some years
later, 'I composed it practically as you see it today. I was full of
my reading of the ancients and of your lessons, and I knew the
Paris stage very little. I worked more or less as though I were in
Athens, I consulted monsieur Dacier[2], the Grecian. He advised
me to include a chorus in every scene in the Greek manner. This
was to advise me to walk about the streets of Paris in the gown of
Plato. I had much difficulty in getting the Parisian actors to consent to perform even the choruses which appear three or four
times in the play. I had even more to get accepted a tragedy almost without love[3]. . . . In a word, the actors who at that time
were little coxcombs and great lords, refused to produce the
play.'[4] The peripeteia of Voltaire's own life also interfered,
though the delay gave him the opportunity to revise his text, but
on 18 November 1718 *Œdipe* was finally produced. It was an
immediate and unique success[5]: indeed its record of thirty almost

1 But 'ce grand génie . . . malgré
Œdipe' ('this great genius . . . notwithstanding *Œdipe*') said Voltaire
unkindly, yet justly, much later (*Commentaires sur Corneille* [1761-62]; Voltaire 55, p. 797).

2 Scepticism has been expressed
about this advice from the famous
classical scholar; but his letter has now
been found (Best.D26; 25 September
1714) and exactly confirms Voltaire's
statement.

3 Rousseau, however, wrote: 'I

have for long been hearing marvels
about the young Arouet's *Œdipe*. I
have a very high opinion of this young
man, but I am deathly afraid lest he
has weakened the horror of his great
subject by mingling love with it'; see
*Correspondance de Jean-Baptiste Rous-
seau et de Brossette*, ed. Paul Bonnefon
(Paris 1910), i.111.

4 Best.D392 (7 January 1731).

5 See the references given in the
general note on Best.D70.

consecutive performances in its first run was not surpassed in Paris by any other eighteenth-century tragedy, and Voltaire's share of the profits, over 3000 francs, exceeded any previous figure.

Nevertheless opinions were acutely divided. At that time no play could be performed or openly printed without official permission. The censor to whom *Œdipe* had been submitted was Houdard de La Motte, whose *approbation*, instead of being couched in the usual formal terms, reads: 'On the performance of this play the public formed hopes of a worthy successor to Corneille and Racine; and I believe that on reading it they will not lessen their expectations.'⁶ So wrote the man whom Voltaire had regarded for a moment as his enemy; and this is the comment on it made by the man whom the youth loved as a friend and respected as a master:

> O la belle approbation!
> Qu'elle nous promet de merveilles!
> C'est la sûre prédiction
> De voir Voltaire un jour remplacer les Corneilles.
> Mais où diable la Motte as-tu pris cette erreur?
> Je te connoissois bien pour assez plat Auteur,
> Et sur-tout très méchant Poëte;
> Mais non pour un lâche Flatteur,
> Encor moins pour un faux Prophète.⁷

What was friendship to Chaulieu in the balance against an amusing epigram, especially as he hated Houdard? This is the dark side of hedonism.

Œdipe is Voltaire's first and most famous play, though by no means his best, and I therefore want to examine it in some modest detail.

This is the story of the play. Jocaste and Philoctète, prince of Euboea, were in love, but Jocaste had been made to marry Laius, king of Thebes. Philoctète goes into exile, but returns after

6 *Œdipe* (Paris 1719), p. [v]. Nevertheless Houdard de La Motte did not hesitate himself to produce not merely a single 'improved' *Œdipe* but two rival performances, one in verse, the other in prose. And why not?

7 *Œuvres de Chaulieu* (La Haye &c. 1774), ii.278. 'Oh the fine approbation! What marvels it promises us! It is the confident prediction of seeing Voltaire replace Corneille one day. But, La Motte, how the devil did you come to make this mistake? I knew you well as a rather dull author, and above all as a very bad poet, but not as a cowardly flatterer, and still less as a false prophet.'

ŒDIPE,

TRAGEDIE.

PAR MONSIEUR

DE VOLTAIRE

A PARIS,

Chez

Pierre Ribou, Quay des Augustins,
vis-à-vis la descente du Pont-Neuf,
a l'Image saint Louis.

AU PALAIS,
Pierre Huet, sur le second Perron de
la Ste Chapelle, au Soleil Levant.
Jean Mazuel, au Palais.
ET
Antoine-Urbain Coustelier,
Quay des Augustins.

M. DCC. XIX.

Avec Approbation, & Privilege du Roy.

3 *Œdipe, titlepage of the first edition,* Paris 1719

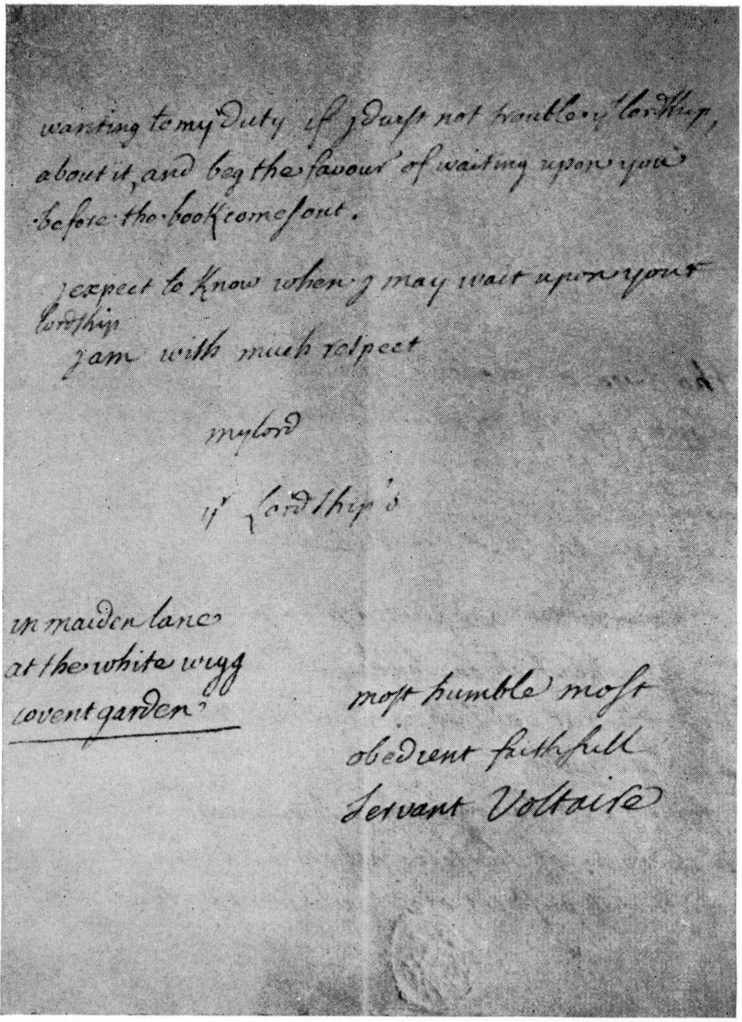

wanting to my Duty if j durst not trouble y^r lord^{ship},
about it, and beg the favour of waiting upon you
before the book come sout.

j expect to know when j may wait upon your
lordship
j am with much respect

mylord

y^r lordship's

in maiden lane
at the white wigg
covent garden

most humble most
obedient faithfull
servant Voltaire

4 Voltaire's letter of *c.* 1 January 1728 to the second earl of Oxford, *from the
holograph in the possession of the marquess of Bath, Longleat*

some years, still loving Jocaste. The curtain rises as he meets his friend Dimas, from whom he learns that Laius was killed four years earlier, that Jocaste was now married to Œdipe, the new king, and that a plague was ravaging Thebes. The high priest (who is not named) declares that the pestilence can be averted only if the slayer of Laius be discovered. Œdipe is told by Jocaste that Phorbas, a follower of the dead king, is suspected of the crime and has been hidden by her because she thinks him innocent. Philoctète is then accused of the murder, but Jocaste, asserting his innocence, admits that he still has a place in her heart, that she never loved Laius, and that she has only affection for Œdipe. The high priest then accuses the king of the crime; Œdipe is indignant, but troubled by vague memories, and finally realises his guilt when the details of the crime are reported by Jocaste and Phorbas. He asks to be executed, but Jocaste maintains that he was not guilty, since he was not aware of his victim's identity. Icare announces the death of Polybe, king of Corinth, the reputed father of Œdipe. It now transpires from the confrontation of Icare and Phorbas that Œdipe was only his adopted son, that he was brought to Corinth from Thebes, and that he is in fact the son of Laius and Jocaste. The high priest, amidst thunder and lightning, ennounces the end of the pestilence. Jocaste stabs herself to death, reproaching the gods who forced her crime upon her.

Of course such an abstract conveys little: the treatment is all. Did Voltaire have a special purpose in writing *Œdipe*? One or two contemporary critics thought that the conflicts in the play represented the deep antagonism between the Jesuits and the Jansenists.[8] The latter had come again to the fore in 1713 with the publication of the bull *Unigenitus*, the object of which was to eradicate once and for all the exclusive doctrine of grace. The rôle of the Jesuits was to maintain to the fullest possible extent the authority of the church, with its apparatus of infallibility and sacraments. This was being undermined by the notions of personal inspiration held

8 [Gabriel Girard], *Lettre d'un abbé à un gentilhomme de province, contenant des observations sur . . . la nouvelle tragédie d'Œdipe* (Paris 1719), pp. 8-9; J. B. Rousseau's remark (Best.D73) that 'the ancients were all perfect Jansenists' was a trivial *obiter dictum*.

by the Jansenists, notions which, unchecked, would have once again split Rome. This view of *Œdipe* has been taken up again recently[9], but it strikes me as highly unconvincing, and even more unlikely. If *Œdipe* had been a contemporary parable references to this aspect of the play would have been the rule rather than the exception. Moreover, Voltaire wrote lengthy dissertations on his play, and frequently referred to it then and later; nowhere is there any trace of such a symbolism and such a purpose.

Nor can Voltaire be said to have added much that is new or profound to the eternal theme of sexual love between mother and son. The reason for the extraordinary success of his *Œdipe* must be sought elsewhere, in the fact that the play expressed profound currents of feelings, so deep-lying that they had not yet come to the surface, though they are perceptible enough to us: an increasing disgust with all forms of absolute authority, and in particular with that of the church and the throne, a disgust of which the regency was an unconscious and impermanent expression. Only a very few years earlier no dramatist would have dared to put into the mouth of one of his heroes such a couplet as:

> Un roi pour ses sujets est un dieu qu'on révère;
> Pour Hercule et pour moi, c'est un homme ordinaire.[10]

Or such lines as:

> Dans le cœur des humains les rois ne peuvent lire;
> Souvent sur l'innocence ils font tomber leurs coups.[11]

Jocaste herself is made to speak lines that have been hundreds of times put into Voltaire's own mouth, because they so exactly reflect his views:

> Nos prêtres ne sont pas ce qu'un vain peuple pense,
> Notre crédulité fait toute leur science.[12]

This couplet, so often singled out, by no means stands alone; thus Araspe, Œdipe's confident, tells him:

9 By René Pomeau, *La Religion de Voltaire*, pp. 87 ff.

10 *Œdipe*, II.iv; 'To his subjects a king is a god to be revered; to Hercule and to me he is an ordinary man.'

11 *Œdipe*, II.v; 'Kings cannot read men's hearts; their blows often fall on the innocent.'

12 *Œdipe*, IV.i; 'Our priests are not what an idle populace imagines, their knowledge is merely our credulity.'

> Ne nous fions qu'à nous; voyons tout par nos yeux;
> Ce sont là nos trépieds, nos oracles, nos dieux.[13]

And even more outspoken are Jocaste's dying words, uttered as the final curtain comes down on her suicide:

> J'ai fait rougir les dieux qui m'ont forcée au crime.[14]

These words echo Œdipe's

> Impitoyables dieux, mes crimes sont les vôtres,
> Et vous m'en punissez![15]

On listening to such sentiments expressed by heroic personages with whom the spectators were intended to sympathise, the audience became aware of their own hidden revolt, which exploded in applause.[16] Yet not only was the play permitted, it was seen more than once by the regent himself, who gave Voltaire permission to dedicate *Œdipe* to his mother[17], ordered the play to be performed at court in the young king's presence, and allowed Voltaire to defend himself in print against his critics. This he did in a series of letters[18] prefixed to the play on publication. Voltaire's defence is most remarkable in this: it includes a detailed criticism of his own play.

There is little to be said about *Œdipe* as literature, and that little may as well be said now once and for all, for it applies to nearly all Voltaire's plays. The strict rules governing the manufacture of plays, as laid down in the seventeenth century, were regarded by him as immutable, and the use of the alexandrine in the more 'serious' kind of plays, that is, in tragedies, as very nearly so.

13 *Œdipe*, II.v; 'Let us trust only ourselves; let us see everything with our own eyes; these are our tripods, our oracles, our gods.'

14 *Œdipe*, v.vi; 'I made the gods blush who compelled me to this crime.'

15 *Œdipe* v.iv; 'Pitiless gods, my crimes are yours, and you punish me for them!'

16 We are told in an editorial footnote that on the first night of *Œdipe* the line 'Qu'eusse-je été sans lui? rien que le fils d'un roi' ['What would I have been without him? nothing but the son of a king'] (I.i) was applauded with rapture; hardly, for this line was not in the original text. Nevertheless Henri Lion, *Les Tragédies et les théories dramatiques de Voltaire* (Paris 1895), p. 17, and other scholars have repeated the assertion; French indifference to the bibliographical aspects of literary research has been particularly harmful to Voltaire.

17 Best.D70, note 1.

18 The first, 'au sujet des calomnies dont on avait chargé l'auteur', is described in the original editions as 'Imprimée par permission expresse de Monseigneur le duc d'Orléans.'

Neither in the least suited Voltaire's literary genius, which consisted essentially in the lucid and elegant expression of humane convictions and a wide-ranging imagination. The combination of a fixed structure, rigid unities of time and place, and a mechanical metre effectively stifled Voltaire's inspiration, and reduced the value of his plays largely to that of their content. He laboured incessantly on the development and writing of his tragedies, but it was to little purpose. Even *Œdipe* contains what Voltaire would have considered to be grave defects had they occurred, say, in Corneille—and if he allowed them to stand it must have been because he was unable to correct them.

Among these defects are such absurdities (particularly numerous in *Œdipe*) as 'un calme heureux écarte les tempêtes'[19]; such padding as 'C'était, c'était assez d'examiner ma vie'[20]; such verbal repetitions as the wearisome recurrence of 'affreux'; such clumsy lines as 'Seigneur, qu'a ce discours qui doive vous surprendre?'[21]; such defective rhymes (even allowing for contemporary pronunciation) as 'couronne' and 'ordonne' with 'trône'[22], 'flamme' with 'âme'[23], 'Philoctète' with 'jette'[24], to cite only one kind of careless rhyming; and such grammatical howlers as

> Et dis-moi si des dieux la colère inhumaine
> A respecté du moins les jours de votre Reine?[25]

It was not for nothing that Voltaire complained with feeling that he was

> soumis à cette loi si dure
> Qui veut qu'avec six pieds d'une égale mesure,
> De deux alexandrins côte à côte marchants,
> L'un serve pour la rime et l'autre pour le sens.
> Si bien que sans rien perdre, en bravant cet usage,
> On pourrait retrancher la moitié d'un ouvrage.[26]

19 *Œdipe*, v.vi; 'A happy calm wards off the storms.'

20 *Œdipe*, iii.iii; 'It was, it was enough to examine my life.'

21 *Œdipe*, iv.i; 'Lord, what has this speech that should surprise you?'

22 *Œdipe*, i.iii and v.i.

23 *Œdipe*, ii.ii and iii.ii.

24 *Œdipe*, ii.iv.

25 *Œdipe*, i.i; this apostrophe, which begins in the singular to conclude in the plural, was afterwards corrected.

26 *Epître au roi de la Chine* (1771), 21-26; 'subjected to the severe law which insists that of the six feet of equal length of two alexandrines marching side by side, one serves for the rime and the other for the meaning. In fact, if custom were ignored, half of a composition could be cut without loss.'

It is particularly interesting that when the best lines in Voltaire's plays are picked out, they often turn out not to be strict alexandrines. Examples in *Œdipe* are the breaking up of the rhythm in the second line of:

> Guidé par la fortune en ces lieux pleins d'effrois,
> Vint, vit ce monstre affreux, l'entendit, et fut roi.[27]

and of

> A leur malignité rien n'échappe et ne fuit;
> Un seul mot, un soupir, un coup d'œil nous trahit.[28]

Not that Voltaire was unable to produce many a perfect alexandrine:

> here and there I see a master line,
> I feel and I confess the pow'r divine.[29]

Among such lines are:

> L'amitié d'un grand homme est un bienfait des dieux.[30]

> Donnez, en commandant, le pouvoir d'obéir.[31]

> Je n'osais à moi-même avouer mes douleurs.[32]

Yet the poet also wrote these lines, which as tragic dialogue could hardly be more comic:

> JOCASTE
> Qu'ai-je entendu, grands dieux!
>
> EGINE
> Ma surprise est extrême! . . .
>
> JOCASTE
> Qui? lui! qui? Philoctète!
>
> ARASPE
> Oui, madame, lui-même.[33]

27 *Œdipe*, i.i.
28 *Œdipe* iii.i.
29 Lady Mary Wortley Montagu on Addison.
30 *Œdipe*, i.i; The friendship of a great man is a blessing from the gods.'
31 *Œdipe*, i.iii; 'Give us, with your orders, the ability to obey'. Jean

Jacques Rousseau did not disdain to quote this line (Leigh 1595).
32 *Œdipe*, ii.ii; 'I dared not admit my sorrows to myself'.
33 *Œdipe*, ii.i; 'What have I heard, great gods / My surprise is extreme!... / Who? he! who? Philoctète! / Yes, madame, himself.'

As for the development of the theme, in his *Lettres sur Œdipe* Voltaire himself pointed out its defects, and I need not nudge the master's elbow. I repeat that these are not so much my criticisms as those that Voltaire would have considered valid and valuable; they represent in fact the kind of treatment Corneille very often received at his hands in later years in his commentaries[34]. And I spare the reader similar observations on vocabulary, imagery, and the like.

Such reforms as Voltaire contributed to the French stage came later. *Œdipe*, technically, made no innovations: all the conventions, which he regarded as laws, remained intact, even the 'noble language' and the monologue addressed primarily to the audience.

Immediately on its production and publication *Œdipe* was discussed in over twenty books, pamphlets and substantial articles. The regent gave Voltaire a gold medal[35] and an annuity of 1200 livres[36], and the British ambassador, John Dalrymple, 2nd earl of Stair, told his minister (James Craggs the younger): 'He's ye best poet maybe ever was in France.' George I responded with a present of a gold medal and watch. Overnight Voltaire had become what he was to remain for sixty years: the chief ornament of French letters.

Yet the play was also a declaration of war against received ideas; the gauntlet thus thrown down was not allowed to lie, and Voltaire was not far out when he told Jean Jacques Rousseau nearly forty years later that there existed 'a gang of wretches determined to ruin me from the day on which I produced the tragedy of *Œdipe*'[37]. On the other hand the young author was consecrated by an event unusual at any time, and perfectly extraordinary in the Paris of 1718: he was celebrated in a long poem by a prince of the blood, Louis Armand de Conti[38], in which a spirit

sans expérience,
Mais dont l'esprit vif, gracieux,

34 Voltaire 53-5.

35 Desnoiresterres, i.158*n*; the manuscript he quotes cannot be identified.

36 See Best.D181 (? end 1723), and the notes thereon; it is mentioned in Voltaire's financial statements to the end of his life; notwithstanding these rewards some writers have found allusions in *Œdipe* to the regent's incest.

37 Best.D6451 (30 August 1755).

38 Great-grandson of Armand de Bourbon, prince de Conti, whose brother was the great Condé; Louis Armand was also, unfortunately, a degenerate nincompoop.

Surpassait déjà les plus vieux
Par ses talents et sa science

is given human form 'sous le nom d'Arouet'.

Ayant puisé ses vers aux eaux de l'Aganippe,
Pour son premier projet il fait le choix d'Œdipe,
Et quoique dès longtemps ce sujet fût connu,
Par un stile plus beau cette pièce changée
Fit croire des Enfers Racine revenu,
Ou que Corneille avait la sienne corrigée.[39]

Voltaire wrote in his autobiography that he could not find his reply[40] to Conti's warm if inelegant compliments: but he remembered, with obvious delight in his own youthful boldness, that he had said: 'Your highness, you will become a great poet; I must get the king to give you an annuity', and on another occasion, as we have seen, while dining at Conti's table: 'Are we all princes or all poets?'[41]

Yet Voltaire did not take himself too seriously. 'The young man', said he of himself, 'who was excessively dissipated and immersed in all the pleasures common at his time of life, was not sensible of the risque he run, nor did he give himself any trouble whether his piece succeeded or not. He indulged himself in a thousand sallies on the stage, and at last wantonly laid hold of the train of the chief priest, in a scene where that pontiff was producing a very tragical effect.'[42] This jest won him the friendship of the maréchal de Villars and his wife, with whom he promptly fell in love.

It was at this time and in this character that Voltaire was painted by Nicolas Largillière[43]. As can be seen in this portrait, reproduced here in colour as plate 3, the eyes are a brilliant brown; the nose is long, and slightly bulbous; the mouth large, sensitive, smiling; the face thin, already showing the lines of humour and, perhaps, of bad health; the whole is crowned by a very high forehead, and

39 See the autobiography, p. 625, below.

40 But we do know a rather dull verse epistle addressed by Voltaire to the prince about this time, the *Epître à s. a. s. monseigneur le prince de Conti.*

41 See the autobiography, pp. 625-626 below.

42 See the autobiography, pp. 624-625 below.

43 The portrait is now Th. B.; another version, the one given by Voltaire to mlle Livry, is in the Musée Carnavalet; and a third at Versailles; contemporary copies were also made.

framed by a full, unusually long, loose, pale wig; a red and buff waistcoat is elegantly unbuttoned at top and bottom to show the handsome shirt and lace jabot; the coat is of dark emerald velvet, with large gold buttons. Of course the youth of twenty-four was sitting for a portrait, and wearing his best clothes. The Genevese councillor François Tronchin, who thirty years later became one of his close friends, painted Voltaire in grisaille: 'In 1722, I was in the pit of the Comédie française, and saw a very thin young man, dressed in black, with a long natural wig, pass in the corridor. I was sitting next to a stranger who asked him how he was. All he replied was: "Always on the go and always ill".'[44]

It seems that the success of *Œdipe*, and perhaps even its merits, gave Arouet *père* a better opinion of his son[45]. At any rate, when Voltaire heard that George 1 had given him a gold watch, he asked lord Stair to send it to his father, who would be delighted by this attention.[46]

Voltaire remained modest. He said in his time many unkind things about Corneille, and he was entitled to say them, but he did not accord the same privilege to the insincere. In his old age he remembered that 'some women told me that my play [*Œdipe*] (which is not worth much) surpassed that of Corneille (which is not worth anything at all). I answered with these two admirable lines from *Pompée*,

> Restes d'un demi-dieu dont jamais je ne puis
> Egaler le grand nom tout vainqueur que j'en suis.'[47]

44 Henry Tronchin, *Le Conseiller François Tronchin* (Paris 1895), pp. 10-11.

45 Longchamps and Wagnière, *Mémoires sur Voltaire* (Paris 1826), i.21-2.

46 Best.D80 (20 June 1719).

47 Best.D18151 (22 January 1773). 'Remnants of a demi-god whose great name I can never equal although I have vanquished him'; the quotation was adapted from act v, scene i of Corneille's *La Mort de Pompée*.

8. *From* Artémire *to* Uranie, *1719-1722*

THE RÔLE OF JOCASTE in *Œdipe* had been taken by mlle Livry, who thus made her début on the stage, not very successfully it would appear. The actor Paul Poisson even hinted that she owed more to Voltaire's bed than to her native talents, and almost provoked the gallant author to a duel[1]. However, the Livry was soon forgotten, for Voltaire fell hopelessly in love with the wife of the maréchal-duc de Villars. She was Jeanne Angélique Roque de Varengeville, and was related to two of Voltaire's closest friends, Courtin and Maisons, a niece of the former, an aunt of the latter. Voltaire spent much time mooning over her at Vaux-Villars (originally and now again Vaux-le-Vicomte), the superb house near Melun created for Foucquet by a combination of genius unparalleled in France: the architect Louis Le Vau, the decorator Charles Le Brun, and the landscape-gardener Le Nôtre. His passion did not prevent Voltaire from visiting Richelieu (which he thought the finest château in France), the duc de La Feuillade at Le Bruel, and Sully, where he spent several months, observing the stars, taking part in the usual country-house amusements, and entertaining his friends with such verse indiscretions as *Le Cadenas*[2] and *Le Cocuage*. It is indeed more than probable, as he told Fontenelle, that

> Nous brouillons tout l'ordre des Cieux
> Et prenons Venus pour Mercure:
> Mais vous remarquerés qu'on n'a
> Pour observer tand de planettes
> Au lieu de vos longes lunettes
> Que des l'orgnettes d'opéra.[3]

---

1 Best.D76-7 (May 1717).
2 That is, in this context, *The Chastity-belt*; see pp. 21-22, above.
3 Best.D92 (1 June 1721). 'We are muddling up the whole system of the heavens, and take Venus for Mercury: but please remember that we have only opera-glasses to observe so many planets instead of your long telescopes.'

His chief occupation, however, was the writing of his next play, another tragedy set in ancient Greece. *Artémire* (of which only fragments have survived) was produced at the Comédie française on 15 February 1720. After the resounding success of *Œdipe* its successor could only be a let-down: it is by no means a good thing in a worldly sense for an artist to be too successful too soon. Anyway, Voltaire withdrew the play after the first performance (though it was put on again at the request of the court), and never allowed it to be published. Yet the famous couplet

> Oui, tous ces conquérants rassemblés sur ce bord,
> Soldats sous Alexandre, et rois après sa mort[4] ...

is from *Artémire*, indeed it forms the play's opening lines. But Voltaire accepted the public's verdict and his own on the play as a whole. Here we see again that as a young man he was already what he was to remain throughout his life: self-critical, modest, and ready—indeed too ready—to listen to the advice of his friends in literary matters. Yet this does not mean that he was not disappointed and depressed. He wrote to Thieriot:

> Le dieu des bons vers m'a quitté
> Pour aller dans ta solitude,
> Et pour comble d'inquiétude,
> Hélas l'amour seul m'est resté.[5]

Voltaire's father died on 1 January 1722, and was buried in Paris on the following day, in Voltaire's presence. He had partly forgiven his younger son, and by his will left him one-third of his residual estate, but in trust. As Voltaire's chief resource had been his expectations from his wealthy father—wealthy, that is, by eighteenth-century standards: the value of the estate, after the payment of all outstanding debts, was 369,345 *livres*; Voltaire's share eventually came to about 150,000 *livres*—had had to make an agonising reappraisal of his position, for the only immediate financial consequence of his father's death was the loss oi his

---

4 'Yes, all these conquerors assembled on this shore, soldiers under Alexander, and kings after his death. . . .' Needless to say, these lines were on everybody's lips in Napoleonic times.

5 Best.D88 (c. 1720). 'The god of good verse has left me for your solitude, and to cap my misgivings, only love, alas, remains to me.'

allowance[6], however modest this may have been. However, he was by no means penniless: he had a small capital put by (from his mother?), *Œdipe* had brought in a respectable sum, he had his annuity from the regent, and another one of 2000 francs a year was added soon after his father's death. On all this he could live in some style if he were careful, but being careful was by no means in the character of this bourgeois poet with the instincts and behaviour of a *grand seigneur*. In any case travelling was expensive, and so was life as a guest in great houses. Fortunately, he in no way changed his mode of life, and managed to get along, no doubt by drawing on his capital and by borrowing.

About this time he formed a liaison with the marquise de Bernières, wife of a *président à mortier* of the Rouen *parlement*. The Bernières lived at La Rivière-Bourdet, a beautiful house near Rouen (now lamentably falling into ruin after passing through the hands of the Montholon and other families), and their town house was at the river corner of the rue de Beaune—the very house in which Voltaire died more than half-a-century later. Mme de Bernières was at this time about thirty-five, good-natured, but greedy, exacting, and perhaps a little too easy-going. Her relations with Voltaire lasted for some years, but when he sadly left for England mme de Bernières went to the opera with the chevalier de Rohan, who was responsible for his exile. However, years after, when Voltaire needed her evidence to refute the slanders of Desfontaines, she more than redeemed herself by supplying it in most handsome terms[7]. For the moment, in 1722, there is evidence that Voltaire engaged with mme de Bernières in some kind of business venture connected with the salt-tax. He was refreshingly offhand about it. 'You inform me that if I am not in Paris today, Thursday, I have missed the business. Tell your gentlemen that only they will have missed it, that it was to me that the licence was promised, and that once I have it I shall choose what associates I please.'[8] Indeed, there is no sign that Voltaire made any serious effort to make money until he reached England in 1726.

He did, however, adopt other methods: he did what he could

6 See Archives nationales: Minutier central, LVII.309, cote 70. François Arouet's will, inventory and related documents are printed as Best.app.D11.
7 Best.D1759 (9 January 1739).
8 Best.D113 (? 1 July 1722).

to ingratiate himself with cardinal Dubois, the prime minister, who had recently negotiated the triple alliance between France, England and Holland. It was a modest exaggeration to write an epistle to his 'sublime intelligence'[9], but this was perhaps not too high a price to pay for the favour of an all-powerful minister at a time when writers held about the same position in France as curates did in England. But when Voltaire went on to make the first of his pathetic efforts to become a diplomat, we can only shake our heads sadly; and even more sadly when we find that the form taken by his effort was a report on an obscure affair of espionage centring round one Solomon Levy, a report containing such phrases as: 'He passed over to the enemy with the facility the Jews have of being received and dismissed everywhere.'[10] This was the first manifestation of Voltaire's anti-semitism (if so anachronistic a term may be used), or rather of his willingness to use any tool that came to hand, for in fact he recognised intellectually the vulgar error of anti-semitic prejudices. Voltaire's language was the language of his time, and we must not expect even the greatest of men always to rise above their environment. Indeed, his language became stronger and stronger as his campaign against the *Bible* and Christianity itself became more violent. And the Jews, as the chosen people of the former and the progenitors of the latter, were an all too tempting target. However, when a Jew wrote courteously to complain of a particularly severe passage, Voltaire replied: 'The lines of which you complain are violent and unjust. Your letter alone convinces me that there are highly cultivated and very respectable men among you. I shall take care to insert a cancel in the new edition. When one has done a wrong one should put it right, and I was wrong to attribute to a whole nation the vices of some individuals.'[11]

Voltaire's fundamental attitude is expressed in an anecdote recorded in his *Notebooks*. When an abbé tried to convert a Jewish lady, she asked: 'Was your god born a Jew?'—'Yes'.—'Did he

---

9 *Epître au cardinal Dubois* (1721).
10 Best.D106 (28 May 1722). Voltaire's charges against Levy appear to have been well founded; see Arthur Herzberg, *The French Enlightenment*

and the Jews (New York 1968), p. 135*n*.
11 Best.D10600 (21 July 1762). It must, however, be said that the passage was not altered.

live a Jew?'—'Yes.'—'Did he die a Jew?'—'Yes.'—'Well then, be a Jew.'[12]

Either at the request of the cardinal, or more probably for the sake of mme de Rupelmonde, in July 1722 Voltaire set off with this lady for Brussels. In her early thirties, daughter of the maréchal d'Alègre, widow of a Flemish nobleman, mme de Rupelmonde was elegantly said by Saint-Simon[13]—it was for him the ultimate insult—to be as 'ginger as a cow', besides her 'unparalleled effrontery' and other defects. Cambrai was on the road to Brussels, and at Cambrai the preliminaries of the peace congress had begun to the accompaniment of balls and dinners galore. Naturally Voltaire stopped for a few days, with the result that everyone clamoured for a performance of *Œdipe*. Unfortunately it had already been arranged to put on Racine's *Plaideurs*. No matter, Voltaire improvised an elegant little petition in verse addressed to prince Windischgrätz, imperial plenipotentiary, and *Œdipe* was duly performed—and not only *Œdipe* but also *Œdipe travesti*! Such parodies later drove Voltaire quite frantic, but now he contented himself with exclaiming amiably 'Demain l'on joue, & la pièce, & l'auteur'[14]. The amorous couple then rolled on to Brussels, where they arrived during the first week of September.

Other things than love and poetry occupied Voltaire on the journey. It will be remembered that his imprisonment in 1717-18 had been directly due to one Beauregard, who had insinuated himself into the young man's confidence, and then betrayed him. When they met again by chance in July 1722 Voltaire duly and, we may be sure, very thoroughly insulted the spy, who reacted in the manner of such creatures: instead of drawing his sword, he waylaid Voltaire and beat him savagely. He then carefully disappeared. Voltaire obtained an order of arrest, and during the following months spent his energy and money in hunting down the wretch until he finally succeeded in getting him into prison.[15] And who shall blame him?

These are trifles. Voltaire soon forgot Beauregard, though the

12 *Notebooks*, i.365
13 *Mémoires*, xii.415.
14 Best.D122 (13 September 1722). The play on words is untranslatable; an approximation would be: 'To-morrow the play will be put on and the author sent up.'
15 Best.D114 (? July 1722) ff.

beating he had received at the hands of the bully was naturally remembered by his enemies. Mme de Rupelmonde, however, must not be forgotten, for by her questions she stimulated her lover to formulate his first substantial declaration of faith, in the long poem best known as the *Epître à Uranie*[16]. During the six weeks he spent in Brussels and at The Hague Voltaire was taken to a brothel[17], rode every day, played tennis, drank tokay, and felt so well that he was astonished[18]. Yet he always spent his time 'between work and pleasure'[19]: among his more serious occupations were visits to learned men and the planning of the illustrations of the *Henriade*[20], plans which he executed in England five years later. He also saw a good deal of J. B. Rousseau, but finished by shocking this reformed rake (the most shockable kind of human animal) by the reading of a poem 'filled with horrors against what is most sacred in religion . . . bearing the hall-mark of the blackest impiety . . . frightful . . . detestable'.[21] This appalling work was none other than the *Epître à Uranie*. Voltaire, already deeply moved by problems of belief, and no doubt by the liberties he thought he found in Holland, 'Calvinist ministers, Arminians, Socinians, rabbis, Anabaptists, all of whom discourse admirably and who, in truth, are all in the right'[22], had for long been revolving these high matters: and his companions questions acted as a final catalyst.

This of course implies that the elements were already there. Some indication that Voltaire had been meditating such a poem since the summer of 1772 is provided by his repeated requests[23] for Louis Racine's *La Grâce*, which he received at the beginning of October[24], and this although he had already read the poem[25]. If

16 also known as the *Epître à Julie* and *Le Pour et le contre*.

17 Best.D121 (11-18 September 1722).

18 Best.D125 (2 October 1722).

19 Best.D128 (7 October 1722).

20 Best.D121 (11-18 September 1722).

21 Best.D1078 (22 May 1736).

22 Best.D128 (7 October 1722).

23 Best.D121 (11-18 September 1722), D125 (2 October 1722).

24 Best.D129 (8 October 1722).

25 In its original suppressed edition of 1720; this is proved by the lines

beginning

Cher Racine, j'ai lu dans tes vers
   dramatiques
De ton Jansénius les erreurs fanatiques.
(*A monsieur Louis Racine*).

These lines have hitherto been dated 1722, but were in fact written in 1721 or even 1720 (see Pomeau, *La Religion de Voltaire*, p. 102, who also gives some account of the interrelations of Voltaire's writings and *La Grâce*). 'Dear Racine, I have read in your dramatic lines about the fanatical errors of your Jansenius.'

therefore Voltaire was so anxious to see *La Grâce* again in 1722, it was not doubt because he was planning his reply.

This reply, once again, was the *Epître à Uranie*, which was at first kept under lock and key, and not published until more than ten years later, and then surreptitiously. It was not included in Voltaire's works until 1772. The poem is in fact a total condemnation of Christianity, as elegant in its form as in its reasoning. 'Tu veux donc', writes Voltaire to mme de Rupelmonde,

> Tu veux donc, belle Uranie,
> Qu'érigé par ton ordre en Lucrèce nouveau,
> Devant toi, d'une main hardie,
> Aux superstitions j'arrache le bandeau;
> Que j'expose à tes yeux le dangereux tableau
> Des mensonges sacrés dont la terre est remplie,
> Et que ma philosophie
> T'apprenne à mépriser les horreurs du tombeau
> Et les terreurs de l'autre vie.[26]

Enter respectfully with me, he goes on, the sanctuary of the god who is hidden from us. I want to love him, and I am shown a monster whom we must hate.[27] He created men in his own image in order to abase them; he gave us evil hearts in order to punish us; he made us love pleasure in order the better to torment us. He created the world and then drowned it, not to create a purer race, but to people it with brigands and tyrants. And then, having drowned the fathers, he died for their children, but without effect, and punished a hundred nations for the ignorance in which he had kept them of his own death on the cross. In all this I do not recognise the god I must adore. l am not a Christian, but it is in order to love him the more. Voltaire then sets out briefly an orthodox view of Christianity, and concludes by asking Uranie to choose.

> Songe que du Très-Haut la sagesse éternelle
> A gravé de sa main dans le fond de ton cœur
> La religion naturelle;

26 'So, lovely Uranie, you want me, become by your command a new Lucretius, to tear away with a bold hand, before you, the blindfold of superstition; to display before your eyes the dangerous image of the sacred lies with which the world is filled; and to learn from my philosophy to despise the horrors of the tomb and the terrors of the other life.'

27 The same feeling is expressed in the poem *A monsieur Louis Racine*.

Crois que de ton esprit la naïve candeur
Ne sera point l'objet de sa haine immortelle;
Crois que devant son trône, en tout temps, en tous lieux,
    Le cœur du juste est précieux;
Crois qu'un bonze modeste, un dervis charitable,
    Trouvent plutôt grâce à ses yeux
    Qu'un Janséniste impitoyable,
    Ou qu'un pontife ambitieux.
Eh! qu'importe en effet sous quel titre on l'implore?
Tout hommage est reçu, mais aucun ne l'honore.
Un Dieu n'a pas besoin de nos soins assidus:
Si l'on peut l'offenser, c'est par des injustices;
    Il nous juge sur nos vertus,
    Et non pas sur nos sacrifices.[28]

    In short, among the innumerable lines of attack open to sceptics, Voltaire chose from the beginning the one that remained most characteristic of him throughout his long life: he was opposed to any system or mode of thought characterised by injustice and unreason.

28 'Consider that the eternal wisdom of the most high has with his hand engraved natural religion in the bottom of your heart; believe that the simple candour of your mind will not be the object of his immortal hatred; believe that before his throne, always, everywhere, the heart of the just man is precious; believe that a modest bonze, a charitable dervish, find grace in his eyes rather than a merciless Jansenist or an ambitious pontiff. Ah! what matter indeed by what name he be implored? Every homage is received, but none does him honour. A god has no need of our assiduous attentions: if he can be offended, it is only by injustice; he judges by our virtues, and not by our sacrifices.' Voltaire developed this theme in his *Poème sur la loi naturelle* (1752).

9. *The* Henriade, *1722*

FROM BRUSSELS Voltaire went on to The Hague to supervise the printing of the *Henriade*, then called *La Ligue*, but though it was set up and subscribed, Voltaire did not publish the poem, the French authorities having declined at once permission to print and a proposed dedication to the king[1]. We have seen that it was at Saint-Ange that the young Arouet began to plan an epic poem in honour of Henri IV, and in the Bastille that he started to write it. In his own words: 'After having finished his Oedipus; but before it had been performed, he began the *Henriade*, when with Monsieur de Caumartin, Intendant of the Finances, at St Ange. I have more than once heard him say, that when he undertook these two performances, he did not imagine he should be able to finish them, and that he was neither acquainted with the rules of the drama, nor Epic poetry; but that he was fired with what he heard of Henri IV from Monsieur Caumartin, who was well versed in history, an excessive admirer of that Prince, and an old gentleman of a most respectable character; and that he began the work from mere enthusiasm, almost without reflection.'[1]

In short, after rivalling Sophocles on the stage, the young poet did not hesitate to measure himself against Virgil in narrative verse. The attempt was all the more daring in that French literature, while it had produced a Racine and a Corneille, entirely lacked even a secondrate epic poem. Apart from the 11th-13th century *chansons de geste* there were only such worthless and forgotten epics as *Moyse sauvé* by Saint-Amant, *Clovis* by Desmarets, *Childebrand* by Carel de Sainte-Garde. During his imprisonment in the Bastille Voltaire set himself seriously to work, composing in his head and memorising several hundred lines. As soon as he had written them down on leaving prison, he started

---

1 See the autobiography, p. 626, below.

to give readings in drawing-rooms and country houses. 'Having one day read several cantos of his poem when on a visit to his intimate friend, the young President de Maisons, he was so teased with objections, that he lost patience, and threw the manuscript into the fire. The president, Hénault, with difficulty, rescued it. "Remember" said mr. Hénault to him, in one of his letters,[2] "it was I that saved the Henriade, and that it cost me a handsome pair of ruffles".'[1]

We need not take the objections too seriously, nor the risk run by the manuscript, of which Voltaire no doubt had more than one copy. By 1721 the poem was so well known among those who interested themselves in such matters that the young man began to be called the French Virgil. References to a poem on Henri IV became more and more frequent in the correspondence for 1721-22, and manuscripts were sent to interested and influential friends, including the regent.[3] Voltaire was indeed working hard at his great undertaking, unhindered by all his troubles, travels and sufferings—for the wretched man, who was sixty years a-dying, was already having trouble with his health. When in the spring of 1722 he asked to be excused from a visit to Villars, the old hero of Malplaquet and Denain, in a kindly letter to his 'great poet', advised Voltaire to come to him rather than put himself into the hands of charlatans. 'Come here to take good soup at regular hours, eat only four meals a day, go to bed early, don't touch either paper or ink or *biribi* or lansquenet.'[4] Voltaire duly went, but then journeyed with mme de Rupelmonde to the Netherlands, afterwards making another round of country houses, among them La Source, near Orléans, where Bolingbroke was spending his exile. It was here that Voltaire finally decided, encouraged by the enthusiasm of the philosopher-statesman, to publish his poem surreptitiously. On 4 December 1722 he wrote to Thieriot from Blois:

2. Hénault refers to this incident in Best.D6598 (24 November 1755) and D7733 (12 May 1758), but not in these exact terms; both allusions suggest that the incident occurred at the house of La Faye, not at Maisons.

3 Best.D96-D99 (15-25 October 1721).
4 Best.D107 (28 May 1722); these are card-games.

I must share with you the enchantment I feel after my journey to La Source, the house of lord Bolingbroke and madame de Villette[5]. In this illustrious Englishman I found all the erudition of his country and all the politeness of ours. I have never heard our language spoken with more energy and precision. This man, who during all his life has been immersed in pleasure and in public affairs, has nevertheless found the means to learn and remember everything. He knows the history of the ancient Egyptians like that of England, he has mastered Virgil like Milton, he loves English, French and Italian poetry, but he loves them differently, because he perfectly discerns their different geniuses. After the portrait I have drawn of lord Bolingbroke it perhaps ill becomes me to tell you that madame de Villette and he were infinitely pleased with my poem. In the enthusiasm of approbation they put it above the whole of French poetry, but I know how much to discount such outrageous praise. I am going to spend three months to deserve some of it. It seems to me that by dint of corrections, the work is finally taking a reasonable form. I will show it you on my return, and we will examine it at leisure. At this moment monsieur de Canillac[6] is reading it and judging me. I am writing to you while awaiting the judgement. Tomorrow I shall be at Ussé[7] where I expect to find a letter from you. I am very ill, but I am accustomed to the disorders of the body and to those of the soul. I am beginning to suffer them with patience, and I find resources against much in your friendship and in my philosophy. And so farewell.[8]

Voltaire by no means exaggerated Bolingbroke's estimate of the *Henriade*; indeed, on the very day on which this letter was written the exiled statesman told a friend (in French) that 'Monsieur de Voltaire has spent a few days here. I was charmed both by him and by his work. I expected to find much imagination in the one and the other, but I did not expect to find the author so judicious, nor his poem so well constructed.'[9]

Voltaire later added a whole book to the *Henriade* (that which is now the sixth), and revised more or less substantially many of the fifty editions that appeared during his lifetime. Yet in the main the poem as first published under the counter in 1723 substantially represents the work his contemporaries regarded as Voltaire's greatest masterpiece. On the poem's publication the

5 Marie Claire Deschamps de Marcilly, Bolingbroke's as yet unrecognised wife, had been the second wife of Philippe de Valois, marquis de Villette.

6 Philippe de Montboisier-Beaufort, marquis de Canillac, an intimate of the regent, whose exile to Blois had been procured by cardinal Dubois a few

months before.

7. The country house of Louis Sébastien Bernin de Valentiné, marquis d'Ussé.

8 Best.D135 (4 December 1722).

9 *The Collection of autograph letters ...formed by Alfred Morrison* (London 1893), 2nd ser. i.323.

critics showered it with superlatives; and even an enemy like the arid lawyer Mathieu Marais, writing his diary for his own eyes, could not help recording with astonishment that France had at last been endowed with an epic poem which was 'marvellous, a masterpiece of intelligence, as fine as Virgil. . . . It is like an inspiration. . . . What surprises, is that everything in it is judicious, systematic, full of morality; there is no enthusiasm, no pretentiousness in it, everywhere there is only elegance, correct language, ingenious turns and simple and grand declamations, which breathe consummate genius'—and more in the same strain.[10]

Of course that is not the whole story. 'All the poets of Paris, and even many of the learned fell foul of him. Twenty pamphlets were let fly against him. The Henriade was play'd at the fair[11]; and it was insinuated to the old Bishop of Fréjus[12], preceptor to the King, that it was indecent and even criminal, to write in praise of Admiral Coligny and Queen Elizabeth. The Cabal had interest enough to engage Cardinal de Bissi[13], then president of the assembly of the clergy, to pass a judicial censure upon the work; but this strange design proved abortive. The young author was filled with equal surprise and resentment at these intrigues. His dissipation had prevented him from making friends among the literati; and he had not the art of combating his enemies with their own weapons, which is said to be absolutely necessary in Paris, if a man wishes to succeed in any kind of pursuit.'[1] This last remark was and, alas, is only too true; Voltaire learnt the lesson so well that it became obsessive, and finally developed into the only serious flaw in his character. We shall see over and over again his violent dislike of personal criticism (as distinct from criticism of his work, which he welcomed), and his ever-increasing passion for intrigue.

Voltaire himself, as we have seen, came to wonder at his own temerity in attempting so difficult an undertaking as an epic poem,

10 *Journal et mémoires* (Paris 1863-8), iii.89.

11 Voltaire means by this that it was parodied; he had in mind, among others, [Louis Charles Fougeret de Montbron], *La Henriade, travestie en vers burlesques* (Berlin [Paris] 1745); this by no means worthless skit went into numerous editions, and has been printed with the *Henriade* itself.

12 Cardinal André Hercule de Fleury, afterwards prime minister.

13 Cardinal Henri de Thiard de Bissy, who issued many *mandements* against, in particular, the Jansenists.

but the opinion of his contemporaries was his own: it was by no mere chance that he entitled his autobiography *Commentaire historique sur les œuvres de l'auteur de la Henriade*; and it was not by chance that the *Henriade* was followed by a flood of imitations: a *Louisiade*, an *Ulissipeade*, a *Colombiade*, a *Pétréade*, and many more with variegated titles and uniformly unreadable contents.

Voltaire's epic is a poem on the model of the *Aeneid*; it is in ten books and about 4300 lines, that is, very roughly a third of the *Aeneid*, and half as long as *Paradise lost*. The subject is technically the siege of Paris by Henri iv at the end of the sixteenth century, but in reality the *Henriade* is a philosophic panorama of fanaticism.

The poem contains great beauties—of that there can be no doubt. But these beauties are not those of the epic. A great crowd of personages fills the canvas, and all those who play any considerable part are brilliantly, penetratingly and consistently characterised. Thus Henri de Guise could not be more happily described than in these lines:

> Téméraire en ses vœux, sage en ses artifices;
> Brillant par ses vertus, et même par ses vices.[14]

The thumb-nail sketch of Mornay is complete in its brevity:

> Il marche en philosophe où l'honneur le conduit,
> Condamne les combats, plaint son maître, et le suit.[15]

With effective alliteration Voltaire describes how Henri iii's *mignons* 'Plongeaient dans les plaisirs ses langueurs léthargiques'[16]; and how Egmont 'Baisa longtemps la main qui fit périr son père'[17].

The peculiarities of Henri iv's character and policy are penetratingly described as he

14 *Henriade*, iii.83-4; Voltaire 2, p.418. 'Bold in his projects, wise in his plans, brilliant in his virtues, and even in his vices.' All references to the *Henriade* are to O. R. Taylor's edition (1970), which is the second volume of *The Complete works of Voltaire*.

15 *Henriade*, vi.225-6; Voltaire 2, p. 501. 'He goes philosophically where honour guides him, condemns warfare, pities his master, and follows him.'

16 *Henriade*, i.38; Voltaire 2, p. 368. 'Plunged in pleasures his lethargic languor.' Voltaire nodded, for 'plongés dans les plaisirs' recurs a little further on (i.204; Voltaire 2, p. 376); it is curious that he, who strongly condemned such repetitions, allowed them to remain in the oft-revised *Henriade*: thus the poppies of sleep occur at least four times (ii.180, iv.230, v.128, vii.24; Voltaire 2, pp. 401, 451, 474, 511).

17 *Henriade*, viii.54; Voltaire 2, p. 545. 'Long kissed the hand that killed his father.'

s'avançait vers sa grandeur suprême
Par des chemins secrets, inconnus à lui-même.[18]

Yet these beauties are neither noble nor particularly poetic: they are epigrammatic. And an unkind critic could match these lines with some pretty bad ones, such as the disagreeable assonances of 'Où Jersey semble aux yeux sortir du sein des flots'[19], and the unbelievably bathetic

Le trouble répandu dans l'empire chrétien
Fut pour eux le sujet d'un utile entretien.[20]

One great quality of the *Henriade*, to which Voltaire himself drew attention[21], is the accuracy with which the most abstract ideas are described. And certainly

La puissance, l'amour, avec l'intelligence,
Unis et divisés, composent son essence,[22]

would be difficult to better as a theological description of the trinity.

But, once more, such compact beauties do not make an epic, and it must be owned that Voltaire's effort to create a French *Aeneid* is a failure—more, it was doomed to be a failure, for the metronomic cadences of the alexandrine couplet are as unsuited to narrative and exposition as they were to the expression of Voltaire's poetic gifts. The genius of Racine sometimes mastered it in tragedy, incidentally imposing on the French theatre a style of declamation which almost succeeded in extinguishing the Comédie française, and which now appears to be ineradicable. But the grandeur and slow development of an epic cannot be chopped up into small and rigid groups of syllables.

The vast success of the *Henriade* (like that of *Œdipe*) was not in fact due to the poetic merits of the poem, but to its ideas. The Voltairean note is struck at the outset: for the poet does not invoke the gods or the muses in the customary way, but truth, and at once

18 *Henriade*, i.85-6; Voltaire 2, p. 371. 'Advanced towards his supreme greatness by secret ways unknown to himself.'

19 *Henriade*, i.191; Voltaire 2, p. 376.

20 *Henriade*, i.219-20; Voltaire 2, p.377. 'The disorder reigning in the Christian realm was for them the subject of a useful conversation.'

21 *Idée de la Henriade*; Voltaire 2, p. 311.

22 *Henriade*, x.425-6; Voltaire 2, p.614. 'Power, love and reason, united and divided, form its essence.'

subordinates all to that. The first book is introductory, but at the very beginning of the second occurs the famous line: 'Je ne décide point entre Genève et Rome'[23], followed by 'J'ai vu des deux côtés la fourbe et la fureur'[24], lines which were revolutionary in that they placed the official religion of France on the same level as that which was persecuted and proscribed. And the general intention is underlined when Henri IV is made to attack the

> chef ambitieux d'un peuple trop crédule,
> Couvrant leurs intérêts de l'intérêt des cieux.[25]

And the description in the same book of the massacre of St Bartholomew, when it was still a living memory, could hardly have been read even by the most hard-bitten Roman Catholic without a shudder. Yet it must be admitted that this episode, precisely because of the failure of its would-be epic style, no longer has the poetic force to move us, and this although Voltaire felt the crime so keenly and intimately that throughout his life he had a temperature on St Bartholomew's day. It is only when Voltaire's strong feelings are united to a poetic treatment capable of expressing it that the *Henriade* comes to life, as when he takes up again one of the principal themes of the *Epître à Uranie*, and asserts of non-Christians:

> Dieu ne les punit point d'avoir fermé les yeux
> Aux clartés que lui-même il plaça si loin d'eux:
> Il ne les juge point tel qu'un injuste maître
> Sur les chrétiennes lois qu'ils n'ont point pu connaître,
> Sur le zèle insensé de leurs saintes fureurs,
> Mais sur la simple loi qui parle à tous les cœurs;[26]

23 'I do not decide between Geneva and Rome'; that is, between the two major Christian sects.

24 *Henriade*, ii.5, 7; Voltaire 2, p. 391. 'I have seen fraud and fury on both sides.'

25 *Henriade*, ii.26-7; Voltaire 2, p. 392. 'ambitious chiefs of a too credulous people, hiding their interests behind the benefits of heaven.'

26 The original text of the *Henriade*, Voltaire 2, p. 515. 'God does not punish them for having closed their eyes to the knowledge which he himself placed so far from them; he does not judge them like an unjust master because of the Christian laws they had no means of knowing, because of the insensate zeal of their sacred rage, but by the simple law which appeals to all hearts.' Voltaire afterwards toned down this passage (vii.103-12; Voltaire 2, p. 516).

when he contrasts the old and the new Romes:

> Un pontife est assis sur le trône des césars;
> Des prêtres fortunés foulent d'un pied tranquille
> Les tombeaux des Catons et la cendre d'Emile.
> Le trône est sur l'autel, et l'absolu pouvoir
> Met dans les mêmes mains le sceptre et l'encensoir;[27]

when he describes, in a passage too long to quote, the resistance of the *parlement* to the religious fanatics[28]; when he sets out the descent of fanaticism from that which

> dans Raba, sur les bords de l'Arnon,
> Guidait les descendants du malheureux Ammon,
> Quand à Moloch, leur dieu, des mères gémissantes
> Offraient de leurs enfants les entrailled fumantes;[29]

when he describes (in one of the few successfully epic passages of the *Henriade*) how easily atrocious crimes can be committed in the sincere belief that they are dictated by god: Jacques Clément, the murderer of Henri III, is shown,

> Son front de la vertu porte l'empreinte austère;
> Et son fer parricide est caché sous sa haire;[30]

And after the assassination he submits peacefully to his death:

> Et, demandant à Dieu la palme du martyre,
> Il bénit, en tombant, les coups dont il expire.[31]

Difficult though it is to define the nature of epic poetry, it will at least be agreed that it must be heroic in subject, in treatment and in language. When Voltaire gave the epic almost unlimited freedom, requiring only that it be 'grounded upon Judgment, and

27 *Henriade*, iv.182-6; Voltaire 2, p. 449. 'A pontiff is seated on the throne of the Caesars; wealthy priests calmly trample underfoot the tombs of the Catos and the ashes of Aemilius. The throne is on the altar, and absolute power places in the same hands the sceptre and the censer.'

28 *Henriade*, iv.399-468; Voltaire 2, pp. 459-63.

29 *Henriade*, v.87-90; Voltaire 2, p. 473. 'In Raba, on the banks of the Arnon, guided the descendants of the unfortunate Ammon, when to Moloch, their god, wailing mothers offered up the steaming entrails of their children.'

30 *Henriade*, v.181-2; Voltaire 2, p.476. 'His forehead bears the austere stamp of virtue; and his parricide blade is hidden beneath his sack-cloth.'

31 *Henriade*, v.325-6; Voltaire 2, p. 482. 'And, begging God for the martyr's palm, he blesses, in falling, the blows from which he dies.'

embellish'd by Imagination'[32], he was arguing *ex post facto*. Only the lyric would fall outside such a definition. And Voltaire recognised the inadequacy of his analysis when he says, at the end of his essay, with his usual wit and good sense: 'To conclude, the best Reason I can offer for our [French] ill Success in *Epick* Poetry, is the Insufficiency of all who have attempted it. I can add nothing further, after this ingenous Confession.'[33] This is the simple explanation of Voltaire's failure: the heroic is necessarily over life-size and artificial, at worst pompous. No qualities were further removed from Voltaire's character: the unrelaxing effort to see things clearly, as they really are, cannot produce the kind of high poetry represented by *Paradise lost*.[34]

---

32 *An Essay upon the civil war of France . . . and also upon the epick poetry of the European nations* (second edition, London 1728), p. 40; I quote Voltaire's original English; all the French editors print only a translation.

33 *Ibid.*, p. 130; this passage has been omitted in the French translation.

34 It must not be forgotten that it was Voltaire who introduced Milton to the French reader. On the *Henriade* in general and its sources and influence, see the above-mentioned edition by O. R. Taylor (1970).

10. *The end of the beginning,*
1723-1725

ON HIS WAY BACK from the Netherlands Voltaire stopped briefly at Mariemont, Cambrai and Orléans, visited even more briefly the duc de La Feuillade, the duc de Sully, and Bolingbroke[1], spent most of the winter at Ussé, and the spring of 1723 at Rouen and La Rivière-Bourdet, occupied with the *Henriade*. But he was never content to work on only one thing at a time, and in the midst of all this hurly-burly he wrote his tragedy *Mariamne*. He leased from the Bernières an apartment in their town house[2], and invited Thieriot to stay there with him. Not content with this he made formal arrangements for half of his royal annuity to be paid to his friend[3]. By the end of May Voltaire was back in Paris, but he was soon off again on visits to Villars and Maisons.

This fine house, now called Maisons-Lafitte, the masterpiece of François Mansart, was the home of the brilliant young président de Maisons. During Voltaire's stay both he and his guest came down with the smallpox, the worst plague of eighteenth-century France. Both recovered, though a few years later Maisons caught it again, with his infant son, and both died, thus extinguishing the family. But now Voltaire was very ill indeed, and was saved only, as he thought, by absorbing two hundred pints of lemonade. He also had a narrow escape from being burned alive in his bed.[4] Voltaire's illness unfortunately deprives us of his comments on the deaths of the prime minister (Dubois; 10 August 1723) and the regent (2 December 1723).

As soon as he was back in the capital Voltaire organised the smuggling into Paris of the *Henriade*, and the production of

---

1 Best.D130 (October 1722) ff.; for the visit to Bolingbroke see pp. 98-99, above.

2 *Mémoire* (1739).

3 Best.D181 (? end 1723).

4 He describes both the illness and the fire in a remarkable letter to mme Du Châtelet's father (Best.D173).

Mariamne. The former reached posterity by way of the furniture of mme de Bernières, the latter was produced in March for a single performance. The actors had insisted on putting on the tragedy although Voltaire was not satisfied with it[5]. He afterwards maintained that the play failed because of the witticisms of the pit[3], but the facts appear to have been a good deal more complex than that. After Voltaire withdrew *Mariamne* another play of the same name, by Augustin Nadal, was put on, and at the same time published with a preface in which the author speaks in very generous terms of his own play, and violently attacks that of Voltaire, and Voltaire himself. Another odd thing happened: at Nadal's first night the public booed, and called for Voltaire's *Mariamne*. If they had recently laughed this play off the stage, as he alleges, would they have called for it a few months later? Or did Voltaire and his friends mount a cabal, as Nadal claims in his preface? This was and long remained a common practice, and I do not think that Voltaire would have hesitated to employ a claque. Anyway, in an open letter he told Nadal that if there had been a cabal it had lasted for forty years[7]—this was unkind, for in fact it was only twenty years since Nadal had first been hissed off the stage. Voltaire did something much more to the point: he revised his own play and put it on again under the title of *Hérode et Mariamne*, which brought it off. 'He is our greatest poet', exclaimed Marais[8].

There can be few parallels in literary history to such a sequence of events: in truth I can think of none. We know both versions of the play, that which failed in March 1724 and that which was cheered in May 1725. A comparison of these texts throws a revealing light on the dramatic values of the French stage two and a half centuries ago. As first conceived Herod presented an image of unrelieved cruelty and tyranny, while Mariamne displayed nothing but pride and hatred. And this was the real reason for the play's failure: for the public would not tolerate such pitiless characterisation. Voltaire also took the revolutionary step of making Mariamne drink poison and die on the stage, which was

5 Best.D184 (? January 1724).
6 See the autobiography, p. 626, below.

7 Best.D226 (20 March 1725).
8 *Journal*, iii.174 (10 April 1725).

contrary to the rules of stage decorum. Voltaire submitted: he transformed these things, and humbly admitted in his preface that he should have followed the tastes of the public rather than his own. Many years were to pass before he again dared to do something new on the stage.

In September 1725 the new queen, Mary Leszczinska, daughter of Stanislas, the former king of Poland, accepted the dedication of both *Œdipe* and *Hérode et Mariamne*,[9] and in the meanwhile the *Henriade* triumphed. After reading it Pope wrote to Bolingbroke with remarkable perspicacity: 'It seems to me that his Judgment of Mankind and his Observation of human Actions in a lofty and Philosophical view is one of the principal Characteristicks of the Writer; who however is not less a Poet for being a man of sense. . . . I conclude him at once a Free thinker and Lover of Quiet; no Bigot, but yet no Heretick: one who honours Authority and National Sanctions without prejudice to Truth or Charity; One who has Study'd Controversy less than Reason, and the Fathers less than mankind.'[10]

Pope's enthusiasm confirmed Bolingbroke in his view of Voltaire's genius, and as soon as he received the English poet's letter he sat down to send the French one a sort of *apologia*[11]. It was clearly intended to direct Voltaire's energies. He recommended him to cultivate his mind, for one left fallow for too long became useless. This and similar passages in Bolingbroke's letter were echoed nearly half-a-century later in the conclusion of *Candide*. The statesman went on to tell Voltaire that he should ignore the public's praise. He was young, but this did not mean that he had time to waste. Nature had endowed him with an inexhaustible fund of imagination and ideas, to which he should join the use of the reason, without which truth could not be found. Bolingbroke strongly urged Voltaire to give Locke's *Essay concerning human understanding* the preference over Descartes and Malebranche, who were poets rather than thinkers.

All this is a little puzzling, for Bolingbroke appears to be forcing

---

9 Best.D249 (17 September 1725).
10 *The Correspondence of Alexander Pope*, ed. George Sherburn (Oxford 1956), ii.228-9 (20 April 1924).

11 Best.D190 (27 June 1724); this letter is in French, which Bolingbroke knew as well as his native language.

an open door. He was in reality exhorting Voltaire to persist on his course without being tempted to take an easier one. Whatever may have been the purpose of this enlightened tory, his recommendation to scepticism and to the life of reason must have been welcome to Voltaire. It endorsed his own inclinations, and seconded a general movement of ideas which had taken place during the regency of Philippe d'Orléans. This was partly a reaction against the lugubrious end of the reign of Louis XIV, a reaction led by the regent himself, who was as free in his behaviour as in his ideas. He gave a striking and beneficent example of his liberalism in accepting the dedication of the 1720 edition of Bayle's *Dictionnaire historique et critique*. It was this great work, rather than Diderot's more famous *Encyclopédie* (1751-72), which first liberated men's minds by claiming and exercising the right to investigate all things in a spirit of scientific inquiry. Since its first publication in 1697 the *Dictionnaire* had influenced only an élite, but the official endorsement given to the 1720 edition sowed the seed far and wide. The strange man and minor poet who was later to be a statesman and Voltaire's friend, the cardinal de Bernis[12], though a child at this time, was perfectly right when he wrote in his old age that disbelief and scepticism were made fashionable by the regent's example.

Part of the summer of 1724 Voltaire, still convalescent, spent at Forges with Richelieu, but the waters disagreed with him. 'There is more vitriol in a bottle of Forges water than in a bottle of ink, and frankly I do not believe that ink is very good for the health.'[13] Braving both the water and the ink, it was at Forges that Voltaire started to write *L'Indiscret*. This one-act comedy was produced a few weeks after *Hérode et Mariamne*. It is in form a conventional construction of lovers' misunderstandings, letters that go astray, disguises, reconciliations. Yet the censor who authorised its publication found in it 'noble and refined humour, which instructs while it amuses'. This was because the public had come to believe that curtain-raisers had to be vulgar farces[14]. Voltaire simply wanted to show that he could obtain popular success, if he wanted to, without indulging the tastes of the pit. *L'Indiscret* was in fact

12 *Mémoires* (Paris 1878), i.41.   14 Best.D246 (20 August 1725).
13 Best.D198 (5 August 1724).

much applauded, and perhaps we can leave it at that, except to remark that in its general tone it anticipated *Figaro*.

On returning to Paris Voltaire took possession of the new apartment, but was soon driven out again by the 'infernal noise of the quay and the street'[15]. He suffered so much from it that he fell ill. During his smallpox he had acquired a taste for doctors and their remedies, and now began his long addiction to this worst of all diseases. From now on he was always a-dying: surely the most energetic moribund of all time!

It was one thing to aspire to the life of reason, it was quite another to attain it. For all the great success of the *Henriade* Voltaire realised that he would never be able to publish this or any other unorthodox work openly in France. He was never again so simple-minded as to believe that in a totalitarian society a ton of merit and sound sentiments could balance a scruple of independent thought. Hardly had the surreptitious *Ligue* been smuggled into Paris than Voltaire sent a copy to George I. 'I have spoken in my work with liberty and truth. You, sire, are the protector of the one and the other; and I dare to flatter myself that you will accord me your royal protection to print in your realms a work which must interest you since it is the eulogy of virtue.'[16] This was not merely a dutiful response to the king's presents: Voltaire really intended to go to England, and very soon he did, though not in circumstances that he could have anticipated.

In the meanwhile he tried hard but unsuccessfully to extract some money from his father's estate[17]; amused himself with the Jansenist miracles which were all the rage, seeing something of a mme Lafosse, who, said he, was cured of a haemorrhage at the price of losing her sight[18]; but perhaps the most significant episode of these months was the beginning of his twenty years' war with Desfontaines[19]. The ex-Jesuit Pierre François Guyot Desfontaines (1684-1745) was a man incapable of original work, but indefatigable in criticising that produced by others more fortunate.

15 Best.D198 (5 August 1724).
16 Best.D250 (6 October 1725).
17 Best.D212 (28 September 1724); D243 (23 July 1725).
18 Best.D241 (27 June 1725); D246 (20 August 1725); *Siècle de Louis XIV*,

xxxvii
19 See Thelma Morris, *L'Abbé Desfontaines et son rôle dans la littérature de son temps* (Studies on Voltaire, xix: 1961).

During the last fifteen years of his life he edited, and largely wrote, successively the *Nouvelliste du Parnasse*, the *Observations sur les écrits modernes* and the *Jugements sur quelques ouvrages nouveaux*. These serial writings are sometimes readable and even amusing, but they lack lasting value. Desfontaines had no particular principles, and seldom went beyond the expression of personal likes and, more often, dislikes. And as he was anything but an interesting character, and only superficially well-read, we are as little interested in his views as in his likes or antipathies.

The earliest encounters between the two men are thoroughly characteristic of Voltaire, who began by being enormously magnanimous to him, and for that very reason came to loathe him unendurably. Voltaire was a man of great, perhaps excessive punctilio. Though there were no limits to his toleration of a man's beliefs and morals, he found it difficult to forgive bad manners.

As soon as the *Henriade* had scored its sensational success Desfontaines not merely produced a pirated edition of the poem but larded it with objectionable and dangerous lines of his own. Voltaire tried to get the edition suppressed, which was virtually impossible, but otherwise made no more than the mildest of comments[20]. Only a few weeks later, when Voltaire was trying to find Richelieu a secretary to accompany him on his embassy to Vienna, Desfontaines did not scruple to recommend a friend for the job, and Voltaire did not hesitate to accept the recommendation[21] after Thieriot had haughtily refused the job. And a few months after *that*, when Desfontaines was in prison for sodomy, he still did not scruple to appeal to Voltaire for help, and Voltaire still did not hesitate to intervene on his behalf. So far as is known, and the documents have survived, he was the first, and very nearly the only one to do so of all those to whom Desfontaines applied. The case was serious, for buggery was a capital offence[22] and long remained one that was universally condemned. Nearly a century and a half later Desnoiresterres (i.325) dared not name the *abbé*'s offence, merely describing it as a nameless infamy. Yet Voltaire was successful in his efforts on the *abbé*'s behalf, and Desfontaines

20 Best.D200 (17 August 1724).
21 Best.D217 (13 October 1724).
22 At just about this time Etienne

Benjamin Des Chaufours was in fact burnt for sodomy (24 May 1726); see the references given in Best.D923, n.5.

was merely exiled. On his release from prison he told Voltaire that he would never forget what he had done for him: 'Your good heart is superior even to your intellect, and you are the best friend any man has ever had.'[23] A year later he was writing and intriguing against his benefactor[24]; and the story will unfortunately have to be continued later on.

Voltaire had the world at his feet, being already recognised as the standard bearer of French letters. He was happy in love, or at least successful. He was the intimate of the learned and the great. Three of his plays were performed at court.[25] He became the lover of the powerful mme de Prie—powerful because she was the titular mistress of the prime minister, the duc de Bourbon—and went with her to Bélébat, where his light-hearted *Fête de Bélébat* was performed. As for the queen, she had wept at *Mariamne*, laughed at *L'Indiscret*, and Voltaire boasted ironically that she called him 'mon pauvre Voltaire' (terms which imply friendly intimacy) and had granted him another annuity[26]. He accompanied the duc d'Antin on a visit to king Stanislas at Bellegarde[27]. And, perhaps most practically useful of all, he was on excellent and profitable terms with the wealthy financier Pâris-Duverney[28]. All this happened in October-November 1725.

So Voltaire triumphantly traversed his nonage: he was no longer an infant prodigy, but at thirty-one he had fame, security, money; 1725 ended with a *magnificat*. He is no longer unhappy at court: 'I begin to have reasonable hopes of being able sometimes to be useful there to my friends.'[29]

Abruptly and violently, a few weeks later, Rohan put an end to all that. Voltaire had long known the chevalier Gui Auguste de Rohan-Chabot, an effete offspring of a family once great, but now they quarrelled. It would appear that Rohan sneered at Voltaire's bourgeois origins and change of name, to which the poet made the obvious retort that Rohan dishonoured his own lineage. So far the incident is insignificant: every society has its

23 Best.D235 (31 May 1725); see Voltaire's own account in the autobiography, pp. 628-629, below.

24 Best.D300 (16 August 1726).

25 Best.D252-3 (both 17 October 1725).

26 The vellum document is now Th. B.

27 Best.D253 (17 October 1725), D254 (18 October 1725).

28 Best.D255 (13 November 1725).

29 Best.D255 (13 November 1725).

boors, but what followed is shocking. Voltaire was dining with the duc de Sully, rue Saint-Antoine, was called to the front door, and was there beaten by the servants of Rohan, who directed the operations from his carriage. When Voltaire rushed upstairs in a rage, the duke shrugged his shoulders: after all, Rohan was a kinsman, Voltaire merely a bourgeois friend of genius. And when Voltaire's subsequent actions (including a stay with a fencing master) made it clear that he would pursue the chevalier until he could bring him to a duel, the Rohan family had the poet thrown into the Bastille (17/18 April 1726).[30]

These facts are so offensive to our notions of fair play that the reader may well suspect my narrative to be partial. Let me therefore quote without comment the account of them given by the maréchal-duc de Villars:

The chevalier was much inconvenienced by a fall which did not permit him to act the bravo. He decided to have Voltaire beaten in broad daylight. Voltaire, instead of appealing to the law, felt that it was more noble to avenge himself by a duel. It is alleged that he sought one assiduously and too indiscreetly. The cardinal de Rohan asked the duke[31] to have him sent to the Bastille; the order was given and carried out; and the unhappy poet, after being beaten, was also imprisoned. The public, disposed to complain of everything, this time was right in finding that everybody was to blame: Voltaire for having offended the chevalier de Rohan; he, for having dared to commit a crime worthy of death in having a citizen beaten; the government for not having punished so notorious a misdeed, and for having the beaten man sent to the Bastille to reassure the beater.[32]

Voltaire wrote to the comte de Maurepas (the responsible minister): 'I would point out very humbly that I was assaulted by the brave chevalier de Rohan, helped by six cut-throats behind whom he had courageously posted himself. Since then I have constantly sought to restore not my honour, but his, which has proved too difficult.'[33] The authorities were little affected by Voltaire's sad irony, but they were more responsive to his offer

---

30 Lucien Foulet, ed. *Correspondance de Voltaire (1726-29)* (Paris 1923), pp. 211-32, gives a masterly account of the whole affair—but he did not know that Voltaire and Rohan were old friends, which of course makes the latter's behaviour even worse.

31 The duc de Bourbon, in effect the regent of France.

32 [Louis Hector de] Villars, *Mémoires*, ed. marquis C. J. M. de Vogüé (Paris 1884-1909).

33 Best.D271 (*c.* 20 April 1726).

to go to England. After all, everybody knew that he was in the right, and he was lionised in the Bastille. All that mattered to the family was that the chevalier should be shielded from the dishonour of being made to cross swords with a commoner. So Voltaire's offer was accepted. This may seem an informal way of doing things, but it is a mistake to suppose that the procedures of the *ancien régime* were always inhuman and bureaucratic. By no means: on many files in the prison archives can be found such endorsements as 'release him if you are satisfied', 'grant his request if you think that he deserves it', 'let her go if she promises to behave herself', and the like. An illustration of this informally and instinctively humane (and of course just as often inhumane) way of doing things is found in the fact that when Voltaire was himself in the Bastille he procured the release from the same prison of Lenglet Du Fresnoy, who had been there for over two years.[34] Anyway, after a fortnight Voltaire was accompanied to Calais, and about the middle of May 1726 he set foot in England. In July he returned secretly and briefly to Paris, still in bootless pursuit of the noble coward, but apart from this remained in England until the turn of the year 1728/29.

Voltaire did not leave France in too melancholy a spirit:

> Je ne dois pas être plus fortuné
> Que le héros célébré sur ma vielle:
> Il fut proscrit, persécuté, damné
> Par les dévots & leur douce séquelle:
> En Angleterre il trouva du secours,
> J'en vais chercher. . . .[35]

It was highly injudicious under the *ancien régime* for a poet, however eminent, to quarrel with a nobleman, however mean: so that when the nobleman and the poet had words, he that was called Rohan was able to order the beating-up of one whose name had been Arouet: and the consequence was that the poet was abandoned by his great friends, and imprisoned at the request of the nobleman's family. Voltaire was not deeply affected by his first imprisonment ten years before: he knew that it was not wholly

34 Best.D298 (? 29 June 1726).
35 Best.D294 (*c.* 8 May 1726); translated below, p. 627.

undeserved, that it was all part of the game, and he took it in his stride although he was innocent of the specific charge. This time he had been made the victim of vulgar injustice, he, the author of *Œdipe* and the *Henriade*, the intimate friend and guest of half the great families in France—and all because he had dared to answer back a Rohan. (One is reminded of Rochester's assault on Dryden: but that was half a century earlier, and Dryden at least was not imprisoned to soften the blows.) Voltaire's reaction was dignified, even stern, and from this moment a new note of gravity enters his writings, never to leave it, and often to be accompanied by a philosophic melancholy.

This change of direction was further emphasised by the immediate result of Voltaire's imprisonment: the hoped for but still involuntary departure for England, which was to become his spiritual home. This time, for once, all was for the best.

11. England and the English letters, *1726-1728*

THE PERIOD 1726-8, marking the transition from the first to the second George, was far from glorious, but a number of circumstances served to make it significant for Voltaire. Politics, it is true, were corrupt, but the squalid scene was relieved by one event: the passing in 1727 of the first of the indemnity acts, which gradually relieved from civil disabilities those who had the misfortune to stand outside the established church. This was to a Frenchman like Voltaire a measure of the highest toleration, and largely accounted for the status in his thinking of England as a symbol of freethought.[1]

Literature was passing through an arid phase, but three works were published during Voltaire's stay in England which strongly appealed to different facets of his temperament: *Gulliver's travels* (1726) to his imagination, the *Dunciad* (1728) to his satirical spirit and love of free speech, the first of Thomson's *Seasons* (1726) to his poetic sensibility; and perhaps the first performance in 1728 of the evergreen *Beggar's opera* is worth noting.

One other happy coincidence was not the least important: Bolingbroke had returned to England a few months before, and was able to introduce Voltaire to the strange society in which he found himself. Yet Voltaire made singularly little impression on England at the time. He printed a lavish edition of the *Henriade*, but not, it must be admitted a really handsome one, a mixture of French and English styles, with its impressive and in many ways significant list of 350 subscribers. He published his *Essay upon the civil wars of France . . . and upon the epick poetry of the European*

---

[1] And so it was, but there were limits: an apprentice in his teens was hanged in 1720 for printing a Jacobite pamphlet; see *State trials* (1812), xv. 1323-1403, quoted by T. C. Duncan Eaves and Ben D. Kimpel, *Samuel Richardson* (Oxford 1971), p. 28.

nations[2]. He fought another campaign in his war against the book-sellers. And that is about all. Voltaire is seldom mentioned in the English memoirs of the time, and few contemporary letters to and even fewer from English correspondents have survived; indeed, although Voltaire undoubtedly met a great many people, including some of the leading figures of the time, he clearly led a retired life and, what is perhaps more important, maintained an attitude of reserve. He was licking his wounds, and he was reading and thinking and writing, as witness the fascinating notebooks of this period, as witness the *Lettres philosophiques*, and as witnesses indeed the rest of Voltaire's life and works. In short, he may not have left any particular personal mark on England, but England influence him profoundly and lastingly[3].

The French establishment was still framed by the social structure which led to Voltaire's departure for England, but was not deluded by it. The comte de Morville, Châteauneuf's successor at The Hague, was now foreign secretary. Far from spurning the persecuted jail-bird he recommended him to the comte de Broglie, French ambassador to the court of St James's, and also asked the British ambassador in Paris, Horatio Walpole (afterwards first baron Walpole of Wolverton), to recommend him to the foreign secretary, the duke of Newcastle, and others[4]. Voltaire did not arrive in England as a man in disgrace, but as an honoured guest, especially as Bolingbroke was now holding court at Dawley.

Yet all this was on the surface: what counted was Voltaire's state of mind. His first and most moving impression on reaching our island was lyrical.

When I landed near London it was the middle of spring. The sky was cloudless, as on the finest days in the south of France. The air was refreshed by a mild west wind, which increased the serenity of nature and disposed the mind to joy: to such an extent are we *machines*, and so much do our souls depend on the feelings of our bodies! I stopped near Greenwich, on the banks

2 But all the French editors have ignored the original English editions.

3 Yet in his autobiography Voltaire's only reference to his stay in England is a short allusion to the publication of the *Henriade*; see pp. 626-627 below. An admirable and detailed account of all this has been published since this chapter was written: André Michel Rousseau, *L'Angleterre et Voltaire* (Studies on Voltaire, cxlv-cxlvii: 1976). This book deals with all Voltaire's contacts with England and all things English.

4 Best.D295-7 (all 29 May 1726).

LETTERS

CONCERNING THE

ENGLISH
NATION.

BY

Mr. DE VOLTAIRE.

LONDON,

Printed for C. Davis in *Pater-Noster-Row*,
and A. Lyon in *Russel-Street*, *Covent-Garden*.
MDCCXXXIII.

5 *Letters concerning the English nation*, London 1733,
titlepage of the first edition

6 Voltaire's letter of 25 October 1721 to Thieriot, *as manipulated by the editors,*
from the holograph in the Bibliothèque nationale

of the Thames. This lovely river, which never overflows, and whose borders are green all the year round, was covered by two rows of merchant vessels to an extent of six miles. All had hoisted their sails in honour of the king and queen, who took their ease on the river in a golden bark, preceded by boats filled with musicians and followed by a thousand little row-boats; each had two oarsmen, all dressed as were our pages formerly, in trunk-hose and doublets with a large plaque of silver on the shoulder. There was not one of these mariners who did not show by his appearance, by his dress, and by his physique that he was a free man and lived in plenty.[5]

Yet, in plainer prose, there is no doubt that at first Voltaire was deeply distressed in his own mind. While his mistress went to the opera[6] (no doubt in the box Voltaire had procured for her) with the man whose vanity and cowardice were responsible for his imprisonment, and his closest friend amused himself at Forges[7], Voltaire was resigned to the conclusion that he was fated to be unhappy. He soon found that the English character was by no means so limpid as he first thought, nor English institutions so uniformly praiseworthy, nor the weather always good. Moreover, though he was by no means penniless, no sooner had he reached our shores than he suffered from a banker's failure; and soon after he received news of his sister's death[8].

This depression lasted well into the autumn. At the end of October he wrote to Thieriot ('J write to you in english, for the same reason that abbot Boylau wrote in latin, j mean that j should not be understood by many over curious people'[9])—the speed with which he had picked up the language is amazing:

Let me acquaint you with an account of my for ever cursed fortune. J came again into England in the latter end of July very much dissatisfied with my secret voiage into France both unsuccessful and expensive. J had about me onely some bills of exchange upon a Jew called Medina[10] for the sum of about eight or nine thousand French livres, reckoning all. At my coming to

5 *A M****; this essay is always dated 1727, but it was probably written later, for Voltaire's chronology is at fault; Sophia Dorothea, the queen of George I, died in seclusion in 1726; Voltaire must have seen George II, who succeeded in 1727, and queen Caroline, and is not likely to have made such a slip immediately after the event.

6 Best.D305 (27 October 1726).

7 *The Miscellaneous works of bishop Atterbury*, ed. J. Nichols (London 1790), [v].72-3.

8 Best.D302 (26 October 1726).

9 Best.D333 (2 May 1728).

10 None of the Medinas seems to have failed, but rather Anthony Mendes da Costa; see Oskar K. Rabinowicz, *Sir Solomon de Medina* (London 1974).

London i found my damned Jew was broken. I was without a penny, sick to death of a violent agüe, a stranger, alone, helpless, in the midst of a city, wherein j was known to no body. My lord and lady Bolingbroke were in the country. J could not make bold to see our ambassadour in so wretched a condition. J had never undergone such distress; but j am born to run through all the misfortunes of life.

But if Voltaire wrote in this vein it was because the tide had in fact turned.

In these circumstances, my star, that among all its direful influences pours allways on me some kind of refreshment, sent to me an English gentleman unknown to me, who forced me to receive some money that j wanted. An other London citizen that j had seen but once at Paris, carried me to his own country house, wherein j lead an obscure and charming life since that time, without going to London, and quite given over to the pleasures of indolence and of friendship. The true and generous affection of this man who sooths the bitterness of my life brings me to love you more and more. All the instances of friendship indear my friend Tiriot to me. J have seen often mylord and mylady Bolingbroke. J have found their affection still the same, even increased in proportion to my unhappiness. They offered me all, their money, their house, but j refused all, because they are lords, and j have accepted all from m^r Faulknear, because he is a single gentleman.[11]

Yet Voltaire clearly had much affection and admiration for Bolingbroke. He recorded in one of his notebooks, it is true, that Bolingbroke 'was as great whoremaster as great statesman. He was in the bloom of his youth, and of his whoring too, when queen Anna made him secretary of war. A swarm of strumpets were walking in St James' park, when a sudden rumor was spred, h. st. [Henry St John] was raised to that place which is worth five thousand pounds a year. All the whores cried out with joy, god bless us, five thousand pounds all among us.'[12] But the eighteenth century was not censorious about such trifles, and Voltaire was entirely sincere when he sang

> toi, cher Bolingbroke, héros qui d'Apollon
> As reçu plus d'une couronne,
> Qui réunis en ta personne
> L'éloquence de Cicéron,

---

11 Best.D303 (26 October 1726); the penultimate word should no doubt be 'simple': the MS. has not been found; the reference is to (sir) Everard Fawkener.

12 *Voltaire's notebooks*, i.61.

L'intrépidité de Caton,
L'esprit de Mécénas, l'agrément de Pétrone.[13]

The relations between the two men became less intimate later on, though when Thieriot was in England in 1732 Voltaire asked him to 'tell chiefly my lord Bolingbrooke j am attachd to them for life.'[14]

For the remaining two years of Voltaire's stay in England, his letters are normal in tone, but they are singularly uninformative. He wrote, to France, for the most part to Thieriot, trying to interest his lazy friend in English books. He recommended the poems of Pope, 'the best poet of England, and at present, of all the world'[15]. He was among the first to recognise the genius of *Gulliver's travels* by the 'English Rabelais'; he had never read anything more amusing and wittier, urging Thieriot to translate the book[16]. Thieriot of course preferred to try his hand at an obscure romance translated from the Arabic, but which Voltaire judiciously found not worth the trouble of being searched for, and he discouraged Thieriot from reading 'that spiritual nauseous romance'[17]. Then he proposed Henry Pemberton's *A View of sir Isaac Newton's philosophy*[18]. All was in vain, even Voltaire's own *Essay* was translated by Desfontaines, very badly as usual.

Voltaire's inland correspondence must have been voluminous. Among the few letters that have survived is a friendly note[19] of sympathy to Pope after an accident:

Sir,

J Hear this moment of your sad adventure. That water you fell in, was not Hippocrene's water, otherwise it would have respected you. Jndeed j am concerned beyond expression for the danger you have been in, and more for your wounds. Is it possible that those fingers which have written the rape of the lock and the Criticism, which have dressed Homer so becomingly in an

---

13 *Epître à monsieur de Gervasi* (1723); 'you, dear Bolingbroke, hero who has received more than one crown from Apollo, who unite in your person the eloquence of Cicero, the intrepidity of Cato, the intelligence of Maecenas, the charm of Petronius.'

14 Best.D492 (26 May 1732).

15 Best.D303 (26 October 1726).

16 Best.D306-7 (*c.* 15 November 1726, only a week after the publication of *Gulliver*).

17 Best.D310 (11 March 1727). As a matter of fact the romance, best known as Edward Pocock's *Philosophus autodidactus* (but see Best.D308, note 2), is not without interest in the history of ideas, for it is about a human suckled by a gazelle on a desert island.

18 Best.D315 (27 March 1727).

19 Best.D301 (September/October 1726).

english coat, should have been so barbarously treated? Let the hand of Dennis, or of your poetasters be cut of. Yours is sacred. J hope ser you are now perfectly recovered. Rely your accident concers me as much as all the disasters of a master ought to affect his scholar. J am sincerely ser with the admiration which you deserve

Your most humble servant

Voltaire

Voltaire also wrote[20] to Swift, enclosing letters of recommendation before the dean's abortive journey to France; but little else has come down to us, except for some business and courtesy letters concerning the *Henriade*, the printing and distribution of which took up much time. Among these a charming note[21] to John Brinsden, Bolingbroke's secretary, must be quoted:

S^r,

J wish you good health, a quick sale of y^r burgundy, much latin and greek to one of y^r children, much Law, much of Cooke, and Littleton, to the other, quiet and joy to mistress Brinsden, money to all. When you'll drink y^r Burgundy with m^r Furneze pray tell him j'll never forget his favours.

But dear John be so kind as to let me know how does mylady Ballingbrooke. As to mylord j left him so well j don't doubt he is so still. But j am very uneasie about mylady. If she might have as much health as she has spirit and witt, sure she would be the strongest body in england. Pray dear s^r write me something of her, of mylord, and of you. Direct y^r letter by the penny post at m^r Cavalier, Belitery square by the R. exchange. J am sincerely and heartily y^r most humble most obedient rambling friend

Voltaire

And I cannot resist quoting *in full* the letter of introduction to the duke of Queensberry which Voltaire gave a little later to mlle Sallé when the actress went to England: 'And shall j be the only one, who will saying nothing to y^r grace about m^{rs} Sallé? Oh per dio no.'[22]

Voltaire even wrote some English verse, of which these conventional lines to Molly Lepell (lady Hervey) have survived:

> Hervey, would you know the passion
> You have kindled in my breast?
> Trifling is the inclination

20 Best.D319 (16 June 1727); see also Best.D323, D328.

21 Best.D338 (summer 1728); 'dear John' is a striking example of Voltaire's adaptability: the use of a person's first name was in France's upper circles almost entirely limited to his family.

22 Best.D382 (*c*. 1 December 1730).

That by words can be express'd.
In my silence see the lover;
True love is by silence known:
In my eyes you'ill best discover
All the power of your own.[23]

From all these letters it is possible to make a list of some of Voltaire's addresses: Everard Fawkener's house at Wandsworth; Half-Penny, the house of a dyer, also at Wandsworth; Cavalier's, Billiter square; the White wig, in Maiden lane, near Covent garden; these are sure, others are probable, of which only Bolingbroke's town and country houses need be mentioned: the former was in Pall Mall, the latter at Dawley, near Uxbridge.

As soon as the arrangements for the *Henriade* were under way Voltaire put in motion the procedures necessary to obtain permission to return to France. His first petition[24] dates from March 1727, and by June he was authorised[25] to spend three months in Paris. He let more than a year pass, and we do not know exactly when he left England. He wrote to Thieriot in August 1728 from London[26]; by November lord Peterborough thought that Voltaire had taken his leave of England and was 'gone to Constantinople in order to believe in the gospels, which he says it is impossible to do living among the teachers of Christianity'[27]—this has the true Voltairean accent, but fortunately the witty sceptic had not gone so far. No further letter from him has survived until February 1729 (an almost uniquely long gap in his correspondence) when he was already at Saint-Germain under a false name, after a stay at Dieppe[28]. In this letter Voltaire tells Thieriot: 'When you see me you shall see and hear things which will please you, recommended to you by the graces of novelty'[29]. And these words enable me to turn with some relief from these scrappy bits of information to the real significance of Voltaire's stay in England.

When Voltaire said that he hoped to learn to think in England[30], this must not be taken literally: he had already reflected to good

23 I have preferred the text of the *Pièces inédites* (Paris 1820), p. 79, misprint and all.
24 Best.D311.
25 Best.D320.
26 Best.D341.
27 Best.D342.

28 See J. C. Guédon, 'Le Retour d'Angleterre de Voltaire et son séjour chez Jacques Tranquillain Féret de Dieppe', *Studies on Voltaire* (1974), cxxiv.137-42.
29 Best.D344.
30 Best.D299 (12 August 1726).

purpose, and had already arrived at the essential ideas characteristic of his philosophy. But certainly his sense of justice, his scepticism and toleration, were confirmed by his reading and experiences here. What he learned in England particularly in the field of politics and government, he never forgot. All his subsequent work, which represents of course the overwhelming bulk of his output, shows this in every line. We must now look at the books which most clearly and most quickly grew from seed planted in England. The chief were indeed drafted there: the *Lettres philosophiques*, first published in English in 1733 under the title of *Letters concerning the English nation*[31]: the *Histoire de Charles XII* (1731), the first 'modern' history: and the tragedy of *Brutus* (1730).

But it is interesting to glance first at Voltaire's notebooks.[32]. He was an assiduous annotator throughout his life, and among the numerous collections and fragments which have survived in manuscript, two[33] date from the English years. Of course such notes must be used with the utmost caution, if only because Voltaire may well have kept others devoted to special subjects. In other words we must not make any negative generalisations, but are free to make proper conclusions from what *is* there.

The first thing that strikes one is the universality of his interests. Philosophical and historical reflections and data abound; but so do notes on etymology, superstitions, anatomy, science, and many other things. Voltaire clearly had a nice taste in bawdy, and kept his eye shrewdly cocked for the absurd. He obviously cared passionately for poetry, and one is amazed by his remarkable memory for major and minor poets in French, English, Latin, Italian: for there is internal evidence that he often quoted and translated from memory. When, here and there, his memory played him false, what he puts down is often an improvement on the original. An example is provided by Pope's famous epitaph on Newton:

> Nature and nature's laws lay hid in night,
> God said let Newton be, and all was light.

31 All quotations are from this edition.

32 These fascinating documents unfortunately remained substantially unknown until 1952, when I published two volumes of *Voltaire's notebooks*, a new and much enlarged edition of which was published in 1968 as Voltaire 81-82; all the references are of course to this new edition.

33 One is in Leningrad, the other in Cambridge.

The hissing sibilants of the first words, as usually pronounced, damage the lapidary effect of the couplet; and in his memory Voltaire transformed them to 'All nature and its laws lay hid in night'[34].

In these notebooks Voltaire quotes Dryden most often among the English poets: and also of course, Pope, as well as Denham, Gay, Rochester, Waller, Milton, Ben Jonson, Temple, Hervey.

The *Notebooks* are full of those elegantly phrased flashes of insight which so distinguish all Voltaire's writing; here are a few examples among those written in English soon after his arrival in England:

We have begun in France to write pretty well, before we have begun to think. English on the contrary.[35]

Seldom brothers agrée together. T'is for this reason sovereigns of Europe are stiled brothers to each other.[36]

Nature, purity, perspicuity, simplicity never walk in the clouds. They are obvious to all capacities and where they are not evident, they don't exist.[37]

A king is in England a necessary thing to preserve the spirit of liberty, as a post to a fencer to coerce himself.[38]

Voltaire made his purpose in writing the *Letters concerning the English nation* perfectly clear, not indeed in the book itself, but in the 'Advertisement to the reader' of *An Essay upon the civil wars*, in which he tells us that he had been 'ordered to give an Account of my Journey into *England*'. And he explains thus his intentions.

The true Aim of a Relation is to instruct Men, not to gratify their Malice. We should be busied chiefly in giving faithful Accounts of all the useful Things and of the extraordinary Persons, whom to know, and to imitate, would be a Benefit to our Countrymen. A Traveller who writes in that Spirit, is a Merchant of a noble Kind, who imports into his native Country the Arts and Virtues of other Nations.

I will leave to others the Care of describing with Accuracy, *Paul's* Church, the *Monument, Westminster, Stonehenge*, &c. I consider *England* in another view; it strikes my Eyes as it is the Land which hath produced a *Newton*, a *Locke*, a *Tillotson*, a *Milton*, a *Boyle*. . . .

The *Letters* deal with religion in England, most space being

34 *Voltaire's notebooks*, i.70, 332.
35 *Voltaire's notebooks*, i.55.
36 *Voltaire's notebooks*, i.61.
37 *Voltaire's notebooks*, i.62.
38 *Voltaire's notebooks*, i.68.

devoted to the Quakers; with government and trade; inoculation; Francis Bacon; Locke and Newton, that is, the new philosophy and the new physics; the stage and literature; individual writers, chiefly Shakespeare, Rochester, Waller and Pope (he discussed Milton in the *Essay on epick poetry*); the Royal society and other academies.

The outstanding feature of the book is seldom explicit, but it was nevertheless so obvious to his contemporaries that the book was persistently condemned and prohibited in France.[39] Voltaire wrote about England, but in a sense he wrote also about his own country. When he praised our institutions it was certainly because he admired them, but it was also because those of France were different. A word of approbation *here* was necessarily one of condemnation *there*; so Voltaire intended, so France understood. Everything in the *Letters* was intended to strike home to French breasts, and did. Consider such a passage as this:

Take a view of the *Royal-Exchange* in *London*, a place more venerable than many courts of justice, where the representatives of all nations meet for the benefit of mankind.[40] There the Jew, the Mahometan, and the Christian transact together as tho' they all profess'd the same religion, and give the name of Infidel to none but bankrupts. There the Presbyterian confides in the Anabaptist, and the Churchman depends on the Quaker's word. At the breaking up of this pacific and free assembly, some withdraw to the synagogue and others to take a glass. This man goes and is baptiz'd in a great tub, and in the name of the Father, Son, and Holy Ghost: That man has his son's foreskin cut off, whilst a sett of *Hebrew* words (quite unintelligible to him) are mumbled over his child. Others retire to their churchs, and there wait for the inspiration of heaven with their hats on, and all are satisfied.

If one religion only were allowed in England, the government would very possibly become arbitrary; if there were but two, the people wou'd cut one another's throats; but as there are such a multitude, they all live happy and in peace.[41]

In praising English religious tolerance, Voltaire is gently ironical about religion itself; he does not miss the opportunity to slip in a hint that business is after all taken more seriously in

---

39 Rome for once was slack, and did not put the book on the *Index* until 1752.

40 The first sentence in the earliest of Voltaire's surviving notebooks reads: 'England is meeting of all religions, as the Royal exchange is the rendez vous of all foreigners.'

41 *Letters*, pp. 44-5.

England than religion; but the sting is in the tail: for in France only one religion was in fact allowed, government was in fact arbitrary, and the Jesuits and Jansenists were in fact at each other's throats. And of course everything is relative: Voltaire found organised religion in England good only by contrast with that of France.

As for the Church of England in itself, the author made some thoroughly Voltairean comments: 'No person can possess an employement either in *England* or *Ireland*, unless he be rank'd among the faithful, that is, profess himself a member of the Church of *England*. This reason (which carries mathematical evidence with it) has converted such numbers of dissenters of all persuasions, that not a twentieth part of the nation is out of the pale of the establish'd church. The *English* clergy have retain'd a great number of the Romish ceremonies, and especially that of receiving, with a most scrupulous attention, their tithes.'[42]

Voltaire deals as elegantly with all the fields of knowledge and reflection into which he enters. Although prohibited, the *Lettres philosophiques* were quickly printed in French and frequently reprinted. The cumulative effect was terrific, and the book has been rightly described as 'the first bomb thrown at the *ancien régime*.'[43]

The book had a wider impact even than this. Of course in England it was very widely read[44], and it was translated into a number of languages. And indeed the *Letters* contain much of universal application. Consider this eloquent and impassioned plea for peace, which Voltaire puts into the mouth of a Quaker:

The reason of our not using the outward sword is, that we are neither wolves, tygers, nor mastiffs, but men and Christians. Our God, who has commanded us to love our enemies, and to suffer without repining, would certainly not permit us to cross the seas, merely because murtherers cloath'd in scarlet, and wearing caps two foot high enlist citizens by a noise made with two little sticks on an ass's skin extended. And when, after a victory is gain'd the whole city of *London* is illuminated; when the sky is in a blaze of fireworks, and a noise is heard in the air of thanksgivings, of bells, of organs,

42 *Letters*, p. 34.
43 Gustave Lanson, *Voltaire* (Paris [1906], p. 52.
44 The English text went into about sixteen editions in the eighteenth century, but since then has been printed only twice: surely a publishing oddity if ever there was one, when one considers that Voltaire's book represents perhaps the most thoughtful and influential tribute ever paid to English institutions.

and of the cannon, we groan in silence, and are deeply affected with sadness of spirit and brokenness of heart, for the sad havock which is the occasion of those public rejoycings.[45]

Voltaire's fame as France's greatest living writer was already established: the *Letters* could do no more than confirm it. Such passages as this established a new reputation, that of Voltaire the humanitarian.

Another work Voltaire started in England was the tragedy of *Brutus*[46] and its important preliminary discourse on tragedy, dedicated to Bolingbroke. By the end of December 1729 the play was finished—so far as Voltaire was ever disposed to consider any of his writings as finished, for he was an obsessional reviser—and the actors were ready to produce it. But it seems that Rohan and others were plotting against it, perhaps because of the alleged republican sentiments of the play, and it was not put on until a year later. Though Voltaire considered it to be his 'most spirited tragedy'[47], it was only moderately successful. However, it steadily increased in popularity, until it became one o. the favourite plays of the revolution—only to be later condemned as reactionary.

The subject of Voltaire's tragedy is not Caesar's friend but the much earlier Lucius Junius Brutus, consul in 509 B.C. The play opens as the Roman senate discuss the offer of Porsenna to send them Tarquin's ambassador. Of course, as always, it is not the subject that counts, it is the manner, and that at once emerges from the opening couplet, spoken by Brutus to the Roman senators:

> Destructeurs des tyrans, vous qui n'avez pour rois
> Que les dieux de Numa, vos vertus et nos lois. . . .[48]

The play is in fact the dramatisation of the conflict between a democracy and external tyranny; and of course the audience, as always, kept their ears open for such outspoken passages as:

---

45 *Letters*, p. 10. Cp. Walpole's 'They now ring the bells, but they will soon wring their hands'; see William Coxe, *Memoirs of . . . sir Robert Walpole* (1798), i.618.
46 Notes for the 'Discours' can be seen in the *Notebooks*, i.82.

47 See the autobiography, pp. 627-628, below.
48 'Destroyers of tyrants, you that have for kings only the gods of Numa, your virtues and our laws. . . .'

Crois-moi, la liberté, que tout mortel adore. . . .
Donne à l'homme un courage, inspire une grandeur,
Qu'il n'eût jamais trouvés dans le fond de son cœur,[49]

and

Arrêtez un Romain sur de simples soupçons,
C'est agir en tyrans, nous qui les punissons,[50]

And when Brutus said that the glory of the senate was to represent the people[51] he uttered an assertion of the democratic idea never before heard on the French stage, an idea which is spelled out most explicitly. Brutus tells Tarquin's ambassador not to plead the innate right of his king. The Romans had taken oaths of loyalty, not of slavery, and for his part the king had sworn to be just. This mutual oath was the bond between the people and the king. 'Il nous rend nos serments lorsqu'il trahit le sien.'[52] In these lines the notion of a public justice transcending authority was heard for the first time. This was strong and inspiring stuff.

Not less permanently valuable than *Brutus* itself, though in a very different way, was the 'Discours sur la tragédie' prefixed to it. This essay on the tragic stage can best be described as an attempt to rationalise the shock Voltaire received on first encountering the English stage, and above all Shakespeare. Voltaire first dealt with this subject in the *Lettres philosophiques*, and returned to it again and again throughout his life. This love-hatred is too complex to bear chronological fragmentation: see the next chapter.

But before dealing with it as a whole, I want to mention a by-product of *Brutus*: by no means the worst thing that came out of it was the letter Voltaire wrote to Marie Ange Dangeville after the first night. She was not quite sixteen when she created the role of

---

49 *Brutus,* I.iii; 'Believe me, liberty, adored by every mortal . . . gives man a courage, inspires a grandeur which he would never have found in the bottom of his heart.'

50 *Brutus,* IV.vii; M.ii.370-1. 'We who punish them act as tyrants when we arrest Romans on mere suspicions'; and the later fate of Voltaire's tragedy is illuminated by the fact that under the revolutionary terror this couplet was altered to

Arrêtez un Romain sur de simples soupçons,
Ne peut être permis qu'en révolution.

'To arrest a Roman on a mere suspicion can be permitted only in a revolution'; A. F. Villemain, *Cours de littérature française* (1828), iv.192.

51 *Brutus,* I.ii.

52 *Brutus,* I.ii; 'He frees us from our oaths when he betrays his own.'

Tullie, and her feelings need no description. Has any dramatist—
even Bernard Shaw—ever written a more admirable letter to a
young actress? What a wonderful mixture of encouragement and
exhortation, reasoned criticism and measured flattery, with the
merest dash of flirtation! And the wise and avuncular Voltaire
himself was only thirty-six:

> Prodigy, here is a copy of the *Henriade*: it is a very serious work for one of
> your age; but a girl who takes the part of Tullie is capable of reading, and it
> is only just that I should give my works to her who embellishes them. I
> thought I was going to die tonight, and I am in a very sad state; otherwise I
> should be at your feet to thank you for the honour you do me today. The
> play is unworthy of you; but be sure that you will acquire much glory in
> covering with your charms my role of Tullie. Any success will be due to you.
> But in order to achieve it remember not to hurry anything, to animate
> everything, to mingle sighs with your declamation, to pause much. Above all,
> perform the final couplet of your first act with much soul and energy. Put
> terror, sobs and long pauses into the finale. Appear desperate in it, and you
> will make your rivals despair. Farewell, prodigy.
>
> Do not become discouraged; consider that you acted marvellously at the
> rehearsals, and that all you lacked yesterday was boldness. Even your
> timidity does you honour. Tomorrow you will avenge yourself. I saw
> Mariamne fall, and I saw her rise up again.[53]
>
> For god's sake, set your mind at rest. Even if things do not go well, what
> does it matter? You are not what you will be one day. As for me, all I have to
> say is to express my thanks: but if you are not a little sensitive to my tender
> and respectful friendship you will never perform tragic roles. Begin by
> having some friendship for me, who love you like a father, and you will act
> the role admirably.
>
> Farewell; it rests only with you to be divine tomorrow.[54]

It is not surprising that on receiving this letter mlle Dangeville
acted 'like an angel'. Voltaire had written some charming lines
warning her not to allow her fruit to be plucked before it was ripe;
on learning how well she had played her role, he hastily added:

> Ma Tullie, il est déjà temps,
> Allons vite que l'on te cueille.[55]

---

53 [This was a compliment at once
bold and subtle, for the role of Mariamne had been created by the great
Adrienne Lecouvreur.]

54 Best.D387 (12 December 1730).
55 Best.D389 (*c.* 20 December 1730).
'Tullie, the time has come, hasten to be
gathered.'

12. Shakespeare and the drama, 1726-1776

I MUST NOW RETURN to one of the most fascinating and significant features of the *Lettres philosophiques*, Voltaire's head-on collision with Shakespeare[1], the reverberations of which continued throughout his life, and can only be dealt with as a whole.

During much of the eighteenth century the day celebrated most solemnly each year by the Académie française was the 25th of August, the anniversary of the death of Louis IX. On the morning of that day the immortals met in the chapel of the Louvre, still a royal palace, where they witnessed the celebration of the mass and listened to a specially composed motet and to a panegyric[2] of the sainted king. All this was limited to the members of the Academy, but each year a public assembly was held in the afternoon, devoted to the distribution of prizes and to a reading or lecture of special importance. In 1776 the *fête de saint Louis* fell on a Sunday. It was therefore kept with special solemnity: the respected composer François Francœur supplied the motet, and the king's preacher, Jean François Copel, famous under the name of père Elisée, pronounced the panegyric. In public, before an audience even more brilliant and cosmopolitan than usual, the Academy transacted some formal business, and then the secretary,

---

1 I have collected all Voltaire's relevant writings in *Voltaire on Shakespeare* (Studies on Voltaire, vol. liv: 1967). The only full-length study yet devoted to this subject is *Shakespeare and Voltaire* (1902) by Thomas R. Lounsbury: unfortunately one of the most insensitive and intemperate books ever published by a scholar. The late professor F. C. Green, whose *Minuet* (1935) contains a stimulating essay on the same subject, lets off Lounsbury very lightly: he calls that author's methods merely 'disastrous' (p. 470). I am bound to add that I disagree with some important details of professor Green's interpretation. Jusserand necessarily writes at length about Voltaire in his valuable but now out-of-date *Shakespeare en France sous l'ancien régime* (Paris 1898).

2 Voltaire himself composed the panegyric in 1749, in very remarkable circumstances; see Best.app.D83 (Voltaire 95, p. 393).

who at that time was none other than Jean Le Rond d'Alembert, read (I translate this description from the original minutes of the Academy) a 'writing by Mr de Voltaire on the tragedies of Shakespeare'. The old sage himself was still far away, in exile at Ferney, and Paris was not to witness the unique, the unforgettable spectacle of his apotheosis until eighteen months later.

To anyone intimate with Voltaire it is obvious that he was not at his ease in this *Discours*; for one thing it is one of the least well written of the master stylist's compositions. He began by reminding his fellow-members that the Academy had formerly been asked to judge Corneille's *Cid*. He now wanted to submit to the Academicians certain foreign tragedies dedicated to Louis XVI. We must remember that such a dedication could not be made without permission, and thus the publication had been given a measure of royal endorsement. As the king was expressly its protector, the strict protocol of the *ancient régime* committed the Académie française in its turn to these foreign tragedies. All those present must at once have realised that it was this aura of official approval which was the direct cause of Voltaire's protest, and they also knew that he was referring to Le Tourneur's translation[3] of Shakespeare, the first two volumes of which, containing *Othello*, *The Tempest* and *Julius Caesar*, had recently been published under the title of *Shakespeare traduit de l'anglois*, which eventually ran to ten times as many volumes.

Some people in the audience must also have reflected that this preamble to Voltaire's discourse was very odd: it is indeed the only really surprising thing in the whole long lecture. The *Cid* has been regarded[4], I think with some exaggeration, as in a sense the most epoch-making play in all literature, and this view was largely shared by Voltaire. Yet when it was first produced in 1637 Scudéry[5] declared that Corneille's tragedy was worthless because its subject was bad, because it violated the rules of dramatic composition, and because its versification was defective. Although Scudéry was himself a writer whose productions match

3 For a first spontaneous reaction to this translation see Voltaire's letter of 19 July 1776 to Argental (Best. D20220); it is on the same lines as the Academy lecture, but more violent.

4 By George Saintsbury, if my memory is to be trusted.
5 In his *Observations sur le Cid* (1637).

in absurdity only the vainglory of their author, his views on Corneille were shared by cardinal de Richelieu. This eminent statesman, who had a high regard for his own literary talent and judgment, had officially created the Académie française just before the production of the *Cid*, and now submitted the dispute to that august body. It promptly sided with the critic against Corneille, choosing as its mouthpiece the inept, the servile Chapelain[6].

These facts were known in 1776 to all literate Frenchmen, and they were intimately familiar to Voltaire, who had discussed them at length in his edition of Corneille's works[7], hardly troubling to disguise his contempt for the author's critics, though he himself dealt faithfully with his shortcomings. How could Voltaire have failed to remember all this when he asked the Academy to judge Shakespeare? It was certainly not that he had greater respect for the living immortals than for those who had gone before. Did he expect them to do greater justice to a foreigner than to a compatriot? and *a fortiori* to one who was infinitely more unconventional than Corneille? Mystery! and 'where mystery begins, justice ends'[8].

Voltaire went on to say that a temple had recently been erected in England to the famous actor-poet Shakespeare, and that a jubilee had been founded—he of course had in mind the goings-on at Stratford of David Garrick, with whom he was in correspondence. Naturally Voltaire thought it a very good thing that such high courtesies should be addressed to a man of letters, but he expressed himself in such a way that the audience could easily have got the opposite impression. And here again he modestly forgot something, the not irrelevant fact that even greater honour had been done to himself, not by one who sought perhaps to acquire a vested interest in a national glory, but by his friends and colleagues, even some of the most envious, who had subscribed for a statue by Pigalle, as we shall see in due course.

Voltaire then protested that some French people had tried to share this English enthusiasm by bringing over an image of the divinity Shakespeare, 'as some other imitators have recently

6 In his *Les Sentiments de l'Académie françoise sur la tragi-comédie du Cid* (1638).

7 Voltaire 54, pp. 44-5.
8 Edmund Burke, *A Vindication of natural society* (1756).

erected a Vaux-hall in Paris, and as others still have distinguished themselves by calling their sirloins *rost-beef*, and prided themselves on serving *rost-beef* of mutton'. The court of Charles II had acquired its polish from that of Louis XIV, but nowadays, he added ironically, it was London that saved the French from barbarism. And now, it was the last straw, there had been announced a translation of Shakespeare, who was, they were told, 'the creative divinity of the sublime art of the theatre', but who had nevertheless remained unknown in France—which in Voltaire's language was tantamount to saying that he had remained unknown to people of good taste.

To prevent any misconception of his wider views, Voltaire next reminded the distinguished audience that he himself, half a century earlier, had been the first Frenchman to learn English, the first to introduce Shakespeare to the continent and to translate him, the first to make known Pope, Dryden and Milton, even the first who had dared to explain the great Newton, and do justice to the profound wisdom of Locke. All these claims are perfectly justified. A substantial treatise could be and should be written on Voltaire's contribution to the dissemination of English thought and English literature.[9] Take only Shakespeare. When Voltaire discussed him at length in the *Lettres philosophiques*, this was the first time that more than half-a-dozen words, written by a Frenchman, had appeared in print on the English poet. Indeed, when Voltaire was at school both the English language and English literature, even in translation, were to all intents and purposes unknown in France, and only a handful of French travellers had ever set a peaceful foot in England. Plays and poems by Shakespeare were first published in the 1590s, and the great posthumous folio is dated 1623. Yet it was not until about 1680 that a Shakespeare volume was first entered in a French library catalogue; and over thirty-five years later still, just about the time that Voltaire's first play was produced, a French guide-book to England could still refer to the author of *Hamlet* as 'un certain Shakespeare'[10]. And though Voltaire condemned Shakespeare in his *Lettres*, the mere fact that he discussed the English poet seriously

9 The groundwork has now been laid; see above, p. 118, note 3.

10 Quoted by Jusserand, p. 131.

so shocked one anonymous critic that he ironically referred to Voltaire's subject as 'his Shakespeare'[11].

In his discourse Voltaire went on to say that his reward for introducing English culture into France was to be persecuted by his compatriots, who thought it high treason to seek for light beyond their frontiers—indeed, they are still under the spell of this amiable delusion. Yet soon they had gone to the other extreme, only English things were fancied, and all English books were translated. Here Voltaire was not far out. So far as I can discover (no real statistics are available), only a few hundred English works appeared in a French dress during the three centuries from the invention of printing to 1750, and perhaps fifteen times as many during the second half of the eighteenth century, a far greater increase than can be accounted for by improved means of communication and the like—and this enormous acceleration took place although England and France were in bitter conflict during much of this period.

To show that this sort of thing had gone too far, and to illustrate the awful kind of stuff that was being introduced into France, Voltaire quoted some of the low and indecent passages in Shakespeare—and of course there are plenty of them. He reserved his most slashing strokes for what is now considered the greatest masterpiece in its kind. 'Some of you, gentlemen', Voltaire said, 'know that there exists a tragedy by Shakespeare called *Hamlet*.' Nor was this allocution at all a rhetorical device: it is in fact certain that not more than two or three of the French people present had ever heard of this play[12], except as the title of a remote adaptation by Ducis (1769). So little was Shakespeare known in France that when Elizabeth Montagu's *An Essay on the writings and genius of Shakespeare . . . with some remarks upon the misrepresentations of mons. de Voltaire* (1760) was translated into French to profit from the notoriety of Voltaire's Academy lecture, the titlepage read *Apologie de Shakespeart* (1777). Those few in the audience who had heard of *Hamlet* no doubt agreed with the others and with Voltaire when he made prolonged fun of this 'monster'. In fact,

11 [Pierre François Le Coq de Villeray], *Réponse ou critique des Lettres philosophiques* (Bâle [Amiens] 1735), p. 79.

12 Strictly speaking this is not true, because of the preliminary reading.

when the paper of the Academy's *enfant terrible* was given a preliminary private hearing a few days earlier, his colleagues decided that some of the passages quoted by Voltaire could not be read in public, and Alembert duly omitted them on the 25th of August. Indeed, the Academy would not even publish the full text containing these passages.

Voltaire next devoted a long passage to the claim that Shakespeare invented the drama, but of course no such claim had been made by anybody competent to express an opinion, and it was easy to show that it was false. Yet Voltaire's punctilio found it insupportable that a French translator should sacrifice France to England in a work dedicated to the French king, and in the preface to which, 130 pages long, not a single French dramatist is named. (As a matter of fact, the introduction does once refer to France as 'the fatherland of Corneille, Racine and Molière'.)

Still, Voltaire acknowledged that Shakespeare, 'so barbarous, so low, so unbridled and so absurd, had sparks of genius'. Some of his plays contain beautiful passages which were taken from nature and belong to the sublime in art, though Shakespeare himself had not the slightest art. Voltaire concluded the essential part of his discourse by saying that the English poet was not to be condemned on this account, he was rather to be pitied for belonging to a nation and a time devoid of taste.[13]

The secretary of the Academy promptly reported to Voltaire that his discourse had pleased and amused the audience, who had even made him repeat several passages. Only a few Frenchmen, Alembert added, had been displeased: not content with being

13 The English dramatist to whom Voltaire most often appealed as a model was Addison, and it is therefore particularly interesting to see what the English essayist had to say in this matter: 'Among great Genius's, those few draw the Admiration of all the World upon them, and stand up as Prodigies of Mankind, who by the meer Strength of natural Parts, and without any Assistance of Art or Learning, have produced Works that were the Delight of their own Times and the Wonder of Posterity. There appears something nobly wild and extravagant in these great natural Genius's, that is infinitely more beautiful than all the Turn and Polishing of what the *French* call a *Bel Esprit*, by which they would express a Genius refined by Conversation, Reflection, and the Reading of the most polite Authors' (*The Spectator*, 3 September 1711, no. 160).

defeated by the English on land and sea, they wanted also to be beaten by them in the theatre.[14]

A good many years before he composed his Academy discourse Voltaire had published a sort of manifesto, an *Appel à toutes les nations de l'Europe* (1761), in which he first declared open war on the tendency, then just becoming fashionable, to praise everything English at the expense of everything French, particularly in literature, and still more precisely on the stage. It must at least be owned that nobody in France had better earned the right to make such a protest against Anglomania, since it was chiefly he who had caused the pendulum to swing from Anglophobia, though not permanently, for it continues to move back and forth—no doubt a good thing, for immobility spells stagnation. Who can

> look into the seeds of time,
> And say which grain will grow and which will not?[15]

In his *Appel* Voltaire gives a minute summary of *Hamlet*, with two translations of the 'To be or not to be' monologue. He provides first a free version in French rhymed alexandrines, and then a literal rendering in blank verse. It is certain that Voltaire regarded his rhymed version as an improvement on the original, and that original as an uncouth piece of work. Yet here again deep called unto deep, and admiration was wrung from Voltaire as it were ineluctably. In seeking to condemn *Hamlet* he in fact pays the tragedy a great tribute. He points out that his literal version is necessarily obscure, since in a rendering of this kind the correct French word cannot be given for every English one. Yet through these obscurities the genius of the English language can easily be distinguished: 'it is natural, and does not fear the lowest notions, nor the most gigantic: it is energetic, though other nations take it to be harsh; it is daring, though those little accustomed to foreign turns of speech regard this as grandiloquence. Yet through these veils can be perceived truth, depth, and an indescribable something that attracts, and that moves us much more than would elegance.

---

14 Best.D20272; Alembert also says that the English members of the audience were displeased, but the evidence is contradictory.
15 *Macbeth*, I.iii.58-9.

And in fact practically everybody in England knows this monologue by heart.' And he concludes with a brilliant image: 'It is a
raw diamond full of flaws: if it were polished it would lose some
of its weight.'

Voltaire points out that there can be no better example of the
differences which exist in national taste. When the merits of
Shakespeare's plays are appreciated there is no point in talking
about the 'rules of Aristotle, and the three unities, and decorum,
and the obligation never to leave the stage empty, and to make
nobody enter or leave it without a valid reason, to devise a plot
with skill, to untangle it naturally, to express oneself in noble and
simple terms, to make princes speak with the propriety they
always exhibit, *or would like to exhibit*, never to break the rules of
language. It is obvious that an entire nation can be enchanted
without so much trouble being taken.'[16]

Just as Voltaire saw the beauties of Shakespeare through the
veils of his own predispositions, so his criticisms, in displaying
his own ambivalent feelings, served to arouse the interest of his
countrymen rather than to disgust them. And one of those whom
he interested was the most prolific contributor to the *Encyclopédie*,
the chevalier de Jaucourt, who promptly wrote for it a long and
enthusiastic article on Shakespeare (1765)—an article which, however, Diderot published under the heading 'Stratford'[17]. Readers
who turn to 'Shakespeare' in the *Encyclopédie* find that there is no
such entry, to the great confusion of those unfamiliar with the
curiously unenlightened ways of the Enlightenment.

Yet, I repeat, Voltaire had made it quite clear that he regarded
Hamlet, for instance, as a monstrosity, a monstrosity of genius to
be sure, but still a monstrosity. His analysis of Shakespeare's
tragedy in the *Appel à toutes les nations* is far too long to quote,
but fortunately he was obsessed by the Shakespeare mystery, as
many are obsessed to this day, by the fact that this ignorant
barbarian had succeeded in holding the attention of successive
generations against all the rules, and that he was becoming more
and more appreciated everywhere, even in Paris, the home of good
taste. So he came back to the problem again and again. He dis-

16 My italics; cp. a similar passage
quoted p. 151, below.

17 In accordance with the usual
practice of the *Encyclopédie*.

cussed it for instance in the *Dissertation sur la tragédie* dedicated to cardinal Quirini and prefixed to *Sémiramis*.

In this dissertation he gives a shorter and even more illuminating abstract of *Hamlet*, that 'vulgar and barbarous play which would not be supported by the lowest public of France and Italy[18]. In it Hamlet goes mad in the second act, and his mistress in the third; the prince kills his mistress's father, pretending to kill a rat, and the heroine throws herself into the river. Her grave is dug on the stage; grave-diggers utter doubtful pleasantries worthy of them, whilst holding skulls in their hands; prince Hamlet replies to their abominable vulgarities with no less disgusting idiocies. Meanwhile one of the personages conquers Poland. Hamlet, his mother and his stepfather drink together on the stage: they sing at table, quarrel, fight, and kill each other. One would take this work to be a fruit of the inspiration of a drunken savage.' But as always, Voltaire struggled to be just, and he at once added that *Hamlet* contains sublime passages, worthy of the greatest genius. 'It seems as if Nature had amused itself by assembling in Shakespeare's head the greatest imaginable power and grandeur, and the lowest and most detestable forms of witless vulgarity.'[19]

It is clear that there must be more in such strictures than lies on the surface. If we can identify these underlying elements we shall have gone a long way towards an understanding of the essential differences between the two cultures. It is not a task that lends itself to summary execution. Still, a rapid effort must be made. Let us consider first the external facts. Is the action of *Hamlet* in fact so abominable? Well, we know today better, certainly, than did Shakespeare, and better even than did Voltaire in his most lucid moments, that there are no absolutes in atrocity, nor in morality, nor in much else for that matter. The only thing we can do in this more humble epoch, having at last succeeded in discarding our certitudes (or have we?), is to seek a standard of comparison. And we have the singular good fortune throughout

18 Italy is dragged in here as a courteous gesture to the cardinal.

19 This essay was printed with *Sémiramis* because in that play, having already done so with disastrous results in *Eriphyle*, Voltaire again tried the revolutionary venture of introducing a ghost into the action; both plays were to that extent suggested by *Hamlet*: Voltaire did not disdain to borrow even from so barbarous a source.

this inquiry of having texts at our disposal which enable such comparisons to be made in a more or less responsible manner— a profoundly difficult thing to achieve when collating imponderables, and an almost impossible one when these imponderables belong to different cultures.

So far as *Hamlet* is concerned, we can contrast this play with a tragedy which not even the most rigid classicist could reject as a touchstone, the *Electra* of Sophocles. We have here two plays which resemble each other to a remarkable degree in their baroque *peripeteia*. These resemblances are not merely superficial, they reach profoundly into the hidden depths of humanity—but that is another story. For our present purposes it is enough to point out that the protagonist of both *Electra* and *Hamlet* is a young prince who seeks vengeance because his mother is implicated in the murder of his father, and has then married the murderer. In the eyes of Shakespeare's Hamlet[20] his mother's crime is even graver than that of Clytemnestra was to Orestes, for the Danish queen is a Christian, and so, in marrying her husband's brother, Hamlet's uncle, she has added incest to murder. Hamlet despatches his stepfather, to say nothing of Polonius and (involuntarily) Laertes, but spares his mother, in this obeying the explicit injunction of his father's ghost, who, incidentally, implies that Hamlet can kill his stepfather with a clear conscience:

> But howsoever thou pursu'st this act,
> Taint not thy mind; nor let thy soul contrive
> Against thy mother ought; leave her to heav'n,
> And to those thorns that in her bosom lodge,
> To prick and sting her.

Orestes, on the other hand, slays his mother, and the tragedy is so contrived by Sophocles that the audience hears Clytemnestra's cries to her husband for help and to her son for mercy, and sees her daughter Electra encourage her brother in the execution of their mother. Is this not more horrifying than all the killings in *Hamlet*? And does it not seem that Voltaire, embedded in the amber of his

---

20 I say 'Shakespeare's Hamlet' because historically the scene of the play is set in pre-Christian Denmark, that is, before the introduction of (late) Christian ideas on forbidden affinities.

traditional prejudices, did here exactly that of which he accused[21] the Greek dramatists, that is, fail to distinguish between horror and terror?

Yet, even allowing for this misconception, it seems to me that the chief reason for Voltaire's profound, almost anguished exasperation with *Hamlet* must be sought elsewhere. If it were not foolhardy to venture on so summary a definition, I would say that the essential difference between the Shakespearean drama and that typified by Racine is this: Shakespeare tells a story, Racine analyses a situation. Of course, 'there are nine and sixty ways of constructing tribal lays'[22], and Shakespeare's way of telling a story penetrates more deeply into the mind of man, and moves us infinitely more, than the flash of Racine's brilliant scalpel. But that is not the point. We are here concerned with an all-important detail of dramatic technique, not with the degree of genius entering into its application.

In Shakespeare's tragedies we are shown the events which lead up to a given situation, the event itself is displayed, and its consequences form the climax of the drama. Racine, on the other hand, assumes the antecedent events to be known, or disposes of them in a brief exposition, and the whole play turns on the hero's behaviour in the given situation. Now the interesting thing here is that *Hamlet* is to a considerable extent a sport among Shakespeare's progeny, for in its general conformation it is more Racinian than Shakespearean. The cause of all the pother is already in the past when the curtain rises, and his father's ghost has to tell Hamlet the facts, because the audience would otherwise be in the dark. Racine hurries through these introductory scenes as expeditiously as possible, and to this day blasé Parisian audiences hardly bother to listen to them. In *Hamlet* the genius of Shakespeare has embodied the indispensable exposition in scenes of sublime poetry and suspense—but that again is another story.

The rest of the play is entirely devoted to one single great query: what is going on in Hamlet's mind? exactly as the tragedy of *Phèdre* concentrates on showing the heroine's feelings about her guilty love. Yet there is an essential, a profound, I venture to

21 *Discours sur la tragédie,* prefixed to *Brutus.* 22 Rudyard Kipling, *In the neolithic age.*

say a cultural difference between the two methods even when they so much resemble each other. Shakespeare presents a mighty human problem, which is not resolved on the stage any more than it would be in life, a psychological enigma which leaves one staring in wild surmise the twentieth time[23] one considers it as much as the first, and the convolutions of which no commentator can map because they are different for every spectator. The performance of a Shakespeare tragedy is a collaboration between author and spectator: is not that the secret of Shakespeare's appeal to every generation and to all peoples?

Beyond the footlights of *Phèdre* the audience is asked only to look and listen. Racine does all its thinking and feeling for it. Every question is answered. No stone is left unturned. The Cartesian light penetrates into every corner. By the end of the play we have witnessed an intellectual strip-tease which leaves Phèdre standing morally naked before us. There is nothing left to feel, nothing to think. At most the audience contributes a measure of what Rebecca West has beautifully called passive empathy[24]. Such at least is the theory—the facts are perhaps a little different.

Voltaire cannot but have perceived the Racinian quality of *Hamlet*, and he must have been all the more scandalised by its profoundly Shakespearean interpretation of so 'classical' a treatment. And I think that this explains why he came back again and again to *Hamlet*, loading Shakespeare's tragedy with exacerbated insults and high if reluctant praise.

Many English critics, and most energetically of all an American one, the ineffable Lounsbury, have thought it necessary to 'defend' Shakespeare against Voltaire: they would have done better to try to understand the one and the other. In fact, instead of 'marvelling at Voltaire's astounding blindness to the grandeur of Shakespeare, we ought to credit him with unusual originality and boldness of judgment'[25]. For when Voltaire first introduced Shakespeare to his own countrymen, bardolatry was almost

23 'Read Hamlet through, the 500th time, & with more relish than ever'; *The Diary of Benjamin Robert Haydon*, ed. William Bissell Pope (Cambridge, Mass. 1963), iv.602 (31 January 1840).

24 *Strange necessity* (1928), p. 102, in a different context.

25 Green, *Minuet*, p. 55.

wholly unknown even in England. Gibbon tells us that he often saw Voltaire act: 'his declamation was fashioned to the pomp and cadence of the old stage and he expressed the enthusiasm of poetry, rather than the feelings of Nature. . . . The habits of pleasure fortified my taste for the French theatre: and that taste has perhaps abated my idolatry for the Gigantic Genius of Shakespeare which is inculcated from our infancy as the first duty of an Englishman.'[26] This ironic reminiscence includes a little hindsight, but if 'infancy' is taken literally this may well be one of the earliest recorded examples of Shakespeare worship, for the significant date here is 1746, when Gibbon first went to school, or perhaps a year or two earlier if the inculcating was done by the aunt who brought him up.

Yet two decades earlier Voltaire had written that Shakespeare's genius was powerful and abundant, natural and sublime, and that his plays included most beautiful scenes, with very grand and terrible passages. Of course he added that Shakespeare had no taste, was ignorant of the rules, and that his fine passages occurred in monstrous farces called tragedies[27]. We are apt to take the praise for granted and to bridle at the criticism. Yet much stronger language was used before Voltaire by Shakespeare's countrymen, and opinions very similar to his were being expressed by his English contemporaries. Voltaire formed his view of the London stage during his stay in England, just after his friend Pope published his edition of Shakespeare (1725). In such an edition a judgment rather more favourable than average is to be expected. Yet the tone of Pope's preface is distinctly patronizing. He begins by saying that Shakespeare affords 'the most numerous as well as most conspicuous instances, both of Beauties and Faults of all sorts'. And he concludes that the plays strike us with great reverence though 'many of the Parts are childish, ill-plac'd, and unequal to its grandeur'. Is this not exactly what Voltaire says in his equally energetic style? Even forty years later, in 1765, only a decade before Voltaire's address to the Académie française, dr

26 Edward Gibbon, *Memoirs of my life*, ed. Georges A. Bonnard (London 1966), pp. 83-4; this did not prevent Gibbon from writing in 1776, but perhaps again ironically: 'A propos nous sommes for en colere contre . . . Voltaire pour les blasphemes qu'il vient d'ecrire contre le Dieu du Theatre Anglois' (see notes on Best.D20392)

27 *Lettres philosophiques*, xviii.

Johnson, in *his* preface to *his* edition, though very hard indeed on Voltaire's criticisms, himself said that Shakespeare had 'faults sufficient to obscure and overwhelm any other merit.' And half-a-century after that, in 1814, Byron found that Shakespeare's reputation stood 'absurdly too high'. 'That he threw over whatever he did write some flashes of genius', he told James Hogg in a Voltairean phrase, 'nobody can deny: but this was all.'[28] All these judgements could serve perfectly as pharaphrases of Voltaire's observations.[29]

Much of this kind of thing is no more than the expression of variations in fashion. The vagaries of taste are indeed perfectly illustrated by our two heroes in their own persons. Voltaire's plays were performed at the Comédie française throughout the eighteenth century more often than those of Racine and Corneille together, and in England more often than those of Shakespeare. It is a literal fact that without Voltaire France's national theatre could not have survived; today he cannot get a hearing at the Comédie française, where his plays have been performed very seldom within living memory. In 1936 there was a production of *Zaïre*[30], perhaps the least Voltairean and consequently the most popular of his tragedies. Since then the Comédie française has put on only the *Orphelin de la Chine*[31]. If the arbiters of taste in Paris today are right, then the whole eighteenth century was wrong, and in that case the theory of absolute good taste, which to Voltaire was an essential article of faith, falls entirely to the ground. I myself believe that theory to be quite unsound, though for other reasons, but I also prefer to trust the taste of several successive generations in the eighteenth century rather than that dictated by small cliques in Paris today.

As for the ups and downs of Shakespeare's reputation, they

28 See my *Voltaire essays,* pp. 132-3, and *Byron's letters and journals,* ed. Leslie A. Marchand (London 1975), iv.84-5.

29 Bernard Shaw was, for once, wide of the mark when he said that Voltaire, as he grew older, was 'less disposed to accept artistic merit as a cover for philosophic deficiencies' in Shakespeare; see his *Collected letters 1898-1910,* ed. Dan H. Laurence (London &c. 1972), p. 552.

30 The 488th performance of *Zaïre* (counting from its first production at the Comédie française) was given on 13 November 1936; see also p. 465, below.

31 The first performance of this new production was given on 22 February 1965, when I had the honour of contributing a preface to the commemorative booklet.

are too well known to require rehearsal. Did not so good a judge as Bolingbroke tell Voltaire that there did not exist a single good tragedy in English[32]? We have just had some glimpses of what English critics thought of Shakespeare. Let me add only one curious example. Shakespeare's sonnets are nowadays regarded as the uttermost peak and pinnacle of lyric poetry: it is difficult to conceive that they will ever be less loved and lauded so long as their language is understood. Have they not resisted the attentions of a hundred critics and even of an historian? Yet, so far as I can discover, Shakespeare's sonnets were not included in his works until Francis Gentleman's edition of 1774, that is, 165 years after they were first published. They were even excluded from the supplementary volume (1725) of Pope's edition, which is devoted to Shakespeare's poems.

A fascinating study could be made of the *comparative* reputations of our two heroes. As we shall presently be discussing the *Mort de César*, I will merely quote a remark on this play made by an English reviewer thirty years before dr Johnson found so much to criticise in Shakespeare. 'The verses', said this critic of Voltaire's play, 'are harmonious and smooth, the sentiments are noble. There is very great art made use of in the design; friendship fills up the place of love; unity of place, and unity of time, are exactly observed.'[33]

And it is not least fascinating to learn that when Aaron Hill translated *La Mort de César* he felt impelled to apologise, in his remarkable prose, because Brutus 'persists in and executes the murder, even after discovering, that it is upon the person of his *father*! I appeal', he wrote to Bolingbroke, 'out of *England*, to the best judge of *England*, whether this would be suffered on our stage? . . . whether, my lord, a people, so rapaciously fond of a quality, that but endears and embellishes *duty*, could support without horror and hatred a scene, that makes war upon *nature*! violating the groundwork, the fundamental obligation of *being*, in behalf of a *collateral* virtue!'[34]

32 Voltaire reports this judgment in the *Discours sur la tragédie* prefixed to his tragedy *Brutus*, and as the 'Discours' is addressed to Bolingbroke himself, the reminiscence can hardly be questioned.

33 *The Literary magazine* (London November 1736), ii.440.

34 Best.D1532 (25 June 1738).

In short, it is not surprising that Voltaire should have shared the views of his English contemporaries. What is surprising is that he, with his Jesuit education, his boundless admiration for Racine, and his immutable canons of 'good taste', should have found any merit at all in Shakespeare.

In considering the causes which led to Voltaire's alleged incomprehension of Shakespeare, the first that leaps to mind is that of language. And indeed, some of the critics who have sought to refute Voltaire, Johnson's friend Baretti[35], for instance, offered his ignorance of English as an explanation of his attitude. That would really be too simple, and in fact it will not do. The available evidence shows that Voltaire knew English very well indeed. Typical is the little-known tribute paid by the Philadelphian fellow of the Royal society John Morgan, who wrote to Samuel Morris in 1764, after visiting Voltaire at Ferney: 'Although at a loss sometimes for an english Word, & that he used many Gallecisms, yet he took pains to articulate his words properly & accent them fully. In this he succeeded beyond what one might expect from his having been but one twelve Month [in fact more than twice as long] in england & that so many years past as in 1726. We meet with few french Men who pronounce english better.'[36]

And now that the authentic texts of Voltaire's letters written in English are available (some have been quoted in earlier chapters), it is incontrovertible that his competence was not limited to the spoken language. Indeed, his feeling for English was so just that he often threw off stylistically engaging phrases.

Here is an example from one of his earliest notebooks, and therefore spontaneous and uncorrected, as witness the spelling and grammar:

How very few are wise enough to admire the daily birth of light and the new creation of all things wich born every day with light; the everlasting regulation of stars, the perpetual miracle of generation, effects of loadstone, of lime burned with water. How very few could fix their eyes upon these usual prodiges, whereof the use is so trivial, and the cause so absconded.

35 In his *Discours sur Shakespeare et sur monsieur de Voltaire* (1777). In a letter of 12 June 1777 (Best.D20695) to an unknown correspondent, Baretti calls Voltaire's address to the Academy 'infamous shitt'.

36 Best.D12089 (? 16 September 1764).

But we see attentively and we admire, a rope danser, a mountebanck, a preecher, a french marquis, a coch in sex.[37]

How many writers whose maternal language is English are capable of throwing off such well-balanced and rhythmical phrases, and possess such an admirable vocabulary?

I have been able to show, and this is even more interesting, that Voltaire quoted much English verse from memory (sometimes after very long intervals) and in at least one context even managed subconsciously to improve a distinguished original by no lesser hand than that of Pope[38].

Thus, apart from occasional lapses, no doubt can be permitted that Voltaire understood what he read in Shakespeare, and was anything but insensitive to the music of his poetry. There is plenty of direct evidence of this, and so no alibi should be sought in that direction. But there is more in language than meaning and sound. This 'more' is easier to illustrate than to define in non-technical terms: it resides in the writer's or the speaker's intentions. Thus, when squire Western, purple in the face and yelling at the top of his voice, calls Sophia a 'blank blank of a blank', the sense and the sound are clear beyond a peradventure, yet Sophia knows that what her father is really saying is 'my beloved daughter, why will you not do what I ask?' This aspect of language is admirably illustrated by a celebrated phrase: the next time some rough character tells the reader to 'smile when you say that', he he can apologise by informing his interlocutor that his injunction is perfectly sound psycholinguistically.

Language, in the sense of meaning, is thus almost irrelevant. What really concerns us is the question of the author's purpose, and that is a much more difficult problem, for I have illustrated it only in its most elementary form. It goes much wider and deeper. I do not propose to demonstrate this point theoretically, but concretely by comparing two tragedies, *Julius Caesar* and *La Mort de César*, the one by Shakespeare, the other by Voltaire[39].

---

37 *Voltaire's notebooks*, i.55-6.
38 See pp. 124-125, above.
39 There is a 1909 Vienna thesis by Johann Patkovic entitled *Voltaires*

Tragödie 'La Mort de César' verglichen mit Shakespeares Julius Cäsar; I must confess that I have not seen it.

Neither play is the author's best, by a long chalk. Nor is either play the most convincing specimen of its kind. The most effective contrast would perhaps be between *Hamlet* and *Phèdre*, at which we have already glanced superficially, but on the one hand we are discussing Voltaire, not Racine, and on the other hand *Julius Caesar* and the *Mort de César* have the advantage for our purpose of dealing with the same subject, thus permitting a more precise confrontation. An additional advantage is that Voltaire himself translated a large part of *Julius Caesar*. In fact, only one important detail prevents the parallel from being entirely satisfactory: Shakespeare's play was written in 1599, Voltaire's in 1731. Put in another way, and apart from the changes in dramatic taste and technique during so long an interval, Shakespeare did not know Voltaire's play, but Voltaire knew Shakespeare's.

Julius Caesar is a tragedy in five acts and in blank verse. The action is first laid in Rome, successively in a street, a public place, a street, Brutus's orchard, Caesar's house, a street, another part of the same street, before the capitol, the forum, a street, a room in Anthony's house; then, in act IV, scene ii, the scene shifts completely to the Roman camp near Sardis, first before Brutus's tent, then inside it; act V takes place in five different parts of the plains of Philippi. The whole action thus evolves in eighteen different places, or it should so evolve, and would if modern producers were somewhat less convinced that they can improve on Shakespeare.

The *Mort de César* is in three acts and in alexandrines. The scene is laid throughout in one and the same place, the Roman capitol.

Shakespeare does not clearly specify the time-scheme of *Julius Caesar*, but the first part of the play appears to take place during the day and night preceding Caesar's murder in 44 B.C., and of course on the day itself; we know historically that the events which are enacted in the last two acts, culminating in the suicide of Brutus, took place at Philippi two years later.

The time-scheme of Voltaire's play is also not specified, for the excellent reason that the action takes place continuously and consequently lasts as long as the play itself.

Julius Caesar has at least forty-eight identifiable speaking parts.[40] *La Mort de César* has eleven in all.[41]

Such statistics may appear sterile, but in reality they are pregnant with meaning. They enable even one who has never seen or read a Shakespearean play or a classical French tragedy to visualise the crowds of *Julius Caesar* milling around, now indoors, now in the open, now in Rome, now on a battlefield, while the personages of the *Mort de César* step solemnly in the capitol about their tragic purposes. These physical conditions enable us also to get a pretty good idea of the nature of each play; but let us examine this a little more closely.

Under a threatening sky the Roman public, in Shakespeare's play, prepares to give Caesar a hero's welcome, to the anger of certain tribunes, who try to stir up discontent. As Caesar walks with his companions a soothsayer warns him to beware, and it becomes clear that the feeling against him is widespread, under the reluctant leadership of Brutus. The report arrives that Caesar has been offered the crown, and although he has refused it, Brutus, egged on by his friends, concludes that their fears are justified. To the accompaniment of thunder and lightning, omens and prodigies, a plot steadily develops to overcome Brutus's love for Caesar. It is successful, and the conspirators decide to kill the ambitious triumvir. Ignoring all warnings and portents Caesar goes to the capitol and is stabbed to death, to the cry of 'Liberty! Freedom!' Mark Anthony, Caesar's loyal friend, had been spared by Brutus, who now also allows him to take part in the funeral ceremonies. Anthony wins the oratorical contest, and Brutus flees Rome as the remaining triumvirs, Octavius and Lepidus, arrive. Two years then pass, and Brutus, tormented by his conscience, by his wife's suicide, and by the behaviour of his friends, prepares to

---

40 In the order of speaking: Flavius, first commoner, Marullus, second commoner, Caesar, Casca, Calphurnia, Mark Anthony, soothsayer, Brutus, Cassius, Cicero, Cinna, Lucius, Decius, Metellus, Trebonius, Portia, Ligarius, Caesar's servant, Publius, Artemidorus, Popilius, Anthony's servant, first citizen, second citizen, third citizen, fourth citizen, servant, Cinna (poet), Octavius, Lepidus, Pindarus, first soldier, second soldier, third soldier, poet, Lucilius, Titinius, Messala, Varro, Claudius, messenger, Cato, Clitus, Dardanius, Volumnius, Strato.

41 César, Antoine, Dolabella, Cimber, Cassius, Brutus, Décime, Casca, Romain, autre Romain, troisième Romain.

resist the assault of Octavius and Mark Anthony. He is defeated, and throws himself on his sword.

In the *Mort de César*, Antoine urges César to reign as king. César agrees that the army, before marching under him against the Parthians, is only waiting for him to assume the crown. He asks Antoine to look after his children, revealing that although Octave, his adopted son, is to succeed him, Brutus is his natural son. Antoine doubts whether even this news will turn Brutus from his stoic ideas. The chief senators enter: César, addressing them seated, assigns to each his responsibilities after his departure, and reminds them that according to an authentic tradition only a king can defeat the Persians. This hint is rejected by the senators, most emphatically by Brutus, who, when alone with César, accuses him of tyranny. Antoine advises severity, but César prefers moderation. The senators discuss the situation, and Brutus's proposal to assassinate César is accepted. César, again alone with Brutus, in vain urges him to change his views, and finally reveals himself as his father. Brutus still persists in begging him to give up his ambition, and César finally turns on him. Brutus is held to his oath by his fellow conspirators, whom he has informed that he is the tyrant's son. Brutus again implores César to withdraw, and warns him that his life is at stake, but in vain. Dolabella also warns him not to appear before the senate, but César leaves. Cries are heard offstage. Cassius enters with a dagger in his hand, and announces César's death. Antoine's funeral oration follows, while the backdrop opens to reveal the body of César, covered with a bloody cloth. Antoine wins over the people, who cry for vengeance while he proposes to Dolabella that they should profit from the Romans' anger by succeeding César.

Such, then, are these two plays. What are their essential themes? *Julius Caesar* shows us how an idealist can be brought to commit an evil action for a noble purpose, and displays the consequences of his crime. Shakespeare's eagle eye sweeps over the offence, its causes and its consequences. The struggle that takes place around and within Brutus is used to illustrate an issue which transcends his person.

Voltaire, on the other hand, was interested chiefly in the personal situation: what happens when a high-minded man learns that the tyrant he has decided to kill is his father? The background has no positive relevance: it is there only because it is needed to give verisimilitude to the situation.

In one sense *Julius Caesar* is an exercise in rhetoric: it is almost as if Shakespeare had set out to illustrate the art of persuasion in all its forms. And with what consummate art he does this! The style and tone are always profoundly characteristic. Nothing of this kind is to be found in the *Mort de César*. Of course Voltaire tries to differentiate the language of his personages to suit their personalities and ideas, but he could not possibly succeed since the dramatic laws to which he submitted ordained that all without exception had to speak with nobility. Hence, when Antoine harangues the crowd, its members are made to respond with such impossibly literary or flat exclamations as 'Puisqu'il était tyran, il n'eut point de vertus' and 'Oui, nous approuvons tous Cassius et Brutus' and 'César fut en effet le père de l'Etat' and 'O spectacle funeste.'[42] Such language is common form in the French classical drama.

Yet Voltaire was very far from insensitive to Shakespeare's flowers of rhetoric. He told his friend Bolingbroke, 'With what pleasure did I see in London your tragedy of *Julius Caesar*, which for a hundred and fifty years had delighted your nation! I certainly do not approve the barbarous irregularities with which it abounds. It is surprising indeed that there are not more in a work composed in an age of ignorance by a man who did not even know Latin, and had had no master but his genius. But, among so many gross defects, with what rapture did I see Brutus, still holding in his hand a dagger wet with Caesar's blood, assemble the Roman people, and speak to them thus from the tribune.' Voltaire then translates Brutus's speech, and goes on: 'After this scene Anthony comes to move to pity the same Romans whom Brutus had inspired with his sternness and savagery By an artful discourse he lowers insensibly these haughty spirits; and when he sees them softened, then he shows them Caesar's body, and using the most pathetic devices, excites them to tumult and revenge.'[43]

42 'Since he was a tyrant, he had no virtues'; 'Yes, we all agree with Cassius and Brutus'; 'Caesar was in fact the father of the state'; 'O wretched sight'.
43 *Discours sur la tragédie.*

At the time when he was working on his edition of Corneille and thus was preoccupied with questions of dramatic technique, Voltaire wrote to his English friend George Keate, contrasting Shakespeare's freedom to do as he chose on the stage with Corneille's 'more difficult' task: 'he was obliged continually to overcome the difficulty of rhyme, which is a prodigious labour; he had to subject himself to the unities of time, place, action; never make an actor come on to the stage or leave it without an interesting reason; devise a plot with skill, and untangle it rationally; make all his heroes speak with a noble eloquence, saying nothing that could shock the delicate ears of a high-minded court or of an academy composed of men who are very learned and very hard to please.'[44]

After comparing Corneille's *Cinna* with *Julius Caesar* he exclaimed that Shakespeare's tragedy was the grossest of extravaganzas.[45] Yet with all this he could not help but be swept away, finding that Corneille, compared with Shakespeare, was icy. One could not help enjoying Shakespeare's plays even though one found them absurd.[46]

To make his point quite clear to the French reader Voltaire translated the first three acts of *Julius Caesar*—and it should be noted that although this was as late as 1764, it was the first French translation of Shakespeare to be published[47]. Voltaire's version is faithful, and it is manifest that he has tried to do his best for the original. A comparison of the two texts line by line would be a liberal education in itself, but it would also be a lengthy business. I must content myself with a single brief example, the beginning of Marullus's harangue[48] to the commoners in the first scene:

> Wherefore rejoice? What conquest brings he home?
> What tributaries follow him to Rome
> To grace in captive bonds his chariot wheels?
> You blocks, you stones, you worse than senseless things!
> O you hard hearts, you cruel men of Rome,
> Knew you not Pompey?

44 Best.D10322 (10 February 1762).
45 Best.D10483 (4 June 1762).
46 Best.D11727 (28 February 1764).
47 La Place had published remote adaptations in 1746.
48 The continuation of which is quoted above.

Pourquoi vous réjouir? quelles sont ses conquêtes?
Quels rois par lui vaincus, enchaînés à son char,
Apportent des tributs aux souverains du monde?
Idiots, insensés, cervelles sans raison,
Cœurs durs, sans souvenir et sans amour de Rome,
Oubliez-vous Pompée, et toutes ses vertus?

Much of the translation is so literal that it might almost be used as a crib. The meaning has been faithfully rendered, the tone is the same, and yet the essential feeling is wanting. And here we approach the heart of the mystery. The difference of course is in the language, not now as meaning but as the vehicle of meaning.

For historical and psychological reasons the development of French and English has differed in recent centuries. The French have long regarded their language with an almost mystical respect, and their aim has been and still is to fix it in an ideally 'perfect' but indefinable form—even if they are obliged to have recourse to the statutes of the realm. The English have been content to enjoy the greatest literature produced in any tongue, and as for their own language, they have allowed it to proliferate as it listed. The most noticeable result is that the English vocabulary is at least twice as copious as the French, and this in turn makes it impossible for a Voltaire to write like a Shakespeare even if he wanted to[49], although Voltaire in fact had a good deal wider vocabulary than any of his non-specialist contemporaries. As for French grammar and the general structure of the language, its use of genders, the difficulties it places in the way of inversion, its rigid use of pronouns, and other more technical features, make it much less pliable, less flowing than English.

But above and beyond that lies the fundamental fact that Voltaire's theories of the drama made it impossible for him to use on the stage the lyric language of which he was capable in other contexts. And beyond even that lies the ultimate fact of poetic genius. Shakespeare had an incomparable gift, facilitated by the English

49 When the late professor Green, in defending Racine's repetitiveness, inferred (I think wrongly) from a line in Boileau, that 'the vocabulary required to express rational ideas must be limited' (*Minuet*, p. 41), I can only rub my eyes. Shades of Voltaire! shades of Descartes himself! Rational ideas require precise expression, and as they get more and more subtle more words have to be created to express them: for instance, 'vocabulary' in the sense used by professor Green is a modern adaptation.

language, for turning words into music, a gift that Voltaire simply did not possess, and that their language has permitted very few French poets to master.

It would be difficult to fault either Shakespeare or Voltaire in matters of stage technique. Each play has a highly effective opening. The first words of *Julius Caesar*:

> Hence! home, you idle creatures, get you home:
> Is this a holiday?

at once convey to the audience the circumstances and tone of the day. The opening of *La Mort de César* is even more effective: as the curtain rises Antoine says to his friend, 'Caesar, you will reign'. And at once an important contrast emerges, one which again underlines an essential difference between the two types of drama: the spectator of *Julius Caesar* need have no special knowledge to understand at once what is going on, whereas the pithy beginning of Voltaire's play, which in four words epitomises what was to be the dramatic transformation of Rome from a republic into a monarchy, cannot be fully savoured without some knowledge of Roman history.

When Voltaire condemned *Hamlet* in his Academy discourse, he objected most energetically to the 'abominable' scene of the grave-diggers, and here his feelings were widely shared[50]. Yet perhaps his most interesting objection, interesting, that is, in giving us an insight into the working of Voltaire's mind in such matters, is the one he had already made more than once in other writings: he found it intolerable that a soldier, on being asked whether he had had a quiet guard, should reply 'Not a mouse stirring'[51]. Yes, exclaimed Voltaire, a soldier can speak like this in a guardroom, but not in the theatre, before the first persons of the land, who express themselves with nobility and before whom others must so express themselves.

And he takes up a comparison made by lord Kames: Racine's

50 See, for instance, the passage I have quoted in my *Voltaire essays*, p. 133n, from an 1818 entry in Haydon's diary.

51 *Hamlet*, I.i.10; Voltaire translated these words 'Je n'ai pas entendu une souris trotter'; this sounds comic to English ears, but it is the correct rendering; cp. 'On entendrait une souris trotter'.

'Mais tout dort, et l'armée, et les vents, et Neptune'[52], which he finds admirably beautiful because the line expresses harmoniously great truths which are at the basis of the play. It is in fact important for the action of *Iphigénie* to know whether or not the sea is calm, but then Voltaire should not have gone on to say that it is perfectly useless to know whether or not the soldier has seen any mice. For of course just as Neptune symbolises the sea, so the silence of the mice conveys the exceptional and highly relevant stillness of the night; and it is at least arguable that Shakespeare's figure is more imaginative than Racine's overworked classical allusion. The trouble really is, to be sure, that a god is 'noble' whereas a mouse is not.

The whole structure of the argument from nobility does not resist analysis, even if one takes only the simple question of fact. Voltaire knew[53] perfectly well that the first persons of the land did not express or even conduct themselves with invariable nobility. Far from it. Let me illustrate this assertion in a manner which Shakespeare would have loved but Voltaire would have disapproved with much energy. When he was given quarters in the royal palace Voltaire complained to mme Denis that his rooms were 'near the most stinking shit-hole in Versailles'[54]: and in fact at the foot of his staircase there was an open sewer which was often flooded. Voltaire would not have used this language to his niece if her mind had not been attuned to the existence of such things at court and elsewhere, and her ears to hearing them referred to in the most straightforward terms.

When Voltaire insisted that everything on the stage must be noble, what he really meant was something like this: it is the duty of a king and his court to give to the nation an example of noble behaviour, and it is the function of the stage to reflect this ideal in theme, in action, and in language.

The insistence on nobility, and in general the conventions of the French classical drama, are supposed to be intimately connected with Cartesian ideas and French rationalism. I believe this

52 *Iphigénie*, I.i; 'But everything is asleep, the army, the winds, and Neptune'.

53 Cp. his 'exhibit, or would like to exhibit' in the passage quoted above

(p. 138).

54 'Vicino al piu puzzolente cacatoio de Versailles'; see Best.D3089; cp. Best.D3419.

view to be mistaken, or at least much exaggerated. Take the famous unities. To listen to Voltaire and to some literary historians one would really think that the unities form an integral part of the French character. What are the facts? The dramatic unities of time, place and action were taken (erroneously) from Aristotle by that same Chapelain who condemned Corneille, a man of decidedly limited ability, the kindest thing that can be said about him being that he talked less badly than he wrote. Cardinal de Richelieu, who thought that the same kinds of methods could be applied to literature as to politics, approved the ideas of his yes-man, and imposed them successively on the Académie française and on Corneille. This at first great dramatist was, in the circumstances of the time, at the mercy of authority. He sulked in his tents for three years, and then submitted, sacrificing his genius in the process. It is as if Disraeli had told Bernard Shaw that he could come to London only if he wrote plays like Pinero or Jones. All this happened at a time when the cardinal sought, as by the creation of the Académie française, to fix good taste and good usage like fossilised flowers. And it also happened that it suited Racine to work within these limits, because they fitted the framework of his own narrow character and sharply delimited talents. All this seems to me a rather inadequate justification for regarding the unities as laws of nature, or of French psychology, or of anything other than illustrations of the folly of thinking that genius can be prefabricated. Anyway, these famous and immutable unities have long since become no more than historical curiosities, insects caught in amber.

If this is how the French classical drama acquired its form, it still remains to discover why its content was so different from that of Shakespeare. Why this concentration on personal problems to the almost entire neglect of great human issues? Why this minute analysis of the individual heart in a particular situation, to the neglect of even more poignant situations at large? Voltaire himself provides the answer to such questions in discussing the differences between the theatres of the two nations: 'The Englishman says whatever he pleases, the Frenchman only what he can'[55], that is, what he is permitted to say. And although Voltaire wrote

55 *Discours sur la tragédie.*

this with special reference to versification, the antithesis has a much wider application. In fact, while Voltaire was bound by a tradition which, though young, had become very powerful, he was even more powerfully bound by the strict control exercised by the government over every form of expression, and most of all over the stage. It was Voltaire himself who gradually outflanked the censorship by indirection, and by writing plays which were printed without being performed. Professor Green was right when he said that 'Voltaire's chief contribution to the French theatre . . . was his annoying habit of using the play, as he did every form of literature, to express his anti-clerical and political propaganda.'[56] The distinguished literary historian was perfectly entitled to find this annoying, but I on the contrary feel profoundly grateful to Voltaire for having burst the shackles that bound French intellectual and artistic life, and thus opening the way to the neoclassical movement.

For although Voltaire held to his dramatic theories throughout his life, yet, such is the unfathomable mystery of human nature, they were his views only in respect of the stage. In everything else, from religion to agriculture, from the biology of the snail to the cosmogony of Sanchuniathon, he judged every case on its merits, and usually came to an enlightened conclusion within the limits of the knowledge then available. Even in literature, and in a field so close to the drama as epic poetry, his views were 'modern'. In England and in English he wrote: 'The same Fancy which hath invented Poetry, changes every day all its Productions, because it is liable itself to eternal Vicissitudes. . . . There are not more Revolutions in Governments, than in Arts. They are shifting, and gliding away from our Pursuit, when we endeavour to fix them by our Rules and Definitions.'[57]

And again: 'I am very far from Thinking, that one Nation ought to judge of its Productions by the Standard of another.'[58] And he concludes: 'the best Reason I can offer for our ill Success in *Epick* Poetry is the Insufficiency of all who attempted it. I can

56 *Minuet*, p. 56.
57 'An Essay on epick poetry', in *An Essay upon the civil wars of France* (second edition, London 1728), pp.38-39; I am obliged to quote this very

rare edition because all the editors of Voltaire's works, in their unanimous wisdom, have ignored this original text of the essay.
58 *Ibid.*, p. 109.

add nothing further, after this ingenuous Confession.'[59] May not this 'ingenuous Confession' be the clue to much else?

The most extraordinary, the most maddening thing of all, to Voltaire, was that Shakespeare is a genius.[60] Those are his very words. He could never get over it, but to suppose that this was due to insensibility, stupidity or envy (to choose only a few of the epithets used by commentators whom, for my part, I will merely stigmatise as ignorant) is a complete misapprehension. Voltaire's attitude to Shakespeare is one of the most striking examples of his fundamental good sense and tolerance. From his point of view, which was shared by almost all his contemporaries, English as well as French, Shakespeare was an uncouth amateur. To Voltaire, who had had a classical education, who venerated Racine, who was impregnated with inflexible notions of taste and punctilio to a degree now hardly credible, and who as a result of this regarded the rules governing the drama as eternally fixed, to see *Hamlet* or *Julius Caesar* must have been an agonizing experience. His feelings must have been like those of Paul v when confronted by Galileo. The pope knew on the highest conceivable authority that the earth was at the centre of the universe, and the evidence of his eyes confirmed the fact. And yet, Galileo was so obviously a genius, his reasoning was so elegant and persuasive. . . . What was one to think? There was an easy way out, tell Galileo to recant and hold his peace. And the church took it. No such comfortable course lay before Voltaire, so he followed the only one open to an intelligent and honest man. He made Shakespeare known to the world beyond the Channel, thus transcending the more foolish forms of nationalism, criticised him as he thought he deserved to be criticised, but never failed to add that though Shakespeare was a barbarian, he was a barbarian of genius. For that we owe Voltaire, not the 'acrimony of a scholiast' from whatever cause it may proceed[61], but an ample meed of respectful gratitude.

59 *Ibid.*, p. 130.
60 'Art dramatique', *Dictionnaire philosophique.*

61 Dr Johnson, towards the end of the preface of his edition of Shakespeare (1765).

13. Charles XII *and the new history,* *1727-1731*

W E D O N O T K N O W positively how Voltaire first conceived the idea of writing on Charles XII, but from
numerous indications the most likely explanation
emerges that what he felt impelled to create was a new kind of
history[1]. Then, casting round for a subject, he must have concluded that Charles XII was ideal for the purpose. He was indeed
the kind of man intellectuals often fall for: a man of action and
courage, who was also well read and not incapable of abstract
thought. Yet he is surpassed in ascending order of villainy only by
Napoleon, Mussolini and Hitler, and therefore before them was
supremely evil in act and consequence. However, the career of
Charles XII had been strikingly exciting and romantic, with violent
ups and downs, and he had only recently fallen in action when still
young (1682-1718). Apart from anything else Voltaire was
fascinated by him as a man rather than a hero[2], but above all he
found him an ideal subject for his prentice hand, for as yet he
lacked the knowledge to write about history at large, and the status
to venture freely on the history of France. Moreover, contemporary witnesses were still there to be questioned.

What we do know more positively is that Voltaire drafted the
book in England, and completed it not long after his return to
France. He went to a great deal of trouble to collect information,
both documentary and firsthand, from those who had participated

1 But here I must for once interrupt
the narrative in order to destroy a
legend; Desnoiresterres, i.28, says (and
his statement has frequently been repeated) that at school Voltaire was
particularly attracted to history, and
above all to contemporary history,
government and politics. He cites as
his authority a letter written to Olivet
in 1738 (Best.D1631); but Voltaire
claims nothing of the kind. He merely
says that he has been criticised because
he first wrote poetry, then history, and
finally philosophy (that is, science).
What was so surprising in that? he
asks. Had not Olivet himself made him
read and learn by heart at Louis-le-grand
poets, historians and philosophers?
2 Best.D1666 (26 November 1738).

in the events, both at the side of the Swedish king, and against him.[3] This extract from an English letter to Thieriot, written soon after his return to France, is typical:

I hope m^r de Brancas will instruct me on the particularities which he knows concerning the late King of Sweden. But there are many more curious things relating to that history, which J conjure you earnestly to enquire of.

You may go to the swedish embassador or to his secretary, or to his chaplain or his whore; ask any of em

1° whether t'is true count Piper had so great a hand in engaging the states to Declare the King *major* at sixteen.

what part the queen grand mother had in the affairs, since her grandson's majority.

what sort of government was established in Sweden after the King's arrival on the turckish dominions.

I begg of you too, to see m^r de Croissy, of whom j made a very honourable mention in my history, and whose family j have much commended as j think it deserves.

Ask him in what tongue the King did speak with him in Stralsund.

But especially sift him about the pretender's interest with that monarck at that time, endeavour to know whether France had any design to help the pretender together with the King of Sweden.

Ask him if he knew the famous baron Goerts, and how far he believes Goerts had carried his vast designs about the pretender, and the empire.

Do not forget to ingratiate me with m^r de Croissy, whom J esteem very much.

When you see m^r de Maisons, tell him you do not know where I am at present, but desire him to forward his remarks, and to restore the manuscripts as soon as he can.

There is another query more weighty than all the rest.

Two or three historians or rather compilers of gazettes have confidently reported, that King Augustus of Poland at his restoration caused to be beheaded one *Fengsten,* his privy councellor, for having signed the shamefull peace of Alrapstad, in order to let the world believe, that, he (the King) had been imposed upon by *Fengsten,* and to load an innocent subject with the whole odium and shame of that treaty. J know Kings are capable of the most outrageous and wiked pieces of barbarity which they call refinement in politiks. Yet I have many reasons to question the beheading of that *Fengsten.* Pray talk to m^r de Brancas about it. Enquire who may give you a true account of that affair.[4]

3 See for instance his correspondence with count La Cerda de Villelongue (Best.D372-5; February-May 1730), and some of the materials he collected and which are now in the Bibliothèque nationale and in his library in Leningrad.

4 Best.D349 (2 April 1729).

Voltaire wrote the book very carefully, and did everything he could to placate the authorities[5], but in vain. He had to print the history surreptitiously at Rouen, where it appeared in 1731, over a fictitious Basle imprint, in two small volumes which mark an epoch, but which had to be black-marketed in Paris. Voltaire was triumphantly justified. In spite of the implacable hostility of the government, the *Histoire de Charles XII* was printed at least ten times in its first two years[6]. Voltaire was back on his throne, with new provinces of literature inscribed on his banner, though in the complex and busy chronology of his life and writings, it must be remembered that the *Lettres philosophiques* had not yet appeared in France.

The literary historian is very fortunate, for even when little information is available about the conception of a work, and even when confronted by so seldom introspective an author as Voltaire, he always possesses the most valuable evidence of all, the book itself. But before we turn to it, let us look at some indirect evidence. A decade later a vast and insufferably boring biography of Charles XII was published by the late king's chaplain Jöran Anders Nordberg. Inevitably, the voluminous dullard found much to criticise in Voltaire's compact lucidity. In fact, although Nordberg's material was far more comprehensive than Voltaire's and occasionally more accurate, his reflections were for the most part purloined from Voltaire, who was not the man to bear this in silence. He wrote Nordberg an open letter[7] of scintillating satire. He lectured the reverend pedant at length about 'useless truth'. He teased him unmercifully because, for instance, he had recorded the doctorates of a number of worthy persons only remotely connected with Charles XII, and because he went into minute details about a chapel burned long before, and about the dais on which the king was

---

5 The correspondence for 1729-31 overflows with details of the negotiations.

6 It has everywhere remained one of the most popular of Voltaire's books; thus, even in Italian more editions have appeared only of *Candide* and *Zaïre*; see my 'A Provisional bibliography of Italian editions and translations of Voltaire', *Studies on Voltaire* (1961), xviii.263-310; and the same thing

naturally emerges from my 'A Provisional bibliography of Scandinavian and Finnish editions and translations of Voltaire', *Studies on Voltaire* (1966), xlvii.53-92. R. M. Hatton, *Charles XII of Sweden* (London 1968), p. xiv, writes that Voltaire's portrait of the Swedish king 'is etched indelibly on the European historical consciousness': true and well said.

7 Best.D2609 (? May 1742).

crowned. 'You tell us . . . at what time Charles XII was crowned;
but you do not say why it was done before the age prescribed by
law; why the queen mother was deprived of the regency', and so
on and so forth. Nordberg calls Voltaire a liar, and points out in
the margin of his book the evidence for this 'flattering allegation'
by proving conclusively that Voltaire was mistaken when he
stated that general Stewart was wounded in the shoulder, for he
was only bruised. It is true that Voltaire for the first time gave
an intelligible and accurate account of the crucial battle of Narva,
but he is a liar because he referred to general Liewen's red uniform,
when in fact it was not red. Voltaire had no difficulty in showing
that Nordberg, however meticulous about such trifles, was uncritical in his use of important evidence. Thus, he demonstrated
from internal evidence (incorrect formulas, wrong terms of address
and subscription, anachronistic terms) that an important letter used
by Nordberg must be a fake—and in fact it is.

Hardly had Sallust shown that the writing of history was something more than the enumeration of events, hardly had Tacitus
brought this realisation to some maturity, than the Christian
philosophy of history undermined the new insight. The historical
process became merely the execution of a divine plan, with a
known beginning and a precisely anticipated end, and the writing
of history was thus hobbled and blinkered: it became a branch of
theology, as ultimately in Bossuet. This absurdity is what Voltaire determined to end, and did end. Of course the classic statement of his view of history is the great and sweeping *Essai sur
les mœurs*: *Charles XII* is no more than a first tentative attempt—
it preceded Gibbon's *Decline and fall* by nearly half a century—
but it was enough to work a revolution. Voltaire replaced providence by natural law. 'The work of Voltaire and his school, in
disrupting the old authority of Church and Bible—bitterly denounced and blackly maligned as it has been—is now recognised
by all thinking minds, at least by all leaders of thought, to have
been an essential service in the emancipation of the human intellect.'[8] And more precisely: 'it was to Voltaire more than any

8 James T. Shotwell, *An Introduction to the history of history* (New York
1923), pp. 325-6.

other man that the new attitude towards the past was due . . .
the crushing weight of authority could only be overthrown by
a whole-hearted champion of the might and majesty of reason. . . .
By allowing his razor-edged intelligence to play freely over vast
ranges hitherto unchallenged by critical thought, he did much to
destroy the blind credulity against which erudition alone was
powerless.'[9]

Two things essentially distinguish the *Histoire de Charles XII*
from all preceding historical writing: first, the undogmatic (or, if
the reader prefers, objective or scientific) attitude of its author;
and second, the freedom with which it is written. Voltaire is no
tacit respector of received ideas on any subject. Every incident is
weighed on its merits. The very first words of his preface (added
in 1748) are: 'Incredulity . . . is the basis of all wisdom.' Voltaire
was still eager to keep on the right side of the authorities; indeed, he
was prepared to take infinite precautions to avoid a third Bastille—
and who can blame him? But throughout his life he had a very
personal way of avoiding trouble: at his most timid he was bolder
than all but the very boldest of his contemporaries. Thus in the
summing-up of *Charles XII* one is astonished to read a set piece
in criticism of kings. There have been few, says he, who deserve
a special history. Only those merit remembrance who have done
good to humanity. And the whole of Voltaire's philosophy
of history is summed up in a remarkable passage to which no
parallel can be found before him: 'During the time that Christian
princes have tried to deceive one another, and make war or conclude alliances, thousands of treaties have been signed and as many
battles have been fought; fine and infamous actions are innumerable. When all this crowd of events and of details comes down to
posterity, nearly all are extinguished the ones by the others. Only
those kings remain who have produced great changes, or those
who, having been described by some great writer, emerge from
the crowd, like the portraits of obscure men painted by great
masters.'[10] In a letter to prince Frederick, Voltaire wished that all

9 G. P. Gooch, *History and historians in the nineteenth century* (London
&c. 1935), p. 7.

10 Cp. Horace's *Exegi monumentum*,
Shakespeare's (sonnet lv) 'Not marble,
nor the gilded monuments Of princes',
and a hundred similar passages.

those histories could be thrown into the sea which merely celebrate the vices and the furies of kings.[11] And Voltaire concludes his *Discours sur l'histoire de Charles XII* on a memorable note—not for him any idea of the historian as a camera: 'If any princes or ministers should find disagreeable truths in this work, let them remember that, being public men, they owe the public an account of their actions; that this is the price at which they buy their greatness; that history is a witness, not a flatterer; and that the only way to compel men to speak well of us, is to do good.'

Nor did Voltaire miss the opportunity to slip in a few glancing blows at religious superstition, as when he described Peter's efforts to civilise the Russian clergy. 'No sooner had the czar introduced the printing press than the monks took advantage of it to announce that Peter was anti-Christ because he made the priests shave and allowed post-mortem dissection in hospitals. One monk, however, who aspired to a bishopric, refuted the accusation because Peter's name did not include the number 666.'[12]

It is also remarkable that in *Charles XII* Voltaire's marvellous style came to maturity. Since his earliest writings it had been impressive by what always remained its outstanding characteristics: lucidity and elegance. But it was not until *Charles XII* that, encouraged no doubt by the subject-matter, there begin to appear regularly those typically Voltairean phrases in which brevity and vocabulary, joined to a carefully chosen word-order, the whole dictated by a perfect ear, produce an effect at once lapidary and natural, and give the reader the *frisson* produced only by words in which the manner perfectly matches the matter. Nothing appears so simple and straightforward, but is in reality more full of art, than such a sentence as: 'Il est vrai que Charles avait donné sa parole, en 1700, de ne se mêler en rien de la guerre de Louis XIV contre les alliés; mais le duc de Marlborough ne croyait pas qu'il y eût un prince assez esclave de sa parole pour ne pas la sacrifier à sa grandeur et à son intérêt'.[13] Or, even more pregnantly, this of

---

11 Best.D1426 (*c.* 15 January 1738).

12 *Histoire de Charles XII*, i.

13 *Histoire de Charles XII*, iii; 'It is true that Charles had given his word in 1700 not to interfere in any way in the war of Louis XIV against the allies; but the duke of Marlborough did not believe that there existed a prince so enslaved by his word that he would not sacrifice it to his greatness and his interests.'

the young Charles: 'Il n'assistait presque jamais dans le conseil que pour croiser les jambes sur la table.'[14]

Other passages well worthy of attention are that in the fourth book in which Voltaire contrasts the character and feats of Charles XII and Peter the great, that in the fifth in which the state of Europe is surveyed after the battle of Pultava, that in the sixth in which the capture of Charles at Bender is described.

14 *Histoire de Charles XII*, ii; 'He hardly ever attended the council but to cross his legs on the table.'

14. The struggle begins, 1728-1734

WHEN VOLTAIRE RETURNED to France one of his first cares was to make himself financially secure. He explained many years later in his *Mémoires*:

I was not born rich, far from it. I am asked by what art I have come to live like a farmer-general: it will be useful for me to explain, so that my example may serve. I saw so many poor and despised men of letters that I decided long ago not to add to their number. In France a man must be anvil or hammer; I was born anvil. A small patrimony becomes smaller every day, because eventually all prices go up, and because the government often lay their hands on both income and capital. The government being always encumbered and always fickle, it is necessary to watch closely its handling of the state's finances. There is always one way or another by which a private individual can profit without incurring any obligation to anyone; and nothing is so agreeable as to make one's own fortune: the first step is painful, the others are easy. . . . After living with kings, I have made myself king of my own domain, notwithstanding enormous losses.

In fact he had succeeded in helping all his family, and very many others, while spending half a million in 'peopling a desert'[1]. Voltaire was extremely proud of this, and made no bones about it. As a matter of fact, his figure is an understatement. His household accounts, recently discovered and published, show that from 1759 to 1768, that is before his work at Ferney had reached its climax, his outgoings were well over a million francs.[2]

Though never poor in the strictest sense Voltaire had always been hard up. Yet he never seems to have cared at all about money. But he had learned his lesson, and he now had a small capital from the profits of the English *Henriade*. With this he proceeded to give a first demonstration of what could be done by measuring his intelligence against that of the professional money-makers.

Before he left for England some of Voltaire's money (from his mother? Ninon de L'Enclos's bequest?) was invested in Paris

---

1 BestD15500 (3 March 1769).
2 See my introduction to *Voltaire's*   *household accounts* (Genève & New York 1968).

municipal bonds, on which the city defaulted. Voltaire took this with the utmost good-humour, as he always took financial setbacks: all he found to say was: 'I have the misfortune to have lost all my annuities upon the town house for want of a formality.'[3] The authorities then decided to reimburse the holders of their bonds, the drawings to be by lot. Owners of bonds could buy lottery tickets to the value of one in a thousand: that is, the holder of bonds having a face value of 1000 francs was entitled to buy ticket at the cost of one franc. The prizes were financed in part by the income from the sale of tickets, in part by a monthly contribution of 500,000 francs from the national government, afterwards increased to 600,000. The drawings were monthly, and consequently each month those who bought tickets made a profit of something over half a million francs, which was distributed among themselves by the luck of the draw. If, however, any one person could obtain all the tickets available in a given month, he would automatically make the whole profit. Voltaire saw this and, in collaboration with the mathematician La Condamine, he organised various groupings and combinations, by means of which he made a profit of six or seven million francs for the syndicate, of which his personal share was about half a million.[4]

A few months later Voltaire made another killing by taking advantage of a loophole in an issue of bonds in Lorraine—an affair of which he has left us a witty if not very explicit account in verse and prose.[5]

Voltaire had taken just a year to attain financial security. And after he had accomplished this feat, and was much better off than his father had ever been, the executor of Arouet's will in handsome terms released Voltaire's inheritance (1 March 1730)[6]. He never looked back, and though all his life he spent prodigiously, maintaining an army of relations, protégés, and servants, building, farming, lending to his tenants free or at nominal rates of interest, and publishing hundreds of books and pamphlets, and although he abandoned the vast profits from his writings to the publishers

3 Best.D330 (11 April 1728); see also Best.D225, D308, D333.

4 For a fuller account of this operation see Jacques Donvez, *De quoi vivait Voltaire?* (Paris [1949]), pp. 37-53.

5 Best.D366 (*c.* September 1729).

6 J. J. Guiffrey, 'La Jeunesse de Voltaire', *Bulletin de la Société de l'histoire de Paris* (Paris 1875), ii.42-50; cp. ii.73-6.

and the actors, he died one of the wealthiest private commoners in Europe.

I think that it was not by chance that Voltaire became more outspoken as soon as his lines of retreat were secured. An example occurred at once. On the 15th of March 1730 Adrienne Lecouvreur played for the last time, in Voltaire's *Œdipe*, and a few days later she died in the author's arms. She was only thirty-seven, the first tragic actress of her time. She was also a woman of intelligence, heart and courage.[7] When the young Argental fell in love with her, she gave him up in a message[8] to his mother: a nobler and wiser letter has never been written in such circumstances. She pledged her jewels and silver to find money for the mad political adventures of the man she loved, Maurice de Saxe. Yet when she died those who had applauded her so enthusiastically refused her at once last rites and consecrated burial—simply because she was an actress, and thus automatically excommunicated. At about the same time that the body of Adrienne Lecouvreur was thrown into quicklime on waste land, the English actress Anne Oldfield was buried in Westminster abbey. The fearful contrast evoked from Voltaire one of his grandest outbursts against fanatical intolerance:

> Que direz-vous, race future,
> Lorsque vous apprendrez la flétrissante injure
> Qu'à ces arts désolés font des prêtres cruels?
> Un objet digne des autels
> Est privé de la sépulture!
> Et dans un champ profane on jette à l'aventure
> De ce corps si chéri les restes immortels! ...
> Ah! verrai-je toujours ma faible nation,
> Incertaine en ses vœux, flétrir ce qu'elle admire;
> Nos mœurs avec nos lois toujours se contredire;
> Et le Français volage endormi sous l'empire
> De la superstition?
> Quoi! n'est-ce donc qu'en Angleterre
> Que les mortels osent penser?
> O rival d'Athène, ô Londres! heureuse terre!

7 Those who share my weakness for such curiosities will be amused to know that she was also the great-grandmother of George Sand.

8 It is printed in the *Lettres inédites de madame la marquise Du Chastelet à m. le comte d'Argental* (Paris 1806), pp. 292-5.

Ainsi que les tyrans vous avez su chasser
Les préjugés honteux qui vous livraient la guerre.
C'est là qu'on sait tout dire, et tout récompenser;
Nul art n'est méprisé, tout succès à sa gloire.[9]

Voltaire also urged the actors to give no more performances until they were treated like other citizens. 'They promised, but did nothing', he told mlle Clairon long after. 'They preferred dishonour with a little money.'[10] Many years passed before the church lifted its excommunication of play-actors, and society its ostracism.

Such a poem was inevitably condemned by the authorities. But Voltaire said that he had to publish these lines 'dictated by indignation, tenderness and pity',

> dût la trouppe des dévots
> Que toujours un pur zèle enflamme
> Entourer mon corps de fagots,
> Le tout pour le bien de mon âme.[11]

He never forgot the fate of this great actress, beloved and rejected by all, and it explains in some measure his unpleasing manœuvres as he saw his own death approaching menaced with a similar fate.

There followed a very active, yet externally rather uneventful period of Voltaire's life. He spent a great deal of time on the surreptitious distribution of *Charles XII*, of which, though it was condemned and seized in January 1731, several[12] editions had appeared by the next year. He began the *Mort de César*[13],

---

9 *La Mort de mlle Lecouvreur*, quoted here in the text of the original edition; 'What will you say, future race, when you hear of the degrading injury done by cruel priests to the arts in mourning? One worthy of altars is deprived of burial! And the immortal remains of this beloved body are thrown at random into a vulgar field! ... Ah! shall I always see my wretched country, feeble in its aims, dishonour what it admires, our customs always conflict with our laws, and the fickle Frenchman asleep under the dominion of superstition? What! is it only in England that mortals dare to think? O rival of Athens, O London! happy land! You have known how to drive out, with the tyrants, the shameful prejudices which warred against you. There all can be said, and all is rewarded; no art is despised, every success is crowned with glory.'

10 Best.D9973 (27 August 1761).

11 Best.D407 (1 May 1731); 'even if the devout gang, always inflamed by pure zeal, roast me alive for the good of my soul'.

12 In Best.D492 (26 May 1732) Voltaire says four, but several editions had been printed without his knowledge.

13 See pp. 145-154, above.

and also wrote and produced his play *Eriphyle*[14] (1731-32), of which, though it had a modest success, he thought so little that he never published it. Apart from the theatre, Voltaire produced little poetry, though he did begin the notorious *Pucelle* as a relaxation during the worst moments of persecution. One poem of 1731 must, however, be mentioned, if only because it is the prime favourite of the anthologists. Mlle de Livry[15], now cutting a great figure thanks to a lucky marriage, snubbed Voltaire, who composed the epistle known as 'Les Vous et les tu' because of the wonderfully effective, but unfortunately untranslatable change in the last line from the formal 'vous' to the intimate 'tu'. It is a graceful piece of rhymed nostalgia, much overrated as poetry[16], but characteristic of Voltaire as a delightful example of the good-humoured, civilised way in which he took such things.

Another of Voltaire's minor writings at this time is a long letter about a point of literary controversy concerning the versification of Campistron. This controversy may now be allowed to remain in the same decent obscurity as that poet himself. What is interesting in this essay is a passage which illustrates Voltaire's punctilio in all matters of social conduct. He says that it is unworthy of French courtesy, and disrespectful, to refer to authors by their names alone, even after their deaths, until they have passed into history. He himself, he explains, would never say Chaulieu (recently dead) or Fontenelle (the old man was still alive); he said 'monsieur Racine' and 'monsieur Despréaux' because they were 'nearly my contemporaries'; but he said 'the great Corneille' because this dramatist had 'the merit of antiquity.'[17] As Boileau died in 1711, Racine in 1699, and Corneille in 1684, it can be seen that Voltaire's practice was governed by the faintest of nuances. But then all such social rules have to be played by ear—that is their charm and their danger. The trouble is that he had a very good ear (except in his dealings with those who arrogated superiority)

14 See p. 139, note 19, above.

15 See p. 75, above.

16 It must be said plainly that Alfred Noyes, *Voltaire* (London 1936), p. 124, is talking nonsense when he compares this charming trifle with Horace.

17 Best.D415 (1 July 1731); this letter is dated from 'Fakener, near Canterbury', because Voltaire was engaged in clandestine printing at Rouen.

and was apt all through his life to get very cross with those who were less lucky.

At the end of 1731 Voltaire went to live with mme de Fontaine-Martel. Their relations appear to have been sexless, and it was in her honour that Voltaire wrote his *Temple de l'amitié*, in which he tells her that only she and he were worthy of it: Voltaire never could play the hypocrite with any success, even when he did it for a laudable purpose. The fact is that he had in the back of his mind the eternal dream of all artists and idealists: 'What a delicious life it would be to share a home with three or four men of letters with talent and no jealousy, who would love one another, live agreeably, cultivate their art, talk about it, enlighten each other! I dream one day to live in such a little paradise.'[18] Voltaire returned to this dream again and again, when he went to Cirey, to Potsdam, to Geneva, but it was never to be. For the moment, mme de Fontaine-Martel was really too exacting: she would not allow her protégés to have mistresses[19]. Moreover, the good lady soon died. Voltaire's report of the circumstances does not betray excessive sorrow:

. . . the illness of the baroness interrupted all our double rhymes. I did not think a week ago that the first verses I should have to compose for her would be her epitaph. I hardly know how I bore all the burdens that have fallen on me during the past fortnight. On the one hand *Zaïre* was seized, the baroness was dying on the other; I had to go to solicit the keeper of the seals and to fetch the last sacrament. I nursed the sick woman all night and did the housekeeping all day. Just imagine, it was I who had to tell the poor woman that she was about to depart. She would hear nothing of the last ceremonies; but I was bound in honour to see that she died in accordance with the regulations. I brought her a priest half Jansenist, half politic, who pretended to confess her, and came back to give her the rest. When this actor of Saint-Eustache asked her aloud whether she was not firmly convinced that her god, her creator was in the eucharist, she answered, *Oh, yes!* in a tone of voice which would have made me burst out laughing in less lugubrious circumstances.[20]

18 Best.D493 (29 May 1732).

19 So Voltaire reports in the letter just quoted; but something seems to have gone wrong somewhere: in later years he quoted mme de Fontaine-Martel as saying that 'when one had the misfortune no longer to be able to be a whore, one should be a procuress' (Best.D14218, 9 June 1767).

20 Best.D563 (27 January 1733). In his *Notebooks* (ii.506) Voltaire added a pleasant detail. A few moments before her death mme de Fontaine-Martel asked what the time was, and when she was told, said: 'Ah, what a comfort it is that at every hour there is always someone who is preventing the race from dying out.'

While all this was going on there suddenly appears this sentence in a letter to Thieriot, who was in England: 'J hope to employ such a studious leisure with Eriphile, the english letters, and the age of Lewis the 14th.'[21] This is the first reference to one of Voltaire's most famous works, the *Siècle de Louis XIV*, which henceforth was never out of his mind until it was published twenty years later.

And some idea of Voltaire's prodigious mental energy and power of work can be gleaned from the fact that only a fortnight later he wrote casually to Cideville that he had started a new play to take his mind off *Eriphyle*[22]. This new play was *Zaïre* generally regarded, though not by me, as Voltaire's best tragedy. Desnoiresterres (i.447) does not hesitate to call it 'the most original, the most inspired of Voltaire's works, which cannot be read 'without emotion and without tears'. It was written in three weeks[23] at once submitted to the actors, and produced 13 August 1732. It was immediately successful. Voltaire was given an ovation, the tragedy was performed thirty-one times in its first season[24], and has since been put on at the Comédie française more often than any other of Voltaire's plays[25]. We must therefore look at it a little more closely, especially as the reasons for the success of *Zaïre* are complex.

Voltaire himself took the play very seriously. 'I want there to be nothing so Turkish, nothing so Christian, so full of love, so tender, so furious.'[26] He took endless trouble with the production; composed a minute analysis[27] of the play; and when he published it, not only took the unprecedented and scandalous step of dedicating it to a commoner, but to a foreign one at that, and went out of his way to specify at the head of the long essay in prose and verse that it was addressed to an 'English merchant'. This was his host at Wandsworth (sir) Everard Fawkener. The dedication was of course suppressed by the authorities, in part perhaps because Voltaire told his English friend and host that although they

21 Best.D488 (13 May 1732).
22 Best.D493 (29 May 1732).
23 See e.g. Best.D8363 (18 June 1759).
24 See Best.D515 (25 August 1732);

see p. 144, above.
25 See p. 144, note 30 above.
26 Best.D463 (29 May 1732).
27 Best.D517 (c. 25 August 1732).

belonged to different nations they were really fellow-citizens since they both loved the arts.

It was also in *Zaïre* that Voltaire introduced the new spelling (now of course universal) of *ai* for *oi* when so pronounced. Thus, 'anglois' had previously been pronounced as written; but by the eighteenth century everybody said 'anglais'; and Voltaire's reform was to make the spelling catch up with the pronunciation. In France it is well-nigh impossible to introduce reforms into the language, but here Voltaire triumphed, and quite quickly at that —within half a century his spelling had been adopted by all but the most conservative.

In short, it is obvious that Voltaire did everything to attract attention to *Zaïre*. The reason is hinted at in a brief note found in only two of the earliest editions. Voltaire says in the preface that he had been reproached with not putting enough love into his plays; he had therefore written *Zaïre*, which was known in Paris as the 'Christian tragedy.' In other words, he had written a tragedy dealing with religion in the guise of a love story. This was seen by Jean Baptiste Rousseau, who, however malicious and hypocritical, was no fool, when he wrote that the purpose of *Zaïre* was to show that grace had no power against passion[28].

Œdipe has been falsely regarded as an anti-Jansenist play[29]: such a description could more reasonably be applied to *Zaïre*. The theme is sounded in the very first scene of the play, when Zaïre says:

> La coutume, la loi plia mes premiers ans
> A la religion des heureux musulmans.
> Je le vois trop: les soins qu'on prend de notre enfance
> Forment nos sentiments, nos mœurs, notre croyance.
> J'eusse été près du Gange esclave des faux dieux,
> Chrétienne dans Paris, musulmane en ces lieux.[30]

This reduces religious belief to a topographic accident, and of course makes nonsense of anything in the nature of innate grace. Such notions of the relativity of ethics and the like recur frequently

28 Best.D561 (13 January 1733).
29 See pp. 81-82, above.
30 'Custom, law bent my first years to the religion of the happy Muslims. I see it too clearly: the care taken of our childhood forms our feelings, our habits, our belief. By the Ganges I would have been a slave of the false gods, a Christian in Paris, a Muslim here.'

in Voltaire's writings: this idea is an essential part of his philosophy.

In 1732 the *Epître à Uranie*[31] was published under the cloak, and as the year drew to an end Voltaire felt ready to continue on all fronts the fight for freedom of thought: he sent the *Temple du goût* to press, and he began to prepare the publication of the *English letters*. I have tried to disengage the life of Voltaire from the morass of legend and worse, and therefore I seldom quote the anecdotes which constitute the vast corpus of Voltairean folklore. But I may here be allowed an exception. The chancellor Daguesseau is said to have asked his secretary at about this time what should be done about Voltaire, and the secretary is quoted as answering that he should be locked up without pen, ink and paper, for he was capable of destroying a state.[32] This may well enough be authentic: if it was not said, it should have been, for it was true.

Voltaire's increasing independence was naturally due, in part, to money. Indeed, by the autumn of 1732 his finances were in such good shape that he planned to become a landed proprietor. But he then lost 12,000 francs at cards, and had to give up this amiable project, which had to wait for a good many years. He little repined, for he was a philosopher in every sense of the word. All he found to say was that he had got what he deserved.[33]

And it is also important to remember that at this time Voltaire still enjoyed the favour of the Court, or at least of the queen. Thus, in October 1732, when the duc de Mortemart, the first gentleman of the chamber then in charge of the theatre, refused to allow *Hérode et Mariamne* to be revived, Voltaire obtained an order from the queen, and the play was put on with great success. The duke revenged himself by getting the Italian theatre to announce a parody of Voltaire's tragedy. The queen promised to forbid this, but forgot to give the order. So she went to the theatre and pointedly rose to leave when the parody came on.[34]

But we must return to the *Temple du goût*, a work unique in its kind: a verse and prose essay in literary and art criticism. The

31 See pp. 94-96, above.

32 Gabriel Brotier, *Paroles mémorables* (Paris 1790), p. 303.

33 Best.D524, D527 (both September 1732).

34 Mathieu Marais, *Journal et mémoires*, iv.438 (28 October 1732).

narrator visits the temple of Taste, and at the very outset Voltaire launches an irrelevant side-swipe at papal infallibility. But soon he meets a cloud of pedants who restore texts, and who compile fat volumes about works they do not understand, who cry out that

> Le goût n'est rien; nous avons l'habitude
> De rédiger au long de point en point
> Ce qu'on pense; mais nous ne pensons point.[35]

Voltaire then hits out at modern fashions in painting and music.

Voltaire then gets down to business. He violently attacks the small talents who make life difficult for the great ones. He laughs at the crowd of poetasters, authors of mathematical novels, academic haranguers, false critics. One by one many then distinguished authors present themselves for admission to the temple. Each of them is judged, a few are admitted, many rejected, all are criticised. Voltaire's judgments have nearly all been confirmed by posterity.

In the eighteenth century good taste was regulated by laws worked out as minutely as those on the statute book. Until nearly the end of Voltaire's life practically all educated people believed implicitly that a masterpiece could be constructed by following these rules. In such circumstances criticism was almost entirely superficial: Voltaire was himself to carry this process to an extreme in his commentary on Corneille. It was far from his intention to destroy these ideas in the *Temple du goût*: for he shared them to the full. All that he wanted to do was to purify the standards of good taste by refining the laws rather than by seeking to abolish them. He was also anxious to drive out of the temple of taste the more obviously worthless writers who had found a place in it by a wholly mechanical observance of the rules. Yet after all genius will out, and Voltaire could not help performing this blameless task in a provocative manner which profoundly dismayed many of his contemporaries. The very structure of his *Temple*, which makes it so interesting to us, annoyed the more witless custodians of good taste: its mixture of poetry and prose, allegory and straightforward narrative, was profoundly disturbing—and it must be

---

35 'Taste is nothing; we are accustomed to record at length and in detail what was thought; but we ourselves do not think.' I return to all this in chapter 33.

owned that it is more baroque than classical. It is a vivid illustration of the intellectual climate of Paris[36] in the 1730s that Voltaire's exercise in literary iconoclasm aroused disapproval almost as violent, even in official circles, as did the *Lettres philosophiques*.

Voltaire cautiously produced the *Lettres* first in an English edition, as we have seen, and then even more cautiously brought the book out in France, and gradually had it distributed in Paris. The elaborate care he took shows that he was well aware of the danger he was running: far from being evidence of cowardice, as has so often been charged, it clearly proves the contrary. The coward runs away from danger, the brave man faces it, taking precautions if he is not a fool. But all Voltaire's care was unavailing. Maurepas ordered his arrest[37], his rooms were searched and his papers taken away[38], and the *Lettres* themselves were ordered to be burnt by the public executioner because the book presented 'the greatest danger for religion and public order'[39]. The official documents concerning the *Lettres* mercilessly reveal where lay the real timidity: as a picture of the intellectual bankruptcy of a decaying order a very long letter[40] from the public prosecutor to the responsible minister would be difficult to match. One pictures him as a blind creature clinging with suckers of pedantry to the slippery rock of tradition.

Yet even if the government perceived only instinctively the real significance of the *Lettres philosophiques* there were plenty of able men in the church and among its supporters who saw it clearly, as witnesses the cloud of articles and pamphlets which now descended on Voltaire. He fought back, with increasing skill and subtlety, and irrevocably became the leader of intellectual and social revolt.

One of the most important sections of the book was not published in the original *Lettres*, though it was written at the same time as the rest. The 'Remarques sur les pensées de M. Pascal' were added in the 1734 French edition of the *Lettres*, and it was

36 On which light is also thrown by the *Vie de Molière* (written in 1733/1734, though not published until 1739), from which it emerges that Molière's comedies were disapproved because they were 'low'.

37 Best.D737 (8 May 1734).

38 Best.D751 (1 June 1734).

39 *Arrest de la cour du parlement, qui ordonne qu'un Livre, intitulé*: Lettres philosophiques . . . *sera lacéré & brûlé par l'Exécuteur de la haute-justice* (10 June 1734).

40 Best.D791 (8 October 1734).

this chapter, perhaps, which aroused the most indignation. The agitation was misconceived, and indeed the reputation the *Pensées* had acquired during the half-century since their publication, and in a measure still possess at secondhand, was equally misconceived. It is perhaps well to recall that the so-called *Pensées* are notes made by Pascal in preparation for a work of Christian apologetics, in which he intended to justify Christianity by arguing against the validity of reason. However desperate the attempt, anything that Pascal had to say on this subject, as on any other, would certainly have merited respectful attention. But we do not know what he would have said: all we have are rough, fragmentary notes, in no particular sequence, many of which would certainly have been discarded or changed. Moreover, only a corrupt version even of this confused text was available in Voltaire's time.[41] Some of Pascal's jottings are quite silly. Others are suggestive, poetic, and even sublime. However, it is absurd to take them as forming a coherent whole, let alone one to be blindly defended against criticism, or deserving sanctification.

Voltaire greatly admired his scientific work and his style, but he thought, rightly, that Pascal represented all the things which to him were anathema: party spirit, dogmatism, intolerance, instinctive pessimism, obscurantism. Pascal indeed 'attacks humanity much more cruelly than he attacked the Jesuits'[42]. Thus, Voltaire quotes this note: 'Let me therefore be no longer reproached for lack of clarity, since I make a point of it; but let the truth of religion be recognised in its very obscurity, in the little understanding of it that we have, and in our indifference about knowing it.' To which Voltaire replied: 'What strange marks of truth Pascal advances! What other marks does falsehood possess? What! in order to be believed it would be enough to say: *I am obscure, I am unintelligible*! It would be much more sensible to offer our eyes only the light of faith instead of these learned twilights.'

Again, another of Pascal's notes, one of the most famous, reads:

41 The importance of this fact has now been brought out by Mara Vamos in a brilliant study, 'Pascal's *pensées* and the Enlightenment: the roots of a misunderstanding', *Studies on Voltaire* (1972), xcvii.97-145.

42 Best.D626 (1 July 1733); the attack was in the *Lettres provinciales*.

'On seeing the blindness and misery of man, and the astonishing contradictions presented by his nature, and seeing the whole universe dumb, and man without light, abandoned to himself, and as it were lost in this corner of the universe, without knowing who has put him there, what he has come to do there, what he will become when he dies, I become fearful, like a man who, transported in his sleep to a deserted and frightful island, awakens without knowing where he is, and without having any possibility of leaving it; and I then marvel that one does not despair of so wretched a condition.'

The organ note is magnificent, but it is false. Voltaire replies, in part: 'What wise man would be full of despair because he does not understand the nature of thought, because he does not know some of the attributes of matter, because God has not revealed his secrets to him? One might as well despair for not having four feet and two wings. Why horrify us because we exist? Our being is not so wretched as you want to make us believe. To regard the universe as a prison cell, and all men as criminals about to be executed, is the notion of a fanatic. To believe that the world is a pleasure ground in which we need only enjoy ourselves is the dream of a sybarite. To think that the earth, men and animals are what they must be in the order of Providence, is, I think, the part of a wise man.'

Voltaire's answer is annihilating, because it is so much more judicious than that of Pascal, whose poetry is devoid of reason, while Voltaire's reason shines in the sun of clarity. He expressed the same view even more elegantly in verse:

> Je lis au cœur de l'homme, et souvent j'en rougis.
> J'examine avec soin les informes écrits,
> Les monuments épars, et le style énergique
> De ce fameux Pascal, ce dévot satirique,
> Je vois ce rare esprit trop prompt à s'enflammer,
>   Je combats ses rigueurs extrêmes.
> Il enseigne aux humains à se haïr eux-mêmes.
> Je voudrais, malgré lui, leur apprendre à s'aimer.[43]

43 *Epître à une dame ou soi-disant telle* (1732); 'I read the heart of man, and often blush for it. I examine with care the half-formed writings, the scattered remains, and the energetic style of that famous Pascal, that pious satirist. I see this rare spirit too ready to excite himself, I combat his extreme

And indeed, when Pascal says that 'if there is a god we should love only him, and not his creatures', how, even leaving the un-believer to his fate, can a Christian not prefer to this pagan state-ment Voltaire's humane and deeply philosophic reply that 'we should love his creatures, and very tenderly: each one should love his country, his wife, his father, his children. So much is it true that we should love them that God makes us love them despite ourselves'? And Voltaire goes on to point out that Pascal applied his sombre beliefs in his own life, treating his sister harshly for fear of seeming to love her. This kind of *argumentum ad hominem* is not usually very pleasing, but in the case of Pascal, as in that of J. J. Rousseau, it is inescapable. And Voltaire points to the obvious conclusion: 'If we were all to behave like this, what would human society be like?'

As for the revulsion felt by the lucid Voltaire against the ir-rationality of Pascal, it is no more obvious than justified. I do not refer here to Pascal's mysticism or to his deliberate obscurantism, for Pascal had a perfect right to choose to be antirational, though it seems odd to arrive by the use of the reason to a decision not to use it. What I have in mind is the element in Pascal of what in anyone else would be called sloppy thinking. Thus, one of Pascal's fragments reads: 'If there were only one religion, God would be too clearly manifest.' Are Christians seriously expected to believe that god deliberately created rivals to Christianity in order that he should be able to hide his face?

Half a century later, in one of his very last writings, Voltaire added further notes on Pascal, and one of these may be left to stand as the summing-up of his reactions to the spirit of dogma-tism and intolerance. In one of his notes Pascal says that it is impossible to doubt that Christianity is the only true religion, because its doctrine explains everything. Voltaire replies, in part:

Remember, wise readers, those . . . horrible times in which the frenzied fanatics called Papists and Calvinists, who at bottom preached the same dog-mas, persecuted each other for two hundred years with sword, fire and poison because they interpreted a few words differently. Consider that it was on the

severity. He taught men to hate them-selves: I should like, in spite of him, to teach them to love each other.'

way to the mass that the Irish massacres and those of St Bartholomew were committed; that it was after the mass and for the mass that so many innocents, so many mothers, so many children were slaughtered in the crusade against the Albigenses; that the assassins of so many kings murdered them only on account of the mass. . . .

Oh Pascal! this is what has been caused by the interminable quarrels about dogmas, about mysteries which could not but cause quarrels. There is no article of faith that has not given rise to a civil war.[44]

In pure literature these years were largely barren, though *Adélaïde Du Guesclin* (1734) is interesting as the first play to put an entirely French historical subject on the stage. This was not generally approved, and though Voltaire more than once rewrote his play under different titles, it never caught on. He also at this time wrote the libretto of *Samson* and *Tanis et Zélide* while ill with an intestinal inflammation. He told Rameau that he had written *Samson* only for the composer's benefit.[45]

If the forging of his philosophic tools was ultimately the most important feature of this period, there was another which in a more limited sense dominated the middle part of his life and activity: his long love affair with Emilie Du Châtelet.

44 From Voltaire's edition of Con-dorcet's *Eloge et pensées de Pascal* (1778).

45 Best.D690 (*c.* December 1733).

7 The marquise Du Châtelet, *from the painting by Jean Marc Nattier*

VUE·DU·CHATEAU·DE·CIREY·
SUIVANT·COMME·JL·DOIT·ÊTRE·
QUAND·JL·SERA·FINY·1742

8 The château de Cirey as planned, *from the central part of a painted triptych*

15. Emilie Du Châtelet, 1733-1749

AFTER VOLTAIRE HAD SETTLED mme de Fontaine-
Martel's affairs, he moved to the rue du Long-Pont (which
has since been re-named the rue de Brosse), opposite the
church of Saint-Gervais. He much admired its portal, by Jacques
de Brosse, which he called a masterpiece of architecture, adding
however that it lacked 'a church, an open place, and admirers'[1].
The church is still largely invisible, though the square has been
created; admirers have not noticeably multiplied, for the portal is
made up of three rows of pillars, one over the other, Doric, Ionic
and Corinthian respectively, huge and elaborate, but not very
satisfying.

It was in this new lodging that Voltaire one day in November
1733 received the visit

> De déesses un couple aimable
> Conduit par le dieu de l'amour;
> Du paradis l'heureux séjour,
> N'a jamais rien vu de semblable[2].

The two goddesses, who had come, says Carlyle, to make Voltaire's 'dim evening radiant for him', were Gabrielle Emilie Le
Tonnelier de Breteuil, marquise Du Châtelet, and her friend the
duchesse de Saint-Pierre. Voltaire had known mlle de Breteuil as
a child in her father's house, but had not met her again until May
or June 1733.[3] They soon became lovers, but for many months
behaved with the utmost discretion. It was not until the following
year that they more or less openly acknowledged their love.
Voltaire had arranged the marriage of Richelieu and the princesse
de Guise, and was present with mme Du Châtelet at the wedding.

---

1 *Le Temple du goût.*
2 Best.D676 (*c.* 15 November 1733).
'An adorable couple of goddesses led
by the god of love; the happy time of
Paradise never saw anything like this.'

The 'god of love' was Louis de Brancas
de Forcalquier, marquis de Cereste.
3 She is first mentioned in the correspondence on 3 July (Best.D627).

The bridal pair were happy, and so were the less official couple, though mme Du Châtelet missed Maupertuis, and Voltaire was anxious about the official reception of the *Lettres philosophiques*.[4] And indeed, hardly had the lovers arrived at Montjeu than hard on their heels followed the king's order for Voltaire's arrest. Luckily they had been warned by friends, and mme Du Châtelet at once announced that Voltaire had gone abroad[5], but not before he offered the newly married couple some grandfatherly advice:

> Ne vous aimez pas trop, c'est moi qui vous en prie;
> C'est le plus sûr moyen de vous aimer toujours:
> Il vaut mieux être amis tout le temps de sa vie
> Que d'être amants pour quelques jours.[6]

Then Voltaire followed Richelieu to the camp of Philippsburg[7], near Karlsruhe, which was being besieged by the French. Richelieu was in their camp, and the ostensible reason for Voltaire's visit illuminates the *ancien régime*: it was to intercede in a threatened duel between his friend and a member of his bride's family. Grand-nephew of France's greatest statesman, himself a duke and already a distinguished soldier, and one, incidentally, whose company in bed had been welcomed by many of the first women of France, it might be thought that Richelieu could carry his head high in any company. Far from it. His family name was Du Plessis, and the title of Richelieu had been acquired in the fifteenth century by marriage. Thus the Guises and Lorraines, who boasted of royal blood, complained of a misalliance when he married one of their number, even though she belonged to a branch which had come down in the world. Henri Jacques de Lorraine, prince de Lixin, grossly provoked the touchy duke. Voltaire could not prevent the duel, and the duke killed the prince.

The siege itself did not fail to provide Voltaire with other specimens of human folly. 'It seems probable', he wrote one day to a neighbour in Champagne, 'that prince Eugene will present

---

4 Best.D727 (28 April 1734).
5 Best.D730 (6 May 1734).
6 *A mademoiselle de Guise dans le temps qu'elle devait épouser m. le duc de Richelieu* (1734); 'I beg you not to love each other too much, that is the surest way to love each other for ever. It is better to be friends for life than to be lovers for a few days'.
7 Best.D766 (1 July 1734).

himself before our pits and trenches tomorrow, Friday, the day of
the virgin, at four o'clock in the morning. It is said that he has a
great devotion for Mary[8], and that she may well favour him
against m. d'Asfeld, who is a Jansenist. You know, madame, that
your Jansenists are suspected of not having enough devotion for
the virgin. You made fun of the congregation of the Jesuits and
of the paradise opened to Pelagia by a hundred and one devotions
to the mother of god.' Voltaire added some details of the casualties
already suffered to no purpose, and concluded that in all this could
be seen 'human folly in all its glory and all its horror'[9].

Voltaire was sung and entertained by his hosts and friends in
the camp, and of course returned the compliment, so that a
wonderful time was had by all. Here we have another example of
the oddly contradictory things that went on in the *ancien régime*,
for the man of whom so much fuss was being made by the princes
of the blood and the field officers at Philippsburg was of course on
the run from a royal order of arrest. The government were furious,
but nobody did anything, and on leaving the camp Voltaire slowly
made his way to Cirey, and so began his long retirement, as notable
for its intellectual as for its amorous activity.

Gildhuin, comte de Breteuil, was the first recorded ancestor of
Louis Nicolas Le Tonnelier de Breteuil, baron de Preuilly (1648-
1728). This high Court official married successively Marie Anne
Le Fèvre de Caumartin and Gabrielle Anne de Froulay. The
latter gave birth, 17 December 1706, to our heroine. Voltaire
wrote after her death: 'From her most tender childhood she had
nourished her mind by the reading of good authors in more than
one language. She started a translation of the *Aeneid*, of which I
have seen several fragments filled with the spirit of its author.
She learned Italian and English. Tasso and Milton were as familiar
to her as Virgil. She made less progress in Spanish, because she
had been told that there is only one famous book in this language,
and that this book is frivolous.'[10] And in his own *Mémoires*
Voltaire added: 'Her father . . . made her learn Latin, which she

---

8 Voltaire made the same remark in
the *Notebooks*, ii.547.

9 Best.D766 (1 July 1734); *Le Paradis ouvert à Philagie par cent dévotions*

à *la mère de dieu* was a very popular
devotional manual by Paul de Barry.

10 *Eloge historique de madame la
marquise Du Châtelet* (1752).

knew as well as mme Dacier; she knew by heart the finest passages of Horace, Virgil and Lucretius; all the philosophic works of Cicero were familiar to her. Her dominant taste was for mathematics and metaphysics.'[11] These details would be surprising at any time: they were unique in the eighteenth century, and what is more, they were perfectly authentic. Nor is the enumeration complete, for Emilie also had a highly cultivated passion for the stage and for music, among other things.

On 12 June 1725, in her nineteenth year, she married Florent Claude, marquis Du Châtelet-Lomont, who belonged to a family nobler, though less ancient, than that of his bride. Born 7 April 1695 at Namur (his father was its governor) Florent Claude entered the army and fought several campaigns. At this time he had reached the rank of colonel, and on his marriage was appointed governor of the city and castle of Semur. The marquis was not a man of mark, but he was gentle, understanding, and easy-going. His wife never failed in her respect and affection for him—and this was rare in a society in which happy and united married couples could be counted on one's fingers.

On 29 September 1725 the Du Châtelets made their ceremonial entry into Semur, and without delay were born (apart from a child who died young), on 30 June 1726, Françoise Gabriel Pauline, who married Alfonso Caraffa, duke of Montenero ('a high-nosed, dwarfish, thin-faced, swarthy, flat-chested Neapolitan'[12]); and, on 20 November 1727, Louis Marie Florent, destined to become duc Du Châtelet, ambassador to the court of St James's (1768-70), and one of the first victims of the revolution. Having done her duty, the marquise accompanied her husband to Paris in 1730, and thereafter seldom saw her splendid house at Semur (now a hospital, but well worth a visit).

In Paris mme Du Châtelet executed what was almost a social obligation: she took lovers. The first was perhaps Louis Vincent, marquis de Guébriant. The account given by the comte de Maurepas of this affair does not sound improbable to anyone who has read the marquise's love letters to Saint-Lambert. Still, it must be remembered that Maurepas had a lifelong hatred for Voltaire,

11 By 'metaphysics' Voltaire means what is now called 'philosophy'.

12 See the autobiography, p. 637, below.

always a thorn in his ministerial flesh. Anyway, whether or not he allowed this hatred to affect his feelings for Voltaire's mistress, this is what he wrote: 'The marquise Du Châtelet ... in despair at being abandoned by the marquis de Guébriant, whom she idolised, wrote him a letter full of eternal farewells, telling him that she wanted to die, since he no longer lived for her. Guébriant, who knew that she was liable to such transports, ran to her house, and, the porter refusing him the door, forced his way in, and found her in bed, sleeping from the effects of an almost mortal dose of opium. He sent for help and saved her life. Not being able to keep him even after this proof of love, she consoled herself with several others.'[13]

Of these 'several others' only the duc de Richelieu and the scientist Maupertuis are known. Mme Du Châtelet, when angry with Voltaire, tried also, though more discreetly, to renew her affair with Richelieu after it came to an end, exclaiming, as she did so, *o felix culpa!*[14] As for her liaison with Maupertuis, it did not cease even during the first and most ardent beginnings of her *grand amour* with Voltaire.[15] For all her excessive sensibility, she had in fact a streak of coarseness in her nature. Later, she had a passing affair in the Low Countries with the lawyer Charlier. And finally came the fatal encounter with Saint-Lambert.

The wretched mme Du Deffand, embittered by her unhappy marriage and her constitutional boredom—the *ennui* that Tolstoy somewhere calls a 'desire for desires'—drew this portrait of mme Du Châtelet:

Imagine a big and dried-up woman, with an over-heated complexion, sharp face, pointed nose. Such is the face of the lovely Emilie, a face with which she is so pleased that she spares nothing to show it off, curls, gew-gaws, precious stones, glass-ware, everything is in profusion; but as she tries to be beautiful in spite of nature, and wants to be magnificent in spite of her means, she is obliged, in order to afford the superfluous, to do without the necessary, such as underwear and other trifles.

She was born with a fairly good mind; wishing to appear even cleverer she

13 *Mémoires* (Paris 1792), iv.173. Raynal gives a similar account in his *Correspondance littéraire*, i.365-6.
14 Best.D871 (21 May 1735).
15 Even fifteen years later, the only

identifiable portrait found in mme Du Châtelet's Paris house after her death, was an engraving of Maupertuis, which hung in her bedroom (postmortem inventory; Best.app.D93).

preferred the study of the most abstract sciences to more agreeable knowledge: she hopes in this peculiar way to attain to a greater reputation than all other women, and to a decided superiority over them.

She has not limited herself to this ambition. She wanted to be a princess, and has become one, not by the grace of god, nor by that of the king, but by her own. This absurdity has been forgiven her like the others. One has become accustomed to regard her as a stage princess, and one has almost forgotten that she is a woman of rank.

Madame works so hard to appear what she is not, that one no longer knows what she really is. Even her defects are perhaps not natural, they may be due to her pretentions, her rudeness to her rank as a princess, her dryness to the fact that she is learned, and her thoughtlessness to her beauty.

However famous mme Du Ch. might be she would not be satisfied if her praises were not sung, and this also she has achieved in becoming the acknowledged mistress of m. de Voltaire. It is he who gives her life its lustre, and it is to him that she will owe her immortality.[16]

There are portraits, whether written or painted, whose subtlety and penetration, or even their intrinsic beauty, render objective precision almost superfluous. Who cares whether Voltaire looked like his bust by Houdon? He is for ever what Houdon has made him. This is not the case here. It is possible that mme Du Châtelet was big, though we cannot be sure. As with Voltaire himself, some witnesses say one thing, others the opposite. It is very improbable that she was dried-up: all the descriptions and portraits contradict this. A high complexion? Quite likely, though Nattier, who painted the best known portraits of mme Du Châtelet, gave all his women brilliant red cheeks. A sharp face? a pointed nose? Everything is relative, but if her nose was a little long, no authentic portrait shows a sharp face. Nancy Mitford concluded that she was 'what is now called a handsome woman'. The marquise was the first to admit her little weaknesses in the matter of gew-gaws and all the rest, and Voltaire teased her a great deal about them. As for her underwear, I must plead an ignorance no doubt equal to that of mme Du Deffand. Miss Mitford admirably summed up that mme Du Châtelet was not 'really elegant. Elegance, for women, demands undivided attention; Emilie was an intellectual; she had not endless hours to waste with hairdressers and dressmakers.'[17]

16 The manucript is in the possession of mr Wilmarth S. Lewis.

17 *Voltaire in love* (London 1957), p. 15. Mme Denis, who cannot be suspected of impartiality, admitted that mme Du Châtelet was 'very pretty' (Best.D1498).

Finally, that the Breteuils and the Du Châtelets were families of modest means, and that Voltaire took pleasure in giving his beloved every comfort and even luxury, was no doubt a cause of envy in mme Du Deffand, but it most certainly was not a crime.

For the rest, it is probable that the giving of precious objects to mme Du Châtelet was Voltaire's delicate way of assuring her future. These are the charming and previously unpublished lines which accompanied one of his presents:

> Pardonne aux diamants qui forment la bordure
> D'un portrait de peu de valeur.
> Je n'ai pas mis tant d'art à te donner mon cœur:
> Il n'a pas besoin de parure.[18]

And below Voltaire added these significant words: 'Here is another piece in case of accident.'

As for the luxury of Cirey, the somewhat vulgar pen of mme de Graffigny[19] has led some readers astray. A report by the président Hénault is more sober and more reliable, not least because he was the intimate friend of mme Du Deffand: 'I also stopped at Cirey. It is a rare sight. The two of them are there alone, plunged in gaiety. One writes verse in his corner, the other triangles in hers. The architecture of the house is romantic and surprisingly magnificent. Voltaire's quarters end in a gallery resembling the picture ... of the school of Athens[20], in which are assembled instruments of all kinds, mathematical, physical, chemical, astronomical, mechanical, etc., the whole surrounded by ancient lacquer, mirrors, paintings, saxon porcelain, etc. In a word, I assure you that it is like a dream.'[21] All this suggests hard work and good taste rather than sybaritic profusion.

18 Best.D2807; 'Forgive the diamonds that frame a portrait of little value. I did not put so much art in giving you my heart: it needs no ornament.'

19 In *La Vie privée de Voltaire et de m^me Du Châtelet* (Paris 1820). The original manuscripts, after being for many years buried in the collections of that most remarkable of baronets sir Thomas Phillipps, were bought by a dealer in New York called Kraus, who did not allow me to collate them—so rare an obscurantism that it deserves to be recorded. Fortunately the Graffigny papers are now in the Yale university library, but without the letters written from Cirey! See English Showalter, *Voltaire et ses amis d'après la correspondance de mme de Graffigny* (Studies on Voltaire, cxxxix: 1975). Mme de Graffigny's description of Cirey will be quoted below in chapter 33.

20 Raphael's fresco in the Stanza della segnatura of the Vatican.

21 Best.D2996 (9 July 1744).

On mme Du Deffand's remarks concerning mme Du Châtelet's intelligence, knowledge and ambitions, there is only one possible comment: she understood nothing of all this, and was perfectly incapable of understanding such things. It is no doubt true that mme Du Châtelet's celebrity is due to her relations with Voltaire, though Voltaire himself may not have thought so, at least in verse:

> Sans doute vous serez célèbre
> Par les grands calculs de l'algèbre
> Où votre esprit est absorbé:
> J'oserais m'y livrer moi-même;
> Mais, hélas! A + D − B
> N'est pas=à je vous aime.[22]

However, we are not particularly concerned with her fame: what we are interested in is the question of her own qualities. And certainly it is not the love of Voltaire that enabled her to accomplish solid work in more than one field, including a paper published by the Académie des sciences; to remain for many years in correspondence with leading men of science; to induce a Mairan to engage in public controversy with her on technical details in physics.

What then were precisely the work and the knowledge of mme Du Châtelet? In literature we must remain at a loss for lack of direct written evidence, but in the field of physics and metaphysics —for to her these two things were closely related—it is not impossible to answer this question. A sceptic could urge that the merits of the *Institutions de physique* (1740), of the *Dissertation sur la nature et la propagation du feu* (1744, but written in 1738), of the commentary on Newton published posthumously as the *Principes mathématiques de la philosophie naturelle* (1759), derive from Maupertuis, König and Clairault. It appears to me impossible to maintain this view after reading the newly discovered letters to Maupertuis, Bernoulli and Jurin. In these letters one can follow, notwithstanding mistakes and technical shortcomings, the reflections of a mind which has very exactly perceived the fundamental principles of natural science and the scientific methodology on

---

22 *A madame la marquise Du Châtelet lorsqu'elle apprenait l'algèbre* (c. 1735); 'The grand calculations in algebra by which your mind is absorbed will no doubt make you famous. I would dare to devote myself to them, but alas A+D−B is not = to I love you.'

which all ascertained truth is based. One can see that mme Du Châtelet was capable of discussing the most abstract points with intelligence and in a critical spirit. And it must not be forgotten—this point is essential—that many of these letters were written precisely to those who are alleged to have held her pen. How inconceivably absurd these disquisitions would have been addressed to those who would have known her to be incapable of them! Even Maupertuis wrote to Algarotti that mme Du Châtelet had triumphed in her scientific dispute with the eminent Mairan.[23]

We must also remember the unique tribute paid to her by Diderot—never exactly lavish with his praise—who said that he could count 'two sweet moments' in his life, one of which was the reading of the letter mme Du Châtelet wrote him about his *Lettre sur les aveugles*[24], a letter which most unfortunately has not survived.

It is impossible to maintain that mme Du Châtelet's learned and scientific pursuits were no more than an eccentricity or a *trompe l'œil*. She was certainly thinking of herself when she said in her *Réflexions sur le bonheur*: 'the love of study is the passion most necessary for our happiness. It is a sure safeguard against misfortune, it is a source of inexhaustible pleasure.' She had indeed 'tried the pure sciences and philosophies, in Books: but how much more charming, when they come to you as a Human Philosopher; handsome, magnanimous, and the wittiest man in the world'.[25]

Voltaire and mme Du Châtelet remained to all intents and purposes 'married' until her death, but their physical passion had waned long before the end of these sixteen years. We shall see more of this later, but we must ask here how this came about. It would be lacking in historical sense to reproach the marquise because she did not devote herself exclusively to Voltaire, even during the first years of their love: rare were the women of her rank who were content with one lover at a time. The husbands of course were out of the picture altogether. They claimed full freedom for themselves, and were civilised enough to grant it to their wives so long as appearances were respected. If the prudish

23 See the general note on Best. D2506.
24 Denis Diderot, *Correspondance*, ed. Georges Roth (Paris 1955), i.115.
25 Thomas Carlyle, *History of Friedrich II of Prussia* (1858-65), x.ii.

Marie Lesczcinska had chosen for her ladies only women as chaste as herself, the queen's existence would have been even more solitary.

Yet it has often been found surprising and even reprehensible that mme Du Châtelet should have abandoned a Voltaire for a Saint-Lambert. The truth is very different. One has only to read with a little empathy this pathetic passage in her posthumous *Réflexions sur le bonheur*:

I have received from God, it is true, one of those tender and immutable souls which do not know how to disguise or to moderate their passions, who know neither weakening nor disgust, and whose steadfastness can resist all things, even the certainty of being no longer loved. But I was happy for ten years in the love of the man who subjugated my soul, and these ten years I passed alone with him, without a single moment of distaste or lassitude. When age, illness, perhaps also the satiety of sensual enjoyment[26] diminished his inclination, it was long before I noticed anything. I loved for both of us, enjoyed the pleasure of loving and the illusion of believing myself loved. It is true that I have lost this happy state, and it was not without costing me many a tear.

It takes terrible shocks to break such chains. The wound in my heart bled for a long time. I had cause for complaint, and I forgave all. I had enough justice to realise that it was perhaps my heart alone in all the world which possessed an immutability capable of annihilating the power of time; that if age and his illnesses had not entirely extinguished his desires, he might perhaps still have been mine, and that my love might have brought him back to me; and finally that his heart, no longer capable of love, felt for me the most tender friendship, and would have devoted his life to me. The certainty that it was impossible to expect the return of his desire for me and of his passion, which is not in nature, as I well know, insensibly led my heart to an untroubled feeling of friendship, and this sentiment, joined to a passion for study, gave me happiness enough.

After making all due allowances for an inevitable minimum of self-deception, these are not merely the reveries of a sensitive soul, they are indubitably a faithful account of what she had experienced and felt. The marquise, however, made one perhaps fortunate mistake by indulging too far her egocentric character: it was not age, nor illness, nor even satiety that diminished Voltaire's sexual

26 mme Du Châtelet wrote 'jouis-sance', which has a specific sexual meaning; this is a sufficient answer to ignorant paradox-mongers who have alleged Voltaire to be impotent, as in the *Progrès médical* for 24 March 1956 (p. 133) and 10 February 1957 (p. 69).

inclination, it was quite simply that he had fallen in love with another woman, and this woman was his niece Marie Louise Denis. His letters to her have survived, they are explicit, but they show also that Voltaire did not for all that abandon mme Du Châtelet, and—it is a moral certainty—never would have left her if she had lived.

This remarkable woman died at Lunéville on the 10th of September 1749, in giving birth to Saint-Lambert's child (which did not survive), and was buried in the church of Saint-Jacques. Her tomb is below a slab of black marble without inscription of any kind.

In some ways she was undoubtedly bad for Voltaire, for she never really understood the forces that moved him. She would have liked to keep him out of trouble, but when trouble inevitably came she made it worse by losing her head; intensely jealous, she yet expected for herself, and received, forbearance of a high order. Yet there is nobody in Voltaire's life who inspires so much affection, and whom one leaves with greater sorrow. Her good qualities far outweighed her little human defects: she was intensely, perhaps a little oppressively, loyal, she stimulated Voltaire, kept pace with him so far as she could in his intellectual adventures, and joined with him in creating at Cirey a refuge which was at the same time an intensely exciting and exhilarating home. The destruction of the correspondence between these two remarkable people was Saint-Lambert's greatest crime.

ELÉMENS

DE LA

PHILOSOPHIE

DE NEUTON,

Mis à la portée de tout le monde.

Par Mᴿ. DE VOLTAIRE.

À AMSTERDAM,

Chez Eᴛɪᴇɴɴᴇ Lᴇᴅᴇᴛ & Compagnie.

M. DCC. XXXVIII.

10 Frederick II of Prussia, *from a contemporary engraving*

16. From Newton to Frederick, 1734-1738

IN THE SPRING OF 1734 Voltaire planned a new tragedy, *Alzire*, 'a very Christian play which may reconcile me with some of the devout'[1]. This tragedy has always been amongst the most popular of Voltaire's plays. Many of his contemporaries, even Desfontaines, esteemed it very highly, and Schelling thought it his best tragedy. Voltaire himself took a cynical view of the success enjoyed by *Alzire*. He said that it was due to the fact that the author was away from Paris, on the principle that absence makes the heart grow fonder.[2]

There are some incidental reasons for the favourable view taken of *Alzire*: it is the earliest surviving[3] French play the scene of which is laid in America (Peru), it was published with an impressive introductory discourse, and it was dedicated to mme Du Châtelet. The preface is notable for the unusually introspective way in which Voltaire explains his purpose. He begins:

An effort has been made in this tragedy, which is entirely born of the imagination and is of rather a new kind, to discover to what extent the true spirit of religion is superior to the natural virtues.

The religion of a barbarian is to offer to his gods the blood of his enemies. An ignorant Christian is often no better. To be assiduous in certain useless practices, and to ignore the true duty of a man; to pay, but to keep one's vices; to fast, but to hate; to conspire, to persecute, such is his religion. That of the true Christian is to consider all men as his brothers, to do good and to forgive evil. . . .

This humanity, which should be the chief characteristic of every thinking being, will be found in nearly all my writings. They show (if I may be allowed to say this) a wish for the happiness of mankind, a horror of injustice and oppression; and this only has so far saved my works from the obscurity in which their defects should have buried them.

1. Best.D804 (c. 1 December 1734).
2 See the autobiography, p. 628, below.
3 A lost *Montézume*, by Louis Ferrier de La Martinière, was produced in 1702. Voltaire's play was stimulated by Dryden's *Indian emperor*, which is several times quoted in Voltaire's note-books. The theme of the 'noble savage' was also taken from Dryden.

Alzire is one of the most 'modern' of Voltaire's plays: it deals with the relations between an occupying power and a subject people, this relationship having at the same time racial and religious overtones. But does Voltaire resolve the problem he has set himself? Does he show whether religion is superior to innate virtue (waiving the question whether there is such a thing)? I think not. Montèze says to Alvarez:

> De tes concitoyens la rage impitoyable
> Aurait rendu comme eux leur Dieu haïssable.[4]

No effective reply is ever made. In fact the conflict is not between grace and nature, it is between men of goodwill, one of whom triumphs because he possesses the ultimate sanction, force. When at the climax of the play Zamore is suddenly converted, touched by an equally sudden gesture of Gusman, he is the victim of a confidence trick. Gusman has not suddenly become a Christian in fact as well as in name, he has merely perceived that he cannot triumph by severity, and therefore tries another policy, which Voltaire makes perfectly explicit in these words spoken by Gusman:

> Montèze, Américains, qui fûtes mes victimes,
> Songez que ma clémence a surpassé mes crimes.
> Instruisez l'Amérique; apprenez à ses rois
> Que les chrétiens sont nés pour leur donner des lois.
> Des dieux que nous servons, connais la différence:
> Les tiens t'ont commandé le meurtre et la vengeance;
> Et le mien, quand ton bras vient de m'assassiner,
> M'ordonne de te plaindre et de te pardonner.[5]

Thus the invader, after admitting that he has committed crimes against his victims, immediately accuses *them* of murder and vengeance, and arrogates to himself pity and forgiveness. The contrast is so gross that the reader is filled with contempt for Zamore for falling into so obvious a collaborationist trap. The

4 I.ii; 'The pitiless ferocity of your countrymen has rendered their god as hateful as themselves.'

5 v.vii; 'Montèze, Americans, who were my victims, consider that my clemency has surpassed my crimes. Teach America, inform its kings that Christians are born to rule them. Realise the difference between our gods: yours teach you murder and vengeance, and mine, when you try to murder me, bid me pity and forgive you.'

key of the whole play is in the words 'Christians are born to rule them'.

It was during these years also that Voltaire wrote one of his most substantial verse sequences, the *Discours sur l'homme*[6]. The seven discourses or sections deal respectively with equality, free-will, envy, moderation, pleasure, happiness, virtue. Remotely suggested by Pope's *Essay on man*, Voltaire's philosophic poem has no universal theme, though a general point of view does emerge.

Voltaire's views on the human condition appear very clearly in the first discourse:

> Tu vois, sage Ariston, d'un œil d'indifférence
> La grandeur tyrannique et la fière opulence;
> Tes yeux d'un faux éclat ne sont point abusés.
> Ce monde est un grand bal où des fous, déguisés
> Sous les risibles noms d'Eminence et d'Altesse,
> Pensent enfler leur être et hausser leur bassesse.
> En vain des vanités l'appareil nous surprend:
> Les mortels sont égaux; leur masque est différent.
> Nos cinq sens imparfaits, donnés par la nature,
> De nos biens, de nos maux sont la seule mesure.
> Les rois en ont-ils six? et leur âme et leur corps
> Sont-ils d'une autre espèce, ont-ils d'autres ressorts?
> C'est du même limon que tous ont pris naissance;
> Dans la même faiblesse ils traînent leur enfance;
> Et le riche et le pauvre, et le faible et le fort,
> Vont tous également des douleurs à la mort.[7]

In the second discourse Voltaire, powerfully influenced by

---

6 The dates usually given to the *Discours* are wrong: all were written in 1737-8. In particular, it has often been said that the last *Discours* was composed a good deal later, but a reference in a letter of *c.* 10 June 1738 (Best. D1515) shows that this is not so. However, several of the discourses contain later additions.

7 'Wise Aristo, you see tyrannical greatness and proud opulence with an indifferent eye; your eyes are not deluded by false glamour. This world is a great dance in which fools, disguised under the laughable names of Eminence and Highness, think to inflate their being and elevate their baseness. We are surprised in vain by the displays of vanity: all mortals are equal, their masks are different. Our five imperfect senses, given to us by nature, are the sole measure of our good and evil. Do kings have six? And are their souls and bodies of a different kind? Have they other springs? All are born from the same mud; they drag out their childhood in the same weakness; and the rich and the poor, and the weak and the strong, all go on equally from sorrow to death.'

Locke, for whom he had nothing less than reverence, concludes that freedom is the power to do what one wishes. There is not and cannot be any other liberty. And to urge this point of view Voltaire brings down a heavenly spirit, whose arguments, however, do not appear fully to have convinced Voltaire himself. At the end of this book, he is about to ask the angel for some trifling additional information:

> Ce que c'est que l'esprit, l'espace, la matière,
> L'éternité, le temps, le ressort, la lumière[8],

when the heavenly being glides away, exclaiming merely 'Be happy'. In fact Voltaire not long after discussed freewill at length with Frederick[9]. His views little by little became subtler, and finally changed. Let him speak for himself, at the end of his life, still to Frederick: 'He who is not able to act is clearly not free to act; he is only free to say: I am the slave of nature. I formerly made every effort to believe that we possess freewill, but I am very much afraid that I was deceived. To want what one wants because one wants it appears to me to be a royal prerogative.'[10]

Envy is treated in the third discourse as the greatest obstacle to happiness. The fourth is dedicated to Helvétius, whose great talents had been immediately perceived by Voltaire, though at this time he was quite unknown; it is devoted to the praise of moderation 'in study, in ambition, in pleasure'. The nature of pleasure is investigated in the fifth discourse. Voltaire tells us in a note that his purpose is to show that all feelings proceed from god. But this is a *trompe l'œil*. Voltaire is in fact concerned to combat the teachings of the Jansenists, and even of Christianity in general.

> Jusqu'à quand verrons-nous ce rêveur fanatique
> Fermer le ciel au monde, et d'un ton despotique
> Damnant le genre humain, qu'il prétend convertir,
> Nous prêcher la vertu pour la faire haïr?[11]

---

8 'What are mind, space, matter, eternity, time, causation, light.'

9 See Best.D1376, D1413, D1469, D1482, D1506, D1521 (October 1737-May 1738).

10 Best.D17409 (18 October 1777).

11 'For how long shall we see this fanatical dreamer [Jansen] close heaven to mankind, and with a despotic voice damning the human race, which he claims to convert, preaching virtue to us by making us hate it?'

On the contrary, god is reached through pleasure; it is pleasure that makes us endure the slavery of marriage, and the agonies of childbirth, and all the other horrors of life. Voltaire does not urge that passions should be unleashed, but returns to the theme of moderation. And he concludes lyrically, with reference to himself:

> Heureux qui jusqu'au temps du terme de sa vie,
> Des beaux-arts amoureux, peut cultiver leurs fruits!
> Il brave l'injustice, il calme ses ennuis;
> Il pardonne aux humains, il rit de leur délire,
> Et de sa main mourante il touche encor sa lyre.[12]

The sixth book deals with the nature of man. Voltaire maintains that complete happiness cannot be enjoyed by man, who should not complain of his lot. With the seventh and last section we come to the most important and most eloquent part of this highly developed philosophic poem. The word virtue is heard on all sides, but what does it really mean? Insensibility is not virtue, nor is asceticism. It is not enough to love god, one should also love man. Religious fanaticism and miracles are all very well,

> mais soulager son frère,
> Mais tirer son ami du sein de la misère,
> Mais à ses ennemis pardonner leurs vertus,
> C'est un plus grand miracle, et qui ne se fait plus.[13]

Humanity compensates all evils. He himself has suffered all his life from the little tyrants irritated by his independence, but virtuous friends have consoled his life.

The year 1735 formed an interlude, perhaps the last period of calm in Voltaire's life, and it was followed by the storm which we heard approaching. True, Voltaire continued peacefully enough the beautification of Cirey; discussed the possibility of having tapestries designed by Oudry, Boucher and others, after scenes in the *Henriade*; debated literary questions with Cideville, Olivet, Louis Racine, and theatrical ones with mlle Quinault; tenderly urged on the lazy Thieriot; created future enemies by befriending

12 'Happy is he who to the end of his life, loving the fine arts, can cultivate their fruits! He puts up with injustice, he calms his difficulties, he forgives his fellows, he laughs at their frenzy, and with his dying hand still touches his lyre.'

13 'but to succour one's brother, but to draw one's friend from the depths of wretchedness, but to forgive one's enemies their virtues, is a greater miracle, and one now never seen.'

Baculard d'Arnaud and other young men; patiently bore with the ineffable Linant family, which Voltaire and mme Du Châtelet took into their service.

Above all, Voltaire began to feel his way into the world of theoretical and even experimental physics. By July 1736 he was able to tell a friend that he was working on a little book which would enable everybody to understand Newton.[14] It was in England that Voltaire had learned to appreciate the beauty of Newton's discoveries, and in the *Letters concerning the English nation* he had devoted several chapters to them. Discussion with mme Du Châtelet no doubt revived his interest, and the *Eléments de la philosophie de Newton* was published in 1738 after the usual difficulties with the authorities, who refused a licence to print. Voltaire tells us that he 'could not obtain a privilege from the Chancellor Aguesseau, who was a man of universal learning, but being bred a Cartesian, discouraged the new discoveries as much as he could. [Voltaire's] attachment to the principles of Newton and Locke, drew upon him a new crowd of enemies. He wrote to mr Falkner . . . "It is believed that the French love novelty, but it must be in cookery and fashions, for as to new truths they are always proscribed among us; it is only when they grow old that they are well received".'[15]

The book finally appeared at Amsterdam in a text neither revised nor authorised by Voltaire, and containing chapters supplied by other hands without his knowledge, all this after he had made a gift of the manuscript to the publishers[16]. Even in this lamentable state (which Voltaire soon put right) the book made an immense impression on laymen and specialists alike, for at this time Newton was practically unknown outside England. Inevitably, it was widely attacked, and Voltaire was involved in the usual battle of the books. He had produced something quite new in literature as well as in science: an attempt by a great humanist to tell the educated public in intelligible language about the new work in science which was transforming man's ideas about the physical world, a transformation which had wide philosophic implications. The impression made by the *Eléments* can only be compared with

14 BestD.1113 (July 1736).
15 See the autobiography, p. 630, below.
16 Best.D1817 (24 January 1739).

the impact, a century later, of the *Origin of species,* for Darwin also had the great advantage of being directly understandable by all (not that one would dream of putting Voltaire's scientific work on the same plane as Darwin's). Voltaire knew that he would have against him the church, as a matter of course, and even most professional men of science, whose devotion to truth does not raise their instinctive reactions above those of other men. Hence Voltaire's sensitiveness to criticism, expressed in a series of pamphlets and open letters, and his anxiety to show, what is indeed perfectly true, that he had at least made no mistakes of fact.

All this, however, must not be allowed to give the impression that the opposition was general: very far from it—indeed, the success of the *Eléments* may properly be described as sensational. The *Bibliothèque françoise*[17], for instance, devotes to it a review of thirty-three pages in which one can sense the reviewer's admiration being wrung from him against his own inclinations. Such examples could be multiplied[18], but I will quote only one passage, and that from a Jesuit publication whose antagonism is above suspicion: 'Nothing shows better the decided efficacity of the printed word, and the superiority of a man who knows how to handle it. Newton, the great Newton, was, it is said, buried in the abyss, in the shop of the first publisher who dared to print him. . . . M. de Voltaire finally appeared, and at once Newton is understood or is in the process of being understood; all Paris resounds with Newton, all Paris stammers Newton, all Paris studies and learns Newton.'[19]

But what gave Voltaire the greatest pleasure was his election as a fellow of the Royal society and the Royal society of Edinburgh, honours which were certainly due in large part to the book on Newton. These elections were to be followed by twenty more to the leading academies in many countries, but these two were the first, a fact of which we can justly be proud. Voltaire's recently discovered letter of thanks to the president of the Royal Society must be quoted in full.

17 xxviii.257-89.

18 See for instance the extract from the leading French scientific review, the *Journal des sçavans* (septembre 1738), p. 534, quoted by Desnoire- sterres, ii.153-4n.

19 *Mémoires pour l'histoire des sciences & des arts* (Paris août 1738), pp. 1673-4.

à Paris 25 n^{bre} n. s. 1743

S^{r},

One of my strongest desires was to be naturaliz'd in England; the royal
society, prompted be you vouschafes to honour me with the best letters of
naturalisation. My first masters in y^{r} frée and learned country, were Shake-
spear, Adisson, Dryden, Pope; j made some steps afterwards in the temple
of philosophy towards the altar of Newton. J was even so bold as to introduce into France some of his discoveries; but j was not only a confessor to his
faith, j became a martir. J could never obtain the privilege of saying in print,
that light comes from the sun and stars, and is not waiting in the air for
the sun's impulsion; that vortices cannot be intirely reconcil'd with mathematics; that there is an evident attraction between the heavenly bodies, and
such trash.

But the liberty of the press was fully granted to all the witty gentlemen
who teach'd us that attraction is a chimera, and vortices are demonstrated,
who printed that a mobile lanch'd out from on high describes a parabola
because of the resistance from the air below, that t'is false and impious to sai,
light comes from the sun. Even some of them printed, *col la licenza dei
superiori*, that Newton ridiculously mistook, when he learn'd from experience
the smaller are the pores of transparent bodies, the more pellucid they are;
they alleg'd very wisely that the widest windows give the greatest admittance
to light in a bed chamber. These things j have seen in our booksellers shops,
and at their shops only.

You reward me sir for my sufferings. The title of brother you honour me
with is the dearest to me of all titles. J want now to cross the sea to return you
my hearthy thanks, and to show my gratitude and my veneration for the
illustrious society of which you are the chief member.

Be pleas'd sir to be so Kind as to present y^{r} worthy bretheren with my most
humble respects. J hope you will sai to mylord duke of Richemont, to m^{r}
Jurin, m^{r} Turner etc. how deeply j am sensible of their favours.

J am with the greatest esteem, and the most sincere respect

s^{r}

y^{r} most humble and faithfull servant, j dare not say brother

Voltaire

I am not a man of science, and if I sang the praises of Voltaire's
book the reader might remain sceptical, and rightly so. What
Condorcet had to say about it a good many years later will no
doubt be more convincing than my protestations. The *Eléments*,
he said,

is still the only book in which men who have not cultivated the sciences can
acquire simple and precise notions concerning the system of the world, and

about the theory of light. . . . Far from containing gross mistakes, as alleged by those incapable of understanding them, it does not contain a single error which can be imputed to m. de Voltaire. . . . When m. de Voltaire published this book, Jean Bernouilli, the greatest mathematician in Europe, still opposed Newtonianism; more than half of the Académie des sciences was Cartesian; even Fontenelle, who was so much above all sectarian and national prejudices, who was not thirty when Newton's system was published, and who was one of the few able to understand it, remained obstinately attached to his original opinion. If to all this is added the fact that the first French school-book in which the theories of Newton were expounded did not appear until ten years after m. de Voltaire's book, one cannot but agree that there was much merit in publishing in 1738 what our illustrious master calls with so much modesty his little catechism of gravitation.[20]

Condorcet's tribute puts into a proper perspective the patronizing judgement of Victor Cousin, who tells us in his *Cours d'histoire* that Voltaire's book displays only 'superficial good sense'.

Alzire was produced with great success in January 1736, and the comedy of *L'Enfant prodigue* was a popular triumph in October —and here we approach the true inwardness of that year. For the *Enfant prodigue* had to submit to censorship at its most inane, the mere use of the words 'patriarche' and 'exorcisme', without the remotest allusion to sacred things, being forbidden. And soon after, grave sanctions were threatened against Voltaire because of the *Mondain*. Beside this Voltaire's crude betrayal by Jore hardly counted, any more than the projected attack on him by Marivaux, the continued enmity of Desfontaines, and the violent, the regrettable polemics with Rousseau.

It was Claude François Jore who had printed the *Lettres philosophiques*. As part of the official campaign against the book he had been deprived of his freedom of the book trade, so that he was unable openly to carry on his business. His living was at stake, he owed nothing to Voltaire but loyalty, and so he is perhaps not too much to be blamed for entering into negotiations with the authorities—indeed the ministry may well have taken the initiative. Jore seems to have been ready to betray Voltaire in exchange for the

20 Letter to La Harpe; Best.D18991 (June 1774). Of course Newton's work was already known to specialists; see, for instance, Pierre Brunet, *L'Introduc-* *tion des théories de Newton en France au XVIIIᵉ siècle avant 1738* (Paris 1931), 1738 being the date of Voltaire's book.

return of his *maîtrise*[21]: it was not that anyone had the slightest doubt that Voltaire was the author, but the authorities wanted irrefutable evidence. But here things went wrong, for Jore, not content with a simple double-cross (he would almost certainly have succeeded in getting away with that, with official protection), also tried to blackmail Voltaire[22]. Legal proceedings followed, with an exchange of *factums* (printed depositions) and all the trimmings. Jore was imprisoned and obliged to publish a disavowal, but the result was in reality inconclusive, nor was this the end of the incident. In 1759 the bookseller sent Voltaire a begging letter[23], and was at once sent 250 *livres*, Voltaire pointing out that Jore ought now to do himself the honour of telling the truth[24]. The bookseller denied that he had anything to withdraw, but offered to do it all the same for 150,000 francs[25]. Perhaps we could leave it at that.

So far as Marivaux is concerned, there is no contemporary writer of similar status to whom Voltaire referred so seldom and so contemptuously. 'Marivaux the metaphysician'[26], about the kindest thing he ever said about him, is a term of abuse in Voltaire's language. For once we may half regret a literary dog-fight, for a book by Marivaux about Voltaire would be worth having. But though it was threatened it was never performed[27].

The row with Desfontaines was a very different affair. Voltaire was ready to forgive and forget, and frequently expressed his friendly feelings[28]. 'I hear', he once said, 'that the abbé Desfontaines is in trouble, and in that case I forgive him. If you know where he is let me know. I may be able to do something for him.'[29] But it was no use. Desfontaines renewed his attacks on Voltaire at the very time that he owed him[30] his liberty, and probably even his life. Every time Voltaire appeared before the public the malicious abbé attacked him more and more venomously, and finally Voltaire exploded in *Le Préservatif* (1738). In this pamphlet

21 Best.D1045 (25 March 1736).
22 Best.D1080 (30 May 1736).
23 Best.D8298 (15 May 1759).
24 Best.D8317 (26 May 1759).
25 Best.D8337 (5 June 1759).
26 Best.D589 (*c.* 10 April 1733).
27 See Best.D1000, D1029, D1035

(February-March 1736).
28 See for instance Best.D931, D937, D990, D1000 (October 1735-February 1736).
29 Best.D997 (29 January 1736).
30 See pp. 112-113, above.

he took the trouble to point out some of the mistakes and other defects in Desfontaines's writings. What a waste of time and energy!

The canny abbé was so sure that he would finally succeed in provoking Voltaire that he had his reply prepared in advance, and now launched it: the *Voltairomanie*, a sort of garbage-can in which he scraped up many of the most scurrilous things ever said or written about Voltaire. Then ensued a wearisome campaign by Voltaire, egged on by mme Du Châtelet, to obtain legal redress, a fight which ended in a stalemate. The most pleasant thing that came out of this protracted battle was a friendly and loyal letter[31] from mme de Bernières; and the most puzzling was the attitude of Thieriot. It was he who had first informed Voltaire of Desfontaines's duplicity, but now, when his great and good friend asked him to put into writing the facts known to him, he not only refused, but persisted in his refusal with a determination otherwise markedly lacking in his character, against the innumerable appeals made by Voltaire and all his friends, and even Frederick[32], during many months. Some of these appeals were perfectly pathetic, for Voltaire was deeply wounded by his old friend's disloyalty: there was no personal defect he found it harder to forgive.

Voltaire's prolonged efforts to persuade Thieriot to act like a gentleman and a friend should not surprise us. Quite apart from his lofty standards of what was fitting, and due to friendship, he had sound practical reasons for his anxiety. Thieriot was known universally (that is, among the few hundred people interested in such things) as Voltaire's friend and spokesman, his *trompette*. In the *Voltairomanie* Desfontaines spoke of Thieriot as one who dragged after him 'the shameful remains of an old attachment'; and the abbé quotes him as denying Voltaire's statement that he (Thieriot) had told Voltaire that Desfontaines had written an attack on Voltaire after the latter had secured his release from prison. If this denial were true Desfontaines would have been not

31 Best.D1759 (9 January 1739).

32 Voltaire had procured for Thieriot a post as the prince's literary factotum in France. On 26 January 1739 (Best.D1823) Frederick wrote to him in his most regal style: 'The sincerity which you seem wishful to profess is incompatible with the tergiversations you affect in your statements. Render justice to the truth if you wish to merit my esteem.'

entirely unjustified in concluding that 'master Voltaire is therefore the boldest and most insensate of liars'. But it is difficult to believe that Thieriot had really made such a denial, for he knew that the letter[33] in which he set out the facts was in Voltaire's hands—and we fortunately know its contents. Certainly, Voltaire could well have ignored such crude stuff, and one wishes that he had: but was he not justified in expecting his friend to confirm the unquestionable facts? Why did Thieriot persistently refuse, in the face of truth and friendship? A detailed answer would take us too far afield, but certain coincident facts can at least be stated. At a time when sodomy was punishable by death, Desfontaines was actively homosexual, and Thieriot's life was singularly devoid of love affairs: there was only mlle Sallé, and she never yielded to him. Of course a fortress can resist because of the determination of its defender, but lack of pressure by the attacker produces the same result. Can we find a clue here to the nature of the powerful hold Desfontaines clearly had on Thieriot?

The acidulous abbé lived on until 1745, but he had shot his bolt. Voltaire paid him no more attention, and so the public also lost interest in this able but unbalanced critic.

The row with Jean Baptiste Rousseau did not fade out so quietly. Which man's grievances against the other were the more justified could be determined, but a detailed inquiry would be unprofitable. Rousseau (1671-1741) was much the older man, and might have been more indulgent and less hypocritically pietistic, but he was embittered by long exile and poverty. Voltaire should no doubt have been more respectful, but it must be remembered that as a boy he had associated on terms of equality with still older and more distinguished men. The simple fact is that the two men 'conceived a strong aversion from each other.'[34]

We have seen[35] the beginning of the vendetta. It was aggravated by a misunderstanding: marshal de Villars complained to prince Eugene that Rousseau had attacked the duc de Noailles. Rousseau in fact had (it was his obsessive habit to write against his friends) and so he was very sensitive to this accusation, for he depended on the patronage of both the prince and the duke. For reasons un-

33 Best.D300 (16 August 1726). below.
34 See the autobiography, p. 630, 35 p. 94, above.

known he thought, quite wrongly, that it was Voltaire who had 'betrayed' him, and he reacted violently[36], and thereafter missed no opportunity to blacken him and all his works. Voltaire said nothing in public for ten years, then, provoked by Rousseau's incessant attacks, finally inserted an allusion in the *Temple du goût*, and this violent outburst in the *Epître sur la calomnie*[37] addressed to mme Du Châtelet:

> Ce vieux rimeur couvert d'ignominies,
> Organe impur de tant de calomnies,
> Cet ennemi du public outragé,
> Puni sans cesse, et jamais corrigé,
> Ce vil Rufus, que jadis votre père
> A, par pitié, tiré de la misère,
> Et qui bientôt, serpent envenimé,
> Piqua le sein qui l'avait ranimé;
> Lui qui, mêlant la rage à l'impudence,
> Devant Thémis accusa l'innocence;
> L'affreux Rufus, loin de cacher en paix
> Des jours tissus de honte et de forfaits,
> Vient rallumer, aux marais de Bruxelles,
> D'un feu mourant les pâles étincelles,
> Et contre moi croit rejeter l'affront
> De l'infamie écrite sur son front.[38]

This language, the strongest Voltaire ever used, incited Rousseau to compose a portrait, which, it is hardly necessary to point out, was written with a pen dipped in hatred, and contains much that is untrue and absurdly unfair. Still, it was very widely circulated, both in manuscript and in print, and is by and large so interesting, and here and there so percipient, that the personal part must be quoted in full:

36 Best.D147 (letter from Rousseau to prince Eugene, 11 February 1723).

37 It was written in 1733, widely circulated in manuscript, and published in 1736.

38 'This old rhymester, covered with shame, impure source of so many calumnies, this enemy of an outraged public, often punished and never corrected, this vile Rufus [Rousseau had red hair], whom at one time your father [baron de Preuilly], through pity dragged out of his misery, and who soon, like a poisonous snake, stung the breast which had restored him to life; he who, mingling fury with impudence, before Themis accused the innocent; the frightful Rufus, far from quietly hiding a life contrived of shame and crime, has just re-lit, in the marshes of Brussels, the faint sparks of a dying fire, and tries to inflict on me the mark of infamy set on his forehead.'

You ask me for the portrait of m. de V., whom you know, you say, only by his works. It seems to me that it is quite an achievement to know the author, but you also want to know the man. I will try to paint one and the other for you. M. de V. is below the measure of great men, that is, a little above mediocrity. I am speaking to a man of science, so I must be quite honest in matters of observation. He is thin, has a parched constitution, a jaundiced appearance, a pinched face, with a witty and caustic air, sparkling and malicious eyes. All the fire that you find in his works is also in his behaviour, so lively as to be irresponsible. It is an ardour that comes and goes, that dazzles you and scintillates. A man so constituted cannot fail to be a valetudinarian, for the blade wears out the scabbard. Gay by nature, serious on principle, open without frankness, politic without subtlety, sociable without friends. He knows the world and forgets it, Aristippus in the morning and Diogenes in the evening. He loves grandeur and despises the great. He is at his ease with them, stiff with his equals. He begins by being polite, goes on coldly, and finishes with dislike. He likes the Court and is bored there, sensitive without love, voluptuous without passion, he is attached to nothing by choice and to everything by inconstance. He is sensible without principles, and his reason has fits like the madness of others. His mind is just, his heart unjust, he thinks all things and mocks everything. A libertine without lust, he also moralises without having any morals. Vain to excess, but even more avid, he works less for fame than for money. He hungers and thirsts for it. In short, he forces himself to work in order to force himself to live. He was made for enjoyment, and he wants to accumulate. . . .[39]

I abstain from comment: the reader will judge. The portrait goes on to discuss Voltaire as a writer, but this part of the satire is much less interesting.

Rousseau followed this up with a very long and vitriolic open letter[40], in which he rehearsed the entire history of his relations with Voltaire, but so inaccurately and with so much animus that Voltaire might well have ignored it. Instead, he published a crushing and equally long reply[41]. Voltaire was right and Rousseau wrong in every factual detail: but right or wrong one cannot but regret that Voltaire thought such a letter worth writing, especially as it did not even serve to work the poison out of his system. At the same time he wrote *La Crépinade*, a verse satire in which he described in great detail how the devil created Rousseau in his

39 Best.D878 (*c.* June 1735); it is only fair to add that Rousseau's authorship is not absolutely certain; see R. A. Leigh, 'An Anonymous eighteenth-century character-sketch of Voltaire', *Studies on Voltaire* (1956), ii.241-72.

40 Best.D1078 (22 May 1736).

41 Best.D1150 (20 September 1736).

own image. And a year or two later he joined with a number of leading French writers in sending Rousseau a sonnet which begins

> Quoy tu n'est pas rayé du nombre des vivants!
> Infâme satirique, et flateur plus infâme.
> Quoy dans ton corps grossier ta lourde et vilaine âme,
> Doit se nourrir encor du fiel de tes serpents![42]

This sort of thing is characteristic of the time, but it is none the less deplorable. Voltaire himself several times expressed regret that he had allowed himself to be dragged down into the mud. In a detailed narrative of the whole affair he wrote in the third person: 'It is said that a man like m. de Voltaire, who until then had had the great merit of never using his talents to crush his enemies, allowed himself to lose this merit.'[43] But the quarrel went on and on, even beyond the grave. In 1763 he still hated Rousseau[44], and even thirty years and more after his death, he still called him his enemy[45]. It is not the prettiest page in Voltaire's life; it cannot be cancelled, but I turn it with relief.

In the meanwhile a bevy of princesses and duchesses were pulling strings, exploring avenues and turning stones on his behalf, for the order of arrest for the *Lettres philosophiques* still ran. Voltaire was quite willing to be pardoned, and quite ready to make conventional gestures. 'They say that I must retract. Very willingly', said he to the duchesse d'Aiguillon. 'I will declare that Pascal is always right; that *fatal laurier, bel astre* is fine poetry[46]; that if st Luke and st Mark contradict themselves, it is a proof of the truth of religion to those with real understanding; that another of the admirable proofs of religion is that it is unintelligible. I will admit that all priests are disinterested, that monks are not proud, and that they neither intrigue nor stink. I will say anything they like so long as they leave me in peace.'[47] And so long, Voltaire

---

42 Best.D1479 (1737/38). 'What! you have not been expunged from the world of the living! Infamous satirist, and more infamous flatterer. What! in your gross body your dull and ugly soul must still feed on the poison of your serpents!'

43 *Vie de m. J.-B. Rousseau* (?1738-1742, but not published until much later).

44 Best.D11271 (19 June 1763).

45 Best.D19363 (1 March 1775).

46 The point is that Voltaire was still being attacked for having said the contrary in the *Temple du goût*.

47 Best.D746 (c. 23 May 1734).

might have added, as he was not expected to change his opinions or to modify his publications. Neither of these things did he ever do under pressure throughout his long life.

At the beginning of March 1735 Voltaire's difficulties with the authorities were ended for the time being by a gracious intimation from the police that he was free to come back to Paris. He was told to behave in a manner worthy of a prudent man who was no longer young[48]. It may be doubted whether Voltaire welcomed this form of words as an appropriate reward for the *Lettres philosophiques*. Fortunately, as he says himself: 'Misfortune never dejected me and my genius grew always bolder when they indeavour'd at submitting it.'[49] And indeed the disputes of the previous years had sharpened his weapons of controversy. This can be seen in his correspondence with Tournemine[50], in which Voltaire ingeniously forces the Jesuit spokesman into an untenable philosophic position, with himself defending the omnipotence of the deity.

Voltaire did return briefly to Paris, but it was only to have himself done in pastel by La Tour[51], who produced a portrait surpassed in beauty and penetration only by the much later busts and statues of Houdon. The pastel is reproduced as the frontispiece of the present volume, and on the jacket.

Otherwise it was a quiet year, a time for study and silent thought. Voltaire wrote no new play, no major verse, not even an essay. Nothing appeared over his name except an unauthorised edition of the *Mort de César*, until Desfontaines broke the charm at the end of the year by his equally surreptitious printing of an epistle to Algarotti. He thus precipitated the final row with his victim.

Voltaire's worst difficulties at this time were those resulting from the circulation in manuscript of the poem *Le Mondain*. This is a defence of luxury as the cradle of the arts. Let who will, said Voltaire, glorify the good old days. For himself, he preferred luxury, pleasure and the arts, cleanliness and good taste. All this is

---

48 Best.D848 (2 March 1735).
49 Best.D829 (? January 1735).
50 Best.D877, D901, D913, D963 (June-December 1735).

51 Two of Voltaire's letters to him have survived: Best.D861-2 (? April 1735).

harmless enough, especially when treated in such a light-hearted way by a man whose humane ideas and capacity for hard work were notorious. But a few provocative passages did slip into the poem, such as the shocking hint that Adam and Eve must have had dirty nails. And the *Mondain* ends:

> C'est bien en vain que, par l'orgueil séduits,
> Huet, Calmet, dans leur savante audace,
> Du paradis ont recherché la place:
> Le paradis terrestre est où je suis.[52]

This is still not very terrible, but the authorities were got at, and grave sanctions were once again threatened against Voltaire. Years later he added a bitter note to the poem, remembering how the mind of cardinal Fleury, the prime minister, had been poisoned against it, and 'the author of the *Henriade, Mérope* and *Zaïre* was compelled to flee his country'.

Voltaire was by now accustomed to persecution, mme Du Châtelet stood staunchly by his side, the sensible Argental sustained him, and it is not impossible that he would once more have ridden out the storm. He might have done so with all the patience of which he was capable but for an event which by chance occurred just at this moment, an event ominous in its consequences for Voltaire, and portentous in its wider meaning: there arrived at Cirey the first letter[53] from the crown-prince of Prussia, the future Frederick II, so-called Frederick the great. Voltaire had been exiled, imprisoned, several times in danger of arrest, beaten, persecuted, spied on, his works regularly prohibited and burnt. He was wellnigh convinced by this time that not even the greatest literary fame, the protection of his eminent friends, the distant retirement of Cirey, his increasing wealth, would make it possible for him to write freely in France. He returned to this theme again and again in later years, more often than not with reference to the events of 1736. Entering into Voltaire's state of mind at this time it is not difficult to understand the effect made on him by Frederick's first letters, in which the heir to what was already one of the most powerful of thrones wrote to him with sincere respect

52 'It is in vain that, seduced by pride, Huet, Calmet, with learned audacity have sought to fix the where-abouts of paradise: the earthly paradise is wherever I am.'

53 Best.D1126 (8 August 1736).

and admiration, with a real appreciation of his ideas, and with the unaffected humility of a disciple paying his respects to his master.

In this first letter the crown-prince told Voltaire that his works were written 'with so much taste, delicacy and art, that their beauties appear as new each time one reads them'. He would cause the moderns to be preferred to the ancients. Frederick hoped that Voltaire would not deny him the benefit of his correspondence. He was the teacher of all men. What could one not expect from the author of so many masterpieces? What new marvels would issue from his pen? He begged Voltaire to send him all his writings, which would make him richer than the possession of any fortune, and concluded his long letter: 'If I am not destined to possess you, at least I can hope one day to see the man whom I have so long admired from a distance, and to assure you face to face that I am, with all the esteem and respect due to those who, taking as their guide the torch of truth, devote their labours to the public benefit, sir, your very affectionate friend, Federic[54], crown prince of Prussia'. So began a correspondence which lasted until Voltaire's death, and extended to nearly a thousand letters, most of which have survived, many of them of prodigious length.

Can it be wondered that Voltaire began to dream again of an oasis of art and freedom, this time under a philosopher-king? How was he to know that in the tortuous mind of the future conqueror an obscure heredity had interwoven strains of true philosophy with ruthless ambitions, and that the sensibility of the flautist-poet was allied to an unmerciful egomania and power complex? He could not know that Frederick shared with George III the terrible 'royal malady'[55].

For the moment Voltaire contented himself with a dignified, even reserved answer: 'One would have to be insensible not to be infinitely touched by the letter with which your royal highness has honoured me. My vanity has been too much flattered by it, but the love of humanity which I have always had in my heart and which, I venture to say, forms my character, has given me a thousand times purer pleasure when I saw that there is in the

<hr>

54 Who always used this spelling, which he found more euphonious than Frederic.

55 See *Porphyria—a royal malady* (British Medical Association: London 1968).

world a prince who thinks like a man, a philosopher-prince who will make men happy.'[56]

He also sent Frederick a long epistle in verse, in which he read the prince a series of admirable moral lessons about the duties of a king; but he was badly inspired indeed to conclude with the line 'Everything becomes a hero except weakness'. The prince responded with almost hysterical—if it was not artificial—enthusiasm. He sent letter after letter, each longer than the last, and accompanied by such princely gifts as a walking-stick the pommel of which was a head of Socrates in gold; expanded in detail his jejune philosophical views; told Voltaire that he awaited his replies with unbearable impatience; and assured him that if he could come to France it would be for him alone, not for the king and Versailles.

Frederick was no doubt sincere in all this so far as he was capable of so pedestrian a sentiment. When he sent his friend Keyserlingk to Cirey bearing gifts he reminded him that he was going to the earthly paradise, to a place a thousand times more delicious than the isle of Calypso, to see the man in whom the human spirit had arrived at its highest degree of perfection.[57] Whatever value is to be attached to such language, the fact is certain: when the innocent *Mondain* aroused reactions grossly disproportionate to the provocation, Voltaire was so deeply wounded that ten years later he still referred to the incident with anguish. He now clearly felt this to be the turning-point, hardly hesitated, and fled—in the direction of Prussia.

56 Best.D1139 (*c.* 1 September 1736). About this time Voltaire first thought of writing about Peter the great (Best.D1334; *c.* 1 June 1737); the book did not appear until 1759-63.
57 Best.D1350 (6 July 1737).

17. Voltaire's god

WE HAVE NOT YET completed our rapid survey of the works poured out by Voltaire during this intensely prolific period: indeed, I have not yet so much as mentioned his most important work since the English letters. This is the *Traité de métaphysique*, probably written soon after he met mme Du Châtelet, and possibly even for her, but never published during his life because it would have led him straight to prison.[1] The primary purpose of his long essay is to answer the question: is there a god? And if so what are his relations with man? This is a subject to which Voltaire often returned and which therefore cannot be treated in a fragmentary way, so I will try to elucidate here in one chapter what I understand Voltaire's answer to have been, taking into account his writings as a whole.

A word of apology even for so brief a survey is perhaps called for. Few people now believe in god, except, as it were, in play. As F. H. Bradley elegantly has it, 'faith is not mere holding a general truth, which in detail is not verified.... Faith is practical, and it is, in short, a making believe.'[2] And of those who do now believe in god, nearly all behave as if they do not. Make believe, even as a form of insurance, does not tend to make its devotees logical or even consistent. In saying this I merely echo many judicious observers, believers and unbelievers alike. Voltaire himself, in arguing against atheism in the *Dictionnaire philosophique* ('Athée'), wrote that 'most of the great ones of this earth live as if they were atheists', and he adds that everyone who has experience of the world knows that belief in god has not the slightest influence on war and ambition, interests and pleasures.

There is no practical difference and little to choose even

---

1 As memories are short, I may be allowed to note that in England, as recently as 1875, a mr Jackson was refused communion because he denied the eternity of punishment and the personality of the devil, a decision which was upheld by the dean of Arches; see *The Times* (17 July 1875).

2 *Appearance and reality* (1893), p. 369.

metaphysically between an atheist and one who behaves as if he does not believe in god. This investigation may therefore appear rather pointless, especially as we are living in an epoch in which men desperately seek a refuge, unable to face the awful and humanly unprecedented fate with which they threaten themselves. As most men, even among the most credulous, have after all been somewhat influenced by scientific modes of reasoning, they no longer at bottom feel quite comfortable, however much they frequent them, in the many-chambered houses of superstition. This is, indeed, one of the rare intellectual advances made in recent centuries: few people now wholeheartedly believe the factually unbelievable. This is why there is such a widespread indulgence in the misty comforts of undefined neologisms and symbolic nonthought. We see even respected humanists taking a Teilhard de Chardin seriously as a thinker.[3] Biosphere and noosphere sound scientific, but I prefer *docta ignorantia* and the 'night of unknowing', which, equally meaningless, at least have the charm of poetry.

There is worse. Far too many ecclesiastics deafen us with lamentations about mini-skirts and four-letter words. One bishop recently informed an abashed world that it was improper for a girl in a short skirt to wear a cross round her neck. Another even more bloody-minded one said publicly that the Aberfan disaster might have been worse, for after all the hundred children had been killed just after saying their prayers. Yet similar learned and reverend gentlemen do not shrink from uttering such indecent formulas as 'religion without god' and 'agnostic Christianity', the worst kind of improprieties, for they are of the mind: they are indeed, in the language of these censors, sins against the holy ghost. Any day now we shall see announced, I dare say, a book by a member of the episcopal bench, entitled *God the agnostic*, or

---

3 I have developed some objections in *The Times Literary Supplement* for 15 June 1962. Teilhard was a palaeontologist, and it is clear from the play made with this fact by his devotees that it is regarded by many as adding weight to his views in other fields. This is a fallacy. Let us not forget that Newton believed in prophecy, that Faraday was a Sandemanian, and Oliver Lodge a spiritualist; and that the distinguished mathematician Michel Chasles collected the autographs, in French, of Cleopatra and Archimedes. 'The greatest men are as subject to error as the narrowest' (Best.D627).

perhaps, why not? *God the great atheist.*[4] Why not indeed? Does not so influential a theologian as dr Tillich assert in his treatise of *Systematic theology*[5], that 'It is as atheistic to affirm the existence of God as it is to deny it'? Nowadays it is not only the scriptures that have to be symbolically interpreted to one's own taste, but also the interpreters. Of course there is a perfectly valid reason for obscurity: Oscar Wilde said that 'to be intelligible is to be found out'. For my part, I think that it is still worth while to give meaning to one's words, and to express one's thoughts as clearly as possible and with the least possible amount of jargon.

Let there be no mistake about it: Voltaire was by no means a man god-obsessed. His references to the subject are relatively few, particularly in his correspondence, far fewer than to many other subjects in which he was more actively interested—and a good many even of these references are pleasantries or purely conventional allusions. Voltaire, like all men, could not help asking himself unanswerable questions, but he was far less interested in philosophic abstractions than in the immediate need to destroy fanaticism and superstition, and to bring about the reign of law and justice. Still, he tried to answer the questions as best he could.

The more academic kind of philosopher thinks that Voltaire's opinions are unworthy of careful examination because they are not formulated in the language of the schools. There is indeed little formally systematic about Voltaire's presentation of his views. His detractors have said so a thousand times. Yet if Voltaire did not compose a system of philosophy it was not because he was incapable of undertaking such a construction: the *Traité de métaphysique* shows this well enough. It was rather because he thought it very foolish to do so. Systems, said he, 'offend my reason'[6]. And again, 'so far as systems are concerned, one must always reserve to oneself the right to laugh in the morning at the ideas one had the previous day'[7]. Voltaire's highest praise of Bayle was that he was wise enough to have no system[8].

---

4 This wild jest was accomplished at the very moment that it was published: Ernst Bloch's *Atheismus im Christentum* (Frankfurt 1969) argues that only an atheist can be a good Christian, only a Christian a good atheist.

5 (1951), i.237.
6 Best.D14117 (c. 15 April 1767).
7 *L'ABC* (1768), xvii.
8 *Poème sur le désastre de Lisbonne* (1759).

Indeed, there was nothing singular about Voltaire's dislike of systems. Since the publication in 1749 of Condillac's *Traité des systèmes* the *philosophes* increasingly disliked philosophic constructions, as can be seen, for instance, in Alembert's preliminary discourse in the *Encyclopédie*. There is also a technical difficulty: Voltaire was utterly incapable of writing a sentence the meaning of which is not pellucid at a first reading[9]. Academic philosophers and theologians naturally take a poor view of such unprofessional conduct.

In short, Voltaire's methods were scientific rather than technically philosophic. And indeed there is nothing monolithic about his thinking: it developed, and even changed in some important respects. This is the first methodological condition we must hold on to. It is possible to say without qualification: 'Voltaire preferred Racine to Corneille', 'Voltaire was against intolerance', but is it possible to make a statement of the same quality about Voltaire's views on god?

It may be urged, though not I think by anyone who has ever tried his hand at this kind of inquiry, that Voltaire's beliefs are already well known. This view may appear particularly well founded in the present context, since we have the good fortune to possess in René Pomeau's *La Religion de Voltaire* by far the best work ever written on Voltaire's religious beliefs, and indeed one of the best books on Voltaire in general. Unfortunately we are disappointed, for while the author endorses the conventional view that Voltaire was a deist, nowhere in his substantial and learned volume does he tell us what he understands deism to be; nor does he make it clear in what sense he uses the term at any given moment, though this sense is by no means always the same.[10]

It may perhaps be said that this is because the meaning of the

---

9 What sir A. J. Ayer said of Hume applies even more cogently to Voltaire: 'The ease and lucidity of his style tend to mask the profundity of his thought'; quoted by Ernest Campbell Mossner, 'The Enlightenment of David Hume', in *Introduction to modernity*, ed. Robert Mollenauer (Austin, Texas 1965), p. 61.

10 In the second edition (1969) of his book professor Pomeau most courteously seeks to refute the conclusions of the present chapter (see particularly pp. 476 ff.), but I cannot feel that he has dealt with the basic problem of ostensible meaning and real meaning in Voltaire; with the utmost respect I can see no reason for modifying my views.

word is self-evident. This is what sir Thomas Browne would have called a vulgar error. 'Everybody' 'knows' what a dog is, yet a treatise on dogs would consist largely and essentially of an attempt to define the nature of a canine, which incidentally, cannot even yet be done completely. There is as great a descriptive range within the notion 'deism'[11] as there is within the notion 'dog', from the fierce, hairy Pekinese to the gentle, naked Great Dane. In any case, no meaning is evident until it has been unambiguously defined by universal consent, and the term 'deism' is among the least self-evident.

It is instructive and amusing to follow certain words through the successive redactions and reductions of the *Oxford English dictionary*, even though the relevant span of these invaluable works is only thirty years, not a long period in the history of ideas and of language. 'Deism' is a case in point. The great original itself in 1894 defined a deist as 'one who acknowledges the existence of a God upon the testimony of reason, but rejects revealed religion'. The indefinite article is surprising, to say the least of it, for the notion that every deist could have each his own god is mildly disturbing. By the time the definition reached the 1924 *Pocket Oxford dictionary of current English* deism had become 'Belief in the existence of God not as a revealed certainty but as a hypothesis required by reason'. The transformation is philosophically complete, and consequently also lexicographically. The indefinite article has been dropped, thus tying deism firmly to monotheism; the acknowledged fact has been downgraded to a hypothesis; and perhaps most significant and surprising of all, 'revealed religion' has been replaced by 'revealed certainty'. Of course some not unimportant details remain unresolved even in the 1924 definition, details each of which presents similar and perhaps even greater uncertainties than deism itself. What, for instance, is the meaning of the term 'god'? What is reason? What is certainty? Is it possible to speak of a 'revealed certainty'? What a fearful chasm opens before the feet of a student innocent enough to believe that the meaning of common words is self-evident! The

11 So early in the debate as 1704-5 Samuel Clarke isolated four types of deism in *A Discourse concerning the*   *unalterable obligations of natural religion* (London 1716), pp. 15-35.

character of his thesis would depend on which edition of the dictionary he happened to use.

Voltaire's compatriots have certainly concluded by now that these difficulties are due to the fog, and that no such obscurities are possible in French. How mistaken they are! Littré, for instance, in his great dictionary, defines deism as a 'religious system', and this is the more significant because he was what was then (1874) called a materialist, who refused to believe even in Comte's so-called religion of humanity. The 'grand Larousse', among various quite bizarre statements, goes one better by telling us that deism is a religious system which rejects all religious belief—a definition which can only be described as a double double-cross, a sort of Tillich *avant la lettre*. It is like saying that a non-bottle is a bottle made to contain non-wine. I dare say the definition was intended to mean something, but to me it means only that the terms deist and deism, far from bearing a precise meaning, are manifestly used in very different senses, and even nonsenses.

Even specialised works do not help us very much. To find anything that even looks like a systematic attempt to define deism we have to go back nearly a century to Leslie Stephen's *History of English thought in the eighteenth century* (1876). In his invaluable though sometimes wrong-headed book Stephen distinguishes between constructive and critical deism. He nowhere tells us precisely what he understands by these categories, and indeed they are no more than convenient channels for the broadest of the many currents of disbelief. Norman Torrey has lucidly described them thus: constructive deism is 'the adoption of a natural religion based on common ideas of morality and including the worship of a rather indefinite Supreme Being whose laws are plain and engraved in the hearts of all men, as opposed to Christianity with its supernatural doctrines and positive religious duties'; on the other hand, critical deists 'were not content with the acceptance of this natural religion, but considered Christianity, in so far as it diverged therefrom, an obstacle to the natural morality and goodness of man'[12]. It is only too obvious that Leslie Stephen's terms do not even adequately describe, let alone define. They are made up of

12 *Voltaire and the English deists*
(1930), pp. 1-2.

question-begging words, and would have very much annoyed
Voltaire in at least one respect: for it is clear that Stephen was
thinking solely in terms of Christian polemics, whereas for Voltaire, and indeed for all philosophers, the problem of god is nothing
if not universal, existed long before Christianity, and must necessarily exist independently of this or that faith.

It is now clear, I hope, that the term deism is not subject merely
to minor nuances: the meanings it is given cover a wide spectrum.
So I will leave there these more or less lexicographic ploys. Words
are tools which change their purposes, and can even become
weapons: cultural revolutions express themselves by the sacking
of libraries, wars are waged under the banner of peace, tyrannies
label themselves democracies, and socialism in becoming national
somehow turns into fascism. I have gone so far only to show
beyond cavil that meaning must not be taken for granted.

Only one further point need be made in this connexion. I make
no distinction of meaning between Voltaire's use of the terms
'deist' and 'theist', for, contrary to the generally accepted view,
no such distinction existed for him. At first he tended to use the
first word, and later the second, but this was simply for prudential
reasons, churchmen having sought to discredit the word 'deist'
by using it synonymously with 'atheist'. Thus, in 1765 Voltaire
wrote of a theist as 'a man firmly convinced of the existence of a
supreme being as good as he is powerful, who has created all
beings . . . who perpetuates their species, who punishes crimes
without cruelty, and reward virtuous actions with goodness'[13],
and efforts have been made to distinguish these terms from those
Voltaire used for deism. Fortunately the still despised handmaiden
bibliography comes to our help. This article in the *Dictionnaire
philosophique* is immediately preceded by one entitled 'Théisme',
which ostensibly dates from 1756, but which in fact was first
published in 1742 under the title 'Déisme'. The mixture was put
up as before, only the label was changed. By entitling the same
text first 'deism' and then 'theism' Voltaire left no room for doubt
that he used the two terms synonymously. And if any doubt could
still linger it is removed by a reference in this article to the English

---

13 'Théiste', *Dictionnaire philoso-* *nature en France dans la première moitié*
phique. Cp. Jean Ehrard, *L'Idée de* *du XVIIIᵉ siècle* (Paris 1963), i.456.

thinkers, which shows that Voltaire in fact had the deists in mind when he was nominally writing about theism.

An amusing example of Voltaire's caution in publishing his views about god can be seen in the manuscripts of his correspondence: bibliography again. Thus, mme Du Deffand once told Voltaire that we have no need to know what we cannot understand[14]. Of course this was no more than a characteristic expression of intellectual indolence born of *ennui*, but Voltaire, with his usual indulgent kindness, exclaimed that this was a great and consoling truth. And he goes on: 'Where there is nothing the king loses his rights, and god also.'[15] But even in such a context Voltaire hesitated. He knew that mme Du Deffand had his letters read out in her drawing-room. Perhaps he had gone too far? Anyway, he altered 'god' to 'nature'; then he restored 'god' and let it stand; but on a final copy, made by his secretary Wagnière, Voltaire with his own hand once more altered 'dieu' to 'la nature'. This caution is another important factor always to be taken into account.

It is indeed by no means easy to pin down Voltaire's views on such sensitive subjects as this. It is necessary, for instance, to distinguish between his avowed works and his clandestine writings at various levels, and between these and many kinds of letters. It is in fact a very delicate matter to judge of the true evidential value of a Voltaire letter. He wrote in every conceivable manner and to every kind of correspondent. It is clearly impossible to assume that all these letters are equally authentic expressions of Voltaire's views. The outpouring of deep feelings in a letter to an intimate friend betrays with evident truth a sorrow or a joy; but what Voltaire felt varied often and sometimes rapidly. The letter may express a genuine feeling, but this feeling may shade away into something very different.

A letter intended to be read also by third persons, perhaps even to be printed, may seem to require prudent interpretation. Yet this is not necessarily the case, for in such letters Voltaire often takes great pains clearly to express his considered views on this or that subject.

In his most intimate letters, written to an Argental, a Thieriot,

14 Best.D15532 (21 March 1769).   15 Best.D15565 (3 April 1769).

a Damilaville, with whom he communicated in a sort of semantic code, Voltaire often intended the contrary of the literal meaning of his words. Once this private language has been learnt, one can distinguish the formulas in which Voltaire, for instance, disavows certain of his writings, indicates that this or that publication is really not by him, or is by him but must on no account be attributed to him, or is by him and can be avowed, or is by him and should be ascribed to another, and so on in almost infinite variety. It is easy to imagine the mistakes that have been made by those who are unaware of these little mysteries, or are merely indifferent to them.

The mistake is often made of attributing to an author the sentiments he has put into the mouths of his personages: the error is gross and recognised as such. But it is almost as grave a mistake to use as evidence what Voltaire says in his letters without taking into account such factors as those I have mentioned, among the least esoteric. The most varied personage created by Voltaire is Voltaire himself. He animates this personage like a puppet, he cannot be contained in a straitjacket of preconceptions.

And beyond the letters again there are the private *Notebooks*, which are invaluable when used with due caution. There is also the often insoluble problem presented by Voltaire's tales, poems and plays: what parts of them can be regarded as expressing his views, and to what extent? And, not least, there is the element of chronology to be considered, for in a long life filled to overflowing with intellectual activity Voltaire showed little sign of mental petrifaction before his very last years, if then. I do not apologise for insisting so strongly on these methodological requirements, the importance of which in the case of Voltaire is paramount: every passage must be weighed and weighted in the light of such considerations as these before it can be used validly to illustrate an inquiry into his opinions.

In a book by an apologist much play is made with the statement, attributed to Voltaire, that there was not a single atheist in all Europe. This is obviously important, and it was necessary to evaluate these words. Not without some trouble, for no reference was given, I found the passage in a courtesy letter[16] written to

16 Best.D9148 (15 August 1760).

Stanislas Leszczinski, the former king of Poland, who had sent Voltaire his book *L'Incrédulité combattue par le simple bon sens*. A very small dose indeed of *simple bon sens*, with perhaps the merest tinge of honesty, would have sufficed to suggest that what is said in an eighteenth-century letter of thanks for such a book by such an author cannot be taken literally. This passage stands alone, but weighed and weighted its statistical value is not even one, it is zero. One need only compare a somewhat more valid source, out of many that could be cited, the article on atheism in the *Dictionnaire philosophique*, in which Voltaire says that 'In England, like everywhere else, there have been and there still are many men who are atheists on principle: for only young and inexperienced preachers, very ill-informed of what happens in the world, maintain that there cannot be any atheists'. And Voltaire was not young nor inexperienced nor a preacher nor ill-informed.

Ideas utterly foreign to Voltaire can be fathered on him by tearing some casual remark even out of a serious context. Thus in his commentary on Malebranche[17] Voltaire seems to favour the theory of continuous creation, because he found it impossible to conceive of a god who remains idle throughout eternity. Yet as this is the only passage of its kind in Voltaire's works, and as there are hundreds that speak in an opposite sense, it has value only as a curiosity.

In a letter Voltaire threw off the epigram, 'Dieu est toujours pour les gros bataillons'[18]. He repeated it in a letter to Condorcet[19], and it has since been used by innumerable opportunists from Napoleon to Stalin, and for equally varied purposes. It would be easy to conduct a long and learned inquiry into Voltaire's exact intention in launching these winged words. The exercise would be a waste of time, for it is obvious to anyone familiar with the Voltairean idiom that this was a mere *obiter dictum*, said and repeated only because it was witty. And luckily there exists convincing evidence for this view. Once more we must have regard to the transmission of the text. Voltaire first recorded the epigram in

17 *Tout en dieu* (1769).

18 Best.D16136 (6 February 1770). 'God is always on the side of the big battalions'. I am inclined to think that the *Oxford dictionary of quotations* is mistaken in attributing this to Voltaire; I believe, though I cannot demonstrate this as a fact, that he was quoting a saying already current.

19 Best.D19856 (11 January 1776).

a notebook, and it then read quite differently: 'Dieu n'est pas pour les plus gros bataillons, mais pour ceux qui tirent le mieux.'[20] When using in his letters the witticism which he had first noted long before, Voltaire improved its literary quality, as he often did when quoting, sometimes from memory, obviously caring not at all that he modified its meaning at the same time. Yet how many pages have been filled with interpretations of Voltaire's famous or notorious 'gros bataillons'!

These are only a very few examples of the way in which it is possible to prove almost anything by quoting the master injudiciously, as the devil quotes scripture.

Having surmounted such difficulties, the first thing we must ask is clearly this: what did Voltaire himself mean by deism? To answer this question adequately with all the supporting evidence such a task requires, would be a long and elaborate task indeed. All I can do here is to present a few key themes and passages, drawing from them the conclusions they seem to impose. So far as I can see Voltaire only once attempted what can be regarded as a clear-cut definition: this was in a letter to Alembert, in which he calls it 'l'adoration pure d'un être suprême, dégagée de toute superstition'[21]. In the published works there is only one substantial passage on deism, as such: it occurs in the *Défense de milord Bolingbroke*. And there he used the term, without explicitly defining it, in very much the same sense. This coincidence is important, because the *Défense* dates from 1752, and between that year and 1757, the date of the letter to Alembert, intervened the fateful year 1755, that is, the intellectual revulsion produced in him by, above all, the Lisbon earthquake[22]. In the *Défense* Voltaire twice described deists as 'philosophers who adore a god'. This *Défense* was a reply to an attack by Formey, and when this susceptible journalist complained, Voltaire replied: 'You have written against the deists . . . and the king [Frederick] and I, who are deists, have taken the part of our religion.'[23] But of course this is 'literary' controversy: it does not mean that Voltaire regarded deism as a religion.

20 *Notebooks*, ii.547, 647. 'God is not on the side of the biggest battalions, but is for those who shoot best.'

21 Best.D7139 (4 February 1757).

'The pure adoration of a supreme being, freed from all superstition.'

22 See ch. 27, below.

23 Best.D5164 (17 January 1753).

225

Voltaire explained that there were two kinds of deists: 1. those who think that god created the world without providing men with a moral law; these deists, he considered, should be called only 'philosophes'. 2. Those who believe that god endowed men with a natural law; these deists have a religion. And Voltaire made it abundantly clear that he regarded any belief beyond these two forms of deism as an evil.[24] These definitions show that Voltaire's sympathies lay with the first kind of deism, obviously, since he was himself the leader and symbol of the *philosophes*. And a little further examination confirms this conclusion: for what does Voltaire mean by natural law? He certainly does not mean anything resembling human law, continuously interpreted and modified by a higher power, which employs sanctions and rewards. He means, broadly, an innate ethic implanted once and for all by the creator, who then has no further power over it. And ultimately Voltaire does not quite mean even this, for his historical work is based implicitly and explicitly on the notion of ethical relativity. As early as 1741 he echoed with approval Pascal's 'What is true on this side of the Pyrenees is false on the other.'[25] And Voltaire was well aware that the notion of a limited liability god is intolerable.

By far the most carefully developed examination of the problem of the existence of a god occurs in the *Traité de métaphysique*, the date of which has made it necessary to examine at this point Voltaire's theological beliefs. He came there to the conclusion from which he never departed, but which is stated in the *Traité* with a calm which underlines its lack of enthusiasm—a lack later obscured by the passions of polemic and propaganda. In the *Traité* Voltaire summed up thus: 'The opinion that there is a god presents difficulties; but there are absurdities in the contrary opinion'[26]. This is, at the highest, to regard the belief in god as a philosophic convenience (not to be confused with political expedience), and it is the tiniest possible step away from atheism.

In his play *Socrate* Voltaire put these words into the mouth of the philosopher: 'There is only one god . . . his nature is to be

24 'Athée', *Dictionnaire philosophique* (1764). It will be seen that these categories are remote from those of Leslie Stephen.

25 See a note on Best.D2513.

26 *Traité de métaphysique* (1734), ii.

infinite; no being can share the infinite with him. Lift your eyes to the celestial globes, turn them to the earth and the seas, everything corresponds, each is made for the other; each being is intimately related to the other beings; everything forms part of the same design: therefore there is only one architect, one sole master, one sole preserver.'[27] A few years later, this time in the guise of a preacher, Voltaire exclaimed: 'What is this being? Does he exist in immensity? Is space one of his attributes? Is he in a place or in all places or in no place? May I be for ever preserved from entering into these metaphysical subtleties! I should too much abuse my feeble reason if I tried fully to understand the being who, by his nature and mine, must be incomprehensible to me.' And this is the dilemma from which Voltaire never managed to escape, because it is inescapable: as the idea of god is stripped little by little of its traditional vestments, nothing finally remains to the theist but an indefinable design, that is, a notion intrinsically contradictory and humanly incomprehensible.

'We have no adequate idea of the divinity', says Voltaire in the article 'Dieu, dieux' of the *Dictionnaire philosophique*, 'we merely drag ourselves from supposition to supposition, from possibilities to probabilities. We arrive at a very small number of certainties. Something exists, therefore there is something eternal, for nothing is produced from nothing. This is a sure truth on which our minds rest. Every construction which displays means and an end announces an artisan; therefore this universe, composed of mechanisms, of means, each of which has its end, reveals a very powerful, very intelligent artisan. Here we have a probability which approaches the greatest certitude; but is this supreme workman infinite? is he everywhere? has he a place? How can we answer this question with our limited intelligence and our feeble knowledge?'

Voltaire often expressed his scepticism. In a letter of 1737 to Frederick he concluded for ontological reasons that the existence of a supreme being is most probable, but he added that he does not believe that there is any proof of the existence of this being[28]. And more than thirty years later he told with evident sympathy

---

27 *Socrate* (1759), III.i.   28 Best.D1320 (*c.* 25 April 1737).

227

the story which he attributed to a Swiss captain who, before a battle, prayed: 'O God, if there is one, take pity on my soul if I have one.'[29]

Voltaire indeed always thought it impossible to prove the existence of god scientifically, and he considered the very attempt absurd. Some of his most scathing sarcasms were directed against the mathematical formula $(m.AR+n.RB)$ which was propounded by Maupertuis as proof of the existence of god[30]. However, this impossibility does not have the consequence that might be supposed. If it were considered possible scientifically to prove the existence of god, then the destruction of a supposed proof would in practice, though not logically, carry with it the destruction of the hypothesis. On the other hand, if it is impossible to prove the existence of god, it is *a fortiori* impossible to disprove it. As Voltaire himself said, in English, in one of the earliest of his notebooks: 'God cannot be proved, nor denied, by the mere force of our reason.'[31]

Perhaps the most compact statement of Voltaire's agnostic views about god occurs in his first letter to Diderot[32], his greatest contemporary. He tells the author of the *Lettre sur les aveugles* that 'It is most impertinent to wish to understand what he [god] is, and why he has made all that exists, but it appears to be very bold to deny that he exists'.

Nearly thirty years later, not long before his death, Voltaire expressed his scepticism in terms the clarity and wit of which are worthy of his swan-song. He had been carrying out some experiments to verify the alleged regenerative powers of the snail, and Spallanzani, sending him the results of his own related investigations of minute aquatic animals, asked Voltaire what he thought about the souls of these creatures. Voltaire, wise and witty as ever, though now well into his ninth decade, replied, in part:

I have long been convinced of the vast and unknown power of the author of nature. I have always believed that he could give the faculty of feeling, ideas, memory to any being he deigned to choose, that he could remove

29 *Homélies prononcées à Londres* (1767). Voltaire may have picked up this story in England; see William King's posthumous *Political and literary anecdotes of his own time* (1818), p. 8, where it is dated 1715.
30 Best.D15600 (20 April 1769).
31 *Notebooks*, i.88.
32 Best.D3940 (? 10 June 1749).

these faculties and cause them to be reborn, and that we have often taken for a substance that which is an effect, a faculty of this substance. Attraction, gravitation is a quality, a faculty. There exist in the animal and vegetable kingdoms a thousand similar mechanisms the energy of which is perceptible, and the cause of which will be for ever unknown. If the rotifer and the tardi-grade, being dead and corrupt, return to life, regain their movements, their feelings, conceive, eat and digest, we should no more know how nature restored them all these things than we know how nature accorded them to these animals in the first place. I admit that I am curious to know why the great being, the author of all, who causes us to live and die, accords the faculty of resuscitation only to the rotifers and the tardigrades. The whales must be very jealous of these little fresh-water fishes.[33]

The soundness of these reflections, and what ensues from them, is in no way diminished by the defects in Voltaire's own experi-mental technique, which invalidated his results, and by his failure to understand the real meaning of Spallanzani's work.

The most common direct or indirect theme of Voltaire's references to god is that of expediency. The work in which Voltaire concentrated the essence of his thought, on which he laboured the longest, and which he wrote with the highest serious-ness, is the *Essai sur les mœurs*. It is there that one would expect to find the clearest exposition of the historical role of god and the belief in god. In fact this great work contains only one substantive reference of this kind, but it is at least clear and emphatic: 'To believe in absolutely no god ... would be a frightful moral mistake, a mistake incompatible with wise government.'[34]

I believe that this conclusion expresses the ultimate truth about Voltaire's convictions. Similar passages abound throughout his works, and I doubt whether a single one could be found to con-tradict it. When writing against atheism in the *Dictionnaire philosophique* Voltaire argued in the same vein that it is morally much better to believe in a god than not to: 'It is certainly in the interests of all men that there be a divinity who punishes what human justice cannot prevent.' In the same article Voltaire ex-pressed this thought even more brutally, saying that if Bayle had had even five or six hundred peasants to govern, he would not have failed to teach them a god who rewards and avenges.

And finally, for these examples could be multiplied indefinitely,

33 Best.D20158 (6 June 1776).　　34 *Essai*, ii.

this is what Voltaire wrote as late as November 1770, with ultimate frankness: 'For the rest, I think that it is always a very good
thing to maintain the doctrine of the existence of a god. Society
needs this opinion.' And he goes on to quote his own famous
line, the meaning of which, so often and so needlessly debated, was
thus established once and for all: 'If god did not exist, he would
have to be invented.'[35]

Another line of argument is often expressed: that from purpose
and intelligence, as we have already seen in passing. In writing to
Condorcet Voltaire repeated once more, and as cynically as ever,
the argument from expediency: 'As for Brahma or Chang-ti or
Oromasis or Isis I do not yet think that I am quite wrong. They
must be accepted when one is dealing with rascals, and one must
shout louder than they.' Yet he went on to add that it was evident
to him that there is intelligence in nature, and that its laws were
not invented by a fool.[36] But it is striking to notice the lack of
conviction with which Voltaire advanced this argument. A couple
of years earlier he had written to the crown prince of Prussia
Frederick William that the ideas of the atheists had always seemed
to him very extravagant. There must be a universal intelligence,
and it only remained to know whether this intelligence was just.
'Now it appears to me', concluded Voltaire, 'that it is impertinent
to accept an unjust god. Everything else is hidden in night.'[37]
And about the same time, in writing to Alembert, he concluded
that the intelligence directing nature must be limited, so full is
nature of imperfections and wretchedness.[38] Much earlier Voltaire
had noted: 'God is the eternal geometrician, but geometricians
do not love.'[39] This lapidary comment pretty well sums up Voltaire's judicious agnosticism about this supposed argument for
the existence of a deity.

I think it hardly necessary to discuss any of the remaining arguments for the existence of a god because none of them is mooted
by Voltaire to any extent or at all effectively. Thus, in two long
letters about freewill written to Frederick, Voltaire argued that
we possess freewill because there is a god, but he seems also to

35 Best.D16736 (1 November 1770);
cp. Best.D16752.
36 Best.D18628(16November1773).

37 Best.D16958 (11 January 1771).
38 Best.D17473(27November1771).
39 *Notebooks*, i.420.

maintain that there is a god because we have freewill. And he asked Frederick why the author of nature gave men the feeling that they are free if in fact they are not.[40] Moreover, Voltaire later changed his views about freewill, without fully exploring the consequences.

Nor is it necessary to deal with the secondary assertions of theism: revelation, miracles, the divinity of this or that religious teacher, and the like. Voltaire, it is true, wrote voluminously on these subjects, but his attitude was invariably one of total disbelief.

Let me now sum up. It turns out that without attempting to devise rigid definitions, and notwithstanding the difficulty of obtaining a true insight into Voltaire's opinions, some affirmations of high evidential quality are after all possible.

If by deism be understood the adoption of a belief having the nature of a law devised by men for their own government, then Voltaire was convinced that men should be deists. But of course such a conviction has nothing to do with philosophy and theology: it belongs to the domain of political science. It is nevertheless permissible to ask whether it throws any light on Voltaire's own beliefs. I think it can hardly be doubted that it does. It is unthinkable that Voltaire could have so consistently urged as merely expedient something he believed to be true. The fact that he insisted so often and with so much emotion on the expediency of belief, and argued so emphatically against atheism as a danger to society, clearly indicates his own disbelief.[41]

If by deism be understood the recognition of any kind of personal, finite or definable divinity, then Voltaire was not a deist.

If by deism be understood any kind of continuing or purposive

---

40 Best.D1432 (23 January 1738), D1468 (8 March).

41 As I read the proofs of the first edition of this book an unpublished letter of 5 October 1770 to the duchesse de Choiseul (Best.D16684) turned up, in which Voltaire expresses even more brutally his view of the belief in god as an expedient: 'I do not believe that there is in the world a mayor, or podesta, having only four hundred horses called men to govern, who does not realise that it is necessary to put a god into their mouths to serve as a bit and a bridle' (Best.D16684). And what could be more revealing than Voltaire's quotation: 'How far does public policy permit the destruction of superstition' ('Superstition', *Dictionnaire philosophique*)?

relationship or interaction between man and a divinity, then Voltaire was not a deist.

If, finally, by deism be understood one of the following propositions: being is infinite, infinity is inconceivable in human terms, it is therefore superhuman, and may for convenience be called god; or alternatively, being is finite and must therefore have a first cause beyond itself, and this first cause may for convenience be called god; then on either of these assumptions Voltaire was a deist.

However, to apply the term deism to these highly abstract philosophic notions is in my opinion to play with words. It is my conclusion that Voltaire was at most an agnostic; and were any tough-minded philosopher to maintain that this type of agnosticism is indistinguishable from atheism, I would not be prepared to contradict him.

18. Life at Cirey, 1736-1741

I WAS WEARY of the idle and turbulent life of Paris, of the crowd of fops, of the bad books printed with official approval and royal privilege, of literary cabals, of the meanness and rascality of the wretches who dishonoured literature: I found in 1733 a young lady who felt more or less as I did, and who resolved to spend several years in the country to cultivate her mind, far from the tumult of the world. It was the marquise Du Châtelet, the woman who in all France had the greatest disposition for all the sciences. . . .

Seldom has so fine a mind and so much taste been united with so much ardour for learning; but she also loved the world and all the amusements of her age and sex. Nevertheless she left all this to go and bury herself in a dilapidated house on the frontiers of Champagne and Lorraine, where the land was very infertile and very ugly. She beautified the house, to which she added pleasant gardens. I built a gallery, in which I created a very fine collection of scientific instruments. We had a large library.[1]

It was superfluous for Voltaire to tell his contemporaries that Cirey was not easily accessible, which is still true to some extent. The nearest big town is Nancy, well over fifty miles away by road, and even Nancy was then little more than a township, for Stanislas had not yet started to create its lovely *place* and other buildings. Paris was normally three or four days away, more in bad weather. It is not surprising that mme Du Châtelet arrived shaken and bruised, in the midst of two hundred packages[2]. Even a century later (1863), the historian George Grote made 'a *détour* for the express purpose of visiting the Château de Cirey', wrote mrs Grote, 'dear to us both as the residence ... of Voltaire and Madame du Châtelet. But in this pious pilgrimage we were defeated by the difficulty of obtaining any manner of conveyance to Cirey. We got within sixteen English miles of it at Joinville; from which pleasant village we could find neither cart nor carriage for love or money during our stay.'[3]

It is thus easy to understand that whenever there was a longish continuous stay in Champagne communications and supplies

1 *Mémoires* (1759), i.7.
2 Best.D793 (October 1734).
3 Harriet Grote, *The Personal life of George Grote* (London 1873), p. 270.

were difficult. The most important agent was Voltaire's Paris man
of business, Bonaventure Moussinot. It is curious to us, though
characteristic of the century, to see an ecclesiastic, not a mere
abbé but a resident canon, acting for a man so antagonistic to his
cloth. He was a faithful and honest servitor if neither very intelligent nor very punctual. No better idea can be given of Voltaire's
activities at Cirey, and even of his character and life in general,
than to translate, with a minimum of explanatory annotation, a
few isolated passages from some of Voltaire's letters to Moussinot,
the manuscripts of which have fortunately survived, for the
wretched Duvernet edited them in the spirit of a butcher gone
berserk, or in the milder language of Desnoiresterres (ii.132*n*),
with a 'monomania for transpositions and deformations'. It will be
seen that Voltaire was not far out when he said in his *Epître à une
dame ou soi-disant telle*, that 'Tous les goûts à la fois sont entrés
dans mon âme'[4]. The earliest surviving one dates from March
1736, when Voltaire was already well established at Cirey.

I don't know why you want me to send receipts to Pinga every day for
such small sums. Hasn't he got a book in which he records all these things,
isn't he an honest man? . . . I will take the Lancrets and the Albanis, and will
let you know when to send them.[5]

I prefer a thousand times your strong-box to that of a notary. There is
nobody in the world in whom I have more confidence than in you. You are as
intelligent as you are virtuous. . . . Consider therefore whether you would
like to take charge of the money of an unbeliever. As opportunity offers you
can use it to make good bargains in the way of pictures. You will tell me, I
need 500 francs, or 600 francs, and you will give me a note.[6]

First of all, have two good copies made [of his portrait by Quentin de La
Tour]. . . . As soon as the first is done, please have it examined and retouched
by La Tour. In the meanwhile send me my original well framed, well packed,
and from the first copy have a miniature made for a brooch. . . . Add a dozen
and a half of oranges to the dozen and a half of lemons. . . . Do you penetrate
the kingdom of Oudry [the painter]? I should very much like him one day
to have tapestries made of the *Henriade*.[7]

To punish you because you did not send for the young Baculard d'Arnaud,
who is in the top form of the collège d'Harcourt, and lives with m. de La

4 (1732); 'All tastes at once have
entered my soul.'

5 Best.D1031 (8 March 1736).

6 Best.D1042 (21 March 1736).

7 Best.D1058 (12 April 1736).

Croix, rue Mouffetard, to punish you, I repeat, because you did not give him the manuscript of the *Epître sur la calomnie* and twelve francs, I condemn you to give him a gold louis, and to exhort him on my behalf to learn to write.[8]

Please buy for me a little screen-table, which can serve at once as a writing-desk and a screen, and have it delivered to madame de Vinterfelt [*née* Olympe Du Noyer], rue Platrière, near the convent of st Agnes.[9]

Among all the services I have asked of you, there is one I forgot, to let me know the subject proposed this year by the Academy of sciences for its prize.[10]

Please read this letter very carefully, and answer point by point.

1. I told you more than two months ago that a bill of exchange for 350 francs would be drawn on you, and you did not reply.

2. It is a month since I asked you to let me know to whom you gave the box of books and of candles. I have heard no more of it and do not know where it is.

3. Is it with my money that you bought the mirrors you mention? Why have these mirrors arrived, and not my case?

4. Would you please have these letters delivered to their addresses, and post those intended to be posted?

5. There is a chevalier de Mouhi, who lives at the Dauphin hotel, rue des Orties. This chev. de Mouhi wants to borrow 200 *pistoles*, and I should like to lend them to him. I dare not ask you to go to see him, but I should be much obliged, then you would be able to tell me what he is. Whether he comes to you or you go to him, please tell him that it is a pleasure for me to help writers when I can, that my affairs are in bad shape at the moment, but that you will try to find the money, and that you hope the repayment can be so arranged that there is no risk.

6 Please let me known whether my miniature portrait is being done.

7. Shall I be getting papers, pens, dressing-gown? I flatter myself that the dressing-gown will be bought by mme Dubreuil.

8. Please forgive me for so many details. I love you with all my heart.

9. I must add that m. Dubreuil will receive a letter addressed to m. Delafosse. It is to be sent to me. . . . Another little word. When m. Dubreuil writes, he always writes via Bar sur Aube. One should write via Vassy. Bar sur Aube is on the road taken by the coach, Vassy on the post-road.[11]

If Boucher would care to work at Cirey we would ask him to do five paintings of the *Henriade*. Then fifteen ells of tapestry would cost about seven thousand francs, and 1500 or 2000 francs for the painter. Perhaps the whole would not come to more than 10,000 francs. . . . Please send me by the coach

8 Best.D1077 (22 May 1736).   10 Best.D1138 (21 August 1736).
9 Best.D1115 (16 July 1736).   11 Best.D1191 (c. 6 November 1736).

two fine and very large diamond shoe-buckles, some diamond garter buckles, two large or four small prints of my little face.[12]

I stick to what I said about the shares. If they are at 2120 let us sell them, if not let us keep them. As for the 43,200 francs and 3690 francs, and everything of mine in your hands, let us divide it into two parts, one ready to be loaned for six months at 5 per cent, the other in hand to buy shares at the favourable moment. . . . I repeat my request for you to give a hundred gold louis to m. Du Châtelet. You can still amuse yourself by buying 6000 francs' worth of pictures if you think you can bring it off. . . . May I now speak frankly? You must do me the kindness to accept a small annual honorarium as a sign of friendship. Let us not stand on ceremony. You used to receive a small payment from your monks. Treat me like a chapter, take twice what your cloister gave you.[13]

I have your letter of six April. Please note that your letters usually take six or seven days to reach me. I think that mine take as long. . . . If they have forgotten . . . a packet of feather-dusters for furniture and three parquet brushes, please remind the agent . . . who should also buy for me, if you please, very good pocket scissors, two little women's toilet pincers, but we don't want the little tweezers from the quai de Gèvres, only those sold in the rue Saint-Honoré, which cost I think 20 or 24 *sous*.[14]

Madame la marquise Du Châtelet has ordered a dressing-case from Hébert [the goldsmith], at the sign of the King of Siam, who has moved I believe and lives in the rue Saint-Honoré, opposite the Oratory. You must give him 1200 francs in advance for the silver he is to use in making it. . . . You must sell shares to get these 1200 francs. . . . I beg you also to buy four concave mirrors of four inches diameter. Take care that all four have the same focus. They cost one *écu* each, and can be found on the quai des Morfondus.[15]

I asked you for thermometers and barometers. I must insist very strongly on this. They are sent all over the world. You can consult m. Grosse about them, or m. Nolet, who lives on the quai des Théatins at the house of the marquis de Locmaria. This m. Nolet sells very good ones. He will give you instructions in writing how to get them safely into the provinces. I think they could very well be sent in a case, the mercury, the glasses, the coloured spirit of wine, each separately, and the thermometers would be filled by following m. Nolet's own method.

What is quite certain is that I must have two good barometers and two good thermometers. If I can have some made according to the method of Fahrenheit I should be very much obliged to you. If they have to be brought to me on foot . . . [the messenger] should also bring some canaries, provided

12 Best.D1201 (17 November 1736). 14 Best.D1313 (14 April 1737).
13 Best.D1306 (30 March 1737). 15 Best.D1336 (5 June 1737).

they are tame . . . and a little parrot with a black collar.[16] . . . What does the parrot say? for we must rehearse it[17]. . . . You can quite safely send the 300 francs [in gold], well packed, by the coach without declaring them so long as the case is well and duly registered, as valuable furniture, to the address of *madame la marquise*. That will do. I think you should obtain a receipt from the office.

To the small parcel please add two little powder-puffs, some scissors, a knife, two or three good sponges.[18] . . . I want a good pneumatic machine, a good reflecting telescope, which is very rare, a perfect Copernican sphere, one of the biggest burning-glasses.[19]

As for Praut [the publisher], he must know that . . . as soon as a book is published in Paris by authority, the Dutch publishers get hold of it, and the one who prints it first in Holland is the one who gets the exclusive rights in that country. In order to secure this right to be the first to print the book in Holland all he has to do is to announce the work in the papers. This is an established usage and is as good as a law. So when I want to favour a publisher in Holland I inform him of the book I am printing in France, and I try to get the first copy to him.[20]

There is a *demoiselle* d'Amfreville, a girl of rank, who has a sort of property near Cirey. I don't know her at all, but she is in great need. This young lady lodges with a madame Damon, opposite the big gate of Saint-Germain. My dear friend, take a carriage, go to her, tell her that I take the liberty to lend her ten *pistoles*, and that when she needs more I have the honour to be at her service. . . . Would you very kindly send me, in addition to paste and a ream of paper, a hundred trimmed quills, two reams of foolscap paper, two reams of large letter-paper, some toothpicks, three or four dozen little flat buttons for shirts?[21]

Your brother would obliged me by procuring for me the abridgement of the philosophic transactions [of the Royal Society] . . . and to charge it to my account. I beg him to obtain for me also *Introductio ad veram fisicam a Joanne Keil* [Oxford 1702], and, if possible, m. de Mairan's dissertation on phosphorus, 1717. . . . I return to the property in question. I have heard that a lot of repairs are necessary, which is very natural in a property under writ. There are vines in a fairly good state, but eleven hundred acres of timber are entirely devastated, and all the big oaks have been sold. I foresee that if the property is sold for 60,000 francs there would be 8000 francs to spend on repairs. Add to this the *quint et requint* [feudal dues of one fifth and one fifth of that fifth], the whole of which would have to be paid out, it would come to over 80,000 francs, and I don't think that the property could ever bring in,

16 Best.D1351 (8 July 1737).
17 Best.D1358 (30 July 1737).
18 Best.D1362 (7 August 1737).

19 Best.D1371 (14 September 1737).
20 Best.D1384 (4 November 1737).
21 Best.D1414 (28 December 1737).

allowing for all the outgoings, more than 3500 francs annually, administered in the most economical way.[22]

I urgently beg your brother to send me all the books I have asked for, either through Praut, or direct, to make a little catalogue of them, and to add to them the elements of Newton published over my name, together with an illustrated book on architecture in which are to be found good drawings of the five orders, either the book of Perrault or Blondel or Scamozzi or Palladio or Vignole, no matter which. It doesn't matter either whether it costs 8 *livres* or ten *écus*.[23]

You will have very much obliged me if you have given the 1200 *livres* to m. Nolet with the courtesies which always accompany the favours you do. Please offer him 100 *louis* if he needs them. He is not an ordinary man with whom it is necessary to keep strict accounts. He is a thinker, a man of real value who alone can supply me with my scientific cabinet and it is much easier to find money than a man like him.[24]

I have received the telescope and the slippers. The telescope has been very well repaired, and the slippers are very well made. My feet and my eyes are very much obliged to you. Send me whenever you like three more pairs of these fine slippers.[25]

So lend the 800 *livres* to monsieur and madame Pitot. They will repay them over five years, nothing the first, 200 the second, as much the third, and so for the rest. . . . Assure monsieur and madame Pitot that if they are pressed later on, I shall not demand the payment and that on the contrary my purse will again be at their service.[26]

I am sending you Le Doux's jewel by the Bar-sur-Aube coach, but if it can be had for 100 *écus* return it to me. I would prefer it to the clock. So your brother consults ill-informed booksellers? The geometry of Daudet is published by Ganeau, rue Saint Jacques, and I lack the 3rd volume. Unless I am much mistaken there is a translation of Boerhave's institutions. Could I have it? Give a hundred francs, or thereabouts to m. Thiriot, but for larger amounts consult me first. The coloured portrait by Vandyk is awaited, but without impatience. Will you please give twelve *livres* to that Bourguignon if he is hard up.[27]

Here is my *certificat de vie*[28] to enable you to collect my life interest on the city for 1738.

22 Best.D1420 (10 January 1738).

23 Best.D1494 (9 May 1738), in the notes of which all these books are identified.

24 Best.D1550 (11 July 1738).

25 Best.D1563 (21 July 1738).

26 Best.D1569 (2 August 1738); Henri Pitot was a distinguished man of science; in fact Voltaire did not press him (see Best.D2928; 4 February 1744).

27 Best.D1674 (4 December 1738).

28 See p. 25, above.

You tell me that since September you have received 31,586 and you have spent 14,410 *livres*. Therefore, say you, you have a balance of 21,500 *livres*. This *therefore* does not appear to me to be very arithmetical, for with a *therefore* only 17,174[29] should remain, unless you received 4326 *livres* in September. No matter. What one has is what is important. . . . Some of the money will serve for the journey we are preparing, the rest for the purchase of furniture for the Lambert palace which we intend to buy in a few years' time.[30]

I asked you to send fifty francs to the chevalier de Mouhy. You will much oblige me by doing so without delay. Let me know whether or not you have any news from the duc de Villars and whether you have received the papers sent to you by the Lille coach.

I have just received very disagreeable news. Messrs Lefevre and company, merchants at Amsterdam, who disposed so badly of our paintings, have pressed our misfortune to its limits. They have gone bankrupt, and I have lost not only the modest proceeds, all charges paid, from these wretched pictures, but also 1400 francs I entrusted to them. They have not written for three weeks. It is from their Berlin correspondents that I learn of their bankruptcy. You may be sure, my dear friend, that I shall put to your credit the entire sum these wretched merchants owe me. They have saddled me with their bankruptcy, but that is no reason why I should do the same thing to you.[31]

I have received your letter of the 9th, in which you tell me of the complete bankruptcy of the banker Michel. He thus takes with him a substantial part of my capital[32]. The lord gave, and the lord hath taken away; blessed be the name of the lord. I don't have the honour to be too much of a Christian, but I am fairly resigned.

> Souffrir mes maux en patience
> Depuis quarante ans est mon lot,
> Et l'on peut sans être dévot
> Se soumettre à la providence.[33]

I admit that I did not expect this bankruptcy, and that I do not conceive how a very rich man, charged with the finances of his very Christian majesty [the king of France], can have fallen so heavily, unless he wanted to be even richer. In that case m. Michel has been guilty of two wrongs. I feel like exclaiming:

29 Voltaire's arithmetic was always erratic.
30 Best.D1944 (*c.* 17 March 1739).
31 Best.D2223 (5 June 1740).
31 Best.D2223 (5 June 1740).
32 Voltaire's loss was about 40,000 francs.
33 'For forty years it has been my lot patiently to bear my woes, and one can submit to providence without being devout.'

Michel au nom de l'Eternel
Mit jadis le diable en déroute,
Mais après cette banqueroute
Que le diable emporte Michel.[34]

But that would be a bad joke, and I don't want to mock m. Michel's losses, nor mine.[35]

You have given fifty *louis* to mme Du Châtelet, and you will give a thousand *livres* to m. Du Châtelet. And I am going to draw on you again and exhaust you. I again thank you for the inviolable secrecy you maintain with everybody concerning my little affairs. In the meanwhile please make your brother a little present of 50 *livres*.[36] . . .

I beg you to buy a small Bohemian crystal chandelier costing about 250 *livres*. I don't want those small old crystals, but the large new ones, similar to those you sent me to Cirey. Please make this little acquisition as soon as possible and send it, well packed and guaranteed by the dealer, to m. Denis, at Lille, military commissioner, with a word of notification. Don't fail to add the silk cord, the tassel and even the hook. Pay the carriage. . . . As for the pictures you want to send to Prussia, the king much likes those of Watteau, Lancret and Pater. I have seen some of his, but I suspect that four little Watteaus in his collection are good copies.[37]

There is no room for hesitation in the matter of m. de Leseau. He now owes me about 5000 francs. His affairs have not been put into order, he refuses to give me an assignment, or to pay me, or even to establish a balance-sheet. After careful consideration please ask m. Begon to take action. . . . When you have the little screen send it to me. Please have an engraving made after the portrait by La Tour, and let it be a little less crude than that of our drunkard. . . . Have you had the kindness to send to the Trévoux editors a little dissertation which I addressed to the academy of sciences and which m. Du Châtelet should have delivered to you?[38]

Voltaire's life was by no means limited to the château itself. Wherever he lived he was always a good neighbour, helpful and generous, and eventually, at Ferney, much more even than this.

---

34 'Once upon a time Michel [Michael] routed the devil in the name of the eternal, but after this bankruptcy let the devil take Michel.'

35 Best.D2268 (21 July 1740).

36 Best.D2401 (8 January 1741), from Brussels.

37 Best.D2407 (17 January 1741), from Brussels.

38 Best.D2502 (20 June 1741). This is the last surviving letter from Voltaire to Moussinot, with one exception, which dates from July 1755 (Best. D6329). That letter shows that the correspondence must have continued in the meanwhile; and it almost certainly went on after 1755. Voltaire's letters may still turn up. As for Moussinot's letters to Voltaire, their discovery would be an incalculable boon to scholars.

It would be boring to enumerate all his kindnesses at Cirey. It will perhaps suffice to quote from a letter written by one neighbour to his son, telling him that Voltaire had 'just left for Brussels with the marquis and marquise Du Châtelet. You can well imagine how sad his absence makes us. There has never been a friend with a kinder heart or more worthy of respect. We look back with regret on the four years he has spent in Champagne. The happy time we spent with him must remind you, my son, as it reminds us, of the tokens of friendship which he has showered upon us. . . . What gratitude you owe him! Nothing obliged him to give us such singular marks of his good will, and I hope that you will never forget his excessive goodness. . . . He leaves adored by the whole countryside, and we all lament his absence.'[39]

39 Best.D2015 (15 May 1739), from Champbonin *père* to Champbonin *fils*.

19. Sensibility at Cirey, 1736-1739

VOLTAIRE DID LEAVE in the direction of Prussia at the end of 1736. He said so himself, and so did mme Du Châtelet[1]. By the first of the year he was at Leyden, two days later at Amsterdam; but then he received an insistent request[2] from the crown-prince not to approach any nearer. In fact the king, his father, would not have tolerated such a visit, as Voltaire well knew. The destination he had given out was merely a smoke-screen to cover his real intentions, which were to distribute the *Défense du mondain* and to set in motion the publication of the Newton book. In March, when he was getting ready to return to Cirey, he let it be known that he was at Cambridge[3].

The *Défense* is not so much a defence of the *mondain* (worldling) as an attack on the arid censors who had found fault with it. It is one of the most attractive of Voltaire's poems, in which he answers with matchless wit and elegance a tirade put into the mouth of a Jansenist. I wish it were possible to quote it in full. Voltaire pointed out that while the priest was condemning Voltaire to roast in hell for having defended 'luxury', he was drinking a cup of coffee. The priest is reminded of the wide implications of this simple fact.

> Ne faut-il pas que l'humaine industrie
> L'aille ravir aux champs de l'Arabie?
> La porcelaine et la frêle beauté
> De cet émail à la Chine empâté,
> Par mille mains fut pour vous préparée,
> Cuite, recuite, et peinte, et diaprée;
> Cet argent fin, ciselé, godronné,
> En plat, en vase, en soucoupe tourné,
> Fut attaché de la terre profonde,
> Dans le Potose, au sein d'un nouveau monde.

---

1 Best.D1209, D1210, D1213, D1224 (November-December 1736).
2 Best.D1244 (*c.* 5 January 1737).

3 Best.D1299 (18 March 1737), D1301 (24 March, letter from Formont to Cideville).

Tout l'univers a travaillé pour vous,
Afin qu'en paix, dans votre heureux courroux,
Vous insultiez, pieux atrabilaire,
Au monde entier, épuisé pour vous plaire.[4]

Voltaire was not content to explore this theme only in verse. Two important books[5] on political science and economics had recently appeared, and Voltaire used them as a point of departure for his own reflections[6], bringing in his memories of the exhilarating days of John Law's epically unsuccessful attempt to save the French economy while lining his own pockets. Voltaire shows a firm grasp of the realities of national finance. He is particularly good on the illusory nature of money, and in distinguishing it from real wealth. Occasionally he falls into a classical fallacy, as when he regards the existence of beggars as a sign of wealth. But his conclusion is impeccable: 'A state which is in debt only to itself cannot be impoverished.'

Voltaire's absence from Cirey was not made more agreeable by mme Du Châtelet's worries and flurries. She was terrified, among many other things, because Voltaire insisted on publishing his Newton. It contained, in particular, she moaned, 'a chapter on metaphysics which is very ill-timed and very dangerous. . . . I have spared nothing to dissuade him. . . . I have to save him from himself at every turn, and I use more guile to conduct him than does the whole Vatican to keep Christianity in its irons. . . . I know this manuscript, it is so rational a metaphysics that it will send its author to the stake. . . . I have not yet got over my astonishment and, I admit, my fury. I have written him a fulminating letter. . . . I must admit that I cannot prevent myself from bewailing my fate when I see how little I can count on a tranquil life. I shall pass it in fighting against him for his own sake, without saving him, and

4 'Does it not have to be ravished by human industry from the fields of Arabia? The porcelain and the fragile beauty of this enamel coated in China, was made for you by a thousand hands, baked and rebaked, and painted and decorated. This fine silver, chased and fluted, whether flat or made into vessels or saucers, was torn from the deep earth, in Potosa, from the heart of a new world. The whole universe has worked for you, so that in your complacent rage, with pious acrimony, you can insult the whole world, exhausted to give you pleasure.'

5 [Jean François Melon], *Essai politique sur le commerce* (1734); Dutot, *Réflexions politiques sur les finances et le commerce* (1738).

6 *Observations sur mm. Jean Lass, Melon et Dutot* (1738).

in trembling for him, in lamenting his mistakes and his absence. Alas, such is my fate, which is yet dearer to me than the happiest. ... I implore you to write to him that you know that the king of Prussia opens all his son's letters'[7], and so on and on and on in a many-paged letter to the angelic Argental.

But Voltaire's love and understanding were great. By 1 March he was back in Cirey[8], and for the rest of the year little more than this fugue was to be visible to the world at large, for no new work was published. The calm, however, was only on the surface: beneath it a new storm was gathering its strength. The visit to the Netherlands had been an escape from persecution at home, but it was not in Voltaire's nature to miss so useful an occasion to learn from the able men of science who lived at Leyden and Amsterdam, in particular the eminent 's-Gravesande. Yet even this pleasure was troubled by the hatred of Rousseau and Desfontaines, who spread the rumour that the purpose of these discussions was to advocate atheism[9]. It was even alleged that he had created a public scandal, and of course plenty of people were only too happy to believe this and to cause Voltaire more trouble with the authorities.

The most significant feature of the year was still Voltaire's correspondence with the crown prince of Prussia. The two men exchanged over thirty letters in 1737, a prodigious number, for communications were slow, the more so because of the Prussian king's distrust. The correspondence, which went far beyond mere question and answer, displays genuine respect and admiration on the part of the prince, while Voltaire's letters are larded with flatteries, perhaps somewhat less sincere, but dictated by generous hopes of what might be accomplished by a philosopher-king. Frederick sent more and more of his dreary verse (for he has a place in the history of French poetry), with increasingly insistent demands for corrections and improvements. The two men discussed literary problems, and above all philosophic ones, but these seldom burst the magic circle of semantics: the correspondents used the same words but they were not seldom talking

7 Best.D1265 (22 January 1737).   9 Best.D1308 (c. 1 April 1737).
8 Best.D1291 1 March 1737).

about different things. Specifically, Voltaire maintained the existence of a limited form of freewill (he changed his mind later), Frederick asserted that all events are determined.

For the rest Voltaire went steadily on with the furnishing and embellishment of Cirey, and particularly of his laboratory and library. He conducted useful experiments in physics, and prepared himself for the work that soon followed. The Académie des sciences had offered a prize for an essay on the nature of fire, and Voltaire and mme Du Châtelet separately decided to enter for it[10].

Voltaire was an amateur only in the sense that he was not a trained man of science, hardly a serious objection at a time when scientific education was rudimentary. He told his old master Olivet that he was trying to work out the weight of the sun. ' "What does its weight matter", you will ask, "so long as we enjoy it?" ' Voltaire explained that it mattered a great deal because of the theory of gravitation. 'Newton', he added, 'is the greatest man who has ever lived, the very greatest, the giants of antiquity are beside him children playing with marbles.'[11]

Voltaire had indeed what is just as necessary as specialised knowledge: a firm grasp of the idea of science, of what science is all about. 'If you want to apply yourself seriously to the study of nature', he wrote to a young scientist (Le Cat), 'allow me to tell you that you must begin by not constructing any system. You should do like the Boyles, the Galileos, the Newtons. Examine, weigh, calculate and measure, but never guess. Mr Newton never erected any system: he saw and he made others see, but he did not replace the truth by his imaginings. We must take for true what is demonstrated by our eyes and by mathematics. As for all the rest, we should say, I do not know.'[12] This would be difficult to fault as a statement of scientific methodology.

A man who could write like this was not likely to waste his time on poets' toys, as the non-scientific reader may instinctively suspect. Voltaire in fact investigated, for instance, the alleged increase in weight of certain substances on calcination. His experi-

10 Best.D1336 (5 June 1737) ff;   11 Best.D1174 (18 October 1736).
Essai sur la nature du feu et sur sa   12 Best.D2463 (15 April 1741).
propagation.

mental work was useful, and his conclusions are sound. The increase in weight does actually take place, and Voltaire was perfectly right in finding that it results from the absorption of matter in the atmosphere. His work takes its place in a long series finally crowned by Lavoisier[13]. Voltaire's *Essai* and mme Du Châtelet's *Dissertation sur la nature et la propagation du feu* were honourably mentioned by the judges but the prize was awarded jointly to three other competitors, one of whom was none other than Leonhard Euler, one of the really great mathematicians. An inspection of the competing essays[14] is instructive: not the least curious detail is the fact that the two papers from Cirey are the only ones reporting experimental work.

Another feature of this period should be noted: Voltaire's efforts to put his financial affairs into order. The letters to Moussinot are by no means easy to follow, especially as we do not possess the priest's replies, but a pattern emerges clearly enough: Voltaire was trying to regulate his affairs in such a way as to provide himself with a sure and regular income, while reserving a substantial amount of cash in hand. He was, in short, clearing the decks. We can see in perspective that he had reached and passed a turning-point in his life. He was himself well aware of this, and he was putting himself in a posture of defence. Complete independence and mobility were in fact Voltaire's only safeguards in his constantly recurring conflicts with the government.

Soon Voltaire returned to the stage with increased zest. The first letter[15] of 1738 is a long one to mlle Quinault, the actress, followed by many more to her and others, in which he discussed the substance and performance of his plays, in particular *Mérope*, to which we will return when it has its public triumph several years later. The comedy *L'Envieux*[16] was written for the benefit of La Marre, but Voltaire thought so little of it that it was never performed nor printed in his lifetime.

During these years Voltaire was also much occupied with

13 See the references given in a note on Best.D1339, and Robert L. Walters, 'Chemistry at Cirey', *Studies on Voltaire* (1967), lviii.1807-27.

14 *Recueil des pièces qui ont remporté le prix de l'Académie royale des sciences*

(Paris 1752), iv.87-221; the two Cirey papers were printed with those of the laureates.

15 Best.D1417 (2 January 1738).

16 *Zulime* was started in 1739, but extensively revised much later.

family affairs. He was in England when his sister died, but among her children were two daughters, Marie Louise (born in 1712) and Marie Elisabeth (born in 1724). Voltaire did not neglect them, and when he was away from Paris more than once recommended them to Thieriot's care. From Leyden he wrote: 'I am delighted that my niece is reading Locke. I am like a worthy old father who weeps with joy because his children are turning out well'[17]. The niece who was reading Locke, or, I dare say, pretending to read Locke, was Marie Louise. It seems that she was already Voltaire's favourite.

A few months later his sister's widower, Pierre François Mignot, also died, and at once Voltaire made himself in large part responsible for the well-being of his orphaned nieces. Again he writes chiefly of Marie Louise, a pupil of the great Rameau, 'and who has an amiable nature'[18], a 'nature full of charm and the head of a real philosopher' according to her uncle Montigny[19]. The two sisters lived in Paris with their aunt mme Paignon or Pagnon, rue des Deux Boules, and Voltaire invited them to make a long visit to Cirey. Mme Du Châtelet pretended to believe that he was interested only in Marie Louise, whom he wanted to marry to the young Champbonin[20]. However, she was not interested in the match, and Voltaire, far from being angry, sent her presents, and wrote to Thieriot: 'I broke it off as soon as she raised the slightest difficulty. Assure her in the strongest terms of my tender affection.'[21]. Rare indeed in that century were uncles so understanding, so tolerant!

The two sisters came to Cirey in a carriage supplied by Voltaire.[22] Marie Louise refused another marriage proposed by Voltaire, although he offered her a dowry of 30,000 francs[23], for she had fallen in love with Nicolas Charles Denis, a notary connected with supplies for the army. She married him with unusual speed on 25 February 1738, in the parish of Saint-Germain-l'Auxerrois. Our astonishing philosopher merely remarked: 'I might complain that the Mignot prefers to live in so abominable a place as Landau

17 Best.D1279 (4 February 1737).
18 Best.D1383 (3 November 1737).
19 Best.D1443 (4 February 1738).
20 Best.D1396, D1406, D1412 (December 1737).

21 Best.D1418, D1419, D1550 (December 1737-July 1738).
22 Best.D1431 (22 January 1738).
23 Best.D1447 (7 February 1738).

rather than in our vale of Tempe, but you know that I want her to be happy in her way and not in mine.'[24] He lived up to his earlier confession of faith: 'God forbid that I should try to interfere with the least of her inclinations. To constrain the freedom of a fellow-creature is to me a crime against humanity. It is the sin against nature.'[25]

In April the young couple came to Cirey, and everybody was extremely pleased, or so said and perhaps even believed Voltaire[26]. This was not quite the opinion of mme Denis, who was in despair, pretending to believe that her uncle was lost to all his friends. She found him 'so shackled that it appears to me almost impossible for him to break his chains'. Why should she have wanted him to break them? The young bride could hardly have been jealous. Was it because Voltaire spent a great deal of money at Cirey, and was even more generous to his mistress than to his nieces? Mme Denis also disapproved of the place chosen by her uncle for his retreat. She found the celebrated couple in a solitude terrifying to human beings. 'Such is the life led by the greatest genius of our century', she moaned. In truth Emilie Du Châtelet put forth all imaginable arts to please Voltaire, but this did not prevent the great man from loving just as tenderly his niece and her husband[27]. Yet certain sides of mme Denis's character soon became all too evident. When Voltaire wrote to Moussinot about his will, he said that his niece went too far 'when she says that she will leave me mistress of all'[28]. The peculiar grammar would have delighted Freud, and the repressed meaning is only too clear. Voltaire evidently had already a pretty shrewd notion of his elder niece's cupidity. Yet he came to transfer to her, little by little, the greater part of his fortune. We shall see why later.

The marriage of Marie Elisabeth to Nicolas Joseph de Dompierre de Fontaine soon followed (19 June 1738). Voltaire gave her also a substantial dowry, though he refused to attend the wedding. He could not face bourgeois marriage ceremonies: 'Gatherings of relations, ambiguous jokes, dull pleasantries, dirty stories which make the bride blush and the prudes purse their lips, a lot of noise,

24 Best.D1462 (22 February 1738).
25 Best.D1396 (6 December 1737).
26 Best.D1483 (23 April 1738).

27 Best.D1498 (10 May 1738).
28 Best.D2136 (9 January 1740).

everybody talking ət the same time, a great deal of food, forced laughter, heavy kisses given without feeling, little girls peeping at everything out of the corner of their eyes.'[29]

Soon after the Denis couple left Cirey an odd and to us highly exasperating incident briefly diverted Voltaire and mme Du Châtelet, the purchase of the Hôtel Lambert. This splendid house, which forms the prow of the Saint-Louis island in Paris, was built by Le Vau and decorated by Lebrun and Lesueur for Lambert de Thorigny. It had been acquired by the famer-general Claude Dupin, from whom it was now bought by mme Du Châtelet (with Voltaire's money of course). It later entered the possession of the Czartorisky family, and still stands as lovely as ever, now in the solicitous ownership of baron Guy de Rothschild. Why the Cirey household ever dreamed of acquiring so large a house is puzzling. Why, having acquired it, they only lived there for a few days before re-selling it[30], is more so, and regrettable, because this beautiful house would have formed a wonderful setting for Voltaire. Besides, had the family settled there many later misfortunes might have been avoided.

Voltaire could scarcely be described as having a placid temperament, nor indeed is the life of reason immune from emotional storm and stress. In Voltaire's case his extreme sensitiveness and punctilio, as well as the dangers to which he was always exposed, made the ups and downs of his affective life abnormally acute. Nor did the well-meant interventions of mme Du Châtelet do anything but aggravate this state of affairs. Still, as a rule Voltaire quickly regained his self-control, and the atmosphere in which he lived was usually serene. For one brief period, however, the turn of the year 1738/39, Voltaire's environment was transformed into a hot-house of sensibility. The great man's rage against Desfontaines was for a time uncontrollable. In 1906 Lytton Strachey wrote to Maynard Keynes: 'I'm reading Voltaire's Correspondence, which is the greatest fun to me imaginable. There's a poor Abbé Desfontaines whom he hated like hell because he criticized his wretched tragedies, and he works himself

29 Best.D1514 (5 June 1738).
30 According to Desnoiresterres ii.344 the Du Châtelets paid 300,000 francs for the house, and sold it for 500,000; both figures are unlikely.

up into a splendid fury. At first he merely says the Abbé had been in prison; then that it was for Sodomy; then that it was for Sodomy with a chimney-sweeper's boy for Cupid—and so it goes on in letter after letter. At last there comes a little poem[31] describing the rape, and how the Abbé was seized by the police in flagrante delicto, stripped and birched—20 strokes for sodomy and 30 for his bad verses. It's really all very scandalous; and I think it's pretty clear that Voltaire himself had had affairs.'[32] This is poor Strachey at his silliest. Nearly all the facts are wrong, and the conclusion is grotesque. It would not worry me in the least if Voltaire had been bisexual, but if he had really had male affairs, would he have said such things about the unscrupulous controversialist Desfontaines, who really was a practising bugger? The very idea is laughable.

It is true, however, that for a time Voltaire's feelings, exacerbated as they were by the behaviour of the ineffable Thieriot, were quite tigerish. Mme Du Châtelet, as usual, at once held Voltaire back and urged him on. She intercepted his letters in order to spare him pain, but he already knew the worst, and was himself trying to keep the details from her. Each pleaded for and against the other in letters to the ever-sure, ever-loyal Argental.

In the midst of all this, mme de Graffigny (*née* d'Issembourg d'Happoncourt) sat in her room at Cirey, vibrating, like her hostess, with sensibility, but somehow ever so insensitively, with ever so little real feeling, though with much emotion, with astonishing lack of insight, and, one is bound to add, rather vulgarly, writing, writing, writing to her lover about herself and her sufferings, about him and his shortcomings, about her other lovers, and of course about her hosts, their virtues and vices, their habits, their quarrels, their furniture, their clothes, their conversation, their private papers. Yet I believe that her picture, whatever one may think of the taste it displays, and though the heat of her colours must be reduced by a good many degrees, and however much filled with mistakes and incomprehension, is substantially a true

---

31 [In Best.D1514 (5 June 1738)]

32 Michael Holroyd, *Lytton Strachey* (London 1967), i.277-8. A little later Strachey still found Voltaire's correspondence 'the only completely satisfactory thing in the world' (Holroyd, i.345).

one. Her narrative is therefore invaluable. For this we must be grateful, and we should be ready to forgive much in her picturesque, racy, slangy letters.

Mme de Graffigny, though she writes like an excitable debutante, was almost exactly the same age as Voltaire: she was born in 1695, he a year earlier. Her husband had been an official of the court of Stanislas at Lunéville, which was about 50 miles by road from Cirey. He was cruelly mad and madly cruel, and after putting up with a great deal of violence, she had left him. Her friends rallied round, and after staying at the château of Stainville she moved on to Cirey, where she arrived on 3 December 1738 on an indefinite visit.

Her best friend at Lunéville was François Antoine Devaux, a young man whose sole achievement was that everybody liked him. Mme de Graffigny wrote him innumerable long letters whenever they were separated, and Cirey being an incomparable subject for gossip, it is not surprising that thirty packets of news sped from Cirey to Lunéville during the nine weeks of her stay, extending to well over 100 pages in my edition.[33]

The first letter was written only a few hours after mme de Graffigny's arrival. The journey had been uncomfortable. She had borrowed horses from one friend, and a chaise from the dowager duchesse de Lorraine, and had left before dawn. At first the roads were good, but finally they became so bad that the coachman refused to go any further. She had to go by public coach from Joinville, and was turned out with her maid at the foot of a mountain (in fact, a slight hill), then tramping through the mud to Cirey. She was received kindly by mme Du Châtelet and enthusiastically by Voltaire. Mme Du Châtelet chatters away, though like an angel. She wears a cotton dress, with a large black apron[34]. Her long hair is piled from behind on the top of her head and curled like a small child's. It suits her very well. Voltaire is powdered and dressed as if he were in Paris. And so to bed.

33 The first is Best.D1675, the last Best.D1876 (4 December 1738-9 February 1739). For the subsequent years see the book cited above in note 19 on p. 189.

34 Her contemporaries were fascinated by this black apron: a sort of inverted snobbery, I suppose.

The next day she writes at midnight. She would like to describe everything and to give her dear Pampan the same pleasure, hour by hour, as she herself enjoyed. Supper was served in Voltaire's quarters. What talk! Poetry, science, all lightly and pleasantly. It is beyond her to describe it all. The meal was not profuse, but well-prepared and elegant, with lots of silver. From her place she saw all the scientific instruments. His blood boiled when he spoke of Rousseau and Desfontaines. She was so tired from her mountaineering that she kept to her bed till noon. Her hostess came to see her, and Voltaire sent her a Newton bound in morocco. A little fat lady (mme de Champbonin) who lives in the neighbourhood came in. She (the little fat lady) loves Voltaire to distraction, and he loves her because she has a good heart.

Voltaire came to mme de Graffigny's room, but it was very cold. However, everything of this kind must not be taken as a fact but as a rendering of what the fact should have been to suit her romantic psychology, like the Cirey 'mountain'; in reality half a cord of wood (about sixty cubic feet) was supplied daily for mme de Graffigny's room. She sent Voltaire away and followed him to his wing of the house. You go through an antichamber, as big as your hand, into his bedroom, which is small, low, hung with crimson velvet, with a little recess. There is little tapestry, but much panelling, in which are framed fine paintings, mirrors, splendid corner-cupboards in lacquer, with porcelain, a remarkable clock, any number of things—everything so clean that you could kiss the parquet. A case contains silver plate, a jewel-box is filled with cameos and diamond rings. From this room you go on to a little gallery of thirty or forty feet. Between the windows are little statues, and on the other side books and instruments, with a stove which heats the room as though it were spring. And mme de Graffigny admires on and on.

But when she comes to describe her hostess's rooms, her lyricism overflows. Voltaire's are nothing to these. Her bedroom is panelled in yellow and pale blue, an alcove has India paper, the bed is in blue moiré, and everything matches, even the dog-baskets. A big mirror-door leads to the unfinished library. There is a small boudoir: one feels like kneeling when one sees it. The panelling is blue and the ceiling is in *vernis Martin* by a pupil of Martin who has been there for three years. All the little panels contain pictures by Watteau. There are brackets by Martin, with lovely things on them, including an amber desk set, a present from the prince of Prussia. There is no furniture other than a large armchair and two footstools in white taffeta. This divine boudoir is paved with marble, panelled in grey, with embroidered muslin curtains. Mme Du Châtelet showed her jewel-box. It is finer than that of mme de Richelieu. She couldn't get over it, for when mme Du Châtelet was at Craon she hadn't so much as a tortoiseshell snuff-box. Now she has fifteen or twenty, in gold, in precious stones, in lacquer, in enamel, and so on and on. But the writer complains of the draughts, and dislikes the arid mountain which she can almost touch and which blocks the view entirely. (Once again, this is a typical pre-Romantic deformation, for the mountain is in fact a modest hill at some distance from the house.) Still, the fireplace is so large a witches' coven could fly through it.

The prince of Prussia has sent one of his gentlemen (it was baron Dietrich von Keyserlingk) to present Voltaire with his portrait. He was welcomed with theatricals, fireworks, illuminations, in short, such things as only fairies or Voltaire could bring off. This evening she will have to read *Mérope*, the history of Louis XIV, and a life of Molière (all three of these works are by Voltaire). It will serve to put her to sleep: the compliment is ambiguous.

The torrent of gossip floods on. One of Voltaire's young protégés (it was the abbé La Marre) wrote to Voltaire: 'Sir, if I am not mistaken I have the pox, and neither friend nor money. Will you let me rot?' Voltaire sent him to a doctor and had him cured. Mme Du Châtelet wants to make Voltaire change his clothes, but he is afraid of catching cold. Voltaire sulks because mme Du Châtelet prevents him from taking a glass of Rhine wine, so he refuses to read out the *Pucelle*. She goes on nagging, he gets irritated, speaks to her sharply in English, and leaves. But they soon make it up, and go on with a reading of *Mérope*. The goddess of the place wants her to go for a drive, but, seeing that their guest is afraid of the frisky horses, Voltaire saves her. And instead the fat neighbour takes her to see the bathroom. What an enchantment! It is all tiled, except for the marble floor. The little *cabinet* is panelled in pale celadon green, gay, divine, admirably carved and gilded. And so on and on.

The next day Voltaire gave a magic-lantern show, and his stories made them die laughing. Really, there had never been anything so funny, but he finished by setting fire to the apparatus. There are theatricals and readings every day. (Once twenty-one spoken acts and two and a half operas were performed between noon and seven o'clock on the following morning.[35])

But soon mme de Graffigny's tone changes. Her room is cold, she is ill, her little bitch is on heat, her maid gives notice, the letters she receives look as if they have been opened. She goes on writing to Devaux, but in addition to the letters she posts, she scribbles away at a private one, interminable, which she keeps by her until she is safely away from Cirey. What had happened? Something of little importance, but that little has been vastly inflated. Voltaire was not an easy man to live with. How could he be? Nor was mme Du Châtelet particularly *vivable*. Besides, he would insist on writing dangerous things, which his mistress even more strenuously insisted on keeping under lock and key. The tensions between them were aggravated by the Desfontaines affair, which was now at its worst. In fact the *Voltairomanie* had just reached Cirey: he kept it from her, and she kept it from him, for both had received it secretly. And just at this moment news reached Cirey that fragments of the *Pucelle* had escaped from a locked drawer. Inevitably mme de Graffigny was suspected. She certainly made free with her host's papers, and admits as much, but the exact degree of her guilt is really of little importance. Voltaire and mme Du Châtelet thought that she was responsible, and made a terrible scene. Later both of them apologised, Voltaire generously, mme Du Châtelet grudgingly, and mme de Graffigny stayed on for another six weeks. Everybody had thoroughly enjoyed a refreshing bath of steaming sensibility.

Mme de Graffigny's troubles were not over. When one of her Lunéville lovers, Desmarets, called for her at Cirey his first words were to tell her that all was over between them, and he then proceeded to flirt outrageously with mme Du Châtelet. When the unfortunate woman left Cirey she was given a home for a few

35 Best.D1872 (12 February 1739).

months by the duchess de Richelieu, until this kind friend's premature death (2 August 1740). For several years thereafter she lived in wretched poverty, then suddenly had two great successes: the novel *Lettres d'une péruvienne* and the play *Cénie*. She went on to write dozens more, all worthless, as the manuscripts testify, for they remained unpublished. But she had had her days of glory, of which those at Cirey were not the least.

In Champagne a relaxation of tension is noticeable after the departure of mme de Graffigny. Voltaire had resigned himself to a less than drastic settlement with Desfontaines, and mme Du Châtelet (who had been furiously angry[36] when Voltaire was merely sad and perplexed) had more or less forgiven Thieriot. Yet it would perhaps be more accurate to say that Voltaire was suffering from a melancholic let-down: the reaction from unusual excitement was always worse for him than the excitement itself. He was unable to concentrate on any major task, though he played with the idea of writing a history of Switzerland[37], which unfortunately came to nothing. In short, he was suffering from a bad attack of boredom and restlessness. Yet there can be no doubt that he had found a new calm. When Prévost d'Exiles, whom he had helped more than once, and whose *Pour et contre* he was now encouraging, offered to write a defence of Voltaire and his works to pay his debts, Voltaire declined the honour with dignity and wit[38]. He pointed out that he could not defend himself without attacking others: he preferred to hide such things rather than publish them. Of course if the proposed book had been an attack on him his attitude would have been the same as on a previous occasion: someone told Voltaire that he had written a book against him, which he would suppress on receipt of 100 *écus*. Voltaire replied that this was not enough, such a book would bring the writer at least 100 *pistoles*, and he should therefore publish it.

This period began with a visit to the Netherlands[39], and ends with another, for the Du Châtelets' law-suit was still dragging on. The party travelled slowly, stopped to have some worldly fun

---

36 See for instance her reply to the *Voltairomanie* (Best.app.D51).

37 Best.D2009 (8 May 1739).

38 (Best.D2143 (15 January 1740), D2112 (c. 30 January).

39 See chapter 16, above.

at Valenciennes and Louvain, and settled down in Brussels at the end of May 1739. In the ample intervals left by the legal procedures Voltaire worked on several things old and new, more particularly on *Mahomet*, while mme Du Châtelet laboured at her mathematics. In June they all went to stay with the duc d'Arenberg at Enghien, where a stone cottage was later to be built for J. J. Rousseau. Mme Du Châtelet wrote mme de Graffigny a glowing letter[40] about their stay. They had put on Molière's *Ecole des femmes*, with Voltaire in the role of Arnolphe, herself as Georgette, and the princesse de Chimay as Agnès. Voltaire had given a party at Brussels, with fireworks and all the trimmings, on the theme of Utopia. Voltaire himself confirms this in a letter to Helvétius, adding that he had never read the book, and that nobody in Brussels even knew the meaning of the word.[41]

In August the travellers, by way of Cambrai, moved to Paris for two months. Mme Du Châtelet stayed with the Richelieus, Voltaire at the hôtel de Brie, in the rue Cloche-perce. All was rejoicing because of the betrothal of the king's daughter Louise Elisabeth to Philip, son of Philip v of Spain: the bride and bridegroom were aged respectively twelve and seventeen. Voltaire found the rejoicings unworthy of France. These things were done differently under Louis xiv.[42] Besides, Paris was huge, filled with noise and dissipation, one had to run after one's friends, one could not live for oneself, and found oneself smothered in flowers and enveloped in whirlwinds vainer than those of Descartes. And no sooner had he arrived than he was involved in the usual gossip and intrigues. Fortunately neither Desfontaines nor Rousseau was there: he pointed out that spiders are not found in well-ordered houses.[43]

As soon as they could the couple left Paris for Cirey, where a visit from the charming mme de Richelieu no doubt produced much gossip. But soon the *ménage* had to return, in Voltaire's wonderfully expressive phrase, 'to bawl in the grotte of the flemish chicane'.[44] Before he left Paris Voltaire invited Helvétius to Cirey in the warmest terms. They had first corresponded a year or

40 Best.D2055 (29 July 1739).   43 Best.D2074 (September 1739).
41 Best.D2040 (6 July 1739).   44 Best.D2175 (2 March 1740).
42 Best.D2062 (12 August 1739).

two earlier, and Voltaire rapidly developed a deep affection for the young man, dedicated to him the fourth *Discours sur l'homme*[45], and took infinite trouble to encourage and advise him[46]. Helvétius at this time was merely a wealthy *fermier général* who dabbled in poetry: *De l'esprit* was not published until twenty years later.

By chance we can see that Voltaire was not suffering from delusions when he felt himself the victim of a police state. Soon after he left Paris the ministry ordered the police to investigate a young man named Ravoisier because he was in frequent contact with Voltaire[47]. This young man was one of those whom Voltaire had helped financially and who expressed his gratitude by robbing him[48]. He is otherwise unknown.

45 See p. 198, above.
46 Not only in his letters, but also in *Conseils a m. Helvétius sur la composition et sur le choix d'une épître morale* and *Remarques sur deux épîtres d'Helvétius*.

47 Best.D2123 (24 December 1739).
48 Best.D2111 (12 November 1739), D2226 (7 June 1740).

20. Mahomet *and* Frederick, 1740-1741

VOLTAIRE NOW ENTERED a calmer period, that is, a period which in any one else's life would be regarded as one of febrile activity. We find no further trace of his malaise. For one thing, he was again hard at work. At the very beginning of 1740 he told Cideville that since they had last met in Paris he had accompanied mme de Richelieu to Langres, and had returned thence to Cirey, and from Cirey to Brussels. 'I have never been so inspired by my gods or so possessed by my demons.'[1] And in fact he had composed *Pandore* and *La Prude* as a relaxation from the revision of *Mahomet*, *Zulime* and the *Anti-Machiavel*.

The exact date of composition of *Pandore* is not known, but Voltaire first mentioned it at the beginning of 1740 in a letter to Helvétius[2]. This little opera forms a curious incident in its author's life. Voltaire was much attached to it, made repeated efforts to get it performed, but never succeeded. He tried to get Rameau and others to set it to music, finally had it done more or less to his satisfaction by Jean Benjamin de Laborde, and gave up his efforts to put it on only when the music of Gluck, as he put it, had crushed that of Laborde[3]. Voltaire's failure with this opera is difficult to understand. His theme is admirably adapted to operatic conventions, and his text is of course far superior to the stock libretto. As the opera was often discussed and at least twice reached the stage of rehearsals[4] one can only suppose that Laborde's music was very bad.

The *Prude*, first called *La Dévote*, is an adaptation of *The Plain dealer* (1674), which is peculiarly interesting, for Wycherley's comedy was itself derived from Molière's *Misanthrope*. Voltaire was of course shocked by Wycherley's language, and perhaps

1 Best.D2137 (9 January 1740).
2 Best.D2130 (3 January 1740).
3 Best.D18997 (20 June 1774).

4 Best.D13920 (4 February 1767), D16014 (29 November 1769).

even more distressed by the fact that words which he refused to print expressed, as he said in his preface, a profound knowledge of the human heart and incomparable wit. It cannot be claimed that in cleaning up Wycherley, and fitting him to ideal sensibilities, Voltaire improved him.[5] The *Prude* was only once performed, in 1747 at Sceaux, the court of the duchesse Du Maine, when Voltaire himself composed and read a prologue.

Mahomet is a very different affair. Conceived in 1739[6], written for the most part in 1740, first performed at Lille in 1741 (Voltaire had gone there to see mme Denis) and in Paris in 1742, this is perhaps the best of Voltaire's plays, certainly one of the best. Voltaire himself thought that it was his best work[7], a tragedy of a new kind, in which superstition and fanaticism were first presented in the theatre[8]. Its purpose is indicated by its alternative title *Le Fanatisme*, and Voltaire's opinion of his play and its theme is sufficiently shown by the fact that he dedicated it first to Frederick (by now king of Prussia) and then to pope Benedict XIV. He once said[9] that if Ravaillac had seen *Mahomet* he would not have murdered Henri IV.

The performance at Lille was a triumph; when Voltaire was in Paris at the beginning of 1742 he read the play in all the drawing-rooms, and he gave a copy to the prime minister, cardinal de Fleury; and the first night at the Comédie française (29 August 1742), at first postponed because a Turkish ambassador was in Paris and might be offended, was a great occasion. Yet a full-scale cabal was at once mounted against Voltaire's tragedy. The censor (Crébillon) refused to authorise the performance; when this difficulty had been overcome, so loud was the outcry that the authorities ordered the play to be taken off after the third performance, although the public liked it more and more.[10] 'Paris City was in transports of various kinds; never were such crowds

5 A student of the mutability of taste could do worse than undertake a comparative study of these plays by Molière, Wycherley and Voltaire.

6 Best.D1862 (9 February 1739); for once I must set the record straight; Beuchot did not often go astray, but he did when he said (M.iv.7n) that Voltaire sent Frederick the first act on

1 September 1738 (Best.D1608): the reference there is to *Mérope*, not to *Mahomet*.

7 Best.D2267 (12 July 1742).

8 Best.D2048 (c. 20 July 1739).

9 Best.13671 (11 December 1767).

10 Pomeau, *La Religion de Voltaire*, pp.151-2n. See also the autobiography, pp. 633-634, below.

of Audience, lifting a man to the immortal gods,—though a part too, majority by count of heads, were dragging him to Tartarus again. "Exquisite, unparalleled!" exclaimed good judges. . . . "Infamous, irreligious, accursed" vociferously exclaimed the bad judges'.[11]

So taken off it was, but the Parisian public usually found some way of revenging itself against arbitrary action, and it would seem that when *Mahomet* was replaced by *Polyeucte* the spectators pointedly applauded its anti-Christian passages[12]. Lord Chesterfield said that he had seen at once that the play was not directed so much against Mahomet as against Jesus Christ, and he was surprised that nobody had noticed this at Lille. It was unforgivable, thought the polite Chesterfield, to take so much trouble to propagate 'a doctrine so pernicious to a civilised society'[13]. The ministry even thought that the play was directed against all religion.

I am not prepared to assert that either he or they were mistaken. If it is shown that a great religion can be and in fact was based on false miracles and ruthless fanaticism, it is impossible to make an intelligent onlooker close his mind to the obvious parallels. Voltaire himself said later that 'he was sorry for having painted Mahomet in more odious colours than he deserved', and that he had done so because 'great passions and great crimes are indispensable requisites in a tragedy.'[14] None of these things discouraged Benedict XIV from assuring Voltaire in his reply to the dedication that he had read his 'bellissima tragedia' ('very fine tragedy') 'con sommo piacere' ('with the greatest pleasure'); nor the dauphin (the son of Louis XV) from learning it by heart[15].

Can the events of the play be reduced to their essentials? Voltaire has done so himself. In the letter to Frederick which he afterwards prefixed to his play, Voltaire says: 'It concerns a young man born virtuous, who, seduced by fanaticism, murders an old man who loves him, a young man who, thinking to serve God, unknowingly becomes a parricide; it concerns an impostor who

11 Carlyle, *History of Friedrich II of Prussia*, XIV.ii.

12 See R. S. Ridgway, *La Propagande philosophique dans les tragédies de Voltaire* (1961), pp. 118-19.

13 *Miscellaneous works of the late . . .* *earl of Chesterfield* (London 1777)' ii.35-6.

14 See the autobiography, p. 634, below.

15 Best.D13586 (24 September 1766).

orders this murder, and who promises the murderer an incest for reward.'[16] But this is not all, for in Voltaire's play Mahomet has a definite and terrifying purpose. The second act, which Jean Jacques Rousseau much admired, contains passages which might represent the political drama of our own time—in other words, its theme is eternal.

Zopire laments the disturbed state of the country, and asks Mahomet:

> Tyran de ton pays, est-ce ainsi qu'en ce lieu
> Tu viens donner la paix, et m'annoncer un dieu?[17]

Mahomet replies that he is ambitious; no doubt all men are,

> Mais jamais roi, pontife, ou chef, ou citoyen,
> Ne conçut un projet aussi grand que le mien.[18]

Many great empires have had their day, now it is the turn of the Arabs:

> Il faut un nouveau culte, il faut de nouveaux fers;
> Il faut un nouveau dieu pour l'aveugle univers.[19]

He had come to bring a more noble servitude to the whole world, to abolish the false gods, to destroy the weakness of his fatherland and to make it great under one king and one god. By what right? By the right of superiority and determination over vulgar humanity.

All in all, by its form, by its content, by the characterisation of the leading personages, by its theatrical quality—including a dramatic and moving curtain—this play is perhaps most worthy of revival of all Voltaire's tragedies. Voltaire once said that *Mahomet* suffered because caution had banked its fire, a sad thing in poetry[20]. One can only wonder what his tragedy would have been had it been written in a free society. In his commentary on Voltaire's plays Flaubert calls him 'one of the first utilitarians in art'[21].

16 D2386 (30 December 1740).

17 II.v; 'Tyrant of your country, is it thus that you bring it peace and announce a god?'

18 II.v; 'But never has a king, pontiff, chief or citizen conceived so great a project as mine.'

19 II.v; 'A new religion, new chains, a new god are needed for the blind universe.'

20 Best.D2148 (26 January 1740).

21 Gustave Flaubert, *Le Théâtre de Voltaire*, ed. Theodore Besterman (Studies on Voltaire, l-li: 1967), i.155.

In his superb letter[22] to lord Hervey Voltaire abstracted the essence of the *Siècle de Louis XIV*; and then, ironically enough, proceeded to spend many weeks of hard work and even harder negotiation in passing Frederick's *Anti-Machiavel* through the press, outsmarting the publisher by thoroughly machiavellian means[23]. Frederick first told Voltaire in March 1739 that he was thinking of writing on Machiavelli's *Prince*[24]. Voltaire at once warmly welcomed the project[25], and Frederick worked on it actively. In the meanwhile the correspondence with the prince flowed on, with much exchange of writings, compliments and gifts. All this continued, indeed, with increased frequency and fervency after Frederick's accession to the throne (31 May 1740). And if Voltaire's adulation strikes a false note now and then, let us reflect that he was doing everything in his power (as by insisting on the publication of an authentic text of the *Anti-Machiavel*) to keep the new king to his princely resolutions. He did not realise that the admirably pacific sentiments of the book were merely a screen behind which very different actions were in preparation. Voltaire was perhaps not as wise—or as cynical—before the event as he might have been, but at the time he had some justification for his hopes. After all, it was no ordinary monarch who, on mounting an already powerful throne, assured his friend that he was disgusted with human vanity and grandeur. 'I beg you to see in me only a zealous citizen, a somewhat sceptical philosopher, but a truly faithful friend. By God, write to me only as a man, and despise with me titles, names and external glamour.'[26] And indeed, even in the first rush of business, the new king found time to write several times to Voltaire, and to summon friends who had been discouraged or worse by his father[27], including Algarotti and the philosopher Wolff. It is pleasant to be able to record these surviving traces of the philosopher-prince—let us at least give him that much credit— for he was soon to be swallowed up by the conqueror-king.

The high expectations nursed by Voltaire did not in fact survive in full bloom the months following Frederick's accession. The

22 Best.D2216 (*c.* 1 June 1740).

23 These are most explicitly revealed by Voltaire in a letter to Frederick of 14 July 1740 (Best.D2269).

24 Best.D1950 (22 March 1739).

25 Best.D1978 (15 April 1739).

26 Best.D2225 (6 June 1740).

27 See the note on Best.D2145.

king almost immediately let fall the mask, and his conduct showed how long and how carefully he had prepared a course of action far removed from the views he had proclaimed, and continued to proclaim. In September 1740 these two remarkable men finally met, not at any of the places proposed and successively agreed, but at the obscure Wesel, on the Rhine, south-west of Cleves. He had a fever, said Frederick, and could see Voltaire only there, and of course mme Du Châtelet not at all. Frederick organised this first encounter with the care he lavished on all his campaigns, and with equal lack of candour. He never intended to meet Voltaire in the presence of the great man's Egeria, and one cannot help admiring the subtle stage-management which finally placed Voltaire in a position from which he could not retire without discourtesy. How mme Du Châtelet must have raged! She sent the king a note which could hardly have been briefer and colder without an offensive disregard for the proprieties[28], following it up with an even curter new year's greeting[29]. And at the same time she started a violent flirtation with her old flame Richelieu.[30]

Yet mme Du Châtelet and Voltaire himself were only minor pawns in this game: Frederick had always intended to go to Wesel, by no means in order to meet Voltaire, but in pursuance of his deviously cunning political and military plans. He was survey-in the territory 'against a certain contingency that may be looked for'[31]: his attack on the prince-bishop of Liège. Frederick came to Moyland, near Cleves, on Sunday, 11 September 1740; Voltaire arrived the same night, after a journey of 150 miles; and 11 September is also the date of Frederick's ultimatum to the prince-bishop. Frederick and Voltaire both left Wesel on Wednesday, the 14th, the day on which the king's troops moved in. All this had been minutely devised in every detail under cover of the philosopher-king's wish to meet the philosopher-poet.

What Frederick thought of Voltaire may be judged from his letter to a friend: 'He has the eloquence of Cicero, the gentleness of Pliny, and the wisdom of Agrippa. In a word, he unites all the best of the virtues and talents of three of the greatest men of

---

28 Best.D2309 (8 September 1740). D2390 (24 December).
29 Best.D2389 (24 December 1740).   31 Carlyle, *History of Friedrich the*
30 Best.D2365 (23 November 1740), *great*, XI.iv.

antiquity. His mind works unceasingly, every drop of ink is a flash of wit sparkling from his pen. He declaimed his tragedy of Mahomet 1. He transported us, and I could only admire him and remain silent. One could make a book of the brilliant things he let fall in his conversation'.[32] In short, Frederick fell even more completely under the charm.

Voltaire's impressions are more difficult to determine: he says less in his letters about the encounter than might have been expected, and expresses himself less freely than we should like. Was he perhaps confirmed in his disillusion? After all, only a few months earlier he had written bitterly to Cideville from Brussels about kings who took themselves for Antonines:

> J'ai vu s'enfuir leurs bons desseins
> Aux premiers sons de la trompette.
> Ils ne sont plus rien que des rois,
> Ils vont par de sanglants exploits
> Prendre ou ravager des provinces.
> L'ambition les a soumis.
> Moi, j'y renonce, adieu les princes,
> Il ne me faut que des amis.[33]

If Voltaire was disillusioned, it must have been on a personal level, for Frederick succeeded in deceiving him about his bellicose intentions: far from protesting when the king's aggression could no longer be disguised, Voltaire wrote and published a defence of Frederick's claims[34]. In short, in the hope that the king would really establish a government by reason, Voltaire was for long willing to accept Frederick's actions at his own valuation; his attitude was later paralleled by Bernard Shaw's admiration for Mussolini's 'efficiency'. However, the evidence for Voltaire's feelings is mainly negative: whatever doubts he may already have acquired, his feet seemed to be set firmly on the road to Berlin. Indeed, before the end of the year Voltaire (to mme Du Châtelet's almost suicidal distress) paid a short visit to Prussia. Seen at home,

32 Best.D2317 (24 September 1741); but this did not prevent the king from expressing less flattering opinions: see Best.app.D60.

33 Best.D2444 (13 March 1741). 'I have seen their good intentions vanish at the first sounds of the trumpet. They are nothing more than kings, they set out to take or ravage provinces by means of bloody exploits. Ambition has vanquished them. I give them up, farewell princes, I want only friends.'

34 *Sommaire des droits de s. m. le roi de Prusse sur Herstall* (1740).

surrounded by his friends, Frederick still further disenchanted Voltaire: and Frederick for his part began to realise that his revered master was not above human frailty. The relations between the two men had many ups and downs for nearly forty more years, but one thing is evident to us by the end of 1740: the honeymoon was over. Henceforth it was Frederick who beckoned, while Voltaire did not always respond.

At the moment, however, as I have said, he did meet the king more than half-way, for after returning to The Hague, where he stayed in Frederick's palace, he paid a short visit to Prussia. There he engaged in a peculiarly heavy-handed verse flirtation with the king, in which the two men reproached each other with being coquettes[35], thus echoing previous exchanges. Before their previous meeting Voltaire wrote to Frederick: 'Were it true that your humanity is coming to Brussels I would implore you to bring some English drops with you, for I would faint with pleasure.'[36] And Frederick replied: 'It would be the most charming day of my life, I think I would die of it; but at least one cannot choose a more agreeable kind of death.'[37] But this was a highly formalised kind of literary love-making. Although Frederick was homosexual, and surrounded by intimate male friends, too much meaning must not be read into such passages. But, in this spirit, before leaving Berlin Voltaire committed perhaps the most outrageously careless indiscretion of his life. He had procured for Maupertuis the important post of head of the revived Berlin Academy[38]. Nevertheless he had no illusions about Maupertuis's tetchy and vindictive character, from which he had already suffered. And yet, when saying good-bye to this ambiguous friend on leaving the Prussian court he was so monstrously imprudent as to refer to his royal host, in writing, as 'the worthy, singular and amiable whore'[39]. Twelve years later Frederick emphatically, even violently, though for no specially evident reason, took the part of Maupertuis in his quarrel with Voltaire. One cannot help

35 Best.D2375 (1 December 1740).
36 Best.D2298 (22 August 1740).
37 Best.D2307 (5 September 1740).
38 On Voltaire's recommendation of

Maupertuis see a note on Best.D2303
(1 September 1740).
  39 Best.D2377 (*c.* 1 December 1740).

wondering whether the former had shown the king Voltaire's reference to him in December 1740.

Voltaire's indiscretion was even greater than appears only too clearly on the surface, for he was not at the Prussian court only for personal reasons. When in rapid succession Frederick ascended the throne of Prussia and Maria Theresa that of the Empire, it was obvious that the political stability of Europe was in danger, not least because Frederick was ruthlessly ambitious and Maria Theresa young and badly advised. Voltaire saw the situation clearly and at once offered his diplomatic services to the aged prime minister Fleury, who responded favourably—no wonder, since Frederick's idol was at that very moment in his company. The cardinal sent Voltaire a letter[40] containing assurances of his pacific intentions. Voltaire 'obeyed the orders your eminence did not give me' and showed the letter to Frederick, who sent a message that he wanted to be the friend of the king of France[41]. For the moment (a short one) all was well, and Voltaire had scored a small diplomatic triumph.

After returning to the Netherlands from Berlin Voltaire started work on his historical masterpiece, the *Essai sur les mœurs*[42]. He also spent a good deal of time in organising a troupe of players which was to go to Prussia under La Noue, but all his efforts were in vain, for in the end Frederick needed the money for less pacific purposes. Naturally enough La Noue was furious, and Voltaire, the innocent intermediary, had to make it up to him professionally. Voltaire also spent an astonishing number of words, with equally little success, on efforts to procure Thieriot an annuity. He also worked hard to smoothe the all too easily ruffled feathers of Maupertuis, but in his correspondence with J. B. Rousseau's editor, conducted for the most part through mme Du Châtelet, he gives a fortunately rare example of the tenacity of his hatred. Yet though he was in the right, even here he finally yielded.

He worked hard on *Mahomet,* and wrote a good deal on kinetic energy[43], though it is clear that he was wearying of his efforts to

40 Best.D2364 (14 November 1740); see the autobiography, pp. 632-633, below.

41 Best.D2368 (26 November 1740).

42 Best.D2493 (1 June 1741).

43 *Doutes sur la mesure des forces motrices et sur leur nature* (1741).

master 'our uncertain science'. As his knowledge increased he perceived ever more clearly the vastness and the complexity of the visible and the hidden universes, and as he did so his agnosticism increased. He realised more and more that he was not likely to discover the truth about these mysteries by dabbling on the sea-shore of the unknown. He was in no mood to accept a friend's advice that he should devote himself to science in order to avoid the annoyances of a literary career.[44]

The correspondence with Frederick continued in spate, but Voltaire's disillusion became explicit in letters to several corre-spondents, and to Frederick himself, when the king entirely threw off the mask by invading Silesia. Voltaire told Cideville that he had returned to his dove-cote after his voyage in search of a sage who had forgotten all his good intentions. As the cat runs after a mouse even when changed into a woman, so Frederick, disguised as a philosopher, had seized his sword as soon as he saw a province at his mercy.[45] Nor did Voltaire hide his feelings from the king. A few years earlier he had composed a dedication to Frederick of the *Henriade*, celebrating him as the peace-loving philosopher-prince. Now Voltaire wrote to the king that he must withdraw these lines, which were no longer true[46], and they were never published. The fact that Frederick abandoned his project for a magnificent edition of the *Henriade*, printed with silver type, may perhaps be chance coincidence. In any case the idea is typically pre-Romantic, poetic but silly. The result of printing with type in silver, which is too soft, would be much inferior, even on a hand-press, to that produced by type cast in a more conventional metal. The use of silver and gold type is a tradition going back to the first century of printing, but there is no real evidence that either was ever used.

<hr />

44 See the verses quoted in the auto-biography, pp. 634-636, below, where Formont advises the contrary.

45 Best.D2444 (13 March 1741);

this is an echo of La Fontaine's *Chatte métamorphosée en femme*.

46 Best.D2520 (3 August 1741).

21. Niece and mistress, 1741-1749

I HAVE ALREADY TOUCHED on what was for long the mystery of Voltaire's relations with his niece Marie Louise Denis, née Mignot. The explanation of his astonishing patience and indulgence was simply that he had long loved her, and then had the misfortune to fall in love with her. For some years, however, they continued merely to be friendly, in a family way, but no more. Presents and gifts of money continued, and Voltaire worked hard for the advancement of monsieur Denis, even to the point of writing very insistently to cardinal de Fleury[1]. Later he complained that the 'accursed hussars have captured all my poor nephew Denis's modest baggage. He is sacrificing body and soul in Bohemia, and is working so hard that he is ill. To make matters worse he sent his wife two fine horses which have been seized here, and I have been unable to drag them out of the grasp of the officials.'[2]

In April 1741 Voltaire and the Du Châtelets travelled to Lille, where Denis was then stationed, chiefly, it is true, to be present at the first night of *Mahomet*; but in November 1743 the visit was renewed, this time for no other than personal reasons. When poor Denis died in April 1744, Voltaire mourned him sincerely, and pitied his niece, who had suffered 'a frightful loss'[3]. Uncle and niece had already made love, but it so happened that at the precise moment of Denis's death the ardour of Voltaire's love for mme Du Châtelet had begun to cool. One of their servants was suborned by the police and made them a report which shows the *ménage* in a cruel but I think pretty authentic light.

Everything is in an uproar in the marquise Du Châtelet's house. Her husband has arrived at Cirey, and writes letter after letter to ask her to return [from Paris]. She had to go to endless trouble to persuade Voltaire to undertake the journey. Since he made up his mind to it he is in an appalling temper,

---

1 Best.D2531 (18 August 1741).   3 Best.D2979 (30 May 1744).
2 Best.D2680 (3 November 1742).

behaves to the marquise with the utmost unkindness and makes her cry all day. The day before yesterday they had an argument that lasted part of the night. Voltaire, expecting to sup all alone, had a narrow table laid. Mme Du Châtelet, having returned to sup with him, wanted to use a more convenient table. Voltaire stubbornly clung to his, and when she insisted, said that he was master in his own house, that he had been made a cat's paw for too long and several other harsh things. These rows, which occur frequently, are mocked by the whole household. The secret cause of these respective bad tempers is Voltaire's passion for mlle Gaussin. This actress comes to see the poet when he cannot go to her, their affair is quite a settled thing, and the marquise is furious about it, but dares not object too violently, lest her lover leave her altogether. A diary of what passes between these victims of love and common sense would be equally singular and interesting.[4]

The spy was not altogether well informed, for Voltaire, in all probability, was discussing stage business with the Gaussin, and using her as a cover for his encounters with mme Denis. Whatever may have been the facts at this time, just before Voltaire left Paris for Cirey, there is no doubt that the next time uncle and niece met in Paris they fell into each other's arms: family affection gave place to sexual passion. Voltaire lamented his niece's misfortune. His concern does him credit, but it was superfluous: never has there been any widow-woman so well able to look after herself as mme Denis. Yet it is impossible to doubt that Voltaire loved his niece sincerely, tenderly, passionately, and often blindly. He was always true to his passion for her (by which I do not mean that he was always technically faithful), even after mme Denis had been guilty of grave offences against her uncle and lover. As for her, did she ever love Voltaire? Scepticism is indicated. Did she not refuse to follow him to Prussia? Did she not rejoin him only at Frankfort on his way home from that ill-starred visit? Did she not then leave him again while he wandered in search of a home, rejoining him only when he had found one? Did she not prefer her other lovers, Baculard d'Arnaud, Marmontel, Ximenès? But all this must await the passage of the years.

In the meanwhile I must make it clear that in the eighteenth century and in Roman Catholic countries incest was not and is not judged with Calvinist severity. Voltaire once said, with perfect

4 *Archives de la Bastille* (Paris 1881), xii.245-6.

accuracy, that 'a man can marry his niece by permission of the pope, for a fee which I believe is normally forty thousand *écus*, including the petty cash. I have always heard it said that it cost monsieur de Montmartel only 80,000 francs. I know some who have gone to bed with their nieces much more cheaply than that.'[5] As well as Paris de Montmartel, the ex-Jesuit Fréron and La Condamine married their nieces, and so did Lamartine, to say nothing of Philip II, Ferdinand of Austria[6], other royal persons, and, in our own times, a member of a distinguished French family.

The beginnings of this love affair were completely unknown until a few years ago, when I had the good fortune to lay my hands on such parts of mme Denis's archives as she withheld when she sold her uncle's papers to the empress Catherine. And this is as good an opportunity as any to illustrate one of the difficulties that had to be overcome in editing the whole of Voltaire's correspondence, the dating. Of the 142 early love letters[7] from Voltaire to his niece, only three are completely dated, and twenty-three partially, that is, they bear a month and a day. At first sight this awkward omission seems to have been partially remedied by mme Denis, who endorsed a year and sometimes an exact date on many of the manuscripts. Alas, these dates, no doubt added much later, have served only to increase the difficulties, for they are usually wrong, and those which are the most circumstantial are liable to be the most wildly inaccurate. Thus a letter dated by mme Denis 2 September 1743 was actually written in the middle of February 1742; and another, dated by her 12 October 1745, can only have been written 7 December 1747.

Voltaire had a far greater knowledge of modern languages than was general in France at that time, or since for that matter. He wrote a large number of letters in English and Italian, and a certain number wholly or partly in Latin, Spanish and German. But they are all isolated letters, though the English ones are fairly numerous during Voltaire's stay in England in 1726-28, and the Italian ones when he was elected to many Italian academies in

5 *La Défense de mon oncle* (1767), vi.
6 See *Notebooks*, i.143.
7 Nearly all these and later love letters to mme Denis are now in the possession of the Pierpont Morgan library, and have been included in Best.D.

1745-46 (he never visited Italy). It is therefore one of the most interesting features of these love letters that a large proportion of them is in Italian, no doubt for prudential reasons.

On learning of the death of Denis Voltaire wrote to his widow: 'My tears moisten the paper as I write. . . . How I pity you, how greatly I feel for you in all your sorrow, how I fear for your health! . . . Leave Lille as quickly as you can. What can you do there but pine away with grief? Go to Paris. . . . Goodbye, be brave and philosophical. Life is a dream, and a sad dream, but live for your friends and for me who love you tenderly.'[8] Several letters of encouragement and advice followed, and in October Voltaire arrived in Paris for the rehearsals of the *Princess de Navarre*. We have already witnessed the agitated life he led at this time, but what did not then emerge was the fact that this agitation was partly due to constant efforts to be with mme Denis. Here are a few extracts from his letters to her in the '40s.

My beloved, I have been seriously ill. Had I not been held up by this mishap I would already have finished all the business that has kept me here [Versailles].[9]

I embrace you a thousand times, my beloved. I hope to dine with you on Wednesday.[10]

I counted on seeing you at Versailles, my dear, after the performance, but the plaguy tricks of the court arranged things quite otherwise.[11]

My dear, I am here as a victim to the duties of friendship, and also to the errors of prejudice. [He had gone to Châlons with mme Du Châtelet, whose son was ill there].[12]

What wretched fiend makes us both suffer, and suffer far from each other? If only we could suffer together! I am afraid to go to Etiole tomorrow [to see mme de Pompadour].[13]

I wish I could see you every day. The temple [his *Temple de la gloire*] does not prevent me from sleeping, but that of friendship is my cathedral and the heart of my religion.[14]

You should be at Versailles next Saturday at three o'clock in the afternoon [for a performance of the *Temple de la gloire*]. I will send you on Saturday a

8 Best.D2958 (18 April 1744).   12 Best.D3105 (20 April 1745).
9 Best.D3303 (1744/45).   13 Best.D3197 (18 August 1745).
10 Best.D3089 (28 March 1745).   14 Best.D3256 (1745).
11 Best.D3091 34 (1 April 1745).

little footman as big as my fist, who will guide you to the hole I inhabit, I will give you back your diamonds, accompany you to the theatre, and put you into your seat. Affectionate kisses.[15]

I don't know yet when my affairs will allow me to leave a place I abhor. The court, society, the great ones of the earth bore me. I shall be happy only when I can live with you. Your company, and better health would make me happy. A thousand kisses. My soul kisses yours, my prick and my heart are in love with you. I kiss your pretty bottom and all your adorable person.[16]

You have written me a ravishing letter, which I have kissed. I am not surprised that you write so well in Italian. It is very right and proper that you should be expert in the language of love. Good heavens! How do you manage? Are so many charms really buried in disuse? You, not going to bed with anyone? Oh my dear one, you insult your god. You tell me that my letter gave pleasure even to your senses. Mine are like yours, I could not read the delicious words you wrote me without feeling inflamed to the depths of my being. I paid your letter the tribute I should have liked to pay to the whole of your person. The pleasures of the senses pass and flee in the twinkle of an eye, but the affection that binds us, the mutual confidence, the pleasures of the heart, the sensual joys of the soul, are not destroyed and do not perish thus. I will love you until death.[17]

My dear, I have been unable to go out, my horses were ill and still are, just like their master.[18]

I intended, my dear, to go this evening to see my beloved, but I am being carried off by force to the other end of town.[19]

Don't come here for I shall be at the Italian theatre. I will come to you tomorrow. No more, I am with the lady [mme Du Châtelet] who watches me.[20]

I am obliged to go out but I shall be home by six o'clock. I will wait for you, my beloved.[21]

You wrote me a marvellously successful letter. I want to thank you for it [mme Denis endorsed this little note 'rimprovero al mio cuore', 'I reproach my heart'].[22]

I also was at the opera, my dear, and my enjoyment would have been redoubled if I had been at your side.[23]

The first thing I did on getting to Paris was to run to you; I spend the

15 Best.D3265 (2 December 1745).
16 Best.D3272 (December 1745).
17 Best.D3277 (27 December 1745).
18 Best.D3282 (1745/1746).
19 Best.D3283 (1745/1746).

20 Best.D3281 (1745/1746).
21 Best.D3286 (1745/1746).
22 Best.D3288 (1745/1746).
23 Best.D3291 (1745/1746).

first moment of the next day in writing to you, and the last will see me at your feet.[24]

My dear one, I have spent the whole day running from street to street. I'm exhausted. I shall not see you today. But my heart flies towards you, I kiss you tenderly, I will love you until death.[25]

Your letter consoles me for my misfortune in being at Versailles, for all the trouble I am obliged to take in order to obtain the most modest favour and to anticipate the harm people are always ready to do. I am very foolish and very unhappy not to live with you, peaceful and forgotten, far from kings, courtiers and mountebanks. These reflections throw me into despair. I blush to be so philosophical in theory, and such a wretched creature in practice.[26]

I beg you to be sober and to make me sober. I ask your leave to bring my limpness. It would be better to have an erection, but whether I have an erection or not, I will always love you, you will be the only consolation of my life.[27]

My dear, the king has given me the vacant appointment [of gentleman of the chamber], but the favours of kings are less dear to me than yours.[28]

Your busy friend and invalid loves you tenderly. His cruel law suit [against Travenol] greatly torments him, but his heart is always full of you.[29]

My angel, I am back from Sceaux, and if I can enjoy a little health today and have a little time I will come to see you, you who are all my consolation.[30]

How is my beloved? I have not yet seen her, but I am afire to see her every day, ever hour.[31]

My dear, I have been to Cirey, and from Cirey here is your vagabond lover at Lunéville, at the court of a king who has nothing of a king but goodness and greatness of soul. But how infinitely I would prefer your boudoir to any court![32]

If the play [*Sémiramis*] is well received at its first performance you will probably see me at the fourth. In any case, I must thank the king. But I shall be coming only for you, and if my miserable condition permits, I will throw myself at your knees and kiss all your beauties. In the meantime I press a thousand kisses on your round breasts, on your ravishing bottom, on all your person which has so often given me erections and plunged me in a flood of delight.[33]

24 Best.D3294 (1745/1746).
25 Best.D3296 (1745/1746).
26 Best.D3305 (January 1746).
27 Best.D3467 (c. 15 October 1746).
28 Best.D3492 (24 December 1746).
29 Best.D3563 (c. August 1747).
30 Best.D3589 (November/December 1747).
31 Best.D3598 (1747/1748).
32 Best.D3610 (1 February 1748).
33 Best.D3726 (27 July 1748).

I am in despair, there is no letter from you, I tremble lest you are ill. To crown all I am staying here [Cirey] until the 20th. I am far from well, and am taking the waters of Tancourt, near Cirey, I am told that they will do me good, but only your letters will do that. I implore you to let me know how you are and what is the affair you mentioned so mysteriously. Console me and love me. You should write discreetly, because letters are sometimes opened. Goodbye my dear muse. Write.[34]

What do you mean by the little fancies etc. which, you say, govern my life? Have I not opened my heart to you? Do you not know that I feel it a public duty not to create a sensation which would be turned to ridicule[35], that I have felt obliged to follow a particular line of action, to respect a union which has lasted for twenty years, and to seek even at the court of Lorraine and in the solitude where I now am [Cirey] a shelter against the persecutions with which I am constantly menaced?[36]

My dear, I fear that I shall not be able to kiss you today, so this day will be lost[37]. I am obliged to run about town, although I am suffering a little from yesterday evening's purge.[38]

How are you? I am very anxious about your health. Write me or have someone write. If you can go to hear the abbé d'Arty on St Louis's day, go with madame Dupin.[39]

My dear, I have just lost one who was my friend[40] for twenty years. You know that for a long time madame Du Châtelet had no longer been a woman to me, and I am confident that you share my cruel sorrow. To have seen her die, and in such circumstances! and for such a reason! It is frightful. I am not abandoning monsieur Du Châtelet in our mutual sorrow. We have to go to Cirey, there are important papers there. From Cirey I am returning to Paris to embrace you and to find in you my sole consolation and the only hope of my life.[41]

We have reached September 1749; we shall see much more of mme Denis, but after the death of mme Du Châtelet everything somehow changed. Let us resume the course of events.

34 Best.D3836 (29 December 1748).

35 By marrying his niece; it will be seen that Voltaire does not speak of a scandal but only of a sensation.

36 Best.D3851 (18 January 1749).

37 According to Suetonius (VIII. viii.1), Titus, having let a day pass without making a gift, exclaimed, 'Amici, diem perdidi', 'Friend, I have lost a day.

38 Best.D3892 (c. March 1749).

39 Best.D3987 (16 August 1749); the abbé's sermon was in fact written by Voltaire, as we shall see.

40 There is an untranslatable *nuance* here: Voltaire wrote 'un ami', in the masculine.

41 Best.D4015 (10 September 1749).

22. *Gentleman and scholar,*
1742-1746

NOW ONCE AGAIN we traverse a period of strife and controversy. The polemics arising out of new publications on Charles XII show Voltaire at his most mordant, but also at his wittiest[1]. But an encounter with the French censorship was less agreeable.

In a letter to Frederick Voltaire hinted that the king had got the better of Fleury in his recent negotiations with the French prime minister[2]. This letter was opened by the French censorship (as was no doubt everything Voltaire wrote to the king by post). Complex manœuvres then followed, the king advising Voltaire to flee to Berlin[3]; Voltaire making pacific gestures[4] to Fleury, partly because he was concerned for the fate of *Mahomet*, partly because he was anxious to be entrusted with a diplomatic mission to Prussia; the king writing him an *ostensible* letter[5] which could be shown to Fleury. The whole affair (which I have much simplified) provides matter for a disquisition on the theme of reality and appearance in eighteenth-century France. After much discussion everybody finally agreed that Voltaire's letter of 30 June had not been written nor received nor intercepted. Yet the authorities knew perfectly well that the open letter of 6 September was a concoction, for apart from anything else Voltaire had clumsily altered the date. The facts, however, were of no importance, for Fleury was just as anxious at this moment, when Frederick had denounced his alliance with France, to use Voltaire, as Voltaire was to be used: and so long as appearances could be kept up, that was all that mattered.

Hardly had all this excitement died down than Voltaire found himself caught up in the Didot-Barois affair, in which he had to

1 See pp. 161-162, above.
2 Best.D2623 (30 June 1742).
3 Best.D2630 (*c.* 1 August 1742).

4 Best.D2644 (22 August 1742).
5 Best.D2652 (6 September 1742).

complain of editions of his works which were not only unauthorised, but contained scandalous writings not by him. In this business, as always in such cases, Voltaire took scrupulous care not to
injure the little men caught up in the machinations of the principal
offenders. Indeed, he finally bought up and destroyed the entire
edition so that nobody (except, of course, himself, the aggrieved
party) should suffer financial loss. In any case, the two offending
booksellers had nothing to fear, for one of them had catalogued
the library of the duc de Béthune's uncle; and as this library was
coming up for sale, the duke asked for and obtained the immediate
release of both men[6].

In a sense Frederick dominates this period, for his offer of
asylum (however selfish), together with his victories in the field,
again aroused hopes that he might after all turn out to be, if a
despot, at least a benevolent one. Yet the little conspiracy between
him, Fleury and Voltaire, provided the last with little comfort,
for there followed immediately the virulent campaign against
Mahomet, in which the French authorities showed as much animus
against Voltaire as the worst of his open enemies.

Still, with great but perhaps regrettable ingenuity Voltaire
turned his disgrace to advantage. He convinced the government
that it would be a good thing for him to accept Frederick's offers
of asylum, for then the king, considering him to be out of favour
in France, would reveal to him his political and military intentions.
Voltaire in the role of a diplomatic 'observer' is not a pleasing
spectacle, not because he did anything particularly disgraceful
(what is a breach of hospitality in the balance of international
affairs?), but because he could have spent his time so much better.
On the other hand, Voltaire must not even here be judged like
other men, for his powers of work and concentration were so great
that he could conduct half-a-dozen careers simultaneously.

Be this as it may, Voltaire was successful enough in his preliminary efforts, though he was less so when he came to real grips
with the king: for Voltaire was too impulsive for this kind of
work, and Frederick was too wily for him. Voltaire sent home a

6 See the notes on Best.D2710 (24
December 1742).

number of well-informed despatches[7], filled with reflections of more than average ambassadorial penetration, and with information derived from excellent sources such as a number of envoys, including Robert Hampden-Trevor, the English ambassador at The Hague[8]. Above all, he had won over, in genuine friendship, Wilhelm van Haren, the Dutch poet and statesman, and had inspired a profound affection in count von Podewils[9], the Prussian ambassador to the states-general. These and many other contacts (such as Frederick, margrave of Brandenburg-Bayreuth), enabled Voltaire to send his minister often valuable details about Prussian and Dutch finances, the movement of the Prussian king's forces and military supplies, and many other things. From Charlottenburg Voltaire sent home a detailed report[10] of a political conversation with Frederick, a despatch which must have been of profound interest to those whose business it was to read the king's mind.

At any rate Voltaire's despatches were agreeable to the French government, who sent him a letter of cordial thanks. They were very pleased with his activities, said Amelot de Chaillou, and owed him all the gratitude he deserved.[11] So Voltaire was not exaggerating when he claimed that he 'performed a singular service to the king his master'[12]. However, when, weary of the king's generalities, Voltaire finally got down to brass tacks by sending Frederick a set of questions, the king amused himself by answering them with marginal comments such as 'I admire the wisdom of France but heaven preserve me from ever imitating it'[13]. And when Voltaire asked him how he could resist the power of Austria, Frederick replied:

> On les y recevra, biribi,
> A la façon de Barbari, mon ami.[14]

7 Best.D2792-D2960 (July 1742-April 1744; some of these letters are in code), and Best.app.D67; in the meanwhile Fleury had died (29 January 1743) and was succeeded by Amelot de Chaillou as foreign minister.

8 The gift of a coach to Bruzen de La Martinière, in a letter containing references to several envoys, is significant; see Best.D2906 (3 January 1744).

9 See his letter to Voltaire of 21 September 1743 (Best.D2846).

10 Best.D2828 (3 September 1743).

11 Best.D2818 (22 August 1743).

12 See the autobiography, p. 637, below.

13 Best.D2830 (c. 5 September 1743).

14 This echo of a popular song is untranslatable, but means roughly 'We shall receive them with firmness and laughter'.

I am not prepared to assert that Voltaire's diplomatic mission was in accordance with the highest principles of friendship; nor do I claim that two blacks make a white; but I must point out that Frederick's treachery was of a far darker character than Voltaire's. After all, the *philosophe*, however famous, was a private person, whereas the king possessed the powers of a throne, and the spectacle of Frederick II, king of Prussia, deploying all his resources to enmesh Voltaire is revolting. There is no doubt that he did deliberately try to disgust the French government with Voltaire in order to get him to leave France. Nor was this infamy a momentary impulse, for the plot was, as usual, most carefully mounted. First Frederick composed some lines of verse, in which, among other things, Louis XV is called 'the most stupid of kings'. The Prussian king then told count von Rothenburg, his ambassador at the French court, that these lines were by Voltaire, and he did not hesitate to add, in clear terms and in writing, 'I want to embroil him for ever with France, so that I can get him to Berlin'. Fortunately for Voltaire, Frederick's literary skill was far below his powers of intrigue, and he made a mess of his plot by joining the fake verse to an authentic line of Voltaire's prose, and this disgusted even Rothenburg.[15] Frederick was so sure that his conspiracy would succeed that he prepared quarters in Berlin for Voltaire, and when the plot failed he almost went down on his knees: 'Choose an apartment or a house; arrange for yourself all you need for the comfort and luxury of your life; let your circumstances be such as you need to make you happy. I will see to the rest. You will always be free and entirely the master of your fate. I seek to claim you only by friendship and an agreeable life.'[16] And when even this did not tempt the fly, the royal spider had to beg his victim not to expose him to the disgrace of having furnished a house for him in vain.[17]

And what did Voltaire say when he learned the details of Frederick's manœuvre? Far from being flattered by the Prussian king's determination to possess him, he wrote to Amelot in prophetic terms which show that he was under no illusions about

---

15 The evidence for this squalid affair is set out in a note on Best. D2813 (17 August 1743).

16 Best.D2855 (7 October 1743).
17 Best.D2885 (14 November 1743).

the king's purpose: 'Not being able to win me over in any other way he thought he could do it by disgracing me in France, but I swear that I would sooner live in a Swiss village than enjoy at such a price the dangerous favours of a king capable of imparting treachery into friendship itself. I have no wish for the palace of Alcina[18] in which one is a slave because one is loved.'[19]

In the midst of all this Voltaire found time to seek admission to the Academy, unsuccessfully, and to respond, with the perspicacity and generosity he always showed in such cases, to the first letter from the young and unknown Vauvenargues, the writings of whose last years owe so much to Voltaire's encouragement. This first letter to the young soldier-philosopher is a model of its kind. He takes very seriously Vauvenargues's literary doubts, answers them at length and with great care, and concludes: 'The mass of judges finally decides in accordance with the views of the en-lightened minority; you appear to me, sir, to be at the head of this enlightened minority. I am sorry that the career of arms which you have chosen keeps you far from the city in which I should be able to profit from your wisdom.' Unfortunately the noble, the serene Vauvenargues was only 32 when he died. Twenty years later Voltaire still spoke of him with tenderness: he lived a sage and died a hero; Voltaire would always cherish his memory.[20]

This correspondence was a pleasant interlude, and Voltaire enjoyed in these troubled times as pleasant a success, the triumph of *Mérope*. This tragedy was inspired by the *Meropa* of Maffei, which had been performed in Paris in 1717. Voltaire began work on his in 1736, revised it almost continuously for several years, and it was finally produced on 20 February 1743. It was an im-mense critical and popular success, and was even accorded the dubious honour of being adapted by Frederick as an opera. The Jesuit Tournemine regarded it as a model of tragedy[21], and this several years before the play was performed. So great was the popular success that the author's share of the proceeds broke all records; and indeed, when the tragedy was first revised in Feb-ruary/March 1744 the attendance was greater than during the first

---

18 In Ariosto's *Orlando furioso*.
19 Best.D2854 (5 October 1743).
20 Best.D2748 (15 April 1743),

D11766 (13 March 1764).
21 Best.D1705 (23 December 1738).

run. All this was the more remarkable in that the tragedy had what was regarded as a fatal defect: it had no love interest. Voltaire himself pointed out in his autobiography that *Mérope* was 'the first piece, not upon a sacred subject, that succeeded without the aid of an amorous passion'. The first night, indeed, was a double first: the author was called for. This had never happened before in the entire history of the French theatre. Mouhy, a police informant who had been much helped by Voltaire, and was therefore no friend of his, reported: 'The success of *Mérope* was one of the most dazzling ever seen. The audience not only brought down the house, but even asked Voltaire a thousand times to appear on the stage.'[22]

All this was not undeserved, though it is difficult to be sure that the most interesting aspects of *Mérope* were in fact perceived. Indeed, there is some reason to suppose that they were not. For instance, no one seems to have noticed that *Mérope* has the same theme, though disguised, as *Mahomet*. Thus, Polyphonte, the tyrant of Messène, is thus described:

> La fière ambition dont il est dévoré
> Est inquiète, ardente, et n'a rien de sacré. . . .
> Il agit pour lui seul, il veut tout asservir.[23]

And there is a repeated insistence on his need for blind zeal and fear in his followers, and even on priestly corruption.[24] Egalitarian sentiments are also expressed in a surprisingly outspoken way. Voltaire went out of his way to reproduce from his early *Eriphyle* the line

> Qui sert bien son pays n'a pas besoin d'aïeux.[25]

And in the same scene Polyphonte adds:

> Le droit de commander n'est plus un avantage
> Transmis par la nature, ainsi qu'un héritage.[26]

22 See the notes on Best.D2727 (21 February 1743), D2744 (4 April 1743); and the autobiography, p. 636, below.

23 I.ii; 'The proud ambition by which he is devoured is restless, fiery, and holds nothing sacred. . . . He acts only for himself, and seeks to enslave all.'

24 See Ridgway, *La propaganda philosophique dans les tragédies de Voltaire*, p. 141.

25 I.iii (*Eriphyle*, II.i); 'One who serves his country well needs no ancestors.'

26 I.iii; 'The right to command is no longer a privilege transmitted by nature like an inheritance.'

Another interesting feature of *Mérope*, at least to us, is the personage of Egisthe, something new on the French stage, the 'virtuous man brought up far from cities and courts in an atmosphere of rustic simplicity' (II.ii). When Egisthe says that his 'virtuous father, under his rustic roof, does good, obeys the law, and fears only the gods', he is speaking the language Rousseau was later to make fashionable.

From about this time dates an amusing little essay which again displays Voltaire's humane and witty curiosity, and his skill in bringing home to men the absurdity of their own prejudices. He writes about a little white animal he had recently seen in Paris, with white wool on its head and face, and pink eyes. 'This animal is called a *man*, because it has the gift of speech, memory, a little of what is called *reason*, and a sort of face.' He then notes that these albinos are despised by their normal fellows. Any black woman making love to one of these creatures would be ridiculed and despised. But, he concludes, if we think ourselves superior to them on that account we are making a terrible mistake.[27]

When the king offered the court the usual splendid celebration of his heir's marriage to Maria Theresa of Spain (who died not long after in childbirth) Voltaire was asked to compose an 'entertainment'. It was a wretched task, done to a precise specification, almost in committee, and in constant conflict with Richelieu, who was in charge of the ceremonies. But Voltaire thought it necessary to seek the favour of the court[28]. *La Princesse de Navarre* was duly put together, and it was produced with much magnificence and some success, to which the splendid decorations by Charles Nicolas Cochin no doubt contributed, although the performance was seen in conditions of considerable discomfort. The king arrived an hour late, no doubt intentionally. The whole thing had been a terrible burden for Voltaire, not relieved, though certainly not appreciably increased by the death of his brother (18 February 1745), who left him a life interest in half his estate, as he was obliged to do by the terms of his father's will.[29] Voltaire had to establish himself for months on end in the palace, where he was

27 *Relation touchant un maure blanc amené d'Afrique à Paris en 1744.*
28 Best.D2999 (11 July 1744).

29 Armand's will and related documents form Best.app.D69.

given vile quarters[30]. He had become, he complained, the king's buffoon at the age of fifty, more embarrassed with musicians, decorators, actors, actresses, singers, dancers, than were all the electors who hoped to become emperors of Germany. 'I run from Paris to Versailles, I write verse in post-chaises. I have to praise the king loudly, *madame la dauphine* delicately, the royal family softly, satisfy the court, without displeasing the town.

> Qu'il vaut mieux obéir aux loix
> De son cœur et de son génie
> Que de travailler pour des rois!'[31]

Still, having set his shoulder to the wheel, Voltaire continued his efforts to get it to the top of the mountain of royal favour. He composed also an ode[32] and an opera[33] in honour of the king's victories in Flanders, more memorable for Rameau's music than for Voltaire's text, which no doubt the composer maltreated, for he had a great contempt for mere words. The new courtier finished up with the popular, if not the artistic, triumph of the *Poème de Fontenoy*. The battle (11 May 1745) had no great strategic consequences. Its outcome was the result of chance and purpose in about the usual proportions. Heroism and cruelty were seen on both sides, but victory was with the French, and this was in itself the real significance of the battle to Voltaire and his fellow-countrymen. The defeat of Cumberland was made to appear as the revenge for the British victory at Dettingen under his father George II. For Voltaire the battle had an additional interest: two of his closest friends since schooldays were the marquis d'Argenson, the foreign minister, and Richelieu, who took a prominent, according to Voltaire a decisive, part in the battle. And moreover Argenson, only four days after the battle, found time to write Voltaire in his own hand a detailed account[34] of it, which he took good care to spread abroad, for the greater glory of the king and his minister. It is therefore understandable that Voltaire should have been inspired to write this patriotic poem, a sonorous roll-

---

30 See p. 155, above.
31 Best.D3073 (31 January 1754). 'How much better it is to follow the dictates of one's heart and one's genius than to labour for kings!'

32 *Discours sur les événements de l'année 1744.*
33 *Le Temple de la gloire.*
34 Best.D3118 (15 May 1745).

call of many of the greatest names of France. It went at once into numerous editions all over France, becoming a genuinely nation-wide best-seller, and was even accorded the very rare honour (under Louis xv) of being printed at the royal press in the Louvre. Voltaire's triumph as a courtier seemed to be complete.

And when all was won, what did Voltaire feel about this fac-titious glory? We need remain in no doubt. When the maréchal de Saxe reported that the king was very pleased, and found the poem to be above criticism, Voltaire ironically commented that this showed Louis xv to be the greatest connoisseur of his kingdom:

> Mon Henri quatre et ma *Zaïre*,
> Et mon Américaine *Alzire*,
> Ne m'ont valu jamais un seul regard du roi;
> J'avais mille ennemis avec très peu de gloire:
> Les honneurs et les biens pleuvent enfin sur moi
> Pour une farce de la foire.[35]

Throughout this time Voltaire maintained that he was not at court, but merely at Versailles[36]: at any rate he was there assidu-ously, and showed every sign of enjoying his favour and of acclimatising himself to the glimpses of the sun.

As a matter of set policy—let there be no doubt about this—Voltaire continued to surround himself with all possible safe-guards. Wealth he had already secured, and this was the most important protection, for only by being rich could he secure mobility. The favour of the king was invaluable if it could be obtained, which was difficult, but had been accomplished in a measure; and it had to be retained, which Voltaire knew to be unlikely. Nor were other measures neglected, and an important one was the membership of famous academies, above all the Académie française, to which he was finally elected at the age of fifty-two, after having been more than once rejected. Even after the triumph of *Mérope* four successive candidates, not one of whom had the slightest literary genius, were given the preference. This time Voltaire was not inclined to go through the manœuvres then

35 Best.D3135 (3 June 1745); 'My *Henriade* and my *Zaïre* and my American *Alzire*, never won me a single glance from the king; I had a thousand enemies and very little glory; honours and benefits at last shower on me for a fair-ground farce'; see the autobiography, p. 640, below.

36 Best.3018 (17 January 1746).

and now inseparable from election to the Academy. He made it clear to the Argentals that others would have to prepare the ground. 'V. is ill, V. is not in a fit state to bustle about, V. is growing grey and cannot decently knock on doors, though he counts on the king's consent. He tenderly thanks his adorable angels. He would be very flattered to be wanted, but he would not care to make advances.' Still, he did after all go through some of the motions, including an eloquent display of his admiration for the Jesuits[37]. The king at last gave his consent, and this time all went smoothly. The voting was as always the most open of secrets: Voltaire said that his election was unanimous[38], though tradition has it that a single vote was cast against him. It was one thing to reject a man who was universally admitted to reign over the republic of letters ('When Louis xv sat on the throne, Voltaire was king'), but it was impossible to deny immortality to a man in favour at court.

Elected 25 April 1746, received 9 May, Voltaire occupied the twelfth fauteuil, and no better indication of the measure by which he towers over French literature can be given than by enumerating those who were elected to his seat before him: Voiture (1634), Mézeray (1649), Jean Barbier d'Aucour (1683), François de Clermont-Tonnerre, bishop of Noyon (1694), Malézieu (1701), Bouhier (1727); and after him: Ducis (1779), comte Raymond de Sèze (1816), baron Amable Guillaume Prosper Brugière de Barante (1828), the Oratorian Alphonse Joseph Auguste Gratry (1868), Saint-René Taillandier (1873), Maxime Du Camp (1880), Paul Bourget (1894), Edmond Jaloux (1936), Jean Louis Vaudoyer (1950), Marcel Brion (1964)—a list which shows that immortality does at least stimulate longevity: only seventeen men have occupied this seat in well over three centuries.

At that time the speeches new members of the Academy had to deliver had already been frozen by tradition into the most boring of forms: a salute to the memory of the founder, cardinal de Richelieu, and a panegyric of the new Academician's immediate predecessor. Needless to say Voltaire's *discours de réception* broke this mould. He disposed of Richelieu and the learned Bouhier in a couple of pages, and the rest of the oration, though laconic

37 Best.3038 (20 March 1746).   38 Best.D3370.

by modern standards, covers a great deal of ground. Voltaire analysed the nature of the French language, and defended its shortcomings in his usual formula: a great part of merit consists in triumphing over difficulties. He then dealt briefly with the greatest of French writers of the past: Corneille, Montaigne, Marot, Boileau, Malherbe, and above all, Racine (who was paid the delicate compliment of not being named). Salutes were then addressed to Frederick, his sister Ulrica (now queen of Sweden), and Elizabeth, empress of Russia, monarchs who admired French culture. Finally, Voltaire devoted a few graceful words to some contemporary French writers: Hénault, Montesquieu, the young Vauvenargues, the elder Crébillon, Fontenelle, Olivet. And the discourse concluded by tactfully reminding the king that the greatest glory of his predecessor, Louis XIV, lay in his encouragement of the arts.

Voltaire was also named at this time to a goodly number of other eminent academies: those of La Rochelle, Marseille, Lyon, Bordeaux, Angers, and probably others in France; he was already a member of the Royal Societies of London and Edinburgh; and he was now elected in rapid succession to the Arcadia, Crusca, Apatisti, Botanica of Florence, Etrusca of Cortona, Intronati.

As a polite way of thanking these last academies Voltaire composed an Italian essay on the changes which the earth has undergone[39]. This essay is decidedly interesting, for it shows once again the width of his interests and reading; but it also shows what was perhaps the most serious flaw in Voltaire's intellectual make-up: his conviction that all problems could be resolved by enlightened common-sense. It was a pardonable mistake on the part of a highly intelligent and erudite man who was sometimes put off balance by the fact that he could establish no scientific truth without destroying a received article of religious faith. And this was particularly true in all matters concerning the earth, its structure, its age and the like.

Thus, geology and palaeontology still being in their infancy, it

---

39 *Saggio intorno ai cambiamenti avvenuti su'l globo della terra*; only the French translation is printed in the standard editions; for the Italian text the original *Saggio* (Parigi 1746) must be consulted until the appropriate volume of the *Complete works* is reached.

was not yet possible confidently to explain the presence of fossil shells far from the sea. Enlightened theologians found the explanation in Noah's flood. Could they not rather have been deposited by the pilgrims and crusaders? asked Voltaire. The suggestion is elegant and sensible, but the theologians were by accident nearer to the truth. The life of reason is not immune from these little mishaps.

By means in part of his membership of so many learned societies Voltaire finally set the seal of conventional approval on his international reputation. He had been widely known abroad since the production of *Œdipe* in 1718, but only to an élite: now his fame had penetrated to the entire reading public of the western world, a fact underlined by the ever-increasing number of translations of his works into foreign languages.

Moreover on 1 April 1745 the king appointed Voltaire historiographer of France, and on 22 December 1746 a gentleman of the bedchamber[40]. The latter of these honours had at least a cash value, for in 1749 the king signed a further warrant, authorising Voltaire to sell the title while continuing to use it: his way of giving a valuable present at no cost to himself. This one yielded Voltaire the useful sum of 53,000 francs[41].

As for his 'historiography', though he called it 'a pompous trifle'[42], and though it had hitherto been regarded as a sinecure, Voltaire took his new title very seriously. Let this English letter witness. Voltaire wrote it when he learned that the duke of Cumberland's secretary during the recent campaign had the same name as his old friend Everard Fawkener. Voltaire wrote:

S^r,

You bear a name that j love and respect; j have these twenty years since the honour to be a friend to Sr Evrard Fawkener. J hope t'is a recommendation towards you. A better one is my love for truth; j am bound to speak it. My duty is to write the history of the late campains. And my king and my country will approve me the more, the greater justice j'll render to the English.

Tho our nations are ennemies at present, yet they ought forever to entertain a mutual esteem for one another; my intention is to relate what the duke of Cumberland has done worthy of himself and his name and to enregister

40 For the texts of the royal warrants see notes on Best.D3092 and D3494.

41 The documents are now Th. B.

42 See the autobiography, p. 639, below.

the most particular and noble actions of y^r chiefs and officers which deserve to be recorded, and what pass'd more worthy of praise at Dettingen and Fontenoy, particularities, if there are any, about general Campbel's death, in short all that deserves to be transmitted to posterity.

J dare apply to you s^r on that purpose. If you are so kind as to send me some mémoirs, j'll make use of 'em. If not j'll content my self with relating what had been acted noble and glorious on our side, and j'll mourn to leave in silence many great actions done by y^r nation which j would have been glorious to relate. . . .'[43]

After this flood of titles and honours, it does not surprise us to find an Italian letter sent through the post to 'Monsieur de Voltaire, very famous Savant, Paris'[44].

> His lockèd, lettered, braw brass collar,
> Shew'd him the gentleman and scholar.[45]

With all this Voltaire still found time to travel, to take part in amateur theatricals at Anet, to settle in their favour the seemingly interminable lawsuit of the Du Châtelets, to prepare in great detail the first Walther edition of his collected works, and to exhaust himself in a senseless law suit with the violinist Travenol[46], who was only a symbol. On Voltaire's election his enemies 'filled Paris, and, to Voltaire's excruciated sense, the Universe, with their howlings and their hyaena-laughter, with their pasquils, satires, old and new. So that Voltaire could not stand it; and, in an evil hour, rushed down stairs upon them; seized one poor dog, Travenol, unknown to him as Fiddler or otherwise; pinioned Dog Travenol, with pincers, by the ears. . . .'[47]

Almost incidentally Voltaire drafted one of the most successful of his tragedies, *Sémiramis* (produced in 1748), and, most astonishing of all, without any outward and visible foreshadowing, he wrote his first story. This came about, with other more immediately significant consequences, as a result of Voltaire's irritated, but probably perfectly justified exclamation that she was playing with cheats, when he saw mme Du Châtelet losing large sums of money gambling at court. Immediate flight was indicated, a refuge

43 Best.D3226 (1 October 1745); the two Fawkeners were in fact one.
44 Best.D3379 (10 May 1746).
45 Robert Burns, *The Twa dogs*, 13-14.

46 For this very complex affair see Best.app.D73.
47 Carlyle, *History of Friedrich II of Prussia*, XVI.ii.

was offered by that 'sublime old personage' the duchesse Du Maine at Sceaux, and there Voltaire wrote his first stories to amuse his hosts. In congratulating the comte d'Argenson on the victory of Lauffeldt, Voltaire began his letter, written in oriental style: 'The angel Jesrad has brought even to Memnon the news of your brilliant successes', and so, out of a blue sky, came the first news of one of Voltaire's greatest achievements, his creation of the French *conte philosophique*[48]. At Sceaux were written *Babouc*, *Le Crocheteur borgne*, *Cosi-sancta* and *Memnon*[49], which later became *Zadig*, one of the best of Voltaire's stories.

With his flight to Sceaux came to an end Voltaire's painful efforts to acquire favour at the French court. During this period he also indulged in the innocent fun of a correspondence with the pope[50]; and at the end of 1745 Jean Jacques Rousseau makes his first appearance on our scene, in an exchange of letters filled with elaborate courtesy and even some regard on both sides. Rousseau's first words to Voltaire were: 'I have been working for fifteen years to become worthy of your attention and of the solicitude with which you favour the young muses in whom you find some talent.' And he goes on to ask for Voltaire's approval of some changes he had made in the *Princesse de Navarre* while setting it to music.[51] Voltaire's first words to Rousseau were: 'You unite two talents which so far have always been distinct. These are already two good reasons for me to esteem you and to seek to love you.' And he goes on to give his usual careful and detailed reply to Rousseau's request.[52]

48 It is hardly possible to say anything of this kind about Voltaire without introducing an immediate qualification; in 1739 (Best.D2033) he mentioned a *Voyage de monsieur le baron de Gangan*, which may well have been the first draft of *Micromégas*.

49 This *Memnon* must not be confused with the much shorter *Memnon* of 1749/50, which is a quite distinct story.

50 Best.D3192, D3193, D3210, D3232 (August-October 1745).

51 Best.D3269 (11 December 1745).

52 Best.D3270 (15 December 1745).

23. Farewell to Cirey, 1747-1750

IN THE *Henriade* (ix.125-8) Voltaire had sung the beauties of
the *chateau* d'Anet, built by Henri II for Diane de Poitiers,
and now the summer home of the duchesse Du Maine. This
ungrateful lady had the talented mme de Launay (baroness de
Staal) in her service, treating her as little more than a waiting-
woman. Her presence at Anet is our good fortune, for in a series
of letters[1] to mme Du Deffand she has left us a sparkling account
of a visit by Voltaire and mme Du Châtelet in August 1747. They
turned up at midnight like two ghosts, smelling like embalmed
corpses risen from the tomb. But they were hungry ghosts, and
also wanted beds, which were not ready. Voltaire was quite
satisfied. Not so mme Du Châtelet, who had to make her own bed,
and complained of the bugs. Still, they would be good value, for
they were going to rehearse a comedy.[2]

The apparitions did not show themselves before the evening,
for one was writing about noble deeds (*Sémiramis?*) and the other
was annotating Newton. They neither played nor walked. Mme
Du Châtelet could not stand her second room, it was noisy and
the chimney had more smoke than fire. So she moved again. She
preferred her studies to all amusements and persisted in showing
herself only as the night fell. Voltaire made up for this by writing
some gallant verse. The comedy was duly performed, the author
providing a special prologue, which he delivered himself. But as
soon as the guests left, Anet was upset by a long letter[3] from Voltaire: he had mislaid his manuscript, forgotten to collect the individual actors' parts, and lost the prologue. All must be found

---

1 Best.D3562,   D3565-9   (15-30
August 1747).
  2 Voltaire's *Le Comte de Boursoufle*,
now known as *L'Echange*; this must
not be confused with *Les Originaux*,
also called at first *Le Comte de Bour-*

soufle; at the time they were referred
to respectively as the *Petit* and *Grand
Boursoufle*.
  3 If it ever existed, it has not survived.

and must be kept under lock and key, not sent by post, because he was afraid that the play would be copied.

After they had left it was found that mme Du Châtelet had collected all sorts of tables in her room: huge ones for her papers, solid ones for her dressing-cases, light ones for gew-gaws. For all that, ink had been spilled on her algebra. Still, mlle de Launay missed the queen and her slave. What would the sprightly Launay have said had she known that Voltaire, in the midst of Newton, noble deeds and theatricals, found time to assure his niece that 'my heart and my prick send you their tenderest compliments'[4]? And how she would have giggled had she known that the chaste Marie Louise altered 'cazzo' in her uncle's letter (for Voltaire, as usual, had written in Italian) to 'spirito'.

Hardly had the strange queen and her still stranger slave returned to Paris than they found themselves involved in one of those pointless and elaborate intrigues which served to occupy the bored courtiers of the *ancien régime*. First of all there was the incident of Voltaire's anger on seeing mme Du Châtelet losing large sums playing cards at the queen's table, hardly the way to become popular at court—I mean of course Voltaire's anger, not mme Du Châtelet's losses. Later the queen, mme de Pompadour, the dauphine, and even, unwittingly, Ulrica of Prussia, were involved in an even more momentous affair. In brief, Voltaire was accused of having lacked in courtesy towards Marie Leszczinska by being too friendly with mme de Pompadour.[5] The whole thing was the absurdest of storms in the most fragile of tea-cups, but at least it is not true, as often alleged, that Voltaire was exiled. Still, exiled or not, he and mme Du Châtelet did leave Paris, Voltaire bidding farewell with profound relief to his career as a man about court.

By this time mme Du Maine had returned for the winter to Sceaux, where the queen and her slave made the apparition mentioned at the end of the previous chapter. Voltaire's comedy *La Prude* was given its first performance on 15 December 1747, and operas were also performed, mme Du Châtelet taking the leading role, Voltaire tells us, 'with nobility and grace. Four thousand

---

4 Best.D3566 (*c.* 25 August 1747).
5 Desnoiresterres devotes many pages to this affair (iii.148-58), not always too accurately.

diamonds formed the least of her ornaments.'[6] This invitation was sent out for *La Prude*:

New actors will perform a new comedy, in verse and in five acts, on Friday, 15 December, in the theatre of Sceaux.

All are welcome, without ceremony. You are requested to be there at six o'clock precisely and to give orders for your carriage to be in the court-yard between half past seven and eight. After six o'clock the door will not be opened for anyone.[7]

It was here also, as we have seen, that Voltaire now wrote his first stories, including *Memnon* and *Zadig*.

When the couple left for Cirey in January 1748, a spring of their coach broke about forty miles out of Paris. Although they had two postilions and two valets with them, more help had to be sent for. It was the middle of the night, and very cold, but the travellers settled down on cushions laid on the snow and contemplated the firmament before resuming their journey. Their talk must have been worth hearing.

Voltaire and mme Du Châtelet then spent some time at the court of Lorraine. Stanislas was perhaps slightly ridiculous, but he was nevertheless an amiable man, whose good taste has left ample traces at Lunéville, Commercy and in the ravishing square named after him at Nancy. The former king of Poland had surrounded himself with a group of courtiers whose wit and elegance exhausted their resources. Nothing is more dreary than ex-courts. And indeed there was little enough here to attract Voltaire, though Stanislas fancied himself as a thinker, with such lamentable consequences that when he published *Le Philosophe chrétien* (*The Christian philosopher*), the queen of France, his daughter, took it to be atheistic, and blamed Voltaire for having corrupted her father. On a more material plane Voltaire found some cause for complaint in the lack of comfort at Lunéville. On 29 August 1749 he wrote to Alliot, the king's steward, at nine o'clock in the morning, to complain in general terms. A quarter of an hour later he wrote again, more sharply. Half an hour passed without a reply,

---

6 Best.D3590 (November/December 1747).

7 [Charles Philippe d'Albert], duc de Luynes, *Mémoires* (1860-5), viii.353.

It can be seen that the duchesse Du Maine's hospitality was not generous: the guests must have been despatched without so much as a cup of coffee.

and Voltaire, his patience exhausted, addressed himself direct to Stanislas. 'Sire', he wrote, 'when one is in paradise one must apply to god.' He was not well, he was working very hard, he lacked necessities. 'When Virgil was in the house of Augustus, Allyotus his aulic counsellor, provided Virgil with bread, wine and candles I am ill today, and I have neither bread nor wine for dinner.'[8]

The reason for Voltaire's prolonged stay at Lunéville and its satellite houses, with Cirey only a few miles away, is found in a farce which turned to tragedy: mme Du Châtelet, now a grand-mother, but still only forty-one, had fallen desperately in love with the self-styled marquis de Saint-Lambert. She prolonged her stay at the court of Lorraine for his sake, and Voltaire remained for hers, for he well knew what was going on, and took it in an admirably civilised way, as can be seen in these characteristic lines he addressed to Saint-Lambert and which, for once, I quote in full, for they paint admirably well the sunny side of this departed civilisation. The lines are too charming and affecting to be muti-lated:

> Tandis qu'au-dessus de la terre,
> Des aquilons et du tonnerre,
> La belle amante de Newton
> Dans les routes de la lumière
> Conduit le char de Phaéton,
> Sans verser dans cette carrière,
> Nous attendons paisiblement,
> Près de l'onde castalienne,
> Que notre héroine revienne
> De son voyage au firmament;
> Et nous assemblons pour lui plaire,
> Dans ces vallons et dans ces bois,
> Les fleurs dont Horace autrefois
> Faisait des bouquets pour Glycère.
> Saint-Lambert, ce n'est que pour toi
> Que ces belles fleurs sont écloses;
> C'est ta main qui cueille les roses,
> Et les épines sont pour moi.
> Ce vieillard chenu qui s'avance,
> Le Temps, dont je subis les lois,
> Sur ma lyre a glacé mes doigts,
> Et des organes de ma voix

8 D3997-D4006 (29 August 1749).

Fait trembler la sourde cadence.
Les Grâces dans ces beaux vallons,
Les dieux de l'amoureux délire,
Ceux de la flûte et de la lyre,
T'inspirent tes aimables sons,
Avec toi dansent aux chansons,
Et ne daignent plus me sourire.
Dans l'heureux printemps de tes jours
Des dieux du Pinde et des amours
Saisis la faveur passagère;
C'est le temps de l'illusion.
Je n'ai plus que de la raison:
Encore, hélas! n'en ai-je guère.

   Mais je vois venir sur le soir,
Du plus haut de son aphélie,
Notre astronomique Emilie
Avec un vieux tablier noir,
Et la main d'encre encor salie,
Elle a laissé là son compas,
Et ses calculs, et sa lunette;
Elle reprend tous ses appas:
Porte-lui vite à sa toilette
Ces fleurs qui naissent sous tes pas,
Et chante-lui sur ta musette
Ces beaux air que l'Amour répète,
Et que Newton ne connut pas.[9]

---

9 *Epître à monsieur de Saint-Lambert;* 'While the beautiful lover of Newton conducts Phaeton's chariot in the paths of light, above the earth, the winds and the thunder, we calmly await by the fountain of Castalia, without sharing her adventure, our heroine's return from her voyage to the firmament, and we assemble to please her, in these valleys and woods, the flowers which formerly Horace made into nosegays for Glycera. Saint-Lambert, these lovely flowers have ripened only for you; it is your hand that gathers the roses, and the thorns are for me. This hoary old man who approaches, Time, to whose law I am subject, has frozen my fingers on the lyre, and makes to tremble the dull cadences of my voice. The Graces of these lovely vales, the gods of amorous frenzy, those of the flute and the lyre, inspire your amiable lines, dance and sing with you, and no longer deign to smile for me. In the happy spring of your days seize the passing favours of the gods of Pindus and of love; it is the time of illusion. I no longer have anything but reason: and even of that I am deprived. But it is evening, and I see our astronomic Emily descending from the height of her aphelion, wearing an old black apron, her hand still stained with ink. She has left her compass, and her calculations, and her telescope; she recaptures all her charms: take quickly to her dressing-table these flowers which grow beneath your feet, and sing her on your pipes the lovely airs rehearsed by Love, and unknown to Newton.'

Saint-Lambert (1716-1803) was a soldier, and a poet more ambitious than talented. He would now be forgotten but for a rare distinction: he joined Voltaire in the heart of mme Du Châtelet, and rivalled Jean Jacques Rousseau in that of the comtesse d'Houdetot. He was the kind of man (Maupertuis was another) not liked by other men, but whose personal charm is evoked by women, with whom he is therefore popular. Saint-Lambert, if he loved mme Du Châtelet at all, certainly loved her less than she loved him. Her letters[10] to him are deeply pathetic, but also, it must be admitted, monuments of incessant, almost hysterical nagging. The hectic, perfervid affair came to an end with mme Du Châtelet's pregnancy, and her death in childbirth on 10 September 1749.

Voltaire had written to several friends that mme Du Châtelet, working at her desk on Newton, exclaimed: 'I feel something.' This something was a little girl, who was laid on a big book. The mother went to bed, and a week later she was dead. This tragedy was probably beneficial in the end to Voltaire and to the world, but still it is deeply moving in the disappearance of a vivid personality in such lamentable circumstances. For twenty years she had been bound to Voltaire by mutual love and esteem, and we cannot part from this exceptional and brilliant creature, this 'great man', as he called her, without shedding a valedictory tear.

This remarkable woman was disposed of in a manner as speedy as it was unseemly: she was buried a few hours after her death, and her tomb in the church of Saint-Jacques, at Lunéville, bears no inscription. Voltaire was shattered. Three times king Stanislas came to weep with him, and no doubt the indecently precipitated business of the funeral occupied him. Then the complicated affairs of the three-cornered household at Cirey had to be settled, Voltaire treating the widower with his usual open-handedness.

But in the meanwhile Voltaire had given minute attention to the production of *Sémiramis*. The French actors hesitated, and it was only after Voltaire left Paris for Cirey and Lunéville that they finally decided to produce the tragedy: a good thing for us,

---

10 Printed in full from the manuscripts in Best.D3635-D4002 (April 1748-August 1749).

because he had to supervise the production by correspondence, and thus many valuable details have come down to us. The king agreed to provide the money for a magnificent setting, Voltaire tried again the innovation of putting a ghost on the stage[11], and finally he accompanied king Stanislas to Paris for the first night (29 August 1748). Yet the play had only modest success, at least by Voltairean standards: fifteen performances were given in the first season, while 1117 spectators paid 4033 francs for admission to the first performance. Justice could not be done to the elaborate production because privileged spectators were still allowed on the stage. It also took time to accustom Parisians to Voltaire's modest innovations, but *Sémiramis* did eventually become one of the most popular of Voltaire's plays, especially in the provinces and abroad, but only after a regular propaganda campaign. As the unamiable diarist Collé said, even if it was a bad play, it was bad Voltaire. 'I couldn't do as well myself.'[12]

One of the oddest features of the production of *Sémiramis* was its censoring, for of course all plays and books still had to be officially authorised. In this case the man appointed to examine Voltaire's tragedy was the septuagenarian Crébillon, himself the author of an earlier *Sémiramis* (1717), who had already reported against several of Voltaire's plays, and who, having done all he could to emasculate *Sémiramis*, promptly authorised the performance of its parody—and this although Voltaire had had the quite superfluous courtesy of asking his permission to use the subject[13]. And he then went to enormous trouble to prevent the putting on of the parody. Voltaire was by no means alone in being revolted by these satires, which were sometimes coarse and brutal.[14] This attitude was a hang-over from the punctilio of the duel.

It is of course inevitable that the stock situations of human life should be used by artists over and over again. Giraudoux did not scruple to name one of his plays *Amphitryon 38*, to indicate that it

---

11 See p. 139n, above. The shrewd Frederick was doubtful about the ghost in *Sémiramis,* saying that a 'public which hardly believes in god must necessarily laugh at demons performing on the stage' (Best.D3525).
12 Charles Collé, *Journal et mé-*

moires (Paris 1868), i.1-2; see a note on Best.D3737 (30 August 1748).
13 Best.D3679 (27 June 1748).
14 See in general Gustave Desnoiresterres, *La Comédie satirique au XVIIIe siècle* (Paris 1885), especially chap. i.

was the 38th on the subject first attempted by Plautus. But now, understandably irritated by Crébillon's attitude, Voltaire proceeded systematically to measure himself against the aged playwright by choosing *Rome sauvée*[15] and *Oreste* as his next plays. One result of this was to stimulate the old man into renewed activity: it is an odd little detail of literary history that Crébillon had seven plays produced in 1705-26, and two more in 1748-54, but none between.

The angel mme d'Argental has left us a sparkling image of Voltaire in Paris during the rehearsals of his *Nanine*, a comedy which was also put on at this time. Her husband was away for the night, and at midnight she wrote to him by special messenger:

Voltaire has just left. He turned up at eleven o'clock in the evening, like a madman. He exclaimed that he had been to Versailles, to Sceaux, to lawyers since he returned, and added a hundred things with prodigious volubility, all the time shouting that he was in despair. Finally, when he had got himself in hand, he told me that he had been able, while running around, to make the cuts you had asked for, and even more, and that, as it was necessary to make these cuts with common sense, providing connecting passages, he had provided them; and that having gone at ten o'clock to give mlle Granval her role, he had found her learning a version which you had sent her yourself, since you never trust him. He asked me in a terrible voice what you were meddling in; told me that this had been put right for mlle Granval, but that he must now wake up Granval and mlle Dangeville at opposite ends of Paris; that he had done fifteen leagues, that he was dead, exhausted; that he had to go tomorrow morning to Plaisance[16] and that he was terrified of the fatigue all this would cause him. In short, I have never seen anyone so beside himself. Still, I calmed him, and in the end he begged me to write to you before going to bed that you must let mlle Granval and mme Dangeville know early tomorrow morning that they are to use his version not yours. And he made me promise that I would make you rehearse Granval, his wife, mlle Dangeville and Minet[17]. The end of all this ruction was that he kneeled to me, laughed at his own rage, told me that exasperation put him into an exaggerated bad temper, but that his heart was not involved, and that he would go on his knees to his angel to thank him for his paternal care; as for me, he loved me to distraction and would never doff his hat to a farmer-general until I had an income of 60,000 *livres*.[18]

15 Which is not to be confused with the *Mort de César*.

16 The country-house of the financier Pâris-Duverney.

17 The prompter at the Comédie française.

18 Best.D3943 (? *c.* 10 June 1749).

A trivial incident leads us into the fateful year 1749, which saw the death of Emilie and Voltaire's departure for Prussia. The *président* Hénault, though dull and deaf, was able to win the affectionate friendship of such very different women as the queen Maria Leszczinska and mme Du Deffand. He had also compiled a pedestrian, though very handsomely printed historical chronology. Otherwise, and apart from his powerful connections, he was a nonentity. Voltaire felt some friendship for him, and flattered him for mme Du Deffand's sake (in vain, for when the wealthy *président* died he left not a penny to his blind and impoverished old friend), and he addressed an elegant epistle to him:

> Hénault, fameux par vos soupers,
> Et par votre chronologie,
> Par des vers au bon coin frappés,
> Pleins de douceur et d'harmonie;
> Vous qui dans l'étude occupés
> L'heureux loisir de votre vie,
> Daignez m'apprendre, je vous prie,
> Par quel secret vous échappés
> Aux malignités de l'envie;
> Tandis que moi, placé plus bas,
> Qui devrais être inconnu d'elle,
> Je vois que sa rage éternelle
> Répand ses poisons sur mes pas.[19]

A good question, for Hénault was deeply offended by Voltaire's verses, and their author had much trouble in smoothing him down. And why was Hénault so annoyed? Because Voltaire had mentioned his suppers before his chronology!

Voltaire became more and more outspoken in his disapproval of Frederick's actions. Thus, when the king wrote some lines deploring the ravages of war, Voltaire replied that one would think the poem was by some wretched citizen. 'Not at all, it is by the king who started the quarrel, it is by him who by force of arms has conquered a province and won five battles. Sire, your majesty

19 See a note on Best.D3838 (3 January 1749). 'Hénault, famous for your suppers and your chronology, for verse bearing the true hall-mark, full of tenderness and harmony; you who spend your happy leisure in study, deign to tell me, I beg of you, by what secret you escape the malignity of envy; while I who in my modest station should be unknown to her, see her eternal rage spread her poisons on my path.'

writes fine verse but pulls our legs.'[20] He made it clear to the king that if their old cordiality were to be resumed it would have to be on realistic terms. It was all very well to write poetry and to send his verse to Voltaire to be corrected. Voltaire did correct it, often very severely, but was it worth while? 'I am very much afraid that you intend to gather laurels at the expense of the Russians instead of cultivating peacefully those of Parnassus.'[21] Frederick ignored the thrust. His skin was thick, his invitations became even more pressing, and finally Voltaire agreed to pay a visit to Berlin after mme Du Châtelet was delivered.

But poor Emilie died, and for some time Voltaire moved about restlessly, being successively at Cirey, Paris, Lunéville, Cirey again, Châlons, Rheims, and finally once more and for almost the last time in Paris, where he set up house with mme Denis, thus exchanging a tiresome but honourable bondage for another less onerous perhaps, but far less pleasing on his part, and merely sordid on hers. 'To the legal Widower, M. le Marquis, [Voltaire] behaves in money matters like a Prince; takes that Paris Domicile, in the Rue Traversière, all to himself; institutes a new household there,—Niece Denis to be female president. . . . A gadding, flaunting, unreasonable, would-be fashionable female—(a Du Châtelet without the grace or genius and who never was in love with you!) —with whom poor Uncle had a baddish life in time coming'—says Carlyle[22] perceptively, who did not dream that the niece was also the mistress.

About this time Voltaire first corresponded with the man who was perhaps his only intellectual rival in the French Enlightenment. Denis Diderot, though he was already thirty-six, was known at this time only for the *Bijoux indiscrets*, an erotic novel with philosophic undertones, but the *Encyclopédie* was only just beyond the horizon. He had now published the anonymous *Lettre sur les aveugles*, in which he ridicules physico-theology, that is, the argument for religion drawn from the marvels of nature. Voltaire at once perceived the interest of this 'ingenious and profound book . . . which says much and implies more'. He told Diderot that he esteemed him as much as he condemned those

20 Best.D3856 (26 January 1749).   22 *History of Friedrich II of Prussia*,
21 Best.D3914 (c. 25 April 1749).   XVI.vi.

who proscribed that which enlightened them.[23] These words no
doubt sustained Diderot when his *Lettre* was made a pretext for
his imprisonment. Fortunately the governor of Vincennes was a
cousin of Emilie's husband, so that mme Du Châtelet was able to
intervene on the prisoner's behalf.[24]

Simultaneously with this correspondence there occurred a little
incident, trivial enough in Voltaire's gigantic life, but still too
extraordinary to be overlooked. Voltaire's correspondence of
June 1749 with mme Dupin in fact reveals the beginning of one
of the most picturesque incidents in literary history. One of the
prizes most coveted by preachers at this time was an invitation to
deliver at the Louvre the annual panegyric of saint Louis, in the
presence of the Académie française[25]. Mme Dupin, whose salon
was influential, had procured this favour for her nephew, the
abbé d'Arty, who also had the advantage of being the son of the
prince de Conti. Dissatisfied with his sermon, aunt and nephew
appealed to Voltaire, who first tore the text to shreds, and finally
wrote an entirely new one[26] in the name of the abbé. Voltaire's
panegyric did not follow the traditional form of such allocutions,
so the abbé divided it into the appropriate parts, added the words
'Ave Maria' in one place, and 'Ainsi soit-il' at the end. This was his
sole contribution; but before delivering the sermon, lest he be
betrayed by Voltaire's well-known hand, he had the manuscript
written out by a tutor who was then employed in mme Dupin's
household: this man's name was Jean Jacques Rousseau.

This, however, is not the end of the story: for in 1752 the abbé
d'Arty again had to deliver an important address, the funeral
oration of the duc d'Orléans, and this time he turned to Rousseau.
In short, the works of the abbé d'Arty consist of two sermons, one
written for him by Voltaire, the other by Rousseau.

It was then, or soon after, that Rousseau's ambivalent feelings
about Voltaire began to take shape. He had heard that a man named
Rousseau had offended Voltaire, and wrote to protest rather
peevishly that he was not that Rousseau. To make his point quite

23 Best.D3940 (? 10 June 1749); for
Diderot's reply see Best.D3945 (11
June 1749).

24 Best.D3972 (30 July 1749).
25 Cp. p. 131, above.
26 *Panégyrique de saint Louis*.

clear he signed himself 'J. J. Rousseau, citizen of Geneva'[27], and this was the beginning of the famous epithet to which such profound significance was later attached by Rousseau himself and by his followers. A trifling detail: Rousseau was no longer at this time a citizen of Geneva, since he had become, though temporarily, a Roman Catholic. Voltaire's reply is worth quoting in full: 'By your probity you rehabilitate the name of Rousseau. The man in question is not a citizen of Geneva but is said to be a citizen of the slough of Parnassus. He has faults of which you are incapable, and does not appear to have your merits.'[28] He could hardly have been more courteous, but the letter angered Rousseau, no doubt by its brevity and lack of effusive protestations. Rousseau's feelings for Voltaire, thus prepared, were soon converted into hatred by the assiduity of the false friends of both men, with Théodore Tronchin and other high-minded Genevese in the van.

During the successful production of *Oreste* we see the master at his best, instructing mlle Clairon in the technique of her art. This tragedy illustrates the sometimes incomprehensible goings-on at the Comédie française. It was produced on 12 January 1750 to a good house. But Voltaire was not satisfied, withdrew the play for a week, after which it was given again in a packed theatre. Seven more performances followed, all to good audiences, but the play was taken off and was not revived until 1761. Some intrigue had clearly been orchestrated, perhaps connected with Crébillon, who was patronised by the queen. But although their hands were forced in the matter of *Oreste*, the players were not slow to take advantage of the public's unsatisfied interest; and it is a most remarkable thing that although as many as 976 persons paid for admission on the last night of *Oreste*, even this number was surpassed by the 1079 who came to see a revival of *Zaïre* two days later. This must have been another demonstration by the Paris public.

Why had Voltaire been less than satisfied? 'You were admirable', he wrote to mlle Clairon, the greatest actress of her time, 'in twenty places you displayed the art in its perfection, and the role of Electra is certainly your triumph; but I am a father, and in the midst of the extreme pleasure I take in the compliments a

27 Best.D4108 (30 January 1750).   28 Best.D4109 (c. 2 February 1750).

delighted public makes to my daughter, I shall still make her a few remarks forgivable because of my paternal friendship.' She speaks certain lines too slowly, with too much languor. 'The impetuous Electra should speak with furious despair. She should vary her diction, like the *allegro* and the *piano* of the musicians, produce her voice in a pompous and terrible way, rising by degrees, and finishing with explosions that touch the soul with horror.' And in sending her a whole series of changes and directives he begs her on his knees to forgive his insolence.[29]

All this is overshadowed by Voltaire's departure in June from his beloved Paris, which he did not see again until the last months of his life, twenty-eight years later.

29 Best.D4095-D4104 (12 - *c*.20 January 1750).

24. Justice and government, 1750-1774

VOLTAIRE HAD A characteristic send-off. The persistent refusal of the church to shoulder any part of the financial burden of the nation had irritated Voltaire into writing *La Voix du sage et du peuple* (1750). In this pamphlet he urged that the government must be master in its own house, and that the wealth of the church should not be used only for selfish purposes. It should be remembered that before the revolution the church owned a quarter or a fifth of the entire wealth of France, and, as in the United States today, was exempt from taxation. *La Voix du sage* roused a perfect storm of pamphlets[1] (fifteen at least) and was of course put on the Roman index. And it is an extraordinary fact, which illustrates the immense power of the ecclesiastic establishment, that it was also condemned (21 May 1751) by the government in whose interest it was written.

The composition of this pamphlet turned Voltaire's mind to the problems of government in general, and he put on paper a series of reflections on this subject[2]. They contain some of Voltaire's most thoughtful and pithy remarks on political subjects, and provide an opportunity to examine briefly his views in matters of society and government. A detailed account of Voltaire's writings on political economy is much overdue, but it would fill a large volume. What I want to do here is to state, very briefly, Voltaire's conclusions in this field, and to show how he arrived at them. I believe that such an inquiry is interesting in itself, and particularly valuable in the case of Voltaire, whose views were based on wide reading and considerable experience, filtered by an exceptional degree of critical intelligence.

1 Such as *La Voix du chrétien, La Voix du fou, La Voix du pape, La Voix du pauvre.*

2 *Pensées sur le gouvernement;* Voltaire did not publish them until 1752, but there is no doubt that they were written in Paris in 1750.

It is true that Faguet's epigram about Voltaire's 'chaos of clear ideas' has done some harm to Voltaire's reputation as a thinker. His writings are numerous and voluminous, and it is much easier to repeat again and again an amusing and easily remembered tag than to reflect over several thousand pages of print. And besides, Voltaire having always been obliged to adopt all kinds of expedients in publishing his writings, some effort is needed to find what he had to say on specific subjects, particularly if these subjects were of a sensitive nature.

Thus, the innocent reader would be much disappointed if he turned to the article 'King' in what now passes for the *Dictionnaire philosophique*[3]. There he could learn what kings are called in many languages, and read some interesting remarks on the power of gold; but when he finally comes to the question: 'What are the limits of royal prerogative and of the liberty of the people?' the only answer offered by Voltaire is: 'I advise you to investigate this question calmly in the town hall of Amsterdam.' This reply, to be sure, contains more than appears on the surface, but as the conclusion of such an article it is not very satisfying. The inquirer will not find much more nourishment in the article 'States, government', though in that Voltaire does at least conclude that the best state is that in which only the laws are obeyed. It is not even in the *Histoire du parlement de Paris* that must be sought Voltaire's views on government, which are hidden in such works as *L'ABC*. Rarely indeed did Voltaire express himself under an 'open' title such as *Pensées sur le gouvernement*, which, however, he was careful not to publish separately, but only more or less hidden in collected editions of his works.

In fact the epigram of the too facile Faguet merely summed up the views of such writers as Tocqueville and Taine[4], a fact which makes it more respectable without adding to its truth. These conclusions, in turn, result from a rather elementary confusion,

---

3 The article was in fact written for the *Questions sur l'encyclopédie* (1771).

4 The relevant passages are quoted by Peter Gay, *Voltaire's politics* (Princeton 1959), pp. 6-8; this is the most interesting of the works devoted to Voltaire's political ideas; but it is a selective biography of Voltaire, not a systematic and technical analysis; and professor Gay's taste for paradox sometimes leads him to say more or less than he means. René Pomeau's selection of texts, *Politique de Voltaire* (Paris 1963), avoids many of the dangers of such anthologies, and has a suggestive introduction.

similar to that caused by the very different meanings borne in different contexts by technical words which have become common coin. Many historians seem indeed to have difficulty in appreciating the fact that a *philosophe* of the Enlightenment is by no means the same kind of animal as a philosopher in modern terms. If a philosopher in the academic sense writes a great deal but a certain unity fails to emerge, one can at a pinch complain of chaos. Even this, however, is by no means certain, for it is perfectly possible to be a philosopher, even a great one, without constructing a system. Leibniz is by no means unique in this respect; and Wolff was not a better philosopher than his master because he took his teaching to pieces and rearranged its elements like a Meccano set.

I do not hesitate to repeat that it is perfectly possible to disapprove constructional philosophy altogether, as did Voltaire. 'Learn', he said towards the end of his life, 'learn that all systems offend my reason.'[5] To use modern terms, Voltaire was a man of science rather than a philosopher. Thus we can see how perfectly irrelevant are the criticisms directed to him because he did not compose formal works of academic philosophy. What is the sense of criticising him for not doing that which he explicitly condemned?

Another factor differentiates Voltaire from conventional philosophers, a factor of paramount importance, and of which he was perfectly conscious. There is no need to argue the obvious fact, a single quotation of a few words will suffice to make the point: 'Jean Jacques [Rousseau] writes only to write and I write in order to act.'[6] He could have said 'to act and to make others act'. Is it necessary to name Ferney and Calas?

During his long life Voltaire was intimately familiar with the Establishment in all its aspects. He saw power in all its forms at work through several generations in several countries, and witnessed changes which were sometimes radical. From time to time he even played a personal role in historic events, and always he was utterly *engagé*. It was a poetical exaggeration, but it was not an absurdity when he wrote in old age that

5 *Dialogue de Pégase et du vieillard*   6 Best.D14117 (*c.* 15 April 1767).
(1774), 153; see also p. 217, above.

vingt têtes couronnées
Daignèrent applaudir mes veilles fortunées. . . .
J'ai fait plus en mon temps que Luther et Calvin.[7]

Having an inexhaustible thirst for knowledge, a deep need for reflection, and the sensibility of an artist, Voltaire grew and developed, sometimes slowly, at other times abruptly by a sudden catalysis. This fact explains why most writings on Voltaire have no permanent value, and endlessly contradict each other[8]. It is futile to discuss Voltaire by quoting him pell-mell, without taking into account the date of each work and the circumstances in which it was written[9].

Of course Voltaire did not derive his political opinions entirely from observation and introspection. Certainly he was not a scholar or a specialist in the sense that he systematically surveyed what had already been written on the subject, but he always read widely and even deeply in several languages. Indeed, very few of his contemporaries had read and remembered as much as Voltaire, not only in his own language, but also in Latin, English and Italian. It would be possible to reconstruct (quite apart from the catalogue of his library) a fairly complete and accurate list of the writings he knew in the field of political thought. Those he had studied minutely were few: *The Prince*, obviously, since he edited Frederick's *Anti-Machiavel*; the *Considérations* of the marquis d'Argenson, his lifelong friend; the works of Bolingbroke, also a friend and by whom he had been much influenced; Montesquieu, whom he could never really admire, put off by his innumerable mistakes and by his disorderly presentation, but whom he had studied with great attention and whom he respected; and the *Instructions* of Catherine II, which he in his turn had influenced. He knew also the relevant writings of, among many others, Bossuet, Boulainvilliers, Chastellux, Daguesseau, Dubos, Gin, Grotius, Hobbes, Hume, Mably, Melon, Quesnay, Saint-Pierre,

---

7 *Epître à l'auteur du livre des trois imposteurs* (1769), 51-4; 'twenty crowned heads deigned to applaud the happy work of my sleepless nights. . . . I have done more in my time than Luther and Calvin.'

8 It also explains why, on the other hand, the biography by Desnoiresterres

has kept much of its value after a century: it is because this graceful writer had little interest in ideas.

9 Gustave Lanson pointed this out in the preface of his admirable little *Voltaire* (1906), but few subsequent writers have heeded his warning.

and such 'political testaments' as that of Belleisle, and that which
he obstinately refused to believe was really cardinal Richelieu's.
He regularly read several periodicals devoted to political economy,
of which I need mention only the *Ephémérides du citoyen*.

It is also important to investigate what works Voltaire did not
know: though a negative can never be proved. Still, it can be
stated with confidence, to give only a few examples, that he knew
but probably never read Bodin; that Filmer seems to have been
entirely unknown to him; and, very surprisingly indeed, that he
did not know the two *Treatises of civil government* by John Locke,
the great Locke whom he once called the wisest man who had
ever lived[10], and to whose European reputation he had so much
contributed. The writings in this field of Rousseau are also missing
from the list of his studies, not because he had not read them, but
because it would never have occurred to Voltaire to take Rousseau
seriously as a writer on such a subject as government.

What Voltaire owed to his precursors is clearly a matter of the
first importance in the history of ideas, and one that can and should
be investigated. It would help us to elucidate Voltaire's own
ideas, even if only indirectly. However, to arrive directly at a
more or less precise understanding of them two main lines of
research must be pursued. First, it is necessary to define the continuity of his thought, to discover what were the basic ideas
which underlie all the rest. Secondly, the structure erected on this
basis must be surveyed in its changing forms. This is what I will
now try to do, very rapidly, limiting myself of course to the
political context.

Although many versions have been given even of Voltaire's
fundamental ideas, there is in my opinion little reason for doubt.
A long, intimate and sympathetic familiarity with his life and
works has convinced me that two ideas dominated Voltaire, two
ideas which form so intimate a part of his make-up that they call
for the attention of the psychologist as much as the historian, two
ideas which are at the base of all he thought and felt and did.
These two things are a passion for justice and a belief in reason.
Everybody knows what Voltaire accomplished to preserve the
ideal of justice, but it seems to me that it has not been sufficiently

10 Best.D646 (*c.* 15 August 1733).

appreciated that his justice-fixation explains much of his life. If he so strongly resented a betrayal by a friend it was because such conduct is unjust; if the malice of a critic or the inefficiency of an official exasperated him beyond endurance it was because malice and inefficiency are contrary to just behaviour; and even in the domain of esthetics, having once made up his mind (often, it seems to us, wrongly) that a certain way of doing things was correct, that is to say, just, all departures from this norm were offences against justice. For Voltaire, in his own words, the fundamental law is to be just.[11]

This conviction is expressed with Voltairean simplicity and finality in the first part of the *Catéchisme chinois* (1764), in a dialogue between prince Koo and the philosopher Cu-Su:

KOO

What must we do to dare to contemplate ourselves thus before the supreme Being, without repugnance and without shame?

KU-SU

Be just.

KOO

And what else?

KU-SU

Be just.

But what is justice? Voltaire several times approached this question, which interested him above all others, but it must be admitted that he fought shy of the difficulties presented by a considered reply. In one of his dialogues he makes the English interlocutor reply 'that which so appears to the entire universe' to the inquiry 'what do you call just and unjust?'[12] a reply in flagrant contradiction of Voltaire's notions of ethical relativity. Yet this reply did clearly reflect his own views, for elsewhere he writes: 'I therefore think that ideas of justice and injustice are as clear, as universal, as ideas of health and sickness, truth and untruth, fitness and unfitness.'[13] There is nothing more false than these analogies, nothing more inadequate than such a view of the nature of justice. So inadequate, indeed, is Voltaire's treatment of the subject that again one is led to psychological interpretations:

11 *L'ABC* (1768), xiii.
12 *L'ABC* (1768), iv.

13 *Le Philosophe ignorant* (1766), xxxii.

quite clearly there was a great deal of affectivity in Voltaire's obsession with justice.

Voltaire has often been reproached for his belief in reason, and if this belief were in fact what it is often represented to be, this reproach would not perhaps be wholly unjustified. However, we must distinguish. Voltaire was not so naive as some of his critics would like to think: he did not believe that men behave rationally, but only that they should so behave, and that if they did the world would be a better place than it is. How can this conviction be contradicted? Where and when has it ever been tried out? It is at least strictly logical.

These two dominant elements in Voltaire's personality united in one concrete expression, just as constant: the conviction that law is the source and basis of civilisation. He said, once and for all, that 'Liberty consists of dependence on nothing but law.'[14] When he went to England, he tells us, it was in order to go 'to enjoy in a free country the greatest benefit I know, and humanity's most glorious right, which is to depend only on men's *laws and not on their whims*'[15]. Much later he expressed the same views: 'That the farmer be not vexed by a minor tyrant; that a citizen be not imprisoned without being immediately tried by his natural judges, who decide between him and his persecutor; that nobody's field or vineyard be taken from him, on the pretext of public necessity, without ample compensation; that priests teach morality, and do not corrupt it; that they raise up the people instead of seeking to dominate them by waxing fat from their substance; that *law reign, and not whim*.'[16] The ideas were so alike that they evoked exactly the same verbal antithesis after thirty-five years: law and not whim. A hundred other passages of this kind could be cited, and I doubt whether a single one could be found in an opposite sense.

This then is the foundation of Voltaire's political ideas: law, born of justice and reason, is the basis of a civilised society. It remains to inquire how Voltaire proposed to apply law to the complexities of such a society. His views were not always the

14 *Pensées sur le gouvernement* (1752), vii.

15 Best.D738 (*c.* 8 May 1734); my italics.

16 *L'ABC* (1768), viii; my italics.

same: the playboy of the regency was not the same man as the courtier of Louis xv, nor were the views of Frederick of Prussia's chamberlain identical with those of the neighbour who supported the disfranchised majority against the self-styled patricians of Geneva.

It is first necessary, however, to bring out one consequence in the domain of politics of Voltaire's dislike of systems: he had a lifelong disdain of utopianism, and was essentially interested only in ideas that produce results, visible results, results now. He could never see that there was any point in constructing ideal solutions if they were impracticable in a foreseeable future. Does it work? was his only question: that is, will it accomplish a good without causing any harm? So emphatic was Voltaire in this respect that he is entitled to be regarded as one of the pioneers of pragmatism. A study on these lines would be valuable.

In order to discover what Voltaire admired politically during his first period, that expressed by the *Lettres philosophiques*, some writers have taken the trouble to analyse the English scene in 1726-28. It is wasted labour. What interests us in this context is not the true nature of English institutions, but only what Voltaire thought they were. To him the essential aspects of English society, even if he was mistaken (and I do not say that he was), were freedom of speech and the press, religious toleration, legality, popular power as expressed by an elected House of commons; and all these things he profoundly admired and advocated with enthusiasm.

Holding these views how could Voltaire adapt them to French conditions? He could and did wage an unremitting warfare against the censorship; he could and did take every opportunity to oppose the power of the church and to defend the Protestants; he could and did fight tooth and nail against injustice, especially when it emanated from the judicial, executive and ecclesiastic authorities. All this was possible, and it would be difficult to exaggerate the effectiveness of Voltaire's propaganda in these fields, which gradually permeated all levels of society, above him and below. But what attitude could he adopt in the field of political power? There was no House of commons in France, and at the time of Voltaire's return from England, there was not the slightest prospect of seeing one established. Voltaire therefore had to choose between the king, the nobles and the *parlement*, a trinity which correspond roughly, very roughly, to the classical one of monarchy, aristocracy and democracy.

Let me add in passing that Voltaire never envisaged a republic as a tolerable form of government. Indeed, he was energetically opposed to such an idea. Some of his most mordant passages are found in his reply to Montesquieu's famous antithesis, which has it that virtue is the active principle of republics, honours that of monarchies. History showed, Voltaire thought, that no republic had ever been created at the dictates of virtue, but only out of ambition, in order to change the receptacle of power. It is true that in a letter written in England Voltaire says: 'All that is King, or belongs to a King, frights my republican philosophy'[17]; but this was written in a special context and in a passing mood; the passage stands alone, and no particular significance need be attributed to it. It is true that Voltaire's arguments against a republican form of government are sometimes difficult to follow. Thus he says that 'small mechanisms do not succeed when enlarged' and concludes that China cannot govern itself like Lucca[18]. The opposite seems to be true: practically, a personal form of government cannot remain effective if its scope extends beyond the radius of one man, and theoretically, if the greater part of the responsibility has to be delegated, the government ceases to be personal.

The choice in Voltaire's mind was in reality even more limited than the classical one, for he was always opposed to the *parlement* precisely because it was not a parliament[19]. When Voltaire arrived in England the power of the nobles had long since been broken, and several constitutional monarchs had succeeded Charles i. There remained only the parliament, which could no longer forfeit public confidence by any imaginable foolishness. In France the nobles had also been diminished to a level of influence from which they could never hope to rise. Voltaire saw this clearly even if

17 Best.D303 (26 October 1726).
18 *Pensées sur le gouvernement* (1752), xxvi.
19 The *parlement*, he said 'has been powerful only under weak ministers. It is ridiculous to say that it represents the nation'; *Notebooks*, i.212.

Montesquieu did not. In every other respect the political situation presented a complete contrast. Voltaire's real choice lay between the *parlement* and the king, and even here the choice was merely academic. Indeed, the record of the *parlement* was such, in Voltaire's view, as to put it out of court. He expressed his reasons very lucidly in one of the notebooks I have had the honour to publish: 'Machiavelli . . . says that the greatest surety of kings is the parliament. That was true when there were dangerous lords whom the authority of parliament could restrain. But since then the *parlement* has itself become very dangerous; what was a defensive arm has today become one that wounds.'[20] And why did Voltaire think that the *parlement* had become dangerous? The answer to this question is implicit in his individualistic passion for freedom. He did not believe in metaphysical systems because they stifle free reflection; he was sceptical of reforms by committee and believed that hardly anything great had ever been accomplished 'but for the genius and firmness of one man'[21]. There was something almost anarchistic in Voltaire's conviction that progress could be attained only by personal effort. Having recited certain notorious actions of the *parlement* (such as their attempts to promote an aristocratic reaction), he continued that 'such is the fate of the wisest bodies which have no rules other than their ancient usages and their formalities: all that is new frightens them. They oppose all the nascent arts, all the truths opposed to the errors of their childhood, all that is not in the old taste and the old form.' And he quotes with approval the remark attributed to Sully: 'If wisdom descended on earth it would prefer to lodge in one head rather than in a body of men.'[22].

Thus it was that Voltaire arrived ineluctably at the conviction that the only possible system of government for France was an absolute monarchy. Why absolute? Voltaire did not believe in absolutism by divine right. This doctrine has indeed been much misunderstood. It is often regarded as one of the bases, if not the chief basis, of monarchy. In fact, it is little more than an historical accident of short duration. Born towards the end of the sixteenth century, it lasted only until kings had successfully opposed their

20 *Notebooks*, i.228.   22 *Essai sur les mœurs*, cxxi.
21 *Essai sur les mœurs*, cii.

divine right to that of the popes. When the latter belief collapsed among thoughtful men, so did the former, which had served only to destroy it. As Voltaire judiciously pointed out, kings sat on their thrones by divine right only in the sense that everything that happens on earth happens by divine right, since god had created man, who can do nothing outside his divine will[23].

Indeed, it was not for any theoretical reasons whatever that Voltaire advocated absolutism, it was because he thought it objectively beneficial to the state that the monarch should be supreme, not first among equals. 'A king who is not contradicted can hardly be wicked.'[24] And Voltaire developed this idea by pointing out that a king who is not absolute has to assert himself, but does not need to do so if he is absolute. He contrasts the reigns of Louis XI and Louis XIV: the former executed thousands of his subjects, Louis XIV very few: 'That was because he was absolute.'[25]

When Louis XV haughtily informed the *parlement* on 3 March 1766, in a *lit de justice* (*séance royale*) which aroused much indignation, that he himself was the sole source of power, Voltaire warmly approved the monarch's stand. Four times on a single day he called the king's tirade a noble idea.[26] Moreover, the choice of the four correspondents is significant: they were Alembert, Damilaville, mme Du Deffand, and Florian: in other words, Voltaire approved the king's flagellation of the *parlement*, and wanted everybody in all circles to know that he did. Why he wanted them to know it is another question.

Voltaire arrived at this conclusion intellectually, against his feelings, for he was no lover of courts. He never mastered the tight-rope art of keeping the favour of a monarch, perhaps because he had no wish to master it. At the height of his courtly career at Versailles, he wrote, as we have already seen, in the intimacy of a love letter to his niece: 'I counted on seeing you at Versailles, my dear, after the performance. But the plaguy tricks

23 *L'ABC* (1768), iii.
24 *Pensées sur le gouvernement* (1752), xvii.
25 *Pensées sur le gouvernement* (1752, strengthened in 1756), xx. Voltaire perhaps remembered also that, strictly speaking, the term 'absolute monarchy', is tautological, since the word monarchy derives from μοναρχία, which in itself means the rule of one.
26 Best.D13205-D13208 (12 March 1766).

of the Court arranged things quite otherwise. I was told that I must run after the king full tilt, and find myself at a certain time in a certain corner. . . . So I was presented to his very gracious majesty, who received me very graciously, and whom I thanked very humbly.'[27] And thirty years later, although he still hoped to be allowed to return to Paris, he wrote to his biographer, the egregious Duvernet: 'Those who told you . . . that in 1744 and 1745 I was a courtier, have asserted a sad truth. I was; I corrected myself in 1746, and repented in 1747. Of all the time I have lost in my life, this is undoubtedly the loss I most regret.'[28] This is not the language of a man who is a monarchist because he loves kings, and the feelings expressed by such passages emerge not infrequently in the language Voltaire puts into the mouths of sympathetic personages in his plays, such as the lines in *Œdipe*:

> Dans le cœur des humains les rois ne peuvent lire;
> Souvent sur l'innocence ils font tomber leurs coups.[29]

Here again is a subject that ought to be investigated: the relation between Voltaire's views as expressed in his prose writings and those revealed in his plays and poetry. Such an analysis might produce interesting results. We can even now venture to think that Voltaire's feelings on this subject sustained him in wishing to limit the absolutism of the monarch.

For indeed, in Voltaire's mind monarchical absolutism was not synonymous with tyranny. He wanted the monarch to be the sole vessel of power, but only on condition that this power was exercised with wisdom and toleration. He distinguished, in short, like Bossuet, between absolute power and arbitrary power. In the *Lettres philosophiques* he had already said: 'The English nation is the only one on earth which has succeeded in controlling the power of their kings in resisting them, and which by effort after effort has finally established the wise government in which the prince, all-powerful to do good, has his hands tied again the doing of evil.'[30] In brief, Voltaire believed in law and in an absolute monarch, a monarch the justification of whose absolutism lay in

27 Best.D3091 (1 April 1745).
28 Best.18772 (7 February 1776).
29 II.v; 'Kings cannot read men's hearts; their blows often fall on the innocent'; cp. p. 82, above.
30 *Lettres philosophiques*, viii.

his submission to his own laws. 'Everything, the monarchy and religion above all, is subject to the law.'[31]

The brief essay entitled *La Voix du sage et du peuple*, written on the occasion of the king's abortive attempt to tax the clergy (1750), contains some of Voltaire's most pungent and profound reflections on government. It is in essence a plea for an absolute but enlightened monarch. Voltaire begins by declaring that the merits of a government consist in the protection and control of all. The government cannot be good unless there is a single power. This theme is developed to show that this single power, the king, must act at the dictates of reason, and that he is best sustained by a nation of *philosophes*. And he concludes: 'The best thing that can happen to mankind is to have a philosopher-prince.' He shows the good such an enlightened monarch could do: 'One could fill a fat book with all the good that can be done; but a philosopher-prince does not need a fat book.'

It is clear that these views are extremely close to those of the physiocrats, and anticipate them, since Cantillon's *Essai* dates from 1755. When Quesnay advised the future king to do nothing and to let the law rule, he by no means had in mind a republican system, and he was therefore advocating exactly the same kind of enlightened despotism that underlay Voltaire's royal thesis. What is 'legal despotism' but 'enlightened despotism'? By an over-simplification of the facts Voltaire has often been regarded as an enemy of the physiocrats, and *L'Homme aux quarante écus* is cited in support of this view. But this is to overlook the dual nature of political economy, the political and the economic. This duality is specially marked in the theories of the physiocrats. There is no doubt that Voltaire rejected the more formal aspects of physiocratic economics; there is equally little doubt that the dominant political ideas of the same thinkers were based on the teachings of Voltaire, and were shared by him.

In order to penetrate the ideas of an author we are obliged to search the nooks and crannies of his publications. The task is particularly difficult in the case of Voltaire because of the multiplicity of his writings and their numerous forms, which call for

31 *L'ABC* (1768), iii; these words are put into the mouth of A, the English interlocutor, but B (Voltaire) clearly agreed.

special caution if we are to avoid false interpretations. Yet in a sense Voltaire has saved us the trouble, for he was after all primarily a poet in the sense Jean Cocteau[32] gave to the word. He was often best able to express his profoundest ideas through his imagination. And in fact, odd though it may appear, the clearest expression of Voltaire's political opinions is to be found in his poetry, in these lines from the *Henriade*, which, though written before 1730, sum up his thinking on these matters:

> Aux murs de Westminster on voit paraître ensemble
> Trois pouvoirs étonnés du nœud qui les rassemble,
> Les députés du peuple, et les grands, et le roi,
> Divisés d'intérêt, réunis par la loi;
> Tous trois membres sacrés de ce corps invincible,
> Dangereux à lui-même, à ses voisins terrible,
> Heureux lorsque le peuple, instruit de son devoir,
> Respecte, autant qu'il doit, le souverain pouvoir,
> Plus heureux lorsqu'un roi, doux, juste, et politique,
> Respecte, autant qu'il doit, la liberté publique.[33]

32 Cocteau once told me that he thought *The Phœnix and the turtle* the greatest 'small poem' ever written, and Voltaire's life the greatest 'major poem'.

33 *Henriade*, i.313-22; 'Within the walls of Westminster one can see at once three powers astonished by the knot which unites them, the people's deputies, the great, and the king, divided in their interests, united by the law. All three are sacred members of that unconquerable body, dangerous to itself, terrible to its neighbours, happy when the people, knowing its duty, respects as much as it should the sovereign power, happier when a king, gentle, just and politic, respects public liberty as he should.'

25. Prussia: hail and farewell, 1750-1753

ON 24 JUNE 1750 Voltaire told the duchesse Du Maine, after the performance of *Rome sauvée* at Sceaux, that the die was cast, and that he was leaving for Berlin at 5 o'clock on the following morning.[1] By the time he reached Compiègne he exclaimed to the Argentals: 'Why am I here? Why do I go on? Why have I left you, my dear angels? . . . Do not scold me, my own remorse is enough.'[2] And on the same day his doubts were expressed even in a letter to Frederick. He reproached the king for the high-pressure methods he had used to get Voltaire to Prussia. Frederick had even invited Voltaire's *protégé* Baculard d'Arnaud, telling him—and making sure that the youth's patron should know of it—that Voltaire's sun was setting and that the young man should come to take his place.[3] But there was no turning back, and though transport difficulties obliged Voltaire to spend a fortnight at Cleves, by 24 July he was at Potsdam[4].

Voltaire went to great pains to detail the reasons for his departure in a very long letter[5] to Richelieu, written only a month after his arrival in Prussia. He told the duke that he could not conceive what Voltaire had been obliged to put up with, the persecutions of all kinds. Why, for instance, had so many people in authority united to chase him from Cirey? Because of the 'very innocent pleasantry of the *Mondain*'. It was then that he had first thought of accepting Frederick's invitations, but he had promised mme Du Châtelet never to leave her, and he kept his word. It is true that he was later appointed to offices under the crown. But what happened? The queen was persuaded that mme

---

1 Best.D4161 (24 June 1750).
2 Best.D4163 (26 June 1750).
3 Best.D4166 (26 June 1750). 'Déjà l'Apollon de la France / S'achemine à sa décadence, / Venez brillez à votre tour.'

4 The time-table of Voltaire's journey presents problems; see Best.app. D100; for his own account of the Prussian adventure see the autobiography, pp. 646-651, below.
5 Best.D4206 (*c.* 31 August 1750).

Du Châtelet and he were responsible for the supposed irreligion of her father, king Stanislas, and for his relations with mme de Boufflers, and it soon turned out that Voltaire's credit at court was non-existent. And after all, the exile asked his old friend, what was he doing in Prussia? It was true that he was helping Frederick with his literary work, but he was also finishing the *Siècle de Louis XIV* for the greater glory of France. The duke had said that the king and mme de Pompadour, who did not spare Voltaire a glance when he was in France, were shocked by his departure. Yet how would he be treated if he came back? Did mme de Pompadour expect that he should give up the intimacy of a great king, who was destined to leave his mark on history, in order to beg for a word at her dressing-table? She and the ministry should at least have been grateful for his *Voix du sage et du peuple*[6]. And she should have recognised that her enemies were the same as his. 'I am by no means an exile who asks to be recalled. I am not a handyman who asks to be bought.' If he could return to France honourably he would leave a court at which he depended on nobody, and had no priests or ministers to fear. 'Here I am not in the anteroom of a secretary of state, but in the apartments of his master.'

And a day or two later Voltaire told Argental that he had secured a haven after thirty years of storms. He had found the protection of a king, the conversation of a philosopher, the charm of an amiable man, of a man who sought only to console and defend him. In Paris he had everything to fear, at the Prussian court a peaceful life lay before him.[7] But Voltaire was whistling in the dark. No sooner had he arrived at the Prussian court than his regrets began to crystallise, and for better cause than he at once realised.

The Prussian king deeply admired Voltaire, and the French one despised him, but now neither behaved like a gentleman. Being an official of the French court Voltaire had to obtain the king's permission to leave the country. While he was making his démarches, Frederick gave the Prussian ambassador, now Le Chambrier, instructions which can only be described as perfidious. He pretended that the removal to Prussia was all Voltaire's doing, and

6 See pp. 305, 317, above.   7 Best.D4207 (1 September 1750).

said that although he was quite willing to receive him, he was equally willing to drop him if the French authorities showed the slightest unwillingness[8]. This, from the man who had fifty times urged Voltaire to come, about the man who had resisted as often, is a measure of the king's sincerity. No wonder that the French ministry treated Voltaire with much coldness, and, in authorising his departure, deprived of his office of historiographer the man who was universally known to be finishing his *magnificat* of Louis XIV. Indeed, the French ambassador in Berlin was told with heavy-handed irony that Louis XV had no regrets in parting from 'an academician some of whose works had made him famous'. The minister doubted whether Frederick would be able to put up with Voltaire's character.[9]

The expendable academician was received in Berlin with much distinction and cordiality.

> They were very great days at Berlin, those of Autumn 1750; distinguished strangers come or coming; the king himself up to entertainment of them, to enjoyment of them, with such a hearty outburst of magnificence . . . as was rare in his reign. There were his Sisters of Schwedt and Baireuth, with suite, his dear Wilhelmina queen of the scene; there were—It would be tedious to count what other high Herrschaften and Durchlauchtig Persons. And to crown the whole . . . there had come M. de Voltaire; conquered at length to us, as we hope, and the Dream of our Youth realised. Voltaire's reception, July 10th and ever since, has been mere splendour and kindness, really extraordinary. . . . Friedrich is loyally glad over his Voltaire; eager in all ways to content him, make him happy; and keep him there, as the Talking Bird, the Singing Tree and the Golden Water[10], of intelligent mankind; the glory of one's Court, and the envy of the world.[11]

Yet it did not take Voltaire long to realise the truth of what he had long suspected, that Frederick's motives were by no means unselfish. The king's enlightened ways were limited to himself and, by extension, to his inner circle at any given moment; but everybody else, beginning with his family, lived in a state of fearful repression. This is how he kept the peace in his court.[12] Besides, Frederick was always happy to betray a friend, even such a one as Voltaire. Still, he gave his talking bird the most emphatic

8 Best.D4184 (8 August 1750).
9 Best.D4194 (22 August 1750).
10 This is the echo of a line in the *Hippolytus* of Euripides.

11 Carlyle, *History of Friedrich II of Prussia*, XVI.v-vi.
12 See p. 329, below.

and unctuous assurances that he would not regret his exile. They were old friends, how could Voltaire fear that the king's house could become a prison?[13] But Voltaire's fears were prophetic, and they were not calmed by the king's assurances. Within five months after his arrival he wrote to mme Denis that the *Mort de César* had been performed at the Prussian court (*Zaïre* followed), but. . . . The king's suppers were delicious, they were feasts of reason, wit and science, where liberty reigned, but. . . . There was the opera, the theatre, suppers at Sans-Souci, study, but. . . . but. . . . And he started to think of returning to France for the winter and of going to Italy. . . .[14]

In the meanwhile Voltaire was put to work on the revision of Frederick's manuscripts and did a good deal of work on a new Walther edition of his own works. 'His apartments were under the King's, and he never quitted them but to go to supper. The King composed works in philosophy, history, and poetry, in the upper apartment, while his favourite cultivated the same arts, and the same talents in the lower.'[15]

Yet Voltaire also got himself involved in a shady business affair. Under the terms of the treaty imposed by Prussia on Saxony in 1745, certain negotiable effects (Steuerscheine) were to be honoured in full by Saxony when they were held by Prussian subjects. The inevitable abuses were apparently not foreseen, and it was not until 1748 that speculation in these effects was forbidden by law. Nevertheless Voltaire entered into an agreement with the Berlin business-man Abraham Hirschel, a 'protected Jew'[16], that is, one who was useful to the state and therefore exempt from the worst oppressions. Voltaire, who had brought a lot of money with him, for he always lived expensively, put a substantial sum at Hirschel's disposal for dealings in the Saxon bonds, Hirschel depositing a quantity of jewellery as security. The transaction fell through, and difficulties followed in connexion with the mutual return of the money and the jewellery. Voltaire brought an action

13 Best.D4195 (23 August 1750).
14 Best.D4256 (6 November 1750).
15 See the autobiography, p. 647, below.

16 Schutzjude was the official term; this is where Hitler got the notion of 'honorary Aryans'.

11 Idealised head of Voltaire,
from an impression of mme Du Châtelet's seal

12 Voltaire and mme Denis, *from a drawing by Nicolas Cochin in the New-York historical society*

against Hirschel, the result of which can perhaps best be described as a technical victory for the plaintiff.[17]

It would be difficult to apportion blame between Voltaire and Hirschel, nor is that the important point. One of the inducements Frederick had offered Voltaire was his appointment as one of his chamberlains, so as to assure his status at court. Thus Voltaire, be he regarded as the king's guest or as an official of his court or simply as himself, should not have engaged in such a transaction. His conduct, though venial by conventional standards, and positively virtuous by comparison with the corruption in business matters of much of the French nobility, cannot and should not be defended, nor do I seek to palliate or extenuate. All that can be said in Voltaire's favour is that he was certainly innocent of the grosser charges brought against him, including forgery.

On arriving in Berlin Voltaire met again an interesting woman whom he had known for some years, and with whom he now formed an *amitié amoureuse*. Indeed, she almost certainly became his mistress—mme Denis, after all, had refused to leave Paris. Charlotte Sophia was born in 1715, the only child and heir of Anthony II, last count of Aldenburg (Oldenburg), sovereign lord of Kniphausen etc., and his wife, princess Wilhelmina Maria of Hesse-Homburg. In 1733, after being courted by several prominent men, including the future king of Sweden, she married William, the third son of John William Bentinck, first earl of Portland, the bridegroom having to be created a count of the Holy Roman Empire to make the marriage acceptable. They separated in 1740, and there followed an interminable law suit turning on the division of their property. The political implications were of some importance, since the destinies of several more or less independent principalities were involved. As these places are on the North Sea, at the boundaries of Hanover, Frisia and Bremen, and included a Prussian enclave, several courts were involved, Denmark, Austria (where at this time count Bentinck was the Netherlands ambassador), Prussia, France, and even

---

17 The sensation-mongering Carlyle, *History of Friedrich II of Prussia*, XVI.vii, saw fit to devote twenty pages to this trivial affair.

Russia and Great Britain; there was a possibility for a moment that war would result.[18]

The future empress Catherine, as a girl of fourteen, went with her family to stay with the Aldenburgs. She found countess Bentinck irresistible, for she sang, laughed and danced like a child, though she was already separated from her husband, of whom she said that she would have been madly in love with him were she not married to him.[19] A few years later, when Voltaire arrived in Berlin, he saw this sprightly and unconventional woman almost every day, wrote her a large number of letters and notes, and got into trouble with Frederick by giving her advice about her law suit. In reading the following extracts it must be remembered that all Voltaire's letters were intercepted and read by the king unless sent from door to door by a sure hand.

Madame la margravine has had a bad night, and I have very bad days when I do not have the happiness to pay my court to madame la comtesse de Benting.[20]

Will you honour with your presence a dress rehearsal [of *Rome sauvée*] we are holding today about four o'clock in princess Amelia's apartment?[21]

I told the king that Thalestris would very much like to settle in the country of Alexander, that you even hoped to persuade your sons to enter his service, and you cannot doubt that I made him feel the value of such an acquisition.[22]

I did not need the singular and painful parallels of my destiny and yours to be devoted to you. Even your kindnesses to me were superfluous. Your lovely soul sufficed.[23]

I have arrived. I have received your orders. I will come to thank you for giving me these orders. If success depended on my zeal you would have the earldom of Oldenburg and the kingdom of Denmark.[24]

18 On all this, and countess Bentinck's life in general, see mrs Aubrey Le Blond, *Charlotte Sophia countess Bentinck* (London 1912); this book, however, is almost a blank for 1750-53; the author, who was descended from countess Bentinck, had access to the family papers (which unfortunately she used in a decidedly amateurish and prudish way, without references, quoting only in translation, often without dates); worst of all, she almost entirely ignored Voltaire's letters of the Berlin period to her ancestress, quoting only a few brief fragments.

19 *The Memoirs of Catherine the great*, ed. Dominique Maroger (London 1955), pp. 43-4.

20 Best.D4212 (*c.* 6 September 1750).

21 Best.D4226 (*c.* 24 September 1750).

22 Best.D4238 (12 October 1750); the image is not very happy, since Thalestris had a child by Alexander.

23 Best.D4277 (*c.* 21 November 1750).

24 Best.D4327 (1750/51).

My heroine who is going to see heroes will find a cup of bad coffee, and some bad food if she wants to eat, at the house of her admirer and her solitary. I have neither furniture nor kitchen, but apart from that I am not badly off when it is fine. I will go at noon to the Marquisat to wait for you on the river-bank. I should prefer to spend my life with you in some cosy château, far from the emperors and the kings of Denmark.[25]

It is true that I pass my life with the dead. They at least do no harm, and besides they are rather suitable company for a sick man like me. If I had good health, if I could indulge my tastes, if I were a man like other men, you would often see me at your feet. . . . I sup with the first of men when I have a little health, I stay at home when I am ill. I take no interest in public affairs, but yours worry me.[26]

Here I am in my desert with your sugar and your big cloak, which I will return if I may the next time I come. I have suddenly taken to my solitude, and I should love it passionately were it not so far from you.[27]

Well or ill, fat or thin, pale or rosy, I truly love you. But I am not lucky in my great passions. . . . I lead a philosophic life which should give me good health. Yet I have none. The king deigns to make me as happy as can be a man attacked by the cruel illness which has been killing me for the last six months, and which has made me lose nearly all my teeth.[28]

A man called La Beaumelle has arrived from Copenhagen. He is a man of letters. He says he is from Languedoc. They say he is from Geneva. . . . If you know anything about this individual, be so kind as to let me know.[29]

If you promise not to laugh during the journey, if you are prepared firmly to resolve to spend the rest of your life with happy philosophy, to despise men who are only shams, wicked and deceitful, to arrange your affairs so that these tigers can no longer bite you, then, yes, madame, I shall have the honour of accompanying you to the queen's with very great pleasure, or rather as a very great consolation, for after all the losses you and I have suffered, only the word consolation suits you.[30]

If you will give me only some soup and two fresh eggs, and no plover, if you will allow me to leave the table if I feel ill, if you forgive my miseries, I will have the insolence to obey your order to call. You are the only person in the world before whom I dare to appear in my present state. You inspire me with as much confidence as you console me.[31]

25 Best.D4421 (15 March 1751); Voltaire had left the king's palace to live in the Marquisat, a small house at Potsdam given by Frederick to Argens; it has unfortunately been allowed to fall into decay.
26 Best.D4448 (24 April 1751).

27 Best.D4465 (*c.* May 1751).
28 Best.D4588 (October 1751).
29 Best.D4603 (?12 November 1751).
30 Best.D4659 (1751/52).
31 Best.D4673 (1751/52).

You have the most beautiful soul I have ever known, and I the most wretched body. I spend my life in bed, and am quite unable to write verse about what is happening in the bed of prince Henry.[32]

Thank you for all your kindnesses. I live with a great king and a great man, in a delightful place, in complete liberty, and I am not at all happy. Far from it. I am far from you, and ill.[33]

I have given your herrings to the king. It seems to me that they are readily eaten at his table. Thank you for sending my portrait, but I am not a fresh herring.[34]

Maupertuis is better, but his book is dead. You cannot imagine how much he is despised in Paris and how much people hate the persecution of König, which he has incited in an affair in which he is himself manifestly in the wrong. There is always an element of the absurd in tyranny.[35]

I think it would be much better for me to have the honour of seeing you after the theatre, for you will not leave the princess of Prussia before 11 o'clock. Nevertheless if you are to be at home at half past ten precisely I am yours to command.[36]

While the wretched Hirschel affair dragged itself through reams of German-Latin jargon, Voltaire played and worked harder than ever. Performances of his tragedies were given, with his active participation, in the apartments of several members of the royal family; and he still struggled to induce Lambert in Paris, and Walther in Dresden, to present his collected works in a more or less adequate form, textually and typographically.

And how did the king feel about Voltaire when the honeymoon was over? It is fair to let him speak for himself. In February 1751 he wrote to Voltaire:

I was very glad to welcome you; I have admired your wit, your talents, your knowledge, and I could not but believe that a man of your age, weary of sparring with authors and of exposing himself to storms, came here to take refuge, as it were, in a calm harbour. But you at once demanded, in a rather singular manner, that I should not employ Fréron to write me news-letters: I had the weakness or the indulgence to grant your request, although it was not for you to decide on those I take into my service. D'Arnaud has behaved badly towards you; a generous man would have forgiven him these wrongs; a vindictive man persecutes those he hates. In short, although d'Arnaud had

32 Best.D4924 (c. 30 June 1752).
33 Best.D4942 (14 July 1752).
34 Best.D4967 (?4 August 1752).
35 Best.D5093 (c. 1 December

1753).
36 Best.D5207 (c. February 1753); this was the last letter to countess Bentinck written by Voltaire in Prussia.

not harmed me, it is because of you that he left. You went to the Russian ambassador to talk to him about things in which you had no business to meddle, and it was thought that I had asked you to do it. You meddled in the affairs of mme de Bentinck, though this was not your business. You have had the most wretched of affairs with the Jew, and created a frightful disturbance in the whole town. The business of the Saxon notes is so well known in Saxony that grievous complaints have been sent to me. For my part, I kept the peace in my house until your arrival, and I warn you that if you have the passion of intrigue and cabal you have come to the wrong place. I like people who are quiet and peaceful, who do not display tragic passions in their conduct. If you can make up your mind to live as a philosopher, I shall be glad to see you; but if you give way to all the heat of your passions, to show ill-will to everybody, you will give me no pleasure in coming here [Potsdam], and you might as well remain in Berlin.[37]

The feasts of wit flowed deep into the nights, and were undoubtedly enjoyed by all. 'It is Caesar, it is Marcus Aurelius, it is Julian, it is sometimes the abbé de Chaulieu with whom one sups.'[38] A contemporary German writer does not exaggerate when he says that these suppers were reputed to be a thousand times more agreeable than the best of books.[39] Yet the contacts between Voltaire and the king began to produce sparks of a different kind. Frederick undoubtedly had cause for irritation in the matter of the Hirschel imbroglio, but elsewhere the provocation was largely imaginary, as in the incidents of the Bentinck law suit and the departure of the Russian envoy. This diplomatic incident was a typically Friderician operation, which Voltaire described in a letter to Wilhelmina of Bayreuth as a vexatious affair which would make a good subject for a comedy. The empress Elizabeth of Russia and the Prussian king decided to break off relations in order to blackmail Maria Theresa. A silly pretext of protocol was therefore invented, and Heinrich von Gross, the Russian resident in Berlin, was recalled. For all his skill in such kitchen intrigues Frederick always tended to gild the lily, as in his Voltaire forgery, and on this occasion he absurdly tried to hold Voltaire responsible for the premeditated incident.[40] The difficulty

37 Best.D4900 (24 February 1751); Best.D4401 (? 25 February 1751) is Voltaire's reply.

38 BestD4248 (24 October 1750).

39 Johann Georg von Zimmermann,

Uber Friedrich der grossen (Leipzig 1788), pp. 190-2.

40 See Best.D4401 (? 25 February 1751), and a note on Best.D4364 (30 January 1751).

with Baculard d'Arnaud had been deliberately created by the king in order to persuade Voltaire to surrender to Frederick's invitations.[41] And so on.

The true inwardness of the growing tension between the two men lay elsewhere. Voltaire had no choice but to swallow the king's vociferous reproaches with the best grace he could muster even when they were undeserved; but he got his own back in his perfectly just but unsparing criticism of his pupil's literary efforts, especially the verse *Art de la guerre*, 'reckoned truly his best Piece in verse', says Carlyle[42], and no wonder, since 300 of its 1600 lines are entirely by Voltaire, and most of the rest were amended or influenced by him.[43] In his turn the royal poet had to accept Voltaire's severities with a smile, but it is only too evident that this smile tended to become somewhat wry. In such a situation something must give, and not even the self-conscious genius and pride of a Voltaire, to say nothing of his irritability, could long withstand the heavy-handed arrogance of an absolute monarch.

However, as the months passed Voltaire continued to take in what he called the king's 'dirty linen'[44], that is, to correct the poetry which Frederick poured out with 'indefatigable pertinacity'. This was no light task. Lytton Strachey, who never could avoid a baroque attitude, was too severe when he found the king's muse 'dreary with an unutterable dreariness, from which the eyes of men avert themselves in shuddering dismay'[45]. Still, even Swinburne, who naturally much admired Frederick, was almost as unkind about the 'supreme demerits' of his verse.[46] But Voltaire toiled away, both by precept and example, and generally a rather feverish peace reigned between the two men. In the little notes he often sent to his host's apartments Voltaire dashed off some of his most elegant occasional verse. When the king expressed his religious scepticism, what could be more graceful than Voltaire's reply?

---

41 See p. 319, above.

42 *History of Friedrich II of Prussia*, XVI.iv.

43 See my edition of 'Voltaire's commentary on Frederick's *L'Art de la guerre*', *Studies on Voltaire* (1956),
ii.61-206.

44 Best.D4956 (24 July 1752).

45 *Books and characters* (London 1922), pp. 169-70.

46 *The Swinburne letters*, ed. Cecil Y. Lang (New Haven 1959), i.116.

Vous nous annoncez avec zèle
Une importante vérité,
Mais vous allez pourtant à l'immortalité
En nous prêchant l'âme mortelle.[47]

Yet Voltaire made it plain to the king that he was aware of the latter's equivocal attitude; he went so far as to tell Frederick that he did not put much trust in his philosophy.

Throughout these growing difficulties Voltaire found some comfort in the composition of a series of prose dialogues of a mildly satirical character, and other short pieces, including the *Eloge historique de madame la marquise Du Châtelet* and the important *Pensées sur le gouvernement*[48]; in friendly correspondence with Wilhelmina of Bayreuth; and above all in the sympathetic presence of countess Bentinck. Wilhelmina, however, was in a state of frightened subservience to her royal brother; while mme Bentinck was herself out of favour because of her awkward law suit and because she had the bad luck to be an attractive woman. Still, Voltaire was no doubt flattered to receive from Frederick an ode addressed to him as 'The mainstay of taste, of the arts, of elegance,/ Son of Apollo, Homer of France . . .'.

In Paris, in the meanwhile, yet another unfaithful secretary had stolen Voltaire's manuscripts, and a police inquiry resulted, to which we are indebted for a fascinating report[49]. In this previously unpublished document Voltaire is described as 'tall, gaunt, with the look of a satyr'. The report then goes on:

He is an eagle in intelligence and a bad lot in character. Everybody knows his works and his adventures. He is a member of the Académie française. Mme Denis is his niece.

In June 1750 he definitely left his fatherland to go to Prussia. His post as historiographer was given to Duclos.

On the previous 15 September he had lost mme la marquise Du Châtelet. . . .

On 29 April 1751 I was instructed by order of the king to search the premises of Longchamp, Voltaire's valet, and Lafond, formerly valet, with his wife, of mme Du Châtelet. . . .

I knew that the real object of this visitation was to try to find the love letters Voltaire had written to mme Du Châtelet and which this lady had

---

47 Best.D4563 (August/September 1751). 'You announce with zeal an important truth, but you are destined for immortality when you preach the mortality of the soul.'

48 See p. 305, above.

49 Bibliothèque nationale, MS. N.a.fr.10781, f.11.

bound in four volumes [more probably, in eight]. They had not been found after her death and it was feared that the maid had taken them in order to get them published, which would be amusing. Voltaire, having feared that this might happen, asked monsieur d'Argenson to have a search made on a pretext. But it was not successful.

On the following 4 May the magistrate told me that he knew for sure that when we searched Longchamp's place a drawer in his desk contained the verses written against the king and mme la marquise [de Pompadour]. . . . How amusing it would have been if verse against the king and mme la marquise, perhaps in Voltaire's hand or in that of one of his entourage, had been found as a result of a search instigated by Voltaire! . . .

It never seems to have occurred to this literate but malicious policeman that Voltaire would hardly have instigated the search if in fact such compromising papers were in existence. It is quite certain that Voltaire never wrote against Louis xv or mme de Pompadour. These allegations were simply echoes of the Frederick forgery.

Voltaire's friends by now realised that he was heading for trouble, and several of them, including Argental and Richelieu, pleaded with him to leave Prussia. Argental reminded Voltaire that his departure had driven him to despair, and warned him that he was at the mercy of one man, and that man was a king. (But was Voltaire's position in France any different?) Voltaire was now regretted at home, even *Mahomet* would be very successful when revived[50]. His glory, his happiness depended on his return. Voltaire knew in his heart that his friends were right. Had Frederick not said, 'I need him for another year at most. One squeezes the orange and throws away the peel'?[51] Voltaire still hoped that the orange would not be utterly squeezed. But the hope soon waned, and at the turn of the year he had made up his mind to leave the court of the all too possessive king. It only remained to find the opportunity, and to make the necessary practical arrangements.

Yet Voltaire's decision by no means implied a return to Paris. With every justification, he felt that his presence there would be unwelcome to the authorities, and soon he knew that he was right when he saw how the *Siècle de Louis xiv* was received. Still,

50 Argental was right; the tragedy was put on again a few weeks later, and the attendance at the eight performances was highly unusual: 1021, 1057, 958, 903, 1102, 996, 882, 1036.
51 Best.D4539 (6 August 1751), D4564 (2 September 1751).

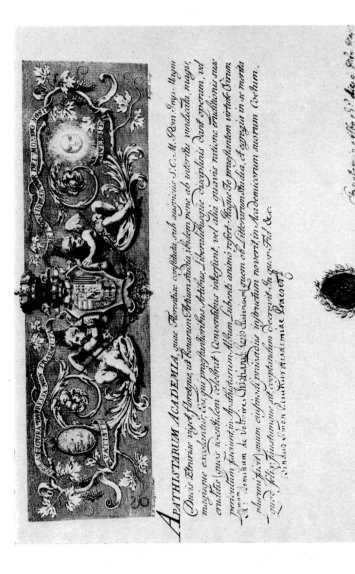

13 Voltaire's diploma of membership of the Apatisti academy, Florence

dévoué pour avoir mangé un peu
d'herbe.

Dans l'école de ces génies, qui feront
les délices & l'inftruction des fiécles à
venir, il fe forma une foule d'efprits
agréables, dont on a une infinité de petits ouvrages délicats, qui font l'amufe-
ment des honnêtes gens, ainfi que nous
avons eû beaucoup de peintres gracieux,
qu'on ne met pas à côté des pouffin, des
le fueur & des le brun.

Cependant, vers la fin du régne de louis
XIV, deux hommes percérent la foule des
génies médiocres, & eûrent beaucoup de
réputation. l'un était la motte-houdart,
homme d'un efprit plus fage & plus éten-
du que fublime, écrivain délicat & mé-
thodique en profe, mais manquant fou-
vent de feu & d'élégance dans fa poëfie,
& même de cette éxactitude qu'il n'eft
permis de négliger qu'en faveur du fublime. il donna d'abord de belles ftances
plustôt que de belles odes. fon talent dé-
clina bientôt après : mais beaucoup de
beaux morceaux, qui nous reftent de lui
en plus d'un genre, empécheront toûjours
qu'on ne le mette au rang des auteurs
méprifables. il prouva, que dans l'art
d'écrire, on peut être encor quelque cho-
fe au fecond rang.

L'autre était rouffeau, qui avec moins
d'es-

Voltaire's relative cheerfulness was no doubt sustained by the publication of the book on which he had been meditating and working for nearly twenty years, and which was to remain one of his favourite children. And he was right, for the *Siècle* is a remarkable combination of insight, humanity and style: in its grasp and graceful presentation of a complex historical subject it has never been surpassed. Even lord Chesterfield was enthusiastic. The *Siècle*, he said, 'showed how history should be written. It is the history of the human understanding, written by a man of parts, for the use of men of parts. . . . He tells me all I want to know, and nothing more. His reflections are short, just, and produce others in his readers. Free from religious, philosophical, political, and national prejudices, beyond any historian I ever met with. . . .'[52]

Voltaire first mentioned the *Siècle* twenty years earlier[53], and it was never long out of his mind. He even recorded unusually full and precise indications of his intentions, perhaps best of all in his letter[54] to lord Hervey, which was promptly published as a pamphlet. He made it clear that he considered Louis xiv to have been a great king, not because but although he deprived France of a million men by his wars. It was not his conquests that entitled the century to be known by his name; it was because he had attracted many able foreigners to France; because he had encouraged and recompensed so many great artists in every field; because he had launched so many scientific researches and explorations; because he had established so many manufactures; because he had made French the universal language.

Of course this picture of Louis xiv's role is incomplete, as Voltaire well knew and clearly said. The king's subservience to the church led to the persecution of the Protestants, probably the most economically and cruelly senseless step taken in the whole course of French history before 1940. His bad administration,

---

52 *Letters written by the late right honourable Philip Dormer Stanhope, earl of Chesterfield* (London 1774), ii.232-5 (13 April 1752).

53 Best.D488 (13 May 1732).

54 Best.D2206 (*c.* 1 June 1740); this was written soon after the publication of John Lockman's translation of a fragment of Voltaire's early draft, *An Essay on the age of Lewis XIV* (London 1739).

ruinous wars, and building mania gave France an uncomfortably close view of bankruptcy.

Many years later, in writing to a publisher about a new edition, Voltaire repeated that his book was a monument to the honour of France, with special reference to literature and the arts[55]. Yet this monument was repudiated by the French authorities, and Voltaire had to publish it in Prussia. Even here the mischief-makers were active, and made some impression on the king. Voltaire told Frederick firmly that the *Siècle* was his just as the Brandenburg history was the king's, and that was that. Outside court circles the *Siècle* made an immense impression, and went at once into a dozen editions, only one or two of which were published surreptitiously in France[56].

Why was Voltaire's glorification of French culture rejected by the authorities? It was because they were so pathologically sensitive to criticism that Voltaire's praise of Louis XIV was seen, by contrast, as a satire on Louis XV. Voltaire himself hoped that his picture of the reign of Louis XIV would be an encouragement to the king's successor. He says so himself[57], and there is no doubt that he wanted to stimulate rather than to criticise, even by indirection. But the reaction of the authorities was inevitable, for it was the expression of an invariable policy. Thus, when Charles Pinot Duclos published (1745-46) an *Histoire de Louis XI*, his comments even on the fifteenth century were regarded as so dangerous in the eighteenth that his book was condemned by the *conseil d'état*. However, he was then rewarded by the succession to Voltaire's 'historiography'. No such compensation awaited Voltaire, other than the admiration and approval of his fellow-countrymen, and indeed of foreigners.

The great man had of course, as usual, taken immense pains to get his facts right[58], and, convinced that the *Siècle* was destined for posterity, he continued all his life to improve it. At the moment he was concerned to get it a hearing, as can be seen from this letter to his old friend Fawkener, which brings out also his meticulous

55 Best.D14341 (7 August 1767).
56 Although the *Siècle de Louis XIV* is now regarded as one of the masterpieces of historical writing, there still exists no adequate critical edition of it.
57 Best.D549 (20 December 1732).
58 See what he says about this in Best.app.D328.

attention to detail in everything he did, and the peculiar charm of his English:

My dear and beneficent friend j send to you by the way of Hambourg, two enormous bales of the scribling trade. J direct them to our envoy at Hambourg, who will dispatch them to you and put my wares to sea, instead of throwing em into the fire, which might to be case in France or at Rome; my dear friend j have recourse to y^r free and generous soul. Some french, good patriots, who have read the book, raise a noble clamour against me for having prais'd Marlborough and Eugene, and some good churchmen damn me for having turn'd a little into ridicule our jansenisme and molinisme. If our prejudic'd people are fools, booksellers and printers, [our] bookjobbers are rogues. J am like to be damn'd in France and cheated by the dutch. The old germanik honesty is gone.

Booksellers of all regions are the same. J'll lose all the fruit of my labours and expenses, but j rely on y^r kindness. You may cause some books to be bound, and chuse an honest man, who will give them to the chief readers of y^r nation. J intreat you to present his highness [the duke of Cumberland] with one of these volumes, and to give some examplaries to those of y^r friends you will think fit. The bookseller you will chuse may do what he pleases with the remainder, and sell them as best as he can, provided he sells not before easter, t'is all j require of him. J beg you hundred pardons for so much trouble, and j wish the book could procure you a pleasure equal to my importunities. My ultimatum is then to teize you with the reading of the book, to pray you to give one to his R. h. the duke and to y^r friends, to commit the rest in to the hands of any man you will think proper to chuse, and to forgive my cumbersom follies. Do what you please. Burn the book in case you should yawn in reading it, but do not forget y^r old friend who will be attach'd to you till the day of his doom.[59]

No sooner was the book published than the pirates got busy. Voltaire spent much energy in confounding them, partly by trying, unsuccessfully of course, to get their editions suppressed, but above all by ceaseless corrections and cancels, and by preparing new authorized versions. Critics of the book also had to be answered, including even a certain La Beaumelle[60], who had the distinction, his sole claim to fame, of achieving some nuisance value in Voltaire's life. Laurent Angliviel de La Beaumelle was born in France in 1726, and moved successively to Geneva,

---

59 Best.D4777 (24 January 1752). The bill of lading for the sheets of the *Siècle* sent to England has survived; see Best.xx, fig. 116.

60 He has left voluminous archives, access to which is steadfastly refused by his descendants, no doubt for excellent reasons.

Copenhagen and Berlin. His stay in each place was brief, his talents and particularly his character being much inferior to his ambition. Thus he almost inevitably became one of the most acrimonious and least scrupulous of Voltaire's enemies. When he arrived in Prussia he had already published a few *trivia*, of which only one survives because of its amiable references to Voltaire: 'Search ancient and modern history, and you will find no instance of a prince who gave an annuity of 7000 *écus* [in fact, 3000] to a man of letters, as such. There have been greater poets than Voltaire, there has never been one so well rewarded, because taste puts no limits to its rewards. The king of Prussia heaps benefits on men of talent for exactly the same reasons that engage a little German prince to heap benefits on a buffoon or a dwarf.' Had La Beaumelle but known it he could have appealed to a distinguished precedent, which luckily was unknown to Voltaire also. Frederick himself, when he reimbursed the expenses of Voltaire's journey in 1740, complained that never had the buffoon of a great lord been paid such wages.[61]

No sooner had La Beaumelle expressed these views, as little flattering to the one as to the other, than he came to Berlin and assiduously sought the acquaintance of the king and his buffoon. And no sooner had Voltaire saved him from penury[62] than he threatened to publish his version of the Hirschel affair[63]. Finally he did publish an edition of the *Siècle* into which he inserted much false and offensive material, for which he was imprisoned as soon as he set foot in France—not, of course, because he had stolen and deformed Voltaire's work, but because he had called the duc d'Orléans a poisoner, and referred disrespectfully to mme de Pompadour.

In his *Supplément du Siècle de Louis XIV* Voltaire refuted the criticisms of La Beaumelle, who then published a ferocious attack on him, the tone and accuracy of which are sufficiently indicated by its opening sentences: 'The whole world abandons you, sir.

---

61 *Mes pensées* (Copenhague 1751), pp. 69-70; Frederick's *Œuvres complètes*, xvii.72. La Beaumelle's essential vulgarity can also be judged by the manner of his choice of a 'suitable' wife and mistress; see for instance Best.D7456a (9 November 1757), D7746a (2 June 1758) in the supplement (Voltaire 130).

62 Best.D14382 (18 August 1767).

63 Best.D5098, D5141, D5192 (December 1752-February 1753).

Disgraced in Berlin, where it only rested with you to be happy, you have been rebuffed at Hanover, where you asked for all recompense only an annuity of a thousand pounds sterling. You have been refused an asylum in Vienna, where they had the weakness a few months earlier to grant you a *lettre de cachet* against me. Your dedicatory epistles have been rejected at Bern. In Holland nowadays they like only calm and peaceful people. I am assured that you cannot return to Paris. You no longer have any friends. Your enemies triumph; the powers crush you; wisdom applauds. What refuge, what expedient remain to you? Colmar and my pity'.[64]

It may perhaps be just worth while to say a word about La Beaumelle's allusions to Voltaire's financial rewards, not because *he* makes them but because they are often repeated by others equally low. It is true that Frederick paid Voltaire's travelling expenses and provided him with pocket-money. This was the usual practice between princes and commoners in the age of patronage, and it was in the same spirit that Voltaire in turn generously reimbursed his *protégés* when they came to see him at a distance. Only a callow provincial like La Beaumelle would have thought of commenting on it. Moreover, Voltaire's removal to Prussia was a costly affair. He immediately lost one of his offices, he had to bear the cost of transferring part of his capital to Berlin and then back again, and because of his absence he had to give up his profitable participation in the enterprises of Pâris Duverney[65]. All this was beyond the comprehension of a La Beaumelle.

To the long list of those who made free with Voltaire's manuscripts must now be added a name that became distinguished, that of Lessing, who does not emerge from this affair with much grace. A local amanuensis had surreptitiously shown the young critic a manuscript of the *Siècle*. Lessing took it away without permission, and when Voltaire complained he replied with perhaps excessive naivety that it was not his fault if his curiosity was greater than

---

64 *Réponse au Supplément du Siècle de Louis XIV* (Colmar 1754), pp. 5-6.

65 Best.D4242 (15 October 1750). See also my introduction to *Voltaire's household accounts* (1968).

his good faith.[66] Longchamps, on the other hand, frankly admitted his own offence, and was promptly forgiven.

Micromégas was published at this time, but an exchange with cardinal Quirini aroused much more contemporary excitement. The cardinal wanted to build a Roman catholic cathedral in Berlin, and asked Voltaire to write about this project. This was a terrible blunder, and he received a vitriolic reply. Frederick, said Voltaire, was an unbeliever, and would have to go to hell with Cicero, Aristides, Plato and Marcus Aurelius. He was guilty of the enormous and cruel sin of tolerance. Voltaire shuddered when he reflected that Muslims, pagans, Quakers, Lutherans, Protestants and Roman catholics were equally well received by him if they were upright. What did the cardinal expect him to do against a prince so hardened in evil?[67]

Even more characteristic was a brief but violent controversy with Formey, over which we need not linger, and his astonishingly minute solicitude for Jean Martin de Prades. This young abbé had submitted a sceptical thesis to the Sorbonne, which the university accepted by some oversight, but they had to reverse themselves when church and *parlement* attacked Prades with the virulence usual in such cases. The young man had to flee the country, and was for a while in difficulties. He was an insignificant personage, and turned out to be also a dishonest one, for when Voltaire persuaded Frederick to give him a responsible job, he soon betrayed his master, and was imprisoned. But in the meanwhile Voltaire had written him a remarkable letter. He gave the persecuted abbé a detailed account of his mode of life in Berlin; described all the difficulties and facilities the Prussian capital had to offer; and invited him to share his roof and board. 'Do not scruple to accept the wretchedness I offer you. Let us be philosophers, as if we had known each other for a long time. . . . You can bring your books, and I would borrow from Leipzig all those you might need. . . .'[68]

The affection of mme Bentinck continued to sustain Voltaire, as did the highly successful revival of *Mahomet*, more particularly because it encouraged the hope that *Rome sauvée* would be equally

66 Best.D4866, D4868 (1 January 1752).

67 Best.D4759 (7 January 1752).

68 Best.D4949 (18 July 1752).

acclaimed—but this was not to be. And now at last, in the summer of 1752, Voltaire began seriously to prepare his departure. An immediate difficulty was presented by the substantial funds he had brought with him to Prussia; this he solved ingeniously by using the money to buy an annuity secured on certain properties belonging to Wurttemberg.

As for a future home, Voltaire made a curiously naive approach to the Bern authorities, which was generously matched by the manner of its even more curious rejection. He asked the Supreme council for permission to dedicate one of his plays to them. 'It is not the greatness of empires that makes the merit of men. Men as respectable as Roman senators formed part of the areopagus of Athens, and the council of Bern contains magistrates as virtuous and as enlightened as those of Athens.'[69] A handsome compliment indeed, but Voltaire made the fatal mistake of beginning his letter 'Messieurs', no doubt because the members of the *parlements* were so designated. On being informed of the magnitude of his error the punctilious author tried again, humbly apologising to the 'Très puissants et très magnifiques Seigneurs'[70] for his ignorance —but to no avail, for his offer was rejected, though in pompous and flattering terms[71], which no doubt amused Voltaire more than they consoled him.

By far the most important event of the autumn of 1752 was the birth of a project for the 'advancement of human reason': the future *Dictionnaire philosophique*, to be published only in years to come, when we shall be able to look at it more closely, though not as minutely as it deserves. More immediately sensational was the still famous quarrel between König and Maupertuis about the authenticity of certain Leibniz letters quoted by the former. The dispute has long since been settled in König's favour, but it is still notorious because of the jealous violence of Maupertuis's behaviour. He was so angry because he was pathologically vain and touchy, because König had discovered passages in Leibniz which appeared to rob him of a trifling scientific priority, because

69 Best.D5064 (8 November 1752).
70 Best.D5177 (26 January 1753).
'Very powerful and very magnificent lords.'

71 Best.D5213 (21 February 1753).

Voltaire took König's part, and because Maupertuis's nose had already been put out of joint by the great man's arrival in Berlin. The king defended Maupertuis because he was the head of the academy[72] and the irascible scientist's arbitrary behaviour and threats were soon overshadowed by the engaging spectacle of a battle of pamphlets between the king of Prussia and his most celebrated guest. Of course such a battle could be won, in the immediate event, only by the king, who adopted an expedient worthy of his heavy-handed ingenuity: he published an anonymous defence of Maupertuis, anonymous, that is, but for the Prussian eagle, the crown and the sceptre on the titlepage. These emblems, commented Voltaire, were surprised to find themselves in such a place. 'Every one shrugs his shoulders, casts down his eyes, and dares not speak.'[73]

Frederick could overawe the public by such means, and he also could and did forbid Voltaire to meddle in the affair, but getting him to obey such orders was beyond the power even of thrones and dominations. Voltaire continued to write and speak in defence of König, and printed the *Diatribe*; the king prohibited its publication; Voltaire circulated it surreptitiously by an ingenious trick; Frederick then had it publicly burnt and brought the ashes to Maupertuis. Small wonder that all this led to the final break between the two men: final in the sense of intimate association and physical proximity. But first Voltaire transformed the whole affair into the wittiest, the most biting of his satires, the *Diatribe du docteur Akakia*. Frederick may have consoled himself and Maupertuis by his *auto-da-fé*, but Europe howled with laughter, both at the *Diatribe* and at the odd goings-on of the philosopher-king.

Voltaire begins his satire by protesting against the conduct of some young and unknown charlatan who had passed off his rubbish as the work of the president of a very illustrious academy. Some of the things that Voltaire found absurd are by no means so ridiculous as he thought them. Thus, Maupertuis was neither the first nor the last to propose that doctors should not be paid if their patients did not recover. However, Voltaire had no difficulty in

72 For another possible reason see pp. 226-227, above.

73 Best.D5067 (15 November 1752).

making fun of much in his publications. But all this is impossible to summarise. Here, however, is the beginning of the peace treaty drawn up by Voltaire:

All Europe having been alarmed by the dangerous quarrel about an algebraic formula etc. the two parties principally concerned in this war, wishing to avoid a further effusion of ink that all readers would ultimately find unbearable, have at last agreed to the following philosophic peace.

The president [Maupertuis] transported himself to the seat of his presidency, and said before his peers:

1. Having had the leisure to recognise my mistake I beg the professor [König] to forget all the past. I much regret that I made so much ado about nothing, and that I accused of forgery a grave professor who has never invented anything but monads and pre-established harmony.

2. I have signed letters patent sealed with my great seal by which I restore its liberty to the republic of letters; and I declare that writers will henceforth be permitted to prove me in the wrong without being accused of dishonesty, etc. etc.

Frederick was now so angry that the philosopher was quite lost in the king. He set a clumsy trap by sending Voltaire a declaration which he was to sign, and in which he was made tacitly to admit that he had written against the government of France and other sovereigns. Once again Frederick overreached himself in at least two particulars. He wrote out the declaration in his own hand, thus revealing its origin; and he betrayed his own state of mind when he imagined that Voltaire could be caught in so crude a snare. Voltaire did not sign, but wrote below the declaration that his heart would make no difficulty about obeying the king's orders, but that he had never written against any government, least of all his own.[74]

However, this time Voltaire saw the light. He told mme Denis: 'I see very clearly that the orange has been pressed; I must now think of saving the rind.'[75] On the first day of 1753 he told the king in formal terms that he wanted to leave, intimating delicately that it was because he felt that he had outstayed his welcome. Yet he ended, 'I had made you my idol, an upright man does not change his religion, and sixteen years of a devotion which knew no limits cannot be destroyed by a single misfortune.' With this letter Voltaire returned his *Pour le mérite* and the chamberlain's key:

74 Best.D5085 (27 November 1752).   75 Best.D5114 (10 December 1752).

Je les reçus avec tendresse,
Je vous les rends avec douleur,
Tel qu'un amant dans sa jalouse ardeur,
Rend le portrait de sa maîtresse.[76]

That Voltaire returned his key is not unnatural, for it was the symbol of an office which he was resigning. The return of the order is quite another matter, since it was an honour. To return such a badge or medal is at worst a deliberate insult, at best the most vigorous kind of protest, a step seldom taken even in wartime. The duc de Luynes said that Voltaire had acted 'as between kings.'[77] It is clear from the tone of Voltaire's letter that neither insult nor protest was intended, and we must therefore conclude that Frederick's award of his highest distinction, the *Pour le mérite*, was conditional on Voltaire's residence in Prussia: a very odd procedure indeed, but at least one that helps to explain Frederick's later insistence on the surrender of the decoration after he had returned it to Voltaire, an insistence which would otherwise have been grotesquely undignified.

On the same day Voltaire wrote a second, informal letter[78] to the king, in which he expressed his sorrow in touching terms. Frederick returned the baubles with sweet words, but it was too late. Voltaire refused to follow the king to Potsdam on the pretext of illness, and insisted on receiving his *congé* to take the waters at Plombières, However, Frederick was not prepared to give up his glittering prize. He sent Voltaire quinine and this message, most ingeniously contrived, it must be owned, to win back the great man:

The king has held his consistory and this consistory discussed whether your case was a mortal or a venial sin. As a matter of fact all the doctors admitted that it is very mortal and proved to be so by lapses and relapses. But nevertheless by the plenitude of Beelzebuth's grace which resides in his majesty he thinks he can absolve you if not of the whole at least in part. This should really be in response to some imposed act of contrition or penitence, but as in the empire of Satan much deference is paid to genius I believe that as a tribute to your talents the faults which might have done some harm to your

---

76 See a note on Best.D5133 (1 January 1753); for a translation see the autobiography, p. 650, below.

77 *Mémoires*, xii.343 ('comme de couronne à couronne').

78 Best.D5129 (1 January 1753).

heart could be pardoned. Such are the words of the sovereign pontiff, which I have gathered with care. It is, indeed, a prophecy.[79]

Once again, it was too late. After receiving this letter Voltaire, writing to the British ambassador (sir Charles Hanbury Williams), described himself as a man who was 'by his madness servant to a king'[80] To the king he held out the hope of a return if his health should improve, but again insisted on his *congé*.[81] He told mme Denis that, not having 150,000 mustachios in his service, he was not contemplating war, but only a decent desertion.[82] Frederick at last conveyed his *exeat* to Voltaire on 15 March, and ten days later the speeding guest left for Leipzig, the brevity of the interval showing that all but the final preparations had already been made. At Leipzig he wrote *Akakia*, and made friends with the publisher Breitkopf and with the learned Gottsched, to whom he wrote letters in Latin and German[83]. Then he visited the courts of Gotha and Cassel, sending from the latter to the former one of his most charming bread and butter letters[84]. Thence Voltaire reached Frankfort on 29 May, being joined there by mme Denis a few days later.

At about the same time Voltaire received a very long letter in which countess Bentinck begged him to make it up with the king. This remarkable letter, vibrant with affection and worldly good sense, deserves to be quoted in full, but it is too long. The gist of it is that Voltaire was at least partly responsible for the rift, and that even if he were entirely in the right he could not expect a king to humiliate himself[85]. Even if Voltaire had been inclined to listen to this advice, which he probably was not, the king's behaviour made any rapprochement impossible. For in the meanwhile Frederick's angry disappointment had again got the better

---

79 Best.D5152 (*c.* 15 January 1753). So anxious was Frederick that he toned down the draft of this judgment by striking out a reference to 'the vices of the heart'.

80 Best.D5161 (16 January 1753).

81 Best.D5229 (11 March 1753).

82 Best.D5114 (18 December 1752). It may have been (but Frederick being what he was it probably was not) a chance coincidence that years later the king told Voltaire that one could write anything one chose with impunity, without having 160,000 soldiers, so long as one did not print it; Best.D8268 (18 April 1759).

83 Best.D5252 (6 April 1753), D5269 (25 April).

84 Best.D5298 (28 May 1753).

85 Best.D5296 (26 May 1753).

of his fundamental good sense, and he gave instructions[86] to his representative in Frankfort to intercept the traveller: instructions so confused, but at the same time so categorical, that when Voltaire in due course reached the free city he was arrested, in defiance of law and decency. His secretary Collini and mme Denis, when she joined her uncle, were also put under restraint.

In order to appreciate the full significance of the instructions given by Frederick to stop and search Voltaire, to remove papers from his luggage, and if necessary to arrest him, all of which was done, it must be remembered that the Prussian king had no legal authority in Frankfort, which was a free city within the domain of the Holy Roman emperor (*freie Reichsstadt*). Frederick was in fact ordering his representative in a foreign state to arrest a subject of a third state. This is hardly the place for a detailed discussion of the matter, but the point has to be made. A German scholar, in a generally judicious and scholarly study, denies[87] that there was any breach of international law, because the mayor and council of Frankfort expressly approved Voltaire's arrest. This defence is unfounded: because the council was unaware of Voltaire's arrest until after it had taken place; because even then the council did not approve the arrest but only tacitly assented to it subject to the production of justificatory documents, which they never received since they did not exist; because they withdrew their assent long before Voltaire was released; because Collini, and later mme Denis, were also arrested without any instructions whatever, and without any assent on the part of the council. All this emerges clearly from the correspondence and documents.[88]

It should also be remembered that Voltaire had not left Prussia for good, but was to return if he could[89]; whether he really intended to do so is a moot point, and an irrelevant one: the essential thing is that his declared intention was to come back after he had taken a cure at the waters, that he had returned cross and key to the king, who had sent them back, and that before leaving Voltaire had explicitly written to Frederick: 'As for the key and the cross

86 Best.D5254 (11 April 1753).

87 Hermann Haupt, 'Voltaire in Frankfurt 1753', *Zeitschrift für französische Sprache* (Berlin Mai 1904) xxvii.173.

88 Printed in full in Voltaire 97-98.

89 See for instance his letters to Frederick of 11 March 1753 (Best. D5228) and 28 April (Best.D5270).

with which your majesty has honoured me, you know, sire, that I am only a man of letters. These decorations, foreign to my condition, are dear to me only because of the hand that gave them to me. I will keep them with the most tender gratitude if you maintain my right to them, and I will return them with the most submissive resignation if you take them back.'[90] If, having written this, and given Voltaire's excessive punctilio, he still had these objects in his possession when he left Prussia, it can only have been by the express desire of the king. Frederick, by then asking for their return (plus a book, and, as an afterthought, his letters to Voltaire—and waiving the manner of the asking), was making it impossible for Voltaire to come back. The king was also publicly accusing him of theft. Over the years Voltaire had called his royal friend Apollo, Socrates, Solomon, Marcus Aurelius[91], but he had never called him Judas.

The king carried his rage to such a pitch that he employed spies to keep track of Voltaire's movements. The evidence for this is circumstantial, but once at least, well over a year later, Frederick betrayed himself. He pretended that Voltaire's visit to Senones meant his return to religion, and implied that Voltaire wore a crucifix.[92] And in fact when he had recently spent a little time in the house of mme Goll, at Colmar, he had found a crucifix hanging in his room, and had of course left it there. But, as Voltaire judiciously inquires, how did Frederick know this?[93]

Voltaire's arrangements for the purchase of a Wurttemberg annuity having been completed, it only remained for him to receive regularly what was due to him: but this was by no means easy, for the officials found it strange, and even reprehensible, that a poet should expect a reigning duke to be punctual in business matters. Voltaire was in the right, but the duke's agents succeeded in wearing him down, and he accepted a substantial reduction in the amounts due to him. The correspondence and documents yield much valuable information about the financial and economic problems of the time.

90 Best.D5229 (11 March 1753).
91 For a further selection of epithets see Adrienne D. Hytier, 'Frédéric II et les philosophes récalcitrants', *The Romanic review* (October 1966), lvii 161.
92 Best.D5983 (14 November 1754).
93 Best.D6013 (6 December 1754).

Voltaire finally managed to escape—it was a flight, not a release—from Frankfort on 7 July 1753. Anybody else would have posted fast and far, but not Voltaire: he merely crossed the Rhine, sat down at Mainz, and on the very next morning launched a paper campaign against his oppressors, pouring out letters and memoranda to join the flood which had already issued from Frankfort. He succeeded only in creating a rift between the king and the Frankfort authorities—not a bad effort for a private individual. As for the king, his anger became still more uncontrollable as his own barbarity and ineptitude came home to him. Slanders of Voltaire flowed from his pen in torrents. He told his sister Wilhelmina that Voltaire had behaved in Prussia like 'the greatest rascal in the universe'. He said that Voltaire had taken up the defence of König only because he himself wanted to be the president of the Academy—in the king's rage he forgot that it was Voltaire who had proposed the appointment of Maupertuis. Voltaire, the king screamed on, had displayed in this controversy his 'baseness, his wickedness and his duplicity'—and so far had the king lost control of himself that he used these terms a second time in the same letter. Voltaire was now distilling new poisons, and, Frederick repeated this also, he was 'the most treacherous rascal in the universe'[94]. I dare say that this was not too unforgivable in a family correspondence, but the king then wrote in similar terms to his ambassador in Paris (now George Keith, 9th earl Marischal), asking him to disseminate these charges quietly in Paris[95]. Keith did his best to calm Frederick, but with little success.[96] And the kindly efforts of Louisa Dorothea of Saxe-Gotha and Wilhelmina of Bayreuth to reconcile the two men were also of no avail. The two men did make it up eventually, not whole-heartedly, but they never again met face to face.

A final detail of the Frankfort affair must be mentioned, because not even the most minute narrative of this infinitely complex and protracted affair could bring home more clearly the atmosphere in which took place these events, of which I have given only the barest outline. When Voltaire was arrested by Frederick's henchmen all his money was taken away, so that he was penniless when

94 Best.D5255 (12 April 1753).   96 Best.D5277 (1 May 1753), D5286
95 Best.D5258 (c. 15 April 1753).   (16 May 1753).

he made good his escape. When he asked for the return of his property he was presented with a bill for all the expenses of his detention. As for the balance, he could have it, he was told, if he applied for it in person.[97]

Long before, after a heated literary debate with Voltaire, Edward Young had said of him:

> You are so witty, profligate, and thin,
> At once we think you Milton, Death, and Sin.[98]

Young remembered this when news of these German events reached him, and his dedication to Voltaire of his *Sea-piece* include the lines:

> 'Tell me', say'st thou, 'who courts my smile?
> What stranger strayed from yonder isle?'—
> No stranger, sir! though born in foreign climes.
> On Dorset downs, when Milton's page,
> With Sin and Death, provoked thy rage,
> The rage provoked *who* soothed with gentle rhymes? . . .

> But such debates long since are flown;
> For ever set the suns that shone
> On airy pastimes, ere our brows were grey
> How shortly shall we both forget.
> To thee, my patron, I my debt,
> And thou to thine, for Prussia's golden key!

Voltaire never forgot 'Prussia's golden key'. It was a salutary lesson. And if Frederick's spiritual heir was Hitler, by the diabolical operation of a sort of Gresham's law, those who resisted him ultimately derived their inspiration from the man who spurned that key for the sake of his liberty of speech and action.

---

97 Best.D5472 (7 August 1753); as this must seem incredible, I quote the actual words, which also provide a modest sample of the linguistic miasma which obfuscates this affair: 'Müssen Ihme sein geldt wen Er sich selbsten melden wirdt ohne anstand nach abzug der kost ausbezahlt werden wirdt.'

98 Quoted by Samuel Johnson in his life of Young (*Lives of the poets*).

26. The road to and from Geneva, 1753-1757

WHILE VOLTAIRE WAS AT Mainz the king of Prussia told George Keith that the escaped prisoner had tried to enter the service of the queen of Hungary and of the king of England.[1] But poor Frederick was simply hitting out blindly in the hope of getting in one good blow. The truth was less romantic. When Voltaire wearied of his anti-Friderician campaign, as of course he soon did, although it was primarily concerned with self-justification, he accepted an invitation from the elector Palatine. Enthusiastic as always, he wrote to mme Denis that the court of Schwetzingen enjoyed the theatre and the opera, good food and conversation, courtesy, grandeur, simplicity[2]. But he soon moved on to Strassburg, where he completed and supervised the publication of the *Annales de l'empire*. This work, composed at the request of Louisa Dorothea, approaches dullness as nearly as Voltaire ever could. If he had undertaken the task at all it was because in these years he sought in the past some relief from the all too disagreeable present. He was quite conscious of this, and told mme Bentinck that he spent his life with the dead, for 'they at last do no harm'[3].

Whatever we may think of it Louisa Dorothea was delighted with the *Annales*, not least with the mnemonic verses with which the book is interspersed. 'What can I say to express all my gratitude?' She had recourse to the standard expedient of persons in her position: she sent Voltaire a present of a thousand *écus*, a substantial sum, for she was not rich. Voltaire had had enough of royal patronage, but it was not easy to refuse without offending the court of Saxe-Gotha. However, Voltaire was not for nothing the greatest stylist French literature has seen. He found an elegant

1 Best.D5421 (13 July 1753). 3 Best.D4448 (24 April 1751).
2 Best.D5469 (5 August 1753).

347

formula for his refusal which transformed it by his deft alchemy into a compliment:

It would have been impertinent of me not to have had a fever since your serene highness had suffered one. It has prevented me from replying sooner to all your kindnesses.

But, madame, can the grand-daughter of Ernest the pious wish to make me fall into the sin of simony? Madame, it is not permitted to sell sacred things. The wish to please you, the joy of obeying your orders are more sacred to me than all the patens of our churches. . . .[4]

Apart from the *Siècle de Louis XIV*, and a number of shorter writings[5] connected with it, Voltaire published another substantial instalment[6] of the future *Essai sur les mœurs*. In fact, what with the pirated editions of this *Abrégé*, of the *Annales* and other works, what with his own publishing ventures and projected editions, what with his correspondence with half-a-dozen present and prospective publishers, Voltaire was immersed during this period in the most tiresome details of authorship. Most of this labour was accomplished at Strassburg (August-September 1753) and Colmar (October 1753-June 1754).

In the meanwhile mme Denis had returned to Paris, where she was supposed to look after her uncle's interests, and in particular to obtain permission for him to return to Paris. But she had other things on her mind, and these things were nearly always connected with her personal interests. She even pretended to be pregnant by Voltaire, and Voltaire pretended to believe her. He also begged her over and over again to send him his papers, but mme Denis was most reluctant to give up this precious cargo. However, her uncle's invention was better than hers, and to flatter her vanity he pretended that he was using her letters as the basis of a novel in the manner of *Pamela*, for translations of Richardson's epistolary novel were enormously popular in France. This did the trick, so flattered was her literary vanity—for she was an assiduous playwright, and an indescribably bad one.

4 Best.D5666 (10 February 1754).
5 *Avertissement sur la nouvelle histoire de Louis XIV, Avis à l'auteur du Journal de Gottingue, Supplément au Siècle de Louis XIV*. The *Examen du testament politique du cardinal Albéroni, A m. de *** , professeur en histoire* and *Doutes sur quelques points de l'histoire de l'empire* should also be mentioned.
6 Under the title of *Abrégé de l'histoire universelle*.

Mme Denis told her uncle that the indignation and horror aroused by his treatment was universal in France. There was nobody whatever in the entire country who did not condemn the violence and cruelty to which he had been subjected.[7] This is a fair specimen of the good lady's honesty, for by this time she knew that permission to return to France had been officially refused to Voltaire in order to placate Frederick.

Neither his correspondence with Malesherbes, the director of the booktrade, nor with Vernet brought much solace, though Voltaire's association with the *Encyclopédie* was a bright spot, and so was a series of delightful letters from the duchess of Saxe-Gotha. Otherwise the period was dull, and even disagreeable: a dispute with the Jesuit Menoux, continued difficulties concerning the Wurttemberg annuity, a brief but bitter quarrel provoked by mme Denis, unsuccessful efforts to obtain permission to go to Plombières. Louis xv still would not allow Voltaire to return to Paris[8], as I have just explained, and even the usually kind and tolerant Stanislas, stimulated by Voltaire's good friend Tressan, refused to have him in Lorraine for fear of offending Frederick[9]. So the wanderer had to continue his search for a permanent home. He sublet part of his house in Paris, disposed of his silver plate, and of some of his pictures and books.

Voltaire found Colmar 'half German, half French, and wholly Iroquois'. An excellent Iroquois Jesuit had preached so fiercely against Bayle that seven copies of the great dictionary had been brought for public burning.[10] In a way the most significant incident of Voltaire's stay in this enlightened city was a letter from the brothers Gabriel and Philibert Cramer, publishers at Geneva. In respectful and dignified terms they put themselves at Voltaire's disposal. 'We will use the finest paper and the best typeface, and above all will pay the most scrupulous attention to all the details of proof-correction'.[11] They promised to do all this with zeal and pleasure, they would do everything to justify Voltaire's patronage. The exiled writer was at this time thoroughly disgusted with all publishers, even Walther and Lambert, the least unreliable he had

7 Best.D5492 (26 August 1753).
8 Best.D5664, D5682 (10, 20 February 1754).
9 Best.D5634 (24 January 1754).
10 Best.D5705 (3 March 1754).
11 Best.D5775 (15 April 1754).

yet encountered, and it is easy to understand with how much pleasure he read this admirable letter. There can be no doubt that it contributed greatly, as well of course as the personal relations soon established with the Cramers and the numerous family of Tronchin, to Voltaire's decision to settle in or near Geneva. 'Chance governs all.'

With or without permission Voltaire enjoyed a few summer weeks of 1754 with the Argentals at Plombières, after spending some little time working in the library of the abbey of Senones, presided over by the learned exegete dom Calmet, an old friend. At Plombières mme Denis (accompanied by her sister) rejoined her uncle, never again to leave him voluntarily. We may deplore the fact for more than one reason, not least because this meant the ending of an illuminating correspondence, in which Voltaire, using code names, expressed himself very freely about a great many people. Voltaire's assent to this union, now made permanent, need not surprise us, for we now know that he was mad (almost literally) about his niece, and so forgave her everything. But mme Denis? Only a few months before she had told her uncle that his troubles had perhaps turned his head, but, she asked, had they also corrupted his heart? She added that he was pierced by avarice (*l'avarice vous poignarde*). And she concluded: 'Do not force me to hate you . . . your heart makes you the lowest of men, but I will hide the vices of your heart as best I can.'[12] If only poor Voltaire had been much less wealthy and a little less famous he might have spent the last and most glorious part of his life in peace. But unfortunately never has any person known so well as mme Denis on which side her bread was buttered. As for Voltaire, there was nothing he did not forgive her, for she was his niece as well as his mistress, and he was very French in his respect for both kinds of ties.

During this time the most notable literary development was a return of Voltaire's interest in the theatre, marked outstandingly by the composition of the *Orphelin de la Chine*. To the continuing difficulties he was having about the pirated editions of his historical works, there was now added what was to be a sore trial for years to come, the unauthorised publication of the *Pucelle*. For the rest,

12 Best.D5714 (10 March 1754).

Voltaire tried to extract an apology from Frederick, the first of many such efforts, all equally unsuccessful. Gossip distorted his efforts: Maupertuis told La Condamine, who told Piron, who told the world, that Voltaire tried again and again to extract from the king a letter he could show. This is nonsense, for Frederick was only too eager to underline his admiration. On 16 March 1754 he told Voltaire: 'Your genius honours humanity too much for me not to be interested in your fate.'

Voltaire was still looking for a home; he returned to Colmar from Plombières, and by the autumn he had more or less decided to live in the region of lake Leman. Nevertheless, when he left Colmar in November he by-passed Geneva and made a great leap south to Lyons, by way of the Franche-Comté and Burgundy, halting briefly at Dijon. At Lyons he is said to have 'lamented very much that his health would not permit him to settle in England, which otherwise would be his choice'. We may take this with a large grain of salt, especially as the unnamed Englishman who reports this found Voltaire 'very much broke and will probably not live long anywhere'[13]. (It was Montesquieu in fact who died about this time, 10 February. Voltaire was asked to write his epitaph, but unfortunately refused, because the president had qualified Virgil and Horace as worthless; Desnoiresterres v.92.) At any rate, whatever he wanted or felt, Voltaire completed the negotiations for a lease of Prangins, and perhaps began those for the purchase of the Délices. In the middle of November he took possession of the handsome house at Prangins, and thus entered the final and greatest period of his life and labour.

The château de Prangins, overlooking lake Leman, north of Nyon, is one of the finest houses in that part of the country. It has since passed through a good many hands, including those of Joseph Bonaparte, and was finally given to the United States as a residence for its ambassadors to the international organisations in Geneva. It is a great pity that Voltaire did not make his home there, but he found the house too big for him, and on 19 January 1755 we find the first reference to what was to become his home

13 de Beer-Rousseau, Voltaire's *British visitors*, p. 25.

for the next few years. Mme Denis announced that on the following day they intended to take a cold chicken to Saint-Jean[14]. In the district so called, then half a league outside the walls of Geneva, the Mallet family had built in 1730-35 an attractive villa in the 'purified' neoclassical style universal in the region at that time. The house was called Sur Saint-Jean, and stood in large grounds in open country. Voltaire fell in love with it. 'It is the palace of a philosopher with the gardens of Epicurus: it is a delicious retreat.'[15]

Difficulties at once arose, for Voltaire was theoretically a Roman catholic, and members of this sect were not allowed to acquire property in the stronghold of that other sect called Calvinist. But where questions of interest are concerned the Genevese are never at a loss. The vendor overcame the religious objections by providing a man of straw, who executed a separate and secret document recognising that he was not the real purchaser. By February all was signed, and the Council graciously gave Voltaire permission 'to live in the republic of Geneva during the good pleasure of their lordships'[16]. 'It was the first instance of a Roman catholic getting an establishment in these Cantons, since the time of Zuinglius and Calvin.'[17] It was not the last, for money has so completely triumphed over convictions that Roman catholics now outnumber Protestants in Geneva.

Voltaire paid 77,200 francs for a life-user of the property and its contents, of which 38,000 francs were to be returned when Voltaire died or gave up his tenure.[18] The smaller figure was much nearer the true value of the property than the larger one; but Voltaire was so happy to have found what he hoped would be a permanent home, that he paid up gladly, took possession, and at once burst into song. His *Epître de m. de Voltaire en arrivant dans sa terre près du lac de Genève, en mars, 1755* is a poem in praise of the beauties of the place and the supposed liberties of Geneva. It is perhaps the most purely lyrical of all his poems.

> O maison d'Aristippe! ô jardins d'Epicure!
> Vous qui me présentez, dans vos enclos divers,
> Ce qui souvent manque à mes vers,

14 Best.D6092 (19 January 1755).
15 Best.D6097 (23 January 1755).
16 See a note on Best.D6127.

17 See the autobiography, p. 652, below.
18 For the documents see Best.app. D145.

15 The château de Prangins, *from a drawing in the possession of P. L. Bader*

Les Délices, *from the engraving by F. M. I. Queverdo after L. Signy*

Le mérite de l'art soumis à la nature,
Empire de Pomone et de Flore sa sœur,
   Recevez votre possesseur!
Qu'il soit, ainsi que vous, solitaire et tranquille!
Je ne me vante point d'avoir en cet asile
   Rencontré le parfait bonheur:
Il n'est point retiré dans le fond d'un bocage;
   Il est encor moins chez les rois;
   Il n'est pas même chez le sage:
De cette courte vie il n'est point le partage.
Il y faut renoncer; mais on peut quelquefois
   Embrasser au moins son image.[19]

Further on he apostrophises 'liberty! liberty! your throne is in this place', and concludes:

Viens m'y faire un destin nouveau.
Embellis ma retraite, où l'Amitié t'appelle;
Sur de simples gazons viens t'asseoir avec elle.
Elle fuit comme toi les vanités des cours,
Les cabales du monde et son règne frivole.
O deux divinités! vous êtes mon recours.
L'un élève mon âme, et l'autre la console:
   Présidez à mes derniers jours![20]

He debaptised the house, and named it Les Délices because, as he told Turgot, nothing is more delicious than to be free and independent[21], and concentrated with his usual energy on its reconstruction and furnishing. On entering the orbit of Geneva Voltaire made the acquaintance of the Tronchins, a leading family. Those with whom he was most involved were Théodore, generally reputed to have been a good doctor, but certainly a most disagreeable and unprincipled man; his cousin François, a city

---

19 'Oh house of Aristippus! oh gardens of Epicurus! you who offer me in your varied parts what my verse often lacks, the merit of art subjected to nature, empire of Pomona and of her sister Flora! receive your new possessor! May he be, like you, solitary and peaceful! I do not boast that I have found perfect happiness in this refuge. Happiness is not hidden in the depths of a wood; it is still less the attribute of kings; not even the wise man possesses it; it is not the lot of this short life. We must renounce it, but at least we can sometimes embrace its image.'

20 'Create for me here a new fate. Embellish my retreat, while friendship calls you. Come, recline with her on simple lawns. She flees like you the vanities of Courts, the world's intrigues and its frivolous life. Oh twin divinities! you are my last resource. One elevates my soul, and the other consoles it: preside over my last days!'

21 Best.D9351 (26 October 1760).

councillor and a man of considerable taste and culture, who might have become a man of mark in a different environment; and Jean Robert, brother of François, a banker and general merchant at Lyons. In 1761 Jean Robert escaped to Paris as a tax collector, but until then he was the general factotum of the 'old Swiss', and as most of Voltaire's letters to him have survived, we have in them as precious a fount of information as that formed for an earlier period by the letters to Moussinot. Here are a few extracts, taken from the period of Voltaire's installation at the Délices, which, Voltaire being Voltaire, inevitably involved much building, decorating, and landscaping, from which I benefited (Genevese authorities notwithstanding) when I lived there for twelve years two centuries later.

I have seen by chance in the Lyons papers of 11 December an advertisement of a little Italian coach with three windows, lined with silk, gilded, well-hung etc., for sale by Bertrand, master saddler. You are so good to a poor sick stranger that I take advantage of your kindness. I venture to beg you to have inquiries made whether this little equipage is still for sale, and what is its price; if it is to your taste, it will most certainly be to mine; and in that case would implore you very kindly to send it to me to Geneva.[22]

Dessert wines and gewgaws are certainly merchandise little worthy of you. So far as the wine is concerned we will drink it to your health; as for the gewgaws, as they will always keep their intrinsic value, and their setting must be changed, I think the best thing to do is for you to have the kindness to return them to me by the hand of the first of your friends who goes to Geneva. A little more important affair will be for you kindly to tell your Paris correspondent to call on m. de La Leu, [Voltaire's] notary, rue Saint-Croix de la Bretonnerie, and to ask him whether he can furnish 24,000 *livres* next March: which 24,000 *livres* will serve for a payment on the Délices.[23]

I have found some very good wine at Versoix which I could not help buying. It is some of the best Burgundy. I shall use it to top up the two tuns of Beaujolais which you are kindly sending me.[24]

Many thanks for the lavender. I promise to have some planted in all the borders of your[25] orchards. I have already had 250 trees planted for you. I have had avenues pierced for you, I am having a little wing built for you....

22 Best.D6091 (19 January 1755).
23 Best.D6186 (27 February 1755).
24 Best.D6207 (17 March 1755); this is still done, though the best Burgundy is not often used.
25 This is literary 'elegance', the Tronchins having a reversionary option on the Délices.

At the moment I am sowing your Egyptian onions; the Israelites[26] did not like them more than I do. In this I shall take advantage of your kindness. I beg you to send me [seeds of] all the flowers and vegetables you can. The garden is absolutely devoid of them. Everything needs to be done here. I am founding Carthage.[27]

Your Serriere wine will be very welcome since you think that I shall live another three years to drink it. All your worthy family, which I love tenderly, has this moment left. We performed nearly the whole of *Zaïre* in the presence of the Tronchins and the syndics. . . . But we have not given up our work on the Délices. We plant, we sow, we build without pause. All your flower seeds are in the earth. The vegetables will be there tomorrow.[28]

What I am now asking you for is for some artichoke suckers, which we lack entirely, for the largest possible quantity of lavender, thyme, rosemary, mint, basilic, rue, strawberries, pinks, and of *thadicée* (?), balsam, saxifrage, tarragon, savory, burnet, sage, and hyssop to wash us of our sins[29], etc., etc., etc., etc., etc., etc. . . . P. S. As we were about to close our letter we reflected, mme Denis and I, that all your trellis should be painted a good green, all your doors white, all your flag-stones red, and some doors a good yellow. I am therefore bold enough, my dear sir, to beg you to give instructions for the despatch to the Délices of 150 pounds of verdigris, 300 pounds of nut-oil, 200 pounds of white-lead, 50 pounds of blue, 50 pounds of yellow ochre, 80 pounds of red for the floors, and 50 of litharge[30], and 80 pounds of strong paste.[31]

I have received from you gold, diamonds and seeds; the last of these are the most precious to me, I owe them to your kindness, and they will increase our real wealth, that of the countryside. We had more need here of lettuce than of brooches, but coined gold will be rather necessary.[32]

You furnish our cellar, you paint our trellis, and you also want us to have good sugar from the fair of Beaucaire. It will serve to make jam with the currants [or gooseberries] that grow at the Délices. You will have to eat some of it. If I am not mistaken it seems to me that I am doing here only what is necessary, and what is necessary appears to be immense. You must admit that one can hardly do without a big poultry-yard, and without rooms for those who come to eat our chickens.[33]

26 In *Numbers* xi.5 the Israelites remember with longing the onions of Egypt.

27 Best.D6223 (28 March 1755). I do not propose to bore the reader with such textual curiosities, but he may be amused to know, for once, that when this letter was first published it was given the date of 13 August, and was conflated with fragments of three other letters: a modest example of Voltaire's sufferings at the hands of his editors.

28 Best.D6231 (2 April 1755).

29 See *Exodus* xii.22, etc.

30 Protoxide of lead, a yellow colouring matter.

31 Best.D6235 (5 April 1755).

32 Best.D6242 (11 April 1755).

33 Best.D6245 (15 April 1755).

The Délices are dear, but will deserve its name. This will take time and care. What annoys me is that it lacks the most necessary things. I have already told you so. The wine-press is in the orangery, the horses are housed with the cows, the greenhouse is below my bedroom, the orchard next to the flower-bed, and that was called good taste. . . . Come, come, courage, we are not done with you. And half-a-dozen no. 4 needles and half-a-dozen no. 18 and a dozen no. 9 and a dozen no. 14; and then you can send me to the devil a dozen times.[34]

[*This extract is from a letter written to Tronchin by mme Denis:*] I have chosen a tapestry of crimson damask to furnish my drawing-room, and I want the chairs to be of crimson Utrecht velvet. Since my uncle saw the velvet-pile fabric which you are sending us he dreams of nothing but this fabric. I have seen the letter he wrote you this evening in which he asks you to send him crimson velvet pile. You will realise that chairs in this fabric will not go at all with damask tapestry. I did not want to vex him, and even pretended to agree with him, but I implore you not to do what he asks, and to send me the 22 ells of Utrecht velvet, telling him that it had already been bought when you received his letter, and that you have no regrets, for there is no velvet pile to be had at Lyons in colours that would match crimson damask. By means of this little precaution the Utrecht velvet will be very welcome and my drawing-room will be charming. On no account mention my letter to him, I should be undone. My uncle likes you tenderly, writes epic poems and tragedies that make one dissolve in tears, but he knows nothing about the furnishing of a drawing-room.[35]

Everything you have sent us has been thoroughly approved, except the rhubarb. Your cousin the doctor gives such marked preference to senna that it is impossible to mention rhubarb to him. We took the liberty to ask you for oil and sugar only in the event of your laying in a stock and seeing fit to send us some. The Utrecht velvet will be very welcome, but we still love your handsome pile, and without daring to compare it with the velvet we would beg you to send us another twenty-six ells of it.[36]

All this was very pleasant and amusing, but Voltaire's euphoria was not allowed to subsist more than a few months. Soon the long-sought Eden became the 'saddened Délices', the 'so-called Délices'. Much could be written about this sudden collapse of Voltaire's hopes: let it suffice to say that the months following Voltaire's arrival at the Délices were among the unhappiest of his life, but also in some way, the most significant.

34 Best.D6251 (18 April 1755).   36 Best.D6271 (16 May 1755).
35 Best.D6266 (6 or 7 May 1755).

The serpent in the garden first took a particularly squalid form: that of an obscure bookseller's assistant who tried to blackmail Voltaire by threatening to publish deformed fragments of the *Pucelle*: this is the notorious *affaire Grasset*. It was the symbol of many other annoyances, present and to come.

The poem he had written with so much joy on arriving at his new home was publicly burned by the Genevese authorities. The modern reader of the Délices poem would have great difficulty in understanding the reason for this characteristic welcome of their distinguished guest. When living at Prangins Voltaire had been struck by the romantic vision of the château of Ripaille on the opposite shore of the lake. In his poem Voltaire apostrophised Amadeus VIII, duke of Savoy, who left Ripaille in 1439 to become the anti-pope Felix. How, asks Voltaire, could he have brought himself to leave such a delicious place and its pleasures for such a purpose? Unfortunately the court of Savoy was trying to get Felix canonised, so this reference to his pleasures was resented, and as Savoy had great influence at Geneva, this was enough, and Voltaire's tribute to liberty and friendship was condemned.[37] Rome was not impressed.

Voltaire was not a man to put up with wrongs in silence. His correspondence is filled with cries of anguish about most of the things that went wrong in his life. But occasionally, when he was really deeply wounded, he said nothing. This was one of those occasions. He was very profoundly hurt and disillusioned by Geneva's treatment of his *exultet*, but not one single word about it has survived in his letters. But traces of his feelings can nevertheless be found. One of the plays performed at the Délices was the *Orphelin de la Chine*, the essential theme of which is resistance to tyranny as a moral imperative. It is not surprising that Voltaire began it during his wanderings after the Frankfort episode, and completed it soon after his arrival at the Délices. Although its subject is eternally topical, the structure and versification of the tragedy are on the whole poor, with great respect to the Comédie française, which recently chose this play for a revival after having silenced for many years the great man to whom they owe so much.

---

37 For the documents see Best. app.D148. 'Faire ripaille' (to carouse) derives from the name of the château of Ripaille.

Yet there is at least one couplet in this play charged with significance when it is placed in the context of Voltaire's life at this time:

> Ainsi la liberté, le repos et la paix,
> Le but de mes travaux, me fuira pour jamais![38]

When the authorities allowed Voltaire to acquire the Délices they of course acquiesced in an illegality. But he was sent an obviously inspired warning through the mouth of the minister Jacob Vernet. He told Voltaire that his views on religion had disquieted the 'wise men' who governed Geneva. 'You know that men need a religion as well as a government', and he added with Genevese modesty, 'you can see that ours, by the grace of God, is so simple, so wise, so gentle, so pure, that a philosopher could not ask for one more rational, nor a policy more fitting for the public good. . . . It would be very agreeable to us to see you enter into our views, and to cooperate, with all our men of letters, when occasion offers, to dissuade our youth from the irreligion which always leads it to libertinism.'[39]

This being how the 'right-thinking bourgeoisie' of Geneva saw itself, the warning was ominous. Voltaire replied that he detested intolerance and fanaticism, and respected the religious laws of the republic. He was too old, too ill and too serious to appeal to young people.[40] But his soft words were wasted.

Almost at once the Genevese were forbidden to attend the theatrical performances Voltaire gave in the theatre he had so lovingly fitted out in the long gallery of the Délices. This disappointment was not immediately devastating, the city fathers disregarding their own regulations, for Voltaire had invited Lekain, and the attraction of the great actor declaiming his host's plays was too strong even for Calvinist consciences. In any case, Voltaire had taken care to have several lines of defence: he simply removed his stage to a Lausanne house, Montriond, which he had acquired as a refuge when the weather at Geneva became unbearable. But the ramifications of the Grasset case proliferated alarmingly. Several unauthorised editions were printed of the *Pucelle*,

---

38 IV.i; 'Thus liberty, tranquility and peace, the object of my labours, will forever escape me!'

39 Best.D6146 (8 February 1755).
40 Best.D6149 (9 February 1755).

and the manuscript of the *Histoire de la guerre de mil sept cent quarante et un* was stolen and published[41]. Both these pirated books were condemned and seized, and involved Voltaire to a distressing and even dangerous extent.

All this exacerbated Voltaire's sensibilities almost to the point of collapse, and his condition was certainly responsible for what I regard as perhaps the most regrettable incident in Voltaire's life. It will be remembered that Olympe Du Noyer passed from Voltaire's arms into those of Guyot de Merville, who then lost no opportunity to attack his mistress's former lover. But whatever his faults may have been this minor writer was an honourable man. He had been guilty of great, and in the circumstances inelegant wrongs, but in April 1755 he sent an ample and apparently sincere apology[42]. Voltaire no doubt knew something that we do not know, but even so he could well have afforded to respond, from the height of his fame, in a spirit of conciliation. Instead he sent a frigidly courteous reply[43]. Let us hope that it did not contribute too much to Guyot's suicide a few days later.

Voltaire was kinder to his monkey. When his pet bit him he refused to have it killed. 'Why should I?' he asked, 'it was my own fault.'[44]

The highly successful production in the summer of 1755 of the *Orphelin de la Chine*, both in Paris and at the court of Fontainebleau, did little to console Voltaire in this sea of troubles, for soon another storm burst to make the atmosphere of Geneva still more unbearable. After the publication of the *Essai sur les mœurs* Voltaire wrote to a local minister, Jacob Vernes (not to be confused with Jacob Vernet) that it was a very honourable thing for Geneva to have allowed him to say in this book that Servet was a fool and Calvin a barbarian. 'You are not Calvinists, you are men.'[45] In fact Voltaire never used the words 'fool' and 'barbarian' in the *Essai*. They are far too forceful an abstract of his text (cxxxiv), and are in fact another illustration of Voltaire's simplicity in such matters. He intended a great compliment to the republic,

41 Mme Denis was again responsible, in collaboration with one of her amorous replacements, the marquis de Ximenès.

42 Best.D6247 (15 April 1755).
43 Best.D6252 (c. 20 April 1755).
44 Best.D7031 (c. 15 October 1756).
45 Best.D7119 (13 January 1757).

and he really thought, after having lived in the heart of Calvinism for nearly two years, that his tribute to Genevese toleration would be taken in that spirit. *Sancta simplicitas!*

Indeed, he went further. In an open letter to Thieriot, that is, one intended for publication and in fact immediately published, and equally intended as a public compliment to Geneva, he wrote that in his universal history he had given expression to impartiality, an extreme love of truth, and zeal for public welfare. 'During all my life I have done all I could to extend this spirit of philosophy and tolerance, which now appears to characterise this century. This spirit, which animates all worthy people in Europe, has grown happy roots in this country, to which I was first led by the needs of my bad health, and where gratitude and the sweetness of a tranquil life retain me. It is not a trifling example of the progress of human reason that the essay on history has been printed at Geneva, with public approval, though it says that Calvin had an atrocious soul as well as an enlightened mind. The murder of Servet today appears abominable.'[46] Here again, though 'atrocious soul' is a fair inference from the facts of Calvin's life, these words do not actually occur in the *Essai*. Voltaire strengthened the terms in order to bring out even more clearly the tolerance of Geneva.

This tolerance existed, unfortunately, only in the writer's wishful hopes. Voltaire's letters aroused violent resentment, and his account of Calvin was formally condemned by pretty well all the civil and religious authorities of Geneva. A great wind of disapproval blew around the Délices, for the Genevese, with inexhaustible gusto, continued to discuss Voltaire's offences against the memory of the 'atrocious soul'. The great man for once had the good sense to look on in silence, but he decided to remove to other pastures. And in the privacy of his library he composed these lines of bitter disillusion, which he entitled *Les Torts* (*The Wrongs*):

---

46 Best.D7213 (26 March 1757). Servet was burned alive in 1553 for theological reasons; Calvin, it appears, would generously have preferred him to be merely beheaded.

Non, je n'ai point tort d'oser dire
Ce que pensent les gens de bien;
Et le sage qui ne craint rien
A le beau droit de tout écrire.

J'ai, quarante ans, bravé l'empire
Des lâches tyrans des esprits;
Et, dans votre petit pays,
J'aurais grand tort de me dédire.

Je sais que souvent le Malin
A caché sa queue et sa griffe
Sous la tiare d'un pontife,
Et sous le manteau d'un Calvin.

Je n'ai point tort quand je déteste
Ces assassins religieux,
Employant le fer et les feux
Pour servir le Père céleste.

Oui, jusqu'au dernier de mes jours,
Mon âme sera fière et tendre:
J'oserai gémir sur la cendre
Et des Servets et des Dubourgs.

De cette horrible frénésie
A la fin le temps est passé:
Le Fanatisme est terrassé;
Mais il reste l'Hypocrisie.

Farceurs à manteaux étriqués,
Mauvaise musique d'église,
Mauvais vers, et sermons croqués,
Ai-je tort si je vous méprise?[47]

All this, far from crushing Voltaire, seemed only to stimulate him. He found time to write, among many outbursts of exasperation, some of his most interesting and amusing letters, including a famous one to Jean Jacques Rousseau. On receiving the discourse on human inequality, Voltaire told its author that never had so much ingenuity been devoted to turning men into beasts.

[47] For a translation see the auto-biography, pp. 656-657, below.

'One is tempted to walk on all-fours when one reads your book.'
He admits that literature and science have sometimes been the
cause of much evil, but after all the greatest crimes had been
committed by celebrated ignoramuses. It is man's insatiable
cupidity and his ungovernable pride that make the world a vale
of tears. Literature nourishes, corrects and consoles the minds of
men. It made Rousseau famous even as he wrote against it. He
understood that Rousseau's health was bad. 'You should come
to restore it in your native air, enjoy liberty, drink with me the
milk of our cows, and browse on our grass.'[48]

As if he did not have enough on his plate, Voltaire now gave
another example of his prodigious powers of work and concentration. In the midst of all his difficulties with the Genevese he
received a letter[49] from the courtier Fedor Pavlovich Veselovsky,
who was in Geneva to visit his exiled brother Avran, inviting him
to write a life of Peter the great. Voltaire at once accepted[50], and
five months later he sent the first eight chapters to Ivan Ivanovich
Shuvalov. Of course Voltaire had already written on Charles
XII, and so was familiar with some parts of Peter's career, but
even so this was an extraordinary tour de force. Nor did he write
a mere impressionistic sketch or an uncritical compilation. As he
told Shuvalov, his chapters were based on the 'manuscript memoirs
of general Le Fort, on accounts of China, on the memoirs of
Strahlenberg and Perry. I have not used a life of Peter the great,
falsely attributed to the so-called boyar Nevestoy and compiled
in Holland by one Rousset. It is nothing but a collection of very
badly digested gazettes and mistakes, and besides, a vagabond
who writes under a false name deserves no credence.'[51]

As Voltaire's difficulties with the *invivable* petty potentates of
the republic of Geneva became known he received some tempting
invitations, but he had learnt his lesson and would never again
sacrifice his independence. He told Thieriot that the queen-em-
press (Maria Theresa) had sent him a most flattering message,
for which he was grateful, but that he would 'adore from afar.
I shall not go to Vienna. I am too comfortable in my retreat at
Les Délices. Happy he who lives in his own house with his

48 Best.D6451 (30 August 1755).
49 Best.D7160 (16 February 1757).
50 Best.D7169 (*c.* 1 March 1757).
51 Best.D7336 (7 August 1757).

nieces, his books, his garden, his vines, his horses, his cows, his eagle, his fox, and his rabbits that caress their noses with their paws. I have all that, and the Alps as well, which are an admirable sight. I would sooner grumble at my gardeners than pay court to kings.'[52]

Voltaire's contentment was progressively eroded, for soon further and even more violent storms in teacups followed. Alembert had come to Geneva to collect information for his article on Geneva in the *Encyclopédie*. This had now appeared and aroused resentment for exactly the same reasons as Voltaire's reference to the 'atrocious soul' of Calvin. Alembert's article was absurdly flattering to Geneva and its clergy, whose morality he found exemplary and who lived in union. Its culminating praise was the recognition by the writer that the church in Geneva had become Socinian, that is, had made of Christianity little more than an ethical doctrine. This was unfortunately far from true, but true enough to bring down on Alembert a flood of accusations and condemnations. As Voltaire put it, 'These ridiculous people dare to complain of the praise you deign to give them'[53], and of course he was also thinking of the similar treatment he had himself received. Voltaire was mixed up in all this because he was thought to have helped Alembert and even to have ghosted his article. This was quite untrue, but Alembert had quoted Voltaire's letter on Calvin in his article, and that was quite enough in Calvinist logic to let slip the dogs of sectarian rage. The Genevese clergy reasserted their belief in an eternity of heaven and hell, the divinity of Jesus Christ, and complete submission to revelation and holy writ. Alembert, disgusted, resigned from the *Encyclopédie*, for he lacked entirely Voltaire's inner fortitude: he complained less than Voltaire, but also resisted far less, and notwithstanding repeated appeals from the Délices, persisted in his betrayal, unloading his burden on to the shoulders of the long-suffering Diderot.

Rousseau now jumped on the band-waggon by writing his *Lettre sur les spectacles*, in which this failed ex-dramatist attacked the stage, and in particular Alembert's defence of the theatre, which he somehow found expressed in the article 'Genève', with

52 Best.D6965 (9 August 1756).   53 Best.D7512 (12 December 1757).

all his usual eloquence and wrong-headedness. And in the meanwhile had been launched the *cacouac* conspiracy, in which a few right-thinking Parisians applied this term to the *philosophes*. A *cacouac* was defined as a monster who has under his tongue a sac of poison which spills with every word, and who does evil for the pleasure of it. Finally, when some of the defenders of the faith became too violent, hounds were called off. The venerable consistory suddenly discovered the 'uselessness of theological disputes' since they redound to the benefit of irreligion.[54] To all of which Voltaire no doubt intoned a heartfelt amen, not forgetting the compliments Rousseau paid him in his *Lettre*. All anti-*philosophe* writers tried this ploy, but they never succeeded in separating Voltaire from his friends and followers.

Among the numerous visitors who lost no time in coming to sit at the feet of the great man now that he had a home, not the least sympathetic was mme d'Epinay, the friend of Grimm and Diderot. She has left us a picture of mme Denis, as amusing as it is malicious: 'Voltaire's niece is enough to make one die laughing. She is a little fat woman, round as a ball, about fifty, more female than one has any right to be, ugly and kind, lying unwittingly and without evil intention, appearing intelligent though she is not, screaming, laying down the law, playing at politics, rhyming, reasoning, talking nonsense, and all this without any pretentiousness and above all without shocking anybody.'[55]

But all the worldliness of the Délices was on the surface. During these years something far more disturbing had come to pass, far more profoundly distressing than anything we have yet seen, because the tragedy was not personal to Voltaire, yet affected him profoundly and permanently: it is the simple truth that during this period our great man became the Voltaire of history. I refer to the Lisbon earthquake and to Voltaire's poem on its lessons, when Rousseau returned to the attack by sending to the Délices his celebrated 'letter on providence'. But before we consider it, we must take a somewhat closer look at the consequences of the disaster and the poem.

54 Best.D7418 (4 October 1757).   55 Best.D7480 (c. 25 November 1757).

27. The death of optimism, 1755

O N THE FEAST OF all saints (1 November) there occurred in 1755 an event which indirectly changed men's thinking about their own place in nature: the Lisbon earthquake[1]. It was a terrible catastrophe, but no more so than many previous ones, and even less disastrous than, for instance, the earthquakes of Villach in 1348, the Abruzzi in 1456, Benevento in 1688, and the central Apennines in 1703, to say nothing of volcanic eruptions, tornadoes and floods.

Moreover man's confidence in his destiny was now at its highest point. Optimism[2] was universal, and the belief in progress had become instinctive. When one is convinced that everything is getting better it is very human to conclude that everything is for the best. And Christian notions of resignation and submission encouraged this feeling. It had recently been powerfully sustained in Leibniz's *Théodicée* (1710), and given its most compact, even epigrammatic expression in Pope's *Essay on man* (1733). In these eloquent lines Pope lucidly crystallised the generally accepted view of evil:

> Cease then, nor Order imperfection name:
> Our proper bliss depends on what we blame.
> Know thy own point: this kind, this due degree
> Of blindness, weakness, Heaven bestows on thee.
> Submit: in this, or any other sphere,
> Secure to be as blest as thou canst bear:
> Safe in the hand of one disposing Power,
> Or in the natal, or the mortal hour.

1 For a fuller treatment of this theme see my *Voltaire essays*, pp. 24-41, and the references given there; to these can be added G. A. Eiby, *Earthquakes* (new edn., London 1967), though the historical part of this book is inadequate. So profound was the impression made by the disaster that for long the Portuguese royal family would not use their palaces, living in wooden huts and in tents; see sir N. W. Wraxall, bart., *Historical memoirs of my own time* (London 1815), i.17-18.

2 The reader is reminded that in this context optimism has nothing to do with one's outlook on life: it is the belief that all that is and happens is for the best.

All nature is but Art, unknown to thee;
All Chance, Direction, which thou canst not see;
All Discord, Harmony not understood;
All partial Evil, universal Good:
And, spite of Pride, in erring Reason's spite,
One truth is clear, Whatever is, is right.[3]

Only a few *philosophes* had sought to undermine the euphoria of a world which regarded itself as the centre of creation. The tremendous impression made by the Lisbon earthquake must therefore have had a special cause. This special cause was the great man who had recently come to live near Geneva, and whose eloquent expression of his deep feelings and unyielding reason moved the world.

On the very day of the Lisbon earthquake the young Patu wrote to Garrick from Les Délices: 'My very dear friend, what a man is this heavenly songster of the *Henriade*, and with what joy one studies so great a mind! Imagine a man who looks near death, but has all the fire of his first youth, and the brilliance of his delightful stories!'[4] This great mind, stimulated by all that it had seen and felt in recent years, was pregnant for the birth of new ideas. The news from Portugal soon reached Voltaire, and on the 24th of November he wrote to the banker Tronchin, then at Lyons:

My dear sir, nature is very cruel. One would find it hard to imagine how the laws of movement cause such frightful disasters in the *best of possible worlds*. A hundred thousand ants, our fellows, crushed all at once in our ant-hill, and half of them perishing, no doubt in unspeakable agony, beneath the wreckage from which they cannot be drawn. Families ruined all over Europe, the fortunes of a hundred business men, your compatriots, swallowed up in the ruins of Lisbon. What a wretched gamble is the game of human life! What will the preachers say, especially if the palace of the Inquisition is still standing? I flatter myself that at least the reverend fathers inquisitors have been crushed like the others. That ought to teach men not to persecute each other, for while a few holy scoundrels burn a few fanatics, the earth swallows up one and all.[5]

For Voltaire, the Lisbon disaster was the last straw. For a long time he had been opposed to Leibniz's ideas and to Pope's simpli-

---

3 *An Essay on man*, i.281-94. 5 Best.D6597 (24 November 1755).
4 Best.D6562 (1 November 1755).

fications. But it was only slowly that he reached his own conclusions. His reactions on the publication of the *Essay on man* in 1733 show that he was completely unprejudiced. He admired the poem, though he found it a little obscure.[6] In the following year, when he wrote the *Traité de métaphysique*, he left aside the problem of evil, considering it to be a human invention and therefore irrelevant. He concluded: 'It is just as absurd to say of God in this connexion that God is just or unjust as to say that God is blue or square.'[7] Pope's *Moral epistles* were to Voltaire a paraphrase of his own remarks on Pascal in the *Lettres philosophiques*[8], and it is certainly true that Pope owed more to Voltaire than the French poet-philosopher derived from the English one he admired so much.

Meanwhile, crown prince Frederick and Voltaire began a wide-ranging correspondence on the subject of freewill; the Cirey group studied Leibniz; mme Du Châtelet finished her *Institutions de physique*, which favoured the German philosopher; and Voltaire completed his *Métaphysique de Newton*[9], which was anti-Leibnizian by implication. This intellectual activity reached a temporary culmination in 1744, with Voltaire's reply to a critic: 'Just show me . . . why so many men slit each other's throats in the best of all possible worlds, and I shall be greatly obliged to you.'[10] Many and many a time did he echo and re-echo this ironic plaint.

There followed all the events we have seen, and then at last the haven of Les Délices, and Voltaire breathed a deep sigh of relief: 'O Maison d'Aristippe! ô jardins d'Epicure! . . .'[11] Alas, we know that even this eloquent hymn to liberty and friendship brought trouble. The persecutions began again, and immediately afterwards came the disaster at Lisbon. In the intellectual and emotional situation in which Voltaire then lived, its effect upon him was decisive. In fact, from that moment the disaster and all it stood for was to haunt his imagination for ever. His *Poème sur le désastre de Lisbonne* was conceived at once, and must have been

6 Best.D635 (24 July 1733).
7 *Traité de métaphysique* (1734), ii.
8 Best.D915 (20 September 1735).
9 Later incorporated into the *Elé-*

ments de la philosophie de Newton.
10 Best.D2945 (March 1744).
11 See pp. 352-353, above.

written straight off, since it was finished before the end of November. Voltaire invited those who claim that 'all is for the best' to consider Lisbon, ruined indiscriminately[12]:

> eut-elle plus de vices
> Que Londres, que Paris, plongés dans les délices?
> Lisbonne est abîmée, et l'on danse à Paris.[13]

'Misguided philosophers' tranquilly seek the causes of the event; they would do better to weep. Is it pride, then, to pity human suffering? How can anyone answer that everything is necessary and good?

> Quoi! l'univers entier, sans ce gouffre infernal,
> Sans engloutir Lisbonne, eût-il été plus mal?
> Etes-vous assuré que la cause éternelle
> Qui fait tout, qui sait tout, qui créa tout pour elle,
> Ne pouvait nous jeter dans ces tristes climats
> Sans former des volcans allumés sous nos pas?
> Borneriez-vous ainsi la suprême puissance?
> Lui défendriez-vous d'exercer sa clémence?[14]

No, answers Voltaire,

> Je respecte mon dieu, mais j'aime l'univers.[15]

Would philosophers have the victims of Lisbon believe that others will benefit from their misfortunes? No,

> Dieu tient en main la chaîne, et n'est point enchaîné.[16]

But why, if he who rules us is just, do we suffer? That is the question:

> Voilà le nœud fatal qu'il fallait délier.
> Guérirez-vous vos maux en osant les nier?[17]

---

12 It was this that also troubled the young Goethe; see *Dichtung und Wahrheit*, I.i.

13 'was she more vicious than London, than Paris, plunged in pleasures? Lisbon is shattered, and Paris dances.'

14 'What! would the entire universe have been worse without this hellish abyss, without swallowing up Lisbon? Are you sure that the eternal cause that makes all, knows all, created all, could not plunge us into this wretched world without placing flaming volcanoes beneath our feet? Would you limit thus the supreme power? Would you forbid it to show mercy?'

15 'I respect my god, but I love the universe.'

16 'God holds the chain and is not chained.'

17 'There is the fatal knot that had to be untied. Can you cure our ills by daring to deny their existence?'

Voltaire went on to insist on the existence of evil, and examined it without reaching a solution.

> Leibnitz ne m'apprend point par quels nœuds invisibles,
> Dans le mieux ordonné des univers possibles,
> Un désordre éternel, un chaos de malheurs,
> Mêle à nos vains plaisirs de réelles douleurs,
> Ni pourquoi l'innocent, ainsi que le coupable,
> Subit également ce mal inévitable.[18]

A single gleam pierces the darkness that seems to shroud the world of living things:

> *Un jour tout sera bien*, voilà notre espérance,
> *Tout est bien aujourd'hui*, voilà l'illusion.[19]

Pope, piling up his epigrams, failed to notice that optimism necessarily entails fatalism, a doctrine hardly less flattering to the supreme being than to man. Voltaire was not so good a poet as Pope, but he reasoned better: he understood more clearly the implications of the philosophy he was attacking. But that is not the main distinction of his Lisbon poem, nor the one which renders it unique in the history of ideas, or contributed the most towards its remarkable effect on Voltaire's contemporaries. The first writings about the Lisbon disaster, I mean the few that were composed without knowledge of Voltaire's poem, take in the whole range of sentiment from total acquiescence to open revolt. Only Voltaire's response derived from a simple, humane impulse of pity. His poem found a response in both the minds and the hearts of his generation, and awakened its latent magnanimity.

In short, men were stirred not so much by the disaster itself as by the event seen through the sensibility of a great man. Once again a poet had become the legislator of mankind.

It is important to observe that with the Lisbon poem Voltaire

---

18 'Leibniz does not tell me by what invisible twists an eternal disorder, a chaos of misfortunes, mingles real sorrows with our vain pleasures in the best arranged of possible universes, nor why the innocent and the guilty suffer alike this inevitable evil.'

19 '*One day all will be good*, that is our hope, *All is good today*, that is the illusion'. Voltaire later added a question mark after 'hope'; see G. R. Havens, 'Voltaire's pessimistic revision of the conclusion of his *Poème sur le désastre de Lisbonne*', *Modern language notes* (Baltimore December 1929), xliv.492.

published his *Poème sur la loi naturelle*[20], which he had written for Frederick a few years earlier, and in which he took up again the theme of the *Epître à Uranie*[21]. It is first worth noting that the poem was written before Frankfort and published after, when Voltaire was still in the white heat of resentment. Nevertheless the flattering allusions to Frederick were allowed to stand. Voltaire still exclaims:

> Philosophe intrépide, affermissez mon âme;
> Couvrez-moi des rayons de cette pure flamme
> Qu'allume la raison, qu'éteint le préjugé.
> Dans cette nuit d'erreurs où le monde est plongé
> Apportons, s'il se peut, une faible lumière.[22]

The purpose of the poem is to show that a natural law underlies religion in all its forms. Men possess an innate sense of justice and morality. To those who object that man

> n'a rien dans l'esprit, il n'a rien dans le cœur;
> De ce qui l'environne il n'est qu'imitateur;
> Il répète les noms de devoir, de justice;
> Il agit en machine, et c'est par sa nourrice
> Qu'il est juif ou païen, fidèle ou musulman[23],

to those, indeed, who advance one of Voltaire's arguments in *Uranie*, he replied by pointing to the instincts of the whole animal creation. Why should man be exempt from this universal law? It is true that man is an enigma, but why should he be a greater mystery than the rest of nature? This of course is to deny the special creation of man, and with it all religion. Voltaire made this conclusion even clearer in the third book, in which he showed the evil done by religions. The gentle inquisitor, cross in hand, kindly burns his fellows and weeps for them. Calvin was personally

---

20 It was of course prohibited and condemned by the authorities; Luynes (*Mémoires*, xvi.108) says that queen Marie Leszczinska was enraged by the mere sight of the title.

21 See pp. 94-96, above.

22 'Intrepid philosopher, sustain my soul; shield me with the rays of the pure flame which is lit by reason, which is extinguished by prejudice. Let us introduce if possible a feeble light into the night of error in which the world is plunged.'

23 'has nothing in his mind, he has nothing in his heart; he is only the imitator of what surrounds him; he repeats the words duty and justice; he acts as a machine; and his nurse determines whether he is a Jew or a pagan, a Christian or a Muslim.' This will be recognized as the theme of *Zaïre*.

responsible for the murder of Servet, but if Servet had triumphed he would have garrotted the trinitarians. The Arminians were martyrs in Flanders, and executioners in Holland. It was said that the virtues of pagans were crimes. 'Pitiless severity! odious maxims!' Dare these rigorists claim that Socrates and Aristides, Trajan and Marcus Aurelius, Leibniz and Locke are condemned to hell?

> Je crois voir des forçats dans un cachot funeste,
> Se pouvant secourir, l'un sur l'autre acharnés,
> Combattre avec les fers dont ils sont enchaînés.[24]

We should do better to help each other to bear our burdens, and it is the duty of government to ensure that we do so, by stopping religious quarrels. And he concludes by again insisting on justice, on the reign of law:

> je prétends qu'un roi, que son devoir engage
> A maintenir la paix, l'ordre, la sûreté,
> Ait sur tous ses sujets égale autorité. . . .
> La loi dans tout Etat doit être universelle:
> Les mortels, quels qu'ils soient, sont égaux devant elle.[25]

And Voltaire's final word is the lapidary 'prejudices are the reasons of fools'.

The stir caused by Voltaire's Lisbon poem was enormous: a score of editions in the course of 1756. All the reviews and gazettes began to publish comments on it, and more or less authentic accounts of the disaster. Pamphlets poured out (I have read a hundred or so just for the years 1756 and 1757); theological, philosophical, and scientific volumes followed, including that of the young Immanuel Kant[26]. Reading this mountain of paper one sees that if this particular event struck so many imaginations it was because Voltaire had provided the impetus. Some of these

24 'We are like convicts in a fatal dungeon, who could help each other, but fight desperately among ourselves with the irons which enchain us.'
25 'I assert that a king, whose duty is to maintain peace, order and safety, has equal authority over all his subjects. . . . The law must be universal in all states: all men, whatever they are,

are equal before it'.
26 *Geschichte und Naturbeschreibung der markwürdigsten Vorfälle des Erdbebens welches an dem Ende des 1755sten Jahres einen grosses Theil der Erde erschüttert hat* (Königsberg 1756). The earthquake even provided a subject for the theatre.

writings are, of course, only conventional reactions: the orthodox cry blasphemy, the followers of Leibniz hoist the master's standard. The majority of these authors, however, share, and share increasingly, Voltaire's agnosticism and doubt. Among his non-sectarian critics it is impossible to find one that opposes him with any real argument. Even Rousseau's reply[27] is an emotional reaction rather than a discussion of a philosophic proposition. Thus he holds men responsible for their own misfortunes because the earthquake would not have killed so many people had they not been gathered together in a big city. The great dreamer's idea provides an elegant subject for controversy, but it does not get us noticeably nearer the truth. It leaves out of account such catastrophes as hurricanes, which can devastate whole countrysides; and worse still, it evades the great problem of freewill, of which optimism is only one aspect.

As for Voltaire himself, the years that followed only increased his pessimism[28]. Immediately after the catastrophe he wrote that men 'do themselves more harm on their little mole-hill than does nature. More men are slaughtered in our wars than are swallowed up by earthquakes.'[29] The horrors of the Seven years' war, including the execution of admiral Byng, aggravated this state of mind. Epithets fly one after another in Voltaire's correspondence for the years 1756-58: the world is 'mad', 'completely mad', there is 'nothing madder or more atrocious'. And each time he expresses his disgust there is a sad or sarcastic allusion to 'all for the best', to optimism, to 'the best of all possible worlds' which 'is certainly ugly enough'; 'the earth is steeped in evil, moral and physical'; 'happy the man who can look with a tranquil eye on all the great events in this best of all possible worlds'. Dozens of similar lamentations could be quoted.

In short, at this period Voltaire had become a man obsessed, tormented by the spectacle of a humanity that suffered and was resigned to suffering. But if he was obsessed, he was also a genius, a creator: it was inevitable that this preoccupation should work upon every level of his consciousness, develop, form, crystallise,

27 Best.D6973 (18 August 1756); Leigh 424.

28 The word itself was not invented until 1794, by Coleridge.

29 Best.D6629 (16 December 1755).

take on an independent life, and be born in the shape a of work of art: and so *Candide* came into the world. The *Poème sur le désastre de Lisbonne* opened the proceedings against optimism; *Candide* closed them with a sentence of death. The Lisbon poem had stirred thinking men and prepared the ground, the furious laughter of *Candide* converted them once and for all. Voltaire had always looked on metaphysics with a doubtful eye, but had occasionally indulged in it himself. It was a poor sort of science, he admitted, but respectable. Now it had become 'metaphysico-theologico-cosmolo-nigology'. Voltaire had abandoned argument for irony. But he left no room for the smallest doubt of his conviction that belief in optimism was a mere straw to which humanity clung so as not to drown in the tempest of misfortunes.

But it is the end of *Candide* which represents the real intellectual revolution of its day: the *Poème sur le désastre de Lisbonne* concluded on a note of hope; later, as we have seen, Voltaire added a questionmark. It may have been at this time that he re-read Pope, and, coming on his exhortation to hope, exclaimed in the margin: 'What can I hope when all is right?'[30] In *Candide* this is all set on one side as irrelevant, and for theories, speculations, and abstractions Voltaire substitutes, through the voice of Candide, a concrete saying: 'We must cultivate our garden.' Voltaire had realised that the doctrine of optimism is in reality the opposite of what it seemed: philosophical optimism is really a doctrine of despair, an antisocial belief, 'a cruel philosophy under a consoling name'[31]. If all is for the best in the best of all possible worlds, what is the use of bothering? Just let events lead us where they will, and let us abandon ourselves to fatalism. No, replies Voltaire, all is not for the best in this world; what is good does not make up for what is bad; the good will not increase nor will evil diminish, on their own, through the operation of laws invented by metaphysicians. On the contrary, it is up to us to haul ourselves out of the slough of despond. We must act. We must cultivate our garden.[32]

30 George R. Havens, 'Voltaire's marginal comments upon Pope's *Essay on man*', *Modern languages notes* (Baltimore November 1928), xliii.435.

31 Best.D6738 (18 February 1756).

32 By a pure chance that is nevertheless striking, the last speech delivered by the sturdiest 'optimist' of the old school, Gladstone, was addressed to a rural society. He ended by exhorting its members to cultivate their garden; but see 'Gladstone on *Candide*', *Studies on Voltaire* (1970), lxx.7-10.

Bolingbroke, whom we have met as a friend of Voltaire's even before his visit to England, was also an associate of Pope, and was soon to suggest his *Essay on man*, had written to Voltaire long before: 'If you succeed in rooting out the tares [from your heart], the good seed will grow abundantly.'[33] Was not this the life Voltaire led after *Candide*? When he saw evil he tried to destroy it. He encouraged the good seed to take root wherever it could.

It was in this way, through the catalytic effect of the Lisbon disaster, that Voltaire became the sage of Les Délices and Ferney, the active conscience of an age, the prophet of justice and of reason and of the offspring of reason—understanding, tolerance, and peace. That was how Voltaire cultivated his garden.

33 Best.D190 (27 June 1724); see also p. 109, above.

17 Silhouette of Voltaire, *from the original by Jean Huber*

18 Medallion of Voltaire, *from the original bronze by Georg Christoph Wächter*

28. Reason and progress,
1755-1778

THE INTELLECTUAL REVOLUTION produced in Voltaire, primarily but not exclusively, by the Lisbon earthquake, had another important consequence. We know by now that he had always been convinced of the value of liberty in every sense, but this conviction now became an obsessive urge to work to bring about the reign of justice as quickly as possible. In other words, Voltaire became utterly committed to the fight for the Enlightenment. But we immediately encounter an awkward difficulty: do we know exactly what was this Enlightenment? It is certainly possible to describe it, and many such descriptions have been published. Yet is it possible to define precisely what it was? I doubt whether this can be done even to the extent that such notions as, say, the renaissance or the dark ages can be defined. The commonest and greatest of misapprehensions is to suppose that the Enlightenment was a coherent body of doctrine or even a consistent mode of thought. In fact there was never anything ordered about the Enlightenment: its foundations were not deep, its structure resembled a maze more than a monolith, and far from being an enduring movement, it did not last, as a self-conscious campaign, even so long as a human life. If this be regarded as a failure, it was due not to lack of acceptance but rather to an over-hasty adoption by an élite of ideas the full implications of which were not always understood.

If a parallel is sought we should perhaps look to the age of Pericles rather than to such slow transitional periods as the renaissance. Yet such comparisons are not particularly helpful. I do not believe that any of the numerous accounts offered of this seminal epoch in the history of ideas can stand up to a resolute analysis. And yet there was a time before the Enlightenment: and there came a time after the Enlightenment; and these two periods were by no means the same. What was the difference? What brought about the change? What caused the catalytic effect?

I do not propose to attempt here a definition or even to offer yet another description of the Enlightenment. I venture to plant only a single signpost: I merely suggest that the Enlightenment had one outstanding characteristic which dominated it and which distinguished it from all preceding history: the belief in progress through reason.

The idea of progress is now so universally accepted that its novelty often surprises. Yet the historical facts are clear. It is with the greatest difficulty that some foreshadowings can be found of this apparently obvious notion. Nor, on reflection, is this really surprising, for so long as man looks inward and upward, and so long as he allows himself to be enclosed by the framework of a fixed time-scheme, the idea of human progress cannot even occur to him.

A particular example of this fact is provided by the belief in metempsychosis and karma. In a sense no more progressive system could well be devised. If a man knows that he is to come back to earth in another body, and in circumstances governed by the state of his own moral balance-sheet, with all his good and evil deeds chalked up on his slate, he would appear to have an overpowering incentive to strain every nerve to do good and to ameliorate the conditions on earth which he himself will have to experience. This would be enlightened self-interest on a macrocosmic scale. Yet the belief has been held for long epochs by many uncivilised peoples[1], from whom it was inherited and developed in particular by Hinduism and Buddhism: and there is no indication that it ever produced anything but inertia. The reason is that in those religions even the majestic march of metempsychosis is not endless, the benefits of the wheel of birth and rebirth are not ultimately sought *here* but *there*. Existence on earth, whether suffered once and for all, as in Christianity, or on the instalment plan, as in other oriental religions, is regarded as an unavoidable but tiresome chore to be got through as patiently

---

1 See e.g. my *Collected papers on the paranormal* (New York 1968), pp. 22-59.

as possible while awaiting paradise, or the ultimate embrace of Brahma, or absorption into nirvana. So why bother? 'Alone, in solitude, he shall meditate upon what is good for himself. By meditating in solitude, he attains the highest good.'[2]

The Greeks and Romans, in varying degrees across the centuries, with the exception of a few of the later philosophers, regarded themselves as the playthings of the gods, by whom they were manipulated like puppets. The *progredior* of the Romans, as in Lucretius's reiterated *pedetemptim progredientis*, 'gradual progress', denoted a succession of events rather than a development: they knew the word but not the thing. The notion even of freewill does not appear until a late stage, and then indistinctly.

The gradual formation of Christian doctrine, even after the slow (but never complete) fading of the belief in a second coming, could hardly change this situation: those who are told to despise life on earth in order to seek eternal salvation in another place, cannot be expected to develop a belief in progress. This idea is, indeed, destructive of religion. Religion would have us believe that virtuous behaviour is that which produces a good in another state of being. Thus, the official Christian view still is that the purpose of life is to ensure the eternal happiness, elsewhere, of a few select human beings. On the other hand, the belief in progress implies, les selfishly, that good behaviour is that which benefits our descendants on earth. As Mary Wollstonecraft said to Burke: 'It is, Sir, *possible* to render the poor happier in this world, without depriving them of the consolation which you gratuitously grant them in the next.'[3]

For the essence of the belief is that progress implies a continuous amelioration of the condition of man within the known framework of his existence. And this notion in turn has vast philosophic implications. By its acceptance the egocentricity of individual men is transmuted into a wider sense of humanity, the continuity and

---

2 *Manu-dharmasūtra*, iv.258; contrast Voltaire's 'To be good only to oneself is to be good for nothing' (*Discours sur l'homme*, vii.28). A different view of what here follows is offered by Ludwig Edelstein, *The Idea of progress in classical antiquity* (Baltimore 1967); but see E. R. Dodds, *The Ancient concept of progress* (Oxford 1973).
3 *A Vindication of the rights of man* (1790), pp. 152-3.

evolution of life have to be accepted, and the notion of degenera-
tion from a primitive ideal is inverted into that of amelioration
to an ultimate 'perfection' on earth. These implications were
perhaps not clearly understood by the authorities when Voltaire
wrote his innocent *Mondain*, but they were certainly felt. The final
line of this charming poem, 'Le paradis terrestre est où je suis'[4],
sealed the impression that Voltaire's ideas were blasphemous and
subversive; he was driven from his retreat at Cirey; and the poem
itself was classed as a satire, an absurd label which still adheres to
it in all the editions.

In short, the reasoning which leads to a belief in progress leads
also to humanism; for humanism is, above all things, the religion
(if this highly coloured word must be used), not of science or of
any particular scientific theory, but of progress[5]. Religion, after
all, is an act of faith. The belief in progress is also an act of faith,
whereas science is a framework within which the notions of good
and evil are irrelevant. The belief in progress is ultimately based
on value judgments which have nothing to do with biologic evolution or even with its not altogether convincing adaptations as the
genetic theories of sociology and history. And this is why the task
of the humanist is the intolerably difficult one of conflating the
apparently contradictory notions of the insignificance and the all-
importance of man.

Since the notion implies such rather difficult conceptions, it is
not surprising that the first explicit presentation of the idea of
progress had to await not only the generalisation of scientific
modes of thought, but also the weakening of religious influence;
had to await, in fact, the eighteenth century, and more specifically,
the popularisation in France by Voltaire of Newton and Locke.
Here we meet at once a rather interesting phenomenon: up to
a given moment the idea of progress can be said to have been
unknown; at another moment, soon after, it had become an
intimate part of thinking men's convictions. We do not know
exactly how this transition came about[6]: the subject deserves

4 'The earthly paradise is where I am'; see p. 211, above.

5 This emerges clearly from such a book as *The Humanist frame*, ed. sir Julian Huxley (1961). Cp. *The Human-ist outlook*, ed. (sir) A. J. Ayer (1968).

6 The rôle of Saint-Pierre has been much exaggerated.

investigation, and I commend it to the attention of historians of ideas. The fact in itself is clear: the idea was absorbed very quickly and thoroughly. On the one hand, if Bayle does not discuss progress it is because the idea was outside the range of his speculations; but on the other hand, if there is no general article on progress in the *Encyclopédie*[7], it is because the idea had not yet been consciously formulated. Yet this is merely superficial, the fundamental difference goes much deeper: Bayle not only does not formally discuss the idea of progress, he hardly betrays any awareness of it; the *Encyclopédie* also does not formally discuss it, but the whole work is penetrated by an unconscious acceptance of the notion as self-evident.

Voltaire provides an even more striking illustration of the total absorption, largely by subliminal osmosis, of this revolutionary new idea. In his voluminous alphabetic essays there is none devoted to progress. Yet nobody could read ten consecutive pages from his pen without realising that belief in perfectibility, or rather in meliorism, was as close to him as his skin, even in his youth.

In short, men's eyes were no longer turned upward and inward. They started to look around them and saw, first, that all was not good, and then that evil can be fought. Once more, the victory of meliorism was sudden and almost complete.

I say 'almost' because the idea of progress soon met with opposition, and from different directions. It was seen by perspicacious men of science that progress in this sense was often thought of as no more than an extrapolation of biologic progress.[8] And even this was questioned. The biologic progress of man is usually taken for granted because it seems obvious that we have become better and better adapted to do what we are doing. Yet is this not begging the question? Are we in fact better

7 There is no entry under 'progress' in the index of the last (11th-12th) scholarly edition of the *Encyclopaedia britannica* (1911-22). Yet writing half-a-century ago, dean Inge opened his essay on 'The Idea of progress' (*Outspoken essays, second series* [1922], p. 158) in terms which confirm my general argument: 'The belief in Progress, not as an idea but as an indisputable fact, not as a task for humanity but as a law of Nature, has been the working faith of the West for about a hundred and fifty years.'

8 Can this notion underlie Browning's apparently meaningless line 'Progress, man's distinctive mark alone'? (*A Death in the desert,* line 586).

able to do what we want to do, or do we merely do what we are
better able to do, perhaps by chance or perhaps to permit a kind
of survival which does not necessarily imply progress?

Nor was it long before another discovery was made. A century
earlier Pascal had written in the fragmentary preface of his
projected *Traité du vide*: 'Not only does every man advance in
the sciences from day to day, but ... all men progress together as
the universe ages, for the same thing occurs in the succession of
men's generations as in the successive ages of one man. So that
the whole succession of generations, throughout the course of so
many centuries, must be considered as a single man who lives for
ever and who learns continuously: whence we see how unjustly
we respect antiquity in philosophers: for, as old age is the time
furthest from childhood, who does not perceive that the old age
of universal man must not be sought in the times near to his
birth, but in those which are the furthest away?' The music of
Pascal is like that of Bach's passion music: the magnificent sound
tempts us to overlook the fact that it outstrips the sense, a fact not
particularly relevant in the sphere of art, but fatal in all others.
What Pascal says in this passage, if carried to its logical conclusion,
would be destructive of his own beliefs; and in a minor key it is
the result of an almost universal confusion between knowledge
and wisdom. And this was the objection soon advanced: that
man's progress seemed to be quantitative rather than qualitative,
that he was mistaking the means for the end. The religion of progress seemed to be little more than a gospel of acceleration.[9]

An even more serious objection to the naive forms of belief in
progress was slower to make itself felt: it is none the less valid, and,
so far, unanswered, perhaps because it is unanswerable. Progress
implies the improvement of man's possibilities of action. Actions,
however, are good and evil, that is, they have good and evil consequences, and merely to improve our ability to perform them is
to improve at once our capacity not only for good but also for evil.

It is not my intention systematically to survey all the objections to the idea of progress. For a notion apparently so obvious,

9 Kingsley Martin, *French liberal
thought in the eighteenth century* (1929),
p. 278.

so universally accepted, so right, so necessary, the objections, philosophic and practical, can be shown to be rather numerous. Yet I must refer to one other difficulty which our own generation has for the first time made plausible. Bury said that 'if there were good cause for believing that the earth would be uninhabitable in A.D. 2000 or 2100 the doctrine of Progress would lose its meaning and would automatically disappear.'[10] This is undoubtedly true, but one feels that Bury noted this possibility simply as a matter of intellectual honesty; he clearly did not envisage the uninhabitability of the earth as a real short-term possibility. Were he alive today his attitude could not but be different. Even the most complacent optimist must now admit as a possibility for tomorrow a final halt in human evolution or at least a catastrophic interruption of its normal course. T. H. Huxley was prophetically right when he said that 'Man is a brute, only more intelligent than other brutes. . . . Even the best of modern civilisations appears to me to exhibit a condition of mankind which neither embodies any worthy ideal nor even possesses the merit of stability.'[11]

Another form of scepticism about the reality of progress was summed up in blinding language and on a high plane of cogency, none the less real because strongly coloured by moral indignation, by the most eloquent prophet of the anti-Enlightenment, William Blake.

> Mock on, Mock on Voltaire, Rousseau:
> Mock on, Mock on: 'tis all in vain!
> You throw the sand against the wind,
> And the wind blows it back again.
>
> And every sand becomes a Gem
> Reflected in the beams divine;
> Blown back they blind the mocking Eye,
> But still in Israel's paths they shine.
>
> The Atoms of Democritus
> And Newton's Particles of light
> Are sand upon the Red sea shore,
> Where Israel's tents do shine so bright.

10 J. B. Bury, *The Idea of progress* (1920), p. 5.   11 Quoted by Bury, pp. 344-5.

One can only bow one's head, leave Blake to 'catch the shrieks of mankind in cups of gold', and pass on, as did his contemporaries. For Blake and his fellows were up against an irresistible force. It was not they who were heard but optimistic sceptics like Gibbon, who felt sure that 'we cannot determine to what height the human species may aspire in their advances towards perfection; but it may safely be presumed that no people, unless the face of nature is changed, will relapse into their original barbarism'. Who, today, would care to echo this sentiment? It is still true, in a sense, but what Gibbon did not foresee was that man himself would acquire the ability to change the face of nature. Yet the wise historian himself added a note of caution: 'We may therefore acquiesce in the pleasing conclusion that every age of the world has increased, and still increases, the real wealth, the happiness, the knowledge, and *perhaps* the virtue, of the human race.'[12]

Nor was the Gladstonian confidence of a Lecky any happier when he wrote a century ago: 'The plain fact is, that the progress of civilisation produces invariably a certain tone and habit of thought, which makes men recoil from miraculous narratives with an instinctive and immediate repugnance, as though they were essentially incredible, independently of any definite arguments, and in spite of dogmatic teaching.'[13] It must be owned that so naive a sentiment nowadays calls up only a smile, if not a giggle. Indeed, just about the time that Lecky wrote these words in his history of rationalism, mlle Soubirous was having interesting experiences in a certain grotto at Lourdes, and since then several score new saints have been canonised, each with his appropriate quota of miracles. Nor has there been any visible sign of that 'undisguised scorn and incredulity' in respect of miracles which Lecky attributes to 'most educated Roman Catholics'[14]. Very few of them indeed, educated or not, in Rome or elsewhere, remember the wise words of Augustine: 'Melius est dubitare de

12 Edward Gibbon, *The Decline and fall of the Roman empire*, at the end of ch.xxxviii (my italics); these sentiments are almost exactly echoed by Condorcet in his *Fragment sur l'Atlantide*.

13 W. E. H. Lecky, *History of the rise and influence of the spirit of rationalism in Europe* (London 1865), i.160.

14 Lecky, i.156.

ocultis, quam litigare de incertis.'[15] Indeed, Augustine himself forgot them. In this respect none of us can afford to be complacent: even in a supposedly secularised and rationalistic society like that of France expenditure on astrology, fortune-telling and the like constitutes a major industry.

The view of progress held by the leaders of the Enlightenment can be not inadequately represented by a single quotation from the noble-minded Condorcet, who wrote, before the revolution, in his biography of Voltaire placed at the head of the great Kehl edition of the master's works:

The history of what has been done in Europe on behalf of reason and humanity is that of his writings and of his benevolence. If the absurd and dangerous practice of burying the dead within the walls of cities, and even in temples, has been abolished in some countries; if in some parts of the continent of Europe men avoid, by inoculation, a scourge which menaces life and often destroys happiness; if the clergy of the countries subject to the Roman religion have lost their dangerous power, and will lose their scandalous wealth; if the liberty of the press has there made some progress; if in Sweden, Russia, Poland, Prussia, the states of the house of Austria, a tyrannical intolerance has vanished; if men have dared somewhat to diminish it even in France and some states of Italy; if the shameful remnants of feudal slavery have been shaken in Russia, Denmark, Bohemia and France; if even Poland today feels its injustice and its danger; if the absurd and barbarous laws of nearly all peoples have been abolished, or are menaced by early destruction; if the need to reform the law and the courts has everywhere been felt; if, on the continent of Europe, men have realised that they have the right to use their reason; if religious prejudices have been destroyed in the upper classes of society, and weakened at court and among the people; if the defenders of these prejudices have been reduced to the shameful necessity of maintaining their political utility[16]; if the love of humanity has become a language common to all governments; if wars have become less frequent; if nobody dares any longer advance the pride of monarchs or pretentions which time has rusted as pretexts for war; if we have witnessed the fall of all the impostures and masks beneath which privileged castes were able to deceive mankind; if for the first time reason has started to diffuse over the peoples of Europe a pure and steady light; everywhere, in the history of these changes, will be found the name of Voltaire, everywhere he will be found beginning the fight or determining the victory.

15 'It is better to doubt the unknown than to quarrel about it.'
16 If Condorcet had not been carried away by his eloquence he would not have said this in a eulogy of Voltaire; see pp. 229-230, above.

This fervent if rather incoherent hymn to the glory of progress and its handmaiden Voltaire is worthy of analysis. Of its eighteen points one refers to a more general love of humanity, two announce improvements in public hygiene, two celebrate a diminution of war, two an increase in the use of reason, five can be described as antireligious, and six glorify one form or another of liberty: personal, social and political. This gives a pretty fair picture of the views held in common by the select band of self-conscious *philosophes*. Liberty was in fact their major preoccupation, and they regarded religion as the chief obstacle to its attainment. Yet we must press the analysis a little further. Reason is specifically mentioned only twice, but this is a purely terminological or even rhetorical fact. For how were the religious and all the other reforms achieved and to be achieved? There was no doubt about that in the minds of Condorcet and his friends: it was by the use of reason. In his preamble Condorcet states explicitly that he is setting out what has been accomplished by Voltaire 'on behalf of reason and humanity'. The *philosophes* were indeed convinced that the progress of humanity would come about by the use of reason, and that Voltaire's major contribution had been to discover this fact and to broadcast it *urbi et orbi*.

Was this conviction justified by the events? In a sense, yes, for all the improvements enumerated by Condorcet had in fact been wholly or partly achieved, and achieved more or less permanently. Even his reference to war was not entirely illusory, for after the consequences of the French revolution had exhausted themselves, Europe did see a century of peace. It is true that we have since more than made up for this strange interlude.

Yet is it not too readily taken for granted that mankind has everywhere progressed? It is certainly not true that progress has been made consistently and uniformly, unless it is measured optimum against optimum, which would be a purely quantitative and non-ethical evaluation. Thus, it is true that today there is less generalised injustice and cruelty than prevailed in former ages: but when these plagues descend upon us our improved means of action have condemned their victims to previously unthinkable abominations. Again, it is certain that many men are better fed in our times than ever before: but a higher proportion of the world's population starves today than ever did before: and even were this not the case, a man can be saved from starvation to die more painfully of a cancer caused by progress in other fields.

This lamentable calendar need not be prolonged, for the facts are only too clear. Let us also remember that in the most vital, the most urgent, the most threatening of all his responsibilities man has made no deliberate progress whatsoever: I refer to his own improvement. We are living on borrowed time, we have mortgaged the future of the race, yet in our immeasurable complacency we make no attempt to do for ourselves what we do for our horses and our cattle, our budgerigars and our dormice. Eugenics is still a dirty word; euthanasia is anathema; and we refuse to take seriously the geometric increase of the world's population. This cognitive dissonance[17] (I apologise for using this convenient jargon) is disastrous. Indeed, the problem is so grave that the horrible solution of state-directed selective sterilisation has become a distinct possibility.[18] Nor has any direct attempt been made (there have of course been incidental by-products) to tackle what I hold to be the greatest of all the tragedies of man: the shortness of his life. What a horrifying waste it is that the decay of human faculties follows so closely on their maturity! The exploration of the atom and of outer space presents no particular urgency, yet we spend in these fields a hundred thousand times as much energy as goes even into the most negative aspects of gerontology.

Such considerations lead ineluctably to the conclusion that in a domain in which much is speculative one thing at least is certain: man's intellectual faculties have not improved since the beginning of recorded history. The quality of Einstein's thinking was not superior to Newton's, nor had Newton a better mind than Galileo, or he than Pythagoras or the author of the *Shu Chung*: each simply had more facts at his disposal than his predecessors. And in the domain of pure thought, thought for its own sake, I do not see that we have surpassed the *Vedanta* in the exquisite *nigologie* of metaphysics. I do not even feel absolutely sure that there has not

---

17 See Leon Festinger, *A Theory of cognitive dissonance* (1957), particularly p. 197.

18 It has, indeed, become a fact in India, and has been proposed to a Canadian royal commission.

been a certain intellectual deterioration, not, perhaps, in man's absolute capacity for thought, but in his respect for certain essential humanistic tones of mental activity. A decidedly distressing example of this is provided by that clarity of which Voltaire was so great a master, and the respect for which has become lip-service rather than profound conviction. In our time obscurity is far too readily mistaken for profundity, and many philosophers, historians and critics acquire fame by chasing the phantasms of ideas down the mirrored perspectives of the imagination. Where in the past ratiocination far too often invaded the domain of the imagination, now the opposite is true: the artist's view intrudes into the realms of the reason. It is perhaps a good thing that a Henry James should write like a psychologist; but few of the psychologists who write like novelists have the genius of William James. Voltaire, in the guise of Acrotal, complained that Bayle was the most abominable of men. 'He explains things with such odious fidelity; he sets out the pros and cons with such cowardly impartiality; he is so intolerably lucid; that he enables those who have merely common-sense to judge and even to doubt: this is unbearable.'[19] Few indeed are the writers who today expose themselves to such an impeachment.[20]

Was Turgot then right in saying that progress consists merely in the growth of knowledge? Marxist dialecticians still think so[21], but they are surely mistaken. It is clearly true that there cannot be progress without increase in knowledge, but whether, given ever increasing knowledge, it is accompanied by progress depends on what we do with that knowledge. The cathedral of Chartres is more than a pile of stones, but the Sacré Cœur is not necessarily a finer structure than the temple of Karnak although it was built thirty-five centuries later.

If we turn to an examination of the idea of progress in itself, we immediately come up against an apparently insurmountable

19 *Entretien d'Ariste et d'Acrotal* (1761).

20 I have come across the following startling *obiter dictum* by the distinguished philosopher George Boas, who, in reviewing a new history of philosophy, describes it as written 'on the whole clearly', which, he adds, 'is almost unique'; see the *Journal of the history of ideas* (New York 1963), xxiv.292.

21 See for instance *Quel avenir attend l'homme?* (Paris 1961), most explicitly in the otherwise admirable essay by Vercors (p. 301).

difficulty, that of discussing it in teleologic terms. The nature of progress is necessarily a function of its purpose. The value of an automobile can be judged by the safety and speed with which it transports us from A to B. In a more general context we know more or less where we are, but where do we want progress to take us? Or, to put the matter less tendentiously, where do we suppose that progress is taking us? Is happiness really—it is an almost universal assumption—the grand goal of man's painful advance? As a fact this cannot even remotely be established, and as an ambition is it not slightly vulgar? In any case, what is happiness? Herbert Spencer, in the introduction of his *Social statics*, has given what is perhaps the most civilised definition: 'Happiness signifies a gratified state of all the faculties.' Perhaps, but how is the quantum of happiness to be evaluated? If behaviouristically, for in this field even more than elsewhere introspection is a hazardous pursuit, Herbert Spencer's definition is manifestly false. Everybody who has lived in the country knows that the happiest man there is the village idiot.

The problem was posed by Voltaire in his epigrammatic apologue, the *Histoire d'un bon bramin*, written immediately after *Candide*, at a moment of acute internal conflict. The wise man is unhappy, unlike the foolish old woman who is his neighbour. 'What is the point?' asks the narrator. 'It is to be happy. What does it matter whether one is clever or foolish? There are more important things: those who are satisfied with their lot are sure to be happy; those who reason are not so sure to reason well. It is thus clear . . . that we should choose not to have commonsense, lest this common-sense contribute to our unhappiness.' And he continues: 'Everybody agreed with me, and yet I could find nobody who was willing to accept the bargain of becoming idiotic in order to be happy. From this I conclude that if we attach importance to being happy, we attach still more to being rational'.

Voltaire would have been well advised to state this conclusion, not as a fact, but as an objective. Should it therefore be concluded that the *philosophes* were mistaken in supposing, again like Herbert Spencer[22], that progress is 'not an accident, but a necessity'? No,

22 *Social statics*, I.ii.4.

for it must never be forgotten that the men of the Enlightenment did not believe merely in progress, but in progress through reason. And it is abundantly clear that men have hardly ever[23] made a serious and sustained effort to apply reason to the problems of life. On the contrary, in recent years, since the black decade of the 1930s, we have only too often seen the kid seethed in its mother's milk, reason used to discredit reason. Such obscurantism is premature, for men have never yet persistently tried to light their way by 'the pure flame lit by reason'[24].

The 'heroes of truth', as the young Wordsworth hoped in *Guilt and sorrow*, have never yet wielded 'th' Herculean mace of Reason'.

> The ruling passion, be it what it will,
> The ruling passion conquers reason still.[25]

Nor is there much sign that mankind is willing to put the philosophy of the Enlightenment to the test. Yet the need for lucid reflection is imperative, and so is its equally lucid expression, for progress is not a six-lane highway; perhaps it is not even a footpath; it is certainly not a one-way street; and I wish I could feel sure that it is not a dead end.

---

23 This qualification may be questioned; but I think it can be shown that the effort was in fact made very briefly during the first days of the French and Russian revolutions.

24 Voltaire, *Poème sur la loi naturelle* (1751-2), *Exorde*, 6-7.
25 Pope, *Epistles*, iii.153-4.

29. La Pucelle, *1755*

VERY many very unkind things have been said about the *Pucelle*[1], which became widely known at this time. The most recent history of French literature, by a French university professor, refers to the 'continuous obscenity' and the 'crushing pornography'[2] of this poem. This was by no means the contemporary view. Distinguished ladies did not hesitate to beg Voltaire for manuscripts, of which they gave readings in their drawing-rooms. Piron said that for many years Thieriot dined out on a single book of the *Pucelle*[3]. Nor did Voltaire hesitate to send it to mme de Pompadour[4], who was said to have read it to the king[5]. Mme Du Châtelet kept both works under lock and key, but thought the poem less dangerous than the *Traité de métaphysique*[6]. The pious duchess of Saxe-Gotha preferred it to the *Orphelin de la Chine*[7]. Even the *président* de Brosses, who comprehensively disliked Voltaire, said that 'this grotesque poem' is one of his good works, in which his epic genius is most marked[8]. All these tributes, which could be multiplied, were written before authentic texts were available. And when Voltaire was given his great triumph on his return to Paris at the end of his life, the crowd shouted 'Vive la Henriade! vive Mahomet! vive la Pucelle!'[9] Certainly, Voltaire's treatment of st Joan was often condemned, but it was usually for religious and patriotic reasons, as in the Inquisition decree of 1757. This controversy has now become unreal, for whether Joan was or was not what she thought she was, Voltaire's irreverence cannot touch her. All that we are interested in is the intrinsic merit of the poem. And here I do not

1 A critical edition has at last been published (1970), by Jeroom Vercruysse, as the second volume of the *Complete works of Voltaire*; all references are of course to this edition.

2 See my review of this book in the *Studies on Voltaire* (1966), xlvii.257-63.

3 Best.D6259 (1 May 1755).

4 Best.D6305 (13 June 1755).

5 Best.D6596 (23 November 1755).

6 Best.D1265 (22 January 1737).

7 Best.D5992 (23 November 1754).

8 Best.D9701 (26 March 1761).

9 According to the Kehl editors, in their preface.

hesitate to assert that the literary merits of the *Pucelle* distinctly surpass those of the *Henriade*.

Voltaire started work on the *Pucelle* certainly by 1730, and possibly several years before. Manuscripts were often stolen and copied surreptitiously, circulated widely almost at once, and eventually became a considerable trade. In 1755 Voltaire said that there were 6000 manuscript copies in Paris[10], and independent evidence suggests that this figure may have been accurate. It would be a great anachronism to imagine that most of these copies catered to the market in *erotica*. Only those who are not aware of the substantial output of deliberate pornography at that time could imagine such a thing. Those who enjoyed the reading of 'curious' literature had no need to buy expensive manuscripts. However, it was inevitable that those of the *Pucelle* should find their way into print (1755), and increasingly corrupt texts soon proliferated. Finally, after more than twenty pirated editions had been poured out (about as many as appeared of *Candide* in a single year) Voltaire was obliged to produce an authorised version (1762)[11].

Voltaire always maintained that the composition of the *Pucelle* was 'an amusement for the intervals between more serious occupations'[12]. No doubt, but this does not mean that this burlesque epic is not worthy of serious examination, even if it were not by Voltaire, whose most trifling scribble deserves attention.

As the form of the *Henriade* is modelled on Virgil, so the *Pucelle* derives from Ariosto. It is in rhymed decasyllabic verse and extends to twenty-one books and about 8300 lines, thus being nearly twice as long as the *Henriade*. Nobody seems to have noticed that the *Pucelle* is unique in at least one respect: it has a complex and flexible rhyme scheme[13], which makes it particularly suitable for reading aloud. The effect is almost musical. Though there is no evidence that Voltaire ever read a word of Chaucer (he never mentions him and possessed nothing by him in his library),

10 Best.D6505 (20 September 1755).

11 Voltaire tinkered with this edition up to and beyond the last moment, so that hardly two copies of it are identical.

12 Best.D885 (26 June 1735).

13 Thus, the opening lines of the poem are rhymed *abbaabba*; book xiii begins *abbaccdedee*, and book xxi *aabbcddcbb*. This sort of thing (which is not to be confused with seventeenth-century *rimes mêlées*) though somewhat reminiscent of Rutebeuf (thirteenth century), was very rare in French poetry.

the *Pucelle* often reminds one of the *Canterbury tales*, both in manner and matter. And Byron's *Don Juan*, in its turn, quite clearly owes a good deal to the *Pucelle*.

Before giving some account of the poem it is perhaps necessary to remind the reader that a poet's views are not to be determined by what he says in a mock-heroic epic. Voltaire more than once wrote seriously about Joan of Arc, with feeling and understanding, and those who revere Joan should realise that he was the first French historian to do so, and that she was not canonised until the present century, so that it is rather silly to call the *Pucelle* blasphemous. Voltaire wrote, for instance, that Joan's execution 'tears the heart and makes common sense shudder. It is difficult to conceive how we dare call any people barbarous after the innumerable horrors of which we have been guilty.'[14] Nor was this revulsion of feeling unique.

Voltaire at once sets the theme and the tone:

> J'aimerais mieux le soir pour mon usage
> Une beauté douce comme un mouton;
> Mais Jeanne d'Arc eut un cœur de lion:
> Vous le verrez, si lisez cet ouvrage.
> Vous tremblerez de ses exploits nouveaux,
> Et le plus grand de ses rares travaux
> Fut de garder un an son pucelage.[15]

Voltaire then describes the loves of Charles VII and Agnès Sorel, of whom he gives a sensually poetic description. When the king makes love to her 'La pudeur passe et l'amour seul demeure'[16]. In the meanwhile the English are ravaging France, whose leaders hold a council at Orleans. To them appears their patron saint Denis, who announces that he intends to look round for a virgin who will liberate the country. The council laugh:

> Quant il s'agit de sauver ma ville,
> Un pucelage est une arme inutile.

14 See *Eclaircissements historiques* (1763).

15 *Pucelle*, i.12-18; Voltaire 7, pp. 258-9. 'I should prefer for my own use in the evening a beauty as gentle as a sheep; but Joan of Arc had a lion's heart, as you will see if you read this work. You will tremble at her new feats; and the greatest of her wondrous works was to keep her maidenhead for a year.'

16 *Pucelle*, i.107; Voltaire 7, p. 263. 'Shame vanishes, and only love remains.'

Pourquoi d'ailleurs le prendre en ce pays?
Vous en avez tant dans le paradis! . . .
Chez les Français, hélas, il n'en est plus.[17]

The saint reaches Domremy and there finds Jeanne working in the stable of an inn. Voltaire describes her with feeling and sympathy, but his frank lines form a remarkable contrast with the painting of Agnès, even when he uses the same terminology. Compare, for instance, of Agnès:

Téton charmant qui jamais ne reposes,
Vous invitiez les mains à vous presser[18]. . . .

with this, of Jeanne:

Ses tétons bruns, mais fermes comme un roc,
Tentent la robe, et le casque, et le froc.[19]

Denis arrived just in time, for the monk Grisbourdin was besieging Joan's chastity. He reveals her destiny to the girl, she is provided with armour and a donkey, and rides to find the king. She comes to the tent of John Chandos, steals his breeches, and draws three fleur-de-lys on his page's bottom. She reaches the king and apostrophises him. Charles is transported, but then asks Joan whether she is a virgin. She invites doctors, matrons, learned men, pedants, apothecaries to examine her, and is given a certificate of chastity. The king leaves Agnès and departs with the blessing of Denis.

A long satirical excursus follows, in the guise of an account of the Palace of Folly. Agnès sets out to find the king, steals Joan's armour, is captured by the English and falls into the arms of Chandos. Joan and Dunois fight the English, and Dunois resists temptation, for he knows that 'the fate of the whole nation depended on her hidden jewel'[20]. They arrive at the château of Hermaphrodix, which gives rise to much erotic badinage, during

17 *Pucelle*, i.344-7, 350; Voltaire 7, p. 275. 'A maidenhead is a useless weapon when it comes to saving a city. Anyway, why seek it in this country? You have so many in paradise! . . . There is none left, alas, among the French.'

18 *Pucelle*, i.116-7; Voltaire 7, p.

264. 'Charming tit, never at rest, you invite one's hands to press you.'

19 *Pucelle*, ii.50-1; Voltaire 7, p. 279. 'Her brown tits, firm as rocks, tempt the robe and the helmet and the gown.'

20 *Pucelle*, iv.206-7; Voltaire 7, p. 327.

which Joan is stripped and whipped, but Grisbourdin arrives in time to prevent the worst. The monk is transported to hell, a long description of which gives Voltaire an opportunity to debate once again the folly of Christian doctrine, which condemns all those who lived before it was possible to be saved. Hell is the

> Sépulcre où gît la docte antiquité,
> Esprit, amour, savoir, grâce, beauté,
> Et cette foule immortelle, innombrable,
> D'enfants du ciel créés tous pour le Diable.
> Tu sais, lecteur, qu'en ces feux dévorants
> Les meilleurs rois sont avec les tyrans.
> Nous y plaçons Antonin, Marc-Aurèle,
> Ce bon Trajan, des princes le modèle;
> Ce doux Titus, l'amour de l'univers;
> Les deux Catons, ces fléaux des pervers;
> Ce Scipion, maître de son courage,
> Lui qui vainquit et l'amour et Carthage.
> Vous y grillez, sage et docte Platon,
> Divin Homère, éloquent Cicéron;
> Et vous, Socrate, enfant de la sagesse,
> Martyr de Dieu dans la profane Grèce;
> Juste Aristide, et vertueux Solon:
> Tous malheureux morts sans confession.[21]

Voltaire then spreads the net wider, and reveals that Clovis and Constantine are in hell, with great preachers, rich prelates, casuists, doctors, Spanish monks, Italian nuns, the confessors of all the kings, the inquisitors. Grisbourdin then tells the story of Joan's adventures, 'and all hell laughed at them with a good heart'[22].

The story then returns to earth and to the adventures of Agnès and Joan. An elaborate description follows of the temple of fame, and of the adventures of Dunois and La Trimouille. During these

21 *Pucelle*, v.72-89; Voltaire 7, p.348. 'Sepulchre in which languishes ancient wisdom, wit, love, knowledge, grace, beauty, and that immortal, innumerable crowd of the children of heaven all created for the devil. You know, dear reader, that the best kings are with the tyrants in these devouring fires. We send there Antonine, Marcus Aurelius, the good Trajan, the model prince; the gentle Titus, beloved by the universe; the two Catos, the scourge of the wicked; Scipio, master of his courage, he who vanquished both love and Carthage. You burn there, wise and learned Plato, divine Homer, eloquent Cicero, and you, Socrates, child of wisdom, martyr of god in pagan Greece; just Aristides and virtuous Solon: all wretches dead unconfessed.'
22 *Pucelle*, v.298; Voltaire 7, p. 357.

picaresque scenes, in which Joan does not figure, occurs a little gem of descriptive characterisation:

> Au cabaret les deux amants dinèrent;
> Et ce fut là qu'à table ils rencontrèrent
> Un brave Anglais, fier, dur et sans souci,
> Qui venait voir la sainte Vierge aussi
> Par passe-temps, se moquant dans son âme
> Et de Lorette et de sa Notre-Dame.
> Parfait Anglais, voyageant sans dessein,
> Achetant cher des modernes antiques,
> Regardant tout avec un air hautain
> Et méprisant les saints et leurs reliques.
> De tout Français c'est l'ennemi mortel,
> Et son nom est Christophe d'Arondel.
> Il parcourait tristement l'Italie,
> Et se sentant fort sujet à l'ennui,
> Il amenait sa maîtresse avec lui,
> Plus dédaigneuse encor, plus impolie,
> Parlant fort peu, mais belle, faite au tour,
> Douce la nuit, insolente le jour,
> A table, au lit, par caprice emportée,[23]. . . .

Even more graphic is the account of a naked duel between this Englishman and La Trimouille, during which their girls are carried off; but it is too long to quote. The two duellists pursue and recapture their mistresses. The story of Agnès Sorel is then taken up again. She finishes up in a convent, where she naturally has an amorous encounter. The English take the convent, and a fight follows between saint Denis and saint George. Joan is still wandering about naked on her donkey. The scene shifts again to the king and Agnès, who consoles herself with Montrose. At last we come back to Joan, now again dressed, who engages in

23 *Pucelle*, viii.213-31; Voltaire 7, p.398. 'The two lovers dined at the inn; and it was at table that they met a worthy Englishman, proud, hard, and without care, who had also come to see the holy virgin to pass the time, in his heart making sport of Lorette and its shrine: a perfect Englishman, travelling without purpose, paying dear for modern antiques, looking at everything with a haughty air, and despising the saints and their relics. He is the mortal enemy of all Frenchmen, and his name is Christophe d'Arondel. He gloomily traversed Italy; and, feeling himself very subject to boredom, took his mistress with him. She was even more disdainful, more impolite, speaking little, but beautiful and shapely, tender by night, insolent by day, capricious at table and in bed. . . .'

single combat with Chandos, who defeats her. He is about to rape her when saint Denis again intervenes, and Dunois vanquishes Chandos.

Voltaire then describes a French banquet at Orleans, followed by a general assault against the English, Charles being encouraged by Joan. The scene of the sixteenth book is laid in heaven, where st Peter appeases his colleagues George and Denis by promising a prize to whichever brings him the better ode. The king, Joan and their companions go mad, and are restored to sanity by the royal confessors. The next two books are filled with picaresque incidents, the most interesting passage consisting of a long excursus in which many of Voltaire's *bêtes noires* are excoriated with equal wit and bite: Frélon (the wasp, that is, Fréron), Coyon (Guyon), Chaumé (Chaumeix), Gauchat, Sabotier (Sabatier), La Beaumelle and other critics and theologians are in turn exhibited.[24]

And so we come to the last two books of the *Pucelle*, which are again devoted wholly to Joan. The devil enters her donkey and tries to seduce her, after first addressing her in eloquent and respectful terms. Joan resists the temptation and chases the devil-donkey. Denis then replaces the devil in the ass. Joan and Dunois defeat the English, and the poem concludes:

> Du haut des cieux Denis applaudissait;
> Sur son cheval saint George frémissait.
> L'âne entonnait son octave écorchante,
> Qui des Bretons redoublait l'épouvante.
> Le roi, qu'on mit au rang des conquérants,
> Avec Agnès soupa dans Orléans.
> La même nuit, la fière et tendre Jeanne,
> Ayant au ciel renvoyé son bel âne,
> De son serment accomplissant les lois,
> Tint sa parole à son ami Dunois.
> Lourdis, mêlé dans la troupe fidèle,
> Criait encore: Anglais! elle est pucelle![25]

24 *Pucelle*, xviii.24-259; Voltaire 7, pp. 533-43.

25 *Pucelle*, xxi.451-62; Voltaire 7, p. 588. 'Denis applauded from the heavens; on his horse, st George shuddered; the ass intoned his grating octave, which redoubled the terror of the British. The king, who was ranked with the conquerors, supped with Agnès at Orleans. That same night the proud and tender Joan, having sent back her fine ass to heaven, faithful to her oath, kept her word to her friend Dunois. Lourdis, mingling with the faithful crowd, still cried: English! she is a virgin!'

It can thus be seen that this light-hearted burlesque does not deserve automatic condemnation. Of course Voltaire could not write about religion, especially in a picaresque poem intended to amuse, without making fun of it. Nor was he in the least inclined to write with conventional respect even about a national heroine. Those who find these things shocking will be duly shocked. But all this is incidental. The main theme is a huge joke: the mystical importance attached to Joan's virginity. Voltaire found irresistibly funny the notion that the fate of France could depend on the preservation of this peasant-girl's maidenhead. And let there be no mistake about it: enormous importance *was* attached by her contemporaries to Joan's virginity. Voltaire developed this theme in fugue and counterpoint, in some of his most successful verse, pausing only here and there to sink his blade into some of man's inhumanities and stupidities. To regard the *Pucelle* as a work of pornography, that is, one intended to titillate, is a judgment a little too lumpish even from those who hate Voltaire.

30. *War on all fronts,* *1756-1760*

WE MUST NOW PICK UP the thread where we dropped it. Rousseau's letter on providence is not celebrated because its views have any special significance, but because it expresses eloquently, if not too clearly, the conventional attitudes Voltaire was most concerned to eradicate. Rousseau found consoling the optimism which to Voltaire seemed so unbearably smug, and he complained that his sufferings were embittered by Voltaire's poem, because it sought to provoke him into protest. That was indeed its purpose, in a general sense, of course, for Rousseau himself was far from Voltaire's mind. This is precisely the fundamental difference between the quietism of Rousseau and the reforming activity of Voltaire. The former preached resignation, the latter's proudest claim on our gratitude is the fact that wherever he saw evil, whether man-made or not, he protested and incited others to protest. Rousseau asked man to suffer because suffer he must; Voltaire sought to replace optimism by meliorism, he asserted that the human condition can become better, and invited mankind to do something about it. This was not merely a philosophical attitude, it was expressed in each man's life. Thus, two examples among many, when Voltaire was asked to do something for the persecuted Protestants, he nearly always responded, often successfully, even though he disapproved of their practices; when similar requests came to Rousseau, he coldly declined, although he was himself (though not always) a Protestant. Voltaire helped and encouraged the young. Rousseau made foundlings of his own children.

Rousseau carried his masochism into his thinking: to such a point that he alleged the consequences of the earthquake to be man's own fault; for, said he, as we have seen, if the inhabitants of Lisbon had not been assembled in a big town the effects of the disaster would have been far less serious. This is unsound even as a statement of fact, for the earthquake spread into many other parts of the peninsula and beyond: those who fled, in addition to their natural fright, felt that they were not merely being struck down, they were being pursued. And Rousseau concluded with a typical *argumentum ad hominem*, for all his thinking was ultimately egocentric: 'I cannot help noticing a singular contrast ... between you and me. . . . Satiated with glory and disillusioned by vain grandeur, you live, a free man, in the bosom of abundance. Very sure of your immortality, you philosophise peacefully about the nature of the soul, and if your body or your heart suffers you have Tronchin for doctor and friend. Yet you find nothing but evil on the earth. And I, obscure, poor, and tormented by an incurable ailment, meditate with pleasure in my retreat, and find that all is well.'[1] Rousseau asserted that nothing could make him doubt immortality and a benevolent providence. 'I feel it, I believe in it, I desire it, I hope for it, I will defend it with my last breath.' Well, it is undoubtedly interesting, it is perhaps even relevant, to know what so eloquent and literate a man as Rousseau felt and believed, but what the soldier said is not evidence.

Rousseau was afraid that Voltaire would be offended by his letter, so little did he understand his correspondent's character. However, Voltaire of course replied very amiably, conveying with the utmost delicacy his opinion of Rousseau's optimistic ramblings. 'Forgive me for dropping at the moment these philosophical discussions, which are merely pastimes. Your letter is very fine, but one of my nieces, who is staying with me, has been in considerable danger for three weeks.' He assured Rousseau of his esteem, and renewed his invitation.[2] Rousseau was charmed, not least perhaps because Voltaire addressed him as 'mon cher philosophe'—and indeed he still regarded Rousseau as one of the small band of superior spirits. 'A man', wrote Rousseau, 'who is able to take my letter as he did deserves to be called a philosopher, and no one can be more inclined than I am to join esteem and friendship for his person to the admiration I have always had for

1 Best.D6973 (18 August 1756); on this letter see R. A. Leigh, 'Rousseau's letter to Voltaire on optimism', *Studies on Voltaire* (1964), xxx.247-309, and Leigh 424.

2 Best.D6993 (12 September 1756).

his works.'[3] By the time he came to write the *Confessions* (ix), this exchange had of course been transformed in Rousseau's mind into a personal triumph over Voltaire, to whom he refers as 'this wretched man, overwhelmed by prosperity and glory but nevertheless bitterly declaiming against the miseries of life'—thus expressing again the crassly materialistic notion that a man's opinions are epiphenomena of his physical condition, as if the difficulties of blindness can be felt only by a blind man, as if only a pauper has the right to be a socialist. All this is not very interesting in itself, but only because of the light it throws on the later rupture between the two men.

All these activities, practical and intellectual, did not exhaust Voltaire, and he began actively to collaborate in the *Encyclopédie*. His contributions were largely on non-controversial subjects, which is odd when one comes to think of it, but the reasons for this have never been adequately explored. Perhaps it was because in the article 'Histoire' Voltaire begins with a definition if impeccable propriety: 'History is the account of facts taken to be true', but goes on to define sacred history as 'a series of divine and miraculous operations by which it pleased God formerly to guide the Jewish nation, and today to exercise our faith.' Still, the volcano obviously could not continue to erupt with the same violence, and indeed the first part of 1756 marks a pause, during which Voltaire spent a great deal of time (though by his standards this was almost idleness) in assembling and revising his works for the first collected Cramer edition, which was to hold the field for twenty years.

As an author Voltaire was now in his element. He had an efficient and intelligent publisher at his door, and one who was only too willing to indulge his patron's slightest whim, for the great man was also a rich and generous one: not only did he take no money from Cramer, he even paid him for special work. As time went on Cramer, not satisfied even with his quasi-monopoly of the vast output of Ferney, became greedy, and exasperated Voltaire beyond endurance by pouring out new editions and collections of his writings, as often as not using inaccurate texts, and even many

3 Leigh 470 (25 January 1757).

apocryphal ones. But in the meanwhile Voltaire generously indulged his passion for elegant typography, good paper and accurate composition. In particular, he had a mania for cancels, and often paid Cramer to substitute amended leaves in books already set up and even printed. He revised, enlarged and transformed this first collected Geneva edition to such an extent over the years that its bibliographical problems will probably never be fully resolved. It is difficult to find two absolutely identical sets.

But, above all, as soon as Voltaire arrived at the Délices, he sent to press, at last, the most remarkable of all his works, the *Essai sur les mœurs*. This eagle's flight must be observed separately, in the next chapter.

For the moment Voltaire devoted his usual meticulous pains to the publication of the Lisbon poem and the older one on natural law, the appearance of which inevitably led to more abuse and persecution. For the rest he went out of his way to renew contact with old friends like mme Du Deffand, Richelieu and Hénault. He was horrified by the feeble attempt of Damiens to murder the king, and referred to it again and again with loathing, attributing it to the poisoning of the assassin's mind by religious controversy. As he told the duke d'Uzès, 'If one goes through the history of Christian murderers, and it is very long, it will be seen that a Bible always accompanied the dagger in their pockets, and never Cicero, Plato or Virgil.'[4]

All normal activity was overshadowed, however, by Voltaire's anxiety about the action at Minorca, in which Richelieu took a leading part, and above all by the breakdown of the alliances and the beginning of the Seven years' war, the consequences of which he saw more clearly than most of his contemporaries. For years to come his thoughts were dominated by the frightful development of this war, which was spreading its devastation over a large part of Europe and into many colonial territories. The horror of these events was fittingly symbolised by the case of admiral Byng, immortalised by Voltaire's bitter witticism in *Candide* (xxiii) that

4 Best.D7135 (28 January 1757). See also the chapter on Damiens in the *Histoire du parlement*, lxvii, in which Voltaire gives a detailed description of the madman's unspeakably cruel execution, but, alas, for once without explicitly condemning it.

in England it is well to kill an admiral from time to time to encourage the others. Byng led his fleet before Minorca irresolutely,
and withdrew it rather ignominiously. When he returned home
he was court-martialled and, though acquitted of cowardice and
disaffection, was condemned to death for neglect of duty. Voltaire had known him in England[5], and now wrote to Richelieu
to ask him to intervene on the admiral's behalf. This the duke
chivalrously did, and Voltaire forwarded his letter to Byng in
these terms: 'Tho' I am almost unknown to you, I think 'tis my
duty to send you the copy of the Letter which I have just received
from the Marshall Duke of Richelieu. Honour, Humanity, &
Equity, order me to convey it into your hands. This noble and
unexpected Testimony from one of the most candid as the most
generous of my countrymen makes me presume y^r Judges will
do you the same justice.'[6] But England was traversing one of
her recurrent crises of self-righteousness, and Byng was duly
executed, though the king was recommended to show clemency.
Voltaire always felt that it was 'diabolic' to have shot the admiral
'for not having killed enough Frenchmen'[7].

As the fearful events of the war multiplied and spread, Voltaire
began the peace negotiations in which he was to persist until the
bitter end. His voluminous correspondence with the duchess of
Saxe-Gotha, of which we now have both sides, is particularly significant. Voltaire also transmitted official and semi-official mes-
sages between the combatants, and himself over and over again
implored Frederick to end the war. 'You are legislator, warrior,
historian, poet, musician, but you are also *philosophe*. . . . To
Sans-Souci, to Sans-Souci, as soon as you can!'[8] All his efforts
were in vain. The war increased in ferocity, Frederick suffered
defeat, appeared to be crushed, and therefore encouraged Voltaire's efforts. He even adopted such frantic measures as the offer
of Neuchâtel to mme de Pompadour[9]. And finally he threatened

5 Best.D7275 (2 June 1757), D15986
(31 October 1769).

6 Best.D7109 (2 January 1757).

7 Best.D16873 (28 December 1770).
Voltaire's part in the Byng affair has
now been told in detail by A. M.
Rousseau, *L'Angleterre et Voltaire,*

i.219-231.

8 Best.D8338 (*c.* 5 June 1759).

9 See A. Du Pasquier, 'La Marquise
de Pompadour et Neuchâtel', *Musée
neuchâtelois* (Neuchâtel 1917), n.s. iv.7-
24.

suicide, evoking a moving and eloquent appeal from Voltaire to hold his hand.[10] Though the king assured Voltaire that he needed no urging to make peace, which was his greatest hope[11], he continued to make war. And suddenly he restored his fortunes by his victory at Rossbach (5 November 1757), one of the most remarkable reversals of fortune known to history. Although heavily outnumbered, Frederick shattered the combined army under Soubise, and lost only 550 men, while the French lost 7000. Though they were knocked out of the continental conflict this by no means ended the war, which continued with the same astonishing instability. The arrival of the at first triumphant Russians had its influence, and Voltaire's peace proposals might then have ended the slaughter if any of the parties had been willing to take them seriously. Voltaire said that he would have done anything to find the smallest stone to serve in the construction of peace.[12] But the Prussian king was determined to keep his conquests even if they had to be devastated in the process, and the French prime minister was a hopeless dilettante. All Voltaire's efforts were therefore in vain, and Frederick had to be left to carry out his threat to 'live and die as a king'.

Nevertheless the long letters written by Frederick and Choiseul to Voltaire, but in reality intended for each other, make remarkable reading. And Voltaire himself, as always, managed to extract some fun even from these painful debates. What would the reader have thought if, in an attic or a forgotten album, he had found the letter[13] here translated?

Nyon, Vaud, via Geneva
15 February

Mademoiselle,

I send you these lines to thank you for your kindness in passing on my letters to Mademoiselle Custrin, my mistress, for whom I still have a secret passion, in spite of her infidelities and her caprice. It is still my purpose to marry her: I am easy-going, and besides I think that in spite of that bad business about the banker she will still have quite a large dowry. She plays very well; my brother Antoine will be able to accompany her on the bass

10 Best.D7400 (*c.* 25 September 1757); Frederick's letter is quoted in the autobiography, p. 665, below.

11 Best.D8650 (13 December 1759).
12 Best.D8620 (30 November 1759).
13 Best.D8758 (15 February 1760).

viol, and we shall lead a very agreeable life, together with my cousin Jacqueline. I should be very grateful, mademoiselle, if you would give my intended the enclosed billet-doux to be going on with until I and my family can write at greater length.

We thank you for the bale of linen you were so good as to send: we are going to make sheets of it. As ever, we commend our cousin Etienne to their serene highnesses, and to madame la grande maîtresse. They say that their highnesses' family is the most amiable possible, and that they act plays in verse to perfection. I'm sorry I cannot see them, for I love the theatre. I was enchanted by their highnesses when you let me see them on their way to dinner. How wonderful the duchess looked, what nobility and goodness! I was in ecstasy. Her children, the little princes, were no higher than my knee. They must be very grown-up now. Dear mademoiselle, how can one help loving such a family with all one's heart, and respecting them as much as one loves them? Be good enough, dear mademoiselle, to lay our service at the feet of our noble mistress, our protectress, and believe me with all my heart your humble and obedient servant

Jacques Sutamier

What charming simplicity, is it not? Nothing of the sort! When deciphered this letter could not be less naïve. Not one word of it means what it seems to mean. There was no such person as Jacques Sutamier, the letter was not written at Nyon, nor addressed to a young lady, and it has nothing to do with a flirt by the name of Custrin.

We are in 1760, in the midst of the Seven years' war. Voltaire was still making passionate efforts to end the murderous and useless conflict. Among other things, we have seen him transmitting the correspondence of Frederick and Choiseul. This was by no means easy; for Voltaire's letters to reach Frederick special messengers had to cross the battlefield. But Voltaire was not easily discouraged: the margravine of Bayreuth[14], the king's sister, was also a great friend, and at first he had transmitted his letters through her. But, alas, this charming lady fell ill and died on the day of Frederick's defeat at Hochkirch (14 October 1758)[15]. Nothing daunted, Voltaire turned to another one, the

14 One of Wilhelmina's letters is quoted in the autobiography, pp. 663-664, below.

15 The king mentioned her death to Voltaire at the same time as his own 'hemorrhoidal and sometimes nephritic colics', and asked Voltaire to 'erect a monument in her honour' (Best.D7966; 6 December 1758). Voltaire responded with an *Ode sur la mort de s. a. s. mme la princesse de Bareith*, the stately periods of which do not altogether disguise the sincerity of his sorrow.

gentle and pious duchess of Saxe-Gotha. But letters may get lost or captured, and a little play-acting was always amusing. And so it was that one day the duchess—we can imagine her surprise—received a letter which addressed her as 'Mademoiselle', and came from a humble stranger who signed Jacques Sutamier. In reality Sutamier was Voltaire; Nyon stood for Les Délices; one young lady was the duchess of Saxe-Gotha; the other, the flirt, was Frederick the great; and Etienne was the duc de Choiseul—that was one of his Christian names. Only 'la grande maîtresse' is almost at once recognisable, and gave me the key to the mystery. In actual fact Voltaire was very fond of mme von Buchwald, lady-in-waiting to the duchess of Saxe-Gotha, and often called her 'la grande maîtresse des cœurs' ('the mistress of all hearts'). And the meaning of the whole can now easily be inferred. As Voltaire wrote to the king on or about the same day: 'It certainly depends only on your majesty to accelerate the peace, and I hope that you will do it'[16].

But the Seven years' war has taken us too far ahead. Thus, at the very beginning of 1756 there had occurred an incident of little interest to the reader but of great importance for Voltaire, to say nothing of his editor and biographer. This was the removal to the court of the elector Palatine of Cosimo Alessandro Collini, who had been Voltaire's secretary since the Prussian fugue. He was not a bad fellow, and had been through much at his master's side, but he was disloyal and grouchy, and mme Denis[17] finally persuaded her uncle to dismiss him. He was gradually replaced by Jean Louis Wagnière, and this meant that Voltaire finally and for the rest of his life had in his service a loyal, honest and efficient secretary, and one who has endeared himself to me, among other things, by dating most of the letters he wrote for Voltaire, who himself continued to write many with his own hand, and, alas, to date few. Wagnière's solicitude for his master's reputation and interests continued after Voltaire's death, often in the face of the selfish opposition of mme Denis. Thus, when she sold his books

16 Best.D8759 (*c.* 15 February 1766).

17 Later on he referred to her in a letter as 'la louche ouvrière', approximately 'shifty busybody' (Best.D7594;

19 January 1758); some such by no means inapt epithet had no doubt come to her ears when Collini was still in Voltaire's employ.

and papers to the empress Catherine, it was he who organised the removal with scrupulous care, cataloguing the books and classifying the manuscripts.

During these very busy months the theatrical performances at Montriond were particularly numerous. We have spirited accounts of these theatricals in letters from the delicious Lolotte to her 'dear child'[18], accounts which are the more touching in their high spirits because Lolotte's pregnancy turned out badly and soon after led to her lingering death. Everybody said that her performance was better than anybody else's. Her hair and jewels were admired, and her 'excrescence' hardly showed. Voltaire, in particular, was enthusiastic. Mme Denis had never acted so badly, didn't know a word of her part, and was the only one who was not applauded—here a little malice must be allowed for, since all the evidence shows that mme Denis was a pretty good actress. 'The intendant of Burgundy was there with fourteen apparitions who didn't look human, and I can assure you that he made the fifteenth. All frightful, all stupid, all untidy and dirty.' They were sixty, seated at three tables, with at least sixty lacqueys. They had arrived with fifty-two horses and expected Voltaire to lodge the whole cavalcade, which he did at Ferney and Tournay, to show off, and led the party there himself at 2 o'clock in the morning.

We have plenty of other evidence of the same kind, which throws light on the standards of comfort and cleanliness still accepted by all even in the middle of the eighteenth century, and long after. Voltaire's family and household servants numbered at least fifty, so that on this occasion there were 175 or so people to lodge in three houses, all of which still stand almost exactly as they were when Voltaire lived in them, and it can be seen that they are relatively modest in size. Between them Les Délices, Ferney and Tournay have about fifty rooms, all told, nearly all the bedrooms being quite small. The conditions can be imagined.

Voltaire sent out copies of the *Essai sur les mœurs*; and much correspondence was devoted to his loans to the elector Palatine and to Saxe-Gotha. The death of the centenarian Fontenelle broke

18 Françoise Charlotte Pictet to her husband François Marc Samuel de Constant Rebecque, Benjamin Con- stant's nephew; Best.D9308 (13 October 1760); cp. p. 59, above.

Voltaire's last link with the *grand siècle,* and a more personal break soon followed because of his ever worsening relations with the Genevese authorities. These petty potentates, having encouraged Voltaire to settle in their midst, now seemed determined to make his life unbearable. Of course, he was guilty of many offences against Calvinist morality. Among far more important ones there was, for instance, his solicitude for a Protestant maid in his service who had become pregnant by a Catholic valet.[19] Anyway, after a final disappointment, Voltaire made up his mind to shake the dust of Geneva from his feet. He made overtures to Stanislas Leszczinski for the purchase of a property in Lorraine. The king was willing if Louis xv had no objection, but as the project fell through it may be supposed that the French king did object.[20] So, before the end of 1758, Voltaire bought the châteaux of Tournay and Ferney, one just this side of the French frontier, and the other just beyond. He explained to Jean Robert Tronchin that he had intended to establish himself permanently by the lake, but unfortunately there were priests in Geneva as elsewhere. They had acted against him, as by spreading the allegation that he had taken *refuge* in Geneva, forgetting that he had done the republic the honour of believing it to be free and worthy to be inhabited by philosophers. He had remained silent, but had acquired other houses. The magistrates of Geneva were respectable and wise, but the people were a little arrogant and their priests a little dangerous.[21]

As usual, Voltaire entered on his new life with hope and gaiety. He told the président de Brosses that he made his entry at Tournay 'like Sancho Panza into his island. I only lacked his belly. Your priest harangued me. Chouet [Brosses's bailiff] gave me a splendid meal in the taste of those of Horace and Boileau. . . . The peasants frightened my horses with musketry and flares. The girls brought me oranges in baskets decorated with ribbons. The king of Prussia tells me that I am happier than he.'[22] And, best of all, Voltaire now had 'four paws instead of two.'[23]

19 Best.D7552 (3 January 1758), D7567 (8 January 1758).
20 Best.D7779, D7787, D7801 (July 1758).
21 Best.D7976 (13 December 1758).
22 Best.D7996 (25 December 1758).
23 Best.D7995 (24 December 1758).

The break with Geneva was complete and visible, but these purchases of properties so far from Paris implied also a spiritual severance from the French capital. The acquisition of Ferney marked also an important development in Voltaire's thinking on social matters. He wrote to a French correspondent:

My land is excellent, and yet I found a hundred acres, belonging to my tenants, which remain uncultivated. The farmer had not sown half of his land. The minister has performed no marriage for seven years, and during this time no children have been produced, because we have only Jesuits in the neighbourhood, and no Franciscans. Geneva absorbs everything, swallows everything. . . . Such are the deplorable consequences of the revocation of the edict of Nantes. But a far more baleful calamity is the rapacity of the farmers-general, and the fury of their employees. Wretches who can hardly find a little black bread to eat are arrested every day, stripped of what they have, imprisoned because they put on this black bread a little salt bought near their cottages. One's heart is torn when one witnesses so much misery. I am buying the estate of Ferney only to do a little good.[24]

This letter can only be described as astonishing. No such language as this is to be found in any previous writing by Voltaire. He had evidently been carefully inspecting the Ferney estates before signing the final contract for their acquisition: and it is as if the condition of the peasants and the land had caused all his thinking suddenly to come to a point, exploding in this trumpet-call of social protest, a call to be incessantly sounded from now on until the end of his life. He did vastly more than 'a little good'. Before the ink was dry on the contract Voltaire set about repairing the road from Geneva to Pregny; wrote the first of the innumerable letters, petitions, memoranda which eventually led to the abolition of the feudal dues attached to the estate; applied to the Dijon *parlement* on behalf of the commune against the oppressive priest of Ferney; employed twenty men to restore the vineyards; asked for drawings of a new kind of wine-press; acquired a sowing-machine with six drills; and prepared to set up a stud-farm.[25] All this was merely an intimation of twenty years of incessant labour which eventually transformed a wretched serflike population into a free and prosperous province.

Soon Voltaire was able to write to lord Lyttelton that he was

24 Best.D7946 (18 November 1758).   D8069, D8265 (December 1758-April
25 Best.D8009,   D8011,   D8020,   1759).

407

not exiled in Switzerland, as the author of the *Dialogues of the dead* had asserted.

J live in my own lands in France. Retreat is becoming to old age and more becoming in ones own possessions. If j enjoy a little country house near Geneva, my mannors and my castles are in Burgundy, and if my King has been pleas'd to confirm the privileges of my lands which are free from all tributes, j am the more addicted to my King.

If j was an exile, j had not obtain'd from my court many a *passeport* for english noblemen. The service j rendered to them intitles me to the justice j expect from the noble author.

As to religion, j think, and j hope, he thinks with me, that God is, neither a presbiterian, nor a lutherian, nor of the low church, nor of the high church; but god is the father of all mankind, the father of the noble author and mine.[26]

Voltaire did not leave Les Délices at once, for of course, he had first to build a theatre at Tournay[27]. In the meanwhile he undertook one of the journeys now become very rare: he went to Schwetzingen to stay with the elector Palatine. As he was about to leave mme Du Bocage, a minor writer of much merit, arrived with her husband, and was charmed by her host. Voltaire appeared to be younger, happier, and in better health than before he went to Prussia. His conversation was as agreeable as ever and even more gay.

At Schwetzingen, in the midst of brilliant festivities, without the sound of a single trumpet, he wrote *Candide*, and soon published it. Like nearly all Voltaire's stories *Candide* glided into the world unheralded. In the midst of his negotiations for Tournay and Ferney, and his various difficulties, he was quietly correcting the proofs of his most famous work, which he had arranged to print simultaneously in several places. Official condemnations followed at once, but within a few weeks Voltaire was able to announce that 6000 copies had been sold in Paris[28]. And even the tepid Thieriot reported that readers were tearing the book from each other's hands: he raved that Voltaire would live longer than Lucian, Rabelais and Swift together.[29]

---

26 Best.D9231 (*c.* September 1760).
27 This was promptly prohibited by the civil and religious authorities of Geneva; see Best.app.D199. For mme Du Bocage see her *Œuvres* (Lyon 1764), iii.403-5.
28 Best.D8172 (*c.* 10 March 1759).
29 Best.D8137 (23 February 1759).

This no doubt helped to console Voltaire during the first months of 1759, after his return from the court of the elector. These months were bedevilled by his efforts to obtain the suppression of the *Guerre littéraire*, another of the more and more numerous publications devoted to the libelling of the great man. He did not object to the book so much because he was attacked in it, but because it had been published in a most compromising form, under the title of *Guerre littéraire ou choix de quelques pièces de m. de V****. It contained only one authentic Voltaire letter, that in which he says that Calvin had 'une âme atroce'[30].

In the meanwhile Voltaire amused himself by denying that he was the author of *Candide*, supplying more and more baroque details about the true authorship. Thus, he wrote to one editor under the name of Démad (the mad? this must surely have been intended?) asserting with a mass of circumstantial detail that *Candide* had been written by his brother, captain in the Brunswick regiment, in order to convert the Socinians. Besides, his brother was the intimate friend of dr Ralph, professor in the university of Frankfurt on the Oder, under whose name he had published it out of modesty[31]. The point of these elaborate jests is lost if one does not realise that 'everybody', and certainly everybody who enjoyed them, knew Voltaire to be the real author of *Candide*: and of course Voltaire knew that they knew. These were family jokes, and Voltaire's literary family was world-wide.

During these same months occurred the renewal of Voltaire's friendship with Frederick, expressed inevitably in frequent and voluminous letters. Brought together by their sorrow at the death of Wilhelmina of Bayreuth, the king's sister, the two men tried rather gingerly to re-establish their former intimacy, but neither could ever again feel quite at ease with the other. Nevertheless the king was insensitive enough to invite Voltaire to return to the Prussian court[32], tempting him with the offer of the same honours whose symbols he had taken from him with such gross indignity only a few years earlier at Frankfort. Frederick was really one of a kind.

30 See p. 360, above.
31 Best.D8239 (1 April 1759).

32 See a note on Best.D8153, and Voltaire's amusing account of the king's offer (Best.D8249; 6 April 1759).

As 1759 drew on into 1760 Voltaire's life became one of almost frenzied activity. Although he had decided to leave he made extensive improvements in the gardens of the Délices (including the terrace and retaining wall which can still be seen[33]) and began to rebuild Ferney. Frederick and Voltaire started to quarrel again, for no adequate reason: it was simply that the king, in Voltaire's words, could not help scratching with one hand while he caressed with the other[34]. After the king had indulged in some bad-tempered outbursts Voltaire told him that his profession of hero and king had not made his heart very sensitive. 'It is a pity, for that heart was made to be human, and without the heroism and the throne you would have been the most agreeable man in the world.'[35] This infuriated Frederick. 'Learn', wrote the philosopher-king, 'in what manner it is fitting for you to write to me. Understand that some liberties are permitted and some impertinences are intolerable on the part of men of letters and fine wits. Become at last a philosopher, that is, sensible.'[36] This was the same man who, when he ascended the throne, had asked Voltaire to write to him as a man, not as a king.[37] So angry was Frederick that he even took a violent dislike (soon overcome) to *Candide.*

Some months later Voltaire's bitterness was expressed in a very outspoken letter[38]. He asked the king to stop troubling the writer's last hours. 'You have done me enough harm. You have embroiled me with the king of France, you have made me lose my posts and my annuities, you ill-treated me in Frankfort, me and an innocent woman, a respected woman who was dragged in the mud and thrown into prison, and then, in honouring me with

33 Though part of it collapsed in 1967 and was restored by the city authorities, over my protests, with rather inadequate taste.

34 Best.D4166 (26 June 1750); and so tenacious was the king's memory for these little truths that he turned the words against Voltaire nine years later (Best.D8304, 18 May 1759); evidently Frederick found this particular charge too true to be good.

35 Best.D8306 (19 May 1759).

36 Best.D8345 (10 June 1759).

37 See p. 263, above.

38 Best.D8866 (21 April 1760). It is important here to make a correction. Desnoiresterres v.384 says that this letter was written with a rage which Voltaire did not try to control. Printed sources can be very dangerous. Had the admirable biographer seen Voltaire's draft of this letter he would also have seen that it was very carefully composed. Every word was deliberate and calculated.

your letter, you poison the sweetness of this consolation by bitter reproaches'[39]. And he went on to tell Frederick that he had done an ill-service to free thought in showing its enemies that philosophers could not live together in peace. And so on at considerable length.

The king reacted as bullies always do when their victims stand up to them. He did not break off relations, replied lengthily and quite pacifically, and simply asked Voltaire to stop pestering him with his niece. 'Molière's servant is discussed, but nobody will ever refer to the niece of Voltaire.'[40]

Among Voltaire's minor works at this time the *Précis de l'Ecclésiaste* and *Précis du Cantique des cantiques* must not be forgotten. Three years earlier the duc de La Vallière had told Voltaire that mme de Pompadour had turned to religion, and would be very pleased if Voltaire converted the psalms into French verse.[41] Unfortunately Voltaire's replies have not come down to us. He did not supply the compositions asked for, but the idea must have germinated in the back of his mind, for in 1759 he suddenly produced these two adaptations of two of the finest poems in the *Bible*, *Ecclesiastes* in an elaborate metre, the *Song of songs* as a dialogue. He dedicated the former to Frederick, telling him that as *Ecclesiastes* had been inspired by the holy ghost, and his own free translation only by reason, it might contain gross errors. Voltaire certainly did not improve on his originals, but equally certainly he did them no injury. Still, anything by Voltaire on the *Bible* must necessarily be dangerous, and his translations were condemned to be burnt.

In the midst of all this, Voltaire managed to continue his controversy with Haller about the 'atrocious soul' until the amiable and learned baron brought the correspondence to an end by beginning a letter in these elegant terms: 'A man behaves like a cannibal when he needlessly torments one of his mortal brethren in order to assuage his vengeance and sometimes solely by insolence.'[42] Why was Haller so angry? Frederick was at least under the fearful

39 Frederick had complained about Voltaire's references to Maupertuis after the latter's death.

40 Best.D8905 (12 May 1760).

41 Best.D6760 (1 March 1756), D6844 (22 April 1756).

42 Best.D8282 (April/May 1759).

strain of a bloody and uncertain war, but Haller spent an idyllic existence in his ivory tower, revered by his compatriots. The explanation is to be found in Haller's own comment when Voltaire arrived at the Délices, to the effect that men could never forgive being made to look ridiculous[43]: many Genevese, from Rousseau down, made the same complaint, but a big fish cannot help creating a stir in a small pond. In the present letter Haller went on to explain, in defence of Calvin, that a man could commit cruelties without being cruel. This was too much even for Voltaire's tolerance for human folly: he neither answered nor ever again wrote to the pious poet.

Yet far surpassing all these things in significance was the invention by Frederick of the symbolic *infâme*[44], immediately taken up by Voltaire as his battle-cry, which he used for the rest of his life with ever-increasing gusto and effect. As Edna St Vincent Millay has it:

> It is the fashion now to wave aside
> As tedious, obvious, vacuous, trivial, trite,
> All things which do not tickle, tease, excite
> To some subversion, or in verbiage hide
> Intent, or mock, or with hot sauce provide
> A dish to prick the thickened appetite;
> Straightforwardness is wrong, evasion right;
> It is correct, *de rigueur*, to deride.
>
> What fumy wits these modern wags expose,
> For all their versatility: Voltaire,
> Who wore to bed a night-cap, and would close,
> In fear of drafts, all windows, could declare
> In antique stuffiness, a phrase that blows
> Still through men's smoky minds, and clears the air.

The 'phrase that blows' was 'écrasez l'infâme' ('crush the infamous'), which Voltaire thenceforth used hundreds of times. It became one of the most famous of all cries of revolt; one example among many: Shelley placed it on the titlepage of *Queen Mab* (1813). There is a slight difference in emphasis in the use of the word *infâme* by Frederick and Voltaire. This nuance is not easy to convey: perhaps it could be said that to Voltaire the infamous, when the word was used in this special sense, was clerical *supersti-*

43 Best.D6205 (15 March 1755).   44 Best.D8304 (18 May 1759).

tion, while to the king it was *clerical* superstition. In other words, though to Voltaire as much as to the king religion was the prime source of the superstition that led to injustice and fanaticism, his hatred of these loathsome phenomena extended to all their forms, whatever their source.

Even in the winter of 1759/60, a season of exceptionally cold winds, of which Voltaire complained bitterly, he was busier than ever. He took very seriously his responsibilities as lord of the manor and 'seigneur haut justicier'. Among his many activities in that capacity was the initiation of a detailed project for the freeing of Gex from the salt monopoly. He tried to buy Tournay outright, but the président de Brosses was to prove too much for him. In the meanwhile Voltaire gave orders for the construction of the now famous church at Ferney on which he announced with ironic braggadocio that he dedicated it to god ('Deo erexit Voltaire'). It was the only church, he asserted, in which there were no intermediaries between man and divinity. Perhaps he still remembered the Quakers who made such an impression on him in England.

While waiting for the production of *Tancrède* Voltaire wrote and published the *Ecossaise*; got involved in the scandal caused by the apparently unauthorised publication of Frederick's poems; discussed Russian history and oriental archaeology; tried hard but unsuccessfully to get Diderot into the Académie française; and managed to find time to attend to the minutest details of his publications, household, money matters, and amateur theatrical productions in his own houses and elsewhere; and incessantly to send 'from the feet of the Alps flying rockets to Paris which burst on the heads of the foolish'[45].

As an example of Voltaire's attention to detail let us take the case of David Duval. This craftsman charged 18 livres for embroidering coats of arms on the shoulder-straps of the Ferney gamekeepers. Voltaire complained that this was twice as much as the cost of such work in Paris. Duval gave his reasons, and Voltaire at once paid his bill.[46]

Extensive building and reconstruction continued at the Délices, Ferney and Tournay. Mme Denis complained that Voltaire spent

45 Best.D9121 (6 August 1760).   46 Best.D8194, D8199, D8200; March 1759.

500,000 francs in two years. This figure is perhaps somewhat exaggerated, but in any case it was only a beginning. After the substantial capital expenditures of 1755-58, Voltaire spent a million during the next decade.[47] As for mme Denis, she contented herself with buying diamonds out of the house-keeping money.

At odd moments Voltaire composed his first frontal attack on Christianity, the *Sermon des cinquante* (of which I shall have more to say a little later), passed through the press the first volume of his history of Russia, continued work on the second volume, engaged in prolonged correspondence concerning *Tancrède* and agricultural subjects, gave theatrical performances at Tournay, and published one of the most scathing of his satires, that on the Jesuit Berthier. The *Relation de la maladie, de la confession, de la mort, et de l'apparition du jésuite Berthier* is also one of the most amusing. Voltaire describes a journey from Paris to Versailles during which Berthier yawns uncontrollably, comes out in a cold sweat, and finally falls into a coma. The doctors and the confessors are about to take extreme measures, when the mystery is finally resolved: some volumes of the Jesuit *Journal de Trévoux* had been loaded in the same coach. Berthier confesses that the *Journal* contains rubbish, whereupon his fellow-traveller exclaims: 'Ah, reverend father, you are a saint; you are the first author who has ever confessed that he is boring; go, die in peace . . . and be sure that you will perform miracles.'

The *Relation* was satirised in a *Relation de la maladie, de la confession et de la fin de m. de Voltaire*[48], purporting to be written by Voltaire's footman; it is mentioned only because it is notable in the flood of anti-Voltairean literature in that it is not entirely unamusing. But Voltaire followed his *Berthier* squib by another even more cruel, the *Relation du voyage du frère Garassise*.

The production of Palissot's *Philosophes* caused an immense stir. In his satirical play Palissot spared Voltaire, but attacked his friends and Rousseau, a situation most men in his position would have enjoyed: but Voltaire sprang to the defence of the *philosophes*,

47 See *Voltaire's household accounts*, p. 72.
48 (Genève 1761), by Joseph Dubois (the pseudonym of Nicolas Joseph Sélis). The two titles are *Narrative of the illness, the confession, the death, and the apparition of the Jesuit Berthier* and *Narrative of the illness, the confession and the end of m. de Voltaire.*

even withdrawing one of his own plays in protest. In a long letter to Palissot he vigorously took the defence of Diderot and the other *philosophes*, and took even Rousseau under his wing by calling him 'my friend Jean Jacques'[49].

In this attitude he was not noticeably deterred by a mad letter from the great misanthrope in which the unhappy genius informed Voltaire that he hated him. Their previous correspondence having got into print Rousseau wrote to tell Voltaire that he was not responsible for the publication. He did so quite rationally, if at rather boring length, when suddenly he burst out: 'Sir, I do not like you.' He told Voltaire that he had done him (Rousseau) grave wrongs. Voltaire had ruined Geneva as its reward for giving him an asylum. He had alienated the Genevese from Rousseau. It was he who made it impossible for Rousseau to live in his fatherland. 'In short, I hate you.'[50]

These words defy comment. They are not the result of a sudden rush of blood to the head, for Rousseau always drafted such letters with the utmost care, sometimes over and over again, until he got them just 'right'. Unfortunately this time no drafts have survived, but only four copies in Rousseau's own hand. Yet there can be no doubt that these words were deliberate, and can only have emanated from a man on the edge of a mental collapse. So they must be judged with understanding and charity. It is hardly necessary to say that they were wholly undeserved at this date, whatever view one may take of the later relations between the two men. It was at about the beginning of 1760 that Rousseau's dislike of Voltaire became uncontrollable. Moultou, having mentioned Voltaire, Rousseau replied (29 January): 'You talk to me about that Voltaire! Why does the name of this mountebank sully your letters? The wretch has ruined my fatherland; I would hate him even more if I despised him less' and so on, in terms which he reproduced in writing to Voltaire six months later. Rousseau's hatred seethed for all this time, until it finally exploded in his letter of 17 June, which even his most enlightened disciple, R. A. Leigh, calls a 'regular declaration of war'.

---

49 Best.D8958 (4 June 1760); Voltaire wrote several more letters to Palissot in defence of his friends.

50 Best.D8986 (17 June 1760); Leigh 1019.

In his *Confessions* Rousseau comments obscurely that Voltaire did not reply to this letter, and that to justify his brutality he pretended to be infuriated.[51] Had Voltaire been infuriated by Rousseau's unprovoked invective one could hardly have blamed him; but in fact he contented himself with expressing brief regret that Rousseau had gone quite mad[52]. It was only a good deal later, when he was convinced that Rousseau had gone over to the enemy, that his references became angry and disdainful.[53]

All this did not prevent Voltaire from corresponding with fifty friends and acquaintances, from offering asylum to the *Journal encyclopédique* when Pierre Rousseau was in difficulties[54], from publishing his usual quota of satires, in particular against Pompignan, and from making final arrangements in connection with the *Ecossaise*, the production of which caused another scandal. Argental was able to report that this play, of which Voltaire had so poor an opinion that he published it before it was performed, had been put on 'with the most prodigious success'. The public applauded and wept.[55] Voltaire's comic satire was in fact given sixteen performances, a large number at that time; and as 738 spectators paid for admission on the last day, the play would probably have been kept on but for the fact that *Tancrède* could no longer be postponed. So great, indeed, was the success of the *Ecossaise* that four other Voltaire plays were revived during its run.

And so, on 3 September 1760, *Tancrède* was at last produced. It was in April 1759 that Voltaire, perhaps stimulated by the forthcoming expulsion of the spectators from their traditional seats on the stage of the Comédie française[56], first mentioned that he was working on 'something strong'[57]. He composed it in three or four weeks, but then revised and rewrote with the most

51 As the reader will no doubt find this difficult to follow, here is the actual text, quoted from Rousseau's manuscript: 'Voici cette seconde lettre [that of 17 June 1760], à laquelle il ne fit aucune réponse, et dont pour mettre sa brutalité plus à l'aise il fit semblant d'être irrité jusqu'à la fureur' (see Best.D8986, note 2).

52 Best.D9006, D9009 (both 23 June 1760).
53 As in Best.D9470 (19 March 1761).
54 Best.D9171 (27 August 1760).
55 Best.D9091 (27 July 1760).
56 Voltaire himself says so in his dedication of *Tancrède* to mme de Pompadour.
57 Best.D8249 (6 April 1759).

19 Theatrical decoration, *gilt wood cartouche from Voltaire's theatre at Les Délices*

20 The château de Ferney, from the engraving by F. M. I. Queverdo after L. Signy

elaborate care, sent out manuscripts for criticism, gave trial performances at Tournay, and later subjected the tragedy to a minute and prolonged postmortem, for the most part in letters to the Argentals, mlle Clairon and Lekain. Voltaire lavished more pains on this tragedy than on perhaps any other of his plays, and it followed on the triumph of the *Ecossaise*, but for all that it was not an outstanding success. Voltaire himself said that it was at first badly received[58], and so did others. Yet these things are relative. *Tancrède* was given thirteen performances in its first run, a figure which does not indeed suggest a real triumph. But the politics of the Comédie française must be taken into account, even if they are often impossible to understand. *Tancrède*, I repeat, was taken off after thirteen performances given between 3 September and 4 October; but during the run the attendance never fell below 816, and at the last two performances rose to 919 and 1052; when the tragedy was revived for a single performance on 26 January 1761 the paid admissions reached 1206, higher than any during the first run; and on the first two nights of the second run, in March 1761, 1211 and 1219 seats were sold.[59] It is thus obvious that *Tancrède* could have been kept on much longer when first produced. And there were indeed many who raved about the play and the performances of Lekain and mlle Clairon, like that foreigner, reported by mme d'Epinay, who wept, cried, and clapped his hands, and whose nationality can be guessed from his comment that 'It's not bad, not at all bad'[60]. Diderot wrote to Voltaire at great length about the tragedy. He found the third act finer than anything in Racine and Corneille, and he positively hymned the performance of mlle Clairon.[61]

The development of this story of medieval knighthood shows nothing Voltairean, nor does its treatment.[62] It is in fact in the

---

58 Best.D13757 (22 December 1766).

59 See a note on Best.D9197.

60 Best.D9216 (10 September 1760).

61 Best.D9430 (28 November 1760).

62 Though its literary form is somewhat revolutionary; Voltaire himself says several times that *Tancrède* is written in *vers croisés*, and all the critics have repeated this; strictly speaking, this is not the case, for the play is in fact written in alexandrines. It is the rhyme scheme that is unusual, for the lines do not rhyme in the usual couplets but in irregular and flexible combinations, somewhat reminiscent of the *Pucelle*. Thus the play opens with this scheme: *abbabababccdd* etc. It is in fact written in *rimes croisées*, not *vers croisés*.

417

tradition that led from *Zaïre* and *Adélaïde Du Guesclin* to Belloy's *Siège de Calais*, and ultimately to the Romantics. The odd thing is that I can find no trace that Voltaire, who usually knew very precisely what he was about, was aware that he was creating a new kind of drama. He wanted to compose a strong and affecting tragedy, and the glorification of *chevalerie* was simply a means to that end.

Voltaire did have a secondary purpose in writing *Tancrède*. He hoped that his glorification of the Norman knights would attract favourable attention at court. But this kind of allusive flattery was far too subtle for Versailles: though years later Marie Antoinette was touched[63]. In the meanwhile Voltaire dedicated the play to mme de Pompadour, but, as usual, he set about it in a most un-courtier-like manner. In his dedication he told her: 'If some fault-finder disapprove the homage I render you, he could only be one born with an ungrateful heart. I owe you much, madame, and I must say it.' This sounds all right, but in the rarefied atmosphere surrounding a royal mistress, this admirable sentiment was not particularly appreciated. As kind friends were not slow to point out to her[64], Voltaire's words could be held to imply that mme de Pompadour was not a suitable object for such a dedication, and that Voltaire overlooked this objection out of gratitude. Poor Voltaire! Instead of sustaining mme de Pompadour's friendship he lost it. He had once again fallen victim to the rancour of the envious, for such an interpretation had not occurred to the Pompadour herself. Naturally Voltaire had not printed his dedication without permission. It had been seen and authorised by the chief minister, the duc de Choiseul (who wept all through a performance of the play[65]), and by mme de Pompadour herself, who wrote explicitly to the minister in charge of the booktrade: 'I have permitted Voltaire to dedicate *Tancrède* to me because I have known him for twenty-five years and because I have found nothing objectionable in his epistle.'[66]

In the autumn of 1760 one of the great dramatic episodes with which Voltaire's life is filled began its majestic course. Ponce Denis Ecouchard Lebrun, who had a considerable reputation as a

---

63 Best.D21030 (7 February 1778).
64 Best.D9715 (March/April 1761).

65 Best.D9242 (19 September 1760).
66 Best.D9192 (4 September 1760).

poet—he was even known as Lebrun-Pindare—wrote to Voltaire to tell him how much he regretted the great man's absence from Paris. 'In what a profound night, in what a vast desert have you left our literature!' And he sent his new ode, which he had dedicated to Voltaire, whom he invited to take an interest in an impoverished girl who was a collateral descendant of the great Corneille, and bore his name. 'It is undoubtedly for genius to protect a family made famous by genius. And in that sense I see only monsieur de Voltaire in Europe from whom a man named Corneille could receive benefactions without demeaning himself.'[67]

Voltaire, though plunged deep in *Tancrède*, at once responded that it was indeed proper for an old soldier in the service of Corneille to make himself useful to the 'grand-daughter' of his general. He was building country-houses and churches, had poor relations to support, and could hardly do what should be done by the grandees of the kingdom. Still, let the young lady be sent to him at his expense, his niece and he would educate her and be her mother and father.[68] He wrote a charming letter[69] to Marie Françoise herself, asked the Argentals to watch over her departure from Paris, requested Tronchin to meet her at Lyons and take care of her there, and organised the whole thing with his usual minute solicitude. When she arrived Voltaire was delighted with the young lady, found her natural and gay, with a little pug-face, fine eyes, an appetising mouth, with pearly teeth. 'If anyone has the pleasure of approaching those teeth, I should prefer it to be a Catholic rather than a Protestant. But I give you my word that it will not be me.'[70] Voltaire said this because the inevitable insinuations were going the rounds of the Paris salons, where there were many guilty consciences about the deplorable state of this branch of the Corneille family[71]. Anyway, by now Voltaire's

---

67 Best.D9349 (*c.* 25 October 1760).
68 Best.D9382 (5 November 1760).
69 Best.D9421 (22 November 1760).
70 Best.D9485 (22 December 1760).
71 Fontenelle was the nephew of the great Corneille; he bequeathed his property to four legatees, two of whom were the grand-daughters of Pierre's brother Thomas; thereupon Jean François Corneille and his sisters, who had been passed over although they were the grand-children of another Pierre Corneille, the poet's cousin, unsuccessfully brought an action for the annulment of Fontenelle's will. This Jean François was the father of the girl whom Voltaire took under his wing.

celebrity was so great that whatever he did attracted its quota of malice mixed with the adulation.

Voltaire did treat the young Marie as his daughter: educated her, introduced her into polite society, and looked after her health. To be fair to mme Denis, she seems for once to have forgotten her own interests and to have participated in her uncle's benevolence. She took a full part in these parental duties. Then Voltaire took fire. He had long urged the publication of standard editions of the French classics, and now he decided himself to undertake one of Corneille, which would also serve—as organised by Voltaire—to provide a *dot* for Marie Françoise. No sooner said than done. The agreement of the Académie française was obtained, and in an amazingly short time Voltaire carried through this vast and often insufferably boring task. The *Théâtre de Pierre Corneille avec des commentaires* duly appeared in twelve volumes in Voltaire's seventieth year. Nearly all Corneille's plays are minutely analysed, almost line by line, in the pedantic spirit of the age, but also with disquisitions on the sources, parallels, etc.[72] The edition eventually brought in nearly 100,000 francs for mlle Corneille's benefit, an enormous figure which was wholly due to Voltaire's business acumen and to his vast prestige and far-flung correspondence, which secured subscriptions for 200-250 copies each from the monarchs of Russia, the Empire, and France. Voltaire not merely did all the work, which was enough to break any other man of his age, he also bought 100 copies, and the rest of the subscription list reads like a miniature *Who's who* and *Almanach de Gotha* in one.

In the meanwhile, as soon as he settled down at Ferney, Voltaire resumed his theatrical amusements. 'Being persuaded that representations of dramatic works contributed as much to soften savage manners, as the exhibitions of the Gladiators formerly did to harden them, he built an handsome little theatre at Ferney, and notwithstanding his bad state of health, sometimes played himself; for his niece, Madame Denis, who possessed uncommon talents for music and elocution, acted several characters there. Mademoi-

72 A critical edition by David Williams forms vols. 53-5 (1974-5) of the *Complete works of Voltaire*.

selle Clairon, and the famous Lekain, performed in some pieces on that stage, and people twenty leagues distant came to hear them. He has oftener than once had suppers of a hundred covers, and balls; but notwithstanding his advanced age, and the appearance of a life of dissipation, he never discontinued his studies.'[73]

In the midst of this hectic life Voltaire, as usual, enjoyed much bad health; but when his death was rumoured Montpéroux, the French resident in Geneva, unkindly reported to his minister that Voltaire had not even been ill. 'His health is very good, and better than it has ever been.'[74]

[73] See the autobiography, p. 657, below. [74] Best.D8877 (25 April 1760).

31. Universal history, 1756

IN 1756 APPEARED, in seven volumes, after many adventures, including the theft of the manuscript and piratical publication, the *Essai sur l'histoire générale et sur les mœurs et l'esprit des nations*[1], on which Voltaire had worked for over twenty years, and on which he continued to work for the rest of his life. This masterpiece, usually known as the *Essai sur les mœurs*, is Voltaire's most complete demonstration of his new principles of historical writing[2]. These are summed up in his final chapter. As he laid down his pen Voltaire wrote: 'A wise reader will readily perceive that he should believe only the great events that present some probability, and contemplate with pity all the fables with which fanaticism, the romantic spirit and credulity have at all times peopled the theatre of the world.'[3] So much for the factual aspect of historiography. As for the dominant theme of all Voltaire's writings on history and government, he stated it himself with his usual lapidary brevity: 'The true conquerors are those who know how to make laws. Their power is stable; the others are torrents which pass.'[4]

The *Essai* is the first universal history in which an attempt is made to treat the development of civilisation as a whole. For all preceding historians the world meant, in effect, Europe, and mankind was held to begin with the *Bible*. Voltaire, after a brief account of the globe itself (already treated more fully in the *Dissertation sur les changements arrivés dans notre globe*[5] and to be discussed again in the *Philosophie de l'histoire*), devotes two chapters to China, two to India, one to Persia, two to the Arabs and their

---

1 The essay often printed as the Introduction is in reality the *Philosophie de l'histoire* (see pp. 495-496, below); the bibliography of the *Essai* is in general most complex; nothing like a definitive edition has yet been attempted; that of René Pomeau is the best (Paris 1963).

2 See p. 162, above.
3 *Essai sur les mœurs*, cxvii.
4 *Essai sur les mœurs*, xxv.
5 See p. 287, above; its original title was *Saggio intorno ai cambiamenti avvenuti sul globo della terra*.

religion, and mentions the Jews only in passing. Only then does Voltaire arrive at the beginning of history as then understood.

In his preface, originally addressed to mme Du Châtelet, Voltaire makes his purpose clear; it was to give a general view of the nations 'who live on the earth and desolate it'. Such a survey should be limited to the spirit, the manners, the customs of the principal nations, supported by such facts as are indispensable. His object was not to make known in which year an unworthy prince succeeded a barbarous one in a boorish country.

Voltaire thus raised his standard in the very first sentence of his vast book. The phrase 'who live on the earth and desolate it' makes it clear that the reader is not to expect a cold uncommitted narrative. And indeed Voltaire has a point of view which the reader is never allowed to forget. Yet he never fails to distinguish between facts and their interpretation. He is amazingly just, impartial and accurate (within the limits of contemporary knowledge, obviously) in his factual narrative. Equally striking is the enormous skill with which Voltaire organised and presented this enormous mass of facts and reflections.

Just as the first sentence of the preface sets the tone, so the first paragraph of the first chapter fixes the framework. To the educated Frenchman in the eighteenth century, brought up on Bossuet, the climax of human history was the empire created by Charlemagne. This is why Voltaire began his book by stating quite simply that the Chinese empire was vaster than that of the Frankish emperor, and had subsisted for 4000 years without sensible alteration.

And of course here as everywhere Voltaire did not limit himself to geography and chronology: he discussed not only the population, but also the problems arising from its rapid increase; and dealt briefly with economics and finance, philosophy and religion, pointing out the special aspects of Chinese civilisation, silk, paper, china, printing, scientific instruments, explaining also the difficulties created by the Chinese system of writing.

Voltaire dealt in the same way with the other oriental and near eastern peoples, devoting, in particular, much space to the religion of Islam. His summing up of Mohammed could hardly be bettered as a description of a religious leader: 'We must suppose that

Mohammed, like all enthusiasts, violently impressed by his own ideas, retailed them in good faith, fortified them with fancies, deceived himself in deceiving others, and finally sustained with deceit a doctrine he believed to be good.'[6]

Voltaire then turned to the establishment of Christianity, in two masterly chapters to which Gibbon owed more than he was inclined to acknowledge. His theme, much simplified, was then quite novel: that Christianity succeeded *in spite* of its religious content, and for reasons foreign to it. How subtly Voltaire insinuated this notion! His ninth chapter is entitled 'That the false legends of the first Christians did not harm the establishment of the Christian religion', and this chapter begins: 'Jesus Christ permitted the false gospels to mingle with the true ones from the beginning of Christianity; and, in order the better to test the faith of the devout, the gospels today called apocryphal even preceded the four sacred writings, which now form the basis of our faith.'[7] And he concluded that Christianity *must* be divine since seventeen centuries of rascality and imbecility had failed to destroy it.[8]

From a relatively brief account of Rome, Voltaire turned to the papacy, but not without, as Flaubert has it[9], a lyrical outburst of sorrow when he thought of the centuries of barbarism to come: 'What was there to prevent these newcomers from putting up regular buildings on the Roman model? They had the stone, the marble, and finer woods than ours. . . . Why were all the comforts unknown that sweeten the bitterness of life, if not because the savages who crossed the Rhine made the peoples they found there as savage as themselves?'[10]

The account Voltaire gave of the papacy, here and throughout the *Essai*, is by no means unsympathetic. He introduced it, indeed, with the obvious implication, thus: 'There are only three ways of subjugating men: that of civilising them by giving them laws, that of using religion to enforce these laws, and finally that of murdering one part of the nation to govern the other.'[11] But he did not fail to give a true account of the Roman church's contribution to the development of the west. Thus, after recording the

6 *Essai sur les mœurs*, vi.
7 *Essai sur les mœurs*, ix.
8 *Essai sur les mœurs*, ix.
9 See my *Voltaire essays*, p. 15.
10 *Essai sur les mœurs*, xvii.
11 *Essai sur les mœurs*, xiii.

14*—V.

execution by Adrian IV (the only English pope) of Arnold of Brescia for opposing the temporal power of the papacy, he still goes on: 'The soul of Adrian IV was all the nobler because his origins were lowly. The Roman church has always had the advantage of being able to accord to merit those things which are elsewhere accorded to birth. . . . Today there are some monasteries in Germany that will receive only nobles into their community. The soul of Rome has more greatness and less vanity.'[12] But of course Voltaire must always be read between the lines. This tribute implies also a characteristically subtle stroke of irony: every French reader of the *Essai* knew that such monasteries were not unknown in his own country.

And so at last Voltaire arrived at the Europe of Charlemagne, from which point the narrative becomes much more detailed. There would be no point in attempting to abstract this summary of a thousand years of history, throughout which Voltaire never misses an opportunity to condemn injustice, fanaticism, war and cruelty, and to uphold the primacy of art and learning. The pages of the *Essai* coruscate with jewelled phrases in which this invariable attitude is expressed. Here are a few.

William the conqueror sent the pope part of the booty he had taken from Harold. Voltaire commented: 'Thus a barbarian, the son of a prostitute, the murderer of a rightful king, shares this king's remains with another barbarian, for take away the names of duke of Normandy, of king of England, and of pope, and the whole thing becomes nothing more than the exploit of a Norman thief and a Lombard receiver: and that in fact is what all usurpation boils down to.'[13]

On Saladin and the earthquake of 1182: 'The Turks were told by their priests that God was punishing the Christians; the Christians were told that God was punishing the Turks; and the fighting continued amidst the ruins of Syria.'[14]

On the supremacy of the artist, in a chapter devoted to science and art in the thirteenth and fourteenth centuries: 'It may appear astonishing that so many great geniuses arose in Italy, without protection and without example, in the midst of dissension and

12 *Essai sur les mœurs*, xlvii.   14 *Essai sur les mœurs*, lvi.
13 *Essai sur les mœurs*, xlii.

war; but Lucretius, among the Romans, wrote his fine poem on nature, Virgil his *Bucolics*, Cicero his philosophical works in the midst of the horrors of civil war. When once a language begins to take shape, it is an instrument which great artists find ready to hand and of which they make use without bothering their heads about who governs or troubles the earth.'[15]

On the cruelty of civil war: England, during the wars of the roses, 'was a vast theatre of carnage, in which scaffolds were everywhere erected on the battlefields'[16].

On the inquisition's persecution of Galileo: 'The manner in which this great man was treated by the inquisition at the end of his life would have endowed Italy with eternal shame, had this shame not been effaced by the very glory of Galileo.'[17]

On the Scottish Presbyterians: 'They swore no longer to obey the king as supreme chief of the Anglican church, never to recognise his brother as king, to obey only the Lord, and to immolate to the Lord all the prelates who might oppose the saints.'[18]

On religious fanaticism: 'Blood has run in wars and on scaffolds for five hundred years on account of theological disputes . . . because morality has always been sacrificed to dogma.'[19]

On the torture and execution of Savonarola: 'One contemplates with pity all these scenes of absurdity and horror; nothing of the sort is to be found among the Romans and the Greeks, nor among the barbarians. It is the fruit of the most infamous superstition that has ever bestialised humanity, and of the worst of governments. But you know that it is not long since we left this darkness behind us, and that all is not yet light.'[20]

On reading such words on page after page of this long universal history the reader could not but be enlightened to a new vision of man's condition.

---

15 *Essai sur les mœurs*, lxxxii.
16 *Essai sur les mœurs*, cxv.
17 *Essai sur les mœurs*, cxxi.

18 *Essai sur les mœurs*, clxxxii.
19 *Essai sur les mœurs*, cxvii.
20 *Essai sur les mœurs*, cviii.

32. The story-teller

IN THIS RAPID NARRATIVE of the years 1756-60 I have mentioned only incidentally what many regard as the most permanently important chapter of Voltaire's life: the writing of *Candide*. It is difficult to deny the verdict of two centuries, nor indeed is there any doubt that *Candide* is a masterpiece, a 'classic'. It is also difficult to oppose to a work of the imagination, and which therefore appeals to all, a *Dictionnaire philosophique* or an *Essai sur les mœurs*, each of which, though also a literary masterpiece, cannot speak to all with an equal voice. Nor do I find it particularly interesting to engage in these pointless comparisons. Yet one thing must clearly be realised: *Candide*, the only one of Voltaire's innumerable writings which is still a best-seller, does not stand alone even within the framework of his imaginative prose.[1]

What did Voltaire himself think about all this? Unfortunately he was the most modest and least introspective of men. Of course like most artists Voltaire was hungry for fame. He never doubted that he would go down to posterity as one of the greatest glories of French civilisation, and the fact that he was quite right is almost irrelevant. But this has nothing to do with vanity, and it is a crude error, of which so many writers on Voltaire are guilty, not to distinguish between one of the basest of qualities and the

---

1 Ignoring the interrelationship of some of these stories, and some doubtful titles, and passing over some trivia and the dialogues usually printed among Voltaire's general writings, his fiction consists of *Le Monde comme il va*, *Le Crocheteur borgne*, *Cosi-sancta* (all 1746), *Zadig* (1747), *Memnon, Bababec* (both 1750), *Micromégas* (1752), *Les Deux consolés, Scarmentado, Le Songe de Platon* (all 1756), *Candide, Histoire d'un bon bramin* (both 1759), *Le Blanc et le noir, Jeannot et Colin* (both 1764), *L'Ingénu* (1766), *L'Homme aux quarante écus, La Princesse de Babylone* (both 1768), *Les Lettres d'Amabed* (1769), *Le Taureau blanc* (1774), *Histoire de Jenni, Les Oreilles du comte de Chesterfield* (both 1775). To these must be added Voltaire's stories in verse, a comparison of which with the prose novels and stories would be profitable. For the reader's convenience the traditional dates of the stories have been shown, but several of them are doubtful.

glorious self-confidence of one who is aware of his own super-
lative powers.

As for introspection, there is no room for doubt here. Seldom
has a great artist shown so profound a dislike for exhibiting in
public the results of self-analysis: he stands at the opposite pole
from a Rembrandt or a Rousseau. Besides, Voltaire never could
throw off the notion that it is ill-bred to talk at length about
oneself.

However, even a Voltaire cannot publish ten million words,
and write in addition twenty thousand letters, without giving
away something of himself. So we do have plenty of evidence
that he regarded himself, as his contemporaries regarded him,
above all as the author of the *Henriade*, then as a dramatist, an
historian, and a *philosophe*. It was not by chance that he gave the
title of *Commentaire historique sur les œuvres de l'auteur de la
Henriade* to his autobiography[2]. The reader of this far too little
known essay must be struck by one odd detail. In it Voltaire tells
us, it is true, very little that is intimate about himself, but he does
say something about his epic poems, serious and burlesque, and
about nearly all his plays, nearly all his historical and scientific
writings, much of his major poetry, and he even mentions a
few of the controversial pieces the authorship of which he had
always disowned; but, and here is the mystery, of the stories not
a word. Almost as complete a silence reigns in his letters, in which
nearly all his works are announced, 'researched', discussed, often
for year after year in minute detail, but in which the tales suddenly
appear, if they are mentioned at all, out of a blue sky.

Thus, in a postscript to a short note sent to his publisher, Voltaire casually remarked that 'The *Ingénu* is better than *Candide*,
for it is infinitely more lifelike'[3]. In a letter to mme Du Deffand
Voltaire says even more casually: 'I am told that the *Princesse
de Babylone* has appeared, with other little works.'[4] These were
Voltaire's first references to his only true novel and to one of the
best of his stories. Similar evidence could be produced for nearly
all the others. Nor did Voltaire mention his tales much more
often once they were published. Thus, in the index of his corre-

2 See p. 621, below.
3 Best.D14279 (July 1767).
4 Best.D14873 (22 March 1768).

spondence, to take an example from a single opening, eight lines dispose of all its author's references to *Micromégas*, while ten times as many are required for the heading devoted to *La Mort de César*.

Dare we see in this some confirmation of the assertion so often advanced, that Voltaire did not take his prose fiction seriously? His silences sometimes have quite a different meaning. Voltaire's letters are filled with complaints, not seldom furious, about a great many annoyances which *we* at a comfortable distance feel that *he* ought to have regarded as trivial. Yet clearly more serious matters are sometimes passed over in silence. Thus, as we have seen[5], when Voltaire made his home at Les Délices after much suffering and unwilling wandering, he felt an almost mystical euphoria, which produced his fine poem on the beauties and liberties of Geneva. Voltaire was profoundly moved by the horrible injustice of the Genevese authorities in condemning this poem, and his disillusion contributed to the complex movement of ideas we have already examined[6]. Yet he is not known to have written a single word about the action of the city council. His silence is in itself more convincing evidence than angry cries would have been that he felt the condemnation very deeply, very intimately.

Voltaire's greatest work was his own life, which happily defies literary exegesis. And there is much of surviving interest in nearly all his writings. We have completely absorbed the ideas of the polemical books and pamphlets. The historical works are now beginning properly to be appreciated again. The poems, including the long ones, are by no means so worthless as fashion would have us believe. The appeal of the tragedies is not exhausted, even if we are now wearied by their faded techniques. A recent revival at the Comédie française of the *Orphelin de la Chine* (by no means the best or most characteristic of Voltaire's plays) was welcomed by the public, especially the younger element, with sustained applause, but was condemned by the critics with dutiful unanimity.

Still, it does now seem clear after two centuries that Voltaire's prose tales are the most likely among all his work to survive.

5 See pp. 352-353, 357, above.   6 See pp. 365-374, above.

Even the great, grey George Saintsbury, whose every second word on Voltaire is an impertinence, said laboriously of *Candide* that 'as a piece of art or craft, the thing is beyond praise or pay … if anybody, having read its first page, fails to see that it is, and how it is, praiseworthy, he never will or would be converted if all the eulogies of the most golden-mouthed critics of the world were poured upon him in a steady shower'[7]. This is true not only of the first page of *Candide*, but in varying degrees of every page of every story, except some of the minor ones thrown off to fill an idle hour and limited to a few pages.

Voltaire invented the *conte philosophique*. Indeed, he invented more: the judicious reader will not fail to notice that Sherlock Holmes must have read attentively the third chapter of *Zadig*, in which the hero, by examining the traces left by these animals, describes the queen's lost pet as a very small spaniel bitch, with long ears, limping on its left fore-foot, and the king's horse as very fast, five feet high, with a small hoof and a tail three and a half feet long, and so on. However, the *conte philosophique* is most intimately Voltaire's child, for he not only invented it but brought it at once to such perfection that only minor writers have dared to imitate him. To suppose that Voltaire brought off so daring a feat as it were unwittingly is to make nonsense of the whole idea of literary creation, and to reduce the artist to mere automatism. However, the argument is academic in the worst sense, for it can be shown by internal evidence that Voltaire's tales are carefully wrought works of art: that is, their forms fit perfectly their content and purpose.

The stories do not fit into any of the ready-made categories: obviously they are not plays, nor poems, nor even dialogues (although they are sometimes superficially in dialogue form); nor, and this is the significant point, can they properly be classed among Voltaire's straightforward prose writings. They are in fact extended dramatic *tirades*[8], and this not only because some of them were originally composed to be read aloud in drawing rooms.

---

7 *A History of the French novel* (1917), i.382.

8 I use the French word, which is not to be confused with the English;

William F. Bottiglia, *Voltaire's Candide* (Studies on Voltaire, viiA: 1964), pp. 53-4, aptly calls the stories dramatic monologues.

21 The view from Les Délices in 1778, from the painting by Simon Malgo

22 Les Délices today

Voltaire was one of the most voluminous writers of all time, but this was because he had much to say, not because he was long-winded. Far from it. He was indeed a fervent advocate of brevity, and a brilliantly successful exponent of this rare art. He wanted Bayle to be reduced to a few pages, and found the *Encyclopédie* so unnecessarily vast that he produced a portable philosophical dictionary to show what could be accomplished in this way. He even applied this principle to his library, in which he sometimes tore out and bound only those pages of a book which he thought of permanent value: a book-lover need not be a bibliophile. In Voltaire's own style nothing impresses so much and so immediately as his ability to cover the ground with complete lucidity however difficult or even technical the matter, in an astonishingly small number of words.

Thus, even a reader totally ignorant of the difficult science of optics, and little caring why or even whether Newton's physics triumphed over the ideas of Descartes, at once understands this explanation of the nature of light: 'Were light a mass of globules [as argued by Descartes], a fluid present in the air and everywhere, a little hole made in a dark room would illuminate it entirely; for the light, pressed in every direction through this little hole, would move in every direction like balls if ivory which, arranged in circles or squares, all scatter when a single one is strongly pushed; but quite the contrary occurs: light arriving through a little orifice, which allows only a small cone of rays to penetrate [as demonstrated by Newton], reaches twenty-five feet, and hardly illuminates half a foot from the spot at which it arrives.'[9]

This clarity, born of a thorough understanding of the subject and a masterful command of the language, strikes home to all in the historical and scientific works, but it is not less present in the stories. The openings of several offer wonderful examples, as in *Candide*. Here is the first sentence of *Micromégas*: 'In one of those planets that turn around the star called Sirius there was a very intelligent young man whom I had the honour to meet during his last voyage to our little anthill: he was called Micromégas. . . .'

9 *Eléments de la philosophie de Newton*, II.i.

Here, without conveying the slightest feeling of haste or compression, the scene is set, the protagonist is introduced, and the whole tone or feeling of the story is established, all in very nearly the minimum possible number of lines. Let us consider rapidly how this is accomplished.

Voltaire's vocabulary is more copious than that of any of his non-technical contemporaries, and this enabled him to avoid much of the circumlocution so often found in French prose. Equally remarkable is Voltaire's choice of words: he had a precise apprehension of the right one needed to convey a meaning or a feeling, and with this he had a probably unique ear for the word which was not only right but sounded right. The resulting style was so flexible that it could be adapted to every purpose. Thus, in argumentative works Voltaire's aim was to arrest the attention, to underline, to emphasise. This was achieved, so far as the vocabulary is concerned, by the tactical placing of a technical, a difficult, or even merely an unexpected[10] word. The stories, on the other hand, were intended to persuade with a smile: their aim was to carry the reader along on the even flow of the narrative, rapid, smooth, the events producing the motive power, never interrupting the rhythm however extraordinary they might be in themselves. Here Voltaire never relaxes his pressure on the accelerator, and seldom touches the brake. Many other devices are used. There is an almost metrical succession and alternation of long and short sentences.[11] Particularly to be noticed is the choice of names, as in the hammering effect obtained by the gutturals in Thunder-ten-tronckh, Candide, Cunégonde, Cacambo, Pococurante; and the liquid polysyllables of Formosante, Amazan, Gangarides, Cimmériens in the *Princesse de Babylone*.

It is often alleged that for all their beauties Voltaire's stories are deficient in characterisation. This is far too hasty and simplified a verdict. First of all, it is necessary to distinguish between a

---

10 All generalisations have their exceptions: one of the best examples of this technique is not in what public librarians elegantly call 'non-fiction', but precisely in *Candide*, where it is said that admiral Byng was executed 'pour encourager les autres', 'to encourage the others'—the reader expects 'discourage', and 'encourage' gives him the intended shock.

11 Two studies by Zakhari Zakhariev on the structure of Voltaire's sentences have now been published in the *Годишник на Софийския университет* (1969).

story like *L'Ingenu*, which is to all intents and purposes a novel, and one like *Zadig*, which is strictly a *conte philosophique*. Voltaire was far too fine a craftsman to use the same methods in the one as in the other. Science-fiction written in the spirit of a novelette would be intolerable. It is true that in the *contes philosophiques* the personages are not closely described or characterised, though the description of Cunégonde as 'rosy, fresh, plump, appetising' is pretty graphic. What is more relevant, all the personages, and not merely the principal ones, display themselves in action, and this is hardly yet to be stigmatised as a defect. We do not know the colour of Candide's eyes[12], but we do know that 'his soul could be read on his face', and as we could hardly know his 'soul' more intimately, the 'face' can be supplied to each reader's taste.

It is thus clear that if Voltaire maintained so complete a silence about the composition of his stories it cannot have been because he regarded them as trivia. A Voltaire is not a Logan Pearsall Smith, and does not so carefully prepare his asides. Yet his silence must surely have some meaning. What is it? I think that the mystery can be penetrated, that the explanation is in reality quite simple: the prose tales are Voltaire's kind of interior autobiography. It is certainly not a chance coincidence that Voltaire never *published* a story until after his flight from the French court[13], when he was finally convinced that he would never be accepted by the entrenched establishment. Four stories then followed in rapid succession, including the new *Zadig*. The next important tale, *Micromégas*, was written in its present form in Berlin. Four more stories in prose, including the profoundly pessimistic *Candide*, followed on Voltaire's discovery that Geneva was a broken reed. Thereafter the pattern is less clear, but one can still be traced. In short, Voltaire felt a profound need to unburden himself, but was temperamentally incapable of doing so openly. Hence the stories. One tells the adventures of a hero who wants to do good but is always misunderstood; another depicts an honest man who visits the earth from afar, and finds men evil and stupid; a third is the story of a simple youth who has faith in

12 Mme Bovary's eyes are sometimes said by her creator to be brown, sometimes black, sometimes blue; see

Enid Starkie, *Flaubert* (London 1967), p. 314.
13 See pp. 292-293, 319-320, above.

justice, only to have his faith destroyed by the unjust; a fourth is the epic tale of an innocent boy who is convinced that all is for the best, but discovers from bitter experience that much in the world is in fact evil, and that this evil can be remedied only by works, not by faith. All these personages are Voltaire, weeping over mankind and his own failure to mould the world to his ideals. And that is why Voltaire, lest he betray himself, never discussed his stories, and did his best to pretend that they did not exist.[14]

Voltaire's tales can be and usually are read for pleasure, as testify the hundreds of editions which still come off the presses in all languages. Yet he hardly ever wrote anything which, however much enjoyment it gives in the reading, does not also give something more. I have no doubt that Voltaire wrote his stories in part to console himself for his own unhappiness. Yet beyond that he was in the fullest sense of the word *engagé*, the first and greatest in that kind. Even some of the lightest drawing-room verse of his youth has body below the surface sparkle. It is understandable that contemporary authority was inclined to attribute to him any satirical writing which was at once well written, witty, and painful. Any discussion, however summary, of the tales must therefore point to the role they played in changing men's ideas about their place in the nation, the world, and the universe. Voltaire put western man in his place by reminding him that there exist other parts of the world, occupied by pagans and savages whose behaviour oddly resembled that of civilised Christians. He compelled his contemporaries to understand that the earth they all alike inhabited was after all no more than a globule scarcely perceptible in the space of infinity. Above all, he never ceased to underscore not merely the horror but the laughable folly of injustice, and its progeny: intolerance, fanaticism, cruelty, and war.

14 For a detailed analysis of the autobiographical element in the stories see Geoffrey Murray, *Voltaire's Candide: the Protean gardener* (Studies on Voltaire, lxix: 1970). This element has been largely overlooked in the generally admirable Jacques Van den Heuvel, *Voltaire dans ses contes* (Paris 1967).

33. *The arts: unity and paradox*

JUST OVER TWO HUNDRED years ago, Diderot got himself involved in a controversy with the sculptor Falconet about art, posterity, and other momentous subjects. It is a tiresome debate, for Diderot was an unwilling correspondent, and the talented but humourless Falconet had a somewhat excessive respect for his own views. In the end the two men quarrelled: Falconet was eager to publish their letters, Diderot wisely declined the honour.[1]

Arguing against Falconet, who was sceptical about posterity, Diderot burst out: 'Pile assumptions on assumptions; accumulate wars on wars; make interminable disturbances succeed to interminable disturbances; let the universe be inundated by a general spirit of confusion; and it will take a hundred thousand years for the works and the name of Voltaire to be lost'[2].

Falconet was already annoyed with Voltaire because he had not received an answer to a letter in which he had sent the great man some corrections of his comments on French art.[3] Diderot's overwhelming eulogy was the last straw, and Falconet in his turn exploded: 'It is Voltaire who knows nothing of architecture or sculpture or painting but who transmits to posterity the views of his century.' In fact Voltaire did not even do that, Falconet went on, and proceeded to prove it at great length, but with singularly poor judgement. The debate is unreal because its norms have

1 In the standard edition (1955-70) of Diderot's correspondence, by Georges Roth (completed by Jean Varloot), some of Falconet's letters have been abridged; see *Le Pour et le contre*, ed. Yves Benot (Paris 1958); and *Correspondance: les six premières lettres*, edd. H. Dieckmann and J. Seznec (Frankfurt 1959); I quote, however, from my own edition (Best. D13184), also based on the manuscripts.

2 Roth 384 (*c.* 15 February 1766).
3 The letter is Best.D12473 (17 March 1765), and Falconet's complaint is in Roth 387 (*c.* 25 February 1766); no reply from Voltaire has in fact survived, but one was almost certainly sent, for Voltaire profited from Falconet's corrections, and in such cases it was his invariable practice to thank his informants: few things are so reliable as Voltaire's punctilio.

437

become meaningless. However, though time has shown that Voltaire was sometimes mistaken in his aesthetic judgements, he was never foolish; but Falconet was nearly always mistaken, and nearly always silly. A very few examples will convince the reader of that.

Voltaire says that Jouvenet was a good painter, though inferior to his master Le Brun; Falconet asserts the contrary. Who knows? Perhaps we shall be able to answer this question in another two hundred years. Voltaire says that Jouvenet must have had a defect in his eyes since all he saw was tinged with yellow; Falconet denies this, and asserts that Jouvenet painted everything yellowish because his first models were sunburnt labourers. Voltaire's theory is possible, but as unlikely as it is superfluous. Jouvenet is not the only painter whose blues have turned yellow because of defective materials or excessive exposure to light. On the other hand Falconet's explanation is plainly absurd. In paintings by African artists are the skies black?

Voltaire says that Vouet had been Le Sueur's only master. Falconet finds this remark 'déprimante', meaning pejorative, because 'Vouet brought back from Italy the grand manner of painting; he developed the great principles, we owe him all'. This is difficult to understand. In any case, Falconet, by a very natural oversight in the heat of controversy, forgot to mention that he is merely echoing, not contradicting Voltaire himself, who went on at once to say that Le Sueur became an excellent painter, and carried the art to its highest point.

Falconet objects to Voltaire's statement that Lebrun's *Family of Darius* is not at all extinguished by the colouring of the Paul Veronese which hangs opposite[4] to it at Versailles, and adds that the drawing and expression should also have been compared. How odd! for this is exactly what Voltaire did. He wrote that Lebrun's picture 'is not extinguished by the colour of the painting by Paul Veronese which is seen beside it, and much surpasses it by the drawing, the composition, the dignity, the expression and the fidelity of the costume'.

The angry sculptor quotes from Voltaire, for once almost

4 Falconet thus extinguishes the argument: in fact Voltaire says 'beside'.

438

accurately, 'Detroyes the younger has produced esteemed historical paintings', and exclaims 'Ah! my master! esteemed pictures! Say that they were filled with the noble, fecund, rich genius
that did so much honour to our school'. We hardly recognize Jean
François de Troy in this panegyric. Here I think we can say
without hedging that Voltaire's judgement was judicious, and
Falconet's perverse.

But enough, for Diderot's judgements are not much more
approved by the posterity Falconet disdained than those of Falconet himself. Nor was Voltaire that much better a prophet than
either of the others. Yet Diderot, though he made no attempt to
answer all this, pointed out tactfully to Falconet that such technical considerations were secondary to the 'ideal of a performance,
on the characters, the expressions, the passions', and that here
Voltaire 'so pronounces that he has nothing to fear'.[5] Yet even
then Diderot says not a word about the essentials of a painting:
colour and form.

The whole controversy was provoked by Voltaire's *Siècle de
Louis XIV*, which includes special sections in which he lists most
of the more or less well-known writers of that time, and the most
celebrated musicians, painters, sculptors, and other artists. An
interesting feature of these lists is that the authors are set out in
alphabetical order, the artists in an unspecified sequence which in
my opinion is clearly intended to be that of merit. The painters
enumerated are, in Voltaire's order, Poussin, Lesueur, Bourdon
and Valentin, Lebrun, Mignard, Claude Gelée, Cazes, Parrocel,
Jouvenet, Santerre, La Fosse, the two Boullongnes, Raoux,
Rigaud, Detroy, Watteau, Lemoine; and he added Desportes and
Oudry as animal painters. The sculptors singled out are Sarasin,
Puget, Legros and Théodon, Girardon, Coisevox, Coustou; and
the engravers, who are merely named: Chauveau, Nanteuil,
Mellan, Audran, Edelinck, Le Clerc, the Drevets, Poilly, Picart,
Duchanges. To discuss the sequence in which Voltaire placed
these artists would be to indulge in futile reflections on the vagaries
of taste. But it is important to realise that these vagaries are not
always the obvious ones. When Voltaire says that Raoux, when
he came off, equalled Rembrandt, it would be natural to assume

5 Roth 392 (15 March 1766).

that this was because Voltaire thought very highly of the French painter: not so, it was because Rembrandt then stood little higher than the rest of the Flemish school.

Chapters XXXII and XXXIII of the *Siècle de Louis XIV* are entitled 'Des beaux-arts'; the former of these chapters, five times as long as the latter, deals only with literature in France, the latter very rapidly with the fine arts. I shall not linger over this chapter and similar parts of Voltaire's works, and for the same reason. They have only historical interest, and can have significance only to the historian of the history of art. Thus, when Voltaire says that painting began with Poussin, and that the mediocre painters who preceded him need not be taken into account, he was not making a statement profoundly indicative of his taste, he was merely confirming what we now very well know, on the most ample negative evidence, that French sixteenth-century painting had been forgotten in the eighteenth.

To confuse matters even more, the next chapter is entitled 'Des beaux-arts en Europe du temps de Louis XIV'. Most of this chapter is not concerned with the fine arts nor even with literature: it deals with England, and is devoted, apart from some deplorable allusions to Milton, almost entirely to philosophy and science in this country.

More interesting is a passage in which Voltaire says that 'le goust manquoit en France jusqu'à Louis 14 parce que le royaume n'étoit pas assez florissant pour que les baux arts qui sont enfans de l'abondance, de la société, et de l'oisivété fussent à la mode'[6]. This entry in his notebooks is particularly valuable because it is unambiguous. The manuscript (preserved at Leningrad) shows that Voltaire first applied this theory to 'les arts' and then inserted 'baux' over the line: an emendation which makes it clear that he was specifically referring to the fine arts.

The great aim of the Enlightenment was to search for truth in all things, and it was inevitable that the freethinkers should seek to make reason triumph even in the artificial world of art.[7] Marc Antoine Laugier, the great contemporary theorist of art who is

6 *Notebooks* (Voltaire 81), i.253.

7 A few sentences in this part of the chapter are based on a section of my 'Art in the Age of reason', *Studies on*

Voltaire (1972), lxxxiii.17-36, which contains references to sources and authorities.

only now coming into his own, expressed this view with elegant clarity when he wrote that it is for the *philosophe* to carry the torch of reason into the obscurity of the principles and the rules. Performance, he said, was the task of the artist, legislation that of the *philosophe*.[8] This may be, in chronological terms, neo-classical doctrine, but it is undistinguishable in content from the so-called classical laws laid down in the seventeenth century. Laugier and his fellow neo-classicists were almost precisely anticipated by so eminent an aesthetic law-giver as Boileau, as in his injunction to the poet:

> Aimez donc la raison: que toujours vos écrits
> Empruntent d'elle seule et leur lustre et leur prix.[9]

Voltaire himself declared, in a couplet as thoughtful as it is elegant, that

> La règle austère et sûre est le fil de Thésée
> Qui dirige l'esprit au dédale des arts.[10]

And it was not by chance that Winckelmann told the painter to dip his brush in intellect.[11] These legislators of taste would have applauded a poet of our own times, Edna Millay, who said exactly the same thing with lapidary insight when she proclaimed that 'Euclid alone has looked on Beauty bare'[12]. Every artist inspired with the principles of the Enlightenment, and not only its visionary architects, would have agreed with her.

The moment in time when the Enlightenment in France began to penetrate those layers of society that were all-powerful (until the middle of the twentieth century) in matters of art—those with social influence or money or both—can be fixed at about 1750, that is, the high tide of rococo. As usual, Voltaire was the pathfinder. Two full decades earlier he had launched his campaign against the false and the feeble in the arts, the *Temple du goût*[13]:

---

8 *Observations sur l'architecture* (1765), preface; see in general Wolfgang Herrmann, *Laugier and eighteenth century French theory* (London 1962).

9 *L'Art poétique*, i.36-7; 'Therefore love reason: let all your writings always take from it their brilliance and their value'.

10 *Stances* (date uncertain); 'The rule that is austere and sure is the thread of Theseus which guides the mind in the labyrinth of the arts'.

11 Quoted by Hugh Honour, *Neoclassicism* (1958), p. 19.

12 *The Harp weaver*, IV.xxii.

13 See pp. 175-177, above.

a work unique in its kind, an essay in criticism composed in verse and prose. Discussing painting, Voltaire is very severe on the imitators of Watteau who paint realistic trifles and think that they are improving on Raphael. In music, he mocks both sides of the fashionable quarrel, finding that 'there is nothing so ridiculous as French scenes sung in the Italian manner, unless it be Italian sung in the French taste'. In architecture he describes with vitriolic fidelity the aesthetic and technical defects of rococo, and its social causes. The *nouveau riche* claims to have much gold, more intelligence, and, most of all, taste. So

> 'il faut qu'on me bâtisse en bref
> Un beau palais fait pour moi, c'est tout dire,
> Où tous les arts soient en foule entassés,
> Où tout le jour je prétends qu'on m'admire.
> L'argent est prêt; je parle, obéissez.'
> Il dit, et dort. Aussitôt la canaille
> Autour de lui s'évertue et travaille.
> Certain maçon, en Vitruve érigé,
> Lui trace un plan d'ornements surchargé,
> Nul vestibule, encore moins de façade;
> Mais vous aurez une longue enfilade;
> Vos murs seront de deux doigts d'épaisseur,
> Grands cabinets, salon sans profondeur,
> Petits trumeaux, fenêtres à ma guise,
> Que l'on prendra pour des portes d'église;
> Le tout boisé, verni, blanchi, doré,
> Et des badauds à coup sûr admiré.[14]

The traveller finally arrives at the Temple of Taste. Voltaire proclaimed that this

> édifice précieux
> N'est point chargé des antiquailles
> Que nos très gothiques aieux
> Entassaient autour des murailles
> De leur temples, grossiers comme eux.

14 ' "a fine palace must be quickly built for me, I need say no more, in which all the arts shall be piled up, in which I insist on being admired all day. The money is ready; I have spoken, obey." He spoke, and slept. Around him the mob pained and laboured. A certain mason, set up as a Vitruvius, traces for him a plan of overloaded ornaments, without vestibule and even less façade; but you will have a long perspective; your walls will be two fingers thick, large rooms, a narrow drawing-room, little pilasters, windows to my taste, which could be taken for church-doors; the whole panelled, varnished, bleached, gilded and most certainly admired by the gapers.'

Il n'a point les défauts pompeux
De la chapelle de Versaille,
Ce colifichet fastueux,
Qui du peuple éblouit les yeux,
Et dont le connoisseur se raille.[15]

Having thus, negatively, brushed aside Gothic architecture and
the *grand siècle*, Voltaire goes on, positively, to describe the
Temple of Taste in these deliberate and significant words, the full
significance of which has not yet been appreciated:

Simple en était la noble architecture;
Chaque ornement, à sa place arrêté,
Y semblait mis par la nécessité:
L'art s'y cachait sous l'air de la nature;
L'œil satisfait embrassait sa structure,
Jamais surpris, et toujours enchanté.[16]

It is not too much to say that these six lines, written in 1732
and published in the following year, laid the foundation of neo-
classicism. All the key words are there: 'simple', 'noble', 'natural'.
So are the key ideas: functional decoration, the art that simulates
nature, pleasure without shock.

All this debate, for and against, was summarized by Voltaire
even more compactly about fifteen years later in the dissertation
prefixed to his tragedy *Sémiramis*, using exactly the same vocabulary: 'Rooms are gilded and varnished; noble architecture is
neglected.'

Even then rococo still had some years to run before wilting to
its decline. It could indeed be argued that no real arrest of the
impulse of rococo took place until the death of mme de Pompadour in 1764. Such overlappings are of course quite common:
history is not made for neat pedants. Thus, it is interesting to note,
for we cannot get away from Voltaire, the cynosure of the age,
that his own fame displays one of the more surprising of these

15 'precious building is not lum-
bered with the antiques, as coarse as
they were themselves, which our very
gothic forefathers piled up around the
walls of their temple. It lacks the
pompous defects of the chapel at Versailles, that gaudy bauble which
dazzles the eyes of the populace and of
which the connoisseur makes fun.'

16 'Its noble architecture was
simple; each ornament, in its appointed
place, seemed to be there because it
was needed: its art was concealed by
seeming natural; the eye, satisfied,
embraced its structure, never surprised,
and always enchanted.'

disorderly processes. The absolute apogee of his reputation, as reflected by bibliography, did not come in the rational neo-classical period, but in the two decades from about 1815. That is, it did not fall where theoretically it should have done, but at the least likely moment, the height of the Romantic movement.

Voltaire's neo-classical convictions came to an intensely personal climax in 1770. The 'purifying' ideas of the Enlightenment inevitably led to neo-classicism by the shedding of ornamental excrescences, by the assimilation of art with science, by purity of line. All these and kindred notions find expression in one particularly fascinating way: the preference of the artist and his clients for the naked body over the clothed. And there is a marvellously poetic aptness in the fact that the first time this principle was applied in modern times to a contemporary portrait was by Pigalle when he was asked by Voltaire's admirers to carve a statue of the old man. Pigalle wanted to represent Voltaire in the nude. Voltaire himself quite saw the point and had no objection. But of course there was the usual difficulty. What about the select body of subscribers, superior men and women one and all? And what about the public at large? All lagged far behind so profoundly revolutionary a notion—none the less so for being an old one brought back to life—and found it unthinkable that anyone but a whore, let alone a great man, should pose naked. Even the faithful Marmontel found the project unreasonable and indecent.[17] So Voltaire had to give in, or at least he pretended to give in, the same thing in that century of 'as if'. He wrote to mme Necker:

> Vous craignez beauté délicate
> Que ce Pigal trop ingénu
> Ne me présente à vous tout nu. . .
>
> Je consens qu'un lourd vètement
> Couvre ma chétive machine . . .[18]

In the end, it is true, Pigalle and Voltaire had their way, by sheer obstinacy one supposes, but although the sculptor represented the

---

17 Best.D17270 (30 June 1771).

18 Best.D17083 (15 March 1771); 'Delicate beauty, you fear lest the too ingenious Pigalle present me to you quite naked. . . . I agree that my puny mechanism be covered by a weighty garment. . . .'

old man naturalistically, only the head was in fact taken from the subject. Even so, for most of its life the statue was hidden in a cellar of the Institut. No progress was made beyond this point until our own times, for Canova's nude portraits were deliberately idealized, those of Napoleon being in a style we find ludicrously heroic.

Voltaire seldom refers to the fine arts, I mean of course relatively seldom: absolutely Voltaire often speaks of them, but for every allusion to art there are a hundred references to each of such abstractions as justice, law, toleration, reason, and other key ideas. Occasionally the two lines converge, and then one gets typically Voltairean exhortations, such as these two, both from the preface of that almost totally unknown play *Les Guèbres* (1769): 'The cultivation of the arts always makes our souls more honest and more pure;' and again 'toleration is needed in the fine arts as in society.' Yet Voltaire does not speak of the arts even as often as he appears to do, for though it is true that the terms 'les arts' and 'les beaux arts' often fell from his pen, they must be treated with much caution, as we have seen. He usually had in mind poetry, the drama, or literature at large[19], sometimes all the arts, occasionally all knowledge. In a recent book on the history of art, the author quotes, to prove a point, from a Voltaire letter to his old friend Thieriot: 'I love the fine arts and . . . I believe them to be always useful', but the words that follow leave no doubt that he is referring to his own particular art: 'notwithstanding all I have suffered from the envy attached to the arts'[20].

This idiosyncratic use of the term 'beaux-arts' is no mere whim or chance. It persisted throughout Voltaire's life, and there is in fact a dominating reason for this apparent ambiguity: it is that Voltaire's powerfully monistic mind operated here as it did in all problems from cosmology to fossils. He was thus strongly inclined to see the arts as one. He shows this in many casual references throughout the years, and sometimes quite explicitly, as in so unstudied a context as a letter of thanks to Charles Eisen, who had illustrated an edition of Voltaire's epic poem: 'I am

19 Similarly, Raymond Naves, *Le Goût de Voltaire* (Paris [1938]), still the best book on the subject, is almost entirely limited to literature.

20 Best.D7433 (26 October 1757).

beginning to believe, my dear sir, on seeing the plates with which you embellish it, that the *Henriade* will pass to posterity. The idea and the execution must do you equal honour. I am sure that the edition containing them will be the most sought after. Nobody takes more interest than I in the progress of the arts, and the more my age and my illnesses prevent me from cultivating them, the more I love them in those who make them flourish.'[21]

(Voltaire, by the way, took a keen interest in the illustration of his books, a subject never yet studied as a whole.[22] And it is not generally known that in 1736, when Jean Baptiste Oudry was the director of the Beauvais works, Voltaire tried quite hard to get him to make a set of tapestries after scenes in the *Henriade*. He even tried to interest Frederick of Prussia in the idea, but it came to nothing.[23] The king preferred the quite unfeasible pre-Romantic idea of printing the epic with type cast in one of the precious metals.)

It can be seen that the form of words Voltaire used to Eisen offers no transition. In writing to thank a draughtsman Voltaire declares that nobody is more interested than he in the advancement of the arts, and only regrets that his age and health prevent him from practising them. There is no hiatus in his mind between the beginning of the sentence, which refers to the pictorial arts, and the end, which relates to poetry and the drama. The fine arts, he said, hold, as it were, each other's hands[24]; all the arts are friends[25], 'The greatest genius, and certainly the most desirable, is that which excludes none of the fine arts. They are the food and the pleasure of the soul'.[26] His profound belief in this unity and brotherhood was expressed in two sets of lines written at an interval of over thirty years. One occurs inevitably in the *Temple du goût*:

> N'avoir qu'un goût est peu de chose,
> Beaux arts, je vous invoque tous.
> Musique, danse, architecture,

21 Best.D14362 (14 August 1767).

22 But see Juliette Rigal, 'L'Iconographie de la *Henriade* au XVIIIᵉ siècle', *Studies on Voltaire* (1965), xxxii.23-71.

23 See Best.D1058, note 5, and D2224 (12 April 1736, 5 June 1740).

24 *Essais sur les mœurs*, lxxxii; for stimulating notes on the theme of *ut pictura poësis* see Warren Ramsay, 'Voltaire and "l'art de peindre"', *Studies on Voltaire* (1963), xxvi.1365-77.

25 'Fable' (1764), *Dictionnaire philosophique*.

26 In the dedication of *Alzire* (1736).

Art de graver, docte peinture,
Que vous m'inspirez de désirs!
Beaux arts, vous êtes des plaisirs.[27]

The other was addressed to Belloy in eloquent, if by Voltairean standards unpolished, lines:

Les neuf muses sont sœurs, et les beaux arts sont frères.
Quelque peu de malignité,
A dérangé parfois cette fraternité:
La famille en souffrit, et des mains étrangères
De ces débats ont profité.
C'est dans son union qu'est son grand avantage;
Mais elle en impose aux pédants, aux bigots,
Elle devient l'effroi des sots,
La lumière du siècle et le soutien du sage.
Elle ne flatte point les riches et les grands,
Ceux qui dédaignent son encens,
Se font honneur de son suffrage
Et les rois sont ses courtisans.[28]

Voltaire's highest praise for Fontenelle in the *Temple du goût* was to say that 'par les beaux-arts entouré'

D'une main légère il prenait
Le compas, la plume, et la lyre.[29]

All in all, Voltaire formulated this unitary conception most beautifully in the lapidary 'We know that all the arts are brothers, that each of them illuminates another, and that a universal light results.'[30]

27 *Le Temple du goût*; variant from Best.D1009; 'It is nothing to have only one taste, fine arts, I invoke you all. Music, dance, architecture, the art of engraving, learned painting, what desires you inspire me! Fine arts, you are pleasures.'

28 Best.D14192 (21 May 1767); 'The nine muses are sisters, and the fine arts are brothers. Some little spite has sometimes disturbed this fraternity: it made the family suffer, and outsiders' hands profited from the argument. Its great benefit is in its unity, it is the light of the century and the stay of the wise man; but it overawes pedants and bigots, and terrifies fools. It does not flatter the rich and the great, those who despise its incense take honour from its suffrage, and kings are its courtiers.'

29 'With a light hand he grasped the compass, the pen, and the lyre.'

30 In the note on the *Ode sur la mort de s.a.s. m^me la princesse de Bareith* (1759). He felt this so strongly that he was always on the verge of false analogies, and did not always remain on the verge. Very early in his career, when defending the dramatic unities, he pointed out with little relevance (in the preface to *Œdipe*, 1729) that Le Brun did not represent Alexander at Arbela and in India on the same canvas.

From the earlier of these poems emerges another strong Voltairean conviction, which I cannot develop here: the close connection between the arts and pleasure. The wisest, he said, are certainly those who cultivate the arts and love pleasure.[31]

At one time Voltaire came very close to a definition of what he understood by the fine arts. This was in the article 'Arts, beaux-arts' (1772) of the *Questions sur l'encyclopédie*. Unfortunately he took it into his head to cast this article in the form of a letter addressed to the dearly hated Frederick of Prussia. He was obviously pulling the leg of Lytton Strachey's 'heavy German muse'[32], but Voltaire's transitions are so subtle that it is difficult to know where in this definition he is serious and where he is merely teasing. Here it is for what it is worth:

'By the fine arts I mean eloquence, in which you have distinguished yourself by being the historian of your fatherland, and the only Brandeburgian historian anyone has ever read; poetry, which has been your pastime and your glory when you have deigned to write French verse; music, in which you have succeeded to such a point that I very much doubt whether Ptolemy Auletes would ever have dared to play the flute after you, nor Achilles his lyre.

Then come the arts in which the mind and the hand are almost equally necessary, such as sculpture, painting, all those based on drawing, and above all watchmaking, which I regard as a fine art since I founded manufacturers on mount Crapack.'

All this is explained by another definition in a different context. Men are agreed, says Voltaire, 'to call *beautiful* all objects that inspire without effort agreeable feelings, that which is only exact, difficult and useful, cannot pretend to beauty. Thus, one does not say a lovely footnote, a lovely criticism, a lovely discussion, as one says a lovely passage in Virgil, Horace, Cicero, Bossuet, Racine, Pascal. A well-made dissertation', Voltaire adds to our relief, 'as elegant as it is accurate, and which strews flowers on a thorny subject, can still be called a *lovely* piece of literature, though at a level very subordinate to works of genius'![33]

31 Best.D7143 (6 February 1757) to Argental.
32 See a note on Best.D1364.
33 'Littérature', fragment incorporated into the *Dictionnaire philosophique*.

Anything more formal than this in the way of aesthetic theory must not be looked for in Voltaire. I repeat that he disliked philosophy in the academic sense, and despised metaphysics.[34] More than once[35] he quoted the well-known line in the *Glorieux* of Destouches, the only one by which this once celebrated poet is remembered: 'Criticism is easy and art is difficult'. The original English text of the *Essay on epick poetry*, which is not to be found in any edition of Voltaire's works, begins: 'We have in every Art more Rules than Examples, for men are more fond of teaching, than able to perform. . . . All those Teachers seem to have much labour'd by their Definitions, Distinctions, &c. to spread a profound Obscurity over things in their own Nature clear and perspicuous; and 'tis no wonder if such Lawgivers, unequal to the Burthen which they took upon themselves, have embroil'd the States which they intended to regulate'. Voltaire was never one to mistake obscurity for profundity. How unhappy he would have been if he lived today!

Much later Voltaire said that philosophers, when questioned about the nature of beauty, answer grandiloquent nonsense. However, when he thought that these same philosophers, when the relativity of beauty was pointed out to them, would abstain from writing long treatises on the beautiful[36], he was for once decidedly too cheerful.

Voltaire himself had no doubts about the function of the rational in the arts: he was also utterly convinced that by the use of the reason all the world's man-made ills could and would be cured. He was not a pessimist, as so many imagine: he was a meliorist, that is, he believed in progress. Yet though this belief was profound it was never explicit, a phenomenon paralleled by the *Encyclopédie*, a work permeated through and through by the

---

34 One of Voltaire's rare 'philosophical' remarks remains a mere *obiter dictum*: in commenting on Pascal's assertation that men choose their trades by chance, Voltaire says 'Il n'y a que les arts de génie auxquels on se détermine de soi-même' (*Remarques sur les pensées de Pascal*, xxi); Voltaire's views on free will were not consistent. I believe that the expression 'arts de génie' occurs only once more in Voltaire's writings, in his letter to Diderot of 20 April 1773: 'It must be admitted that all the arts of genius are the work of instinct'.

35 As in Best.D3866, D10310, D12874, D13923.

36 'Beauté', *Dictionnaire philosophique*.

belief in progress, but in which there is no article devoted to it, any more than in Voltaire's *Dictionnaire philosophique* and *Questions sur l'encyclopédie*, or in Bayle's *Dictionnaire* for that matter, where it would have been a terminological anachronism, since the unqualified use of *progrès* appears to date from the middle of the eighteenth century.[37]

Has there been any progress in the arts? Voltaire did not doubt that for a moment. It was self-evident to him that our ancestors were 'très gothiques' and 'grossiers'.[38] Orpheus was no doubt a great musician, but if he returned to earth to compose an opera he would have to learn from Rameau.[39] The Capitol was admirable, but St Peter's is much bigger and finer; and the Louvre is a masterpiece compared with the palace of Persepolis. Perhaps, but Voltaire is cheating a little in comparing the best of the moderns with the second-best of the ancients; and when he went on to imply and even to state categorically that anything modern is better than anything ancient, for instance, that every picture shown in the Paris *salon* was superior to the then newly discovered paintings of Herculaneum[40], comment becomes painfully superfluous.

Yet here we are confronted by a strange paradox. Voltaire was convinced that, while everything was not good, man's condition was steadily getting better: yet at the same time he was almost as obsessed as Max Nordau, though in a very different spirit, by the notion of the decadence in the arts. During his last years he told a correspondent: 'I perceive that among all the nations of the world the fine arts have only a single moment of perfection, and that after the century of genius everything degenerates because of too much thinking (à force d'esprit).'[41] In a once celebrated letter to the duc de La Vallière, which might well be regarded as a key to the Enlightenment[42], Voltaire said that 'genius has necessarily declined, but knowledge has multiplied. A thousand me-

37 Ferdinand Brunot, *Histoire de la langue française*, vi.i.109-10, quotes only Turgot (1750) and Mirabeau (1757). See ch. 28, above.
38 See p. 442, above.
39 Best.D12070 (2 September 1764), to Chabanon.
40 'Antiquité, v' (1770), *Questions sur l'encyclopédie*.

41 Best.D19011 (5 July 1774), to La Touraille; see *Notebooks* (Voltaire 81), i.407, note 2, the references given there, and the index of the *Notebooks*, s. v. 'decadence'.
42 Cp. Werner Krauss, *Studien zur deutschen und französischen Aufklärung* (Berlin 1963), p. 98, 157-8.

diocre painters of Salvator Rosa's time were not the equal of Raphael and Michelangelo. But these thousand mediocre painters, who had been formed by Raphael and Michelangelo, constituted a school infinitely superior than that found by these two great men.'[43] When he revised this letter for publication in his autobiography, Voltaire strengthened this view still further by altering 'genius has declined' to 'genius declines and will decline'[44]. The whole passage raises important philosophical questions. It is an odd statement to come from a man whom I have described as a fervent believer in progress. Voltaire really seems to have believed that the wider diffusion of the arts was lowering their level. I do not often disagree with the great man, but here I most certainly do. The genius of man is not a fixed quantity like his blood: it proliferates. And yet . . . which of us has not been moved by strange disconcerting doubts when looking at certain vestiges of early art? Who, to stand Voltaire's pronouncement on its head, would not exchange an entire Summer exhibition at Burlington house for a single painting at Altamira? Is it not somehow indecent that the temple of Karnak should be so much finer than Westminster cathedral? Most disconcerting of all is the fact that retrogression has been most marked in those arts that most depend on technology. The first books printed in the middle of the fifteenth century were also the finest, aesthetically and even technically, that have ever been produced. Gothic stained glass has never been equalled. So, could Voltaire after all have been right when he asserted so often that 'The first who trace a path always remain at the head in the eyes of posterity. There is no glory but for the inventors. . . .'?[45]

This paradox suffuses the whole of Voltaire's life and work. With diffidence I suggest that it can be resolved. I believe the explanation to be this: Voltaire was convinced that man's condition was steadily getting worse in the world as he knew it: not only literature and the arts feebler, wars also more terrible, intolerance more vexatious, injustice more oppressive, but he was also convinced that this process could be reversed by the use of

43 Best.D9754, (*c.* 25 April 1761). 45 Best.D18962 (3 May 1776).
44 See the appendix to the autobiography.

the reason, and would be so reversed if men willed it so. He was not a passive quietist looking upward and outward for salvation, he was an active meliorist, convinced that man could save himself by his own efforts.

Was Voltaire personally involved in the arts? A distinguished authority[46] says that our philosopher-poet was very ignorant of the techniques of the fine arts, but his allegation is not quite clear. If taken in the narrowest sense there is certainly no reason to suppose that Voltaire knew how to handle a brush or a chisel. In a wider sense, Voltaire had an extensive technical awareness of at least the visual arts. One need only read his criticism of Bouchardon's sculpture *Amour se faisant son arc de la massue d'Hercule*[47], or the innumerable passages in the correspondence about the staging of his plays, in which he shows a constant awareness of colours, shapes, and proportions—far more so than any other pre-Romantic dramatist.

One thing is certain, whatever his technical competence may have been Voltaire was highly sensitive both to natural and to man-made beauty, and to their interplay. A volume of aesthetic theory is summed up in the pellucid couplet

> Songez que le secret des arts
> Est de corriger la nature.[48]

I will not deny myself nor the reader the pleasure of quoting nearly the whole of a short letter in which these qualities are elegantly illustrated. It was written from the Délices, 25 April 1760 (Best.D8875), to thank Claude Henri Watelet for sending Voltaire a copy of his still instructive and still agreeable poem *L'Art de peindre*:

I do not know, sir, whether you sent me through a book-lover that handsome present for which I have the honour to thank you. But this book-lover is not named *il far' presto*. I received only three days ago this instructive and agreeable poem, these lessons given modestly, in prose, these fine plates drawn by your hand which add a new merit to the work, and which are one of the most precious monuments of the fine arts.

46 Naves, p. 370.
47 Best.D1757 (? 9 January 1739), to Caylus.
48 Best.D404 (2 March 1731), to Cideville; 'Reflect that the secret of the arts is to improve nature'. 'A madame la marquise d'Ussé' (1730) is a charming epigram on art and nature.

I do not know why there were so many great painters in the sixteenth century, and why we have so few today. I imagine that the manufacturers of mirrors, Chinese trifles and snuff-boxes costing a hundred gold louis have harmed painting. May your work, sir, form as many good artists as it will win you praises. I wish I could find some Claude Lorrain to paint what I see from my windows. It is a vale closed opposite to me by the city of Geneva, which rises as an amphitheatre. The Rhône leaves the city as a cascade to join the river Arve, which descends on the left between the Alps. Beyond the Arve there is yet another river on the left, and beyond that river four leagues of country-side. On the right is the lake of Geneva, beyond the lake the plains of Savoy, the entire horizon closed by hills which merge, twenty-five leagues away, into mountains covered with eternal ice, and the whole territory of Geneva scattered with country houses and gardens. I have nowhere seen such a situation. I doubt whether that of Constantinople is as agreeable.

The reader will not have needed this letter to learn that Voltaire was a marvellous correspondent: but he will not perhaps be displeased to know that Voltaire's reputation as an arid and heartless man, without eyes, ears and heart for the beauties of nature belongs to that great clan of accepted slanders which our more obtuse Panglosses think it unscrupulous to expose. Because Voltaire did not wear his heart on his sleeve like Diderot, or appear to pour it out like Rousseau, it must not be supposed that he had no inner life. The anguish of the artist has never been more tellingly expressed than in his 'In all the arts, there is a point beyond which one can no longer advance. One is confined within the limits of one's talent; one sees perfection beyond one's self and one makes futile efforts to attain it.'[49] Voltaire was utterly committed to the primacy of reason, but he was none the less a man of sensibility and of feeling.[50]

When Voltaire sat to the great pastellist La Tour[51] in 1735 the result was his best portrait until Houdon created his masterpieces in the great man's last year. Voltaire undoubtedly appreciated the beauty of the picture, but our own awed respect, perhaps due to Whistler, for works of art as physical objects was unknown in the eighteenth century. When Voltaire installed the Délices

49 In the preface of *Mariamne* (1725).
50 These words have been endorsed and amplified by R. S. Ridgway, *Voltaire and sensibility* (Montreal &c. 1973).

51 A letter asking for an appointment has survived: Best.D861 (April 1735).

he did not hesitate to send to Paris for his two Albanis simply because they fitted into available spaces[52]; nor was he embarrassed to say that he was waiting for the 'coloured portrait' by Van Dyck, but without impatience[53]. As for the La Tour, Voltaire, without the slightest regard for the art historian and for future composers of certificates of authenticity, instructed his Parisian man of affairs: 'First of all have two copies made, and then we will make others. But here is what I should like: that the first copy be made with all the skill and ability of the copyer, so that it can serve as an original for the others. As soon as this first copy is done, I would beg you to have it examined and retouched by La Tour. In the meanwhile you would send me the original well framed, well packed, and have a miniature, suitable for a ring, made from the first copy.'[54] A few months later the work was done, and Voltaire received the so-called original (or was it the first copy?) presumably touched up by La Tour. He was not very pleased. 'I could have wished that it was a little more *empâté* and in brighter colours.[55] Could you have a rather more animated copy done?'[56] After this, who would care to identify the true original preparation?

Elsewhere Voltaire does not hesitate to write: 'You remember that picture in my Paris library? Send me something of the same kind and of about the same size.'[57] What fun one could make of such examples of apparent nonchalance and even philistinism! But it is perhaps more profitable to look below the surface. It must be remembered that Voltaire wrote such letters to those who knew him very well, and who also knew his tastes. It must be remembered above all that the standard of craftsmanship was so high that one could only with difficulty get bad work done. But the best test is the pragmatic one: what was the end result? Luckily we know Voltaire's taste in architecture, and the work he did at Cirey, Les Délices, and Ferney, all surviving and identifiable, to say nothing of his acquisition of the Hôtel Lambert, one of the half-dozen loveliest houses in Paris, show that

52 Best.D6329 (3 July 1755).
53 Best.D1674 (4 December 1738).
54 Best.D1058 (12 April 1736).
55 La Tour's portrait is thin and pale even for a pastel.
56 Best.D1201 (17 November 1736).
57 Quoted from memory, and certainly not verbally accurate.

he had a good eye. And as for the minor arts, we equally possess
a description of the quarters built and decorated under Voltaire's
direct supervision at Cirey. Mme de Graffigny may have been a
bit of a vulgarian, but she was familiar with fine houses, and was
an intimate of Lunéville, the court of that singularly art-conscious
prince and ex-monarch Stanislas Leszczynski, the initiator of
perhaps the finest thing of its kind, the place Stanislas at Nancy.
Mme de Graffigny was therefore no open-mouthed tourist when
she visited Cirey. The wing Voltaire added to the small renaissance château can still be admired. The interior has long since
been pretty well transformed. This is how mme de Graffigny
described it as she saw it.

Voltaire's little wing, she wrote at the time to her friend at
Lunéville, François Etienne Devaux,

is so much part of the house that the door is at the foot of the main staircase.
There is a little antechamber as big as your hand, then his bedroom, small, low,
hung in crimson velvet, with an alcove of the same with gold fringes. This is
the winter installation. There is little tapestry and much panelling, in which
admirable pictures are framed, and mirrors, as you can imagine, with fine
lacquer in the corners, porcelain, shrines, a clock supported by birds of strange
shape, an infinity of things in the same taste, dear, rare and above all so clean
that one could kiss the parquet, an open casket containing silver plate, all that
a taste for the superfluous—that necessary thing—could invent, and what
silver! what workmanship! There is even a jewel-box in which there are ten
or twelve rings with engraved stones, besides two very thin ones with diamonds.

Thence one goes into the little gallery, which is only thirty or forty feet
long. Between the windows there are two most beautiful little statues on
lacquer[58] pedestals, one of that famous Venus, the other of Hercules. The
other side of the window[59] is divided into two cupboards, one containing
books, the other physical apparatus. Between the two is a stove against the
wall which makes the air spring-like. In the foreground is a big stone pedestal,
on which stands a fairly large eros aiming an arrow. The room is not finished.
A carved alcove is being made for the eros, to hide the stove. The gallery is
panelled and lacquered in pale yellow. Clocks, tables, desks, you can easily
imagine that nothing of the sort is lacking. Beyond this is the dark room,
which is not yet finished, like that in which his apparatus will be placed. That
is why they are all still in the gallery. A single sopha, no easy armchair, that
is, they are good but only covered. Apparently the comfort of the body is not

58 'Vernis des Indes', the meaning
of which is doubtful.

59 But surely she meant the wall
facing the windows?

his form of sensuality. The panels of the woodwork are of very fine Indian papers, so are the screens, the screen-tables, the porcelain corners, the whole very elegant. In the middle is a door giving on the garden.[60]

Mme de Graffigny also describes the apartments of mme Du Châtelet, but I will spare the reader the tears of envy her lyric would bring to his eyes.

Of course such effects were not obtained by chance. Everything was directed and ordered by Voltaire. With what affectionate poetry he later decorated and furnished the ill-named and ill-fated Délices. Having decided to paint the trellis-work green, the doors white and yellow, the floors red, he ordered '150 livres de verdet, 300 livres d'huile de noix, 200 livres de céruse, 50 livres de bleu, 50 livres d'ocre jaune, 50 livres de rouge . . . et 50 de litarge'[61], to which he later added 'blanc de Troye'[62], not forgetting the brushes[63]. Such orders also illustrate one of the most charming aspects of Voltaire's genius, his wonderful ear for the right word even in the most technical contexts. He had a far wider vocabulary than any other contemporary French writer.

Long before, in 1733, Voltaire went to live in the rue du Long-Pont opposite Saint-Gervais, and it was then no doubt that he added to the *Temple du goût* his reference to that church, a masterpiece of epigrammatic comment. Whether one agrees with him or not about the merits of the portal of Saint-Gervais, it would be difficult to better his comment that it is a 'masterpiece of architecture, lacking a church, a square, and admirers.'[64] A *place* has since been created, but the church is still largely invisible, and admirers have not multiplied.

Voltaire was in fact deeply sensitive to urban architecture, and to the planning of towns, particularly Paris, to which he devoted the essay *Des embellissements de Paris* (1749). He concluded sadly that if nobody were found to undertake the work of beautifying Paris they would soon have to weep over the ruins of Jerusalem.

We have seen what happened when he wrote the *Mondain* to

60 Best.D1677 (6 December 1738).

61 Best.D6235 (5 April 1755); in Best.D6257 'verdet' is called 'verd-de-gris'; cp. Best.D9143 (13 August 1760).

62 Best.D8096 (10 February 1759).

63 Best.D6237 (8 April 1755).

64 By Jacques de Brosse; see Best. D606, note 1.

advocate the graces of urban civilization as the cradle of the arts. Do not the lines already quoted[65] form a little treatise on the sociology and the economics of art?

Voltaire was never able unreservedly to admire Versailles, because its luxury and cost were disproportionate even to the celebrity it brought to France. He thought that the most glorious and grandest monument of the king's reign was the canal of Languedoc.[66] How often and how sadly Voltaire spoke of the king's neglect of Paris! If only he had spent in completing the Louvre and in beautifying Paris the enormous sums wasted on bringing water to Versailles!

Voltaire was indeed one of the very few men of his generation who was convinced of the fact that the arts could not be divorced from the society in which they existed. He had, in our modern jargon, a social conscience. Here at least we have Voltaire's monism without paradox. And in a man so utterly committed to the primacy of the arts this is perhaps the ultimate paradox. Or is it?

65 See pp. 243-244, above. 66 *Le Siècle de Louis XIV*, xxix.

34. *The Calas case, 1761-1763*

A T FIRST SIGHT the early months of 1761 might appear to
have been exclusively filled by disputes: an agreeable and
victorious conflict with a group of Jesuits who wanted to
dispossess an old-established family with the connivance of a
Genevese magistrate[1]; a heated attack on the curé of Moëns who
had beaten up a parishioner of whose conduct he disapproved; a
preposterous row with the président de Brosses about the ownership of a parcel of wood, a row set off, it is too often forgotten,
by a deliberately provocative letter[2] from the président. Voltaire,
'arm'd with more than complete steel The justice of my quarrel'[3],
much enjoyed these little wars.

As was so often the case these conflicts were merely Voltaire's
safety-valves. In reality he was meditating much work of import-
tance. Indeed, on the first day of the year he wrote to the Académie française offering to edit the works of Corneille for the benefit
of the little Marie; and soon the Ferney dynamo was working at
full power: before the end of the summer letters, explanations,
appeals had gone out in all directions; nor were they stereotyped
circulars, as can be seen from this letter to lord Chesterfield,
typical in its elegance and attention to detail:

> Mylord,
> Give me leave to apply from the foot of the alps to the english noble man
> whose wit is the most adapted to the taste of every nation. J have in my old
> age a sort of conformity with you. T'is not in point of wit, but in point of
> ears. Mine are much hard too. The consolation of deaf people is to read, and
> some times to scribble. J have as a scribler, made a prety curious commentary
> on many tragedies of Corneille. T'is my duty since the gran daughter of
> Corneille is in my house.
> If there was a gran daughter of Shakespear, j would subscribe for her. J hope
> those who take Pontichéri will take subscriptions too.

---

1 See the autobiography, pp. 659-
660, below.
2 Best.D8582 (*c.* 9 November 1759).
3 From a couplet which occurs both

in *Lust's dominion* (IV.iii), sometimes
attributed to Marlowe, and in Aphra
Behn's *The Moor's revenge* (IV.v.).

The work is prodigiously cheap, and no money is to be given but at the reception of the book.

Nurse receives the names of the subscribers. Y^r name will be the most honourable and the dearest to me.

J wish y^r lordship long life, good eyes and good stomak.

Mylord souvenez vous de votre ancien serviteur Voltaire qui vous est attaché comme s'il était né à Londres.[4]

The first subscriptions were soon received, and the foundations of the vast undertaking well and truly laid. Many of the letters he wrote in connection with the Corneille edition are filled with discussions of poetic and dramatic principles and practice, for it was not in Voltaire's nature to write even begging letters without giving their recipients good value.

As usual when Voltaire was busy, he was very busy indeed. He presented to what is now the Bibliothèque nationale the manuscript of what he took to be an ancient commentary on the *Vedas*, but which is in fact a modern and tendentious concoction by a Christian missionary.[5] And now he complained for the first time[6] of snow-blindness, from which he was to suffer henceforth every winter. Indeed, so poor was Voltaire's health that rumours again got abroad of his death. Dupan told a correspondent that Voltaire could recover if he wanted to, 'but he behaves like a poet', whatever that may mean. And he added: 'His death would have overjoyed many people.'[7]

Undeterred, Voltaire still found time and concentration to do much work on the second volume of his Russian history, continuing his patient efforts to extract authentic materials from his Russian correspondents, who were more concerned with glorifying Peter I than with the painful responsibilities of the historian. Voltaire also produced his defence of the French stage against the English[8]; and his justly famous epistle on agriculture which begins

Qu'il est doux d'employer le déclin de son âge
Comme le grand Virgile occupa son printemps!

4 Best.D9929 (5 August 1761); 'My lord, remember your old servant Voltaire, who is as attached to you as if he were born in London.'

5 See Best.D9892 (13 July 1761) and the notes thereon.

6 Best.D9559 (19 January 1761), although he writes of it as of a mishap he had already experienced every year.

7 See a note on Best.D10429.

8 The *Appel à toutes les nations*; see pp. 137-138, above.

Du beau lac de Mantoue il aimait le rivage;
Il cultivait la terre, et chantait ses présents.
Mais bientôt, ennuyé des plaisirs du village,
D'Alexis et d'Aminte il quitta le séjour,
Et malgré Mævius, il parut à la cour.
      C'est la cour qu'on doit fuir, c'est aux champs qu'il faut vivre.[9]

In a remarkable letter[10] to Deodati de Tovazzi Voltaire analysed the relative merits of the French and Italian languages, and
in another[11] to the duc de La Vallière, the development and decay
of good taste. It was in this letter that Voltaire made the famous
pronouncement, a thousand times quoted: 'Genius has necessarily
diminished, but enlightenment has multiplied.'[12]

Voltaire continued to bombard Pompignan with pamphlets.
The episode of his quarrel with the pompously pious poet is
too trivial for discussion, but it gives me the opportunity to clear
up a misunderstanding of some importance. Voltaire is often
accused[13] of having crushed the reputations of worthy writers.
This is quite untrue. That Voltaire devoted a great deal of time
and energy to these polemics appears to us regrettable, but of
course what we think is not necessarily just. Voltaire was engaged
in a crusade for what were unquestionably true and noble causes,
a crusade in which he had the whole establishment against him.
Those who stood in his way could therefore expect short shrift.
But Voltaire belaboured only two men of real talent, both also
of very different character, Rousseau and Maupertuis, and then
only after intolerable provocation: both men's reputations now
stand higher than ever. The notion that Voltaire was responsible
for the presentday obscurity of men like Pompignan, and of others
even more completely forgotten, is absurd. Good work is not so

9 *Epître à madame Denis sur l'agriculture*; 'How sweet it is to spend the
decline of one's days as the great Virgil
spent his spring! He loved the shores
of the fine lake of Mantua. He cultivated the land, and sung its fruits. But
soon, weary of village pleasures, he
left the abode of Alexis and Aminta,
and, notwithstanding Mævius, appeared at court. It is the court one
should flee, it is in the countryside
that one should live.'
10 Best.D9572 (24 January 1761).

11 Best.D9754 (c. 25 April 1761).
12 This is one of the few ambigu-
ously oracular remarks made by Voltaire, and has inevitably tempted the
exegetes; see most recently the excellent paper by Roland Mortier, 'L'Idée
de décadence littéraire au XVIIIᵉ siècle',
Studies on Voltaire (1967), lvii.1013-
29.
13 Most recently by Theodore E. D.
Braun, 'Voltaire's perception of truth
in quarrels with his enemies', *Studies
on Voltaire* (1967), lv.287-95.

easily buried for two centuries, and the fact is that even the qualified survival of such writers is due to Voltaire himself, without
whose polemics their very names would now be known only to
specialists. Voltaire's writings on them have in fact led to the
regular rereading of their works, and the fact that in no case has
this led to a revival of interest in them is a clear demonstration
that Voltaire's judgment was sound.

Although once again news of Voltaire's death sped through the
Paris drawing-rooms and academies, the exiled poet preferred to
publish the *Conversation de m. l'intendant des menus*, in the main
a satire on the automatic excommunication of stage-players; the
Lettres de Charles Gouju, a squib in which Voltaire shows that
priests are false Christians; *Les Chevaux et les ânes*, another protest,
this time in verse, against the decay of taste and manners; the
Sermon du rabbin Akib[14], a deeply felt jeremiad against priestly
fanaticism, in particular condemning the execution of the aged
Jesuit Gabriel Malagrida, publicly strangled by the Portuguese
inquisition; to say nothing of other miscellanea, and an ample
letter[15] to Olivet comparing Corneille unfavourably with Racine
—in fact, the more he worked on the former the more he liked the
latter.

Not least amusing among the trifles Voltaire composed at this
time is his *Lettre de m. Clocpicre à m. Eratou*, a pastiche of the
kind of biblical criticism indulged in by the pious, and in particular by dom Calmet. Taking as his text 'Ye shall eat the flesh of
the mighty, and drink the blood of the princes of the earth. . . .
And ye shall be filled at my table with horses and chariots, with
mighty men, end with all men of war, said the Lord God'[16], Voltaire inquired with persuasive innocence 'whether the Jews ate
human flesh, and how it was prepared'. Was it in a stew or roasted
on a spit? In the end this important issue is lost sight of, it is
pointed out that a cossack was eaten during a siege, and Voltaire's
personage concludes: 'Really, gentlemen, you are very delicate;
two or three hundred thousand men are killed, and everybody
approves; one cossack is eaten, and everybody cries out.'

14 The full title is *Sermon du rabbin
Akib prononcé à Smyrne le 20 novembre
1761 (traduit de l'hébreu)*.

15 Best.D9959 (20 August 1761).
16 *Ezekiel*, xxxix.18-20.

But perhaps most interesting among the minor writings of this period is a long letter[17] to Choiseul in which Voltaire expounds his sceptical view of history, in a sweeping survey of the immediate past and of short-term prospects. He maintains that political action does not dictate events, it is the events that dictate the reactions of the statesman. 'You have had Prussia for ally, you now have her for enemy. Austria has changed her policy, and so have you. Twenty years ago Russia had no weight in the balance of Europe, and now she has a great one. Sweden has played a great role and now plays a very small one. Everything has changed and will change.' And he concludes that alliances are like a quadrille, in which one changes partners at every moment, and these changes are due to causes beyond the volition of the statesman. With daunting realism Voltaire concludes that in international negotiations only money and victories count: if one commands success and money one can do as one pleases. These words being addressed to the leader of a nation which was singularly unsuccessful on the field of battle, and which approached ever nearer to bankruptcy, it is not surprising that in Choiseul's reply[18] he refers only to a passport requested by Voltaire for a friend, to the death of cardinal Passionei, to his application to the papal nuncio for an authentic relic for Voltaire's church[19], to the proposed removal of the Ferney cemetery, to Voltaire's plan for fewer public holidays, and to the subscription for Corneille. As for matters of high diplomacy, not a word. Such was the prime minister of France at this critical time.

Voltaire was now satisfied that Rousseau, far from being an

17 Best.D9894 (? 13 July 1761).

18 Best.D9913 (25 July 1761).

19 Voltaire, who never could resist a chance to pull a sacred leg, had written to Clement XIII to ask for such a relic, in a letter which begins, in Italian: 'François de Voltaire, gentleman of the Chamber of his very Christian majesty, count of Tournay in the province of Gex near Geneva, lord of Ferney in the same province, and Marie Louise Denis, his niece, lady of Ferney, place their parish and all their vassals at the sacred feet of his beatitude' (Best.D9841; 23 June 1761). Voltaire got his relic, but most unfortunately Choiseul, in forwarding it to Ferney, does not specify its nature, referring only to bones (Best.D10041; 28 September 1761). Lolotte de Constant writes of relics in the plural, telling her husband that for the moment they were spread out on the chimneypiece (5 October 1761, in a note on Best. D10055). To complicate this grave problem even further, Voltaire himself says that the relic was the hair-shirt of st Francis (Best.D10067, c. 10 October 1761; D10098, 26 October).

asset to the advocates of intellectual liberty, was a positive danger to them. For the first time he wrote against him, in the *Lettres à m. de Voltaire sur la Nouvelle Héloïse*[20]. He stigmatised Rousseau as the most conceited of living authors, but this would hardly have offended him. He was no doubt much more wounded by Voltaire's strictures on his style and grammar, and on the structure and development of the novel. In passing, Voltaire ironises about the 'aristocratic' atmosphere of Rousseau's novel, for it must not be forgotten that Julie was the daughter of a baron of Vaud, and that milord Edouard was proud, hard and a drunkard, in short 'a worthy peer of Great Britain'. But what Rousseau found most offensive was certainly Voltaire's references to his platitudinous moralisings. 'Never', says Voltaire inelegantly, 'has a whore preached more, and never has a valet, seducer of girls, been more philosophic.' Alembert found this too personal[21], and Voltaire then made it clear that he regarded Rousseau as a dangerous renegade[22] and a bastard of Diogenes[23]. Perhaps we can leave it at that.

The interests of the landowner were not forgotten, and were promoted by the accession to the highest offices of Choiseul and his cousin Praslin, whose new powers were ultimately of greater advantage to their friend Voltaire than to France. But the patriarch's motives were not altogether selfish, for the negotiations concerned the liberation of the province of Gex as a whole, the debate getting ever wider, until it embraced questions of taxation, import duties, and the like. On a more domestic scale, Voltaire tried once again, in vain, to curb his niece's extravagance by limiting her pocket-money to 2400 francs a month, in addition to her income from his various gifts, including the revenues from the estates of Les Délices and of Ferney, which was in her name. Apart from this Voltaire estimated his monthly domestic expenses at 6000 francs.[24]

20 Voltaire published them over the name of the marquis de Ximenès, a former lover of mme Denis, but as usual the true authorship was an open secret.

21 Best.D9674 (9 March 1761).
22 Best.D9682 (19 March 1761).
23 Best.D9684 (19 March 1761).

24 Best.D10259 (10 January 1762). Mme Denis almost at once exceeded her allowance: in April she spent 2784 francs, which Voltaire of course paid (Best.D10448; 6 May 1762). Soon after he gave up the struggle, and resigned himself to footing all her bills as before (Best.D10639; August 1762).

Voltaire was of course as preoccupied as ever with his own plays. By October 1761 the theatre at Ferney was ready[25], and henceforth Voltaire's plays were rehearsed and performed in it, as well as many other plays. In Paris, on the greater stage of the Comédie française, the fact emerges incidentally that during the season 1761/62 the great man's plays were performed more than twice as often as those of Corneille and Racine put together[26]. After long preparation *Olympie* was produced; the tragedy was successful, but was nevertheless taken off.

And now Voltaire first heard of an event which, following rapidly on the decapitation of the pastor Rochette[27], was to have as profound an effect on him as had the Lisbon earthquake some years before: the torture and execution of the Protestant Jean Calas, found guilty at Toulouse of the murder of his son, because, it was alleged, he suspected him of seeking conversion to Roman Catholicism. Voltaire was informed almost at once, was sceptical at first, then curious: 'An event so appalling as the accusation of an entire family of a parricide[28] committed for religious reasons; a father expiring on the wheel for having strangled his son with his own hands on the bare suspicion that this son wanted to abandon the opinions of Jean Calvin[29]; a brother violently accused of having helped his father to strangle his brother; the mother accused; a young lawyer suspected of having served as executioner in this unheard of assassination . . . forms an essential part of the history of humanity and of the vast panorama of our furies and our weaknesses.'[30] It was in this spirit that Voltaire embarked on his investigation. Eventually he was convinced—

25 Best.D10052 (3 October 1761).

26 The figures are given in a note on Best.D10065 (see also p. 144, above):
Corneille: 16 performances of 5 plays, total paid attendance 11,285; average 705.
Racine: 18 performances of 6 plays, total paid attendance 12,097, average 672.
Voltaire: 76 performances of 16 plays, total paid attendance 42,330, average 557.

27 Preaching by Protestants was forbidden under pain of death, but François Rochette, arrested by accident at Caussade (14 September 1761), disdained to conceal his identity, and was executed (18 February 1762).

28 At that time this word was not limited in French to the murder of a father.

29 According to Calvin Calas would have been entitled to put his son to death for filial disobedience; see the *Institutio religionis christianae*, II.viii. 35 (5).

30 Best.D10414 (15 April 1762).

and he was quite right—that there had been a terrible miscarriage of justice.

Soon nearly all his thoughts and energies, and much of his writing, were devoted to this legal assassination provoked by religious hysteria. It was to dominate his life for three years, and his labours in their turn profoundly affected public opinion throughout the western world. Indeed, it can plausibly be maintained that by his activity in the Calas case Voltaire created public opinion as a new and increasingly weighty factor in the life of a civilised community.[31] It was Voltaire who first used the term in this sense, and it is certainly no coincidence that in *Olympie*, which he was completing at this time, is to be found the line 'L'opinion fait tout; elle t'a condamné.'[32] And he soon showed that he had absorbed the moral: 'Laws are made by public opinion'[33]; and even more directly: 'Opinion governs the world, and in the end the *philosophes* govern men's opinions'[34].

At any rate Voltaire's incessant propaganda and his unique influence soon reached the innermost circles, and produced, among many others of the same kind, this remarkable letter[35] from mme de Pompadour, in terms never seen hitherto over such a signature.

You are right, the affair of the unfortunate Calas makes one shudder.

He should have been pitied for being born a huguenot, but he should not on that account have been treated like a highwayman.

It seems impossible that he should have committed the crime of which he was accused: it is against nature.

Yet he is dead, and his family is branded, and his judges refuse to repent.

The kind heart of the king has much suffered at the recital of this strange adventure and all France cries vengeance.

The poor man will be avenged, but not revived.

These people at Toulouse are hot-headed, and have more religion of this kind than they need to be good Christians. May God convert them and make them more human.

31 According to Rulhière the power of public opinion was born exactly in 1749! See his *Œuvres* (Paris 1819), ii.26 quoted by Arthur M. Wilson, *Diderot* (New York 1972), pp. 94-5.

32 IV.ii; 'Opinion does all; it has condemned you.'

33 *Remarques pour servir de supplément à l'Essai sur les mœurs* (1763),

xvii; the whole of the *Remarques* is a commentary on the role of public opinion.

34 Best.D13639 (27 January 1766). In English the term 'public opinion' appears to have been first used by Gibbon (*Decline and fall*, xxxi.iii), which is equally significant.

35 Best.D10677 (27 August 1762).

At first, however, Voltaire's general activities were hardly affected, especially as his *Droit du seigneur* was produced in Paris, and *Olympie*, a little later, was performed at Ferney, to the accompaniment of the usual technical discussions. Among a number of publications in 1762 the most notable was the *Extrait des sentiments de Jean Meslier*, one of Voltaire's most influential works—for he can fairly be said to have made it his own. Voltaire had known since 1735[36] the extraordinary 'testament' left by this anti-Christian priest (1664-1729). He did not mention him again for a quarter of a century, but then came a flood of references to him, the only priest, in the mass of rascally theologians, 'who asked God's forgiveness when dying'[37] for having taught Christianity. The book he left behind him, and of which Voltaire for the first time published a part, is a thoughtful and tormented and ferocious attack on Christianity as an outrage against god and humanity.

Routine activities continued as usual: the Corneille edition, the Russian correspondence, theatrical performances. Rousseau published his *Emile*, of which Voltaire disapproved very forcefully as a whole, while just as forcefully commending one part of it, the 'profession of faith of the Savoyard parson'. Friends equally faithless to both profited from this situation by poisoning the minds of Voltaire and Rousseau against each other: a sad spectacle. The wretched Théodore Tronchin, in particular, may have been a good doctor for all I know, though one would hardly think so after reading his consultations, but he certainly had a most Calvinistic character. He encouraged the natural antagonism of the two men by quoting extracts from their letters, each at the other, and by blackguarding both to mutual friends.[38] Voltaire discussed Rousseau with several of his regular correspondents, especially with mme Du Deffand, and it was to her that he made a formal declaration on his relations with the Genevese misanthrope. In his letter he points out that Rousseau, out of the blue, had written to say that he did not like Voltaire because he gave theatrical performances and corrupted the morals of Geneva as a reward for the asylum he had been given.

36 Best.D951 (30 November 1735).
37 Best.D10039 (28 September 1761).

38 See for instance his letter to Grimm of 15 September 1762 (Best. D10707).

Such a letter from a man with whom I was not in correspondence appeared to me wonderfully mad, absurd, and offensive. How could a man who had written plays reproach me because I gave performances in my house in France? Why does he outrage me by telling me that Geneva had given me a refuge? I certainly need no refuge, and sometimes even offer asylum to others. I live on my own estates, and never go to Geneva. In a word, I cannot understand under what pretext Rousseau can have written me such a letter. He no doubt felt that he had given me offence and thought that I would avenge myself. And in this he showed that he knew me very ill.'[39]

Needless to say Rousseau was well able to keep his end up. When he received a mad letter from a crank he at once attributed it to Voltaire[40]; and soon after he composed an amusing little dialogue[41] between Voltaire and a workman, in which the former is made to appear a calumniator and a hypocrite. And thenceforth he lost no opportunity to exercise his bile at Voltaire's expense. Worse was to come. In the meanwhile he implacably vetoed an attempt at a reconciliation initiated by Moultou.[42] Voltaire, on the other hand, was always sympathetic when he heard of Rousseau's misfortunes. Thus, when the latter was in conflict with the Genevese authorities and renounced his citizenship, Voltaire wrote to Louisa Dorothea of Saxe-Gotha: 'This poor devil drags out a wretched life and the pope is a sovereign with an income of 15 millions. So wags the world.'[43]

So far as Corneille was concerned, difficulties continued to the last minute, the Académie française not finding the terms of Voltaire's dedication sufficiently respectful. But he pressed on, and the great edition was duly published, its editor supervising every detail of manufacture and distribution with all the care he had lavished on the work itself. The edition was a great success, though dissentient voices were inevitably raised. When mlle Corneille married[44] she was assured of a handsome *dot*.

Yet this period had two features of great hope: the Seven years' war finally drew (*de facto*) to an end[45], and Catherine II mounted the imperial throne of all the Russias by getting rid of

39 Best.D11951 (27 June 1764).
40 See Best.D10611 (27 July 1762).
41 Best.D10785 (30 October 1762).
42 See the correspondence quoted in a note on Best.D11114.
43 Best.D11313 (19 July 1763).

44 In February 1763; for the marriage contract see Best.app.D225.
45 To the sound of violins and the firing of rockets at a grand ball at Ferney (Best.D10918; 17 January 1763).

her husband, Peter III. Not long after, she sent a friendly message to Voltaire, subscribing to the Corneille[46]. Voltaire responded that 'Catherine the second is assuredly the unique Catherine'[47]. The empress then wrote direct to Voltaire, begging him not to praise her until she deserved his approval, and telling him how much she owed to his writings. She would like to know almost every page of the *Essai sur les mœurs* by heart.[48] Soon Catherine's image replaced that of Frederick in Voltaire's dream of a philosopher-king, an illusion fortified by the empress's offer of hospitality to the *Encyclopédie*, now banned in France. It is impressive to see how polite monarchs could be when they wanted something, especially when that something was the friendship of the eminent publicist Voltaire.

While the Calas case dragged on and work now wearily continued on Corneille, Voltaire persisted in his unavailing efforts to get *Olympie* performed in Paris. The second volume of the *Histoire de l'empire de Russie* was published, together with the new edition of the *Essai sur les mœurs*, and its *Additions*[49] as well as *Saül*, the anti-biblical play for which the young Goethe would have liked to strangle its author. The printing of the *Traité sur la tolérance* was finished, but publication was held up in order not to injure the prospects of the Calas campaign. Among the minor publications of this period were several verse *contes*[50], in which Voltaire tried his hand for the first time in a new manner, and in which he eschewed the libertinism of La Fontaine.

As if all these manifold occupations were not enough Voltaire turned to the new trade of reviewer for the *Gazette littéraire* newly established by Choiseul. Among the twenty or so books he dealt with were Algernon Sidney's republican *Discourses concerning government* (they 'cost him his life, but immortalised his memory'); lord Kames's *Elements of criticism*[51]; the *Letters of lady Mary*

46 Best.D11210 (*c.* May 1763).
47 Best.D11296 (4 July 1763).
48 Best.D11421 (*c.* September 1763).
49 A substantial volume later merged into the main work.
50 In rapid succession Voltaire wrote *Ce qui plaît aux dames* (after Dryden's imitation of Chaucer's *Wife of Bath*); *L'Education d'un prince* (on which Voltaire afterwards based his play *Le Baron d'Otrante*); *Gertrude ou l'éducation d'une fille*; *Les Trois manières* (in which three Greek girls compete to tell the most affecting love story); *Thélème et Macare* (which Alembert in Best.D11720 found charming, wise and ravishingly written).
51 See p. 154, above.

Wortley Montagu (there reigns above all in her book 'a spirit of philosophy and of liberty which characterises her nation'); the *Poems* of Charles Churchill ('satires full of bitterness, ardour and energy'); David Hume's *History of England* ('perhaps the best written in any language . . . a spirit superior to his matter, who speaks of weaknesses, errors, and barbarities as a doctor speaks of epidemic diseases'); the works of Conyers Middleton ('He is one of the most learned men and best writers of England'); and the *History of lady Julia Mandeville* [by Frances Brooke] ('perhaps the best novel of its kind to have appeared in England since *Clarissa* and *Grandisson*'[52]).

No wonder Voltaire wrote despairingly to his publisher: 'I no longer know where I am with the general history. What is your last page? Where am I? Ah, Gabriel, Gabriel, I am up to my eyes in it, history, chapters, Peter the great, the great Corneille, plays, plays to perform, plays to compose. And after all I have only one brain five inches deep'[53].

Rousseau's letter to Christophe de Beaumont and the law against inoculation produced much wry amusement, but more than ever underlying Voltaire's thoughts during this period was the wish for all lovers of toleration to unite: hence the bitter tone of his references to the 'apostate' Rousseau.

It was in the summer of this year that Gibbon, in Voltaire's house, met again Suzanne Curchod (the future mme Necker) for the first time since the breaking of their engagement five years earlier. This, however, he does not mention in his vivid description of this visit:

I made a little excursion some days ago to Geneva, not so much for the sake of the town which I had often seen before, as for a representation of Monsieur de Voltaire's. He lives now entirely at Ferney, a little place, in France but only two Leagues from Geneva. He has bought the estate and built a very pretty tho' small house upon it. After a life passed in courts and Capitals, the Great Voltaire is now become a meer country Gentleman, and even (for the honour of the profession) something of a farmer. He says he never enjoyed so much true happiness. He has got rid of most of his infirmities and tho' very old and lean, enjoys a much better state of health than he did twenty years ago. His playhouse is very neat and well contrived, situated just by his

52 Voltaire also wrote an unpublished review of Sterne's *Sermons*.

53 Best.D10842 (December 1762).

Chappel, which is far inferior to it, tho' he says himself, *que son Christ est du meilleur faiseur, de tout le pays de Gex*. The play they acted was my favourite *Orphan of China*. Voltaire himself acted *Gengis* and Madame Denys *Idamé*; but I do not know how it happened: either my taste is improved or Voltaire's talents are impaired since I last saw him: He appeared to me now a very ranting unnatural performer. Perhaps indeed As I was come from Paris, I rather judged him by an unfair comparaison, than by his own independent value. Perhaps too I was too much struck with the ridiculous figure of Voltaire at seventy acting a Tartar Conqueror with a hollow broken Voice, and making love to a very ugly niece of about fifty. The play began at eight in the evening and ended (entertainement and all) about half an hour after eleven. The whole Company was asked to stay and set Down about twelve to a very elegant supper of a hundred Covers. The supper ended about two, the company danced til four; when we broke up, got into our Coaches and came back to Geneva just as the Gates were opened. Shew me in history or fable, a famous poet of Seventy who has acted in his own plays, and has closed the scene with a supper and ball for a hundred people. I think the last is the more extraordinary of the two.[54]

A more sympathetic view is offered by John, lord Spencer, who told lord Nuneham that 'I pass'd a whole day with ye great Voltaire, & had ye luck to find him in very good humour. We went to dine with him at his country house, from which ye view is really very fine, but he has a rage of wishing to lay out every thing in ye English taste, & fancies that all he has done there is so. I accordingly when he shew'd us his place, admired everything extremely, & took notice at every *allé*, *parterre*, & *bosquet* I came to, how perfectly English it was. He in return, shew'd away as much as he could, & was very entertaining.'[55]

Yet by far the most important literary and philosophical event of this prodigiously productive period has not yet been so much as mentioned, the distantly reverberant publication of the *Dictionnaire philosophique*.

54 Edward Gibbon to Dorothea Gibbon, 6 August 1763 (Best.D11343).

55 Edward William Harcourt, ed. *The Harcourt papers* (Oxford [1889-1905]), viii.71-2.

23 The Calas family, *from the engraving by Delafosse after C. de Carmontelle*

DICTIONNAIRE

PHILOSOPHIQUE,

PORTATIF.

MDCCLXV.

24 *Dictionnaire philosophique, titlepage of an early edition, with the design representing the five senses*

35. *The* Dictionnaire philosophique, *1764*[1]

FIRST PLANNED IN BERLIN in 1752 during the last months of Voltaire's bitter-sweet stay with Frederick of Prussia, the *Dictionnaire philosophique* became one of his most cherished writings. Held up by the exile's long search for a home (the evil star that led him to Geneva caused also long prudential delays) and a thousand other activities, the first edition finally came off the press in 1764. Published a few weeks before Voltaire's seventieth birthday, it is in many ways a young man's book, angry, hard-hitting, uncompromising. Its impact was prompt, powerful and lasting. However, the most immediately perceptible though least important result was its condemnation by all the establishments, religious and governmental, drawing from Voltaire the usual flood of protestations and disavowals. However, also as usual, these disavowals were accompanied by new editions of the 'alphabetic abomination', containing additions which, like the inevitably anonymous original *Dictionnaire*, could obviously have come from no other pen than his. As we have already seen more than once, Voltaire was always happy to play the formal game of denial, as required by the unwritten laws of governmental and even ecclesiastic censorship, according to which a protestation of not guilty was accepted as evidence of innocence unless some police spy like Fréron[2] could produce positive evidence of guilt. But though Voltaire went through the motions, and gleefully played this charade of 'as if', he never unwillingly withdrew a word he had written or an opinion he had advanced.

In short, the book was condemned by the authorities, but read

---

1 This chapter, in a different form, serves also as the introduction to my translation of the *Philosophical dictionary* (Penguin ed. 1971).

2 See M. R. Bruno, 'Fréron, police spy', *Studies on Voltaire* (1976),cxlviii. 177-99.

by 'all', that is, by the few who could read and the still fewer who had access to books. 'Few', 'fewer', these are relative terms, and it would be a mistake to imagine that the French reading public in the second half of the eighteenth century comprised only a tiny élite. By no means, for the *Dictionnaire* went into numerous editions, rivalling *Candide* (published five years earlier) which sold 6000 copies in a few weeks[3].

The *Dictionnaire philosophique* is not what we now understand by a dictionary, least of all a dictionary of philosophy, for its alphabetic arrangement is little more than a literary *trompe l'œil*. This epoch-making little book is in fact a series of essays on a wide variety of subjects, sometimes arranged under convenient headings in alphabetic sequence, but sometimes placed under deliberately misleading or even provocative catchwords. Thus, under 'Catéchisme chinois', the reader will find nothing whatever about any kind of Chinese catechism, but instead he will be able to enjoy a far-reaching demonstration of the superiority of ethics over religion.

To say further that the *Dictionnaire* is even less a treatise on philosophy than a dictionary is not a paradox but, in our time, a necessary explanation. This gloss was not needed in the eighteenth century: the contemporary reader of a new work which, though anonymous, showed on every page the unmistakable hallmark of the sage of Ferney, and the titlepage of which bore the words *Dictionnaire philosophique*, knew exactly what to expect. For in the language of Voltaire and his fellow *philosophes*, a language by then quite widely understood and even accepted, the term philosophy was used in such a context in the sense of what we now call freethought or rationalism—either one a better and more accurate term than the now fashionable humanism, a word as vague as it is ambiguous. In other words, philosophy in the language of the Enlightenment was a state of mind, not a discipline of the schools. But of course the eighteenth-century use of *philosophe* in French can be as misleading as the humanism of twentieth-century English. Every time it occurs the reader has to determine whether it is being used in the general or its special sense, and the translator has to decide whether to render it as

3 See Best.D8172.

philosopher or as freethinker; and as Voltaire was rightly convinced that the only true philosopher was a *philosophe* in the
special sense, the difficulty is much compounded. Generally
speaking, what we today understand by philosophy was usually
referred to by Voltaire as metaphysics. As for our metaphysics,
he stigmatised it as nonsense. Pangloss, it will be remembered,
taught Candide metaphysico-theologo-cosmolo-nigology.

What is certain is that the *Dictionnaire philosophique* is a world
away from the academic or even the systematic. Voltaire wrote
what his preoccupied genius impelled him to write, and the result
could turn out to be a play or an epigram, a letter or a poem, a
controversial dissertation or a treatise in several volumes. If it
was a fairly short piece of 'non-fiction' in prose, he would sometimes print it as a pamphlet or even a leaflet, but more often he
would file it in a series of folders marked *Mélanges* (miscellanies).
From the contents of these folders Voltaire built up his innumerable volumes of essays, published both separately and as parts of
his various, ever more voluminous sets of collected works. When,
however, Voltaire's writings were of this kind but of a still more
precise type, consciously hortatory or propagandist, they found
their way, beginning with essays composed in 1752 and added
to thereafter without interruption until the end of his life, into
volumes eventually destined to be entitled *Dictionnaire philosophique portatif*[4] (from 1764), *Opinion par alphabet* (this title never
appeared in print), *La Raison par alphabet* (from 1769), *Dictionnaire philosophique* (from 1770), *Questions sur l'encyclopédie*[5] (from
1770).

Voltaire's wider object in publishing these works is evident,
and he made his specific purpose clear beyond a peradventure in
a lapidary remark on the great *Encyclopédie*: 'Twenty folio

4 This title, now so utterly Voltairean, was not new. A compiler and
journalist named Didier Pierre Chicaneau de Neuvillé had published in
1751 an anonymous *Dictionnaire philosophique*, which became in its second
edition a *Dictionnaire philosophique,
portatif, ou introduction à la connais-
sance de l'homme* (1756). It has no
resemblance whatever to Voltaire's

book, and I know of no evidence that
he knew it; but Voltaire knew everything and even possessed in his library
the same writer's *Considérations sur les
ouvrages d'esprit* (1758).

5 This title should always be written
thus, not with a capital *E*, for it means
Encyclopedic questions not *Questions
on the Encyclopédie* of which Diderot
was the architect.

volumes will never make a revolution. It is the little portable volumes of thirty *sous* that are to be feared. Had the gospel cost twelve hundred sesterces the Christian religion would never have been established'[6].

Voltaire acted on this conviction. His alphabetic essays, dialogues, skits and other papers, and even more the mixed volumes containing them, vary in tone and emphasis, but all quickly became enormously popular in their collected forms, and were frequently revised and reprinted. Some of these editions were prepared under Voltaire's supervision, but most often they were pirated by the booksellers. They are interrelated in so complicated a pattern that it would be a considerable critical and bibliographical enterprise to disentangle the various states of many of the texts. So one cannot but sympathise with Condorcet and Beaumarchais. When, after the great man's death, they were preparing the so-called Kehl edition of his works they were confronted with a vast mass of miscellaneous material, most of it in print, but some left by Voltaire only in manuscript. Unwilling or unable to cope with it logically, or even, it must be said, intelligently, and finding that a good deal of it could be forced into an alphabetic semblance, they poured as much as they could into a vast cornucopia for which they purloined the label *Dictionnaire philosophique* which had been used by Voltaire for a very different kind of work, short and cheap.

It is true that in adopting this desperate procedure they imitated up to a point Voltaire's own example, for he was decidedly casual in such matters, like most of his contemporaries. Yet Beaumarchais and his collaborators went far beyond anything authorised by Voltaire's practices. Indeed, the title they used was even less justified since they included a great deal of not even ostensibly alphabetic material, and even a complete book (the *Lettres philosophiques* or *English letters*) that has nothing remotely alphabetic about it, to say nothing of many long essays, and contributions published or intended for Diderot's *Encyclopédie*. For good measure they also went so far as to throw in a number of lexicographic notes written for the *Dictionnaire de l'Académie*. All this makes up the wretched and unnaturally distended rag-bag which

6 Best.D13235 (5 April 1762).

is nowadays accepted as Voltaire's *Dictionnaire philosophique*.

As I have said, the original *Dictionnaire philosophique* was repeatedly condemned by the civil and religious authorities in several countries, but nowhere with more congenial venom than in Geneva, whose unco guid still hate Voltaire. Thus, when the *procureur général* (public prosecutor) of that little town, Jean Robert Tronchin, was asked by the city council in 1764 to state his opinion of Voltaire's book, with a view to a prosecution, his very long report[7] described it as a 'deplorable monument of the extent to which intelligence and erudition can be abused'. Among the terms the *procureur* used to describe the *Dictionnaire* are 'baneful paradoxes', 'indiscreet researches', 'audacious criticism', 'errors, malignity and indecency', 'contagious poison', 'temerarious, impious, scandalous, destructive of revelation', and so on and on. The book was to the end included in the unlamented official Roman index of forbidden books. This fate was only to be expected, and indeed it can almost be said to have been invited, for Voltaire deliberately planned the *Dictionnaire* as a revolutionary book, in which the most liberal ideas were to be expressed openly and lucidly, and made available to all who could read. Most decidedly Voltaire did not regard himself as a 'harmless drudge': his intention was to be as harmful as possible to superstition and all forms of conventional thought. Dangerous undertaking! Did not the presence of the *Dictionnaire* among the books of the chevalier de La Barre contribute to his frightful execution for blasphemy?

The *Dictionnaire philosophique* also provoked widespread condemnation by the Jesuits and other religious polemists. The abbé Louis Maïeul Chaudon's *Dictionnaire antiphilosophique* (re-named even more explicitly *Anti-dictionnaire philosophique*), first published in 1767, went into several editions. Three years later appeared *Observations sur la Philosophie de l'histoire et sur le Dictionnaire portatif* and a *Dictionnaire philosophico-théologique portatif*, respectively by the abbés Laurent François and Aimé Paulian. The egregious Nonotte contributed his mite in four volumes entitled *Dictionnaire philosophique de la religion* (1772). Voltaire's general purpose being to undermine credulity, all

7 Best.D12093 (20 September 1764).

these attacks and many more of the same kind can be ignored. It is more interesting to see whether Voltaire's more precise intentions in launching the *Portatif* can be determined from the contents of the little book. Here is a list of the articles contained in the first edition of 1764 (in French these are of course in alphabetical sequence): Abraham; Soul; Friendship; Love; Socratic love; Self-love; Angel; Anthropophagi; Apis; Apocalypse; Atheist; Atheism; Baptism; Beautiful; Beauty; Beasts; Good, sovereign good; All is good; Limits of human understanding; Character; Certain, certainty; Chain of events; Chain of created beings; the Heaven of the ancients; Circumcision; Body; China; Chinese catechism; Japanese catechism; Catechism of the clergy; Historical researches on Christianity; Convulsions; Criticism; Destiny; God; Equality; Hell; State, government (which is the best?); Ezekiel; Fables; Fanaticism; Falsity of human virtues; End, final causes; Folly; Fraud; Glory; War; Grace; History of the Jewish kings and paralipomena; Idol, idolator, idolatry; Flood; Jephte, or sacrifices of human blood; Joseph; Freewill; Laws; Civil and ecclesiastic laws; Luxury; Matter; Wicked; Messiah; Metamorphosis; Metempsychosis; Miracles; Moses; Fatherland; Peter; Prejudices; Religion; Resurrection; Solomon; Feeling; Dreams; Superstition; Tyranny; Tolerance; Virtue.

It is clear that Voltaire's preoccupations in the first *Dictionnaire philosophique* were overwhelmingly theological and philosophical. Indeed, although we have seen that it is not a systematic treatise, the *Portatif* does contain preponderantly philosophical writing in the widest sense. This is evident in the articles themselves even more than in their titles, which, I repeat, do not always define very exactly the texts that follow them. Even such essays as 'Friendship' and 'Beautiful' have religious or ethical overtones. And this tendency is strongly confirmed by the second edition of 1765, in which Voltaire added articles entitled Abbé; Confession; Dogmas; False intelligence; Faith; War; Idea; Letters, men of letters; Martyr; Paul; Priest; Sect; Superstition II; Theist; Theologian.

Voltaire's treatment of the religious subjects, indeed of all subjects, is above all scientific: that is, he was concerned to establish the truth. Here and elsewhere his first question is always: did an

alleged event really occur? He never fell into the universal theological error of examining a thing before knowing whether it
exists. This fact explains what so many people find disconcerting:
the destructiveness of Voltaire's writings on religion. This negative kind of approach is no longer necessary, thanks very largely
to Voltaire himself. Besides, in the twentieth century mere facts
have become almost irrelevant: theologians have learned the subtle
art of selective symbology. Educated laymen, of course, learned
it even more quickly.

One of the bitterest complaints made by the *procureur général*
of Geneva was that Voltaire quoted from the *Bible* passages which
'taken literally would be unworthy of Divine Majesty'. Tronchin,
mercifully for him, was not conscious of the fact that he had himself swallowed a large dose of the 'contagious poison' of Voltaire's
thought, and had been affected by it to an extent amply revealed
by the innocent confession I have just quoted. It must be remembered that it was then quite exceptional even to envisage the mere
possibility that there could be things in holy writ considered unworthy of 'Divine Majesty', or that these things could be taken in
any other way than literally. Indeed, when the *Dictionnaire* was
first published men were still simple and logical enough to believe
that scriptures proclaimed to be sacred and inspired must be taken
to mean what they say. They could not but hold it to be blasphemous to select for belief what was convenient to believe, and
to ignore or 'interpret' the rest. Voltaire often satirises this tendency, as when he inquires in 'Pierre' whether, if a reference to
Babylon is interpreted to mean Rome, we must assume, when
Rome is really named, that Babylon is in fact intended. At the end
of 'Prophètes' Voltaire makes a sustained attack on this kind of
selective pseudo-symbolism. He sums up in 'Résurrection': 'To
give clear passages arbitrary meanings is the surest way to prevent
people from understanding each other, or rather to be regarded
by honest people as people of bad faith.'

The fundamental task of the freethinker was therefore to throw
the light of reason into this murky backwater of belief, an undertaking well within Voltaire's capacity and knowledge, to say
nothing of his courage.

In most cases it was of course impossible for Voltaire to

determine positively whether or not a given Biblical narrative was historically true, and often this is still impossible. But he always tried to establish the truth in the light of the available facts. Whether or not he succeeded, he never wavered in the scientific certainty that the effort should be made. And if he felt unable to arrive at any conclusion he did not hesitate to admit his ignorance.

Having pushed the factual investigation as far as he could, Voltaire proceeded to a second inquiry: even if the Biblical story is true, were the events depicted good? In other words, Voltaire added an ethical judgement to a primary scientific evaluation. The whole of his work, in the *Dictionnaire philosophique* as in all his writings, is indeed an illustration of his notion of reason: the search for the true and the good. This general idea can be even more briefly subsumed: Voltaire's master idea, one can almost speak of an obsession, was the notion of justice, for to him that which is just is that which is true and good. It is not too much to say that Voltaire was also obsessed by man's ignorance of himself, his world and his universe.

These being Voltaire's guiding principles, and his interests being universal, it was inevitable that the range of subjects treated in the *Dictionnaire philosophique* should steadily widen, until it finally took in nearly everything of 'philosophical' interest in the widest possible sense. Thus it was that Voltaire's little 'portable' finally came to have profound influence on men's thinking in all fields of reflection and public policy.

The very first words of the first edition of the *Dictionnaire philosophique* characterise the whole: 'Abraham is one of the names famous in Asia Minor and in Arabia, like Thoth among the Egyptians, the first Zoroaster in Persia, Hercules in Greece, Orpheus in Thrace, Odin among the northern nations, and so many others whose fame is greater than the authenticity of their history'. This opening paragraph appears to us simple, direct, innocuous: but this is only because we have completely absorbed the Voltairean idiom and mode of thought. In the middle of the eighteenth century all readers were staggered, and most of them horrified, to find so distinguished and respectable a Biblical personage as Abraham quietly classed, without fuss or apology, with pagan and even mythological figures who are described as more famous than authentic. Voltaire then added that he of course, though perhaps not quite consistently, excluded from this category the Jews, about whose history he felt as he must, since it had manifestly been written by the holy ghost in person. This double irony emphasised what was being denied, and it served also to underline the revolutionary nature of his comparative and critical method of religious investigation.

Voltaire goes on to explain that he is concerned only with the Arabs (he means the Mohammedans—for he hardly distinguished between them), who boast of their descent from Abraham. Yet, as he shows all that is doubtful about this claim, he cannot but demonstrate also the doubtful historicity of the Jewish patriarch, and the mistakes and contradictions of the references to him in the *Bible*. Of course Voltaire does not expect the reader to follow him blindly; he concludes his original article on Abraham by referring the reader to the many volumes published to resolve the difficulties: 'They are all written by delicate wits and discerning minds, excellent philosophers, unprejudiced, no pedants'.

Such was always, in a literary sense, Voltaire's method: he tried to ascertain the facts, then drew ethical conclusions from them, and finally presented these conclusions with the lucidity and elegant irony which were the secrets of his unique style. In the *Dictionnaire philosophique* Voltaire did indeed follow his own precepts: 'I think the best way to fall on the infamous is to seem to have no wish to attack it; to disentangle a little chaos of antiquity; to try to make these things rather interesting; to make ancient history as agreeable as possible; to show how much we have been misled in all things; to demonstrate how much is modern in things thought to be ancient, and how ridiculous are many things alleged to be respectable; to let the reader draw his own conclusions'[8]. What was the 'infamous'? Here Voltaire clearly means Christianity. Was this always what he intended? That is another story[9].

No wonder Alembert begged for another copy of the 'dictionary of Satan' which had issued from the 'printing press of Beelzebub'; and that Grimm widely distributed this 'precious *vade mecum* which all the elect should carry in their pockets'. Voltaire, I repeat, was of course obliged to disavow the book, which he did

8 Best.D11978 (9 July 1764).   9 See p. 412-413, above.

481

frequently and energetically. His view was always that the infamous should be crushed but that the hand which did the crushing should remain unknown[10]. His friends agreed, and anyway it appeared to them obvious from internal evidence that the *Dictionnaire* had at least four authors: Beelzebub, Astaroth, Lucifer and Asmodeus, whom the angelic doctor (saint Thomas Aquinas) had so ably demonstrated not to be consubstantial one with the other. Voltaire himself from the very beginning accepted the title of 'theologian of Beelzebub'[11], but the article 'Théologien' is a rather more faithful self-portrait of the author of the *Dictionnaire philosophique.*

One is struck by Voltaire's high standards of accuracy in his search for historical truth. To be sure, modern notions of textual fidelity were unknown in the eighteenth century. The words Voltaire places within quotation marks are not always accurate or even direct quotations. True, they are seldom so inaccurate as those quoted by, say, Montesquieu or Diderot, but still every quotation has to be checked, especially as Voltaire often relied on his wonderful memory, as can be seen in his *Notebooks.* On the other hand, an intrinsically interesting point has to be made before one condemns Voltaire: it will be found that often, when Voltaire has been criticised by the devout for misquoting the *Bible,* he has in fact faithfully translated the Latin Vulgate, which he regarded (wrongly, as we now know) as the best available text.

However, when it comes to objective facts, Voltaire can seldom be faulted. Even his references to sources are usually accurate, a rare thing in the eighteenth century. In his Introduction (p. xxiii) to his edition of Voltaire's *Essai sur les mœurs* (1963) René Pomeau has analysed the references to authorities in sample sections of that wonderful book[12]. The results are remarkable: 351 substantially accurate references, 32 wrong or unverifiable ones have been counted. This compares very favourably indeed with his contemporaries, and not unfavourably with a great many more recent scholars.

10 Best.D12208(25 November 1764).
11 Best.D5053 (October/November 1752).
12 See also his 'La Documentation de Voltaire dans le *Dictionnaire philo-*

sophique', Quaderni francesi (Napoli 1970), i.395-405. But Byron found Voltaire 'dreadfully inaccurate frequently', *e. g. Letters and journals* (1976), v.199, 215.

Moreover, Voltaire's knowledge of these sources can justly be described as exceptional, both in the *Essai* and the *Dictionnaire*. Specialists had of course read more widely in their own fields. Those who knew the Biblical languages enjoyed an evident advantage, but they were very few. On the other hand Voltaire read English and Italian fluently, and Latin of course, and above all, if his reading was deep only in limited fields, it was amazingly wide. This is reflected, for instance, in his vocabulary, possibly unsurpassed by any other French writer, other, of course, than those who were specialists.

It is not too difficult to know what Voltaire had read. His own works, his library, his letters provide ample evidence. What is more difficult is to evaluate all this information in eighteenth century terms. A few generalisations can be ventured. The English reader will take Voltaire's Biblical quotations and references as matters of course. But the position on the other side of the Channel was different. Indeed, Voltaire probably knew the *Bible* better than any other layman in France, and better even than most ecclesiastics. It must be remembered that Rome discouraged, and still discourages, the reading of the *Bible*.

As for the secondary sources, such as the church fathers. Voltaire read some of them at first-hand, others in such works as Louise Ellies Du Pin's *Bibliothèque des auteurs ecclésiastiques* and Augustin Calmet's *Commentaire littéral sur tous les livres de l'Ancien et du Nouveau testament*. And he also obtained much information from experts and even, in non-theological fields, from eye-witnesses, for he knew everybody. Many of his more than 1800 known correspondents were exposed to his insatiable curiosity and passion for authenticity.

Voltaire's scrupulous exactitude is amusingly illustrated by his account of the miracles of saint Francis Xavier. In 'Convulsions' he says that this Jesuit missionary 'exhausted the society's grace by resuscitating nine dead men by exact count'. Now Voltaire's library catalogue shows that he possessed a copy of *La Vie de saint François Xavier* (1754) by the Jesuit Dominique Bouhours. He described this book on the titlepage of his copy as 'a masterpiece of fanatical folly', for he was a passionate annotator, and his library contains many hundreds of his marginalia, very few of which have yet been published. It was in Bouhours that Voltaire found the story of the nine miracles attributed to the future saint. In 'Miracles' the number was reduced to eight, no doubt an error of memory—yet not, as might have been expected from a man holding his views, an error of exaggeration. However, when he was writing 'Christianisme' Voltaire extended his researches, as can be seen from a passage towards the end of that essay: 'Saint Francis Xavier, who carried the holy gospel to India and Japan when the Portuguese went there to search for merchandise, performed a very large number of miracles, all attested by the reverend Jesuit fathers. Some say that he resuscitated nine dead men, but the reverend father Ribadeneyra limits himself to saying in his *Flower of the saints*[13] that he resuscitated four: which is quite enough'. The reference is perfectly correct. What minute computation of non-events!

And when it comes to things verifiable and to contemporary history it is enough to say that Voltaire is a reliable guide. Thus, all the books and events mentioned in 'Etats, gouvernments' were intimately known to him. However, though it is so obvious it must still be repeated that the words 'verifiable' and 'contemporary' are used in the context of more than two hundred years ago: Voltaire must not be blamed because he had no access to the authentic Pali and Chinese classics, which were then for the most part known only in the original languages, and often as mere titles.

The literary methods used by Voltaire to sweeten the bitter pill of reason or to shock the reader into swallowing it, are varied, complex, and often very subtle. Everybody knows that admiral Byng was executed to encourage others. Why has this witticism become so famous? Because it is a firmly rooted superstition that society punishes offenders to discourage the others. Hence every time a reader encounters Voltaire's 'encourage' he is startled, stops, reads again, and perhaps begins to think and wonder.[14]

These little shocks are felt on every page of the *Dictionnaire*. Each paragraph of 'Concile', for instance, administers one. Thus, Voltaire tells us that 600 bishops 'after four months of quarrels, unanimously deprived Jesus of his consubstantiality'. Every word

---

13 Voltaire possessed a French translation of this book.

14 See p. 400-401, above.

is a dart. 'Deprived'? The contemporary reader at once reflected that these men were bishops *because* Jesus is the son of god. If he is divine is it for his servants to take away or to award him his essential nature? Besides, if they quarrelled for four months the bishops must have disagreed pretty deeply. How then could their unkind deprivation have been unanimous? They must have compromised. A compromise about an eternal verity? If Voltaire had said all this, his essay would have been merely another contribution to Christian polemics. But by stating the implications in this particular way, in these particular words, he made the inevitable conclusion as it were melt into the reader's consciousness by means of the reasoning that follows empathy—what is vulgarly called intuition.

A still more subtle procedure can be seen in the immediately preceding paragraph of 'Concile': 'It is reported in the supplement of the council of Nicaea that the fathers, being very perplexed to know which were the cryphal or apocryphal books of the Old and New Testaments, put them all pell-mell on an altar, and the books to be rejected fell to the ground. It is a pity that this elegant procedure has not survived.' The attention of the reader is at once pulled up by the amusing invention 'cryphal', and he is thus made even more receptive by this pregnant pause to the shocking character of the grotesque anecdote that follows, and Voltaire's ironic comment on it.

This kind of treatment often goes beyond the mere surface of the words. Our thinking, as mirrored by the words we use, is too often painfully banal. Clichés become polished to invisibility by incessant use. It is so commonplace to say that man makes god in his own image, that the implications of the words are no longer felt. Voltaire knew exactly how to remedy this: by defining man in a particular way the contrast becomes shocking, and arrests the attention, and so we get: 'Two-legged, featherless animals[15], how long will you make god in your image?'

This oblique way of obliging the reader to make his own case is occasionally replaced by a direct exhortation. So in 'Prêtre' Voltaire exclaims: 'What things could be said about all this!

---

15 Voltaire particularly liked this image, and frequently used it.

Reader, it is for you to say them to yourself' or when he ends 'Sensation' with the injunction: 'What are we to conclude from all this? You who read and think, conclude'. Sometimes this kind of approach is overwhelmed by a thunderclap, all the more devastating by being so rare and so, as it were, out of character. Every so often Voltaire's indignation does indeed become uncontrollable, leaving no room for literary and rhetorical devices. He begins by guffawing at 'the humbug we are told about the martyrs', but as he goes on he becomes more and more indignant, and finally bursts out: 'Do you want good, well-attested barbarities? good well-authenticated massacres? rivers of blood that really ran? fathers, mothers, husbands, women, children at the breast really butchered and piled upon each other? Persecuting monsters [Christians], seek these truths only in your annals: you will find them in the crusades against the Albigensians, in the massacres of Mérindol and Cabrières, in the appalling day of saint Bartholomew, in the Irish massacres, in the valley of the Waldenses. . . .'. Note the 'good' barbarities, the 'good' massacres. This passage is immediately preceded by yet another example of the 'shocking' word: a little boy was condemned to have his tongue cut out because he stuttered; the emperor's chief physician, adds Voltaire, 'had the decency to perform the operation himself'.

The first of these nerve-tingling blows is struck without a moment's delay, for proper receptivity is produced by the very first amusingly satirical sentence of the book, that on Abraham, quoted above.

Let there be no doubt about it, all these techniques were deliberate, self-conscious, meditated. Voltaire did not write his masterpieces by accident, as some have maintained. A thousand passages could be quoted in proof. In a letter of 1764, the year that saw the first publication of the *Dictionnaire philosophique*, he wrote to his disciple, the marquis d'Argence: 'I implore you, my dear sir, not to argue with obstinate people. Opposition always irritates them instead of enlightening them; they jib, they get to hate those whose opinions are cited against them: argument has never convinced anyone. They can be made to change their minds only by being made to think for themselves, by appearing to share their doubts, by leading them as it were by the hand without their being aware of it'[16]. And Voltaire even printed the same sentiments in the preface of an early edition of the *Dictionnaire*, though of course in a less outspoken form: 'The most useful books are those to which the readers contribute half; they develop the ideas presented to them in seed; they correct what appears to them to be defective, and strengthen by their reflections what seems to them to be weak'[17].

Another aspect of Voltaire's mind and style, for the two things are inseparable, must strike the reader: his acute sense of humour, very nearly unique in the French Enlightenment. Examples can be found on nearly every page. If I single out this one it is because its secondary implications may escape the modern reader. In 'Prophètes' Voltaire writes: 'It is thought that king Amaziah had the prophet Amos's teeth drawn to prevent him from talking. In fact it is not absolutely impossible to speak without teeth. Very talkative old and toothless ladies have been known. But a prophecy must be pronounced distinctly, and a toothless prophet is not listened to with the respect that is his due'. Here Voltaire's fun did not spare himself: by this time he had lost all his teeth, and he could safely assume that this fact was known to 'everybody'.

It was Voltaire who taught the world the lesson beyond price, that high seriousness is not merely compatible with a sense of humour, but runs with it in tandem with elegance and speed. Bernard Shaw and Bertrand Russell were among those who acknowledged that they had learned that lesson at his knee. Voltaire is indeed one of the most *enjoyable* of all great writers. 'Unless you have signed a pact with the infamous, I defy you to not to admire, not to love Voltaire.'[18]

---

16 Best.D11769 (14 March 1764).
17 These two quotations have also been used by Jeanne R. Monty, *Etude sur le style polémique de Voltaire: le* *Dictionnaire philosophique* (Studies on Voltaire, xliv: 1966), p. 176.
18 [René] Etiemble, *Mes contrepoisons* (Paris 1974), p. 182.

36. The end of some chapters, 1764-1766

MORE THAN ONE CHAPTER now closed. The publication of the *Dictionnaire philosophique* brought to fruition twelve years of reflection and research. The massive corpus of the annotated Corneille was the crown of an enterprise in which Voltaire's erudition, benevolence and acumen joined to achieve a massive success. The setting aside of the judgment against Calas ended years of incessant effort by the old gentleman, of which he often wearied. He was exasperated by the way in which the case dragged on, complaining that 'it seems easier to break people on the wheel than to do justice to innocence'[1]. But he persisted, writing hundreds of letters, a dozen pamphlets, and one substantial book, the *Traité sur la tolérance*. Written in 1762, but not published for tactical reasons until 1764[2], it takes as its point of departure the juridical assassination of Jean Calas, but then broadens out into a comprehensive examination of intolerance through the ages.

Voltaire points out at the outset that public opinion puts up with 'the inevitable fatality of war', because the dead at least fall with weapons in their hands—luckily Voltaire did not live to see what improvements the twentieth century has made in this respect. But 'if the accused has no defence but his virtue; if the arbiters of his life in murdering him risk only a mistake; if they can kill with impunity by decree, then the public cries out'. This is why Voltaire took up the case, and this is why he wrote his treatise on toleration, in which he concludes, in utilitarian terms, that men's errors are crimes only if they disturb society, and this happens only when the errors are due to fanaticism. Men must therefore cease to be fanatics in order to merit toleration.[3] 'May

---

1 Best.D11726 (28 February 1764).
2 A few copies reached Paris in December 1763.

3 Ch.xviii.

all men remember that they are brothers! May they abhor the tyranny which seeks to enslave the mind. . . !'[4]

Having unburdened himself of the *Traité sur la tolérance*, and brought to so remarkable an end his campaign against religious fanaticism sustained by judicial partiality, Voltaire merely remarked that the bones of poor Calas has been broken for all that —and at once began to widen his attack on injustice. The name of Sirven came to the fore. This was a case less fearful in its consequences—for luckily it came to Voltaire's notice in time—but even more preposterous juridically. Elisabeth, one of the daughters of Pierre Paul Sirven, had been kidnapped and handed over to the bishop of Castres, who tried by violence to convert her to Roman Catholicism. She went mad under this benevolence, was released, and was later found dead in a well (4 January 1762). The Calas case was then notorious, yet the Sirvens were accused, the father and mother were condemned to death, and the two remaining daughters were ordered to witness the execution of their parents, and then to be exiled. However, warned in time, all four succeeded, with much suffering, in making their escape to Ferney. Voltaire at first played for time, but as soon as the Calas family was definitely rehabilitated, he took up the Sirven case with all his usual energy. For technical reasons the struggle was particularly difficult, and it was not until November 1771 that the Sirven family was acquitted, in the terms of the decree, of the 'false and calumnious accusation brought against them'. These official terms might seem conclusive but even so the Sirvens' rehabilitation was not completed until 11 May 1775.

Voltaire was much affected by the deaths of mme de Pompadour and Algarotti[5], by the vision of death in its most horrible aspects in such cases as that of Calas and the incessant wars, and by his own seventieth birthday. Yet this man, so often accused by his enemies of living in fear of death, wrote at this time an admirable letter to mme Du Deffand, who had complained that life was too short. He agreed, but he also agreed with Seneca and La Fontaine that it was better to suffer than to die.

I agree with you that life is very short, and quite unhappy; but I must

4 Ch.xxiii.

5 He contributed an obituary of his old friend to the *Gazette littéraire*.

tell you that a member of my household is a relation of twenty-three, hand-some, well-built, vigorous, and this is what happened to him.

One day he fell from his horse while hunting, and hurt his thigh a little. A small incision was made, and there he is paralysed for the rest of his life, not paralysed in one part of his body, but so paralysed that he cannot use any of his limbs, cannot raise his head, with the absolute certainty that there can never be any improvement. He has got used to his condition, and loves life to folly. . . .

As to death, I beg that we may reason a little. It is very certain that we do not feel it at all, it is not a painful moment, it resembles sleep like two drops of water, all that gives us pain is the idea that we shall not awaken. What is horrible is the apparatus of death, it is the barbarism of extreme unction, it is the cruelty of warning us that all is over. . . . It is sometimes said that a man dies like a dog, but really a dog is very happy to die without all the abominable paraphernalia with which the last moments of our lives are persecuted. . . .[6]

Indeed, more than by thoughts of mortality, Voltaire was afflicted by the publication, unauthorised of course, of the first considerable collection of his letters[7], which set the pattern for nearly all future compilations of Voltaire's correspondence in its utter disregard for authenticity and accuracy. He also continued to have difficulties with the duke of Wurttemberg, and was finally obliged to buy another annuity so as to make sure of receiving his payments on the first. But none of these worries, nor his entry into his eighth decade, in the least affected Voltaire's light touch and unerring ear for words, as can be seen from this letter to Arthur Hill-Trevor:

This is my answer to the *anonime* letter j have receiv'd.

If it is reported in a pamphlet impos'd upon me, that a minister of state under Charles the second, was a candid and good husband to two wives at once, and that he wrote a pretty book on those patriarcal good manners, j know neither that pamphlet nor that statesman, but j should be very glad to peruse the pretended book writ on the plurality of wives, tho j am no way concern'd in the business of poligamy or bigamy or even monogamy.[8]

---

6 Best.D11866 (9 May 1764); the sick man to whom Voltaire gave a home was Charles Hyacinthe Daumart, son of his second cousin.

7 *Lettres secrettes de mr. de Voltaire* (Genève 1765); this volume actually appeared towards the end of 1764.

8 Best.D11758 (8 March 1764). As a matter of fact, Voltaire's memory misled him, as he soon realised (see Best.D11767), for in the 1761 edition of the *Essai sur les mœurs* (ch. cxxx) he had written: 'Trevor [in later editions altered to Cowper], chancellor of England under Charles II, secretly married a second wife, by consent of the first;

It may be doubted whether Boswell's visit provided adequate consolation in this sea of troubles, but the letter[9] to mme Denis in which he wheedled an invitation to Ferney must be quoted:

I address myself to you, Madam, as to the friend of the Stranger. I have the honour of knowing you to be such from most agreable experience; for, yesterday at dinner you not only entertained me with easy and chearful conversation, but took care that I should have a double portion of the sweet tart which I am so extremely fond of. You may remember, Madam, that I exprest my affection for that dish in the strongest manner; Je suis attaché à la Tourte; I spoke in character; for I spoke with that honest frankness with which I declare my sentiments on great & on small occasions. At no time shall I ever deny by Faith, my friend, my mistress or my tart[10].

I present myself in my natural character, which I find suits me the best of any. I own that I have in some periods of my life assumed the characters of others whom I admired: But, as David found the armour of Saul, I found them by much too heavy for me, and like David was embarrassed, and unable to move with freedom. I hope, Madam, I may be allowed to quote the old Testament once to the niece of a Gentleman who has quoted it so often.

I do not however think lightly of my own character. No, Madame, I am proud enough. The French say: Fier comme un Ecossois; It shall not be my fault if that Proverb goes out of use.

I must beg your interest, Madam, in obtaining for me a very great favour from M. de Voltaire. I intend to have the honour of returning to Ferney Wednesday or Thursday. The gates of this sober City shut at a most early, I had very near said a most absurd hour, so that one is obliged to post away after dinner, before the illustrious Landlord has had time to shine upon his Guests. Besides I believe M. de Voltaire is in opposition to our Sun, for he rises in the evening. Yesterday he shot forth some rays. Some bright sparks fell from him. I am happy to have seen so much. But I greatly wish to behold him in full blaze.

Is it then possible, Madam, that I may be allowed to lodge one night under the roof of M. de Voltaire? I am a hardy & vigourous Scot. You may mount me to the highest & coldest Garret. I shall not even refuse to sleep upon two chairs in the Bedchamber of your maid. I saw her pass thro' the room where we sat before dinner.

I beg you may let me know if the favour which I ask is granted, that I may

he wrote a little book in favour of polygamy, and lived happily with his two wives.' Voltaire not only maintained this statement, but repeated it in the *Honnêtetés littéraires*, XXII.ix. He may have heard the story of the alleged bigamy of William Cowper, first earl Cowper, from Swift, who seems to have been responsible for giving it currency (in the *Examiner*, xvii, xxii). What is certain is that Cowper did not publish a book in favour of polygamy.

9 Best.D12258 (25 December 1764).

10 No pun was intended, for at this time the word had only its gastronomic meaning.

bring a nightcap with me. I would not presume to think of having my head honoured with a nightcap of M. de Voltaire. I should imagine that like the invisible cap of Fortunatus, or that of some other celebrated magician, it would immediately convey to me the qualitys of it's master; and I own to you Madam, my head is not strong enough to bear them. His Poetical cap I might perhaps support; but, his Philosophical one would make me so giddy, that I should not know which way to turn myself. All I can offer in return for the favour which I ask is many many thanks; or if M. de Voltaire's delicate french ear would not be offended, I might perhaps offer him a few good rough english verses. Pray, Madam, give me your interest. I would also beg the Assistance of my Reverend Father the young man of sixty, The Student of our language, the disbanded soldier of the Company of Jesus. Sure a Lady and a Priest must prevail.

Voltaire replied (in the name of his niece): 'You will do us much honour and pleasure, we have few beds, but you will not sleep on two chairs. My uncle, tho very sick, hath guess'd at y^r merit. J know it more, because j have seen you longer.'[11] Unfortunately Boswell's stay was of little interest to posterity: he was too overawed to speak to Voltaire as he spoke to Rousseau and even to Johnson, and instead engaged his host in a highfaluting conversation about natural religion. Boswell found Voltaire's talk the most brilliant he had ever heard.[12] He wrote again, still trying to tempt Voltaire into 'lofty conversation'. But the old man was not to be seduced:

My distempers and my bad eyes do not permit me to ansuver with that celerity and exactness that my duty and my heart require. You seem sollicitous about that pretty thing call'd soul. J do protest you j know nothing of it. Nor wether it is, nor what it is, nor what it shall be. Young scholars, and priests know all that perfectly. For my part j am but a very ignorant fellow.

Let it be what it will, j assure you my soul has a great regard for your own when you will make a turn into our deserts, you shall find me (if alive) ready to show you my respect and obsequiousness.[13]

In his reply Boswell told Voltaire that 'abstracting from your fame, I venerate you for your antiquity'[14]. This ambiguous compliment seems to have discouraged Voltaire, and Boswell could not extract any further letter from Ferney.

11 Best.D12259 (25 December 1764).
12 He says so, with ineffable tact, in a letter to Rousseau of 31 December 1764.
13 Best.D12397 (11 February 1765).
14 Best.D12525 (4 April 1765).

Another episode came to an end at this time. In recent years Voltaire, disgusted with the behaviour of the Genevese, whose unctuous moralisings differed so vastly from their behaviour, had lived less and less at the Délices, and though he still served as an occasional intermediary between Choiseul and Geneva[15], in 1765 he sold this whilom house of Aristippus and garden of Epicurus. Voltaire's decision was well-timed, for there now began another period of political trouble in Geneva, or rather, for these troubles were incessant, a period of their outward and visible manifestation, leading even to violence. By 1766 little short of civil war had broken out in Geneva between the forces of reaction and those which were liberal only by contrast. Voltaire's efforts to make peace were hopeless, for interference by one who, however eminent, was after all a private foreigner, was even less welcome to Genevese xenophobia than official mediation. If it was tolerated at all it was only because somehow or other the Genevese quarrels were mixed up with jurisdictional troubles in Gex and with the usual difficulties with Rousseau, in both of which Voltaire was intimately concerned. The 'guerre de Genève' may well have bored Choiseul to tears, as he admitted, but Voltaire did not weary in his efforts to bring the parties together. Although he had now become more prudent in his methods, he was no more successful, and continued to be in trouble with both the French and the Genevese authorities. The confused state of mind of the latter is illustrated by a despatch from their representative in Paris, who recommended them not to use Voltaire as an intermediary, giving two mutually contradictory reasons: first, because Voltaire had no influence; second, because he would do great harm if he wrote against Geneva[16]. This so typically Genevese opinion reminds one of a story told by an oriental sage: a woman sued her neighbour because she had returned a pot in a damaged condition. The defence was that no pot had been borrowed, that it was already damaged when received, and that it was in perfect condition when returned.

Fortunately Voltaire was now out of reach of Genevese resentment. Henceforth he was to be the patriarch only of Ferney. And indeed, as soon as it became known that the great man was in

15 Best.D11643 (15 January 1764). 16 See a note on Best.D13029.

continuous residence there visits to Geneva from distinguished foreigners diminished and those to nearby Ferney became more and more numerous. Among the most interesting guests entertained by Voltaire at this time were mlle Clairon and Damilaville. The actress's passage inevitably led to much theatrical activity, which in its turn stimulated Voltaire to take more interest than usual in the revivals of his plays at the Comédie française.

The tiresome controversies concerning the *Dictionnaire philosophique* continued unabated, for the book was still being condemned on every hand, and going into numerous editions. So did the discussions concerning Voltaire's relations with Rousseau, largely in correspondence with Alembert, whose book on the Jesuits Voltaire saw through the press. Voltaire's admiration for Catherine knew no bounds when he heard that the empress had bought Diderot's library, leaving him in possession of it during his lifetime, a regal gesture indeed even if the motives that inspired it were not altogether pure. 'Who would have thought fifty years ago that one day the Scyths would so nobly recompense in Paris the virtue, the knowledge, the philosophy treated by us so shamefully.'[17]

This period continued to be one of the most prolific of Voltaire's life. He initiated the great quarto edition of his collected works, but this was a mere parergon, for at this time he wrote and published several of his most important works. The *Philosophie de l'histoire*[18] is not a philosophy of history, nor an introduction to universal history: it is a handbook of history for the use of free-thinkers. In other words, it is not what Voltaire himself would have regarded as a piece of historical writing, which must be objective and impartial. By this I do not mean that Voltaire distorted the narrative. On the contrary, he went to a great deal of trouble to get his facts right, plunging into folios the very titles of which made him tremble[19]. But, as every universal historian must, he chose to follow those threads which led to the point at which he wanted to arrive. How dangerous such a method

17 Best.D12568 (24 April 1765).
18 A critical edition by J. H. Brumfitt forms volume 59 (1968) of the *Complete works*.

19 Best.D11985 (13 July 1764).

can be has been demonstrated by professor Toynbee in his *Study of history*, following, at a distance, in the footsteps of Bossuet. But the truth was safe in Voltaire's hands.

The book begins with geology, goes on to ethnology, and then plunges into a discussion of the beginnings of philosophy and religion. A survey of history from its earliest times follows, down to the decadence of the Romans. The essential theme is defined in Voltaire's theory of the origin of religion. The idea of god as we understand it is not held by Voltaire to be innate, it is the product of reason or revelation. Primitive religion is explained as the attempt by men to explain and propitiate the natural phenomena by which they were surrounded and which they found incomprehensible. The conception of this kind of animism became generally accepted a century ago on the publication of E. B. Tylor's *Primitive culture*. Frazer's definition of religion is almost word for word the same as Voltaire's: 'a propitiation or conciliation of powers superior to man which are believed to direct and control the course of nature and of human life.'[20] But in the eighteenth century the idea was novel, and though Voltaire certainly got some hints from earlier writers, he seems to have worked out the theory himself; nor did he fail to see how this central idea leads insensibly to the vast theological systems of organised religion. Voltaire concludes (ch. liii) that 'Every profane legislator who dares to pretend that divinity has dictated his laws was obviously a blasphemer and a traitor'. In the words of J. H. Brumfitt: 'This is a final condemnation of Judaism and Christianity.'[21] Pomeau is therefore quite right when in the simplest terms he calls the *Philosophie de l'histoire* the 'corner-stone of the Voltairean doctrine.'[22]

None of Voltaire's works was more persistently persecuted in Geneva than the *Questions sur les miracles*. This was another example of the hypocrisy which so exasperated Voltaire, for few even of the Genevese clergy believed in miracles any more than the sage of Ferney. It is true that Voltaire's book, as usual, contains more than one would suppose from the title. Thus, he gets in some side swipes at Geneva itself, by introducing Covelle[23] as

20 Sir J. G. Frazer, *The Golden bough*; cp. the beginning of chapter v of *La Philosophie de l'histoire* (Voltaire 59, pp. 99-100).

21 Voltaire 59, p. 322.
22 *La Religion de Voltaire*, p. 344.
23 See p. 526, below.

25 Henri Louis Lekain, *from the painting by Simon Bernard Lenoir of Voltaire's favourite tragedian, in the role of Orosmane in Zaïre*

26 Jean Jacques Rousseau, *from the contemporary painted plaster
by an unknown sculptor*

one of the interlocutors; at Rousseau; and at the English Jesuit Needham on account of his alleged spontaneous generation of eels. But these things are incidental. Voltaire began by appearing, in the guise of a postulant, to defend the authenticity of miracles, and it can readily be imagined what scope this gave to his irony and erudition. Not least telling is the passage in which a sceptic is made to say that the church has never been in a worse state, and so more in need of a miracle. The greatest miracle, replies the naive postulant, would be to give us charity and love. And Voltaire concludes by hoping with, for him, rather heavy sarcasm, that priests will keep the right to excommunicate and anathemize as they see fit, 'this right being divinely attached to their divine ministry. We even hope that not only will these learned men work miracles, but that they will hang all those who do not believe in them. Amen!'

Le *Philosophe ignorant* is on a very different plane. It was written in a mood of exasperation and disgust produced by the impossibility of resolving the great metaphysical problems. In a series of brief sections Voltaire tries to answer the questions with which he begins: 'Who are you? whence do you come? what are you doing? what will you become?' Or rather, he more and more irritably points out how unanswerable they are, and how insignificant is man when confronted by them. It was maintained that the heavenly bodies had been created for the earth and the earth for man. But as the celestial motions would go on without man, and as on the earth there were infinitely more creatures than man, he felt rather that he was the slave of his environment, not its king. We do not know how or why we think. Aristotle has taught us only to disbelieve all he says. Descartes talks very positively about things he does not understand. Man does not always think. One might as well suppose that birds always fly because they can fly. We do not know the nature of matter, nor of mind. Our intelligence is as limited as the strength of our bodies. Why and how do the latter obey the former? We have no idea.

In a Pascalian section entitled 'Well-founded despair', Voltaire points out that we can measure the distance of the sun, but we do not know what is the sun, why it turns on its axis, and in one direction rather than another. He goes further and attempts to show that it is impossible for us to know the first principle which makes us think and act. We are not free, but we are eternal, for even if there has been creation something cannot be created out of nothing. Nevertheless there must be one supreme artisan, says Voltaire, making little attempt, however, to square this conclusion with the contradictory one which precedes it. He then examines in more detail the theories of Leibniz and Locke, to whom he again resorted as a prodigal son returns to his father, and here he arrives at a purely sensualist conclusion: there are no innate ideas, nothing becomes known to us but through our senses. Voltaire then becomes a little diffuse, dealing pell-mell with ethics, justice, truth, turning to Hobbes and some ancient thinkers. The idea of justice he finds so natural, so universal as to be independent of law and religion.

As usual, Voltaire himself best explained what he was doing. He at one time intended to include a frontispiece in the published *Philosophe ignorant*, and this is how he described the subject to be illustrated: 'The thing is to represent three blind men who grope after a fleeing donkey. This is the symbol of all philosophers who run after the truth. I consider myself one of the blindest, and I have always run after my donkey. So it is my portrait for which I am asking you.'[24]

Yet perhaps the most important of Voltaire's writings at this time, at least in its practical effects on society, is the *Commentaire sur le livre Des délits et des peines*. The then practically unknown marquis Cesare Bonesana Beccaria had published in 1764 his essay *Dei delitti e delle pene* (*On crimes and punishments*). It made a considerable impression, which was multiplied by the publication of Voltaire's commentary—and it is worth noting that this commentary was written or at least finished during an anxious fugue to Rolle[25], such were his self-control and powers of concentration. This is the more remarkable in that Voltaire's essay is not so much a commentary on Beccaria as an independent book stimulated by the reading of the Italian work, which it procured an international reputation.

Hitler and Stalin notwithstanding, in this field reform has gone so far that there would be no point in summarising what Vol-

24 Best.D13194 (3 March 1766).   25 See Best.D13456 (28 July 1766).

498

taire has to say about torture, the punishment and extirpation of heretics, witches and traitors, the death penalty (Voltaire concludes against it), suicide (even here Voltaire was far in advance of his time, arguing that it is wrong to consider suicide a crime). He concluded by making a number of detailed recommendations for reforms in France. At a time when nearly all judicial offices were bought and sold, Voltaire urged that a lawyer should be able to advance by merit. The law should not be applied differently in different parts of the country. Limits should be fixed between civil and ecclesiastical authority. Nobody should be arrested without cause shown. All these reforms were introduced during Voltaire's life or soon after.

The outstanding event of these years in its impact on Voltaire's life was, however, none of these things, it was something not particularly important in itself in the scale of the cruelties inspired by religion, but of the utmost significance because of the dimensions it acquired in passing through the crucible of Voltaire's horror and indignation.

The chevalier de La Barre, though he was little more than a boy, was officially done to death in July 1766 because he had failed to doff his hat to a religious procession. He was alleged to have been guilty of other blasphemies of similar importance. He was spared no torture, and his horrible death, so utterly out of proportion to his offence, affected Voltaire even more violently than the Calas and Sirven cases: it was never long out of his thoughts during the remaining years of his life. Voltaire was dangerously implicated, for the *Dictionnaire philosophique* had been found among La Barre's effects, evidence enough, for the fanatic, of its demoralising influence. Voltaire had suffered so much from persecution brought on by similar offenses that he found it necessary to flee Ferney. However, he soon overcame his fears, and not only returned from Rolle after a few days, but immediately launched a vigorous campaign in defence of La Barre's memory and on behalf of the *chevalier*'s companions, who had escaped.

Rousseau would not allow himself to be forgotten. His obsessive hatred of Voltaire became uncontrollable, exacerbated by the persecutions he himself suffered, and for which in his blind anger he held Voltaire responsible. In June 1764 he accused the scoundrel (*scélérat*) Voltaire of being the author of an underhand swindle (*fourberie*), in the shape of a pamphlet in which Rousseau was attacked, but of which an obscure lawyer was in fact the author[26]. And about the same time he did something that Voltaire with great moderation described as the action of a man who is 'neither a *philosophe* nor an honourable man'[27]. In his *Lettres écrites de la montagne* Rousseau put into Voltaire's mouth a speech in which he is made to boast of his attacks on religion, with special reference to the *Sermon des cinquante*. This essay was then the most direct and outspoken of Voltaire's condemnations of Christianity, in which the attempt is made to show it to be the result of a priestly conspiracy to have Jesus recognised as a god. As I have pointed out before, the police of the *ancien régime* operated on the principle of 'as if' and those who claimed the right to hink for themselves could get away with their attacks on received ideas only by anonymity and persistent denials of authorship. By printing what he did Rousseau blew the gaff on this civilised pretence and exposed Voltaire to the greatest dangers. No wonder that Voltaire, with his usual punctilio, told Alembert sadly: 'It is a pity for freethought that Jean Jacques is a madman, but it is still sadder that he is dishonourable.'[28] Voltaire's feelings against Rousseau now exploded. He had always been reluctant to quarrel with the man some of whose work he respected, but he now began to write against him at every opportunity, nearly always with a note of sadness. The most telling of Voltaire's retorts is not the *Sentiments d'un citoyen*, his part in which is doubtful, but perhaps the *Lettre au docteur Pansophe*, in which he attempts, in his own words, to teach Rousseau good faith, common sense, and modesty. He does this by bringing out, with pointless perspicacity, some of the many internal contradictions in Rousseau's writings, and the even graver differences between his teachings and his practices.

As for Rousseau, he plaintively inquired: 'What have I done to deserve the persecutions of M. de Voltaire?'[29] The fact that he could ask such a question shows that he is not to be judged by normal standards. Rousseau had now reached the stage at which

26 See a note on Best.D11927.
27 Best.D12276(31 December 1764).

28 Best.D12296 (9 January 1765).
29 Best.D12365 (31 January 1765).

not only Voltaire, but all and sundry were out of step but Jean Jacques.

This was a troubled time. Geneva refused the proposals of the mediators, Voltaire made untiring efforts to urge on the lawyers who were acting for the Sirven family, another and even worse collection of his letters[30] was published, and towards the end of the year Voltaire faced the serious consequences of his attempt to smuggle his subversive pamphlets into France. Yet he found time and energy to solicit his friends for help and money for the Sirven family; to prepare *Octave*[31] for publication with his usual meticulous care; to receive numerous visits; and to write scores of letters to his friends on these and other subjects, including one of his most amusing pastiches in the character of an ignorant clerk[32]. And when he met with an accident he reported it light-heartedly: 'You will remember than when Luc bit my leg[33], I declared that I was in the wrong. I owe the same justice to Collette. Wagnière and I were attending to our cushion and dropped the reins. Collette encountered a milestone, and took the gig over it. We all fell on each other, that is, Wagnière, Collette, the gig and I, we picked ourselves up as best we could, Collette begged my pardon and gave me the most charming smile in the world, and we continued our drive with the greatest gaiety.'[34]

A vivid account of Voltaire during these years has been left by the traveller and zoologist Thomas Pennant. In May 1765 he called at Ferney, and reported that Voltaire had bought there

an extensive manor. He found an antient Chateau on the Estate, which he pulled down, and built a very moderate house in its room. It commands a fine view of a flat country well cultivated: Mount Jura, part of the lake of Geneva and the snowy Alps of Savoy. We were at first introduced to his niece, Mademoiselle Dennis, a sedate, worthy looking woman about fifty. Voltaire made his appearance out of an adjacent study, and came into the room with more affectation of bodily infirmity than was requisite: not but that he really was as meagre and as arid a figure as ever I saw. His dress was a sky blue ratteen coat, lapelled, a blue turned up cap over a long flowing brigadier

30 *Lettres de m. de Voltaire à ses amis du parnasse* (Genève 1766).
31 Also known as *Le Triumvirat*.
32 Best.D13537 (5 September 1766).
33 Voltaire's monkey bit him in October 1756, and the old gentleman remembered very accurately what he had said eight years before; see p. 359, above.
34 Best.D12261 (c. 25 December 1764).

grey wig, his knees without buckles, his stockings coarse, his shoes thick and large. After a short address on the honor we did a weakly old man, his countenance brightened, his eyes, which were the most brilliant I ever saw, sparkled with pleasure at the attention paid to his fame. He repaid with interest our flattering visit; spoke in our own language, which he seemed almost to have forgotten except our imprecations, which he denounced most liberally on himself if he did not love the English, aye better than his own country-men: 'By G— I do lov de Ingles G-d dammee, if I don't lov them bettre dan de French by G—'. Our victories had made a full impression on the old man. He proposed a walk in his garden, which was extensive but in a wretched taste,—with strait walks and espalier hedges, but as it was not inclosed with a wall he informed us that it was flung open in conformity to the English taste. His avarice appeared in his very walks, which were now in mowing for hay, and would have been inaccessible by reason of the grass a few days before. When we returned into the house we found assembled a niece of M. Corneille, whom he had just married to a pert young frenchman, and portioned with a new edition of her uncles works; a gentleman from Geneva, the poor skeleton Le Pere Adam his constant butt, and mademoiselle Dennis. A finical young monk joined us. No sooner had the latter entered than Voltaire instantly attacked him, wondering at his imprudence at venturing into the company of the damned,—'You see, sir, two Englishmen of the reformed church whom you must allow are in a state of damnation: a Genevese Calvinist not a bit better, Le Pere Adam a Jesuit damned at least in France, and myself a free thinker. So Reverend sir, let me beg you to retire from such dangerous society'. His conversation was the whole time extremely lively, for fortunately for us this was not one of his gloomy days, when I was informed he was captious and disagreeable to a high degree. His theatre at this time down; his theatrical entertainments were formerly very frequent. He performed his own pieces and usually acted a part himself. Adjacent to his house is one half of the parish church. He had pulled down the other, and giving the remainder a new front, had the assurance to put in golden letters,—Deo erexit Voltaire.[35]

35 Thomas Pennant, *Tour on the continent 1765*, ed. sir G. R. de Beer (London 1948), pp. 76-7.

37. The prodigal years, 1767-1768

A S SOON AS GENEVA declined the plan of mediation, the French ambassador left, stopping at Ferney on his way, and French troops proceeded to invest the republic. Although Ferney was and is in France politically, it was and is economically tied to Geneva, and the blockade caused much discomfort and some hardship in the château—Voltaire even talked of famine. All this, and the repercussions of Voltaire's attempt to pass some of his pamphlets over the frontier at Collonge, caused him to enjoy a minor stroke. Very feeble at the age of seventy-three, he tells Argental, surrounded by a hundred mountains of snow, assailed by troubles, he had experienced also a 'sort of little apoplexy'[1]. It certainly laid him low, provided a congenial subject for correspondence, but did not otherwise affect his intellectual activity. A bookseller told Beccaria that Voltaire, though working more than ever, still found time to entertain with theatrical and dinner parties the French officers who were blockading Geneva. 'You would be astonished, on seeing that he is little more than a skeleton, to find in it so much gaiety and vivacity. He is a sparkling light, his eyes speak for him. Will you not come to enjoy his laughter and his charm?'[2]

The quarrel with Rousseau went on apace. The great egotist had always been ill-advised, in every sense of the term, in his relations with Voltaire. Given half a chance the great man would have been, what for long he tried to be, Rousseau's friend, but by now he had become fixed and violent in his dislike of the wretched Jean Jacques, ailing in mind and body. He told the young poet Dorat that Rousseau's behaviour went beyond mere literary quarrelling, it was the result of 'the blackest ingratitude and wickedness'. Nobody had ever wished more ardently than he himself for the unity of men of letters. 'The infamous trade of vilifying one's colleagues to earn a little money should be left to

1 Best.D13931 (9 February 1767).   2 Best.D14385 (19 August 1767).

cheap journalists, to the Desfontaines and the Frérons. It is those wretches who have made of literature an arena for gladiators.'[3] And about the same time Voltaire spoke what was, in effect, his last word in this matter: 'Jean Jacques Rousseau, who could have been useful to literature [Voltaire meant to the advanced school of thought], has become its enemy by his ridiculous pride, and its shame by his frightful behaviour.'[4] This compact summing-up contains the key to the supposed mystery of Voltaire's attitude to the renegade and rejected *citoyen de Genève*. It is true, of course, that if Voltaire had been a twentieth century psychologist instead of an exceptionally punctilious eighteenth century 'aristocrat', his attitude to Rousseau would have been more indulgent. However, if the author of the *Nouvelle Héloïse* could not but be what he was, nor could the author of *Candide*—which is where we came in.

The Sirven campaign was continued with ardour, and Frederick was persuaded to do something for one of the companions of the unfortunate La Barre. Nor did Voltaire cease to watch over the Calas family, especially when Sirven went to Paris, and echoes of all these tragic cases reached Ferney through the blockade. Nor did this prevent the flow of events and visitors, who included so exotic a personage as the farmer-general of the king of Patna[5]. As the king of Poland (Stanislas Poniatowski) told Voltaire: 'Every one of your contemporaries who can read and who has travelled, but has not met you, must be unhappy.'[6]

Voltaire's innumerable activities continued as usual. Still 'panting Time toil'd after him in vain'. He even found time to launch another campaign, against the condemnation of Marmontel's *Bélisaire* by the 'satanic rabble', of which he wrote in a white heat of indignation. In *Bélisaire* Voltaire's disciple made a plea for civil and religious toleration, and although the book had been passed by the censors, Marmontel was at once attacked violently by the Sorbonne and the establishment generally. *Bélisaire* was in fact the kind of book most disliked by the church: it was not an attack on religion, but rather an appeal for a return to a purer and simpler Christianity. Voltaire at once poured out a stream of letters in defence of Marmontel, and a number of pamph-

3 Best.D13978 (20 February 1767).   5 Best.D14579 (8 December 1767).
4 Best.D14048 (16 March 1767).   6 Best.D13988 (21 February 1767).

lets of which the *Anecdote sur Bélisaire* was merely the first. As usual, until Voltaire showed the way Marmontel stood alone, but now the affair developed into an 'embittered dispute of imposing and unparalleled proportions between the *philosophes* and the church'. The battle ended in a 'complete rout of the Sorbonne and its apologists' and in a 'personal triumph for Voltaire'[7].

After being printed, performed at Ferney, and endlessly discussed, Voltaire's allegorical play on Geneva, *Les Scythes*, was finally produced in Paris, whereupon its inexhaustible and indefatigable author redoubled his improvements and corrections. *Les Scythes* was not a popular success, and has indeed been generally condemned, even the judicious Lanson calling it a 'false and hypocritical tragedy'[8], an oddly intemperate judgment, and one quite undeserved. But there is no accounting for critical vagaries, some of the contradictions in this case being particularly striking. Thus, Collé writes that 'even his brilliance [*coloris*] has faded. The verse is as feeble as that of Corneille's last tragedies.'[9] While Grimm, using exactly the same word, comes to a contrary conclusion: 'Although the brilliance [*coloris*] of the author of the *Henriade* is still evident, the style appears a little feeble. . . . There is no getting away from the fact that the old age of m. de Voltaire is very different from that of Pierre Corneille', meaning that it was much better.

The essential feature of the play is that it deals with the Genevese in the guise of the Scythians, and that Voltaire has projected himself in the role of Sozame. Nor did he make any mystery of this, for the preliminary epistle opens with the words: 'Once upon a time there lived in Persia a good old man who cultivated his garden; for all must come to that; and this garden was accompanied by vineyards and fields, *et parvulum silvæ super erat*[10]; and this garden was not near Persepolis, but in an immense valley surrounded by the mountains of the Caucasus, covered with eternal snow; and this old man wrote neither on population nor on agriculture, as was done in Babylon to pass the time . . . ; but he

7 John Renwick, 'Reconstruction and interpretation of the genesis of the *Bélisaire* affair', *Studies on Voltaire* (1967), liii.222.

8 *Nivelle de La Chaussée et la comédie larmoyante* (Paris 1903), p. 294.

9 Charles Collé, *Journal et mémoires* (Paris 1868), iii.133.

10 Horace, *Satires*, ii.vi.3; 'and above them a little wood'.

had reclaimed uncultivated land, and tripled the number of inhabitants around his hut.' And when Voltaire goes on to refer to Choiseul and Praslin under transparent anagrams, he can hardly be taxed with having put out even a *drame à clef.* Ridgway is much nearer the mark when he describes *Les Scythes* as a 'philosophic allegory, a sort of Voltairean *conte* in five acts and in verse'[11].

Nor is there really any mystery about Voltaire's specific purposes in this tragedy. He makes them perfectly plain in his prefaces. He explains that, to provide playgoers with new sensibility, he had already shown on the stage ancient chivalry (*Tancrède*) and the contrast between Mohammedans and Christians (*Zaïre*), Americans and Spaniards (*Alzire*), Chinese and Tartars (*L'Orphelin de la Chine*). Now he offered a conflict between the Scythians and the ancient Persians, and moreover dared to associate on the stage the peasant and the prince. As always, or nearly always, he knew exactly what he was doing, by defining his play as a confrontation between natural man and artificial man. And to leave no doubt at all about the implications, he says explicitly that his tragedy 'is perhaps the depiction of certain modern nations'[12].

Let us now drop the stage-names, and give the protagonists their real identities. At the very beginning of the play the Genevese are made to say:

> Nous sommes tous égaux sur ces rives si chères,
> Sans rois, et sans sujets, tous libres et tous frères.[13]

But it is not to be supposed that this complacent claim is accepted by Voltaire. He makes another personage say to Sozame in quite remarkably bad verse:

> Je sais que les humains sont nés égaux et frères;
> Mais je n'ignore pas que l'on doit respecter
> Ceux qu'en exemple au peuple un roi veut présenter;
> Et la simplicité de notre république
> N'est point une leçon pour l'état monarchique.[14]

11 *La Propagande philosophique dans les tragédies de Voltaire*, p. 203.

12 In the *dramatis personae* Hermodan is openly described as an inhabi-of a 'Scythian canton'.

13 I.i; 'We are all equal in this beloved place, without kings and without subjects, all free and all brothers.'

14 I.iii; 'I know that men are born equal and brothers; but I am not unaware that we should respect those who wish to offer a king as an example to the people; and the simplicity of our republic is by no means a reproach to monarchy'.

And the final conclusion is put into the mouth of Obéide before she kills herself:

> Moi, complaire à ce peuple, aux monstres de Scythie;
> A ces brutes humains pétris de barbarie,
> A ces âmes de fer, et dont la dureté
> Passa longtemps chez nous pour noble fermeté,
> Dont on chérit de loin l'égalité paisible,
> Et chez qui je ne vois qu'un orgueil inflexible,
> Une atrocité morne, et qui, sans s'émouvoir,
> Croit dans le sang humain se baigner par devoir! ...
> J'ai fui pour ces ingrats la cour la plus auguste,
> Un peuple doux, poli, quelquefois trop injuste,
> Mais généreux, sensible, et si prompt à sortir
> De ses iniquités par un beau repentir![15]

and so on for another eighteen lines. 'I had a little fun with these imprecations', Voltaire told Argental, 'I painted a little portrait of Geneva to amuse myself.'[16] And here indeed Voltaire discharged himself of all his disillusion about the Genevese, all his horror of the 'atrocious soul' of Calvin, and the hypocritical narrowness of the Calvinists. When the *Scythes* was performed in Geneva (for a company was now tolerated in the suburbs) Voltaire was afraid that the actors would be stoned[17]. The complacent Genevese, however, failed to recognise themselves: all Voltaire's efforts to save them from themselves were lost.

The year 1767 is chiefly remarkable for the number of Voltaire's more important parerga which came to fruition. Apart from such works as the *Essai sur les dissensions des églises de Pologne* (in which Voltaire makes these theological dissensions responsible for the partition of Poland), there are several books and pamphlets about which a few words must be said.

In the *Questions de Zapata* a professor of theology in the

---

15 v.iv; 'I humour this people, these Scythian monsters, these human brutes moulded in barbarism, these souls of iron, whose hardness was long taken by us for noble firmness, and whose peaceful equality was cherished from afar, but in whom I see nothing but inflexible pride, dismal atrocity, who coldly believe it their duty to bathe in human blood! ... For these ingrates

I fled the most august of courts, a gentle and polite people, sometimes too unjust, but generous, sensitive, and always prompt to disown its iniquities by a splendid repentance!'

16 Best.D13719 (8 December 1766). 1766).

17 Best.D14003 (February/March 1767).

university of Salamanca puts a number of difficulties to a junta of theologians, in order that the answer may guide him in his teaching. He first asks how he is to explain the fact that the Jews, now burned in their hundreds, were for 4000 years god's chosen people. In the sixty-seventh and last question Zapata inquires whether it is his duty to announce such miracles as those of Maria of Agreda (better known as sor Maria de Jesus), who in her ecstasies showed her backside to little boys; and if so how he is to deal with the contumacious who dared to doubt: should he put them to the question ordinary and extraordinary? Voltaire adds in a postscript that Zapata, having received no reply, simply preached god. 'He isolated truth from falsehood, and separated religion from fanaticism. He taught and practised virtue. He was gentle, benevolent, modest; and was roasted at Valladolid in the years of grace 1631.'

Voltaire begins the *Honnêtetés littéraires* with a remark he often made, and which some critics of his polemics would do well to ponder: 'It is ridiculous to defend one's prose and one's verse, when they are no more than verse and prose. In matters of taste one should write and then keep quiet.' And he added that no one was obliged to read the *Henriade* if he did not like it, or go to see his plays if he found them boring. 'But if you accuse an impartial historian, a lover of truth and of men, of bad faith and of printing lies; if you print and reprint lies . . . then I hold that the facts should be elucidated. It is right that the public be instructed, because it is to their advantage.' Voltaire then proceeded to set out a number of case-histories, ranging from geographical and historical inaccuracies, to such monstrosities as the ecclesiastic who published a book in defence of the assassination of the Protestants, and of the Jesuits who advocated regicide, and to the journalists who had called Alembert a stinking beast and the publisher who had sought to blackmail Voltaire.

I cannot resist enlarging on an earlier attempted blackmail, for it produced not the least amusing of Voltaire's letters, one which requires no explanation or comment. He wrote to the publisher:

In your letter of 30 April from Avignon you offer to sell me for a thousand *écus* the entire edition of a collection of my errors *in matters of history and faith*, which, you say, you have printed in papal territory[18]. I am obliged in conscience to warn you that on recently re-reading a new edition of my works, I found more than two thousand *écus'* worth of mistakes in the preceding one; and as I am the author I have probably erred by half in my favour, so here we have twelve thousand francs' worth. It is thus evident that I would wrong you to the extent of nine thousand francs if I accepted your offer.

Besides, consider what you would earn in publishing the collection. It is a product which particularly interests all the powers that are at war, from the Baltic to Gibraltar. So I am not surprised when you tell me that *the work is sought after universally*.

General Laudon and the whole imperial army will not fail to take at least 30,000 copies, which you tell me that you sell at two livres a copy, say	60,000
The king of Prussia, who loves dogmatics passionately, and who concerns himself with them as much as ever, will sell about as many, say	60,000
You should also count a great deal on *monseigneur* prince Ferdinand [of Brunswick], for I always noticed, when I had the honour to pay him my court, that he was delighted when my dogmatic errors were pointed out; so you can send him 20,000 copies, say	40,000
As for the French army, in which even more French is spoken than in the Austrian and Prussian, you will send them at least 100,000 copies, which, at 40 *sous* each, make	200,000
You have no doubt written to admiral Anson, who will procure you the sale of 100,000 of your collection in England and the colonies, say	200,000
As for the monks and the theologians more particularly concerned with dogmatics, you could not sell them less than 300,000 copies, which makes at a stroke an amount of	600,000
Add to this list about 100,000 amateurs of dogmatics among the laity, which comes to	200,000
total	1,360,000 livres

You will perhaps have some expenses, but your clear profit will be at least a million.

I therefore cannot enough admire your disinterested attitude in sacrificing so great a gain for a single payment of three thousand *livres*. . . .

As for your anonymous author, who has devoted his vigils to this important labour, I admire his modesty. I beg you to present him with my tender compliments, and also your ink-merchant.

18 The implication being that Voltaire would be unable to prevent the publication; Best.D10451 (17 May 1762).

The purpose of the *Examen important de milord Bolingbroke* is indicated by its subtitle: 'the tomb of fanaticism'. It is one of the series of Voltaire's more and more learned and vigorous condemnations of Christianity, which is attacked root and branch. Beginning with the most pointed doubts about the historicity of the *Old testament*, going on to Jesus and the *New testament*, passing rapidly through the fathers of the church, Voltaire reserves his most violent criticisms for the various sects and persecutors, and above all the Roman catholic church. 'I conclude that every sensible man, every man of goodwill, must have the Christian sect in horror.'[19] And Voltaire's last word is: 'The more laymen are enlightened, the less harm can be done by priests. Let us try to enlighten even these, to make them blush at their errors, and to induce them little by little to become citizens.'

The *Lettres à s. a. mgr le prince*[20] is a survey, as stated in its full title, of authors accused of having written against Christianity. Voltaire discusses in some detail Rabelais and his precursors, Vanini, the English deists, Swift, rather miscellaneous groups of German and French writers, the *Encyclopédie*, Spinoza, and, perhaps the most original feature of this essay, a number of Jewish writers, with special reference to Isaac Balthasar Orobio and Uriel Acosta. The latter had a most remarkable life, abandoning Christianity to become a Jew, and finally rejecting both only to commit suicide. The whole is in effect a tract against intolerance and fanaticism.

In the *Fragment des instructions pour le prince royal de* *** Voltaire turns to government. He first warns the prince against the Christian sect which calls itself universal because it has sent missionaries to America and Asia. This is, comments Voltaire, as if the king of Denmark called himself lord of the entire world because he possesses an establishment on the coast of Coromandel and two little islands in America.

The prince is advised never to persecute anyone for his religious

19 And yet whole libraries have been written (most notably Alfred Noyes's *Voltaire*) to show that Voltaire's polemics were not directed against Christianity as such.

20 The full title is *Lettres à s. a. mgr le prince de* ***** *sur Rabelais et sur d'autres auteurs accusés d'avoir mal parlé de la religion chrétienne*; this is usually abridged to *Lettres sur Rabelais*, which is rather misleading.

beliefs. 'Show all superstitition to be ridiculous and odious, and you will never have anything to fear from religion.' He should sustain justice and be himself the first to submit to it. He should never condemn without due process of law. 'The wretch is a man, and you are responsible for his blood.' If the prince needed money he should sell his woods, his silver, his diamonds, but never legal offices. Torture should never be used. And so on, for in these matters Voltaire was always on the side of the angels, and hardly ever put a foot wrong.

Voltaire returned to religion in the *Homélies prononcées à Londres*, in which he deals broadly with atheism, superstition and the interpretation of the *Old* and *New testaments*. However often he deals with the same subjects there is always something new in the exact point of view and in the evidence and reasoning adduced. The *Homélies* are no exception, and the first two sermons, in particular, throw a rather brilliant light on the exact nature of Voltaire's beliefs. Here we see again how extremely tenuous is Voltaire's oft-proclaimed belief in a divinity. What, for instance, could the faithful make of such a passage as: 'To adore the supreme being, to love him, to serve him, to be useful to mankind, this is nothing: it is even, according to some, a false virtue which they call a splendid sin'?

The *Homélies* concludes with another of those splendid perorations of which Voltaire was the master: 'Let us therefore reject all superstition in order to become more human; but in speaking against fanaticism, let us not imitate the fanatics: they are sick men in delirium who want to chastise their doctors. Let us assuage their ills, and never embitter them, and let us pour drop by drop into their souls the divine balm of toleration, which they would reject with horror if it were offered to them all at once.'

La *Défense de mon oncle*[21] ranks among the most significant of Voltaire's polemical writings on history. It is a link in a long controversial chain. The *Philosophie de l'histoire* had been answered by one Pierre Henri Larcher, in a *Supplément à la Philosophie de l'histoire*, who alleged in his preface (p.34) that Voltaire had exposed himself to the hatred of mankind and deserved to be hunted

21 The *Défense de mon oncle* was so called because the *Philosophie de* l'histoire purported to be by one Bazin, edited by his nephew.

like a ferocious beast. The ferocious beast replied in his *Défense de mon oncle*, to which Larcher then retorted in a *Réponse à la Défense de mon oncle*, and this elicited a *Lettre à l'auteur d'une brochure intitulée Réponse à la Défense de mon oncle*, which, however, was not by Voltaire. And the controversy continued and continues.

The *Défense de mon oncle* is, inevitably, much more than a defence against an attack. Voltaire shows, for instance, that this defender of the faith had himself been inoculated with the new philosophy. 'It is very painful for Christian eyes to read in his book, page 298, *that sacred writers may have made mistakes like others*.'[22] He shows how the defence of traditional beliefs through thick and thin leads to the most outrageous absurdities. Thus, Voltaire showed by quotations from the *Zend Avesta* that Sextus Empiricus was mistaken when he said that pederasty was obligatory among the Persians. Larcher found this scepticism unjustified, even though Voltaire pointed out that no government would order a practice which would lead to the extermination of the nation.[23]

And so Voltaire goes on from point to point, opposing the critical spirit and common-sense to blind acceptance of the printed word. Finally he quotes what he had written long before about stupid pedants:

> Nous rédigeons au long, de point en point,
> Ce qu'on pensa; mais nous ne pensons point.[24]

This survey by no means exhausts Voltaire's publications during this extraordinary year 1767; but after all this it is hardly worth mentioning various trifles, to say nothing of the comedy *Charlot*. As for *L'Ingénu*, like all Voltaire's stories it appeared unheralded: quite suddenly, in a postscript to a letter, its author says casually that it is better than *Candide*—posterity does not agree, but Voltaire may well have been right. The author also spent much time in correcting his plays and historical works for

22 Cp. the similar remark made above, p. 479, about the attorney-general of Geneva.

23 *Philosophie de l'histoire*, xi; *Essai sur les mœurs*, v; *Défense de mon oncle*, v.

24 See p. 176, above.

27 Articulated figure of Voltaire, the head after Houdon,
made to fit his clothes

28 *Le Lever du philosophe, from the painting by Jean Huber*

new editions. I add almost with relief that he wrote no poetry in 1767, but on the other hand more letters than ever: hundreds have survived from this prodigal period. Not the least interesting is that in which he tells prince Golitsuin: 'There will always be ignorance, folly and envy in my fatherland, but also there will always be knowledge and good taste. I even venture to tell you that in general our leading soldiers and the members of the council, the councillors of state and the judges, are more enlightened than they were in the great century of Louis XIV. Great talents are rare, but knowledge and reason are common. I see with pleasure that an immense republic of cultivated minds is taking form in Europe. Enlightenment is gaining ground everywhere.'[25]

Among the letters he received is one from George Keate, in which this interesting personage apostrophises Voltaire:

> Why talk of Age?—the same bright Fire
> Breaths still in ev'ry Line,
> The Muses still as much inspire,
> Thy Arts as strongly shine.
>
> True Genius, like the Orb of Day
> Time's Hand can never tame;
> The Form it dwells in may decay,
> Its Blaze remains the same.[26]

And Keate followed this up with his *Ferney, an epistle to mon^r de Voltaire* (1768).

In the midst of weighty literary and historical discussions, we see Voltaire trying hard to keep a straight face when Richelieu refused to answer a letter from the French resident in Geneva because he had been addressed as 'Monsieur le Maréchal' instead of 'Monseigneur'[27]. Nothing astonishes one more than the patience Voltaire showed in his dealings with the wretched Wurttemberg officials, who had the unenviable job of saving their prodigal duke from dishonour. La Beaumelle now reappeared on the scene, sending Voltaire a threatening letter[28]. He was in fact preparing a series of publications against the sage of Ferney, who, as usual, was well informed. He replied, in the name of his valet:

25 Best.D14363 (14 August 1767). 27 Best.D14413 (9 September 1767).
26 Best.D14349 (10 August 1767). 28 Best.D14234 (22 June 1767).

'My master does not answer the insults of calumniators. The particulars of your threats are known to him. He awaits your chastisement and authorises you to print this letter at the head of your libels.'[29]

If Voltaire's activity in 1767 was astonishing, that of 1768 approached the miraculous. It was now that began to take shape an important project born of Voltaire's creative imagination. The province of Gex and the French countryside behind Geneva was being stifled for lack of an outlet within the frontiers of France. Voltaire saw the problem comprehensively and proposed the perfect solution. In a letter to the chevalier de Beauteville, the French ambassador to the Corps Helvétique (that is, Switzerland, of which, it must be remembered, Geneva was not part), Voltaire argued that instead of taking direct measures against Geneva (that is, the blockade) France should 'establish a port in the province of Gex; open a main road to Franche-Comté; do business directly between Lyons and Switzerland by way of Versoix; draw there all the trade of Geneva; and thus put a stop to the enormous contraband traffic operated by the Genevese'[30]

Even Choiseul was able to see the immense strategic and commercial interest of this proposal, Versoix being on lake Leman, only a few miles from Geneva. By April he was threatening the republic with the construction of the port, to the great alarm of the Genevese resident in Paris.[31] Geneva did not take the hint, and throughout 1768 work continued with great energy, a post office was opened[32], a road was completed, a frigate was built on the lake, and had Choiseul not fallen from power in 1770 the whole economy of the countryside would have been transformed. For one thing, Versoix would not have been ceded to Switzerland in 1815, and Geneva would have been much reduced in importance. All this was not to be, for Choiseul's successors cut off supplies, and the port of Versoix collapsed far more rapidly than it had been developed. It is now an archaeological site. What a

---

29 Best.D14239 (?24 June 1767); see also Best.D14292 (c. 18 July 1767), in which we behold the extraordinary spectacle of the government coming to Voltaire's defence, and ordering La Beaumelle to put a stop to his 'in-

numerable anonymous letters'.
30 Best.D13937 (10 February 1767).
31 See a note on Best.D14162.
32 By June 1768 Voltaire dated a letter 'au château de Ferney par Versoix' (Best.D15104).

pity Choiseul did not commission Voltaire to nurture his own brain-child!

It was now also that Voltaire again took an interest in experimental science, though this time in the field of biology. For the same kind of reasons that caused the theories of Darwin to create such an uproar a century later, the biological controversies of the Enlightenment centred around the notions of regeneration, spontaneous generation and the like.[33] Voltaire tried the experiment of cutting off the heads of snails, and reported on his work in *Les Colimaçons du révérend père L'Escarbotier*. He worked in a genuinely scientific spirit, with reasonable precautions and controls; but of course knowledge of the physiology of the snail was altogether inadequate, and when he concluded that these animals do regenerate their heads he was as mistaken as were most of the inferences of nearly all the professional biologists two centuries ago, like those of his *bête noire* Needham about the spontaneous generation of eels.

At the same time as the *Colimaçons* Voltaire composed his long essay *Des singularités de la nature*, in which he examined some of the mysteries and peculiarities of nature, with special reference to geology. And it was here that he gave notable evidence of his greatest intellectual weakness, the conviction that enlightened common-sense is a sufficient guide in science. He began well enough by insisting that all theories should be distrusted until they have been demonstrated beyond doubt to our eyes or our reason. He quoted with approval the Spanish proverb 'De las cosas mas seguras, la mas segura es dudar'[34], but his fundamental error, which he shared with nearly all his contemporaries, was to equate sensory perceptions with the inferences to be drawn from them. Thus Voltaire could not believe that a stone apparently bearing the imprint of a plant which did not grow at the place where the fossil was found, could really be what it appeared to be; that coral reefs were really the product of insects; that polyps were really animals; that bees had queens; and so on. And thus, confronted by the presence of sea-shells on mountain tops, he

33 See, most recently, Colm Kiernan, *The Enlightenment and science in 18th century France* (Studies on Voltaire, lixA: 1973); and ch. 28, above.

34 Ch. xxiii; 'Doubt is the surest of certainties.'

inquired whether they could not have been dropped there by the pilgrims from St James of Compostella (ch. xii): a most 'sensible' suggestion which is nevertheless absurd.

Voltaire was on surer ground when he pointed out that most scientific theories had turned out to be false, and that many which were sound had been rejected. And it must not be forgotten that many of the obscurities which so exasperated Voltaire that he devoted a chapter to 'ignorances éternelles' are still just as obscure. We still do not know how mind and body interact, or even whether there is such a thing as mind. What and why is life? What and why is matter? (ch. xxiv). And Voltaire concluded that there had certainly been progress, but that it was shameful that society had not improved as much as our knowledge. 'Our light is only a dawn. We have come out of a dark night, and we await the light of day' (ch. xxxviii). Indeed, Voltaire's systematic scepticism was justified ninety-nine times out of a hundred, as in nearly all the examples he gives in the *Singularités* and many other works.

Yet by far the most numerous and impressive of Voltaire's writings in 1768 were in different fields. The *Princess de Babylone* also has its advocates as perhaps the best of Voltaire's tales. *La Guerre civile de Genève*[35] is perhaps the wittiest of his verse satires. Among the outstanding general writings of the year are such masterpieces as *L'Homme aux quarante écus*. This has a special technical interest. Voltaire wrote many stories and much verse, and also a great deal of what the public libraries, in one of the worst question-begging labels of all time, call 'non-fiction'. But none of his fiction, although extremely readable, is limited to the telling of a story; and none of his non-fiction lacks literary genius. Occasionally the two genres are unified to such an extent that one is hard put to it to determine which is which. Voltaire even inserted dialogues into the *Dictionnaire philosophique*. Perhaps the outstanding example of this conflation of genres is *L'Homme aux quarante écus*, a serious treatise on political economy cast in the form of a story.[36] But within this framework *L'Homme* is one

35 See pp. 526-527, below.

36 The literary status of this work has recently been examined at length, the author coming to the conclusion that '*L'Homme aux quarante écus* is a work of philosophic rhetoric in which literary techniques are employed to persuade a universal audience to adopt a certain philosophic and practical outlook on life'; Robert Ginsberg, 'The

of the most complex of Voltaire's writings, composed partly in the first person, representing at least three narrators; partly in the third person in various forms and tenses; partly expository. Nearly all the subjects broached are discussed and rediscussed from each point of view, in an intricate counterpoint so ingeniously worked out that it nearly always passes unperceived. The whole is closely akin to Diderot's masterpieces, of which Voltaire had no knowledge, and which he therefore anticipated by a wide margin of time.

On his way Voltaire discusses a variety of social and economic problems, including education. Poverty is unjust, and this injustice is due to government, including the church. What are the direct causes? The neglect of agriculture, the unproductiveness of the church, luxury, spending abroad, war. All these things are explored from various points of view, and illustrated by anecdotes. Throughout the narrative Voltaire, in his current mood, runs a thread of scientific reflection. Everything outside geometry and mathematics should be doubted. But whatever the detours and intricacies of the literary maze created by Voltaire, the goal is always the same: the slow but irresistible advance of reason, accompanied by her two intimate friends experience and toleration (ch. xiv).

The *Dîner du comte de Boulainvilliers* is a series of dialogues about religion. The first is a conversation before dinner between an abbé and a count, who maintains that freethought[37] is superior to the Roman catholic religion. When challenged he defines freethought as 'the enlightened love of wisdom, sustained by love of the eternal being, who rewards virtue and avenges crime'. When the abbé claims that the same is true of his religion, the count quotes many passages from *Matthew* and *Luke* to prove the contrary. And when the abbé makes the standard reply, the count exclaims that it is a strange god who requires interpretation and who perpetually advances contradictory propositions. He is also revolted by the eternal damnation of the great men of

Argument of Voltaire's *L'Homme aux quarante écus'*, *Studies on Voltaire* (1967), lvi.622. See also Nuci Kotta, *L'Homme aux quarante écus: a study of Voltairian themes* (The Hague 1966).
37 Voltaire uses the word *philosophie*; but see pp. 474, 307, above.

antiquity. The abbé regrets that there is in fact no salvation outside the church.

Dinner is served, and the conversation broadens into light-hearted but extremely outspoken fun about the grosser absurdities of the *Bible* and religion. When the learned Fréret is made to stig-matise communion as monstrous and ridiculous idolatry, de-scribing it as the practice of eating and drinking god only to excrete him thereafter into a chamber-pot, the abbé proclaims himself unmoved by such trifles, with which he has long been familiar. The countess tells him that he reminds her of a duchess who, when she was called a whore, replied: 'So I have been told for thirty years, and I hope that they will go on saying it for another thirty.'

After dinner the conversation takes a practical turn. Is religion necessary to enforce morality? The general conclusion, in which even the abbé eventually joins, is that human nature requires religion, but only when purified from superstition and the priest-hood.[38]

Le Pyrrhonisme de l'histoire[39] is the application of Voltaire's doctrine of doubt to history, where it naturally had even greater play than in other fields of human knowledge. Voltaire made it clear in his very first sentence that his scepticism was not mere obscurantism. 'I seek neither an extravagant pyrrhonism, nor a ridiculous credulity.' And he gave a number of elementary ex-amples—though they were by no means obvious at the time—to underline this attitude. There was never an Egyptian prince called Sesostris, but this did not exclude the possibility that some-one may have existed whose name and attributes had been de-formed by historians. On the other hand, should this be the case it would not follow that all the events connected with Sesostris actually apply to his prototype. In the same way the most cele-brated monuments and the most solemn commemorations do not prove the historicity of the events they are supposed to celebrate.

38 On the utilitarian function of religion see pp. 229-230, above.
39 'Pyrrhonisme', after Pyrrho of Elis, was the favourite eighteenth-century term for generalised scepticism. This essay was probably published at the beginning of 1769, but it was writ-ten in 1768.

Voltaire surveyed rapidly the whole course of history, from the beginnings to his own times, letting the brilliant searchlight of his critical curiosity play into corners left in sombre obscurity by prejudice or ignorance.

He dealt first with Bossuet, then regarded as the most authoritative of modern historians, and showed how ingeniously and ingenuously he slipped the most monumental untruths into his narrative. When writing of various Christian sects Bossuet said casually: 'These heresies, so often foretold by Jesus Christ...' The fact is that nowhere in the *New testament* does either the word or idea of heresy occur, nor even the word or idea of dogma (ch. ii).

We need not linger over Voltaire's strictures on ancient history, including that recorded in the *Bible*, for these have become commonplaces. His judgment of Herodotus is typical of his judicious attitude: 'Nearly everything that he says at secondhand is false, but all that he has seen is true' (ch. vi). But Voltaire goes on to show that the alleged facts of the middle ages, in particular the legendary history of France, are almost as dubious, even when they appear to be documented. Thus, it was then a cornerstone of the French historical tradition that Pepin III was made king by order of the pope—and this conviction derived from a passage in an ancient manuscript. Voltaire pointed out that in the middle of the eighth century the papacy was in no position to do anything of the kind, and he was quite right, for we now know that it was in fact Pepin who obliged Boniface to crown him, in exchange creating the papal state.

Coming to modern times, Voltaire showed that historical writing was as corrupt as ever, but now because of prejudice, dishonesty, and the spirit of the schools. Such calumnies, he concluded, were the greatest and commonest of crimes after murder and poison (ch. xliii).

One of the most interesting books produced at this time is the *ABC*. This is a dialogue between three personages (one an Englishman, another Voltaire himself) designated by the first three letters of the alphabet. Under the anodyne title of *L'ABC* Voltaire has set down some of his clearest and most outspoken statements on government[40].

40 See pp. 310, 311, 315, 317, above.

This long enumeration by no means exhausts the list of Voltaire's publications in 1768, to say nothing of new editions. In the *Entretiens chinois* Voltaire, in a dialogue between a mandarin and a Jesuit, told his own compatriots some painful truths. The mandarin, for instance, tells with horror of an Indian rajah whose priests praise conquerors from their pulpits, and even bless their standards. The *Profession de foi des théistes* concludes: 'Muphti of Constantinople, sherif of Mecca, great brahma of Benares, dalai lama of Tartary who are immortal, bishop of Rome who art infallible ... enjoy in peace your goods and your honours without hating, without insulting, without persecuting the innocent.' *Les Droits des hommes et les usurpations des papes* is sufficiently described by its title.

A number of shorter pieces I must pass over in silence, but not two of Voltaire's best verse *contes*, which appeared in this miraculous year: *Le Marseillais et le lion* and *Les Trois empereurs en Sorbonne*. The former, in which a pact of non-belligerence is made between the lion and the man, both influenced by self-interest, cannot easily be quoted, for much of the fun is in the footnotes. The *Trois empereurs* is a by-product of the great *Bélisaire* ruction. Trajan, Titus and Marcus Aurelius are shown the sights of Paris. They finally arrive at the Sorbonne, and burst out laughing when they hear the Latin there prevalent. The man who had condemned *Bélisaire* informs the three emperors that they are doomed to eternal damnation, while Ravaillac and Clément (the assassins of Henri III and Henri IV) may well be in heaven if they confessed before they were executed. The emperors conclude that a mistake has been made: they had not been taken to the Sorbonne as they thought but to a lunatic asylum.

It is doubtful whether a mass of writing of such quality and range can be matched by anyone else in any literature. And this was the output of a man of seventy-four, in bad health, and most of the year in deep distress because of the events that led to the dismissal of mme Denis to Paris, events which can without exaggeration be said to have broken Voltaire's heart. They made him in reality what he was already on paper, an old man. If there is still anyone left so obtuse that he regards Voltaire as an avid and heartless man, let him read the next chapter, and let him consider, among other things, the astounding magnanimity of his behaviour to La Harpe.

The recovery of Voltaire's correspondence with his niece, and of many of her letters to their friends in and around Ferney, reveals much of the first importance. These letters justify the unkind remarks I have often made about mme Denis and prove once again that I am not indulging in hero-worship when I insist on Voltaire's profound goodness.

It is sad to see the old man alone, but the absence of his niece had its benefits: a little peace is good for the soul even of a Voltaire. He took advantage of it to disentangle the confused web of his affairs, and to have a good look at himself and his manifold activities. Neither his sorrows nor his varied labours prevented Voltaire from pursuing all his usual activities, not forgetting the Sirven and La Barre cases and, unfortunately, the wretched Wurttemberg affairs.

Most obsessive was the fate of La Barre. As he told Beccaria, Voltaire found this case even worse than that of Calas, for typically subtle reasons, for Voltaire was not incapable of sharp thought even when his feelings were most deeply engaged. He pointed out that Calas would have deserved his fate had he been guilty. At bottom what had happened was a miscarriage of justice. In the case of La Barre his guilt was not in question, and the judges made no mistake in that sense. What they had done was to commit a juridical crime in punishing by death, preceded by appalling torture, an offence that deserved, even by contemporary standards, at most a few months in prison. 'What an abominable jurisprudence is that which sustains religion only by means of the public executioner. This is what is called a religion of love and charity.'[41]

Voltaire made a special point of begging his friends not to attribute to him all the intellectually revolutionary publications that came off the press more and more frequently, and even went so far as to partake of the sacrament at easter, and to exhort his parishioners from the pulpit, in the hope of deflecting persecution.

41 Best.D15044 (30 May 1768).

17*—V.

The bishop of Geneva told Voltaire that he (like most of Voltaire's friends) was by no means edified, though, he added with heavy sarcasm, he did not believe that Voltaire, the great man of his century, could have been capable of betraying his beliefs by an act of hypocrisy. 'You confessed, you took the sacrament, so you did it in good faith, you did it as a true Christian.'[42] I am not often in the unhappy dilemma of agreeing with Voltaire's enemies, but this time I am. Voltaire justified his action on the usual grounds of expediency[43]. He was not content merely to rescue his vassals from the horrors of poverty, and to do what he could to make them happy, he felt that it was also his duty to edify them. It would be extraordinary, said he, for the lord of a parish not to do so.[44] All this made no difference: all the anti-religious works that now flooded the market were attributed to him, and he was accused of infecting with deism the French officers and engineers in his neighbourhood.[45] The bishop complained to the king of Voltaire's behaviour, and in consequence the sage of Ferney received a reprimand from the comte de Saint-Florentin, minister for home affairs, who did not disdain to use offensive terms and even to adopt so childish a procedure as to address Voltaire as a 'former gentleman in ordinary to the king'[46], though he of course well knew that Voltaire still held the office.

Voltaire received this letter at eleven o'clock in the morning, and at noon he replied, with dignity, expressing his astonishment that the king should so readily believe calumnies and lies, and enclosing formal certificates from the *curé* of Ferney and other local dignitaries, attesting that Voltaire had done nothing improper, and paying tribute to all that he had done for the good of the province.[47]

Voltaire's efforts to pass himself off as theologically respectable were inevitably abortive. After all one cannot spend a lifetime in arguing that Christianity is a poison and expect the world to take at its face value a moment's well-publicised conformity. So strong was the animus against Voltaire that his writings in defence of a

42 Best.D14944 (11 April 1768).
43 See p. 229, above.
44 Best.D14950 (15 April 1768).
45 Best.D15048 (31 May 1768).
46 Best.D15083 (18 June 1768).
47 Best.D15093 (23 June 1768).

deity were condemned as heartily as the openly atheistic writings of Holbach. And indeed when Voltaire published a refutation of Holbach, that also was condemned, as when the public prosecutor Antoine Louis Séguier delivered a *Réquisitoire* which led to the public burning of works by Holbach and Voltaire's *Dieu et les hommes*, which was directed against them. When a speaker (Antoine Léonard Thomas) at the Académie française seemed to criticise the *Réquisitoire* his speech was seized, and he himself was condemned to silence for two years.[48]

Rumour again advertised the death of our great man: the wishes of many fathered the thought. On the contrary, Voltaire wrote letters during these months to an unusually large number of correspondents, and even began again to play with the idea of a visit to Paris, perhaps encouraged by the intense cold at Ferney, where the temperature fell twelve degrees below zero in January.[49] Indeed, the château was completely cut off for some time.[50]

Had Horace Walpole not been so conventional and so timid intellectually the correspondence[51] of these two great epistolarians might have developed into something remarkable: as it is it died newborn. Voltaire asked Walpole to send him his *Historic doubts on the life and reign of king Richard the third*, for he was already meditating his own essay on *Le Pyrrhonisme de l'histoire*. Walpole answered in reminiscent vein:

It is true, sir, I have ventured to contest the history of Richard the third, as it has been delivered down to us: and I shall obey your commands, and send it to you, though with fear and trembling; for though I have given it to the world, as it is called, yet, as you have justly observed, *that* world is comprised within a very small circle of readers—and undoubtedly I could not expect that you would do me the honour of being one of the number. Nor do I fear you, Sir, only as the first genius in Europe, who have illustrated every science; I have a more intimate dependence on you than you suspect. Without knowing it, you have been my master, and perhaps the sole merit that may be found in my writings is owing to my having studied yours: so far, sir, am I from living in that state of barbarism and ignorance with which you tax me when you say *que vous m'êtes peut-être inconnu*. I was not a stranger to your reputation very many years ago, but remember to have then thought

48 See a note on Best.D16649.
49 Best.D14643 (4 January 1768).
50 Best.D14687 (18 January 1768).

51 Best.D15063, D15089, D15140, D15161 (June-July 1768).

you honoured our house by dining with my mother—though I was at school and had not the happiness of seeing you.

And he went on to tell Voltaire that he had found fault with his criticisms of Shakespeare. Voltaire then, at considerable length, explained his attitude; but Walpole timorously backed away, substituting worldly courtesies for arguments. And to mme Du Deffand he insensitively attributed Voltaire's attitude to wounded pride, because Walpole's preference for Shakespeare over Racine and Corneille implied also that he put Shakespeare before Voltaire himself.[52]

[52] See the note on Best.D15161.

38. This long weary day,
1 March 1768

IT IS A DESPERATELY difficult thing to display any man as he really was, and impossibly difficult in the case of the polymorphic chameleon, the omniscient polymath Voltaire. Yet the material is so abundant that it would be unforgivable not to make the effort. Let us try to put a single day in Voltaire's life under the microscope.[1]

I have not chosen this day in his sparkling youth, nor in his maturity at Cirey or in Prussia, nor during the vital transformation at the Délices, after which Voltaire became the patriarch of Ferney. I have taken one of the saddest, most painful periods of his life. He is seventy-four, for some years his activity at Ferney has been unremitting, quite apart from his writing: his labours have been on the one hand destructive of intolerance and of religion, that is, of superstition; on the other hand constructive, benevolent, humane. He has living with him a member of his mother's family, paralytic and dying (Charles Hyacinthe Daumart); the little Marie Corneille, her husband Dupuits, and their children—for, as we have seen, he had not merely taken her into his house, he had educated her, provided her with a substantial dowry, found her an excellent husband, and kept the entire family under his wing; an unfrocked Jesuit (Antoine Adam) to whom he entrusted minor clerical work and with whom he played chess; the young writer La Harpe and his wife; the architect Racle; the freethinking lawyer Christin; the ever-faithful Wagnière, his secretary; the amanuensis Bigex; fourteen officers in charge of the French troops which were blockading Geneva; sixty indoor and outdoor servants; five, twenty, fifty, a hundred guests come to Ferney to take part in Voltaire's private theatricals

---

1 The letters of 1 March 1768 are
Best.D14785-D14799; cp. p. 559, note
1, below.

or to watch them, to dine, to spend a night or many nights, or simply to see for a moment the most famous man in the world; and finally she who, above all, must not be forgotten, the widow Denis, niece, housekeeper and mistress of the lord of the manor.

It is Tuesday, 1 March 1768. The dissensions between Paris and Geneva had been somewhat pacified. Voltaire served as a link between the two countries, and did all he could to encourage and to maintain those improved relations. He tried hard to do nothing to awaken fears and suspicions, but this was impossible in Geneva. Voltaire often laughed when he felt most serious, most unhappy, and this time the laughter was entitled the *Guerre civile de Genève*. In this long poem Voltaire made fun of a recent incident: one Robert Covelle (a Burns *avant la lettre*, for Calvinism knows no boundaries), having been found guilty of fornication, was obliged to receive his sentence kneeling before his judges. Although the *Guerre* is in reality a plea for toleration, it contains some well deserved shafts of satire, such as:

> Près d'une église à Pierre consacrée,
> Très sale église, et de Pierre abhorrée,
> Qui brave Rome, hélas! impunément,
> Sur un vieux mur est un vieux monument,
> Reste maudit d'une déesse antique,
> Du paganisme ouvrage fantastique,
> Dont les enfers animaient les accents
> Lorsque la terre était sans prédicants,
> Dieu quelquefois permet qu'à cette idole
> L'esprit malin prête encor sa parole.
> Les Genevois consultent ce démon
> Quand par malheur ils n'ont point de sermon.
> Ce diable antique est nommé l'Inconstance;
> Elle a toujours confondu la prudence:
> Une girouette exposée à tout vent
> Est à la fois son trône et son emblême;
> Cent papillons forment son diadème,[2] etc. etc.

2 *La Guerre civile de Genève*, ii.145-161; 'Near a church dedicated to Peter [the cathedral of Geneva], a very dirty church and abhorred by Peter, which, alas, braves Rome with impunity, there is an old monument on an old wall, an accursed remnant of an ancient goddess, a fantastic product of paganism. God sometimes allows the devil again to lend his voice to this idol, given speech by hell when there were no preachers on earth. The ancient devil is named Inconstance: she has always confounded prudence: a weathercock

It will readily be understood that Voltaire did not want to expose France or himself to the reactions of Genevese sensibility when wounded by such allusions—the reactions were in fact violent. Voltaire kept his manuscript under lock and key, but suddenly part of the poem appeared in print. Voltaire was furious and anxious in the extreme, but he remained just. He pressed his inquiries calmly and methodically, and it emerged that the guilty man, without the least shadow of doubt or ambiguity, convicted indeed out of his own mouth, was La Harpe, the young writer whom he had welcomed at Ferney, with his wife and children, for many months, and whose praises he had sung for the past two years. It was he who had stolen the manuscript, and carried it off to Paris in the same bag as that in which it was Voltaire's habit to slip a roll of gold pieces on the departure of his protégés. There was worse. La Harpe had been encouraged, perhaps seduced, by mme Denis. How? We shall never know, but her vulgar avidity and undiminished sensuality authorise a guess.

Voltaire forgave La Harpe with astonishing indulgence, as he always forgave those who offended him in his person—he had less forbearance for intellectual offences. Not only did he forgive an action particularly dishonourable on the part of a guest, but, being convinced of La Harpe's talent, and not wishing to harm the impoverished young man, Voltaire sent the newspapers a statement completely exonerating him. He clearly thought him more sinned against than sinning, and at once resumed their correspondence, soon writing in the same affectionate terms as before.

But as for mme Denis, whose first offence of this kind dated from long before, he simply showed her the door. She played the innocent. In a letter to Henri Rieu[3], she pretended not to know the reason for the separation. She blamed everything on her uncle's domestic Jesuit.[4]

exposed to every wind is at once her throne and her emblem; a hundred butterflies form her diadem.'

3 Best.D15027 (19 May 1768); Rieu was later to inherit the English books in Voltaire's library, a number of which have recently gone to the Dé-

lices, by the generosity of Rieu's descendants, now English, in particular the distinguished man of letters E. V. Rieu.

4 Desnoiresterres vii.203 for once goes badly astray. He misrepresents Wagnière's words, and then concludes

It was in these circumstances that mme Denis left Ferney on 1 March 1768. That very evening Wagnière sent to her at Lyons, this letter:

I thought at a quarter past twelve that monsieur de Voltaire would kill me. After he had been alone for an hour with father Adam I was surprised when he said that you were sleeping very late. I cried out that you had left at ten o'clock, and that I thought father Adam had told him. He was furiously angry with me, although I told him that you had all knocked for a long time at his doors, which were closed on both sides, and that monsieur Dupuits tried three times to get into his rooms. I was so upset that I still feel quite ill. Still, he has calmed down a little.

He tore up the promissory note by which he undertook to give you twenty thousand *livres* a year. I think he will send you another when you are in Paris. Master Nicod has returned the power of attorney. My heart thumped a little when I gave it to him. He looked through it calmly and put it into his desk, saying that it was quite in order.

Thus, madame, passed this sad day. My heart wishes you a good journey, and I hope that we shall soon have the happiness to see you again at Ferney.

It would be possible to comment on this letter at great length, but that would take us too far afield. Two words must suffice. After the death of her uncle mme Denis behaved very badly to the amiable Wagnière, and with great meanness. She said that it was because he had always been her enemy and had stirred up her uncle against her. From all that we knew of Jean Louis's character, the accusation seemed improbable, and this letter now shows that it was indeed false. Wagnière's letter betrays only genuine friendship, and indeed it could be claimed that it shows some indiscreet tenderness.

Then, and this is much more important, the words 'He tore up the promissory note' suggest that Voltaire, in the first flush of his indignation about his niece's unceremonious departure, and its causes, had decided to do no more for the woman to whom he had already given a large part of his fortune[5] and whom he had main-

that mme Denis was expelled because she took La Harpe's part: a notion factually without a shred of evidence and psychologically untenable on both sides.

5 To such an extent was this the case that on the morning of her departure mme Denis had to execute a power of attorney in favour of her uncle in order to enable him to administer Ferney (see

29 *Voltaire à la canne, from the ivory by or after Joseph Rosset*

30 Voltaire, *from the painted plaster by Lucas de Montigny*

tained in luxury for thirty years. However, Wagnière could not divine what was in Voltaire's mind; but we now can, for Voltaire's intentions emerge from yet another previously unpublished letter written on the same day. This was addressed to the président d'Hornoy, son of the first marriage of Voltaire's younger niece, who was now marquise de Florian; *maman* is mme Denis's nickname[6]; mme Dupuits was Marie Corneille; the business concerning the duke of Wurttemberg was the annuity Voltaire had bought from him and which he always had difficulty in collecting; Blet was the duc de Richelieu's man of business, responsible for the affairs of the Guise family, which was heavily indebted to Voltaire, who had advanced them the money they needed when the princess de Guise married his friend Richelieu.

Maman and *madame* will soon do what I should like to do, embrace you. *Maman* must absolutely spend a little time in Paris for the benefit of her gums, which are in a dangerous state, and I shall have to go myself to put some permanent order into my business with the duke of Wurttemberg, who will never owe me twelve years like the marshals of France.

I should like to share with her the whole of marshal de Richelieu's debt to me, which amounts I believe to 27,425 *livres*. It would be well if the whole were paid at one time. *Maman*, who knows him intimately, will get him to pay up more easily than a bailiff. It is true that she is no longer at an age that opens the purse of dukes and peers, but an old liaison is always respected. Between you, you will certainly manage to get something out of the abbé Blet.

One cannot but admire the discretion, the loyalty, the self-control of the old gentleman writing to his grand-nephew about the latter's aunt. Mme Denis's gums! And it must not be forgotten that the maréchal-duc's debt which Voltaire so gaily shared with his niece amounted to well over £10,000 at today's values. It is true that if Richelieu had had to reward all his old flames in this way he would have had to multiply his marauding campaigns.

But now we are going to learn what Voltaire really felt on this day, in his heart of hearts. It will be remembered that mme Denis left at 10 o'clock in the morning, without saying good-bye. I have

Best.app.D297-298); Voltaire did try to sell the property on her behalf, and it emerges incidentally that it had cost him to date 500,000 francs (Best. D14820; 8 March 1768, to mme Denis). 6 See p. 59, above.

had the good fortune to discover a letter[7] Voltaire wrote to his niece at two o'clock on this fateful day, one of the most moving letters he ever wrote:

There is no doubt a destiny, and it is often very cruel. Three times I came to your door, and you knocked at mine. I wanted to take my sorrow into the garden. It was ten o'clock, I moved the needle of the globe to ten o'clock, I waited for you to wake up. I met there monsieur Mallet. He told me that he was unhappy because of your departure. I supposed that he had just left your rooms. I thought that you would dine at the château as you had said you would. No servant told me anything, they all thought that I knew. I sent for Christin and father Adam. We talked until noon. Finally I returned to your door. I asked for you. Wagnière said, 'Why! don't you know that she left at ten o'clock!' More dead than alive I turned to father Adam. He gave me the same answer as Wagnière, 'I thought that you knew'. I sent at once to the stables for a horse. There was nobody there. So, in the same house, with twenty servants, we looked for each other in vain. I am in despair, and this persistent ill-luck foreshadows a most sinister future. I know that the moment of separation would have been frightful, but it is still more frightful that you should have left without seeing me, while we were looking for each other. I quickly sent for mme Racle to weep with her. She is dining with Christin, Adam and her husband; and I am very far from dining. I suffer, and I write to you. . . .

You will see monsieur de Choiseul, de Richelieu, d'Argental. You will appease my sorrows: that also is your destiny. You will succeed in your affairs and in mine. You will see again your brother and your nephew. If I die, I die wholly yours; if I live, my life is yours. I tenderly kiss monsieur and mme Dupuits. I love them, I regret them, I am cut to the heart.

Such, in part, is the letter Voltaire wrote to this niece who owed him all, who had a hundred times betrayed him, who had been guilty of the most vulgar wrongs, and who had left without a word of farewell after forty years of friendship and love. Such is the letter of the man whom his enemies paint as vindictive and heartless.

It is thus two o'clock or half past two on the afternoon of Tuesday, 1 March 1768. Voltaire found only one consolation in his sorrow: he plunged into even greater activity than usual, with a noble and sad serenity. The good Wagnière must have gone to bed that night with a fine writer's cramp.

We find first of all a correspondence with the French resident

7 Best.D14789; this letter, like all Voltaire's letters to his niece, and many others of great importance, is now in the Pierpont Morgan library.

in Geneva, Pierre Michel Hennin. I say correspondence because on this day the courier's horse must have made four, perhaps even six, times the journey between Ferney and the resident's *hôtel* in Geneva. In the morning Voltaire had already written a long letter to assure Hennin that a certain 'Languedocienne with fine eyes' could not have seen the second book of the *Guerre civile*, and that it was La Harpe who was responsible for the publication. He also asked for the newspapers. Hennin sent them, and asked Voltaire to let him know if he would like to have company. 'You cannot doubt that it would be a pleasure to prove to you my devotion at any time and any way.' The same evening Voltaire returned the papers to his 'dear minister'. '*Maman* has gone, I have turned hermit. You know that the devil became one in his old age. But whatever they may say, I am not a devil.'

Between the first and last of these letters there was a regular avalanche of correspondence. Here is one to his 'divine angel' comte d'Argental, sending him a little pamphlet which he disavows, as usual, but the title, style and subject of which all bear his hall-mark, the *Lettre de l'archevêque de Cantorbéri à l'archevêque de Paris*, published on this very day. This is one of his tracts in defence of Marmontel's *Bélisaire* against the intolerant thundering of the church. As for the voyage of mme Denis and the Dupuits, it is necessary. He wishes that he could have gone with them. But in this letter to his most intimate friend Voltaire does not so much as mention La Harpe. Why? Precisely because the loyal Argental would have had a lively and dangerous reaction. A few weeks later, in reply to an inquiry from his friend, Voltaire explained that he did not mention the La Harpe incident because he was convinced that, however badly the young writer had behaved, he had not intended to injure his host. 'He is young, he is poor, he is married; he needs help, and I did not want to deprive him of your esteem.'[8]

To the duchesse de Choiseul Voltaire wrote one of his most gracefully complimentary letters, sending her his *Dîner du comte de Boulainvilliers*, telling her that she could and should read every-thing: 'conversation amuses, but books instruct'. This sounds platitudinous to us: it was anything but that in eighteenth century France, addressed by a man to a beautiful and pious duchess.

8 Best.D14954 (16 April 1768).

Next we have a letter to the young Chabanon, whose play *Eudoxie* had been written at Ferney, under the great man's eyes: 'So *maman*, my dear colleague, will see *Eudoxie* before me. She is leaving for Paris, she will let mme Dupuits judge whether plays are better acted in Paris than at Ferney. . . . She is going to attend to her health, her affairs and mine. Everything has gone to wrack and ruin during the twenty years she has been far from Paris. . . . Ferney has now again become a desert, as it was before I took it in hand. I abandon Melpomene for Ceres and Pomona. Noble youth, cultivate the fine arts and surfeit yourself with pleasure, I have had my day.'

Then we have a letter to the charming Dorat. La Harpe had previously been guilty of a milder indiscretion: he had sent to Paris from Ferney an epigrammatic dart intended for the graceful poet:

> Bon Dieu, que cet auteur est triste en sa gaîté!
> Bon Dieu, qu'il est pesant dans sa légèreté!
> Que ses petits écrits ont de longues préfaces!
> Ses fleurs sont des pavôts, ses ris sont des grimaces.
> Que l'encens qu'il prodigue est plat et sans odeur!
> Il est, si je l'en crois, un heureux petit-maître;
> Mais, si j'en crois ses vers, qu'il est triste d'être
> Ou sa maîtresse ou son lecteur![9]

This is not at all in the style of Voltaire, but it is amusing, and so was automatically attributed to him. But the great archer preferred to manufacture his own darts, and above all to choose his own targets. He had not the slightest wish to hurt the feelings of the young Dorat, and this is why he went into great detail in writing to him, concluding: 'In short, sir, I am too sincere and too frank to be disbelieved when I swore to mme Necker that I had no share in this mischievous affair. It is for you to know who are your enemies. I am not one of them. . . .'

Here is a letter to François Louis Henri Leriche, a high government official at Besançon. Voltaire complains that his letters have

9 'Good god, how sad is the gaiety of this writer! Good god, how heavy is his lightest touch! How long are the prefaces of his little writings! His flowers are poppies, his smiles are grimaces. How flat and odourless is the incense with which he is so lavish! If he is to be believed he is a lucky lover; but to judge by his verse how sad it is to be his mistress or his reader!'

been impudently seized at Saint-Claude. He protests that the insolent inquisitions of certain persons are against the laws of the kingdom, and he concludes: 'A very great revolution is taking place in men's minds in Italy and Spain. The whole world is shaking off the chains of fanaticism, but the shade of the chevalier de La Barre cries in vain for vengeance against his murderers.'

Here is a letter to the supreme trusteeship council of Montbéliard, which had become by marriage the property of the duke of Wurttemberg. We know that Voltaire had bought an annuity from the current duke on the security of Montbéliard and other properties. The duke and his council found it shocking that a poet should expect to be paid regularly and punctually. Voltaire was obliged to write over and over again to receive the money due to him, and he even had to threaten to go to law. This time he tried pathos: 'I find myself in a difficult situation, in an abyss from which I shall never be able to extricate myself without the arrangements you have so kindly made.' And he adds: 'If I were alone, you may be sure, gentlemen, that I would not importune you; but I have a numerous family which has no other resource than the income in question.'

Here is a letter to the duc de Richelieu, to announce to this old friend the arrival of mme Denis. 'My adopted daughter Corneille is accompanying her to Paris, where she will witness the massacre of her great-uncle's plays. As for me, I remain in my desert. Somebody must look after the country household. This is my consolation.' For the rest: 'I already regard myself as a dead man although I enliven my death-throes as much as I can.'

Here is a letter to the chevalier de Rochefort d'Ally to thank him for a present. 'You have sent me champagne whem I am on diet of herb-tea; it's like sending a girl to a eunuch.'

I have given only short extracts from most of these letters; but here is a note to the pastor Jacob Vernes, which is exceptional among the letters of this 1 March in that it is short, so that I can quote it in full.

Priest of a God father of all men, preacher of reason, tolerant priest, if you want to have the philosophic soldier by the late saint-Hiacinthe[10] your

---

10 That is, *Le Militaire philosophe, ou difficultés sur la religion* (1768), published by Naigeon and Holbach under a pseudonym.

illustrious and worthy friend monsieur de Moultou has it and will lend it to you on presentation of this note.

Have you read the sermon preached at Basle? I think it is by your little brother.

Mme Denis is going to Paris on temporal affairs. When are you coming here to discuss spiritual ones?

The little brother, author of the *Sermon prêché à Bâle le premier jour de l'an 1768, par Josias Rosette, ministre du saint evangile*[11], was Voltaire himself, who had written it to render thanks for 'the greatest event which has distinguished the century in which we live', that is, the expulsion of the Jesuits.

And with this letter, the fifteenth, we come to the end of Voltaire's 1 March 1768, a long weary day on which he gave a noble example of toleration and self-control. Seldom indeed is it possible to follow a great man's thoughts and feelings on a single day in such intimate detail. I hope the reader will agree with me that Voltaire emerges as a very human, a kindly and a lovable man.

11 It had been published a few days earlier.

39. *A busy pause, 1769-1771*

IN 1769 VOLTAIRE celebrated his seventy-fifth birthday; he referred more and more frequently to his dissolution and impending death, but there is little trace of old age either in his work or even in his handwriting. It is true that these years were almost entirely barren of substantial books, barren, that is, by Voltairean standards, for they did after all see the publication of one of his most important books, the *Histoire du parlement de Paris*.

This book, like all Voltaire's major works, went into numerous editions, and had considerable influence, as its author intended. It was, however, exceptional in that it was never officially prosecuted, though more than once threatened with condemnation. Voltaire showed in much detail how the *parlements*, at once legislative and juridical, come into being, and how their scope and power had developed since their ancient beginnings. Perhaps their most valuable function was the right of registering, that is, of approving, the king's decrees. The system is inverted today in the United States: the enactments of Congress become law only when the president signs them. He can refuse to do so but only at the cost of conflict with the legislature, which must eventually win by the exercise of political power. In the *ancien régime* the *parlements* could remonstrate (this was the official word) against royal laws which they did not approve. The king could then call a *lit de justice* (a plenary meeting which he attended in person) at which he tried to bully them. If this did not succeed he could and did arrest or exile the members. Such a system naturally produced a permanent state of tension, which now and then exploded into fierce conflict.

In its judicial capacity the record of the *parlement* of Paris, with which Voltaire was chiefly concerned, was bloodstained and grotesque. Voltaire described its conduct after the massacre of St Bartholomew, and its ideological edicts, as when it declared in favour of Aristotle and against inoculation (as he recorded also in his *Notebooks*), though he recognised that it performed valuable services, as when it saved France under Henri IV. Voltaire concluded that a reform of the institution had become indispensable.

Nor is the *Collection d'anciens évangiles* by any means negligible. It is a systematic survey and partial translation of the apocryphal books of the *Bible*, with a great display of erudition, much of it at secondhand, to be sure. Voltaire shows the absurdities contained in these writings excluded from the sacred canon, nowhere explicitly stating but everywhere clearly implying that after all these absurdities are no worse than those in the approved books of the *Bible*. Voltaire is at his most dangerous in his pose as a defender of sacred scripture, as when he points out that *Matthew* xxiii.35 refers to Zachariah, son of Barachiah, although Zachariah was killed long after the supposed date of the gospel; but, says Voltaire, the objection is specious.[1]

This relative paucity of long writings was not due to a slackening of energy: on the contrary, it was because Voltaire was devoting more and more of his time to what became *La Raison par alphabet* and, in due course, the *Questions sur l'encyclopédie*, pouring out articles of every description. As an unkind wit said of a far lesser man, Voltaire was reading with his left hand, and writing with his right hand. Although there is no lack of letters to all and sundry on an equally wide range of subjects, Voltaire may be said with little exaggeration to have been almost wholly preoccupied with 'âme' and 'ange' and 'adorer'. The first batch of volumes appeared towards the end of 1770, and Voltaire continued his work on the rest of the alphabet, though now with increasing weariness. The thinning of the material as the *Questions* advance is striking.

Even so, the year is remarkable for the quantity of his minor publications, both as author and editor. In the latter capacity he produced the first editions of the *Journal de la cour de Louis XIV*, which are the memoirs of Philippe de Courcillon, marquis de Dangeau (1638-1720) and of *Les Souvenirs de madame de Caylus*[2],

1 Voltaire's reference to *Matthew* is incorrect, but every editor has reproduced it.

2 Voltaire's editions of Dangeau and mme de Caylus are both dated 1770 in their first editions, but both were published in 1769.

that is, Marguerite La Vallois de Villette-Mursay, marquise de Caylus (1673-1729). The former journal was described by Voltaire as the work of an old imbecile who had gathered together all the gossip of the antechambers of the great[3]. Yet such sweepings have value for the historian, and it is thoroughly characteristic of Voltaire that for all his disdain it was he who first printed extracts from Dangeau's diary, which was not fully published until 1845-1860.

As for mme de Caylus, Voltaire's edition of her memoirs was also the first. Much shorter than those of Dangeau, but much better written and more reliable, they also throw interesting light on the court of Louis xiv. But it must not be imagined for one moment that Voltaire the editor was different from Voltaire the author. Opportunities for an elegant thrust occur not infrequently. Thus, living so far from Paris, Voltaire suffered a great deal from the systematic examination of his correspondence by the 'black office'. A reference by mme de Caylus to the imprudence of a courier gives him the opportunity to add a quiet footnote: 'All letters were opened. This breach of trust, as everybody knows, is no longer committed anywhere.'

The *Lettres d'Amabed,* the *Canonisation de Saint-Cucufin, Tout en dieu, Dieu et les hommes, Le Cri des nations,* the *Défense de Louis XIV* and the *Requête à tous les magistrats du royaume* are most notable among Voltaire's shorter original writings in prose in these years, but only a few words can be devoted to the works listed in this catalogue.

Les Lettres d'Amabed is an oriental tale, the first letter in which is dated from Benares, on the second day of the month of the mouse in the year 115,652, that is, in A.D. 1512. It is the story of an encounter between simple orientals and the civilisation of the west, including the inquisition of Goa and a lecherous Father Fa tutto.

The *Canonisation de saint Cucufin* is a *jeu d'esprit* concerning in the main contemporary notions of the sacred. Voltaire pointed out that the ancients respected their gods so much that no empress, for instance, would have dared to take the names of Juno,

3 At the end of the *Dissertation sur la mort de Henri IV.*

Minerva, Latona, Venus or Iris, whereas in our society any Tom, Dick or Harry is given the name of John or Matthew, and even, Voltaire might have added, of Jesus. He then explores the principles of canonisation, but instead of making all too easy fun of them, he points out how agreeable it would be if we followed the examples of the Romans. They had their Divus Trajanus and Divus Antoninus, why should we not have our saint Bayard and saint Montmorency? When he turned to the female saints, Voltaire thought that he was being wildly funny when he suggested the canonisation of Joan of Arc, but of course the church has caught up with him in our own century.

The subtitle of *Dieu et les hommes* describes this treatise as a 'theological but rational work', and the first chapter is entitled 'Our crimes and our follies'. It is thus easy to guess the nature of the book. In yet another passage that reveals Voltaire's profound convictions he describes the recourse to a god who rewards and avenges as the most powerful antidote against men's wickedness. In so doing Voltaire offers a bitter and disillusioned definition of civilisation, which is to be wicked and unhappy in towns instead of in the open air or in caves (ch. ii). Yet, oddly enough, *Dieu et les hommes* purports to be a demonstration of the existence of a god. Voltaire achieved this by implying that an atheist is one who maintains that one can lie, murder and the like if one is the strongest in a society. This was so obviously absurd that the reader no doubt drew his own conclusions about Voltaire's real intentions.

Voltaire then proceeded to make yet another survey of the history of religion, showing that in so far as it is not absurd it is universal and ancient. He makes the implication quite clear by heading one chapter 'On India, the Brahmans and their theology, imitated much later by the Jews and then by the Christians' (ch. v). He also shows that the notion of a Jewish religion is unhistorical, since that religion changed continually until the captivity. He also has no difficulty in showing that if Moses ever existed, and if he wrote the pentateuch, then he was a plagiarist, since much that is found in those books was clearly borrowed from Sanchuniathon (ch. xiii ff.). However, Voltaire was not aware that what Philo says about this Phoenician is just as dubious as the statements of the *Bible* about Moses.

When he comes to Christianity Voltaire exclaims that only a fanatic or a rascal could maintain that the history of Jesus must not be submitted to the light of reason. How else should it be examined? By the light of folly? he questions in his purest anti-Pascalian mood (ch. xxxi). He concludes with judicious ambiguity that Jesus had really existed, although everything we are told about him is untrue and although no contemporary reference to him is known. As for the 'innumerable frauds of the Christians', they did not prevent the success of the new religion, which was due to the pagan beliefs absorbed by the early devotees. In fact Christianity brought great evils to the world, including the murder in its name of 9,468,800 human beings (ch. xlii).

Tout en dieu is a very different sort of essay: a commentary on Malebranche, but with the same purpose. Voltaire quotes ancient writers, including st Paul, who maintained that all existence is in god. So did Malebranche, but his commentary is even more obscure than the original texts. Voltaire therefore set out to make the notion intelligible. He examined the laws of nature, the mechanics of the senses and of ideas, and concluded that none of these things can exist in themselves and must therefore be part of a prime cause. But Voltaire despised metaphysics, and could not take such inquiries seriously. Thus he was led inevitably to circular arguments which are quite meaningless. An example is his discussion of light, in which he maintained quite seriously that light is useless unless apprehended, that light extends throughout the universe, and therefore that there must be life throughout the universe.

As usual evil is the stumbling block. What is virtue? An act of will, my will derives from god, therefore virtue is divine. In that case evil must also derive from god. Voltaire faces the issue squarely, and concludes that since evil is, and therefore derives from god, this can only be so because evil is necessary. This from the man who wrote the Lisbon poem and *Candide*! Such an argument in Voltaire's mouth is so absurd that one is again driven to the conclusion that he meant it to be seen to be absurd. And of course the whole essay is in fact a prolonged exercise in irony, as he allows to transpire from the final paragraph of *Tout en dieu*, where he says that he submits his feeble understanding to 'the superior penetration of those whose duty it is to illuminate my steps in the darkness of this world'.

Among the more simply literary works of these years are the plays *Sophonisbe* and *Les Pélopides*, and a dozen verse epistles, including some of the most important. The *Epître à Boileau* is sub-titled 'my testament', and it is indeed one of the very rare writings in which Voltaire speaks of his childhood[4] and life. In the main, however, the poem is a survey of the public events of the past half-century. In the *Epître à monsieur de Saint-Lambert* Voltaire bemoaned the lot of the peasant, whose son has to go to Paris to wait on the rich, and comes back an officer of the law to oppress his own family. He concluded by asking for how long the virtuous tiller of the soil will continue to feed his oppressors. A better time would no doubt come in another world. As for this one, he had no hope.

The *Epître au roi de la Chine*, who had published a volume of verse, turns out to be a satire of the French literary scene. The *Epître au roi de Danemark* celebrated Christian VII's edict according liberty to the press. In the *Epître à l'impératrice de Russie*, the last of these royal epistles, Voltaire apostrophised Catherine:

> Elève d'Apollon, de Thémis, et de Mars,
> Qui sur ton trône auguste as placé les beaux-arts,
> Qui penses en grand homme, et qui permets qu'on pense;
> Toi qu'on voit triompher du tyran de Byzance,
> Et des sots préjugés, tyrans plus odieux,
> Prête à ma faible voix des sons mélodieux;
> A mon feu qui s'éteint rends sa clarté première:
> C'est du nord aujourd'hui que nous vient la lumière.[5]

The Russo-Turkish war produced much Russian correspondence, for Catherine was anxious to secure Voltaire's public sympathy, and succeeded. The political and military events also led to a formidable revival in the correspondence with Frederick of Prussia, in its tone and volume almost reminiscent of old times.

---

4 See p. 28, above.

5 'Pupil of Apollo, Themis and Mars, who has placed the arts on your august throne, who thinks as a great man, and who allows others to think; you whom we see to triumph over the tyrant of Byzantium and stupid prejudices, even more odious tyrants; lend melodious sounds to my feeble voice, give back to my inspiration its former clarity: light now comes to us from the north.'

But the royal star at this time was undoubtedly Catherine. In February 1769 an embassy arrived at Ferney from Russia, bearing gifts. By a lucky chance James Callandar (afterwards sir James Campbell of Ardkinglas, bart.) was present when the Russian embassy was received at Ferney, and has left this account of the ceremony:

When at Geneva I was invited to Ferney to assist at the presentation of the Prince Dolgouroukie, a young man of very high rank in Russia, who came to Voltaire at the head of a deputation from the Empress Catherine the Second, than whom, perhaps no one has ever been more anxious as to what should be said of her by the world. Voltaire had contributed to foster, at the same time that he gratified, this passion, by writing a great deal in the Empress's praise; and the presents which were bought by the Prince Dolgouroukie were probably intended either as a reward for past praises, or as a retaining fee for the future. I say nothing of the truth of what he has written, but content myself with recording what I witnessed at the reception of the embassy.

The presents were produced by the Prince in succession, and exhibited with great state and ceremony. The first was an ivory box, the value of which consisted in its being the work of the Empress's own hands. The next was her Imperial Majesty's portrait, brilliantly set in diamonds, of very great value; and I could not resist the idea that the eyes of the philosopher sparkled with delight at the splendid setting of the picture, rather than at the picture itself. Then followed a collection of books in the Russian language, which Voltaire admitted that he did not understand; but he admired them, and very justly, as rare specimens of typography, and as being bound in a style of magnificence befitting an Imperial gift. The last of the presents was a robe, the lining of which was of the fur of the black fox, from the Curile Isles. It was certainly of immense value, and such only as the Empress of Russia could give. The Prince, on producing it, begged to be shown into a darkened room, where, on drawing his hand across the fur, it produced so much electrical fire, that it was possible to read by it. This was ascribed to the extreme closeness or thickness with which the hair was set on the skin.

In return for these princely gifts, Voltaire had his portrait drawn by my friend Huber, in which he was exhibited in rather an extraordinary position, rising out of bed in an ecstasy upon the presents being presented to him. The picture was accompanied by a copy of verses in the Empress's praise, in the taste of the period, and of course sufficiently nauseous and fulsome.[6]

Callandar's prince was in fact Fedor Alexeevich Kozlovsky, and his enumeration is incomplete, for the empress had also sent a

6 *Memoirs of sir James Campbell of Ardkinglas* (London 1832), p. 186.

French translation of the new code of laws, a manuscript account of Catherine's inoculation, and letters. The new laws were, at least in intention, compiled under the influence of Voltaire, and the inoculation was a personal triumph for him and the campaign he had waged on this subject since the *Lettres philosophiques*. In exchange for all this Voltaire sent not only some feeble verse, but also plans for a war-chariot which was to astonish and subjugate the Turks[7]—but the military declined his proposal without thanks.

More agreeable were the charming exchanges with the duchess de Choiseul, Voltaire writing as if he were a Lyons compositor, and the duchess sometimes assuming the character of her maid. Voltaire, in order to diversify the economy of Ferney and to set up the young Calas in trade, had created a silk factory. He told mme Du Deffand with pride that he learnt how to breed silk-worms in a country covered with snow for seven months in the year; and the silk he produced was better than that of Italy.[8] To show what he could do, he asked mme de Choiseul for one of her shoes. To tease him she sent a huge one, whereupon she became mme Gargantua, but nevertheless found that the silk stockings he made specially fitted her. When Voltaire dropped the mask of Guillemet she expressed her regret. She was quite willing to correspond with the leading printer of Lyons, but she would blush if she dared to correspond with 'the greatest genius of all time'. She enjoined him to continue in his efforts to diminish the sum of human folly, notwithstanding all the annoyances this caused him: he should console himself by thinking of the altars posterity would erect in his honour.[9]

Less amusing was the tug of war between Voltaire and mme Denis. The uncle tried hard to discourage the niece from returning to Ferney, reminding her how horrible she had found country life. Her unpaid bills were still flooding in, he told her ruefully, but he would look after her if she remained in Paris. If she returned to share his solitude, he asked her, 'Could you bear it? What consoles me, would it console you? I tremble lest you be not happy. Are you not frightened by a solitude in a desert in the midst of

7 Best.D15487 (26 February 1769).
8 Best.D15876 (6 September 1769).
9 Best.D15933 (30 September 1769).

the snows? No festivities, no play-going, not even any society. Could a parisienne like you put up with me?'[10] Mme Denis, on the other hand, tempted Voltaire to return to Paris. She even held out to him the prospect of obtaining the king's consent, which, she hinted, she was on the point of securing. 'You were born gay, nature prodigally endowed you with all her gifts, don't lose that of gaiety. . . . Why sadden one's life when one possesses every facility to make it agreeable? You may be sure that there is no man of any kind who would not like to be in your place. Would you change with another? Certainly not.'[11] All this was true enough in the kind of worldly context which is all that mme Denis was capable of understanding. To her one could be happy only in the dissipation of Paris, but she need not have concerned herself. Voltaire's gaiety was deeper than she realised, and resistant to old age and a sea of troubles, as testifies, among many others, his letter to cardinal de Bernis, in which he asked him to obtain the pope's permission for Voltaire's domestic Jesuit Adam to wear a wig when saying mass. In view of the enmity of the bishop of Geneva the poor rheumatic priest could not do so without the full plenitude of apostolic power.[12]

Another beautiful example of wit and gaiety is the letter (which I translate in its entirety) Voltaire wrote to the duke of Grafton on the publication of a forged letter: 'I see in *The Whitehall evening post* of the 7th of October 1769, no. 3668, an alleged letter written by me to his majesty the king of Prussia. This letter is very foolish, nevertheless I did not write it.'[13]

The result of the debate between uncle and niece was a draw, for if Voltaire resisted the blandishments of mme Denis and remained at Ferney, she equally resisted Voltaire's strongest hints, and soon after left the capital and returned (complete with what she regarded as a suitable retinue) to Ferney (27 October 1769). Not that she was eager to return to the 'frightful solitude' of which she had so often complained, but she was anxious about her inheritance. At any rate, uncle and niece were again reunited, this time

10 Best.D15786 (31 July 1769).
11 Best.D15603 (23 April 1769).
12 Best.D15681 (12 June 1769). Although there was a technical defect
in Adam's petition Bernis duly sent the authorization (Best.D15764, 19 July).
13 Best.D15977 (29 October 1769).

for good, so far as physical proximity was concerned. Mme Denis at once reported to mme d'Argental that Voltaire seemed fairly well. His passion for work was as great as ever. He worked fifteen hours a day, and would be in hell if he could not work. He had more imagination than ever and had some charming things in preparation. Mme Denis added that her uncle was very pleased to see her back.[14] This we may take leave to doubt, but perhaps Voltaire was a little consoled by a company of marionettes who came to show him Corneille and Racine waiting for him in paradise.[15]

In the midst of continued preoccupation with the Sirven case, the victim of which in his turn (luckily still alive) approached rehabilitation, Voltaire found time to take immense pains on behalf of Durey de Morsan, a less meritorious object of his benevolence.

Voltaire's ever increasing interest in purely social problems is eloquently expressed in a remarkable letter to Du Pont de Nemours, his most explicit statement in this field since that contained in the remarkable outburst[16] of November 1758. Writing to Du Pont (whose revolutionary and American adventures were to make him famous) about Saint-Lambert's pastoral poem *Les Saisons*, Voltaire was carried away to a wider disquisition on the miseries of the French countryside. But in the midst of this he indulged in a lyrical description of the farm he had created at Ferney, which he described as a

vast rustic house, entered, through four great gateways, by chariots heaped with all the spoils of the countryside. The oak columns which support the whole framework are placed at equal distances in stone sockets. Long stables stretch to the right and left. Fifty well-kept cows occupy one side with their calves: the horses and oxen are on the other. Their fodder falls into their troughs from lofty granaries.

In the middle are the barns in which the grain is beaten. . . . In the midst of these fine monuments of agriculture are the poultry-yard and the sheepfolds. To the north are the presses, the store-rooms, the fruit stores; to the east the lodgings of the bailiff and of thirty servants; to the west extend the great meadows grazed and fertilised by all these animals, man's labouring companions.

The trees of the orchard, loaded with different kinds of fruits are yet another source of wealth. Four or five hundred beehives are set up by a little stream that waters this orchard—

14 Best.D15994 (12 November 1769).

15 Best.D15784 (30 July 1769).

16 See p. 407, above.

and much more in the same vein.[17]

Voltaire continued to have financial difficulties with the Wurttemberg authorities—we can echo Jane Austen's 'an annuity is a very serious business'; and life at Ferney went on as usual, on the principle *labor ipse voluptas*. The correspondence with Frederick had lapsed for a year or two, but now resumed with much of its old vigour. When Clement XIII died Voltaire remembered that Matthias was chosen by lot to succeed Judas[18], and proceeded to throw dice for a new pope[19]. And after Ganganelli had been elected he told Bernis that the new pope appeared to be a good fellow, since he had not committed any folly since his reign began[20]: as this reign had then lasted only a few months the tribute was not even as warm as might appear. Yet the cardinal did not hesitate to repeat the jest to the pope, who heard it with pleasure, and praised Voltaire's superior talents.[21]

Voltaire may well be the only man of letters in modern times to whom his contemporaries raised a statue during his lifetime. Mme Necker told him that he had erected his own countless monuments: his works would convey his glory to all the centuries, but his contemporaries wanted themselves to immortalise the delirium of their hearts.[22] The idea was taken up with enthusiasm, even Rousseau offering a subscription, which Voltaire regrettably declined. As for Frederick, he waxed positively lyrical. 'Voltaire's finest monument', he told Alembert, 'is the one he has erected to himself, his works, which will remain longer than the basilica of st Peter, the Louvre and all the buildings consecrated by human vanity to eternity. When French is no longer spoken, Voltaire will still be translated into whatever language has succeeded it.'[23] The more than respectable sum of nearly 19,000 francs was subscribed.

Voltaire asked the sculptor what he could make of his emaciated form, and made him a prophetically neoclassical proposal:

> Sculptez-nous quelque beauté nue,
> De qui la chair blanche et dodue

17 Best.D15679 (7 June 1769).
18 *Acts* i.26.
19 Best.D15482 (20 February 1769).
20 Best.D15996 (13 November 1769).

21 Best.D16188 (28 February 1770).
22 Best.D16284 (*c.* 9 April 1770).
23 Best.D16552 (28 July 1770); the letter is quoted in full in the autobiography, pp. 667-668, below.

Séduise l'œil du spectateur,
Et qui dans son âme insinue
Ces doux désirs et cette ardeur
Dont Pygmalion le sculpteur,
Votre digne prédécesseur,
Brûla, si la fable en est crue.[24]

Pigalle cruelly took the hint to this extent: his famous statue shows Voltaire in the nude. However modest he may have been Voltaire could not but be pleased by this extraordinary testimonial. But when he learned that the inscription 'To the living Voltaire' had been proposed he objected that it should be to the dying Voltaire.[25]

This gratifying event provided some badly needed consolation during a period of acute tension in his relations with the Genevese authorities. The political situation continued to involve Voltaire and his neighbours in material difficulties, and the authorities seemed for a while disposed to aggravate them. They should have been grateful to the sage of Ferney, whose generosity and hospitality kept many watchmakers near Geneva, to return there in due course. The future of the republic would have been less prosperous had these skilled men dispersed to more distant places. On the other hand, Voltaire's active support of Versoix was distinctly unwelcome in Geneva, and for better reasons. One can almost sympathise with the devout Genevese scientist Charles Bonnet when he exclaimed that providence had permitted earthquakes, floods, heresy and Voltaire.[26] But it was in vain that Voltaire cried to Choiseul with the voice of John in the desert. If Choiseul had built even fifty houses at Versoix 400 homeless emigrants from Geneva could be housed, who would not be obliged to go to England or Holland. But Voltaire, in his most biblical vein, submitted such considerations in vain to the dull eye and the ophidian prudence of Choiseul.[27] The old man offered to put up his own money and to start building at Versoix himself.[28]

24 *Epître à monsieur Pigalle*. The poem is quoted and translated in full in the autobiography, pp. 668-671, below. See also pp. 444-445, above.
25 Best.D16316 (27 April 1770).

26 In a letter to Haller of 6 November 1767 (Bibliothèque publique et universitaire, Geneva, MSS Bonnet).
27 Best.D16159 (18 February 1770).
28 Best.D16227 (14 March 1770).

But it was all useless. He was obliged to limit his efforts to his own Ferney.

And Voltaire now discovered that it was no small matter to establish an industry in a village. He came to be more and more caught up by the practical problems of housing and feeding the watchmakers whom he had welcomed at Ferney, of finding gold and other raw materials for their workshops, and finally of discovering new outlets for their products. He dealt with all these difficulties with his usual energy, efficiency and success, for all his bad health. He wrote pathetically to one of his doctors: 'An old man of seventy-six has long since been attacked by a scorbutic humour which has always reduced him to a very great emaciation, which has lost him nearly all his teeth, which sometimes attacks the tonsils, which often gives him the rumblings, insomnias, etc. etc. caused by his illness, begs m. Bouvard to have the kindness to write at the foot of this note whether he thinks that goat's milk could procure him some relief.'[29]

Voltaire overcame all the difficulties, practical, economic and political, and by 9 April 1770 the first consignment of watches left for Spain, for the Cadiz trade. When one of the Genevese politicians brought him a 'masterpiece of eloquence' Voltaire told him that he would have done better to bring him a watch-pinion.[30] A high official, sent by the French government to inquire into the state of affairs at Versoix, said in his report: 'I must do m. de Voltaire the justice of stating that he has welcomed eighty emigrants on his Ferney estate, has built there four houses, and lent them money, and the watch-making workshops have been set up in such a way as to give a very favourable notion of the benefit that can be drawn from the emigrants. This is an obligation we owe to m. de Voltaire, and it is not the only one that the province of Gex owes him.'[31]

By 1770 Choiseul's urbane incompetence led France to the brink of renewed war, which was indeed averted only by his dismissal. His fall deprived Voltaire of a powerful supporter, and also of a friend, for the fallen minister and his charming duchess

29 Best.D16198 (5 March 1770).
30 Best.D16281 (9 April 1770).
31 Best.D16459, note (29 June 1770); eventually Voltaire built ten times as many houses.

found Voltaire's loyalty inadequate because he refused to condemn automatically all the measures of the new government. This Voltaire could not do. He followed the changes with the closest attention, and approved some of them, in particular the reforms in the administration. All this makes the correspondence of this period specially interesting even by Voltairean standards. The political crisis in fact involved Ferney in much stimulating discussion with the new and the old leaders of affairs. The international situation brought some particularly notable exchanges apart from those with Catherine and Frederick.

In addition to the usual literary and philosophical discussions, there was an unusually wide range of family correspondence, and a spate of letters to and from publishers. One proposal unfortunately fell through: an offer from Baskerville, the great Birmingham printer, to produce an edition of Voltaire's works, although 'the old scribbler' promised to send 'his poor sheets duly corrected' and promptly did so.[32] And as if this were not enough, these months produced some particularly interesting contributions by Condorcet, Alembert, and others. Voltaire seemed to be more than ever the radiant centre of intellectual influence. 'His head and his hairs were white like wool, as white as snow, and his eyes were as flame of fire; . . . and his voice as the source of many waters.'

Apart from the *Pélopides*, the literary merits of which are not conspicuous, most of Voltaire's writings at this time were devoted to political affairs, and to seemingly local ones at that. However, the wider implications of his campaigns were never long absent from his thoughts. He also spent a great deal of time in preparing the new edition of his collected works.

The last months of this period marked a sort of pause in Voltaire's life. Perhaps the outstanding event, important enough to be the culminating point of any ordinary man's career, was the final rehabilitation of Sirven. This victim of fanatical intolerance told Voltaire: 'I owe you my life, and what is more, the restoration of my honour and my reputation. . . . You judged me, and the

---

32 Best.D17347, D17451, D17490, D17548, D17613 (September 1771-February 1772); Baskerville's matrices were later bought by Beaumarchais, and the type cast from them was used for the great Kehl edition of Voltaire's works.

informed public dared not differ from you. In enlightening mankind you have succeeded in making them humane.'[33] Alas, not so,
but in saying that he owed Voltaire his life and his honour Sirven
did not exaggerate.

Charles Burney, the musicologist and the father of Fanny
Burney, has left a fascinating account of his visit to Voltaire at
this time. It is too long to quote in full, but I cannot resist repro-
ing at least this passage:

I sent in to enquire whether a stranger might be allowed to see the house &
was answered in the affirmative. The servant soon came & conducted me
into the cabinet or closet where his master had just been writing, which is
never shown when he is at home; but being walked out, I was allowed that
privilege. From thence to the library. Not a very large one, but well filled.
Here I found a whole length figure in marble of himself[34] recumbent in one of
the windows; & many curiosities in another room; a bust of himself not 2
years since; his mother's picture; that of his niece, Madᵉ Denis; her brother,
M. Dupuis; the Calas family, &c. &c. It is a very neat and elegant house, not
large, or affectedly decorated. I should have said, that close to the chapel,
between that and the house, is the theatre, he built some years ago and which
he used as a receptacle for wood and lumber, there having been no play acted
in it these 4 years. The servant told me his master was 78, but very well.
His words were these, Il travaille pendant dix heures chaque jour. He studies
ten hours every day; writes constantly without spectacles, and walks out with
only a domestic, very often a mile or two—'Et le voilà, là bas!'

He was going to his workmen. My heart leaped at the sight of so extraordinary a man. He had just then quitted his garden, and was crossing the
court before his house. Seeing my chaise, and me on the point of mounting
it, he made a sign to his servant, who had been my *Cicerone*, to go to him,
in order, I suppose, to enquire who I was. After they had exchanged a few
words together, he approached the place where I stood, motionless, in order
to contemplate his person as much as I could when his eyes were turned
from me; but on seeing him move towards me, I found myself drawn by
some irresistible power towards him; and, without knowing what I did,
I insensibly met him half-way. It is not easy to conceive it possible for life
to subsist in a form so nearly composed of mere skin and bone, as that of
M. de Voltaire. He complained of decrepitude, and said he supposed I was
curious to form an idea of the figure of one walking after death. However his
eyes and whole countenance are still full of fire; and though so emaciated, a
more lively expression cannot be imagined. He enquired after English news,
and observed that poetical squabbles had given way to political ones; but

33 Best.D17479 (27 November   34 [No such statue is known, and
1771).   Burney certainly made a mistake.]

seemed to think the spirit of opposition as necessary in poetry as in politics. 'Les querelles d'auteurs sont pour le bien de la littérature, comme dans un gouvernement libre, les querelles des grands, et les clameurs des petits sont nécessaires à la liberté.' (Disputes among authors are of use to literature; as the quarrels of the great, and the clamours of the little, in a free government, are necessary to liberty.) And added, 'When critics are silent, it does not so much prove the age to be correct as dull.' He enquired what poets we had now; and I told him we had Mason and Gray. They write but little, said he, and you seem to have no one who lords it over the rest like Dryden, Pope and Swift. I told him that it was, perhaps, one of the inconveniences of periodical journals, however well executed, that they often silenced modest men of genius, while impudent blockheads were impenetrable, and unable to feel the critic's scourge: that Mr Gray and Mr Mason had both been illiberally treated by mechanical critics, even in newspapers; and added, that modesty and love of quiet seemed in these gentlemen to have got the better even of their love of fame. During this conversation, we approached the buildings he was constructing near the road to his château. These, said he, pointing to them, are the most innocent, and, perhaps, the most useful of all my works. I observed that he had other works, which were of far more extensive use, and would be much more durable than those. He was so obliging as to show me several farm-houses he had built, and the plans of others; after which I took my leave, for fear of breaking in upon his time, being unwilling to rob the public of things so precious as the few remaining moments of this great and universal genius.[35]

35 British library, Add. MSS. 35122, ff. 26-7.

40. *Old man in a hurry, 1772*

AS IF TO MAKE UP FOR the busy pause of 1769-71, Voltaire from now on was very much an old man in a hurry. In his seventy-eighth year he turned again to the writing of narrative poems, the *Bégueule* and *Jean qui pleure et Jean qui rit* being by no means his worst efforts in this kind. He also published his tragedy of the *Pélopides*, which Frederick at least classed among its author's masterpieces, singling out in particular the elegance of its versification[1]. It must be owned that this judgment merely underlines the king's uncertain taste.

Voltaire also published two of the most effective of his verse satires, *Les Systèmes* and that most unpacific 'œuvre pacifique' *Les Cabales*. In the former he teased the inventors of metaphysical systems, and in the latter he approached the same subject from a wider point of view, excoriating intellectual and political cliques, intrigues and fashions, concluding:

> Des charmes de la paix mon cœur était frappé;
> J'espérais en jouir: je me suis bien trompé.
> On cabale à la cour, à l'armée, au parterre;
> Dans Londres, dans Paris, les esprits sont en guerre;
> Ils y seront toujours. La Discorde autrefois,
> Ayant brouillé les dieux, descendit chez les rois;
> Puis dans l'Eglise sainte établit son empire,
> Et l'étendit bientôt sur tout ce qui respire.
> Chacun vantait la Paix, que partout on chassa.
> On dit que seulement par grâce on lui laissa
> Deux asiles fort doux: c'est le lit et la table.
> Puisse-t-elle y fixer un règne un peu durable!
> L'un d'eux me plaît encore. Allons, amis, buvons;
> Cabalons pour Chloris, et faisons des chansons.[2]

1 Best.D17708 (22 April 1772).

2 'My heart was struck by the charms of peace; I hoped to enjoy them; I made a great mistake. They intrigue at court, in the army, in the pit; the wits are at war in London, in Paris; they always will be. Once upon a time Discord, having embroiled the gods, descended among the kings; then established her empire in holy church, and soon extended it over all who breathe. Everyone praises peace,

Above all, the spate of pamphlets and of encyclopedic articles resumed its normal energy. Neither war nor rumours of the plague, nor even a real though minor earthquake at home, put any stop to the old man's incessant work, though they did affect his health, and created panic in Geneva and at Ferney. Still, Voltaire's activity was to suffer no further interruption until the end, though now he was much affected by the death of Helvétius, whom at one time he had regarded as his successor. But he still refused to take himself and his prodigious career with undue seriousness. When one of his numerous biographers wrote to him for information he was told that life was short and that Voltaire intended to find better things to do in the little time that remained to him than to answer his commentators. More than four hundred attacks on him had been published, he added.[3] This the commentators have, as usual, treated as rodomontade, but, as usual, the figure is an understatement if substantial articles in journals be included. However, it is a very near estimate limited to French writings. Indeed, a list of books and pamphlets published in French on Voltaire to 1830 runs to 629 items.[4]

During this period Voltaire devoted a great deal of time and energy to the endless and somewhat squalid Morangiés case; to the far more touching one of mme de Bombelles (mlle Camp), whose husband repudiated her on the plea that their marriage was invalid because she was a Protestant; and to that of the serfs of Saint-Claude, this being by far the most important of his general campaigns in its political implications. Most of the peasants of France still lived in a state of feudal servitude, subject to lay as well as ecclesiastic tithes and innumerable taxes, obliged to sacrifice much of their time to road-building and other *corvées*. Voltaire had already pointed out all these grievances in his eloquent *Requête à tous les magistrats du royaume* (1770), and he now discovered that a community of monks in his own province, at Saint-Claude, used their feudal rights to such a point that their peasants were little

which is everywhere chased away. It it said that only two most agreeable refuges were indulgently left to her: the bed and the table. May she there establish a durable reign! One of them still attracts me. Come friends, let us drink; let us intrigue for Chloris, and sing songs.'

3 Best.D17653 (23 March 1772).
4 J. Vercruysse, 'Bibliographie des écrits français relatifs à Voltaire, 1719-1830,' *Studies on Voltaire* (1968), lx.7-71.

more than slaves. They had even enforced the *jus primae noctis*, and confiscated the goods of a bride's father because she had slept with her husband on the night of their marriage.[5] This inflamed Voltaire's indignation to such an extent that he launched a whole fleet of memoranda and petitions against the ferocious monks. These were not without effect, and some of the worst abuses were eventually remedied; but the real reform had to wait for the revolution.

The old gentleman still found time to spend endless energy, to no purpose, on the hoped-for production of the *Lois de Minos*, which one of his friends was getting ready to steal; to deal with innumerable other incidents: a letter to the pope which was attributed to Voltaire only because it was well written; the political upheaval in Sweden; a minor writer who suspected Voltaire of literary misconduct if not worse; the production of his plays in Geneva and in a girl's school in St Petersburg; a Parisian ceremony in his honour; his own and his family's business affairs; the allegation that he had tried to seduce a young woman.

Among the family affairs perhaps the most interesting was the marquis de Florian's wish to marry a divorced Protestant. Florian, the widower of Voltaire's younger niece, inevitably appealed to him to use his influence, and just as inevitably Voltaire did his best. The difficulties were enormous. This time not even so old a friend as the cardinal de Bernis could help, although Voltaire told him pathetically that he 'who was no longer able to commit mortal sins, was anxious to preserve the innocence of these two souls'[6]. Bernis wrote from Rome that the thing could not be done, that such a marriage could not even be proposed.[7] And in the end the couple had to have recourse to the services of a Lutheran priest.

Voltaire's protestations of impotence did not prevent the drawing-rooms from buzzing soon after with a most savoury story. Voltaire, now in his seventy-ninth year, was said to have tried so hard to seduce a young woman that he fainted three times, although some people did say that it was she who had tried to seduce him. It was true, Voltaire protested to Richelieu, that the

5 *La Voix du curé sur le procès des serfs du Mont-Jura* (1772).

6 Best.D1757 (23 January 1772).
7 Best.D17615 (25 February 1772).

appetising Judith de Saussure had come to his bedside, but it was fear and respect that had made him faint.[8]

Literary flirtation was perhaps more appropriate to Voltaire's age, and here at least he had not lost any of his skill. When the king's new mistress, mme Du Barry, asked a friend to kiss Voltaire on both cheeks on her behalf, Voltaire answered in terms that remind us of the most brilliant epigrams of his nonage:

> Quoi! deux baisers sur la fin de ma vie!
> Quel passeport vous daignez m'envoyer.
> Deux! c'en est trop adorable égérie,
> Je serais mort de plaisir au premier.[9]

None of these things, and many others, impeded the usual flow of letters concerning Voltaire's publications, his preoccupations with international affairs, his concern with humanitarian causes, and so on in endless profusion. At Ferney itself Voltaire's energy was unabated. He installed a lace-making industry, built more houses, and installed a marble bath in the château.[10] But much of his love of the place was still concentrated on the grounds. When sir William Chambers sent him his *Dissertation on oriental gardening*, in his mania for *chinoiserie* the future architect of Somerset house very ignorantly expressed his regret that 'Monsieur de Voltaire, amidst the great variety of subjects he has so successfully treated, has never employed his thoughts' on gardening[11]. Voltaire replied that a prince would ruin himself in trying to follow Chambers's precepts, but that he himself, so far as his ignorance and means allowed, had everything in his gardens: 'flower-beds, small lakes, formal walks, very irregular woods, valleys, lawns, vineyards, kitchen-gardens with walls covered with fruit-trees'[12]. It is a pity Voltaire did not know that sir William's grandfather had financed Charles xii. What questions that knowledge would have evoked!

---

8 Best.D18098 (21 December 1772) and the notes thereon; Richelieu, whose sexual prowess was legendary, refused to believe his old friend, and sent him a pleasantly bawdy reply (Best.D18107; 29 December 1772).

9 Best.D18456 (*c.* 5 July 1773). 'What! two kisses as I come to the end of my life! What a passport you deign to send me! Two! It is one too many, adorable Egeria; I should be dead of pleasure at the first.'

10 Best.D17841 (21 July 1772).

11 Best.D17810 (3 July 1772).

12 Best.D17848 (7 August 1772).

Even more aptly than Whitman Voltaire could have said: 'I am large, I contain multitudes.' And he was no doubt gratified when he received a testimonial from the inhabitants of Ferney, in which they told him that it must be a great satifaction to his noble soul, after so glorious a career and in the midst of such universal admiration. 'May days so precious to humanity be prolonged to the greatest possible extent! That is the wish of our hearts, in which you have inspired sentiments of the most lively gratitude.'[13]

This may well have given him even greater pleasure than the more sophisticated ceremony at which his friends in Paris crowned his bust with a laurel-wreath while mlle Clairon recited an ode by Marmontel in which Voltaire was told that he possessed 'graces, virtues, reason, genius', had surpassed Corneille and Racine, was equal to twenty illustrious men, and in addition to all this was the defender of innocence against the law.[14]

I wish I could insert John Moore's account[15] of his visit to Voltaire in July 1772, for a reliable eye-witness is worth a hundred of pages of reconstruction. Here at least are the first few pages of his narrative:

This extraordinary person has contrived to excite more curiosity, and to retain the attention of Europe for a longer space of time, than any other man this age has produced, monarchs and heroes included.—Even the most trivial anecdote relating to him seems, in some degree, to interest the Public.

Since I have been in this country, I have had frequent opportunities of conversing with him, and still more with those who have lived in intimacy with him for many years; so that, whatever remarks I may send you on this subject, are founded either on my own observation, or on that of the most candid and intelligent of his acquaintance.

He has enemies and admirers here, as he has everywhere else; and not unfrequently both united in the same person.

The first idea which has presented itself to all who have attempted a description of his person, is that of a skeleton. In as far as this implies excessive leanness, it is just; but it must be remembered, that this skeleton, this mere composition of skin and bone, has a look of more spirit and vivacity, than is generally produced by flesh and blood, however blooming and youthful.

13 Best.D17886 (? 25 August 1772).
14 Best.D17931 (*c.* 25 September 1772); and *Mémoires de mlle Clairon* (Paris 1822), pp. lxii-lxvi.
15 In his *A View of society and manners in France, Switzerland, and Germany* (London 1783), i.261-85; it can most conveniently be read in de Beer and Rousseau, *Voltaire's British visitors*, pp. 158-68; in the same book are reproduced the narratives of other British visitors in 1772.

The most piercing eyes I ever beheld are those of Voltaire, now in his eightieth year. His whole countenance is expressive of genius, observation, and extreme sensibility.

In the morning he has a look of anxiety and discontent; but this gradually wears off, and after dinner he seems cheerful:—yet an air of irony never entirely forsakes his face, but may always be observed lurking in his features, whether he frowns or smiles.

When the weather is favourable, he takes an airing in his coach, with his niece, or with some of his guests, of whom there is always a sufficient number at Ferney. Sometimes he saunters in his garden; or if the weather does not permit him to go abroad, he employs his leisure-hours in playing at chess with Père Adam; or in receiving the visits of strangers, a continual succession of whom attend at Ferney to catch an opportunity of seeing him; or in dictating and reading letters; for he still retains correspondents in all the countries of Europe, who inform him of every remarkable occurrence, and send him every new literary production as soon as it appears.

By far the greater part of his time is spent in his study; and whether he reads himself, or listens to another, he always has a pen in his hands, to take notes, or make remarks.

Composition is his principal amusement. No author who writes for daily bread, no young poet ardent for distinction, is more assiduous with his pen, or more anxious for fresh fame, than the wealthy and applauded Seigneur of Ferney.

He lives in a very hospitable manner, and takes care always to keep a good cook. He has generally two or three visitors from Paris, who stay with him a month or six weeks at a time. When they go, their places are soon supplied; so that there is a constant rotation of society at Ferney. These, with Voltaire's own family, and his visitors from Geneva, compose a company of twelve or fourteen people, who dine daily at his table, whether he appears or not. For when engaged in preparing some new production for the press, indisposed or in bad spirits, he does not dine with the company; but satisfies himself with seeing them for a few minutes, either before or after dinner.

All who bring a recommendation from his friends, may depend upon being received, if he be not really indisposed.—He often presents himself to the strangers, who assemble almost every afternoon. But sometimes they are obliged to retire without having their curiosity gratified.

As often as this happens, he is sure of being accused of peevishness; and a thousand ill-natured stories are related, perhaps invented, out of revenge, because he is not in the humour of being exhibited like a dancing-bear on a holiday. It is much less surprising that he sometimes refuses, than that he should comply so often. In him, this complaisance must proceed solely from a desire to oblige; for Voltaire has been so long accustomed to admiration, that the stare of a few strangers cannot be supposed to afford him much pleasure.

It was in June 1772 that Diderot, the only *philosophe* who approached Voltaire in universal genius, wrote an eloquent defence of the master. A friend had repeated some of the allegations often made about Voltaire's jealousy, ingratitude[16], and all the rest. All this may or may not be true, said Diderot,

> But this jealous man is an octogenarian who during all his life has raised his whip against tyrants, fanatics, and the other great malefactors of this world.
>
> But this ungrateful man, steadfast friend of humanity, has more than once succoured the unfortunate in their distress, and avenged oppressed innocence.
>
> But this madman introduced to his fatherland the philosophy of Locke and of Newton, attacked the most revered prejudices in the theatre, preached freedom of thought, inspired the spirit of tolerance, sustained expiring good taste, performed a number of praiseworthy actions, and produced a multitude of excellent writings. His name is honoured in all countries, and will endure throughout all the centuries. . . . [17]

16 As the reader may well be surprised by this accusation, I must explain that it arose from Voltaire's refusal to subscribe unconditionally to Choiseul's policies; see pp. 547-548, above.

17 Best.D17783 (*c.* June 1772); see also one of the epigraphs of the present book, quoted again on p. 437, above.

41. Exile, 1773-1775

VOLTAIRE'S chief, even obsessive personal wish ever since he left Berlin in 1753 had been to return to Paris. For nearly twenty years he had turned every stone and explored every avenue to this end. His most recent hope had been that the king's animosity might be stilled by a successful production of the *Lois de Minos*, quite certainly a vain hope. Such as it was, this last possibility, as he thought it, was now destroyed, not entirely by the disloyalty of Richelieu, who declined to use his powers to have the play put on, and the dishonesty of Marin, who sold to a publisher the manuscript entrusted to him for official purposes. Voltaire, soon to become an octogenarian, resigned himself to a permanent exile—but his resignation was preceded by an outburst of rage and indignation on 1 February 1773. On this day Voltaire wrote no fewer than fifteen surviving letters[1] of complaint about the treachery which had destroyed his hopes. These fifteen letters, the largest number that has come down to us from a single day, run the whole gamut of emotion. To Alembert he expressed philosophic resignation; to Argental he described himself as a hare pursued by greyhounds; in a letter to Chabanon, striking out wildly, he hit on the exact truth about the manner of his betrayal, though he still failed to identify the criminal as his friend Marin, to whom the manuscript had been sent as censor; to Condorcet he cried for help, 'A mon secours les philosophes!'; and so on.

Yet on this very day Voltaire also wrote to Frederick an endless letter including a long verse commentary on the decadence of contemporary taste, lines which the censorious mme Du Deffand described as the gayest and most charming thing he had ever written.[2]

Voltaire's immediate public reaction to the collapse of his hope

1 Best.D18164-D18178; once before Voltaire had written the same number   (see p. 525, note 1, above).
2 See a note on Best.D18170.

559

was characteristic: he produced an edition of the *Lois de Minos* into which he stuffed a collection of some of his most disapproved short pieces, from the *Loi naturelle* to the *Cabales*.[3]

Voltaire was exceptionally busy during this period as a land-owner, buying, selling, leasing, lending, litigating. He also had a set-to with his man of business, in which the client showed himself the better lawyer of the two. The old gentleman no doubt sought consolation in this way for what he now regarded as a permanent exile. This same feeling expressed itself also in a wide renewal of contacts: the recipients of Voltaire's letters were unusually numerous during this period, and in ten or a dozen countries. The correspondence deals with almost the entire range of Voltaire's interests.

As 1773 drew on the *parlement* decided in favour of Morangiés, and Voltaire was freed from an unworthy cause and one of which he had long since wearied. He was thus able to redouble his efforts on behalf of the far more serious Lally case, in which he was also to triumph in due course. This was one of the grossest miscarriages of justice in the *ancien régime*, because the victim (for all his faults of character) was so obviously deserving of his country's gratitude and was so utterly helpless in the toils of political and court intrigues. Thomas Arthur, comte de Lally-Tollendal (son of the Jacobite sir Gerard O'Lally), had formed the project of reconquering India from the English. He did everything humanly possible in the face of overwhelming difficulties, of which the worst were those created by his own superiors and subordinates. After a long resistance he was defeated and taken prisoner by the English, obtained his parole when he heard that he was being accused of treachery, and was executed by his countrymen with every ignominy, a scapegoat of Louis xv's ineptitude. There was widespread indignation, but as usual it was Voltaire who first took up the case, pursued it with all his usual energy and skill, and finally was able to write to the victim's son that the news of his father's rehabilitation had revived him. But he added that he could now die happy.[4] And he did, for this was the last letter he ever wrote.

In the meanwhile, as he entered his eightieth year, Voltaire

3 For a full list see Best.app.D365.   4 Best.D21213 (26 May 1778).

complained more and more of his decrepitude, both intellectual and physical. He was much troubled, literally, by a retention of urine, a double tertian ague, and gout; and metaphorically he was as deaf, blind and helpless as a badly conserved Egyptian mummy.[5] He regularly announced his impending death, with some conviction. He even fainted and remained unconscious for three-quarters of an hour.[6] Frederick, however, found that gout at Voltaire's age prognosticated a long life[7]—as good a medical judgement as any other. However, Voltaire survived, and he explained that it was because he discovered, as he was about to expire, that too many trinities awaited him.

> J'allais passer les trois rivières
> Phlegeton, Cocyte, Acheron.
> La triple Hecate et ses sorcières
> M'attendaient chez le noir Pluton.
> Les trois fileuses de nos vies,
> Les trois sœurs qu'on nomme furies,
> Et les trois gueules de leur chien
> Allaient livrer ma chétive ombre
> Aux trois juges du séjour sombre
> Dont ne revient aucun chrétien.
>   Que ma surprise était profonde
> Et que j'étais épouvanté
> De voir ainsi de tout côté
> Des trinités dans l'autre monde![8]

However, there is little sign of senility in Voltaire's work, except for an occasional failure of his remarkably retentive memory. He even turned again to verse satire in *La Tactique*, which contains one of his most passionate attack on war.

> J'achetai sa *Tactique*, et je me crus heureux.
> J'espérais trouver l'art de prolonger ma vie,
> D'adoucir les chagrins dont elle est poursuivie,

5 Best.D18373 (17 May 1773).

6 See the note on Best.D18553 (18 September 1773).

7 Best.D18292 (4 April 1773).

8 Best.D18331 (22 April 1773). 'I was about to pass the three rivers Phlegeton, Cocytus, Acheron. The triple Hecate and her sorceresses awaited me in the home of the black Pluto. The three spinners of our lives, the three sisters called furies, and the three mouths of their dog were about to deliver my feeble shade to the three judges of the sombre dwelling from which no Christian ever returns. How profound was my surprise and how appalled I was to find trinities everywhere in the other world!'

De cultiver mes goûts, d'être sans passion,
D'asservir mes désirs au joug de la raison,
D'être juste envers tous, sans jamais être dupe.
Je m'enferme chez moi, je lis; je ne m'occupe
Que d'apprendre par cœur un livre si divin.
Mes amis! c'était l'art d'égorger son prochain.

    J'apprends qu'en Germanie autrefois un bon prêtre
Pétrit, pour s'amuser, du soufre et du salpêtre;
Qu'un énorme boulet, qu'on lance avec fracas,
Doit mirer un peu haut pour arriver plus bas;
Que d'un tube de bronze aussitôt la mort vole
Dans la direction qui fait la parabole,
Et renverse, en deux coups prudemment ménagés
Cent automates bleus, à la file rangés.
Mousquet, poignard, épée ou tranchante ou pointue,
Tout est bon, tout va bien, tout sert, pourvu qu'on tue.[9]

Voltaire seldom quoted himself, but he reproduced the complete text of *La Tactique* (146 lines) in a letter[10] to Voisenon, and throughout the year he came back again and again to the horrible notion of writing a book to teach men how to kill. Yet he concluded his poem with a sad reference to the 'impracticable peace' of Saint-Pierre.

The failure of *Sophonisbe* (15 January 1774) depressed Voltaire, and was followed by some slowing-up of his intellectual activities. In his correspondence there is an unusually high proportion of family and business letters; and though there is the usual quota of difficulties of one kind and another, Voltaire seems to have been more interested in Beaumarchais's quarrels than in his

9 The satire was provoked by comte Jacques Antoine Hyppolyte de Guibert's *Essai général de tactique* (1772). 'I bought his *Tactique*, and thought myself fortunate. I hoped to discover the art of prolonging my life, to assuage the sorrows which pursue it, to cultivate my tastes, to be passionless, to subject my desires to the yoke of reason, to be just to all, without ever being dupe. I shut myself up in my room, I read, I sought nothing better to do than to learn by heart a book so divine. Great heavens! it was the art of butchering one's neighbour. I learned that once upon a time a good priest in Germany amused himself by kneading sulphur and saltpetre; that an enormous ball, flung with a crash, must be aimed rather higher in order to arrive lower; that death flies instantly from a bronze tube in the direction formed by the parabola, and knocks down, in two blows prudently husbanded, a hundred blue automata set up in rows. Muskets, poniards, swords, whether cutting or pointed, all is good, all is acceptable, all serves, so long as it kills.'

10 Best.D18635 (19 November 1773).

31 Watch made at Ferney

the justice j expect from the noble author

as to relligion; j think, and j hope, he

thinks with me, that God is, neither

a presbiterian, nor a lutherian, nor

of the low church, nor of the high

church: but god is the father of all

mankind, the father of the noble

author and mine ——

　　　j am with respect

　　　　　　　his most humble serv
at my castle of　　Voltaire gentleman of
fernex in　　　　the King's chamber
burgundy

32 Voltaire's letter of September 1760 to lord Lyttelton, *from the holograph
in the Bibliothèque municipale, Nantes*

own. On the other hand the Frederick correspondence was particularly active, the king pretending to be much amused by Voltaire's hatred of war: 'I would as soon declaim against the quartan ague as against war. It is a waste of time. Governments allow cynics to bray and go their ways, and the fever pays no more attention. All that remains are some well-written lines, which testify, to the astonishment of Europe, that your talent does not age. Preserve your renewed youth, and even if you were to satirise me in scathing verse at the age of a hundred, I assure you in advance that I would not be angry, and that the patriarch of Ferney can say what he pleases about the freethinker of Sans-Souci.'[11] In reality, he was very angry about the clearly implied criticism in Voltaire's *Tactique* of his warlike behaviour, and even said that it had given him the gout.[12]

The death of Louis xv (10 May 1774) once again made Voltaire's friends hope that he might safely return to Paris, and Voltaire's *Eloge funèbre de Louis XV* was perhaps not entirely foreign to these hopes. As soon as the news of the king's death reached Ferney Voltaire told Argental that only his health could now prevent his return to Paris. After all, he said, it was ridiculous that 'Jean Jacques the Genevese' should be free while he himself was unable to visit his own birthplace. But he asked for secrecy, for perhaps he could slip in unobserved in present circumstances.[13] All this led to a revival of the old man's interest in outside events, though he still published little.

Unfortunately the late king's undisguised and acidulous dislike for the man who was his most eminent subject was merely replaced by the new one's dull hatred. Ample evidence of this can be found in the scandalous official correspondence[14] which followed so soon on the accession of Louis xvi, and which has every appearance of having been personally initiated by him. The purpose of the very elaborate and detailed plans, devised to cover all eventualities, with a full panoply of royal and ministerial open and sealed orders addressed severally to all the officials who might conceivably be concerned, was to take possession of all Voltaire's papers as soon as he was dead *or dying* ('sans ressource'). News of these

11 Best.D18733 (4 January 1774).   13 Best.D18945 (18 May 1774).
12 Best.D18808 (10 February 1774).   14 Printed in Voltaire 125.

orders inevitably came to Voltaire's ears, and in April 1777 the king cancelled, probably obliged to do so by the changes in the government, the indecent measures he had taken in anticipation of Voltaire's death. But this does not alter the fact that a monstrous illegality and abuse of power was deliberately and minutely prepared by Louis XVI and his ministers: an example of the *ancien régime* at its worst.

For all that, Voltaire now continued to watch with passionate interest the political upheavals and economic controversies in Paris. He no longer seriously hoped to be allowed to return, and his concern was therefore even less egocentric than usual. He was always torn between his hope that almost any change would be an improvement in the country's lamentable condition, and the fear that constant change would hamper steady reform. He was in that most sociably desirable of all states of mind: chronic indignation. In general, a slight increase in Voltaire's general cheerfulness can be detected after the first of Turgot's proposals for reform, but even here hope was dashed by the difficulties these soon began to encounter.

For all that, his eightieth birthday found Voltaire in an almost melting mood. He becomes even more affecting in writing to his oldest friends and in lamenting the deaths of his contemporaries. He tells Argental with tenderness how much he longs to take refuge under his wings in Paris. But it was a physical impossibility for him to leave his hole, and besides he was surrounded by doctors, notaries, lawyers, masons, carpenters, labourers, watchmakers. He would die in harness.[15] Yet nowhere is there to be found the slightest trace of complacency about his almost incredible career. He continued to work, to produce 'squibs, Pamphlets and Volumes' (to say nothing of elegant drawing-room verse at the request of the unappreciative mme Du Deffand), and to fight for his pet causes, above all for Etallonde, particularly in letters written on his eightieth birthday, which he does not even mention. His concern for Etallonde led to a multiplication of his correspondence with Frederick. Indeed, the La Barre case continued to weigh on Voltaire year after year.

But although this cannot be eternally repeated it must be

15 Best.D19161 (24 October 1774).

remembered that none of these things prevented life from going on normally at Ferney. Hundreds of letters continued to arrive from all and sundry and of every kind; hundreds continued to be written in reply, letters as witty, as learned, as graceful, as consoling as usual; all the normal duties of a large landowner continued to be carried out; and weekly dances were given by mme Denis, which Voltaire thought preferable to consulting urologists[16]— though he continued to need one, for his strangury made him suffer like damnation[17].

Yet the incessant stream continued of adoring or merely inquisitive visitors, a multitude that made Voltaire what he himself called the innkeeper of Europe, and all were received appropriately, and sometimes in state. Thus when the rulers of Darmstadt[18] arrived at Ferney they fell into the midst of the celebration of the anniversary of st Louis. The court of the château was lined with vassals, accoutred some in green, others in red. Cannon were fired on the arrival of the guests, who were led through 'a long suite of rooms' filled with ladies and gentlemen[19]. Voltaire wore a red costume with broad gold embroidery, crimson silk stockings, and a long powdered wig. Stolberg found him a handsome old man, with splendidly fiery eyes. He was as vain as he was witty. The German courtier feared that Voltaire would live several years more to spread his poison, 'which would certainly still drip from his mouth at the moment of death'. Ferney and its gardens were delicious, and in his library, in which Voltaire lived, there was a cage of canaries.

Voltaire did indeed live in his library, for his output in the period around his eightieth birthday was again prodigious: nearly forty distinct writings. Not even an enumeration can be attempted. They included such major works of minor calibre as the tragedy *Don Pèdre*; the *Fragments sur l'Inde*, an exhaustive analysis of the French presence in India; another essay in historical doubt, the

16 Best.D18806 (9 February 1774).
17 Best.D18864 (21 March 1774).
18 George William of Hesse-Darmstadt, his wife Louisa, and one of their daughters; the account that follows is based on a German letter by one of his suite, Friedrich Leopold, count zu

Stolberg (Best.D19623, 22/27 August 1775).
19 This is only another example of the caution with which all such accounts must be received; there is not at Ferney anything that could be described as a 'long suite of rooms'.

Fragment sur l'histoire générale; and his last three tales, *Le Taureau blanc*, the *Histoire de Jenni* and *Les Oreilles du comte de Chesterfield*, which deserve to be ranked among his best work.

A recent discovery has shown the quite unsuspected and unique fact that about this time the tiny hamlet transformed by Voltaire into a flourishing township was given his name, not during the nineteenth century as had always been supposed, but during his own lifetime.[20] This honour was no doubt a spontaneous tribute to Voltaire's efforts not only on behalf of Ferney but of the whole country of Gex. The French resident in Geneva, Hennin, reporting to his minister, now the comte de Vergennes, on some recent festivities at Ferney, exclaimed: 'When one reflected that a dozen years ago this place held only twenty families of wretched peasants, it was a singular spectacle to see a ceremony many cities of the kingdom would be unable to equal in its elaboration and cost. And yet it is the presence of one rich and benevolent man that has operated this change in a few years.'[21]

The middle of 1775 is dominated by the personality of mme Suard. She was the wife of the writer and editor J. B. A. Suard[22], talented but lazy and unprincipled: a couple whose name became ignominious because they refused to shelter their close friend Condorcet when he was in flight from the extremists in 1794[23]. But in 1775 the young woman was still carefree and gay. Her letters[24] from Ferney to her husband in Paris offer an exceptionally vivid picture of the great man, his entourage, his doings and his sayings. These letters deserve to be quoted in full, but this being impossible, here are a few extracts:

My hopes have at last been fulfilled, and the aim of my journey accomplished. I have seen m. de Voltaire, and I no longer know how to express the feelings he inspires in me. The greatest of men appears to me to be also the best and the most amiable. My heart beat violently when I entered his house, and for all my extreme wish to see him, I almost felt relieved when I was told

20 See a note on Best.D19658 (15 September 1775).

21 Best.D19492 (23 May 1775).

22 The greater part of whose archives is now Th. B.

23 A pathetic folder has survived: it contains a letter from Voltaire to mme Suard, and on it Condorcet's

daughter, who was collecting materials for an edition of his works, wrote that she wanted the letter to be excluded, so that the name of the Suards need not appear in her father's works (see a note on Best.D20538).

24 See Voltaire 126.

that he had gone out with mme Denis, for whom we [she and her brother] had first asked. . . . I expected to see a decrepit face, a caricature, but I saw a physiognomy full of fire, grace and expression. In truth, I find him charming but his tone, his politeness are even better than that. . . . Although I was enchanted to see him, I implored him to retire, for he seemed tired. I kissed his hands, an attention which he returned with sensibility. He went into his study, but a moment later he joined me in the garden. I walked with him for a long time and spoke with the greatest freedom. I told him how much we hope to see him in Paris.[25]

He put on his wig today for my sake, because I had told him that I found him very good-looking and twenty years younger than in his night-cap. In fact he has the air of a courtier of Louis XIV. He holds himself marvellously, is not round shouldered, and walks very nimbly for a man of his age. He has the most beautiful eyes in the world, still so brilliant that one can barely support their lustre. And with it all he has an air of goodness. . . . His woods are very vast, and he has pierced most agreeable vistas everywhere. Then we went to his farm, which is in the finest condition in the world, a charming farm-yard, many fine and well-cared for cows. I drank some warm milk which m. de Voltaire presented to me himself. He wanted to leave early, although it was very hot. He said that he was ill. I gave him my arm to his coach, but as soon as he reached it he wanted to reconduct me to mine. . . . I saw with pain that those who surround him, and even his niece, have no indulgence for such things as are due to his age and his weakness. He is often treated as a capricious child.[26]

And after leaving Ferney she wrote to Voltaire:

With what transports, with what rapture have I seen the glory and the honour of my century! How affected I was on seeing him as good, as amiable as he is great, on seeing that he does around him the good he would have liked to do to the whole of humanity! Sir, what a delicious memory I shall conserve all my life of the moments I have passed in the study to which you deigned to admit me and to talk to me with so gentle and sympathetic a familiarity! How tempted I was to run in again when leaving Ferney. The door was open, I heard the sound of your voice, I wanted to throw myself at your feet, but I was held back by the fear of robbing you of one moment of the time you devote to our pleasure and our happiness.[27]

Some allowance must of course be made for all the obvious reasons, but the sincerity of these letters seems clear, and, written as they were by a rather hard-boiled and independent young

25 Best.D19499 (2 June 1775), to her husband.

26 Best.D19505 (9 June 1775), to her husband.

27 Best.D19519 (c. 20 June 1775).

woman, are a remarkable illustration of Voltaire's effect on his contemporaries down to the youngest generation.

A neighbour reported that it was Voltaire's habit to get up at noon, work or see visitors until two o'clock, ride in his coach until four alone with his secretary, take only coffee or chocolate instead of dining, work until eight, then come down for supper when his health permitted. What this friend did not realise was that Voltaire worked also when he was in bed. Anyway, he goes on to give particulars of his host's library (6210 volumes—this figure is about right), his income (150,000 francs a year—it was actually about double), and his building activities (he ordered houses as others order a pair of shoes—and in fact in July 1774 he had twenty houses[28] in hand, making about a hundred[29] in all). He administered everything himself.[30]

28 Best.D19021 (14 July 1774).   30 Best.D19217 (8 December 1774).
29 Best.D19639 (1 September 1775).

42. *Apotheosis, 1776-1778*

A S THE LAST EPOCH of Voltaire's life opens, one has the
impression that he was engaged in a kind of summing-up
of his life-work, though it is not clear that he was himself
conscious of this process. Be this as it may, during this period
Voltaire published the *Commentaire historique sur les œuvres de
l'auteur de la Henriade*, a contemporary translation of which is
printed at the end of the present volume; *La Bible enfin expliquée*,
in which he gathered together the conclusions of a lifetime's
critical reading of the *Bible*; and the *Lettre à l'Academie francaise*[1],
in which he put into sharp focus all his arguments on behalf of
what he regarded as the classical theatre, and against the encroach-
ments, in particular, of Shakespeare.

The same thing is true of Voltaire's more mundane affairs. This
period was marked by feverish activity in the development of
Ferney. It was almost as if he deliberately sought to complete the
little town before his death, well knowing that mme Denis hated
the place and would get rid of it at the earliest opportunity, as in
fact she did. Voltaire (whether in his own name or that of his niece)
now owned nearly all the land surrounding his house for a considerable distance. He could easily have built and then sold or leased
any number of houses, thus still further increasing his large fortune.
Instead, he adopted the most enlightened and least profitable
method: he encouraged craftsmen and labourers to settle at Ferney
by selling them land, and then, if necessary, lending them money,
often on very favourable terms, to pay for it and to enable them
to build their own houses. The documents concerning a large
number of such transactions have been found.[2]

Much of Voltaire's energy was also absorbed during the early
months of 1776 by his efforts to put the affairs of Gex on a sound

1 See pp. 131-137, above.
2 They have been published in
numerous appendixes of Best.D.

569

basis, now that he had succeeded in liberating the province from arbitrary burdens. He had to overcome the vested interests of his neighbours as much as the opposition of the farmers-general. No vituperation was too strong for the backwoods-squireens to direct at Voltaire, and he even suspected an attempt to poison him.[3]

He found time nevertheless for much correspondence about more general political and economic problems, in particular the reforms of Turgot, whose rise to power in 1774 was greeted by Voltaire with enthusiasm. Nearly everything Turgot tried to do was in line with the policies Voltaire had urged for many years. The new comptroller-general tried to suppress all the privileges enjoyed by one class at the expense of others. Thus he sought to abolish the *corvées* imposed on the peasants, and to subject the clergy to the same taxes as the laity. And all this he tried to do in edicts written so clearly that even a village magistrate or a peasant could understand them. But privilege was too strongly entrenched, Turgot was rejected by all but the *philosophes*, and in May 1776 he was dismissed.[4] Voltaire was deeply distressed (though Turgot had turned down most of his requests), and began to despair of the future of France, especially when Trudaine died before Necker had accomplished very much. In the meanwhile Voltaire at once wrote to Turgot: 'An old man of about eighty-three is ready to die when such news reaches him; but he will use the few moments that remain to him in respecting you, in loving you, and in pitying France very sincerely'[5]; and the next day he added that it only remained for him to die on the ending of Turgot's twenty months, which would be eternally celebrated.[6] Nor was he much consoled by the more and more cordial letters he again received from Frederick.

Voltaire's discouragement was, however, a little relieved by a visit from Lekain, his favourite tragic actor, who performed at Ferney and, like all Voltaire's visitors, found him miraculous, as when he only just lost a foot-race against his nephew. Lekain found that Voltaire still worked ten hours a day, not only in

3 Best.D19837 (2 January 1776).
4 His fall was fully analysed by Condorcet in a very long and remarkable letter to Voltaire (Best.D20194; June/July 1776).

5 Best.D20125 (17 May 1776).
6 Best.D20130 (18 May 1776).

writing but as his own manager and bailiff.[7] In addition to the usual topics, one finds at this time letters more appropriate to the pen of an orientalist. On the other hand, the *Lettres chinoises, indiennes et tartares*, which appeared at the beginning of the year, are not as oriental as the title.

At about this time (April 1776) Martin Sherlock visited Voltaire, and has left us a very interesting account, which again is unfortunately too long to quote, but the end of which must be reproduced:

His house is convenient, and well furnished; among other pictures is the portrait of the Empress of Russia, and that of the King of Prussia, which was sent him by that monarch, as was also his own bust in Berlin porcelain, with the inscription IMMORTALIS!

His arms are on his door, and on all his plates, which are of silver: at the dessert, the spoons, forks, and blades of knives, were of silver gilt: there were two courses, and five servants, three of whom were in livery: no strange servant is allowed to enter.

He spends his time in reading, writing, playing at chess with Father Adam, and in looking at the workmen building in his village.

The soul of this extraordinary man has been the theatre of every ambition: he wished to be a universal writer; he wished to be rich; he wished to be noble; and he has succeeded in all.

His last ambition was to found a town; and if we examine, we shall find that all his ideas tend to this point. After the disgrace of M. de Choiseul, when the French ministry had laid aside the plan of building a town at Versoix, in order to establish a manufactory there, and to undermine the trade of the people of Geneva, Voltaire determined to do at Ferney what the French government had intended to do at Versoix.

He embraced the moment of the dissentions in the republic of Geneva, and by fair promises he engaged the exiles to take refuge with him, and many of the malcontents followed them thither.

He caused the first houses to be built, and gave them for a perpetual quit-rent; he then lent money, by way of annuities, to those who would build themselves; to some on his own life, to others on the joint lives of himself and Madam Denis.

His sole object seemed to me to have been the improvement of this village: that was his motive for asking an exemption from taxes; that was the reason why he endeavoured every day to inveigle workmen from Geneva to establish there a manufactory of clock-making. I do not say that he did not think of money; but I am convinced that it was only a secondary object.

On the two days I saw him, he wore white cloth shoes, white woollen

7 Best.D20245 (5 August 1776).

stockings, red breeches, with a night-gown and waist-coat of blue linen
flowered and lined with yellow: he had on a grizzle wig with three ties, and
over it a silk night-cap embroidered with gold and silver.[8]

As the months wore on into 1777 Voltaire's correspondence
became particularly rich and various, even for him, and, what is
surprising, includes letters to and from a surprising number of
new personages. Yet in contrast with the preceding months there
is a distinct relaxation of tension, though Voltaire did write a good
deal about his last two plays, *Irène* and *Agathocle*. He was very
hesitant indeed about the former. Mme Denis wept when she
read the tragedy, and this reassured Voltaire, but, he said, he had
against him the English party (because of his campaign against
false Shakespearean ideas), the Jewish party (because he had been
criticised for his attitude to them and had replied in his *Un chrétien
contre six juifs*), the devout, and all the writers and journalists.
'Heaven knows what joy it would give all this *canaille* to unite to
hiss an old fool who in his eighty-third year abandons all his
occupations to present to the public the embryo of a tragedy.'[9]
All this must not be taken too seriously: there was, for instance,
no such thing as a Jewish party, and many (perhaps most) writers
were by now Voltaireans. As for going to Paris, he had lost the
use of his eyes, his ears, his legs, his teeth, his tongue. There
could be no question of his presenting himself in such a state. It
is true that he suffered another slight stroke at this time, but a
year later he did go to Paris, and *Irène* was produced, and in
circumstances as wildly different from those feared by Voltaire as
can well be imagined.

In the meanwhile he was not without honour at Ferney. It
would be wearisome to describe the festivities organised in his
honour on suitable occasions: most engaging is an incidental
picture of him in the sun, seated in his armchair on the lawn,
surrounded by his sheep, a pen in one hand and printer's proofs in
the other. But the day was ruined because he discovered that the
pet pigeons of his little 'belle et bonne' had been killed, and he

8 *Letters from an English traveller*
(London 1780), pp. 166-9; the full text
has been reproduced by de Beer-

Rousseau, *Voltaire's British visitors*,
pp. 186-7.

9 Best.D20493 (1 January 1777).

flew into a violent rage.[10] This girl, mlle de Varicourt, daughter of an impoverished neighbour, was soon married, very advantageously by worldly standards, for the marquis de Villette was very rich, though dissolute. Voltaire told Argental: 'Our cottage of Ferney is not made for the safe-keeping of maidens; we have now married off three, mlle Corneille, her sister-in-law mlle Dupuits, and mlle de Varicourt, who is being carried off by m. de Villette. She has not got a penny, but her husband has made an excellent bargain. He has married innocence, virtue, prudence, taste for whatever is good, an invariable serenity of soul, with sensibility, the whole adorned by the lustre of youth and beauty'.[11]

All this did not, however, prevent Voltaire from doing much work, including the writing in a week of his elaborate commentary on Montesquieu[12]. The manuscript[13], written as clearly and firmly as ever, shows at once all his usual ease and clarity, and his passion for minute revision; and so does the metaphysical essay *Dialogues d'Evhémère*[14]. Nor did Voltaire's state of health destroy his sense of humour. He whispered into the ear of an English child: 'One day you will be a Marlborough; as for me, I am only a dog of a Frenchman.'[15] When an official sent him an actuarial table, on which Voltaire must have figured as a minus quantity, the old man accepted his condemnation without a murmur. He went so far as to say that everybody died at the same age, for when a man died it was all one to him whether he had lived twenty hours or twenty thousand centuries. 'I have placed my balance sheet at the head of my bed, and I am very much obliged to you for it. Nothing is more apt to console me for the wretchedness of this life than to reflect continuously that all is nothing.[16]

Later in the year Voltaire devoted much attention to the prize he had offered for a new criminal code, and to the essay he himself composed for this purpose, but which he did not submit: the *Prix de la justice et de l'humanité*.

On 3 February 1778 mme Denis left for Paris, with the Villettes, to attend to some necessary business, and to feel out the possibility

---

10 Best.D20826 (*c.* 15 October 1777).
11 Best.D20881 (5 November 1777).
12 *Commentaire sur l'Esprit des lois.*
13 Now Th. B.

14 The original manuscript is also Th. B.
15 Best.D20780 (1 September 1777).
16 Best.D20715 (1777).

of a visit by Voltaire to the capital. The old gentleman had no intention of following them, at any rate not until they had reported; but between the morning and the evening of that same day his longing to see Paris again became irresistible, and he decided to leave. He set off on the 5th, with Wagnière, by way of Nantua, Bourg-en-Bresse, Dijon and Joigny, and reached the capital on the 10th. He lodged with the Villettes in the house in which many years before he had shared an apartment with Thieriot, at the corner of the rue de Beaune and the quai des Théatins (now quai Voltaire). His arrival was saddened by the burial of Lekain on the very same day, but this was soon compensated by the delirious welcome he received from all except of course the court and the church. The populace ran after his coach, cheering the defender of Calas, and he was paid unique honours by the two companies with which he had been most closely associated, and whose fame he had multiplied: both the Académie française and the Théâtre français immediately sent deputations to wait on him and signify their respect and affection.

Soon hundreds of callers came to the rue de Beaune to pay their respects; all his old friends of course called, as well as many new ones, including Benjamin Franklin and Gluck, and, I am glad to say, the British ambassador[17], who had been present at Voltaire's Shakespeare discourse. Mme Du Deffand reported that he suffered from his bladder, and had haemorrhoids and diarrhoea, but had been overjoyed to see her. The blind old lady seems to have made a trifling mistake, for when Voltaire consulted Théodore Tronchin on the very next day, he complained of a retention of urine, it is true, but also of diabetes and constipation[18] —though the first two of these have mutually contradictory symptoms, so I dare say that Voltaire was no nearer the mark than mme Du Deffand. The whirlwind of activity in which he was living, which included the casting and rehearsal of *Irène*, was indeed too much for him, but Voltaire was determined to drain to the last drop this intoxicating cup for which he had longed for a quarter of a century.

17 David Murray, viscount Stormont (later earl of Mansfield).
18 Best.D21049 (17 February 1778).

Now started the church's attempt to take over its greatest enemy, for the marriage-bed and the death-bed are its favourite battlegrounds. Priests, carefully instructed by the hierarchy, kept up a daily bombardment of letters and visits. Sometimes Voltaire responded, sometimes he did not. He signed various contradictory declarations as his last moments approached—in the intervals becoming a freemason in the lodge of the nine sisters—but rational men, unlike professionals of mortality, will pay little attention to statements and declarations made in such circumstances.[19]

In the meanwhile Voltaire promised his true friends (who did not include mme Denis and m. de Villette) to return to Ferney to save his life; but at the same time he looked for a house in Paris. And nobody who realised how passionately and how long he had hoped to return to the capital could have imagined that, once there, he would ever leave on his feet.

Anyway, Voltaire was dying very actively. In the minutes of the Académie française for 30 March 1778 can be read: 'M. de Voltaire arrived at the Academy about 4 o'clock. The Director and all the Academicians present met him in the first room. He came into the Assembly room and the Director begged him to take the first place and to preside over the sitting.' Other honours were paid to him, so unusual that the minutes particularly specify that they were not to be taken as a precedent.[20] Voltaire was also actively making notes for the new edition of the French dictionary he had asked the Academy to undertake, and on which it is still working.

On the same evening there occurred the famous 'apotheosis' of Voltaire at the Comédie française, when, in his presence, his bust was placed on the stage and crowned with a laurel wreath, to the accompaniment of a verse apostrophe, drowned by loud and universal applause, echoing the sentiments of 'seven hundred thousand amiable Frenchmen'[21].

A vivid and accurate, though compressed and restrained account of all this was given two days later by the marquis de Saint-Marc

---

19 I have printed them and the related documents in Voltaire 129. See also René Pomeau, 'La Confession et la mort de Voltaire', *Revue d'histoire littéraire de la France* (Paris 1955), lv.299-318.

20 See a note on Best.D21127.

21 Voltaire's terms in a letter to the empress Catherine, Best.D21168 (30 April 1778).

in a letter to the advocate Linguet. Everything that concerned Voltaire, he said, was deserving of fame, not least the previous day's events, when the great man came to the Comédie française to see the sixth performance of *Irène*.

Having been to the Academy he came from the Louvre to the Comédie française. His carriage was surrounded all the way by a double row of the curious. Having arrived in the courtyard of the Tuileries, his carriage had the greatest difficulty in getting through the crowd which overwhelmed him with applause, and the whole of the French guard had to make the greatest efforts to find a way for him to the box of the first gentleman [of the bedchamber]. You can imagine the applause he received when he appeared in the theatre! Nothing like it has ever been seen or heard. There has never been so flattering a triumph. An actor came to bring him a crown of laurel and gave it to mme de Villette, who sat next to him. She placed it on Voltaire's head, and the applause redoubled. But M. de Voltaire tore it from his head and returned it to mme de Villette, who made vain efforts to replace it. The play began, and was continuously applauded.... The play ended, the curtain came down, then came up again, and the bust of M. de Voltaire became visible, crowned with laurel, and surrounded by most of the actors, who extended more crowns to the bust. The whole stage was filled with spectators who, exceptionally had been allowed to see the performance of the tragedy from the wings. The entire theatre applauded with enthusiasm for more than five minutes. Mme Vestris came forward, and read the verse....[22]

Mme Denis now managed to separate Voltaire from Wagnière, finding an expedient for sending the devoted secretary to Ferney. A pathetic correspondence between them followed, but now Voltaire was deprived of proper care, and really had nothing more to live for. He begged Wagnière to return. He set out at once, but it was already too late. Voltaire wrote his last letter[23] and died between 11 o'clock and midnight on Saturday, 30 May 1778.

> Death be not proud, though some have called thee
> Mighty and dreadful, for, thou art not so,
> For, those, whom thou think'st, thou dost overthrow,
> Die not, poor death.

But everything about Voltaire was above life-size. He had already enjoyed his apotheosis, but the church's revenge was swift,

22 Best.D21139 (1 April 1778). Notwithstanding the excitement, his great age and his failing health, Voltaire did not relax his punctilio, and the very next morning sent a charming letter of thanks to the author of the complimentary lines read by mme Vestris (Best.D21131; 31 March 1778).

23 See p. 560, above.

and Voltaire had to die a double death. The night after his physical death, Sunday, 31 May 1778, a coach drove away before midnight from the quai Malaquais. If the torch of some linkboy or the lantern of a watchman on his rounds, for it was a dark, moonless night, had for a moment thrown a wavering light into this coach, great indeed would have been the surprise of the beholder, for he would have seen features known to the civilised world by a thousand portraits, and most recently moulded by the immortal hand of Houdon, the features of the man who is said to have been king of France when Louis xv occupied the throne, the features of the most celebrated, the most honoured, and the most hated man in Europe, the features of François Marie Arouet de Voltaire. The passer-by would have gone on his way wondering why this grand old man of eighty-three was stealing away so quietly, even secretly. He was obviously leaving Paris, that was evident from the coach and six, but why like this, in darkness and silence, behind the backs of the innumerable friends and applauding crowds by whom he had been surrounded since his return to Paris not many weeks before? Our imaginary idler might well wonder. Had he known the truth his surprise would have given way to horror: for the features he had glimpsed were those of a dead man. Voltaire in fact had died twenty-four hours before, and his embalmed body, decked in the famous dressing-gown and night-cap, accompanied by a servant whose duty it was to make the corpse simulate life, was being smuggled out of Paris to escape the indignities prepared for it. The plot to deny Voltaire decent burial had failed, and it only remained for the church to besmirch his deathbed and to poison his memory. They did their best, and for long succeeded.

43. *The letter-writer*

THE NEOPLATONIST PROCLUS, in his learned Περὶ ἐπιστολιμαίου χαρακτῆρος established forty-one categories of letters. It was a worthy effort, but civilisation, we are told every day, has made vast progress since the age of innocence, and so limited a number of pigeon-holes would really not suffice nowadays. Where, for instance, could we file certain pastoral letters and the fan-mail of a sex-kitten? Besides, such a category as that comprising love-letters presents in reality no more than a metaphysical homogeneity. There are as many kinds of love-letters as there are kinds of love, and I leave it to those who feel able to classify the latter, to establish the former in a decimal or duodecimal classification.

Cicero, Erasmus, mme de Sévigné, Horace Walpole, Voltaire, Bernard Shaw: these are the great names of the epistolary style, and the mere enumeration is enough to show to what an extent Voltaire out-tops the others. Cicero is not far from the elegance of the Voltairean style, but the relatively small number of his surviving letters gives little idea of the Roman's universality. Erasmus paints a whole era, but his correspondents are few, his letters written in an almost barbarous style, accessible only to the most skilled Latin scholars, and even then. . . . One can admire all the grace, the charm, all that is truly literary in the letters of mme de Sévigné, without having any illusions about the narrowness of her knowledge and preoccupations. As for Horace Walpole, he is the tiniest of great men: never has anyone so deeply and at such length explored the surface of things. No true judgement is yet possible of the epistolary art of Bernard Shaw, for his letters are being published slowly and incompletely: but we can see already that it is a treasure. Yet how far Voltaire surpasses Cicero in his style, Erasmus in the width if not the profundity of his erudition, mme de Sévigné in grace and friendship, Walpole by the universality of his interests and the number and variety of his correspondents!

A few months before his death Renan was questioned by a journalist about literary evolution. The old man answered, surprisingly enough: 'Literary fashions...how puerile, how childish', but then he pulled himself up, and went on, 'Excuse me, excuse me, I withdraw what I have just said, it is exaggerated. Racine has done some very fine things, and Voltaire! Ah! Voltaire's letters, do you see, are divine, what treasures do they not contain! They are admirable....'[1]

And indeed there can be no doubt that Voltaire's letters constitute the greatest of all *biblia abiblia*, literature in spite of itself. There are many reasons for this supremacy. Apart from a childhood letter[2] signed Zozo, the oldest surviving epistles[3] were written in 1711, when Voltaire was a schoolboy. Four sombre years of decline still remained to Louis xiv, followed by the too short regency of the duc d'Orléans and the interminable reign of Louis xv, beloved in name only; and Voltaire still had a few very active years before him when Louis xvi mounted the throne. In short, he was born at the height of the *ancien régime* and died only a decade before the French revolution. His correspondence thus extends over sixty vital years, during which the modern world was conceived.

This by no means exhausts the historical scope of Voltaire's life. The brilliant gifts and personality of the boy and young man captivated much older people. As a small boy he impressed so strongly Ninon de Lenclos, born eighty years before him, in 1615, that she couched him, not in her bed, as so often and so ill-advisedly alleged, but in her will. When still at school he was treated as an equal by Chaulieu, the last of the 'libertine' poets, his senior by sixty years. Some of the delightful letters[4], in prose and verse, they exchanged, have luckily come down to us. Through a Chaulieu, a Caumartin, a prince de Vendôme, the boy penetrated far into the 'grand siècle'. All this we have already seen in successive chapters.

And in 1718 the unprecedented success of his first play *Œdipe*

1 Jules Huret, *Enquête sur l'évolution littéraire* (Paris 1891), pp.400-21; I owe this quotation to Henri Guillemin.

2. Best.D1 (29 December 1704); the authenticity of this letter is not certain.

3 Best.D2-D6 (8 May-c. 7 August 1711).

4 Best.D32, D33, D35, D38 (summer 1716).

made Voltaire at 24 the recognised head of French literature, after eighteen months of prison and exile, with all that this meant in fact and in symbol. People already kept, bought, stole, exchanged his letters, and even printed them. When adolescent he had a love-affair with a young woman, whose mother, a journalist of low degree, hastened to print the letters[5] he wrote to her daughter. How mortifying! It is not surprising that he always loathed the publication of his letters. One wonders that he was ever again capable of writing one.

Voltaire's publications shone so brightly visible with genius even when he discussed the most forbidding subjects, that his reputation quickly extended very widely in his own country, and beyond it. Although above all a creator, Voltaire was much more, as we have abundantly seen: an original historian, a scientific populariser, a social reformer, an adversary of religion as a superstition, a militant of liberty and tolerance. This is what makes his works, and not least his correspondence, as remarkable for its content as for its temporal duration, and thus uniquely remarkable. And this is reflected by the astonishing quality, variety and quantity of his correspondents. They include of course, first of all, his fellow-geniuses, or near enough: Fontenelle, Alembert, Diderot, Helvétius, Vauvenargues, Rousseau, Buffon, Condorcet, Beaumarchais, Pope, Swift, even Lessing, as well as minor writers, many of them minor only by contrast with the giants: Algarotti, Goldoni, Maffei and Spallanzani; Bernouilli and Haller; George Keate, Boswell and Horace Walpole; Sumarokov; Mayáns y Siscar; Jean Baptiste Rousseau, Maupertuis, Destouches, La Condamine, Moncrif, Voisenon, Prévost d'Exiles, Tressan, Piron, Mairan, Saurin, Marmontel, Delisle de Sales, mme de Graffigny, La Harpe, Du Pont de Nemours, mme d'Epinay, mme Du Deffand, Ximènes, Suard, Sedaine, Palissot, Chamfort, mme Du Bocage, Florian, Duclos, Dorat.

I do not wish to emphasise too much this aspect of the correspondence, but I must underline one little detail that emerges from this enumeration: Fontenelle was born in 1657, Suard and Du Pont de Nemours died 160 years later, in 1817. And there is even

5 Best.D7-D13, D15-D18, D20-D23 (November 1713-February 1714).

better: in 1769 Voltaire wrote to the duc d'Aumont: 'Your great-grandfather was my first patron'[6], and this great-grandfather[7] was born in 1632, thus representing a bridge of 185 years.

Voltaire also corresponded with a good many of the leading statesmen of Europe, from Dubois, Fleury, the Argensons, Amelot, Bernis, Maurepas, Richelieu, Choiseul and Turgot, to Bolingbroke and Wilkes; the Austrian Kaunitz; the Dane Bernstorff; the Germans Podewils and Cocceji; the Swiss François Tronchin; the Hungarian Fekete de Galánta; the Spaniard Miranda; the Russians Shuvalov, Vorontsov and Golitsuin.

The anything but arid Voltaire was on friendly, sometimes intimate, terms with many of the great ladies of that time—to mention only those with whom he also corresponded—including the marquise de Bernières, the duchesse d'Aiguillon, mme Dupin, the duchesse Du Maine, the marquise de Pompadour, the duchesse de Choiseul, mme Necker, mme de Saint-Julien, countess Bentinck, and above all the learned, the scintillating, the beloved Emilie Du Châtelet, whose long love-affair with Voltaire has become one of the most celebrated in history[8].

As for the crowned heads to whom he wrote as an equal, for all the divinity that still hedged even the pettiest throne, Voltaire was the favourite correspondent of two of the most remarkable monarchs of all time. Frederick II, king of Prussia, and Catherine II, empress of all the Russias: Frederick, his disciple, his dear friend, or rather his beloved enemy; Catherine simply his disciple, perhaps because they never met. A complete list of the reigning princes whose names figure among Voltaire's correspondents would be tedious: I will mention, apart from English, French and Prussian kings and queens, only Ulrica of Sweden, Christian VII of Denmark, Wilhelmina of Bayreuth, the elector Palatine Charles Theodore, Louisa Dorothea of Saxe-Gotha, Carolina Louisa of Baden-Durlach, the prince de Ligne, Stanislas Leszczynski and Stanislas Poniatowsky, kings of Poland, Charles Eugene and Louis Eugene of Wurttemberg; and many more, together with such

6 Best.D15807 (9 August 1769).

7 Louis Marie Victor, duc d'Aumont (1632-1704); it is not known what he did for the little boy.

8 Nancy Mitford's *Voltaire in love* (1957) is regarded by many as her best book.

princes of the church as Benedict XIV and Clement XIII, and numerous cardinals and bishops, notably Tencin, Passionei and Quirini, not to speak of such exotic personages as Gabriel Podosky, prince-archbishop of Poland and Lithuania, and Jean Pierre Biord, prince-archbishop of Geneva.

These enumerations by no means reveal the extent of Voltaire's correspondence—naturally enough since he wrote and was written to by well over 1800 persons, and a number of corporate bodies. I have said nothing of his letters, including some of the finest he ever wrote, to actors and actresses; nor of those to artists, doctors, publishers, financiers, bankers; nor of those he wrote to the many academies of which he was a member; I have said nothing of his letters to his quite extensive family, and I can only briefly mention the long and profoundly interesting series of letters he wrote to the friends of his youth and of all his life: Argental, Cideville, Richelieu, Thieriot. And something very remarkable must not be overlooked here, so remarkable that it should in itself suffice to prove how wrong are those who represent Voltaire as a quarrelsome man with whom it was impossible to get on. I have recorded here the names of only four friends: but what is so impressive is that in the list of Voltaire's correspondents are found the names of thirty-five people with whom he exchanged letters continuously for over twenty years, and a score of those, outside his family, with whom he corresponded for more than thirty years. How many men could say as much?

It is worth noting in passing that Voltaire's letters were not written only in French: he wrote a good many in English and Italian, and some Latin, German and Spanish texts are also encountered.

All this is by no means banal, it is indeed unparalleled. A correspondence covering so long a period of time, so voluminous, and of such profound and wide interest, could be historically important, without being literature. And yet this is precisely the uniqueness of Voltaire's letters. What makes a mere document into a piece of literature is the personality of the author, the quality of what he has to say, and the manner in which he says it. There is a distinction to be drawn here. There are some who in general write well, even superlatively, and who are incapable of writing a good letter. The correspondence of Baudelaire, for one, proves this contention. On the contrary, there are those who write very good letters while quite incapable of composing a story or a novel, for all that these forms appear to be in a sense developments of letters. We all know such people among our own acquaintances. It is not a question of style. Even writers whose style is extremely artificial, such as Henry James, Proust, James Joyce, have written admirable letters, as have a few, like Flaubert, who went to enormous trouble to achieve simple and flowing effects. I think that the problem is essentially a psychological one. The author writes for the public, be this public very limited or indifferent; the letter-writer addresses himself to a particular person; and not many people are capable of doing both.

It is self-evident that the characteristic qualities of the good letter-writer are varied and precise, some of them being perhaps unexpected. The essential thing is clearly an ability to put oneself into rapport with the person to whom one is writing, to get into his skin. Voltaire had this gift to an almost miraculous degree. To see him describe the same event, make the same reflection to an old friend, to an academic colleague, to a woman, to a young protégé, to a country neighbour, is a liberal education. It is not that he necessarily seeks to please—there are innumerable letters far removed from any such aim—but to touch, to interest each one by the aspect of the matter most closely corresponding to his own interests, tendencies, beliefs. 'Accuse me if you wish of an excess of vanity', mme Du Deffand once wrote to Voltaire, 'but you tell me nothing I do not believe I have already thought.'[9] Could a good letter be better defined? And Voltaire replied: 'One easily adopts the tone of those to whom one speaks; it is not so when one writes; it is by luck that one hits it off.'[10] Luck! strange luck that always favoured Voltaire when he took his pen in his hand! unless one chooses to call it luck to be endowed with such a degree of empathy.

Much generosity of spirit is equally required, and even just plain generosity, for a great man to write good letters. Consider Bernard Shaw, who received astronomical fees for whatever he put his pen to, the smallest scrap of his writing having become a

9 Best.D15497 (1 March 1769).   10 Best.D15517 (15 March 1769).

valuable merchandise to collectors or publishers both—such considerations did not prevent him from answering very often and at great length young writers and actors who sought his advice and help. This was not exactly the case of Voltaire, who never accepted a penny of his literary earnings, but consider this man's occupations; lord of the manor, justiciary of high and low justice, farmer, builder, business man, head of a family, and even, at odd moments, author of some thousands of compositions published under 150 pseudonyms. All this did not prevent him from writing letters to a Helvétius or a Chabanon, commenting at length on the writings they submitted to him; to a Damilaville or an Argence to encourage them to crush the infamous; to mme Du Deffand to console her for her malice and her blindness; to Frederick to discourage him from suicide; to Catherine to encourage her to liberate the serfs or to crush Mustapha; to the whole world to solicit subscriptions for Marie Corneille, and to agitate public opinion on behalf of Calas, Sirven and many more; to his bankers and agents about money matters; to his publishers and printers to complain of their work, their delays, their misprints, the poor type they used, their excessive or inadequate margins; innumerable letters of simple friendship, neighbourliness, consolation or congratulation.

It has become a commonplace nowadays to say that the art of letter-writing is simply a function of distance, that people do not write what they can say, and that speed of communication, and above all the telephone, enable us always to communicate by speech, consequently that the art of the letter is dead. It seems to me that this belief, like most received ideas, is false. I have already mentioned Shaw, and many more examples could be cited. What about Proust's letters? and the Gide-Claudel correspondence? and the letters of D. H. Lawrence? and the extraordinary epistolary eruptions of Thomas Wolfe? to cite only a few.

It is not even true that fewer letters are written, as we shall see in a moment. It is true only that certain very limited kinds of letters are no longer written, or much less than they were. A large proportion of Voltaire's delightful notes to his publishers would certainly now be replaced by even more frequent telephone calls. That would be a pity, but it hardly justifies the total pessimism affected by so many writers about the future of the epistolary art.

585

It is true that in those days the arrival and the departure of the courier were great events; people prepared themselves to send and receive their letters; pains were therefore taken in the writing of them, especially as it was usually the recipient who paid the postage, often very heavy. But what letters have lost in consequence have they perhaps not gained in naturalness? Alas, the transformations of social and family life have also had an opposite tendency: the fear of spontaneity. Many are those who nowadays are haunted by the dread, even when writing the most intimate letters, or particularly when writing such letters, of having them read out in a law-court.

In any case, it must not be imagined that the absence of the telephone and the difficulties of travel automatically produced good letters. In fact, even in the French eighteenth century, the fine flower of polite manners, it must frankly be admitted that Rousseau, Diderot, Frederick II, mme Du Deffand, mlle de Lespinasse, mme Du Châtelet, Catherine II, are the only ones a few of whose letters have entered French literature by the side of the great mass of Voltaire's—and it is not uninteresting to observe that this short list includes the names of a Swiss, a Prussian, and a Russian of German birth.

The miracle, one of the miracles, of Voltaire's letters is that among so many it would be very difficult indeed to find a single boring one. For indeed, although a letter may well be very interesting even if it is badly written, it will not resist the corrosion of time: *a fortiori* a correspondence of scores, hundreds, and indeed thousands of letters. To survive, that is to become literature, it is after all indispensable that a letter should have literary qualities. And this is precisely where Voltaire triumphs. He had an instinctive feeling for words and phrases, feelings so refined by incessant practice and discipline, that it was impossible for him to write or dictate a banal sentence—for he wrote as he spoke and dictated as he wrote: there is no difference or only the slightest except in relatively minor details of punctuation and spelling between a letter written by his own hand and one dictated to a secretary.

There are also few differences between the letters of the youth and the old man. The early ones are perhaps more poetic, the later ones more energetic though no less graceful, but in general the same vocabulary is found, constantly enriched by the experiences of a long life, but remaining always of the same kind, a vocabulary in which the echos of the Latin learned at Louis-le-grand, the reading of the old French poets and the new English thinkers, mingle most happily with the technical terms of law, medicine, and the arts and crafts, the idioms of Burgundy and Geneva. Everywhere is found the same flowing grace, the same passion, the same sincerity, the same seriousness, the same reasoning sensibility, the same spontaneity, the same love of antithesis, the same wit, in short, the same style. His most trifling business notes often evoke a smile or a sympathetic grimace.

And what a course of epistolary technique! How to complain to one's publisher because proofs have not been received that day: 'I am stupefied not to have received anything from my dear Gabriel. I am not accustomed to such forgetfulness. A day without a sheet is a day lost and it was not worth while to come to the Alps and become a chamois in order to suffer such disappointments. To what are you sacrificing Jeanne, the history, Oreste? This is killing me.'[11]

How to respond to a forgery: 'I see in *The Whitehall evening post* of the 7th of October 1769, no. 3668,' wrote Voltaire to the duke of Grafton, 'an alleged letter written by me to his majesty the king of Prussia. This letter is very foolish, nevertheless I did not write it.'[12] This is the entire letter, which I cannot resist printing a second time.

How to consult one's doctor: 'An old man of seventy-six has long since been attacked by a scorbutic humour which has always reduced him to a very great emaciation, which has lost him nearly all his teeth, which sometimes attacks the tonsils, which often gives him the rumblings, insomnias, etc. etc. caused by his illness, begs monsieur Bouvard to have the kindness to write at the foot of this note whether he thinks that goat's milk could procure him some relief. It is perhaps ridiculous to hope for a cure at this age; but the patient having some business in hand which cannot be finished

---

11 Best.D19271 (1774/1775); this 'a day lost' was one of Voltaire's favourite classical allusions: according to Suetonius the emperor Titus exclaimed 'Amici, diem perdidi' when-ever he let a day pass without giving someone a present.

12 Best.D15977 (29 October 1769); see p. 543, above.

before six months, he takes the liberty to ask whether goat-milk could make him last that long? He inquires whether there is any evidence that goat-milk, with some absolutely necessary purges, had done any good in similar cases?'[13]

Finally, for this course in the art of letter-writing, the most universal of the arts, could be prolonged indefinitely, this is how Voltaire, at the age of 83, a few days before his death, on a scrap of paper, refused the invitation of a lady: 'I well know what I desire, but I do not know what I shall do. I am ill, I am suffering from head to foot. Only my heart is sound, and that is no good for anything.'[14]

In addition to all this Voltaire's letters contain much verse, including some of his most charming occasional lines, and here and there a deeper touch of poetry: more than one example has been quoted in these pages.

It is true that the quite special circumstances of Voltaire's life vastly contributed to make him a great letter-writer. In this context his life falls into three parts which are quite sharply defined. First was his wordly epoch. Voltaire lived in Paris and thence visited his friends, as can be seen from the map (p. 69 above), as far as Forges and La Rivière Bourdet to the north; Caen to the west; Richelieu, Ussé, La Source and Sully more to the south; in addition to Sceaux, Maisons, Vaux and many more in the immediate environs of the capital.

Then came the time of Voltaire's absence from the capital, the stay in England, then at Cirey, in the Netherlands, in Prussia; in this period were written the major philosophic and scientific letters, addressed to Frederick, Maupertuis, Mairan, and a hundred others.

Finally, there is the period of exile. Voltaire was completely absent from Paris for a quarter of a century, and these are the years of the most voluminous correspondence with the whole of Europe, since letters had become nearly his sole means of communication with the outside world. He became the great reformer and propagandist.

It is obvious that if Voltaire had remained quietly at home, his

13 Best.D16198 (5 March 1770).
14 Best.D21195 (? May 1778, to mme de Saint-Julien).

correspondence would have been very different, much more limited, and infinitely less interesting.

A word of warning is called for. To judge the true meaning of a Voltaire letter is a task full of nuances. All kinds of genres are found among his letters: the mere list of his correspondents shows that this must have been so. In these circumstances it is evident that they do not all express equally the true thoughts and feelings of the writer. The overflowing emotions of a letter addressed to an intimate friend in a moment of sorrow or of joy betray Voltaire with obvious truth: but what he felt often varied, even very rapidly. The effect may be one of profound truth, and usually is, but this truth is sometimes a passing one.

On the other hand, a letter which Voltaire knew to be destined to be read widely, and even printed, might at first sight be regarded as having to be read with prudence. But this is not invariably so, because in such a letter Voltaire often takes a great deal of trouble to express his ideas clearly and accurately. Even here there are shades to be taken into account. Voltaire was not unaware that certain of his correspondents, mme Du Deffand for one, for all their protestations to the contrary, read his letters to the faithful of their salons. In such cases Voltaire wrote letters which were indeed intimate, but expressed in such a way that they could be seen by other eyes. It was a delicate task, and the drafts of his letters to the blind misanthrope show how much trouble Voltaire took to perform it.

And then, in his most intimate letters of all, written to an Argental, a Thieriot, a Damilaville, with whom he communicated in a sort of secret language. Voltaire very often said the opposite of the literal meaning of his words. Of course some letters were written in an actual code, needing a key, but this is not what I mean here. I am talking of the sort of hidden language of allusion and indirection which can be learnt only by the most attentive and prolonged study of the texts. Once this internal language has been absorbed it becomes possible to distinguish the formulas which indicated to his Parisian friends that certain works must be disavowed, that others were really not by him, that yet more were by him, but that this must absolutely not be admitted, or could be avowed if necessary, or admitted tacitly, or attributed to another, and so with almost infinite variations. It is easy to imagine how many mistakes have been made by commentators unaware of these little mysteries.

The mistake is often made of attributing to a writer the sentiments he puts into the mouths of his personages: this is recognised to be a vulgar error. But anyone who quotes Voltaire's letters without taking into account the often subtle difficulties I have only lightly outlined, is guilty of almost as grave an error. The most innumerable personage created by Voltaire is Voltaire himself, who agitates this personage like a marionette. He cannot be forced into a straight-jacket.

How many letters did Voltaire write? My definitive edition of the correspondence, including the supplement, extends to about 21,350 numbers, or about a quarter of a million leaves of papers: for many of the letters extend to two or more pages, and some of the letters have survived in several, even as many as twelve or fifteen texts: drafts, originals, file copies, contemporary copies, variant editions, variants often due to Voltaire himself when preparing certain of his letters for printing—though these were all open or formal letters, for he never printed a personal letter. Certain periods of his life provide a great number of letters; but these periods are rare and brief. At other times, particularly in the early years, we have relatively few. At others still, when Voltaire was actively promoting some cause or other, many letters have come down to us, but we know that he wrote many more. Thus, in October 1748, Voltaire made great efforts to prevent the staging of a parody of his tragedy *Sémiramis*. We have the letters[15] he wrote on this subject on the 10th to the queen of France, to the chief of police, and to the angel Argental, but he tells us himself—not vaguely that he has written thirty letters, a purely symbolical remark cited a thousand times as if it had a statistical value—he tells us very precisely that he wrote also to mme de Pompadour, to the duchesse d'Aiguillon, to Maurepas, to the duc d'Aumont, to the duchesse de Villars, to the duc de Fleury and to the duc de Gèvres[16]: it was a very ducal correspondence that day. All these

15 Best.D3775-D3777.   16 see the note on Best.D3778.

letters are unknown, but it is probable that some at least still exist in unsearched archives.

All this does not mean that Voltaire wrote a relatively enormous number of letters. About 20,000 written by Voltaire himself survive. However, apart from childhood letters, his correspondence extends over 67 years, that is, 3484 weeks, or 24,380 days, ignoring leap years. We thus arrive at an average of not even one letter a day. I estimate that we possess about half of Voltaire's epistolary output. Let us therefore say that he wrote an average of two letters a day. It is little, whether absolutely or relatively. We are asked to believe that ex-President Hoover wrote 55,952 letters in his 84th year.[17] This is frankly incredible, for it makes an average of 155 letters a day if mr Hoover worked 365 days in the year. But even if the figure is grossly exaggerated or very loosely defined, this total of 55,000 letters in one year puts into the shade the wretched 20,000 written by Voltaire in his entire life.

In fact what is remarkable is not the number of letters Voltaire wrote, but the number his correspondents kept from his early youth. Of how many people could it be said that half their letters have survived? And apart from archivists driven by official obligations or collectors of the most avid kind, who would want to keep a letter from mr Hoover for enjoyment?

17 *Time* (international edition), 18 August 1958, p. 31; see also the note on p. 13, above.

33 Voltaire at the age of 82, *from the marble head by François Marie Poncet
in the possession of Theodore Besterman*

34 Voltaire at the age of 83, *from the original terracotta statue by Houdon*

44. *The summing-up*

I

GOETHE WAS SELDOM at a loss for an abstract and sweeping generalisation. Once, however, he was so overcome that he quite lost his breath: it was when he wanted to express what he thought of Voltaire. He only managed to gasp out: 'Profundity, genius, intuition, greatness, spontaneity, talent, merit, nobility, imagination, wit, understanding, feeling, sensibility, taste, good taste, rightness, propriety, tone, good tone, courtliness, variety, abundance, wealth, fecundity, warmth, magic, charm, grace, urbanity, facility, vivacity, fineness, brilliance, boldness, sparkle, mordancy, delicacy, ingenuity, style, versification, harmony, purity, correctness, elegance, perfection'. Then, taking a deep breath, he added, to leave the reader in no doubt about his feelings, that Voltaire was the greatest writer of all time, the most astonishing creation of the author of nature.[1] How well I understand Goethe's almost horrified awe! How often have I myself experienced this rush of superlatives to the head!

II

When François Marie Arouet was born into the professional bourgeoisie of Paris, the reign of Louis XIV still had two decades to run before it descended to its gloomy close; and when this younger son of an obscure and arid attorney died, he had long since become Voltaire—the most famous, the best loved and the most fanatically hated man in Europe—the American revolution was already in the past, and the French one was not far over the horizon. As a boy Voltaire knew well, some even intimately, men and women born in the early years of the seventeenth century; as an old man he helped writers and others destined to become

1 From Goethe's notes on his edition of Diderot's *Neveu de Rameau*.

famous far into the nineteenth. The middle part of this long span of time saw a revolution in men's thinking, for Voltaire's maturity was contemporary with the end of one epoch of history and the beginning of another. Indeed, this end and this beginning, in short, this revolution, were more than merely contemporary with this man. They were largely his work. Let so impeccable an authority as the *Dictionnaire de théologie catholique* bear witness. Its article on Voltaire concludes: 'It was principally by the efforts of Voltaire that there came into being the modern world . . . in which the state, liberated from the church and purely secular, guarantees to every citizen the freedom of his person, of thought, of speech, of the press, of conscience and of religion.' Of course the erudite author was thinking only of France, for it is unfortunately not true that the state has everywhere been liberated from the church.

This tribute is the more remarkable in that Voltaire was all his life a mercilessly unremitting enemy not only of the church but of Christianity and of all religion. He did, it is true, try very hard to convince the authorities that he was at least a deist, that he did at least believe in a kind of god. But as I have shown[2], although in his aristocratic way—for this bourgeois was an aristocrat by instinct and conviction—Voltaire was convinced that public order could not be maintained without religion, he did not consider that the need to have faith extended to the enlightened few. His ostensible belief was, in short, pure expediency. I do not advocate or defend Voltaire's attitude: it was what it was.

It is indeed obvious that Voltaire did not believe in religion. To him religion, not being based on reason, was no more than superstition. He held that in a civilised state law must be just and supreme, and religion consequently useless—hence in such a state expediency becomes irrelevant. It was therefore false and dangerous to maintain a church, an authoritarian, dogmatic and intolerant organisation created to maintain a superstition made superfluous by social advance. This conclusion was consecrated by Voltaire in his lucid and lapidary exhortation, which seemed for a time to triumph: *Ecrasez l'infâme*, Crush the infamous.

2 See chapter 17, above.

Such was the negative, the destructive side of Voltaire's philosophy: in order to build the ground must be first cleared. All great truths, said Bernard Shaw, begin with blasphemies; and Voltaire's blasphemies were precious and indispensable. By tearing down the infamous he showed his contemporaries that the system they saw as an iron cage was in fact a mere spider's web.

But of course in the long run it is the positive, the constructive element of his teaching that is important.

What, then, according to Voltaire, is a society based on reason and utilitarian morality? First of all, it assures to all freedom of thought. This seemed to him perfectly obvious, as indeed it is, since truth emerges from reflection. Truth is therefore injured the moment any limit is placed on the free play of speculation. And here again Voltaire offered one of his lapidary insights, which in a few words resume and perpetuate a whole philosophy: 'Freedom is the health of the soul.'

He saw that the fundamental principle of freedom of thought determines a long series of other liberties. Or rather, freedom constitutes an interlocked whole: break one link and the entire system collapses. Thus, although reason is a vital discipline for every individual, it becomes directly useful to society only when its findings are communicated: hence freedom of expression is an indispensable corollary of freedom of thought. But what would be the use of possessing these freedoms if they were exposed to sanctions? That would be a Barmecide feast indeed. Voltaire was therefore led to insist on the freedom of the individual under law, and to do all that he did in the fields of legal and penal reform. Man must be free; freedom depends on law; hence the best government is that which guarantees to all, without distinction, the utmost liberty he can enjoy without harm to his fellows. And so the chain of liberties comes, link by link, to an end without end.

The philosophy of Voltaire can be summed up thus: man's behaviour must be governed by reason, completed by social morality and aesthetic sensibility. 'Wisdom excelleth folly as far as light excelleth darkness.'

It will at once be objected that these liberties have often and seriously been infringed. This is only too true, and yet it is undeniable that a fundamental change has taken place in human society. What is this change which is due in such large part to Voltaire? I think it can be expressed, with a high degree of accuracy, thus: up to a certain moment intellectual freedom occasionally existed by the indulgence of the establishment; since that moment, when it does not exist it is because the power of the state has been abused. What was a privilege has become a right. We still have dictators, but they take care that a cloak of legality covers the abomination of desolation. Thus analysed, it is clear that the importance of the change can hardly be exaggerated.

Of course such a transformation, which gave to every man the right to use his reason, and to the common man his dignity, was ultimately the work of many generations of human effort and suffering: the seekers, the artists, the scholars contributed their several parts. It may therefore seem extravagant to give one man so much credit for the change. Yet when the picture of the physical universe, built up during long centuries of reflection and research, was ready to take form and colour, a man was needed to crystallise this long development, and this man's name was first Newton and then Einstein. So, the parallel is almost complete, this catalytic instant in man's long struggle to become himself, for man simply *sapiens* to become *philosophicus*, this moment in the history of humanity is called Voltaire.

III

Two and a half centuries ago, in 1718, Voltaire was twenty-four. Louis XIV, at last, was dead, Louis XV was still a child. The unprecedented success of Voltaire's first play, *Œdipe*, following on his eighteen months in the Bastille and in exile, made him in that year what he remained throughout his long life, the head and forefront of French literature and the international symbol of free thought. He was imprisoned because of a ferocious satire on the corruption and inefficiency of the government. It so happened that he had not written this particular squib, but no matter. The significant fact is that the young man could reasonably be supposed to be its author. In his tragedy of *Œdipe* Voltaire did nothing to contradict this reputation. Far from it, for the play contains strongly anti-monarchical and anti-clerical lines, the most famous of which accuses the church of trading on the public's ignorance. Such notions could be expressed on the stage only because they were already dormant throughout the nation, and because the regency of Philippe of Orleans was giving France a brief glimpse of intellectual light between the obscurantist reigns of Louis xiv and his great-grandson Louis xv.

At this time France was the most powerful and, superficially, the wealthiest country in the world. But this power and this wealth had been mined by megalomaniac kings and a corruptly incompetent nobility and governing class. Such as it was it was based on a population of peasants who lived in misery and ignorance. Even when their poverty was intermittently relieved by temporary rises in the price of farm produce, they were still wretched, for they were broken by numerous and complex taxes and obligations. They were little more (sometimes nothing more) than serfs of absentee feudal landlords, who were themselves responsible only to an autocratic king, since in many respects they were not effectively subjec. to taxation and the law. This same law, on the other hand, was as slow as it was costly. If a private citizen (the word already existed, the thing hardly at all) was suspected of a crime he must expect to be put to the question ordinary, and all too often extraordinary, on the still popular principle that a man will say what you think he ought to say if you hurt him enough. As for the freedoms of thought and of speech, they did not exist, since hand in hand with the king there reigned an even more partisan intolerant and unjust power, the church. Victor Hugo said, with a passion which in no way disfigured the truth, that in the eighteenth century France was ruled by religion and the law, a religion which was intolerance, and a law which was injustice.

Much of this intolerance and injustice Voltaire saw at close quarters and even experienced in his own person. He was never, it is true, poor, and he soon became very rich, deliberately, in order to be free to write and to say what he chose, and to go where he pleased. And as nothing is easier for an intelligent and well-informed man than to make money, Voltaire, who was both to a high degree, made a great deal while he was about it. But before he thus became footloose he was twice imprisoned and thrice exiled because of his satires on the establishment. When he quarrelled with a member of a great family he was publicly beaten by the nobleman's servants, and then sent to the Bastille by the government to console him. And later, though he was always able, not without considerable effort, to keep his own person one jump ahead of the latest *lettre de cachet*, he could not prevent the authorities, civil and ecclesiastic, from censoring, condemning, prohibiting, lacerating, burning nearly all his innumerable publications. Not even his glorification of Louis XIV was exempt, for to the Byzantine mentality of Louis XV and his minister Maurepas praise of the fourteenth Louis was equivalent to criticism of the fifteenth.

All this was the result, not the cause, of Voltaire's revolt against the society in which he was born. Even as a very young man he showed that the mysterious processes of heredity had bred in a commonplace family one endowed with an eye that saw things as they are, the ability to reflect independently, the courage and the patience to give effect to his conclusions, and the gift to express what he had to say with unique clarity, passion and persuasiveness. Nothing could silence a man so constituted and so endowed.

IV

About fifteen million of Voltaire's written words have come down to us, enough to make twenty *Bibles*. This vast quantity of writing is in almost every conceivable form: plays and dialogues, novels and stories, epic and lyric poetry, encyclopedic essays, scientific and learned papers, polemics and squibs of every description, book reviews, and of course, most numerous of all, letters, and again letters, since twenty thousand have survived, addressed to 1800 correspondents ranging from popes to peasants and from ministers to mistresses, and perhaps as many again have perished—and what letters! The subjects dealt with in these twenty *Bibles* and these twenty thousand letters correspond broadly to the entire range of knowledge in the eighteenth century, from paleontology to economics, from history to biology, from biblical criticism to semantics, from abbeys to Zoroaster.

Nor should it be assumed that all this was, as it necessarily would be today, mere journalism. Or, to put it in another way, it would be a violent mistake to imagine that Voltaire produced a few great works which have to be extracted from the mass like a precious metal from the bulky ore. No, if Voltaire wrote much it was because he had much to say. He was essentially a *serious* writer. It is true that Matthew Arnold[3] could not take Voltaire seriously because the great man laughed—which only goes to show that even a most powerful poet and critic runs the risk of making a fool of himself if he lacks a sense of humour. After all, Wordsworth, an even greater poet, but with even less wit than Matthew Arnold, went so far in the opposite direction as to find, he possibly alone in all humankind, that Voltaire was dull[4]. Far from underrating Voltaire because he laughed, I should prefer to say that his laughter compels us to take him seriously. Because he smiled while destroying superstition he did not replace it by some equally virulent system. As Bertrand Russell said when I asked him to define Voltaire's influence on him, what had most impressed him was the great humanitarian's ability to attack even the worst of abuses with ironical laughter. 'This', he went on, 'is the great merit of ridicule in controversy. Ridicule does not substitute one dogma for another, but suggests the absurdity of all dogmas in regions where only doubt or a confession of ignorance is rational.'[5] This is a notable tribute from the man who has most closely resembled Voltaire in modern times as the 'voice of passionate reason'. George Steiner has most elegantly brought this out: 'Like Voltaire he cultivated a mordant style and a cool delight in polemic. His distaste for the raw vehemence and exhibitionism of D. H. Lawrence recalls Voltaire's fastidious condescension towards Rousseau. Both men were tireless in taking up unpopular causes, in regarding the whole spectrum of human social nastiness and political misconduct as their own very personal business.'[6]

Always grimly though smilingly determined to extirpate the infamous, everything that Voltaire wrote, except perhaps some of the most brittle of his drawing-room verse, has meaning and purpose as well as form. And in addition Voltaire was sublimely endowed with the gift of language. His style was not a fragile shell enclosing a void. If he expressed himself with transparent

---

3 *Mixed essays* (1924), p. 107.
4 *The Excursion*, ii.443.
5 'Voltaire's influence on me', *Studies*

on Voltaire (1958), vi.161.
6 George Steiner, in *The Sunday Times* (London 8 February 1970), p. 12.

lucidity it was, I repeat, because he thought lucidly. Others have reasoned with clarity, and some have been able to express their conclusions intelligibly, but, in the whole extent of the world's literature it has been given to few, if any, to express so much worth saying, so well documented, and with the charm, the elegance, the biting wit, with which Voltaire animated all that came from his pen. Open his works anywhere (I do not exclude even his far too comprehensively despised plays or his theological commentaries or his business letters) and nowhere will a page be found which does not contain something worth saying said just about as well as it can be. Nor should the vulgar error be made—I am afraid it very often is made nowadays—of mistaking clarity for superficiality. It is one of the greatest curses of the irrational times in which we live that obscurity is so widely taken for profundity: hence the popularity of writers like Teilhard de Chardin, who, ironically enough, is a collateral descendant of Voltaire. The great man would certainly not have approved the fashionable Jesuit who closely shared his ancestry. When Pascal made a virtue of obscurity, urging that this very obscurity was evidence for the truth of religion, the young Voltaire exclaimed: 'These are strange signs of truth that Pascal advances! What other signs are shown by falsehood? What! is it then enough, in order to be believed, to say, I am obscure, I am unintelligible!'[7]

When Voltaire wrote these words nearly all his intellectual life was still before him, but they already breathe the essence of the man. They contain nearly all the key-words of the Voltairean outlook. Our great man was in fact for light, and against obscurity; for truth, and against falsehood; for lucidity, and against unintelligibility. 'Nothing', said Voltaire in a letter, 'so distinguishes a just and upright mind as the ability to express itself clearly. A man's words are confused only when his ideas are muddled.'[8]

V

Of course all this has not gone unperceived. Although it is true that Voltaire is not particularly in fashion these days, since we are traversing an age of unreason and even of anti-reason, even

7 *Lettres philosophiques*, xxv.xviii.
8 Best.D4115 (19 February 1750).

today only a few fanatics would refuse him a place among the world's greatest men. Yet the curious thing is that Voltaire's reputation has been achieved as it were in spite of itself. Thus, he is universally recognised as the greatest of all letter-writers, yet for nearly two centuries after his death his correspondence was known only in fragmentary and corrupt texts. Everybody knows that Voltaire was one of the most directly influential thinkers of all times, and easily the most internationally diffused writer during the century beginning around 1740: witness the thousands of editions of his writings in all languages. Yet a critical edition of his collected works has only now been initiated. Yet how many general readers have so much as heard, to take a few titles in D, of the *Défense de Louis XIV*, the *Défense de milord Bolingbroke*, the *Dialogues d'Evhémère*, the *Diatribe du docteur Akakia*, the *Doutes sur la mesure des forces motrices*? Yet the last three of these essays are respectively: the *Evhémère* Voltaire's most considerable discussion of metaphysics; the *Akakia* the most ferociously witty attack ever made by one writer on another (it makes H. G. Wells on Henry James appear, in his turn, elephantine); and the *Doutes* a significant contribution to the downfall of Cartesian physics.

An even more specific witness of the hazards Voltaire's reputation has traversed is the extraordinary fact that during much more than his lifetime his plays were constantly performed all over Europe (not excluding England), and more often in France than those of Racine and Corneille together. Yet how many theatre-goers alive today have ever seen a Voltaire play?

I do not mean that Voltaire has not been much exposed to the scholars. Indeed, to anticipate the next chapter, in which all this is described in detail, the standard bibliography of his own writings, now three-quarters of a century old, extends to four substantial volumes. It is nevertheless very incomplete, since I have myself published a supplement to this bibliography, in which are set out 361 unrecorded eighteenth-century French editions of works by Voltaire. The standard biography, still older, fills eight even larger volumes. It is nevertheless just as incomplete, since it hardly deals at all with Voltaire as a writer and thinker. The books and scholarly papers written about him are numbered by the thousand. Yet the great bulk and infinite variety and range of his works have undoubtedly terrified those who might have been competent to do so from undertaking a systematic analysis of the corpus as a whole. Only now is the effort being made, if only aspect by aspect.

VI

Among the innumerable portraits of Voltaire is an engraving which bears the legend, 'The man unique in all times'. This is true. The epigrapher no doubt meant that Voltaire was the greatest of all men. I do not go so far. Such a pretension would be odious and foolish. Shakespeare is the unique poet. Bach is unique as a composer. The novelist Tolstoy is unique. Rembrandt is perhaps unique as a painter. Yet each man is in some measure the distilled essence of his own fatherland. Shakespeare, for instance, is known to all *although* he is English and even though he cannot be adequately translated. Voltaire certainly stands for all that is most characteristically French, for good and ill, but he was also the most universal genius of modern times. He was so because he spent half his life in England, in the Netherlands, in Prussia and other parts of Germany, and in what is now Switzerland; because of his numerous friendship in these and many other countries; by the visits of many hundreds of foreigners come to do him homage; by his innumerable correspondence, which includes letters written by him in English, Italian, German, Spanish, Latin; by his wide and deep reading in all these languages. But above all he was universal in himself, because he felt for all men and spoke a language all could understand. He was, in Byron's words,

> A wit as various—gay, grave, sage, or wild—
> Historian, bard, philosopher combined:
> He multiplied himself among mankind. . . .

If we look at this universality a little more closely, we find that Voltaire was a great and greatly influential historian, the first to write a universal history in which the whole extent and duration of human activity was for the first time liberated from the straitjacket of theology. Voltaire wrote tales which are amongst the world's finest, and in some of which, incidentally, an entirely new kind of story-writing was at once invented and brought to perfection. Voltaire's plays, I repeat, occupied the stage with great distinction for many years throughout Europe. He composed two epic poems, of which one, though it is fashionable to despise it, is still the best the French language has to offer, and of which the other does not deserve its scandalous oblivion. Voltaire also wrote many shorter poems, only a few of which can be described as great, but which, taken as a whole, are, again, unique in their content, their elegance and their occasional lyricism. Voltaire made Newton and Locke known on the continent of Europe. He had the immense merit of recognising the awesome beauties of Shakespeare and of introducing him to France, even though he regarded the author of *Hamlet* as a barbarian, a barbarian of genius, to be sure, but still a barbarian. Voltaire wrote a vast mass of polemical and propagandist books and pamphlets, in which he is always on the side of justice and tolerance, always against superstition, fanaticism and cruelty, but without himself becoming intolerant or dogmatic, and without ever losing the magic of his incomparable style.

Almost incidentally, he was the greatest letter-writer of all times, his surviving correspondence forming the greatest single source of information about a significant epoch of human history, as we have seen.

VII

And when all this has been said, we observe so astonishing a fact that once again it can only be described as unique. This enumeration of Voltaire's claims to greatness, however rapid and foreshortened, has, after all, evoked his life and his writings. And when one has spoken of a writer's thoughts, work and life, what is left? In the case of Voltaire there is this left, that which has had the greatest influence of all his labours on the intellectual evolution of mankind: I mean of course his actions. Voltaire was in fact the first great man of letters who used his fame and literary skill in the active promotion of his social convictions.

It was in this spirit that he always encouraged and sustained the young and the talented, that he built, planted, manufactured; that he created the prosperous township of Ferney, soon to become Ferney-Voltaire; that he helped those who had become the victims of injustice. When religious fanaticism, hand-in-hand with a subservient magistrature, tortured to death a father falsely accused of hanging his son for religious reasons, and who unsportingly refused to confess though his limbs were being broken one by one on the wheel; when another father was falsely condemned for murdering his daughter, who had in fact been driven to suicide by the missionary rage of a bishop; when a boy in his teens had his hand cut off, his tongue torn out, and the remnant done to death because of suspected blasphemy; when these things and many others of this kind took place, Voltaire's voice was the first to be heard in protest, and Voltaire's pen alone was taken up and never again put down until the king, the church and the judiciary were compelled to bow their heads before the storm of public opinion—for in the process Voltaire had indeed created what was to become the touchstone of all government, even the most dictatorial. He had shown, by evoking a vast response throughout the civilised world, that there was such a thing as public opinion, and that this opinion could be formed and harnessed. And all these things were done not only, at first, without any encouragement, but in the face of opposition fanatical and unscrupulous to a degree unimaginable to succeeding generations until the twentieth century achieved the apparently impossible by breeding a new epoch of self-destructive barbarism. I repeat, Voltaire did not destroy injustice, but he took the first step, he put the unjust on the defensive.

Of course all this was not accomplished without a price. The horror of injustice which was Voltaire's deepest conviction and most deeply felt emotion, was an inestimable boon for the world at large: but for himself it was the cause only of anguish. He was intimately convinced, like Martin Luther King, that injustice is indivisible. The repulsion he felt against it was not a current that could be switched off and on. It was always there, he always vibrated with it. The ingratitude of a friend, the malice of a censor, the stupidity of an official, all these wretched trifles exasperated him and made him suffer and react to a degree incomprehensible by smaller men. We must try to understand: even a Voltaire cannot always rise above the shadows of his qualities. A rather confused admirer, damning with ill-considered praise, says that

Voltaire's 'love of justice is not rational, it is passionate'[9]. It would not have been a merit in Voltaire to have loved justice with his heart rather than his head, nor did he. The truth is that this most profound conviction was the fruit of Voltaire's reason, but it was expressed with all the deepest passions of his being. It is no doubt true that 'Voltaire's crusade was at all times motivated by a warm heart'[10]. How could it not have been? But this warm heart, though it sometimes led Voltaire into impulsive and even regrettable actions, was always directed, in matters of principle, by a wise, cool, powerful and experienced head.

Indeed, Voltaire was utterly a man of the mind. He lived by the mind, his mind forced his ailing body to accomplish miracles of hard work. He was indeed the most absolute kind of rationalist. He was not prepared to accept the notion that mankind depends on external forces and influences, and therefore he placed squarely on man's shoulders the responsibility for his own moral evils. He was convinced that evil, that is, injustice, was the result of bad thinking.

Pascal was to Voltaire the symbol of all the things he most hated: the spirit of the schools, dogmatism, intolerance, pessimism, obscurantism. There is a famous passage in which the sombre genius deplores the blindness and wretchedness of man, and his fearful condition in the universe, like that of a man who awakes to find himself on a deserted and frightful island which he cannot leave. Voltaire has given an annihilating reply to this attitude of mind in his *Lettres philosophiques*[11]; but he also gave another thrown off in a poem[12] addressed to a lady and which I do not apologise for repeating:

> Je lis au cœur de l'homme et souvent j'en rougis.
> J'examine avec soin les informes écrits,
> Les monuments épars et le style énergique
> De ce fameux Pascal, ce dévot satirique,
> Je vois ce rare esprit trop prompt à s'enflammer.
> Je combats ces rigueurs extrêmes:
> Il enseigne aux humains à se hair eux-mêmes,
> Je voudrais malgré lui leur apprendre à s'aimer.

9 André Delattre, *Voltaire l'impétueux*, ed. R. Pomeau (Paris 1957), p. 101.
10 Charles Vereker, *Eighteenth-century optimism* (Liverpool 1967), p. 119.
11 XXV.vi.
12 *Epître à une dame ou soi-disant telle* (1732).

'I often blush when I read the heart of man, I carefully examine the shapeless writings, the monumental ruins and the energetic style of that famous Pascal, that satirical believer, I find that rare spirit too ready to be inflamed. I dispute his extreme rigours: he teaches men to hate themselves, I would sooner teach them to love one another.'

35 Voltaire, *from the head of Houdon's statue*

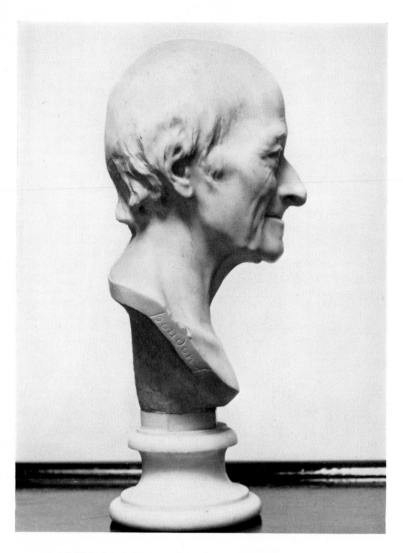

36 Voltaire at the age of 83, *from a marble bust by Houdon in the possession of Theodore Besterman*

45. *Bibliographical note*

I

THE FIRST separately published Voltaire bibliography appeared in 1817, nearly forty years after his death. This pioneering work was by J. J. E. G., that is, Gabriel Peignot, a very voluminous bibliographer and antiquary, none of whose works was good enough to survive, though the *Répertoire des bibliographies spéciales, curieuses et instructives* (1810) still has some interest as a bibliophilic curiosity. The most interesting part of Peignot's Voltaire bibliography is its full title, which shows the spirit in which allegedly scholarly work was done at that date: *Recherches sur les ouvrages de Voltaire, contenant . . . une notice raisonnée des différentes éditions des ses œuvres . . . l'indication raisonée des principaux ouvrages où l'on a combattu ses principes dangereux.* When I mention that a work with so comprehensive a label sets out only 150 titles in all, it will be seen at once that it is quite absurdly inadequate, even by the standards prevailing in that generation, and even though the publications on Voltaire listed by Peignot are limited to those that were written against him.

A quarter of a century later Peignot was succeeded by a far better scholar, Joseph Marie Quérard, a limited edition of whose *Bibliographie voltairienne*[1] appeared in 1842. The author is famous for his massive *La France littéraire* (1827-39), a bibliography which is still of much value, and his *Les Supercheries littéraires dévoilées* [1845-60], a new edition of which would be welcome. His Voltaire bibliography sets out 1131 titles, clearly much fuller than Peignot, but still grievously incomplete, even though Quérard took his material almost in its entirety from the admirable edition of Voltaire's works by A. J. Q. Beuchot. He admits as much in his own preface.

1 Bengesco's copy, with his notes, is in the Bibliothèque nationale.

Bibliographical note

All the early bibliographies of Voltaire's own writings, among which I mention only these separately published works by Peignot and Quérard, though there were many more, slighter ones, were superseded by the labours of the Romanian diplomat Georges Bengesco (more correctly Bengescu), whose intelligent masters allowed him to remain *en poste* in Paris for many years. He was thus enabled to produce in 1882 his preliminary *Notice bibliographique sur les principaux écrits de Voltaire, ainsi que sur ceux qui lui ont été attribués*, which is in reality no more than an off-print of the bibliography in vol. 50 of Louis Moland's edition of the *Œuvres complètes de Voltaire*, which is only now being superseded as the standard edition. Bengesco followed this immediately with the work of which the *Notice* is an abridgement, his four-volume *Voltaire: bibliographie des ses œuvres* (1882-90), to which I return below. Since then no general bibliography of Voltaire's works has been attempted, and from what follows it is easy to understand the reason for this lack of enterprise.

On the other hand, specialised bibliographies have multiplied. The most direct supplement to Bengesco is my own book entitled *Some eighteenth-century Voltaire editions unknown to Bengesco*[2]. This sets out full-dress descriptions, with many facsimile title-pages, ornaments etc. of no fewer than 361 French eighteenth century Voltaire editions unknown to Bengesco—and I have already discovered more[3]—a figure that gives some idea of the extent to which he is incomplete.

A still more specialised supplement, which partly goes beyond the limits of Bengesco's bibliography, is volume lxxvii (1970) of the *Studies on Voltaire and the eighteenth century*, which contains a 'Calendar of Voltaire manuscripts other than correspondence' by Andrew Brown, and William H. Trapnell's 'Survey and analysis of Voltaire's collective editions, 1728-1789'. The former of these studies excludes the correspondence because that is dealt with in Voltaire (135). In that volume the listing of the manuscript sources of Voltaire's correspondence occupies about 400 columns, and that of the printed works in which letters have been

2 Vol. cxi of the Studies on Voltaire (1973), with a supplement in vol. cxliii.105-112.

3 See *e. g.* my 'Three additions to Voltaire bibliography' in the Robert Niklaus homage volume.

published for the first time a similar amount of space. These statistics speak eloquently of the sheer crushing volume of the material. To put it another way, at the date of publication of Voltaire 135 I had found no fewer than over 1200 publications in which Voltaire letters had been printed for the first time.[4] As for manuscripts in general, such publications as Fernand Caussy's *Inventaire des manuscrits de la bibliothèque impériale de Saint-Pétersbourg* (1913) together with my 'The Manuscripts of the Institut et musée Voltaire'[5] must not be forgotten.

Bengesco is limited to French editions, though he did not admit as much until his book was finished, but Voltaire when still quite young attained an international reputation of a kind now, *mutatis mutandis*, inconceivable. In consequence I have paid much attention to the foreign editions and the translations of his works, previously ignored by nearly all bibliographers, though without them it is not possible to arrive at just conclusions about Voltaire the writer and the *philosophe*. First I commissioned 'A Provisional bibliography of English editions and translations of Voltaire' by Hywel Berwyn Evans[6], which describes no fewer than 578 editions with English imprints. Since then, without any systematic search, I have found about forty more English editions to add to this number, and an even fuller, though only short-title list, limited to genuinely British imprints, appears in André Michel Rousseau, *L'Angleterre et Voltaire* (Studies on Voltaire, cxlv-cxlvii: 1976), pp. 976-1032. It is difficult to appreciate such a figure absolutely. May I therefore give it some relative status, much though I hate such invidious comparisons, by mentioning that this figure of well over 600 English editions of Voltaire very far exceeds the number of French editions of Shakespeare, though the latter had a century's start. What this proves invites critical attention. At least, it is a fact.

To this English bibliography should be added Keith I. Maslen's discussion of 'Some early editions of Voltaire printed in London'[7].

---

4 André Delattre's *Répertoire chronologique des lettres de Voltaire* (1952) has of course been superseded; see my review in *Travaux sur Voltaire et le dix-huitième siècle* (1955), i.220-4.

5 In *Studies on Voltaire* (1958), vi.293-5.

6 In *Studies on Voltaire* (1959), viii.9-121.

7 In *The Library* (1959), 5th ser. xiv.287-93.

With it is also connected by language the earlier *Voltaire in America, 1744-1800* (1941), by Mary Margaret Barr, which contains about 500 references of every kind, including writings on him.

I myself followed up the English bibliography with 'A Provisional bibliography of Italian editions and translations of Voltaire'[8] (212 titles), 'A Provisional bibliography of Scandinavian and Finnish editions and translations of Voltaire'[9] (157 titles), and a 'Provisional bibliography of Portuguese translations of Voltaire'[10] (63 titles). A similar 'Bibliographie provisoire des traductions néerlandaises et flamandes de Voltaire'[11] (169 titles), by Jeroom Vercruysse followed. It will be noted that this last bibliography is limited to translations, unlike the others, which include editions. This is because the complex structure of the French book-trade in the eighteenth century requires much more investigation before French books produced in France can be accurately distinguished from those printed in the Netherlands. A provisional Spanish bibliography is in the press.

It thus appears that well over 1200 translations of Voltaire have so far been recorded, not including such earlier bibliographies of a similar kind as D. D. Yazuikov's *Вольмеръ зь русскcй лимерамурѣь* (1879) and *Die Deutsche Voltaire-Literatur des achtzehnten Jahrhunderts* (1921) by Paul Wallich and Hans von Müller.

In general, a good many booksellers' and auction catalogues devoted to Voltaire must also be taken into account, and of course such library catalogues as the *Collection voltairienne du comte de Launoit* [1955], now in the Bibliothèque royale of Brussels. To this must be added J. Vercruysse's 'Notes sur les imprimés et les manuscrits de la collection Launoit'.[12] Not without interest is Andrew R. Morehouse's 'The Voltaire collection in the rare book room'[13] at Yale. Unfortunately, the heading 'Voltaire' in the Bibliothèque nationale catalogue is still awaited, by me with resigned despair; the whole of my work on him has been done

---

8 In *Studies on Voltaire* (1961), xvii.263-310.

9 In *Studies on Voltaire* (1966), xlviii.53-92.

10 In *Studies on Voltaire* (1970), lxxvi.19-35.

11 In *Studies on Voltaire* (1973), cxvi.19-59.

12 In *Studies on Voltaire* (1962), xx.249-59.

13 In the *Yale university library gazette* (1943), xiii.66-79.

without access to this, the finest Voltaire collection in existence, thanks to Beuchot and Bengesco. It will be by far the longest entry in the catalogue, and will occupy an entire volume. Its dimensions can be inferred from the Voltaire heading in the British library catalogue, which extends to nearly 100 columns, though not strictly comparable. Obviously of far less value, but still not without interest, are such exhibition catalogues as *Le XVIIIᵉ siècle à Lyons: Rousseau, Voltaire et les sociétés de pensée* (1962), by Alice and Henry Jolly, and *Voltaire et la culture portugaise* (Paris 1969), an exhibition organised by, oddly enough, the ultra-conservative Gulbenkian foundation.

There are also numerous studies of Voltaire's individual editions and works. Thus, the great Kehl edition organised by Beaumarchais, and which ruined him, perhaps because of the fulminations of the church, has attracted a great deal of attention; see for instance Giles Barber's 'The Financial history of the Kehl Voltaire'[14] and the references he gives. The Kehl edition is so famous that no French book-collector's library is complete without a set. It is one of those quite unusual books with a market value greater than it deserves, I mean of course by purely commercial considerations, since after nearly two centuries the supply is still inexhaustible. Several thousand copies were printed, and most of them still exist, on various papers, with the plates in various numbers and states, and of course in all sorts of bindings, from the original stitched paper, usually blue, to the most ornate contemporary morocco. Yet, and this is surely a great reproach to French erudition, the Kehl edition has never been adequately examined. Bengesco (number 2142; iv. 105-46) devoted forty-one pages to it, but without suspecting the bibliographical problems of a textual nature which fill it. There are all sorts of variants in the octavo edition, and for all I know in the duodecimo also (but I think not), that should be sorted out. However, the labour involved is so great that even Trapnell (p. 138) contented himself

14 In *The Age of the Enlightenment: studies presented to Theodore Besterman* (1967), pp. 152-70. Cp. F. J. Crowley, 'The Walther edition of Voltaire (1748)', *Modern language notes* (1954), lxix.331-4; this is now of little interest, because I have since published Voltaire's correspondence with Walther, which was not known to Crowley.

611

with the frankly laughable statement[15] that the Kehl edition is so 'well-known and widely accessible' that there is 'no need to give a detailed description of it'.

The Kehl edition is not the only collective one badly in need of critical attention. In fact, Trapnell took the first and most important, but still only the first, step towards adequate knowledge of all the collected editions produced during Voltaire's lifetime, and their inter-relations. Nor is this a small matter, for at least a hundred such editions, 'complete' or selective, appeared in the half-century from 1728, the date of the first. An important study of Voltaire's annotated copy of the 'édition encadrée' is Samuel Taylor's 'The Definitive text of Voltaire's work'.[16]

As for other individual works, the still unresolved problem of the first edition of *Candide* has spawned dozens of more or less valuable studies. I have myself distinguished about twenty editions, impressions, issues dated 1759, a fact unique in the five centuries of the printing press. The analysis[17] I have made of some of these editions is merely a first contribution. Much more investigation is needed. Nor is *Candide*, though supremely complex, entirely alone. There are other and various studies of individual works, such as 'La Première édition française de *La Princesse de Babylone*'[18] by Madeleine Fields, H. J. Minderhoud's *La Henriade dans la littérature hollandaise* (1927), D. W. Smith's 'The First edition of the *Relation de Berthier*'[19] and, rather wider, Durand Echeverria's 'Some unknown eighteenth-century editions of Voltaire's political pamphlets of 1771'[20], to take very diverse examples. And of course it must be remembered that critical editions usually contain bibliographies. Thus the best enumerations of the editions of the *Henriade* and the *Pucelle* are in the editions by, respectively, O. R. Taylor and Jeroom Vercruysse in Voltaire 2 and Voltaire 7.

In a more general way, Voltaire's own library, sold by his

15 But his study is nevertheless invaluable not least for the great Voltaire edition now in progress.

16 In *Studies on Voltaire* (1974), cxxiv.7-132.

17 In the work cited in note 2, above, nos. 237-53, and figures 20-40.

18 In *Studies on Voltaire* (1961), xviii.179-82.

19 In *Studies on Voltaire* (1975), cxxxvii.47-54.

20 In *Studies on Voltaire* (1974), cxxxvii.61-4.

greedy niece to the empress Catherine, must not be forgotten. A great deal has been written about it, and the Leningrad librarians, though they took their time, did finally produce a reasonably adequate catalogue: *Бпблиомека Вольмера: Камалог Книг* (1961). As for the works cited in the annotation of Voltaire's correspondence, a listing of them is in Voltaire 135, extending to over 400 columns.

II

Turning now to writings on Voltaire, some of the bibliographies already mentioned incidentally include a few, but by far the most voluminous listing is Mary Margaret Barr's *A Century of Voltaire study: a bibliography of writings on Voltaire, 1825-1925* (1929). This is unfortunately marred by being entirely uncritical and technically inadequate. Also, in order to make a neat century, she made the basic error of beginning in 1825, a particularly inconvenient date in Voltaire studies. The author's supplements to this bibliography were cumulated by her and Frederick A. Spear under the title of *Quarante années d'études voltairiennes ... 1926-1965* (1968), with the same technical defects. The two volumes together list about 3700 entries, but their inadequacy can be judged from Vercruysse's 'Bibliographie des écrits français relatifs à Voltaire'[21], which sets out no fewer than 629 books and pamphlets in French published on Voltaire from 1719 to 1830—Barr, of course not being limited to separate publications.

There are many other specialised bibliographies of writings on Voltaire. Thus, we have the admirable 'Etat présent des études voltairiennes'[22] by René Pomeau, and J. H. Brumfitt's 'The Present state of Voltaire studies'[23]. Louis Mohr, *Les Centenaires de Voltaire et J.-J. Rousseau* [1880] lists no fewer than 270 titles of writings published on the occasion of these two centenaries in 1878. Still more specialised are two surveys of Voltaire texts and criticism in particular reviews, one French, one English. These

21 In *Studies on Voltaire* (1968), lx.7-71.

22 In *Travaux sur Voltaire et le dix-* *huitième siècle* (1955), i.183-200.

23 In *Forum for modern language studies* (1965), i.230-9.

are 'Voltaire et le *Mercure de France*'[24] by Madeleine Fields, and the rather amateurishly compiled index by J. A. R. Séguin, *Voltaire and the Gentleman's magazine* (1962). A valuable article by Samuel Taylor, 'La Collaboration de Voltaire au *Théâtre français* 1767-1769'[25] must not be overlooked.

III

I now return to what is by very far the most useful Voltaire bibliography so far published, that by Bengesco. The first volume appeared in 1882, and was partly destroyed in a fire at the printers, being then re-issued with the date 1882-85, the fourth and last volume being published in 1890. Of the whole work 550 plus copies were printed.

The third volume (1889) is entirely devoted to Voltaire's correspondence; but although it is by far the biggest of the four (609 pages) it is also much the most incomplete, being, except for one hundred additions, based on the Moland edition. This is a rather bizarre fact, for Bengesco knew of many more uncollected letters.

These volumes nevertheless represent a prodigious labour of love. Unfortunately Bengesco abandoned (see the 'Avertissement' to the fourth volume) the further volume or volumes he had intended to devote to translations of Voltaire's writings and to those about him. The whole work as published extends to two thousand pages—everything connected with Voltaire is larger than life—and can be superseded only by another work conceived on the same majestic scale, and which therefore would have to be very much larger still. Bengesco's is in fact a bibliography in the widest sense of the word. He gives detailed, often minute information—which does not mean of course that it is necessarily accurate and scientific—about the first edition and the successive printings of each distinct work. When he knew of no separate edition Bengesco tells us in what book, periodical or other publication Voltaire's text was first published. In a rough and ready way, he analyses the series and the collected editions. Not content

24 In *Studies on Voltaire* (1962), xx.175-215.   25 In *Studies on Voltaire* (1961), xviii.57-75.

with this he has narrated the history of each work, told us when and how and why it was written, and what Voltaire said about it. He even goes so far as to describe the controversies surrounding many of his works.

It is only fair to say all this—and very impressive it is—but it is now necessary to add that all this was done—a century ago it must be remembered—in an utterly unscientific way. Moreover, the bibliographer took no account of manuscripts. Of course all this was not poor Bengesco's fault. He could not use bibliographical techniques not yet invented. Besides he knew only a few thousand Voltaire letters, and over 21,000 have now been published (including those addressed to him). The fact remains that Bengesco presented his research in so unmethodical a way that as a first step I had to commission an index[26] of his bibliography, for the general index he himself promised (as in the 'Avertissement' of vol. ii) never saw the light. Only then could it be used to any effect, for Bengesco discusses the same work under different headings, he retraces his steps, he corrects himself (his book contains five lists of additions and corrections, totalling 65 pages); his classification is arbitrary and even whimsical, waiving the absurdity of describing an author's works in any other way than chronological, although it is true that the chronology of Voltaire's works presents exceptional difficulties: writings published and continuously revised over a period of years, sometimes decades, are only one of the many problems presented by our tireless and voluminous polymath. However, I need not enlarge on Bengesco's classificatory vices, for I have elsewhere[27] analysed the contents of his bibliography, and here merely record one's astonishment that such a disorder should have been created by the man who was himself so severely critical (vol. i, pp. xi-xii) of Quérard's deficiencies in that respect.

It is even stranger that although Bengesco, born in 1848, lived until 1922, he never replaced his hand on the Voltairean plough, except for some editions of little importance. The great work on

26 Jean Malcolm, *Table de la Bibliographie de Voltaire par Bengesco* (1953).

27 In the preface (pp. 7-10) to the index cited in the previous note.

Moldavia on which he worked for many years was never completed, but he published studies and bibliographies on Romanian
and near eastern subjects, in particular on Carmen Sylva, and
translated a few Romanian works into French, but he left his
great Voltaire bibliography untouched. It is easy to believe that
he must have been exhausted by his great effort.

IV

Voltaire's earliest known work, the *Epître à monseigneur*,
'Noble sang du plus grand des rois', dates from 1706 or 1707,
and he went on writing until a few days before his death in 1778.
The output of this extraordinary man thus extends over more
more than seventy years, and unpublished work still turns up
from time to time. This great span of active life may have been
exceeded once or twice in the history of mankind, but the even
vaster scope of his work never has. It is difficult to think of any
kind of writing that he did not attempt. In verse he wrote an
epic poem and a burlesque epic, odes, epistles, and every kind
of medium-length and shorter poem, from the lightest drawing-
room epigram to some of the most profound and philosophically
influential poems of modern times; and he also composed numerous tragedies, comedies, operas, and light entertainments. In
prose he wrote novels, stories, and dialogues. And this is far
from emptying the cornucopia, for Voltaire also composed
scientific treatises, diplomatic papers, legal documents, historical
works, articles, book reviews, dictionaries, lectures, commentaries, and of course letters, more letters, always more letters. He
wrote, edited, revised, annotated, reviewed, compiled, translated.

As for his subjects, on what did he not write, from the ABC
to Zoroaster, by way of love, snails, freewill, madness, music,
convulsions, and the stercorists?

If his letters be included it may be estimated that about 23,000
separate pieces of writing were born of Voltaire's prodigious
fecundity, pieces ranging from the briefest of epigrams to the
Dictionnaire philosophique, which in its present-day form extends
to 2400 large pages. When it is remembered that most of Voltaire's works were printed clandestinely, under about 150 pseudo-

nyms or entirely anonymously, with false dates and false imprints, under the names of imaginary publishers and printers, or with no name at all, in two or more places simultaneously, not always in the same country; when it is realised that many of his works, including the correspondence, went into several, even dozens, sometimes hundreds of editions and impressions, that he ruthlessly corrected and revised successive editions of many of his works to the point of extensive transformation, consolidation and separation; and that many of them are now known in very numerous more or less contemporary foreign editions and translations into many languages; it will be appreciated that the task of creating a Voltaire bibliography is one of such enormous difficulty that I have not used excessive poetic licence in naming it elsewhere an impossible dream. And of course the more difficult the task the more necessary it is. The bibliography of no other writer is at once so complex and so difficult as Voltaire's, because of its enormous size and the innumerable, often subtle, problems it presents. Indeed, a considerable proportion of my work has consisted in laying the bibliographical groundwork on which adequate editorial work can be done; and as that groundwork is still most lamentably incomplete, the labour of those who are now collaborating in the great critical edition of Voltaire's works is made even more difficult.

There are many other *desiderata Voltaireana*. I have, for instance, collected much material towards a Voltaire iconography, but I can see little prospect of it being completed. I should like to see a listing of books dedicated to Voltaire, and an anthology of contemporary poems written about him. Why has nobody yet attempted a study of Voltaire's influence in various countries? or of the attitude to him at home in contemporary periodicals? Important and fascinating books remain to be written on Voltaire's influence on particular writers, such as Bernard Shaw. A chronology of his life and writings already exists in draft, and awaits revision. We need a dictionary of the personages in Voltaire's tales and plays, a study and index of his vocabulary[28], an analysis of his sources as indicated by his familiar quotations[29].

28 I have laid the basis for this in Voltaire 135.

29 I have listed these in Voltaire 135.

Volunteers are needed for a vast general index of the critical edition of his works now in progress. These are only a few samples of the work that remains to be done, chosen among the most obvious.

Above all, however, a full-dress bibliography of Voltaire is needed, and I hope I may succeed in stimulating erudite emulation. If any scholar anywhere feels competent and courageous enough to dream this impossible dream, he can count on my fullest help, including access to all the material assembled for the critical edition of Voltaire's works now in progress, assured publication, academic fame, and even a little money. Nor are these offers limited to my life-time, for I have made arrangements to ensure that the work will be continued after my death.

V

The most comprehensive English work on the French eighteenth century in general is the relevant volume of the Cambridge modern history, though unfortunately the new edition is not as good as the old. The soundest brief treatment is by John Lough, *An Introduction to eighteenth century France* (1960). Stimulating books of somewhat wider scope are R. J. White, *Europe in the eighteenth century* (1965) and David Bayne Horn, *Great Britain and Europe in the eighteenth century* (1967).

More specifically on the Enlightenment the chief works are Ernst Cassirer, *The Philosophy of the Enlightenment* (translated in 1951 from the German original of 1932); Lester Crocker, *An Age of crisis* (1959-63); Peter Gay, *The Enlightenment* (1966-69), pretentious, but unsound and humourless; *The Age of the Enlightenment: studies presented to Theodore Besterman* (1967).

No editions of Voltaire's writings are cited here since the first critical edition has only recently been launched by the Voltaire Foundation at the Taylor institution of the university of Oxford: *The Complete works of Voltaire;* the following volumes have appeared so far:

2. *La Henriade,* edited by O. R. Taylor. 1970.
7. *La Pucelle,* edited by J. Vercruysse. 1970.

53-55. *Commentaires sur Corneille,* edited by David Williams. 1974-75.

59. *La Philosophie de l'histoire,* edited by J. H. Brumfitt. 1968.

81-82. *Notebooks,* edited by Theodore Besterman. 1968.

85-135. *Correspondence and related documents,* edited by Theodore Besterman. 1968-76.

The standard work on Voltaire is that by Desnoiresterres (see p. 14, above). The most stimulating biographies at the moment available in English are those by Richard Aldington (1925), A. N. Brailsford (1935), George Brandes (1930), Gustave Lanson (1906), John Morley (1872), Alfred Noyes (1936), N. L. Torrey (1938); in each case the date shown is that of first publication.

Voltaire's family is discussed, so far as the scant evidence permits, by Jacques Renaud, *Les Ancêtres poitevins de Voltaire* (Niort 1960), and Guy Chardonchamp, *La Famille de Voltaire: les Arouet* (Paris 1911).

Many other specialised works are mentioned in the footnotes, the most important being the series of *Studies on Voltaire and the eighteenth century,* over 160 volumes of which have now been published.

37 This 18th century gold box in the Wallace collection has just
been found to have a secret slide, with a miniature of
mme Du Châtelet on the other side

Appendix

[The *Mémoires* written by Voltaire in 1759 (but published posthumously) is a controversial work, consisting in large part of an account of his relations with Frederick. Its value is therefore limited. On the other hand his *Commentaire historique sur les œuvres de l'auteur de la Henriade* is an important and in all essentials accurate autobiography, which does not deserve the almost total neglect into which it has fallen (by accident, because it is buried in the preliminary documentation of the Moland edition). Though in the main composed in the third person, it was almost certainly written by his own hand in 1776 or 1775/76, or at least dictated by him: his style is unmistakable, apart from many other indications. The disguise often becomes perfectly transparent, as when the writer says, in the first person singular, that he was present at the first performance of *Zaïre*, in 1731. When Voltaire writes in the first person, it is sometimes in the singular, at other times in the plural: clearly another reflection of half-hearted anonymity. But the result is confusing, and I have therefore restored the normal English singular everywhere.[1]

Among the many other details pointing to Voltaire's personal responsibility for the *Commentaire* is a rather odd one: the not infrequent wrong dates, an almost invariable feature of Voltaire's autobiographical allusions in his letters and other writings; and the occasional defective sequences of events, clear evidence of a man writing from memory in old age.

The original edition of the *Commentaire* was printed in Geneva in 1776, with a false Basle imprint. All subsequent texts in Voltaire's works (the *Commentaire* has not been reprinted separately

---

[1] At least once, in an endorsement he wrote on Best.D8455, Voltaire's secretary claimed that the *Commentaire* had been 'fait par Wagnière'; but, for all my faith in his integrity, this cannot outweigh the clear evidence.

since 1777, nor has it ever been edited) must be used with caution. The startling abuses Voltaire's writings have suffered at the hands of his editors have not spared the *Commentaire*. Thus, the Kehl editors inserted into it large chunks of the *Mémoires*. That Voltaire wrote those in a very different spirit, nearly twenty years earlier, and in the first person, were trifling difficulties which the editors overcame by freely adapting both texts.

A translation of the *Commentaire* was published in 1777 under the title of *Historical memoirs of the author of the Henriade*. This has never been reprinted, but has now been faithfully reproduced below, after having been corrected where necessary from the original: only misprints and literal mistakes in translation have been put right. Both are numerous, though in general the translation is excellent. I have added a minimum of explanatory notes within square brackets.

In the original edition of the *Commentaire* 160 pages of Voltaire's letters were appended. These have been omitted, but those printed in the text itself have been here translated in full.]

HISTORICAL MEMOIRS, &C.

In these Memoirs, the subject of which is a literary man, I shall endeavour to avoid every thing which may not in some degree tend to the advantage of letters, and particularly make it my care to advance nothing, except on the authority of original papers. No use shall be made of the almost innumerable satires and panegyrics which have been published, unless they are found to be supported by facts properly authenticated.

Some fix the birth of FRANCIS DE VOLTAIRE to the 20th of February, others to the 20th of November, 1694, and there are extant medals of him bearing each of these dates.

He has several times told me, that at his birth it was thought that he could not live, and that having been privately sprinkled by the midwife, the ceremony of baptism was put off for several months.

Although I think nothing is more insipid than the details of infancy, and the time spent at school, yet it ought to be mentioned, from the authority of his own writings, and the voice of the public, that at about twelve years of age, having written some verses that appeared to be superior to what could have been expected so early in life, he was introduced to the celebrated Ninon de l'Enclos, by the Abbé Chateauneuf, her intimate friend, and that extraordinary woman bequeathed to him the sum of two thousand livres to buy books; which legacy was punctually paid.

The little piece in verse here alluded, is probably that which he composed for an Invalid who had served in the regiment of the Dauphin, under the only son of Louis XIV. The old soldier had gone to the Jesuits College to entreat one of the Masters to oblige him, by writing a petition in verse, to be presented to the Dauphin. The Master told him he was then too busy, but that there was a young scholar who could do him the favour he requested. Here follow the verses composed by the child.

> Digne fils du plus grand des Rois,
> Son amour et notre espérance,
> Vous qui, sans régner sur la France,
> Régnés sur le cœur des François;
> Souffrez-vous que ma vieille veine,
> Par un effort ambitieux,
> Ose vous donner une étrenne,
> Vous qui n'en recevez que de la main des Dieux?
> On a dit qu'à votre naissance
> Mars vous donna la vaillance,
> Minerve la sagesse, Apollon la beauté:
> Mais un Dieu bienfaisant, que j'implore en mes peines,
> Voulut aussi me donner mes étrennes,
> En vous donnant la libéralité.

Which may be thus paraphrased:

Illustrious offspring of the first of Kings,
The Monarch's joy, the peoples future stay,
    To whom each Frenchman's heart its tribute brings,
Tho' France to thee no regal honours pay.

Now chilling age has damp'd my generous fire,
    Yet deign t'accept this gift without a frown,

This *martial* gift, which dares thus high aspire,
    For thou receivest gifts from Heaven alone.

'Tis said, their choicest influence to dispense,
    Around thy infant couch the powers combin'd:
Mars gave thee valour, and Minerva sense,
    His lineaments divine, Apollo join'd.

One friendly power that oft has heard my woe,
    Then deign'd to me a noble boon t'impart,
He gave your eyes with pitying tears to flow,
    And to relieve distress, a generous heart.

This trifle of the young scholar put some Louisdores into the pocket of the old invalid, and made a considerable noise both at Versailles and Paris; and 'tis probable that from that time the youth determined to follow his natural bent for Poetry. But I have heard from his own mouth, that he was principally, and indeed solely, engaged to addict himself entirely to the cultivation of the Belles-lettres, by the disgust he conceived against the method of teaching Jurisprudence in the law schools, to which his father (who was treasurer of the chamber of accompts) had sent him immediately after he left school.

Notwithstanding his extreme youth, he was admitted to an intimacy with the Abbé Chaulieu, the Marquis de la Fare, the Duke of Sully, and the Abbé Courtin; and he has often told me that his father believed him entirely ruined, because he kept company with people of fashion, and made verses.

At the age of eighteen, he began the tragedy of Oedipus, in which he proposed to introduce choruses after the manner of the ancients[1]. The players were very unwilling to appear in a tragedy, the subject of which had been already treated by Corneille, whose performance was what is commonly called a *Stock Play*. It was not acted till 1718, and even then, not without bringing influence to bear.

The young man, who was excessively dissipated and immersed in all the pleasures common at his time of life, was not sensible of the risque he run, nor did he give himself any trouble whether his piece succeeded or not. He indulged himself in a thousand sallies on the stage, and at last wantonly laid

1 We have a letter of the learned Dacier, dated 1713, in which he advises the author, who had then finished his piece, to add singing choruses, in imitation of the Greeks; but it was impracticable on the French stage. [André Dacier's letter is dated 25 September 1714; Best.D26.]

hold of the train of the chief priest, in a scene where that pontiff was producing a very tragical effect. Marshall Villars's lady, who was in the first box, enquired who the young man was that had play'd that trick, as it seemed to be done with a view to ruin the piece; and being told that he was the author, she sent for him into the box, and the attachment he formed from that time to the Marechal and his lady, continued during their lives, as may be seen by a poetical epistle, which has been printed and begins:

> Je me flattais de l'espérance
> D'aller gouter quelque repos
> Dans votre maison de plaisance;
> Mais Vinache a ma confiance,
>
> Et j'ai donné la préférence
> Sur le plus grand des Héros,
> Au plus grand Charlatan de France, &c.[2]

At Villars he was presented to the Duke of Richelieu, whose friendship he acquired, and which has subsisted uninterruptedly for sixty years.

What is as singular, and a fact scarcely known, is, that the Prince of Conti, the father of him who gained so great reputation by the battles at the blockade of Demont and Château Dauphin, addressed some verses to him, which conclude thus:

> Ayant puisé ses vers aux eaux de l'Aganippe,
> Pour son premier projet il fait le choix d'Œdipe,
> Et quoique dès longtems ce sujet fut connu,
> Par un stile plus beau cette piece changée
> Fit croire des Enfers Racine revenu,
> Ou que Corneille avait la sienne corrigée.[3]
>
> From Aganippe's source, his strains he drew,
> Then brought old Oedipus again to view,
> A theme well known—yet such correctness shines,
> Such easy grace adorns his polish'd lines;
> We think Racine had left the shades below,
> Or Corneille's rugged numbers learnt to flow.

I have not been able to find the answer of the author of Oedipus. I asked him one day if he did not jestingly say to the Prince, 'My Lord, you will be a great poet; I must procure you a pension from the King'; and whether, as is also pretended, he did not once put this question to his Highness at supper.

2 [The first line was here omitted, and so was the translation, 'I flattered myself with the hope of taking some rest in your country house; but Vinache has my confidence, and I have given the preference to the greatest charlatan of France over the greatest of its heroes.']

3 [This is not the full text, for which see Moland edition, i.302-3.]

Are we all princes? or are we all poets? He replied, *Delicta juventutis meæ ne memineris Domine. Remember not the sins of my youth, O Lord.*

After having finished his Oedipus; but before it had been performed, he began the *Henriade,* when with Monsieur de Caumartin, Intendant of the Finances, at St. Ange.

I have more than once heard him say, that when he undertook these two performances, he did not imagine he should be able to finish them, and that he was neither acquainted with the rules of the drama, nor Epic poetry; but that he was fired with what he heard of Henry IV from Monsieur Caumartin, who was well versed in history, an excessive admirer of that Prince, and an old gentleman of a most respectable character; and that he began the work from meer enthusiasm, almost without reflection.

Having one day read several cantos of his poem when on a visit to his intimate friend, the young President de Maisons, he was so teazed with objections, that he lost patience, and threw his manuscript into the fire. The President, Henaut, with difficulty rescued it. 'Remember', said Mr Henaut to him in one of his letters, 'it was I that saved the Henriade, and that it cost me a handsome pair of ruffles.'

Some years after, several copies of this poem were handed about, while it was only a sketch, and an edition of it with many chasms was published under the title of *The League.*

All the poets in Paris, and even many of the learned fell foul of him. Twenty pamphlets were let fly against him. The Henriade was play'd at the fair; and it was insinuated to the old Bishop of Fréjus[4], Preceptor to the King, that it was indecent, and even criminal, to write in praise of Admiral Coligny and Queen Elizabeth.

The Cabal had interest enough to engage Cardinal de Bissi, then president of the assembly of the clergy, to pass a judicial censure upon the work; but this strange design proved abortive. The young author was filled with equal surprize and resentment at these intrigues. His dissipation had prevented him from making friends among the literati; and he had not the art of combating his enemies with their own weapons, which is said to be absolutely necessary in Paris, if a man wishes to succeed in any kind of pursuit.

In 1722[5], he gave the tragedy of Mariamne. That Princess was poisoned by Herod. When she drank the cup, the faction cried out, *the Queen drinks,* and the piece was damned.[6]

These continual mortifications determined him to print the Henriade in England, as he could neither obtain privilege nor patronage for it in France. We have seen a letter[7] in his own hand writing, to Mr Dumas d'Aiguebere,

4 [Better known as cardinal André Hercule Fleury.]

5 [Or rather, on 6 March 1724.]

6 Probably this alluded to some report circulated at that time, which has not come to the knowledge of the translator, otherwise the expression could not have had such an effect. [The explanation is simply that drinking was 'noble' only when taking poison, and the interruption broke the spell.]

7 [Best.D294 (*c.* 8 May 1726).]

since that time counsellor in the parliament of Tholouse, in which he speaks of that journey in the following manner:

> Je ne dois pas être plus fortuné
> Que le Héros célèbré sur ma vielle:
> Il fut proscrit, persécuté, damné
> Par les dévots & leur douce sequelle:
> En Angleterre il trouva du secours,
> J'en vais chercher. . . .

> If fortune frown, should I complain?
> The great have had their share of pain;
> Even he, the hero of my page,
> Oft felt the malice of her rage;
> The victim of a bigot crew,
> To England for relief he flew,
> I'll seek that hospitable shore. . . .

The rest of the Poem is torn off. It ended thus:

> Je n'ai pas le nez tourné,
> A être prophète en mon pays.[8]

> At home a prophet is despis'd.
> Howe'er in distant regions priz'd;
> My dear experience proves the point,
> For here my nose is out of joint.

He was right; King George the First, and more particularly the Princess of Wales, afterwards Queen of England, raised an immense subscription for him. Their liberality laid the foundation of his fortune: for on his return to France in 1728, he put his money into a lottery established by Mr Desforts, Comptroller General of the Finances. The adventurers received a rent charge on the *Hotel-de-Ville* for their tickets; and the prizes were paid in ready money; so that if a society had taken all the tickets, it would have gained a million of livres. He joined with a numerous company of adventurers, and was fortunate. I was furnished with this anecdote by a member[9] of the same society, who verified it by producing his registers. Mr. Voltaire wrote to him as follows: 'To make a fortune in this country, nothing more is requisite than to read the arrets of the Council. It is seldom but the Ministry is obliged to make such arrangements in the Finances, as turn to the advantage of individuals.'

This change of circumstances did not weaken his ruling passion for the cultivation of the Belles-lettres. In the year 1730, he gave his Brutus, which I

8 [This 'couplet' is in fact prose.]
9 [La Condamine.]

look upon to be his most spirited tragedy, not even excepting Mahomet. It was violently criticised.

I was present at the first representation of Zara, in 1731, and although it drew tears from a great part of the audience, it narrowly escaped being hissed. It was parodied at the Italian comedy and the fair, where it got the name of the Foundling, and Harlequin on Parnassus.

About that time one of the Academicians having proposed Mr. Voltaire to fill a vacancy, of which he did not entertain the least thought, Mr. de Boze declared that the author of Brutus and Zara could never deserve a place in that society.

He was then intimately acquainted with the illustrious Marchioness of Chatellet, with whom he studied the principles of Newton, and the systems of Leibnitz. They retired to Cirey, in Champagne, for several years, two of which Mr. Kænig, an eminent mathematician, passed with them. Mr. Voltaire caused a gallery to be erected, where they performed all the experiments on light and electricity.

Notwithstanding these employments, on the 27th of January, 1736, he brought out his tragedy of Alzira, or the Americans, which met with great applause. He ascribed his success to his absence, saying, *laudantur ubi non sunt, sed non cruciantur ubi sunt*[10].

The most virulent censurer of Alzira, was the Ex-Jesuit Desfontaines.—That affair was attended with some uncommon circumstances.—Desfontaines had been employed in the *Journal des Savans*, under the direction of the Abbé Bignon, from which he had been dismissed in 1723. He then set up a kind of Journal of his own, and was what Mr. de V. . . calls un Folliculaire (a venom spitter[11]). His character was well known.—He had been taken in the fact with some Savoyard boys, and imprisoned in the *Bissetre*. His indictment was begun to be drawn up, and it was intended to burn him alive, as it was said Paris stood in need of an example. Mr. de Voltaire prevailed upon the Marchioness de Prie to use her interest in the criminal's favour. There is still extant one of the letters written by Desfontaines to his deliverer[12]; it has been printed among those of the Marquis d'Argens Deguille, page 228, vol. 1: 'I shall never forget the obligations I lie under to you: the goodness of your heart is still superior to your genius. I ought to employ my life in giving you proofs of my gratitude. I conjure you likewise to obtain for me a revocation of the *Lettre de Cachet*, by which I am delivered from the *Bissetre*, and banished thirty leagues from Paris.'

In a fortnight after, this same man wrote a defamatory libel against the person in whose service he ought to have employed his life.—This fact is authenticated by a letter[13] of Mr. Tiriot's, dated the 16th August, and taken from the same collection.—This Abbé Desfontaines is the person who, in a

10 [Roughly, 'distance makes the heart grow fonder'.]
11 [No, merely a hack.]
12 This letter was the 31st May: the date of the year is not affixed, but it was written in 1724. [No, in 1725; see Best.D235.]
13 [Best.D300; 16 August 1726.]

conversation with the Count d'Argenson, attempted to vindicate himself by saying, *I must live,* to which the Count replied, *I see no necessity for it.*

After the affair of the *Bissetre,* this Priest desisted from paying his addresses to chimney sweepers. He bred up some young Frenchmen to his double trade of non-conformist and Folliculaire; he taught them the art of writing satires, and in conjunction with them composed a number of defamatory libels, under the title of *Voltairomanie* & *Voltairiana.*—They were a farrago of absurd stories. An estimate of them may be formed from a letter signed by the Duke de Richelieu, the original of which we have recovered. Here follow his own words. 'That book is very dull and very ridiculous. What seems to me most extraordinary is, his assertion that the Duchess de Richelieu gave you a hundred Louisdores and a coach, with some circumstances unworthy of you, however worthy of the author, for this excellent fellow forgets that I was then a widower, and did not marry again till fifteen years after, &c. Signed, the Duke de Richelieu, 8 February 1739.'[14]

Mr. V . . . made no use of so many authentic testimonies; and they would have been of no service to his memory if I had not recovered them, with great difficulty, in the chaos of his papers.

I likewise lighted on a letter from the Marquis d'Argenson, who was Minister for Foreign Affairs: 'He is a villainous fellow, this Abbé Desfontaines', says he, 'his ingratitude is still blacker than those crimes, the commission of which gave you an opportunity of laying him under an obligation. 7th February, 1739'[15].

Such were the people with whom Mr. de Voltaire had to do, and whom he called *the rascallity of literature: they live,* said he, *upon pamphlets and foul deeds.*

I likewise find a man of the same stamp who went by the name of McCarty giving himself out to be one of the noble family of the McCarty's in Ireland, and assumed the character of a man of letters. He borrowed a considerable sum[16] from M. de V . . . , with which he went off to Constantinople and turned Mahometan; upon which our author said, *McCarthy is only gone to Bosphorus, but Desfontaines is gone farther—he has fled to the lake of Sodom.*

It appeared that the opposition, malice, and abuse, which he met with at the representation of every new piece, could not make him desist from indulging his taste; for on the 10th of October that same year[17], he produced his Comedy of *The Prodigal Son,* though not under his own name; and he gave the profits to Messrs. Linant and Lamarre, two young pupils, whom he had formed, and who came to Cirey while he resided with Madame de Chatellet.

---

14 [The translator omitted the '8 February' of the French text, but this only made the error more precise, for the letter is in fact dated 8 January 1749 (Best.D3864).]

15 [Best.D1860.]

16 I have seen in the hands of the Notary, Perret, a bond for five hundred livres, but I could not find the other of two thousand.

17 [1736.]

He appointed Linant Preceptor to that Lady's son, who has since been Lieutenant General of the army, and Ambassador at Vienna and London.

The Comedy of The Prodigal Son had great success. The author wrote to Mademoiselle Quinaut: 'You can keep other people's secrets as well as your own. Had I been known to be the author, the piece would have been hissed. Men cannot bear that the same person should succeed in two kinds of writing. I made enemies enough by Oedipus and Henriade.'

However at that time he commenced a study of a very different nature. He wrote *the Elements of the Newtonian Philosophy*, a philosophy then scarce known in France. He could not obtain a privilege from the Chancellor Aguesseau, who was a man of universal learning, but being bred a Cartesian, discouraged the new discoveries as much as he could. My author's attachment to the principles of Newton and Locke, drew upon him a new crowd of enemies. He wrote to Mr. Falkner, to whom he dedicated his Zara. 'It is believed that the French love novelty, but it must be in cookery and fashions, for as to new truths they are always proscribed among us; it is only when they grow old that they are well received.'

I have recovered a letter which he wrote a long time after to Mr. Clairaut on these abstract sciences; as it seems worth preserving, the reader will find it in its proper place in this collection[18].

By way of relaxation from his studies in Natural Philosophy, he amused himself in writing his *Maid of Orleans*. I have proofs that this piece of drollery was composed almost entirely at Cirey, Madame de Chatellet loved Poetry as much as Geometry, and was a very good judge of it. Although this Poem was only comic, yet there was found to be much more fancy in it than in the Henriade; but it was vilely disgraced by some shameless scoundrels, who printed it with horrid lewdnesses. The only good editions are those of Messrs Cramer.

He was obliged to go to Brussels to solicit a suit which the family of Chatellet had for a long time maintained against the House of Honsbrouk, a suit which might have ruined both families. Mr. Voltaire, jointly with Mr. Raesfeld, President of Cleves, accommodated this old dispute, on condition of a hundred and thirty thousand French livres being paid to the Marquis de Chatellet.

The celebrated and unfortunate Rousseau was then at Brussels, Madame de Chatellet refused to see him, because she knew that Rousseau, when a domestic of her father, the Baron de Breteuil, had written a satire against that nobleman, of which we have proof in a paper entirely written with Madame de Chatellet's own hand.

The two Poets had an interview, and soon conceived a strong aversion from each other. Rousseau having shewn his antagonist a lyric epistle addressed to posterity, met with this repartée: *my friend, this letter will never be delivered*

18 [In the appendix mentioned above, p. 622; the letter is Best.D8455 (27 August 1759).]

according to its direction. Rousseau never forgave this piece of raillery. There is extant a letter from Mr. de Voltaire to Mr. Linant, containing the following passage: 'Rousseau despises me because I am sometimes careless in my rhimes, and I despise Rousseau because he is only a rhimer.'[19]

The uncommon kindness which the King of Prussia had for him, soon made him forget Rousseau's enmity. That Monarch was likewise a poet; but he possessed all the talents of his rank, with many others which are seldom found in a king. While he was Hereditary Prince Royal, a regular correspondence had been long carried on between him and our author. Some of their letters have been printed in the collections of Voltaire's works.[21]

This prince had just finished visiting his frontiers, after his accession to the Crown, and a desire of seeing the French troops, and of travelling incognito to Strasbourg and Paris, induced him to undertake a journey to the first of those places, under the name of the Count du Four, but being recognised by a soldier who had served in his father's army, he returned to Cleves.

Several curious persons have preserved in their collections, a letter in verse and prose, after the manner of Chapelle, written by that Prince on the subject of his journey to Strasbourg. The study of the French language and poetry, Italian music, philosophy and history, had been his consolation during the hard treatment he met with in the earlier part of his life.

That letter is a remarkable monument of a man who has since gained so many battles. It is written with elegance and ease. Here follows some passages of it.

---

19 I observe that a letter of Mr. de Médin, to a Mr. de Messe, of the 17th February, 1737 [Best.D1288], shows well enough that the Poet Rousseau had not corrected himself at Brussels; we here give it: 'You will be surprised at my misfortune—some of my bills have been protested and returned:—on Wednesday night I was arrested and thrown into jail. Would you believe it, that rascal Rousseau, that scoundrel, that monster, who, for six months past never eat or drank, except at my table, to whom I have done numberless services of the greatest importance, was the cause of my being arrested? He irritated the holder of the bills against me, and at last this monster, this offspring of Satan, after drinking with me at my table[20], kissing and embracing me, served as a spy to the officers, who dragged me out of my house at midnight. Never was villainy so black, I cannot reflect upon it without horror.—If you knew all that I have

done for him!—Patience!—I hope this accident will make no alteration in our friendship.—What a difference between that hypocrite and Mr. de Voltaire, who has honoured me with his friendship and assistance!'

It must be acknowledged that such an action tends greatly to vindicate Saurin, as well as the sentence and decree by which Rousseau was banished; but he let us not dive into the depths of an affair so horrid and so disgraceful.

20 *The Reader cannot but recollect the same fulsome behaviour of Rousseau to his benefactor the late David Hume, and that too when he had formed a scheme for blasting his friend's reputation.* [This note was added by the translator, rather unfortunately, for he confused Jean Jacques with Jean Baptiste.]

21 [The translator here inserted in a footnote a rendering of Frederick's long first letter to Voltaire (Best. D1126).]

'I am just returned from a journey, where I have met with several singular adventures, some disagreeable, but many of the pleasing kind.

You know that I set out for Brussels, in order to pay a visit to a sister for whom I entertain an equal affection and esteem.—On the road, Algarotti and I consulted the map in order to settle our return by Wesel.—Strasbourg was not much out of our way, and in preference we made choice of that route. 'Twas resolved to travel incognito;—at last every thing being arranged and concerted in the best method possible, we reckoned upon reaching Strasbourg in three days.

> Mais le ciel qui de tout dispose
> Régla différemment la chose.
> Avec des coursiers efflanqués,
> En droite ligne issus de Rossinantée,
> Des paysans en postillons masqués,
> Nos carosses cent fois dans la route accrochés,
> Nous allions gravement d'une allure indolente.

> But Heaven, whose high despotic sway,
> Disposes all—had barr'd our way.
> Coursers, which by their wind and speed,
> Seem'd of the true la Mancha breed;
> Postillions taken from the plough,
> Our coaches sunk in every slough;
> With gentle pace along we trudgd'd'[22]

'Tis said that scarce a day passed in which he did not write some of these agreeable letters, which were the extempore effusions of his pen. But he had just finished a work of a nature more serious and more worthy of a great Prince; it was the refutation of Machiavel. He had sent it for publication to Mr. de Voltaire, whom he arranged to meet at Meuse, a small castle near Cleves;—when they met my author, paid him the following compliment: 'Sire, had I been Machiavel, and been permitted to have access to a young King, my first advice to him would have been, to write against me.'

From that time the King of Prussia redoubled his kindness to the French man of letters, who in the year 1740, went to pay his court at Berlin before the King was prepared for invading Silesia.

At that time Cardinal Fleury used every art of flattery to cajole him; however, my traveller does not appear to have fallen into the snare.—I shall here present my readers with a very singular anecdote, which may throw great light on the history of the present century. On the 14th of November, 1740, the Cardinal wrote a long ostensible letter, of which I have a copy, containing the following words:

'Corruption is so general, sincerity and faith so shamefully banished from every heart in this unhappy age, that if we do not keep ourselves steady in the

22 [Best.D2305 (2 September 1740).]

superior motives which oblige us not to depart from *them*, we should be sometimes tempted to fail in them on certain occasions. But the King, my master,
shews at least that he does not imagine himself entitled to *have* such sort of
reprisals; and the moment of the Emperor's death, he assured the Prince of
Lichtenstein, that he would faithfully keep all his engagements.'[23]

It is not my province to examine how it was possible, after such a letter, to
form an enterprise, in 1741, for stripping the daughter and heiress of Charles
the Sixth of her paternal dominions. Either Cardinal Fleury changed his
opinion, or that war was entered into against his inclination. This work has
no connection with politics, to which I am an absolute stranger; but as a
literary man, I cannot conceal my surprise, that a courtier and member of the
academy should make use of such a phrase as, 'if we don't keep ourselves
steady in the *motives* which oblige us not to depart from *these motives*;—
that we would be tempted to fail in *those motives*, and that a man is justly
entitled to *have* such sort of reprisals'. What a number of errors in stile within
the compass of a few words!

However, it plainly appears to me that my author had no design to make
his fortune by politics; for on his return to Brussels, he dedicated himself
entirely to his beloved Belles-lettres. There he composed the tragedy of
Mahomet, and soon after went with Madame de Chatellet to get it represented
at Lisle, where there was a very good company, under the management of
Mr. Lanoue, an author and actor. The famous Mademoiselle Clairon play'd
there, and at that early period gave specimens of her great theatrical talents.

Mr. Denis, commissary at war, and captain in the regiment of Champagne,
had married my author's niece, who lived in some splendor at Lille, that
place being within her husband's department.—Madame de Chatelet resided
in her house;—we were spectators of all these diversions, and Mahomet was
extremely well play'd.

Between the acts, the author received a letter[24] from the King of Prussia,
acquainting him with the victory at Molwitz: he read it to the audience, who
received the news with a general clap. *You will see* (said he) *that this piece of
Molwitz will insure success to mine.*

It was play'd at Paris the 19th of August the same year. Upon that occasion
appeared stronger proofs than ever of the excess to which literary jealousy
may be carried, especially in theatrical matters. The abbé Desfontaines, and
one Bonneval, whom M. de Voltaire had relieved in his necessities, not being
able to prevent the piece from succeeding upon the stage, lodged an information against it before the attorney general, as containing some things contrary
to the Christian religion. Things went so far, that Cardinal Fleury advised
the author to withdraw his performance. This advance was equivalent to a
command; however, the author published his play, with a dedication to
Benedict XIV (Lambertini), who had already shewn him particular marks of

23 [Best.D2364(14November1740).]
24 [Best.D2464 (16 April 1741).]

regard. He had been recommended to this Pope by Cardinal Passionei, a man distinguished in the literary world, and with whom he had long maintained a correspondence. We have some of that Pope's letters[25] to M. de Voltaire. His Holiness was desirous of drawing him to Rome, and he has always expressed a regret for not having seen that city, which he used to call the capital of Europe.

Mahomet was not play'd again till long after, when it was revived by the credit of Madame Denis, notwithstanding Crebillon, then licenser of theatrical pieces, under the direction of the Lieutenant of the Police. It was found necessary to appoint M. d'Alembert licenser. This procedure of Crebillon was highly disapproved by people of fashion. The piece has continued in possession of the theatre, even when that species of entertainment has been most neglected. The author acknowledged that he was sorry for having painted Mahomet in more odious colours than he deserved. 'But had I only made him a hero and politician', he wrote to one of his friends, 'the piece would have been hissed. Great passions and great crimes are indispensable requisites in a tragedy.' Some lines after he added, 'the *genus implacabile vatum*[26], persecutes me more violently than Mahomet was persecuted at Mecca. People talk of jealousy and intrigues disturbing courts, but they abound more among men of letters'.

After all these squabbles, Messrs. de Reaumur and de Mairan advised him to renounce poetry, which only exposed him to envy and vexation; to addict himself entirely to natural philosophy, and to sollicit a seat in the Academy of Sciences, as he already had one in the Royal Society at London, and in the Institution of Boulogne [Bologna]. But M. de Fourmont, his friend, a man of letters, and of a most amiable character, having exhorted him in a poetical epistle not to bury his talent, he wrote the following reply:

> A mon très cher ami Fourmont,
> Demeurant sur le double-mont,
> Au-dessus de Vincent Voiture,
> Vers la taverne où Bachaumont
> Buvait et chantait sans mesure,
> Où le plaisir & la raison
> Ramenaient le tems d'Epicure.
>
> Vous voulez donc que des filets
> De l'abstraite Philosophie
> Je revole au brillant palais
> De l'agréable Poësie,
> Au pays où regnent Thalie
> Et le cothurne & les sifflets.

25 [Only one has survived: Best. D3210 (15 September 1745).]

26 [Adapted from Horace, *Epistles*, II.ii.102: *'genus irritabile vatum'*, 'the sensitive race of poets'.]

Mon ami, je vous remercie
D'un conseil si doux & si sain.
Vous le voulez; je cède enfin
A ce conseil, à mon destin;
Je vais de folie en folie,
Ainsi qu'on voit une Catin
Passer du Guerrier au Robin,
Au gras Prieur d'une Abbaye
Au Courtisan, au Citadin:
Ou bien, si vous voulez encore,
Ainsi qu'une abeille au matin
Va sucer les pleurs de l'aurore
Ou sur l'absinte ou sur le thim;
Toujours traveille & toujours cause;
Et vous paitrit son miel divin,
Des gratte-cus & de la rose.[27]

Which is thus imitated:

To Fourmont, friend, I hold most dear,
Who lives upon the forked hill;
Above Voiture's, that tavern near
Where Bachaumont was wont to swill,
And stretch'd in careless ease along,
Maudlin pour'd th' unmeasur'd song.
Where of yore join'd hand in hand,
Sober reason, sprightly pleasure,
Lightly trip'd in frolic measure,
And Epicurus led the band.
'Quit that thorny road', you say,
'Quit Philosophy's dark gloom,
Resume the long forsaken way,
Where Posey's sweet flow'rets bloom,
Melpomene with sober air,
And sportive Thalia wait you there.
Nor dread the surly Critics frown,
Whose only talent is to rail,
Your merits weigh'd in even scale,
You'll grow the fav'rite of the town.
Throw off the philosophic frock,
Put on the buskin or the sock.'

My friend, I'll do what you advise,
Your counsel seems right, sound, and wise.
Besides, it suits my inclination,

27 [Best.D1410 (23 December 1737).]

635

So I'll resume my occupation.
Adieu then to these barren shades,
Welcome again, ye charming maids.
Fate will'd I should be ever changing,
From folly still to folly ranging.
So easy Phillis will admit
Th' embroider'd courtier, or plain cit,
The humble clerk, the lordly rector,
The peaceful quaker, bullying hector,
By turns she hugs them in her arms,
Each has for her resistless charms.
Or, if you choose a different strain,
So when Aurora gilds the plain,
Forth flies the bee to suck her sweets,
And settles on each herb she meets;
Unwearied plies her nimble wings,
Incessant works, incessant sings;
Eager t'increase her honey'd store,
Or from the weed, or from the flower.

And immediately he begun his Merope. The tragedy of Merope is the first piece, not upon a sacred subject, that succeeded without the aid of an amorous passion, and which procured my author more honour than he hoped from it, was play'd on the 16th of February, 1743. We cannot better describe the singular circumstances attending its reception, than by inserting his letter of the 4th of April following, to his friend Mr. L'Aiguebere, then at Tholouse.

'Merope is not yet printed, I am afraid it will not succeed so well in the closet as on the stage.—The piece is not mine; it is Mademoiselle Dumenil's.—What think you of an actress that kept the audience in tears through three successive acts?—The public have run into a little mistake, and given me credit for a part of the extreme pleasure given them by the actors. The seduction was so great, that the pit, with loud shouts, insisted upon seeing me.[28] I was seized in the hiding place, where I had squatted for shelter, and brought by force into the box of Marshal Villars's lady, who was there with her daughter-in-law.—The pit was mad; they called out to the Duchess de Villars to kiss me, and they made so much noise, that she was oblig'd to comply by order of her mother-in-law.—Thus have I been kissed in public, as was Alain Chartier by the Princess Margaret of Scotland; but he was asleep, and I was wide awake. This popular favour, which probably will soon pass, has a little consoled me for the petty persecution I have sustained from Boyer, the former Bishop of Mirepoix, who is still more a Theatin than a Bishop. The Academy, the King, and the Public, destined me to suc-

---

28 Hence the ridiculous custom of crying the author, the author, when a piece, whether good or bad, succeeds the first night.

ceed Cardinal Fleury, as one of the forty[29]. Boyer was against it; and at last, after ten weeks search, he found a Prelate to fill the place of a Prelate, in conformity to the Ecclesiastical Canons[30]. I have not the honour of the Priesthood; I suppose it is proper for a profane person as I am, to give up all thoughts of the Academy.

Letters are not much favoured. The Theatin has told me that eloquence is expiring; that he endeavoured in vain to resuscitate it by his sermons, but that nobody had *seconded* him; he meant nobody had listened to him.

The Abbé Langlet is just imprisoned in the Bastile for having published documents, already well known, serving for a supplement to the history of our celebrated de Thou. The indefatigable and unhappy Langlet did a signal service to good citizens, and to the lovers of historical researches. He deserved a recompense, and at the age of sixty-eight he has been cruelly thrown into prison. 'Tis tyrannical.

Insere nunc Meliboee piros pone ordine vites.[31]

Madame de Chatellet desires her compliments.—She marries her daughter to the Duke de Montenero, a high-nosed, dwarfish, thin-faced, swarthy, flat-chested Neapolitan.—He is now here, and is going to rob us of a jolly plump-cheeked French girl.—*Vale et ma ama.*

V . . . .'[32]

Soon after we see him again taking a journey to the King of Prussia, who was always inviting him to Berlin but could never prevail on him to quit his old friends for any considerable time. In this journey he performed a singular service to the King his master, as we see by the letters which passed between him and Mr. Amelot, the Minister of State. But these particulars come not within my present design.—I view him only in his literary character.

At this time the famous Count de Bonneval, whom he had formerly seen at the house of the Grand Prior de Vendome, and was become a Turkish Pacha, wrote to him from Constantinople, and their correspondence continued some time, but nothing of it has been recovered except a single fragment which we shall transcribe.

'I am the first saint that was ever given up to the discretion of Prince Eugene. I was sensible, that by submitting to circumcision, I should expose myself to a kind of ridicule; but I was soon assured that I should be excused from undergoing that operation, on account of my advanced age; but I was still with-held by the ridicule of changing my religion. It is true that I have always thought it a matter of indifference to the deity, whether a man was

29 The Academy consists of forty members. [Translator's note.]

30 By a letter dated the 3rd March, 1743, from the Archbishop of Narbonne, it appears that that Prelate gave up his pretensions in favour of M. de Voltaire. [See Best.D2729.]

31 [Virgil, *Eclogues*, i.73. 'Now graft your pears Meliboeus, plant your vines in rows'.]

32 [Best.D2744 (4 April 1743).]

Mahometan, Christian, Jew, or Guebre: on that subject I have always maintained the same sentiments with the Regent Duke of Orleans, my dear friend the Marquis de la Farre, the Abbé Chaulieu, and all the men of sense and honour with whom I have passed my life. I know that Prince Eugene thought as I did, and that he would have done the same thing in my situation. In a word, I was reduced to the alternative of losing my head, or covering it with a turban. I communicated my perplexity in confidence to Lamira, a domestic of mine, my interpreter, whom you have since that time seen in France with Said Effendi. This man brought me an Iman, who possessed a fund of knowledge superior to the generality of his countrymen. Lamira presented me to him as a Catechumen, whose faith was very wavering. Hear what this good Priest dictated to him in my presence;—Lamira translated it into French;—I shall preserve it while I live. "Our religion is indisputably the most antient and the purest in the known world: 'tis the religion of Abraham, unsophisticated by the least mixture, and this is confirmed by our holy Koran, where it is said, *Abraham was a true believer; he was neither Jew, Christian, nor Idolater.* Like him, we believe in only one God, like him we are circumcised, and we regard Mecca as a holy city, only because it was reverenced as such even in the time of Ismael, son of Abraham.

God hath certainly poured his blessing on the race of Ismael, for his religion has spread over the greatest part of Asia and Africa; and the race of Isaac has not been able to preserve an inch of ground in either of them.

It is true, that our religion is perhaps somewhat mortifying to the flesh; Mahomet has repressed the licence in which all the Asiatic Princes indulged themselves;—that of having an undeterminate number of wives. The Princes of the abominable sect of the Jews had carried this licence farther than any other: David had eighteen wives; Solomon, according to the Jews, had seven hundred, but our Prophet reduced the number to four.

He has forbidden the use of wine and strong liquors, because they disorder both body and soul, occasion diseases and quarrels, and because it is much more easy to abstain from them entirely, than to keep within bounds.

But what above all renders our religion holy and excellent, is its being the only one which makes alms-giving an essential duty. Other religions recommend charity, but we expressly command it, under pain of eternal damnation.

Our religion is likewise the only one which forbids games of chance, and under the same penalties, which proves the profound wisdom of Mahomet. He knew that gaming rendered men incapable of applying to business, and but too often transformed society into assemblies of dupes and knaves, etc.

In this place there are several lines so blasphemous that I dare not copy them. They may be pardonable in a Turk, but a Christian cannot transcribe them.

If this Christian has a mind to abjure his idolatrous sect, and embrace that of the victorious Musselmen, he has only to pronounce our holy formulary in my presence, to repeat the prayers, and perform the ablutions which are ordained'.

Lamira having read this writing to me, he said, Monsieur the Count, these

Turks are not such fools as they are believed to be at Vienna, Rome, and Paris.—I replied, that I felt an inward impulse of Turkish grace, which consisted in the firm hope, that I should have the command of some Turkish battalions.

I pronounced the formulary word for word, after the Iman: *Alla illa allah Mohammed resoul allah*. They then made me repeat the prayer, which begins with these words; *Benamyezdam Bakshacier dadar*, in the name of the most merciful god, &c.

This ceremony was performed in the presence of two Musselmen, who went immediately to acquaint the Pacha of Bosnia. While they were gone on this errand, my head was shaved, and the Iman covered it with a Turban, &c.'[33]

I might join some songs of the Count Pacha to this curious fragment, but, though his verses are lively, they are not so interesting as his prose.

I have nothing to mention that happened in the year 1744, except that my author was admitted of almost all the Academies in Europe, and what is most singular, into that of *La Crusca*. He had carefully studied the Italian language, as may be seen by an eloquent letter of Cardinal Passionei, which begins with these words.

'I have read your charming and learned Italian letter over and over again, and always with new pleasure. It is difficult to conceive how a man, who professeth such a fundamental knowledge of other languages, could acquire such perfection in this.

The remarks which you make in your letter upon the errors of the greatest men, comes very apropos; for the sun has his spots and eclipses; they are mentioned in the most petty almanacks; and as you very properly observe, they who censure too severely, have often greater need of our indulgence than those whom they reprove. Homer, Virgil, Tasso, and several others, can lose but little by some slight faults, covered with a thousand beauties; but the Zoiluses will be ever ridiculous, and incapable of distinguishing the pearls from Ennius's dung, &c.'[34]

Cardinal Passionei wrote, as is evident, almost as well in French as Italian, and thought very judiciously. Our Zoiluses did not escape him.

About the end of the year 1744, M. de Voltaire had a warrant appointing him Historiographer of France, which he called a pompous trifle. He was already known by his History of Charles XII, which has been so often printed. This history was chiefly composed in England, when he was in that country with Mr. Fabricius (Chamberlain to George I, King of England, and Elector of Hanover) who had lived seven years with Charles XII, after the battle of Pultowa.

Thus was the Henriade begun at St. Ange, after his conversation with M. de Caumartin.

That history was much praised for its stile, and as much criticised for the

33 [Best.D2844(*c.* September 1743).]   34 [Best.D3336 (9 March 1746).]

incredibility of its facts: but when King Stanislaus sent the following authentic testimony to the author, by the Count de Tressan, his Lieutenant General, the criticisms ceased, and the facts were credited.

'Mr. de Voltaire has neither forgotten nor misplaced a single fact or circumstance; all is truth and properly ranged. He has spoken of Poland and all the events which happened there, as if he had been an eye witness.

Given at Commercy, 11th July, 1759.'[35]

Since he had got the title of Historiographer, he was not willing to hold it in vain, lest that should be said of him which was said by one of the Clerks of the Royal Treasury concerning Racine and Boileau, *We have as yet seen nothing of these gentlemen but their subscription*. He wrote his History of the War of 1741, while in its utmost rage, which may be found in his age of Louis XIV and XV.[36]

He was then at Etiole, with the charming Madame d'Etiole, afterwards Marchioness of Pompadour. The Court gave orders for some grand festivals in the beginning of the year 1745, when they were about to marry the Dauphin to the Infanta of Spain. They desired to have interludes with singing music, and a kind of comedy, which should connect the songs. It was given in charge to my author, although it was a kind of entertainment for which he had no relish. He chose the story of a Princess of Navarre for his subject. The piece was written superficially. Mr. Popeliniere, one of the Farmers General, but a man of letters, introduced some airs, and the music was composed by the famous Rameau.

Madame d'Etiole at that time freely obtained the employment of Gentleman in Ordinary of the Chamber, for Mr. de Voltaire. It was a present worth sixty thousand livres, and the more pleasing, that a little after he obtained the singular favour of being permitted to sell this employment, and to preserve the title, privileges, and functions of it.

Few people know the little impromptu which he made upon this favour being granted him, without being twice asked.

> Mon Henri quatre et ma Zaire
> Et mon Américaine Alzire
> Ne m'ont valu jamais un seul regard du Roi.
> J'avais mille ennemis avec très peu de gloire;
> Les honneurs & les biens pleuvent enfin sur moi,
> Pour une Farce de la Foire.

> Alzira, Zara, Henry writ in vain,
> Not ev'n a smile could from our Monarch gain;
> A thousand critics rose to blast my name,
> At last a farce has brought me wealth and fame.

35 [Best.D8390.]

36 It has been printed separately, and most ridiculously adulterated.

Nevertheless he had been given long since a pension of two thousand livres from the King, and one of fifteen hundred from the Queen, but he never asked for payment.

History being now a duty, he began his *Age of Louis XIV*, but did not persist in it:—he wrote the Campaign of 1744[37], and the famous Battle of Fontenoy, entering into the whole detail of that important action, even to the number of the killed in each regiment is mentioned. The Count d'Argenson, Secretary of War, had communicated all the Officers' letters to him, and the Marechals Noailles and Saxe, gave him their materials.

I believe it will give singular pleasure to those who wish to know men and events, if I transcribe a letter written on the field of battle, to Mr. de Voltaire, by the Marquis d'Argenson, Minister for Foreign Affairs, and eldest brother of the Secretary of War.

He addresses him, Monsieur, the Historian, and says: 'You must have been informed by Wednesday of the news on which you so heartily congratulate us. A Page set out from the field of battle, to carry the dispatches, at half past two o'clock on Tuesday. It was a glorious spectacle to see the King and the Dauphin writing upon a drum, surrounded by the conquerors and conquered, the dead, dying, and prisoners. I made the following remarks:

'I had the honour of meeting the King near the field of battle, having arrived at Chin from Paris on Sunday. I was informed that the King was gone to take an airing, and having got a horse I joined his Majesty near a place which was in view of the enemy's camp. I then learnt for the first time, what was supposed to have transpired recently. I never saw a man so chearful as he was upon the occasion. We discussed that point of history that you have handled in a few lines: which of our Kings gained the last royal battles; and I assure you that his courage did not wrong his judgment, nor his judgment wrong his memory. We then went and lay upon straw;—never was there a ball-night more gay, nor so many *bon-mots* uttered. We slept all the time, which was not interrupted by Courtiers and Aids-de-camp. The King sung a droll song of several verses. As to the Dauphin, he went to the battle, as to a hare hunting, and almost said, what! is this all? A cannon-ball struck in the mud, and bespattered a man near the King.—Our masters laughed very heartily at the person that was spattered. One of my brother's grooms, who was behind the company, was wounded in the head with a musket ball.

What is true and certain, and without flattery, is, that the King gained the battle by his own determination and courage. You will see different accounts and details, and you will be informed that there was a terrible hour in which we saw a second volume of Dettingen, the French were prostrated before the English steadiness; their rolling fire resembled the flames of hell, which I own stupified the most unconcerned spectators, and we began to be in despair about the state.

37 [or rather, of 1741].

Some of our generals, who have more heart and courage than abilities, gave most prudent advice. They dispatch'd orders all the way to Lisle;— they doubled the King's guard;—they had every thing packed up, &c. The King laughed at all this, and going from the left to the center, he asked for the corps-de-reserve, and the brave Lowendahl; but there was no occasion. One group of reserves gave battle, consisting of the same cavalry which had already made an unsuccessful attack, the King's household, the Carabineers, those of the French guards who had not moved, and the Irish, who always distinguish themselves when they march against the English and Hanoverians. Your friend, Richelieu, is a real Bayard; it was he who gave the advice to attack the infantry like hunters, pell-mell, the hand lowered, the arm shortened, masters, servants, officers, cavalry, infantry altogether, and he executed it. Nothing can withstand this French vivacity which is so much spoken of, and in ten minutes the battle was gained by this unforeseen stroke. The heavy English batallions turned their backs; and, in short, there were fourteen thousand of them kill'd.[38]

Certainly the artillery had the honour of this terrible slaughter;—there never were so many or large cannon fired at one battle, as at the battle of Fontenay. There were a hundred. It would seem as if the poor enemy were willing to let every thing arrive which could be unfavourable for them: the cannon from Douay, the foot-soldiers, the musketeers.

Do not forget one incident which happened at the last attack which I spoke of. The Dauphin, from a natural impulse, drew his sword in the most graceful manner, and insisted upon charging, but he was begged to desist. After that, to mention the bad with the good, I observed a habit too easily acquired, of looking calmly upon the naked dead, the dying enemies, and the reeking wounds upon the field of battle. For my part, I own that my heart failed, and that I wanted a restorative. I attentively remarked our young heroes, who seemed too indifferent upon this head.—I am afraid for them that this inhuman carnage may encrease that turn of mind in the course of a long life.

The triumph is the finest thing in the world.—Shouts of God save the King; hats in the air and upon bayonets; the compliments of the Sovereign to his troops; visiting the entrenchments; villages; and intact redoubts; joy, glory, and tenderness; but the ground of the picture is human blood, and fragments of human flesh.

At the end of the triumph, the King honoured me with a conversation about the peace, and I have dispatched some couriers.

The King was much entertained yesterday in the trenches;—they fired a good deal at him, but he remained there three hours. I was employed in my closet, which is my trench, for I own I have been much retarded in business by all these dissipations. I trembled at every shot I heard fired. In my own modest

---

38 In fact, there were fourteen thousand men missing at the muster, but about six thousand returned that day. [*Note by Voltaire.*]

person I went the day before yesterday to see the trenches. It is not very entertaining by day. We shall have a *Te Deum* sung to-day under a tent, and there will be a general salve of the whole army, which the King will go to see from Mount Trinity;—it will be very fine.

I present my humble respects to Madame Chatellet. Farewell sir.'[39]

It was this same Marquis d'Argenson, whom some trifling courtiers used to call the blockhead d'Argenson. This letter shews that he was of an agreeable turn of mind, and had a tender heart. They who were acquainted with him, saw more of the philosopher than the politican in him, but chiefly valued him for his being an excellent citizen. He may be judged of by his book, entitled *Considerations upon the Government*, printed in 1664[40], by Marc Michel Rey. Attend chiefly to the chapter on the sale of offices. I cannot resist the pleasure of quoting some passages.

'It is astonishing that a book, which is called The Political Testament of Cardinal Richelieu, has met with such general approbation. It is the work of some church pedant, and unworthy of the great genius to whom it has been ascribed, if only for the chapter where the sale of offices is consecrated. It is a wretched invention, which has been productive of all the mischief, the remedies for which, though most indispensibly necessary, is almost become impracticable; for it would require the whole revenues of the state only to reimburse the principal Officers, who do the greatest harm.'

This important passage seems to have foretold, at a distance, the abolition[41] of this shameful venality, which was accomplished in 1771, to the astonishment of all France, where such a reformation was thought impossible. In the above passage we discover the same opinions entertained by Mr. de Voltaire, who has shewn the absurd errors with which that libel swarms, that has been so ridiculously ascribed to Cardinal Richelieu, and who has wiped away from the memory of that able and respectable Minister, the stain with which his names was covered, by ascribing such an impertinent work to him.

Let me likewise transcribe a part of the picture which the Marquis d'Argenson has drawn of the wretchedness of the peasants.

'To begin with the King; the higher the rank at Court, it is the more difficult to persuade one's self of the wretchedness of the country. The nobility who have great possessions in the country, sometimes hear a good deal said upon the subject, but their hard hearts feel nothing in these miseries, but the diminution of their revenues. Those who come from the country, and were affected with what they saw, very soon forget it, by being immersed in the

39 [Best.D3118 (15 May 1745); this letter was written by René Louis de Voyer de Paulmy, marquis d'Argenson.]

40 [or rather, 1764.]

41 This abolition in 1771, was only transitory.

delights of the capital. *We must have steady souls and tender hearts to be able to preserve compassion for objects at a distance.'*

That truly patriotic Minister had always a tender friendship for Mr. de Voltaire, from his infancy. We have seen a great deal of their correspondence; and the consequence was, that the Secretary of State employed the man of letters in several important affairs during the years 1745, 1746, and 1747, which is probably the reason of our not having any theatrical pieces from our author during that period.

I observe by his papers, that the secret of the proposed descent upon England, which was undertaken in the year 1746, was trusted to him. The Duke of Richelieu was to have commanded the army. The Pretender had already gained two battles, and a revolution was expected. Mr. de Voltaire was employed to write the following Manifesto, which I have copied from a draft in his own hand.

MANIFESTO

Of the King of France in favour of Prince Charles Edward.

The most serene Prince Charles Edward having disembarked in Great Britain, without any assistance but his courage, and all his actions having procured him the admiration of Europe, and the hearts of every true English-man, the King of France joins in the same sentiments. He esteems it his duty, at the same time, to assist a Prince who is worthy of inheriting the Throne of his ancestors, and a generous people, of whom the worthiest part have joined in recalling Prince Charles Stuart to his country. He sends the Duke of Richelieu at the head of his army, only because the English, of the purest intentions, have sollicited this assistance; and he sends only the precise number of troops which have been demanded, because he will be ready to withdraw them as soon as the English nation shall require it. His Majesty, in affording this just assistance to his relation, the descendant of so many Kings, and a Prince so worthy of a Throne, takes this step for the people of England, only with the design, to restore peace to them and Europe, fully persuaded that the most Serene Prince Edward depends upon the good will of the people, and looks upon the support of their liberties, laws, and happi-ness, as the purpose of all his undertakings; and, lastly, because the greatest Kings of England have been those, who, like him, being bred in adversity, have deserved the love of the nation.

It is in these sentiments that the King assists their Prince, the son of him who was born the lawful heir of three kingdoms, a warrior, who comes to throw himself into their arms, and notwithstanding his valour, expects nothing from them and their laws, but a confirmation of his most sacred rights: who never can have a separate interest from theirs, and whose virtues have at length softened the souls that were the most prejudiced against his cause.

He hopes that such an opportunity will reunite two nations that ought mutually to esteem one another;—who are naturally connected by their commercial wants, and ought to be so upon this occasion, by the interests of a Prince who deserves the goodwill of all nations.

The Duke of Richelieu, commander of the army of his Majesty the King of France, adresses this declaration to the faithful people of the three kingdoms of Great Britain, and assures them of the constant protection of the King his master. He comes to join the heir of their ancient Kings, and like him to shed his blood for their service.'

It is evident by the expressions in this piece, what were the sentiments of esteem and inclination, which the author had at all times entertained for the English nation, and in which he has always persisted.[42]

It was the unfortunate Count Lally who projected the scheme of this descent, which was afterwards laid aside. He was born in Ireland, and detested the English as much as my author loved and esteemed them. I have several times heard Mr. de Voltaire say, that this hatred was even a violent passion in Lally. I cannot help testifying my profound astonishment at that General having been accused, since that time, of betraying Pondicherry to the English. The decree which condemned him to death, is one of the most extraordinary sentences which has been given in our days, and was a consequence of the misfortunes of France. This instance, and that of the Marechal de Marillac, plainly shew that whoever is at the head of armies or affairs of state, is seldom sure of dying in his own bed, or in the bed of honour.

It was in the year 1746 that Mr. de Voltaire was admitted into the French Academy. He was the first who deviated from the insipid custom of filling the introductory discourse with nothing but hackneyed praises of Cardinal Richelieu. He embellished his discourse with new remarks upon the French language and upon taste. They who have been admitted since his time, have generally followed and perfected this useful practice.

He accompanied Madame du Chatellet to the Court of King Stanislaus at Luneville, in 1748, when he sent to the actors the Comedy of Nanine, which was played on the 17th of July in that year. It did not succeed at first, but some time after, it had a very considerable and continued run. This whimsicalness of the public can be ascribed only to the secret desire of humbling a man who has too much reputation: but after a time pleasure restores them to the proper channel.

The same thing happened at the first representation of Semiramis on the 29th of August of the same year, 1748, but at last it had greater success upon the stage than either Merope or Mahomet.

It was an extraordinary thing in my opinion that he did not declare himself

---

42 *By the composition of this manifesto, we may see Mr. Voltaire's affection for the English nation, and his gratitude to the family of Hanover, to whom he owed the foundation of his fortune.* [Translator's note.]

to be the author of the panegyric upon Louis xv, which was printed in the year 1749[43], and was translated into Latin, Italian, Spanish, and English.

The disorder which alarmed the public so much for the life of king Louis xv, and the battle of Fontenoy, which occasioned still greater fears for the King and the nation, rendered the work interesting. The praise which the author bestowed was supported by facts, and there was that philosophic turn in it, which characterises whatever has come from his hands. This work was as much the panegyric of the Officers as of the King, yet he did not present it to any one, not even to his Majesty. He knew very well that he did not live in the age of Pelisson. He wrote to his friend Mr. Fourmont:

Cet éloge a très peu d'effet.
Nul mortel ne m'en remercie.
Celui qui le moins s'en soucie
Est celui pour qui je l'ai fait.

My panegyric meets neglect,
None shews it ev'n the least respect;
No, not the object of my praise,
Regards the Author or his lays.

He was at the court of Stanislaus, in the palace of Lunéville, in that same year 1749, with the Marchioness of Chatellet, when that illustrious Lady died there. The King of Prussia at that time gave Mr. de Voltaire an invitation to come and live with him. I see that it was not till towards the end of the month of August, 1750, after having for six months combated the opinions of all his family and all his friends, who strongly dissuaded him from this removal, that he resolved to quit France, and attach himself to his Prussian Majesty for the rest of his life. He could not withstand the letter which the King of Prussia wrote to him the 23d of August from his apartments to the room of his new guest, in the palace of Berlin: a letter which has been often printed and is universally known.

'I have seen the letter which your niece wrote to you from Paris. The friendship which she expresses for you, commands my esteem. I should think as she does if I were Madame Dennis; but being what I am, I think otherways. I should be distracted if I thought myself the cause of making my enemy wretched; how then could I desire the unhappiness of the man whom I esteem and love, and who, for my sake has given up his country, and whatever has been thought dear among men? No, my dear Voltaire, I should be the first to dissuade you from it, if I could foresee that your transplantation could in the smallest degree prove a disadvantage to you. Yes, I should prefer your happiness to the excessive pleasure I have in your company. But you are a Philosopher, and so am I; what can be more natural, more simple or

43 [or rather, 1748.]

reasonable, than that those Philosophers who were formed to live together, who are united by the same studies, who have the same taste, and the same manner of thinking, should enjoy that satisfaction?

I respect you as my master in eloquence and learning, and I love you as a virtuous friend. What slavery, what unhappiness, what change, what inconstancy of fortune, is to be dreaded in a country where you are as highly valued as in your own, and with a friend who has a grateful heart? I have not the foolish presumption to think Berlin equal to Paris. If riches, grandeur, and magnificence, make a city agreeable, Berlin must yield to Paris. If there is a particular place to be found in the world, where fine taste more generally prevails, I know, and allow it is Paris; but do not you carry that taste with you wherever you go? We have powers sufficient to praise your merits, and as to sentiment, we will not yield to any country upon earth. I respected the friendship which attached you to Madame du Chatellet, but after her, I am one of your oldest friends. What! because you consent to retire to my house, shall it be said that that house becomes your prison? What! shall I become your tyrant because I am your friend? I confess to you I do not understand that logic, and I am firmly persuaded that you will be very happy here, as long as I shall live: you will be looked upon as the father of letters, and of men of taste; and you will find all the consolations which a man of your merit can expect from one who values him. Good-night.

FREDERIC'[44]

After this letter, the King of Prussia asked the consent of the King of France, by his Minister at that Court, which was readily granted. My author was presented at Berlin with the order of merit, the key of Chamberlain, and a pension of twenty thousand livres. However he did not give up his house at Paris, and by the accounts of Mr. Delaleu, Notary in Paris, I find that Mr. de Voltaire was at an expence of thirty thousand livres a year there. He was attached to the King of Prussia by the most respectful regard, as well as by their conformity of taste. He has a hundred times said, that that Monarch was as agreeable in company, as he was formidable at the head of an army: and that he had never more pleasing suppers at Paris, than those to which that Prince kindly admitted him every day. His enthusiasm for the King of Prussia rose to a passion. His apartments were under the King's, and he never quitted them but to go to supper. The King composed works in philosophy, history, and poetry, in the upper apartments, while his favourite cultivated the same arts and the same talents in the lower. They communicated their works to one another. The Prussian Monarch wrote his history of the House of Brandenburgh at Potzdam; and the French author having carried his materials with him, wrote his Age of Louis XIV, at the same place. Thus did his days glide along in tranquility enlivened by such agreeable employments.

His *Orestes*, and *Rome Preserved*, were performed at Paris. *Orestes* was

44 [Best.D4195 (23 August 1750).]

played about the end of the year 1759[45], and *Rome Preserved* in 1760[46]. These two pieces, like his *Merope* and *The Death of Caesar*, are entirely free from any love affair. He wished to purge the stage of every thing which was not capable of producing the emotions proper to Tragedy. He looked upon *Electra* in love as a monster dressed in dirty ribbons; and in different works he has shewn that these were his sentiments.

I have recovered a letter of his in verse, which he sent to the king of Prussia with his manuscript of Orestes.

> Grand juge, & grand feseur de vers,
> Lisez cette œuvre dramatique,
> Ce croquis de la scène antique
> Que des Grecs le pinceau tragique
> Fit admirer à l'univers;
> Jugez si l'ardeur amoureuse
> D'une Electre de quarante ans,
> Doit dans de tels événements
> Etaler les beaux sentiments
> D'une heroine doucereuse
> En massacrant ses chers parents
> D'une main peu respectueuse.
>
> Une princesse en son printems,
> Qui surtout n'auroit rien à faire,
> Pourait avoir par passe-tems
> A ses pieds un ou deux amants
> Et les tromper avec mistère.
> Mais la fille d'Agamemnon
> N'eut dans la tête d'autre affaire
> Que d'être digne de son nom,
> Et de vanger le roi son père.
> Et j'estime encore que son frère
> Ne doit point être un Céladon.
> Ce héros fort atrabilaire
> N'était point né sur le Lignon.
> Apprenez moi mon Apollon,
> Si j'ai tort d'être si sévère,
> Et lequel des deux doit vous plaire
> De Sophocle ou de Crebillon.
> Sophocle peut avoir raison,
> Et laisser des torts à Voltaire.[47]
>
> O thou in whose capacious mind
> The Poet with the Critic join'd,

45 [Or rather, 1750.]
46 [Or rather, 1752; but it had been performed privately in 1750.]

47 [Best.D4128 (17 March 1750).]

Unite their mingled fires,
These homely lines deign to peruse,
Faint transcript of a Grecian muse,
Whose strains the world admires.

Say if it would the scene improve,
Should old Electra talk of love,
And languishing complain,
Or frantic for her slaughter'd Sire,
With fell revenge her bosom fire,
Till blood efface the stain?

'Tis granted that at warm fifteen,
A sighing Princess might be seen,
To burn in am'rous flame;
But past the hey day of the blood,
Now cool'd the lusty youthful flood,
At forty—is't the same?

Nor should Orestes sigh and whine,
And for a mistress idly pine,
Or weep because he's scorn'd;
By fury stung he madly drew
His falchion, and his mother slew;
With other flames he burn'd.

Now, my Apollo, deign to tell,
If I have reason'd ill or well,
And which will stand the test?
Crebillon and the Grecian bard
Humbly sollicit your award,
Say, which will please you best?

It must be owned, that nothing could be more agreeable than this kind of life, or any thing do more honour to philosophy and the Belles-lettres. This happiness would have been more lasting, and would not have given place to a still greater happiness, if it had not been for a dispute on a subject in mixed Mathematics, which arose between Maupertuis, who likewise lived at that time with the King of Prussia, and Kœnig, librarian to the Princess of Orange, at the Hague. This dispute was a continuation of that which for a long time had divided the Mathematicians about the living and dead forces. It cannot be denied but that a little quackery gets into this subject, as well as into theology and medicine. It was a most trifling question at best, for let them entangle it as much as they will, they must always return to the plain laws of motion. The tempers of the disputants were sowered, and Maupertuis, who ruled the Academy at Berlin, procured a condemnation of Kœnig's opinion in the year 1752, because he had arrived at it on the authority of a letter of the late

Leibnitz, without being able to produce the original of that letter, which however had been seen by Mr. Wolf. He went still farther,—he wrote to the Princess of Orange, to beg her to dismiss Kœnig from his employment of Librarian; and represented him to the King of Prussia, as a man who had been wanting in the respect due to him. Voltaire, who had passed two whole years at Cirey with Kœnig, during which he had contracted an intimacy with him, thought it was his duty openly to espouse the cause of his friend.

The quarrel became violent, and the study of Philosophy degenerated into cabal and faction. Maupertuis was at some pains to have it reported at Court, that one day while General Manstein happened to be in the apartments of Mr. de Voltaire, who was then translating into French, *The Memoirs of Russia*, composed by that Officer, the King, in his usual manner, sent a copy of his verses to be examined, when Voltaire said to Manstein, *Let us leave off for the present, my friend, you see the King has sent me his dirty linen to wash, I will wash your's another time*. A single word is sometimes sufficient to ruin a man at Court; Maupertuis imputed such a word to Voltaire, and ruined him.

At this very time Maupertuis published his very strange Philosophical Letters, in which he proposed to build a Latin city; to fare by sea in quest of discoveries at the Pole; to *perforate* the earth to the centre; to go to the Streights of Magellan, and dissect the brains of a Patagonian, in order to investigate the nature of the soul;—to cover the bodies of the sick with pitch, to prevent the danger of perspiration: and above all, not to pay the Physician.

Mr. de Voltaire discussed these Philosophic ideas with all the railery which so fine an opportunity presented, and unfortunately the learned all over Europe were amused with these raileries. Maupertuis was careful to join the king's cause to his own: and this pleasantry was looked upon as a failure in respect to his Majesty. My author in the most respectful manner returned the key of Chamberlain, and the cross of his order to the King, with the following verses.

> Je les reçus avec tendresse;
> Je vous les rend avec douleur.
> Comme un amant jaloux, dans sa mauvaise humeur,
> Rend le portrait de sa maîtresse.[48]

> With rapture I those gifts receiv'd,
> Now to return them much I'm griev'd;
> Such pangs the jealous swain attack,
> Who sends his mistress' picture back.

The King sent back the key and ribbon. Voltaire then set out to pay a visit to her Highness the Duchess of Gotha, who continued to honour him with her friendship while she lived. It was for her that he wrote *The Annals of the Empire*, about a year after; a work which was entirely new modelled in his *Essay upon the History of the Genius and Manners of Nations*.

48 [See Best.D5132, note.]

While he remained at Gotha, Maupertuis employed all his batteries against my traveller, which he was made sensible of when he came to meet his niece, Madame Denis, at Francfort on the Mayne.

On the first of June, an honest German[49], who neither loved the French nor their verses, came, and in bad French demanded the works in *poeshy* of the King his master. My traveller replied, that the works in *poeshy* were with the rest of his property at Leipsic. The German informed him, that he was confined to Francfort, and would not be allowed to depart till these works arrived. Mr. de Voltaire gave him the key of Chamberlain, and the cross of the order, and promised to restore what he had demanded; upon which the messenger wrote the following billet[50].

'SIR,

So soon the large package from Leipsic shall be here, where is the work of poeshy of the King, my master, you may depart wherever you think proper. Francfort, 1st June, 1753.'

The prisoner wrote at the bottom of the note, *Good for the work of poeshy of the King, your master.*

But when the verses were returned, it was pretended there were some Bills of Exchange expected, which did not arrive.—The travellers were detained fifteen days at the Goat inn, on account of these pretended Bills; and at last were not permitted to depart without paying a considerable ransom. These are details which never come to the ears of Kings.

This adventure was very soon forgotten by both parties, and with great propriety. The King sent back his verses to his old admirer, and soon after a considerable number of new ones. It was a lovers' quarrel;—the bickerings of a Court soon die away; but a laudable passion will long continue. My French traveller, on reading over again with emotion that eloquent and affecting letter of the King's, which I have transcribed, felt his former tenderness return, and cried, *After such a letter I must certainly have been greatly in the wrong.*

The fugitive from Berlin possessed a little estate in Alsace, in the territories of the Duke of Wirtemberg. He went there and amused himself as I have already said, by publishing the *Annals of the Empire*, which he made a present of to John Frederic Shoeflen, bookseller at Colmar, and brother to the celebrated Shoeflen, Professor of History of Strasbourg. This bookseller's affairs were much out of order, and Mr. de Voltaire lent him ten thousand livres. Upon this occasion I cannot help expressing my astonishment at the meanness of those scribblers, who gave it out, that he had made an immense fortune by the constant sale of his works.

Mr. Vernet, a French refugee, and minister of the gospel at Geneva, and

49 [Baron Franz von Freytag.]
50 The translator, that the spirit of the original might not evaporate, has rendered it word for word.

651

Messrs. Cramer, old citizens of that famous city, wrote to him while at Colmar, begging him to come and print his works there. The two brothers, who were booksellers, were preferred, and he gave them to these gentlemen on the same terms he had done to Mr. Shoeflen, that is to say, in a present. He therefore went to Geneva with his niece, and his friend Mr. Coligni, who acted as his secretary, and who has since been secretary and librarian to the Elector Palatine.

He purchased a lease for life of a charming country-house near that town, where the neighbourhood is extremely agreeable, and there is the finest view in Europe. He bought another at Lausanne, and both of them upon condition that a certain sum should be returned him when he quitted them. It was the first instance of a Roman Catholic getting an establishment in these Cantons, since the time of Zuinglius and Calvin.

He likewise purchased two estates in the *Pays de Gex*, about a league from Geneva. His principal residence was at Ferney, of which he made a present to Madame Denis: it was a Seignory, which had been absolutely free from all royal duties and imposts from the time of Henry IV. In all the other provinces of the kingdom, there are not two which have the same privileges; the King confirmed these privileges to him by a warrant, which was an obligation conferred upon him by the interest of the most generous and worthiest of men, the Duke de Choiseul, to whom he had not even the honour of being personally known.

The little *Pays de Gex* was at this time almost a savage desart. Fourscore ploughs had been laid aside ever since the revocation of the edict of Nants; half the country was a morass, which produced infections and diseases. My author's ambition had always been to settle in some forsaken Canton, and to bring it to life. As I advance nothing without authentic proofs, I shall transcribe only one of his letters to a Bishop of Annecy, in whose diocese Ferney is situated. I cannot recover the date of the letter, but it must date from the year 1759.

'Sir,

The Parson of the little village of N . . . ., in the neighbourhood of my estate, has commenced a process against my vassals of Ferney, and having frequently left his Cure to carry it on at Dijon, he has easily overpowered the farmers who are kept at home in order to labour, for their daily support. He charges them fifteen hundred livres costs of suit, and has the cruelty to include in those costs the expence of the journeys he took on purpose to ruin them. You, Sir, know better than I, how the holy fathers in the early ages of the church were incensed against the Clergy who sacrificed to temporal affairs that time which should have been dedicated to the altar. But if they had been told that a Priest came with officers of justice to extort money from poor families, to obliged them to part with the only meadow which they had to feed their cattle, and to take the milk from their children, what would the Ireneuses, the Jeroms, and Augustins, have said? This is what a Parson has done at the gate of my castle. I sent to let him know that I would pay the greatest part of what he exacted from my tenants, but he answered that that would not satisfy him.

You, no doubt, sigh at the thought of any Pastors of the true church setting such horrid examples, while there is not a single instance of a Protestant Clergyman having entered into a law suit with his[51] parishioners about money matters, &c.'[52]

This letter, and the issue of that affair, may suggest some very important reflexions. Mr. de Voltaire put an end to the process, and the whole affair, by paying the claims which oppressed his poor vassals out of his own pocket; and this wretched district very soon changed its appearance.

He extricated himself more agreeably out of a dispute in the Protestant country, where he had two very agreeable possessions, the one at Geneva, which is still called the House of Delights [Les Délices], and the other at Lausanne.

It is sufficiently known how dearly he loved liberty; to what degree he hated persecution, and with what horror he at all times looked upon those rascally hypocrites who, in the name of God, dare to destroy, by the most dreadful punishments, those people whom they accuse of differing from them in sentiment. It was upon such occasions that he sometimes repeated,

Je ne décide point entre Genève et Rome.[53]

I pretend not to decide between Rome and Geneva.

One of his letters happened to be made public by too common an indiscretion, in which he said that that Picard, John Chauvin (called Calvin), the assassinator of Servetus, had *an atrocious soul,* and some canting humbugs were offended, or pretended to be offended, at the expression. A gentleman of Geneva of the name of Rival, who was a man of genius, addressed the following lines to him upon that occasion.

> Servet eut tort, & fut un sot
> D'oser dans un siècle falot
> S'avouer antitrinitaire.[54]
> Et nôtre illustre atrabilaire
> Eût tort d'employer le fagot
> Pour réfuter son adversaire.
> Et tort nôtre antique sénat

51 What occasions the Protestant Clergy having no suits with their flocks, is their being paid their salaries by the States. They have no dispute with miserable wretches about their eighth or tenth sheaf. The Empress Catharine has taken the same method in her immense dominions, where the plague of tythes is unknown.

52 [Best.D7981 (16 December 1758).]
53 [*La Henriade* (Voltaire 2), ii.5.]
54 Servetus might rest on Calvin's own words, who says in one of his works, *in case that any one is heterodox, and scruples at the words* trinity *and* person, *we do not believe there is sufficient reason for rejecting that man, &c.*

D'avoir prêté son ministère
A ce dangereux coup d'état.
Quelle barbare inconséquence!
O malheureux siècle ignorant!
Nous osions abhorer en France
Les horreurs de l'intolérance
Tandis qu'un zèle intolérant
Nous fesait bruler un errant!
    Pour nôtre prêtre épistolaire
Qui de son pétulant effort
Pour exhaler sa bile amère
Vient réveiller le chat qui dort,
Et dont l'inepte commentaire
Met au jour ce qu'il eût dû taire,
Je laisse a juger s'il a tort.
    Quant à vous célèbre Voltaire
Vous eûtes tort, c'est mon avis.
Vous vous plaisez dans ce pais,
Fêtez le saint qu'on y révère.
Vous avez a satieté
Les biens où la raison aspire;
L'opulence, la liberté,
La paix (qu'en cent lieux on désire),
Des droits à l'immortalité.
Cent fois plus qu'on ne saurait dire.
On a du goût, on vous admire,
Tronchin veille à vôtre santé.
Cela vaut bien en vérité
Qu'on immole a sa sûreté.
Le plaisir de pincer sans rire.

Servetus in a bigot age,
'Gainst orthodoxy turn'd his rage,
He was not over wise;
Calvin with equal madness led,
Devotes to flames the guilty head,
And poor Servetus dies.
Our antient senate aids the cause,
Abets those sanguinary laws,
And lights th' inhuman fires;
Our antient senate sure was wrong,
To join a blinded frantic throng,
Whom barbarous rage inspires.
We mourn'd the Frenchmen savage zeal,
Destructive of the public weal,

By which their victims bled:
And yet at home, we did the same,
And madly to the raging flame
A hapless wanderer led.
The meddling priest to purge his bile,
Who kindles fresh th' extinguish'd pile,
And bright religion stains,
By commentaries, which reveal
What he for ever should conceal,
Shews too his heated brains.
E'en thou Voltaire, so justly priz'd,
If thou by men might be advis'd,
Forbid thy pen to stray;
Nor honours to our saint refuse,
With us, since your abode you choose,
'Tis sure the prudent way.
Nature and fortune both combine,
In you their choicest gifts to join,
With wealth, with genius blest;
Nor want we sense your works to prize,
If they have merit, we have eyes,
By all their worth's confest.
Here peace and freedom crown your age,
Here Tronchin too a friendly sage,
Your health incessant guards;
Then while such blessings you enjoy,
Would you your happiness destroy,
For Satire's lean rewards?

Our author replied to these pretty Verses by the following

Non, je n'ai point tort d'oser dire.
Ce que pensent les gens de bien.
Et le sage qui ne craint rien.
A le beau droit de tout écrire.

J'ai quarante ans bravé l'empire
Des lâches tirans des esprits.
Et dans vôtre petit pais
J'aurais grand tort de me dédire.

Je sais que souvent la malin
A caché sa queue & sa griffe
Sous la tiare d'un Pontife
Et sous le manteau de Calvin.

Autobiography

Je n'ai point tort quand je déteste
Ces assassins religieux
Employant le fer & le feux
Pour servir le Père céleste.

Oui, jusqu'au dernier de mes jours
Mon âme sera fière & tendre,
J'oserais gémir sur la cendre
Et des *Servets* & des *Dubourgs*[55].

De cette horrible frénésie
A la fin le tems est passé;
Le fanatisme est terrassé,
Mais il reste l'hipocrisie.

Farceurs à manteaux étriqués,
Mauvaise musique d'Eglise,
Mauvais vers & sermons croqués,
Ai-je tort si je vous méprise?[56]

No sure, I can't be in the wrong,
Loud to proclaim with daring tongue
    The thoughts of every sage;
The man whose heart for virtue glows,
Nor dastard fears, nor danger knows,
    But stems fanatic rage.

Full forty years I've boldly fought
The wretches that would fetter thought,
    And tyrannize the mind;
And surely in this petty state,
Now to recant, the blame were great,
    'T would speak me mean and blind.

Full oft mankind's insiduous foe,
Leaving the dreary realms below,
    To Peter's chair has shuffled;
And oft his claws and tail conceal'd,
So close they cou'd not be beheld,
    In Calvin's cloak been muffled.

Still keen resentment fires my breast,
Those holy murd'rers I detest,
    Who sword and fire employ;

55 Dubourg, Counsellor and Clerk of Parliament was served at Paris, as Servetus was at Geneva.

56 [These lines are known under the title of *Les Torts* (1757).]

Who in our heavenly father's cause,
Breaking his fundamental laws,
    His images destroy.

So long as life informs my heart,
I'll constant act my wonted part,
    Be proud and tender still;
O'er Dubourg and Servetus pour
With equal zeal the pious shower,
    Nor dread the threaten'd ill.

But now those horrid scenes are o'er,
The blazing pile we see no more;
    That frantic zeal is fled;
Hypocrisy now fills its room,
Whose train diffusing sullen gloom,
    Their baneful influence shed.

Ye base unsightly crew avaunt,
Silence your vile unmeaning cant,
    That cheats the gaping throng;
Your stupid hymns, your sermons vile,
I do not think them worth the while,
    And, am I in the wrong?

We may see by this answer, that he was neither of Apollos, nor of Cephas, and that he preached toleration to the Protestant churches, as well as to the Romish. He always said, that it was the only way to make life tolerable, and that he would be content to die, if he could establish these maxims in Europe. It may be said that he has not been altogether mistaken in his design, and that he has contributed not a little to render the clergy, from Geneva to Madrid, more gentle and humane, and especially to opening the eyes of the laity.

Being persuaded that representations of dramatic works, contributed as much to soften savage manners, as the exhibitions of the Gladiators formerly did to harden them, he built an handsome little theatre at Ferney, and notwithstanding his bad state of health, sometimes played himself; his niece, Madame Denis, who possessed uncommon talents for music and elocution, acted several characters there. Mademoiselle Clairon, and the famous Lekain, performed in some pieces on that stage, and people twenty leagues distant came to hear them. He has oftener than once had suppers of a hundred covers, and balls; notwithstanding his advanced age, and the appearance of a life of dissipation, he never discontinued his studies. On the 20th of August, 1755, he brought his *Orphan of China* upon the stage at Paris, and *Tancred* on the third of September, 1760. Mademoiselle Clairon, and Mr. Lekain, displayed all their abilities in these two pieces.

The Coffee-house, or the Scotchwoman, a comedy, in prose, was not intended for the stage, but it was played with great success that year. He amused himself in composing this piece to chastise the hack Freron, whom he mortified, but did not correct. This comedy, translated into English by Mr. Colman[57], had as great a run at London as at Paris. These works took no time; the *Scotchwoman* was written in eight days, and *Tancred* in a month. While he was in the midst of these employments and amusements, Mr. Titon du Tillet, who had been long master in ordinary of the Queen's household, and eighty-five years of age, recommended to him the granddaughter of the great Corneille, who being entirely without fortune, was forsaken by the whole world. It was this same Titon du Tillet, who being a great lover of the fine arts, without cultivating them, caused a figure of Mount Parnassus to be constructed in bronze, at a considerable expence, in which are seen the statues of several French poets and musicians. This monument is in the King of France's library. He had bred up Mademoiselle Corneille at his own house, but seeing his fortune spent, he could do no more for her, and imagined that Mr. de Voltaire could take care of a lady of so respectable a name. Mr. du Mallard, a member of several Academies, known by his learned and judicious dissertation upon the ancient and modern tragedies of Electra, and Mr. Le Brun, Secretary to the Prince of Conti, wrote a joint letter to Mr. de Voltaire. He thanked them for the honour they had done him in casting their eyes upon him, and observed, *that it was no more than the duty of an old soldier, to serve the grand-daughter of his General*[58]. The young lady came to his country house of the Délices, near Geneva, in 1760, and from thence to his castle at Ferney. Madame Denis most chearfully undertook to finish her education, and at the end of three years Mr. de Voltaire married her to Mr. Dupuis of the *pays de Gex*, a Captain of dragoons, and since that time a Staff Officer. Beside the portion which he gave them, and the pleasure he had in having them to live with him, he proposed to write a commentary on the works of Pierre Corneille, for the benefit of his descendent, and to print them by subscription. The King of France was pleased to subscribe eight thousand livres, and some other Princes followed the example. The Duke de Choiseul, whose generosity is so well known, the Duchess de Gramont, and Madame Pompadour, subscribed considerable sums. Mr. de la Borde, the King's Banker, not only took a number of copies, but occasioned so great a number to be sold, that by his zeal and liberality he was the principal founder of Mademoiselle Corneille's fortune; so that in a little time she had fifty thousand livres for a wedding present.

There happened a very singular occurrence during this rapid subscription. Madame de Geofrin, a lady remarkable for character and genius, had been executrix of the famous Bernard de Fontenelle, the nephew of Pierre Corneille. Mr. Fontenelle unfortunately had forgotten this relation, who not

---

57 Colman's play is entitled The English Merchant. [*Translator's note.*]

58 [Best.D9382 (5 November 1760).]

being presented to him till too short a time before his death, was dismissed, along with her father and mother, as unknown pretenders that had assumed the name of Corneille. Some friends, affected with the fate of this unfortunate family, but excessively indiscreet, and very ill informed, commenced a rash prosecution against Madame Geofrin, and found a Counsellor, who, abusing the privileges of the Bar, published a very scurrilous memorandum against this lady. Madame de Geofrin, who was most injustly attacked, gained her cause unanimously. Notwithstanding the bad treatment she met with, she had the magnanimity to forget it, and was the first to subscribe a considerable sum.

The Academy as a body, the Duke de Choiseul, the Duchess de Gramont, Madame Pompadour, and a number of the nobility, gave Mr. de Voltaire a power to sign the contract of marriage for them. This is one of the occurrences which reflects the greatest honour on literature.

While he was making preparations for this marriage, which has proved very happy, he enjoyed another singular satisfaction, by being the means of having a paternal estate restored to six gentlemen, who were almost all minors, which had been purchased by the Jesuits at an under rate. But it is necessary to give the particulars of the affair from the beginning.—It is the more interesting, as it began before the famous bankruptcy of the Jesuit Lavallette and Company, and in a manner was the first signal of the suppression of the Jesuits in France.

There were six brothers of the ancient and noble family of Deprez de Crassi, in the *Pays de Gex*, on the borders of Swisserland, and all in the King's service. One of them, who was a Captain in the regiment of Deux-Ponts, in conversation with his neighbour, Mr. de Voltaire, gave him an account of the sad condition of the family estate; told him it was of considerable value, and might have been a resource to them, but had been a long time mortgaged to some people in Geneva.

The Jesuits had purchased some lands adjoining to this estate, in a place called Ornex, worth about two thousand crowns a year. They wanted to have the estate of the Messrs. de Crassi, joined to their domain. The superior of the Jesuits, whose real name was *Fesse*, which he changed to *Fessi*, settled matters with the Genevan creditors, so as to purchase the lands. He procured leave of the Council, and was upon the point of getting it confirmed at Dijon. He was told that there were minors, who, notwithstanding the leave of the Council, might recover their rights; but he answered that the Jesuits run no risk, for the Messrs. de Crassi never could be able to pay the money which was requisite for them to get possession of the ancestral estate.

Mr. de Voltaire was scarcely informed of the extraordinary method that Father Fesse was taking to serve the company of Jesuits, when he instantly went to the Clerk of the Precinct of Gex, and deposited a sufficient sum in his hands, to answer the claims of the original creditors, so that the family of de Crassi might recover their rights. The Jesuits were obliged to desist;—the family were put in possession of the estate by a decree of the Parliament of Dijon, and enjoy it at present

The best of the whole affair is, that in a little time after, when France was delivered from the Reverend Jesuit fathers, these very gentlemen, whose property the good Fathers were desirous of seizing, purchased the lands of the Jesuits, which were contiguous to them. Mr. de Voltaire, who had always combated the Atheists and Jesuits, wrote upon that occasion that we must acknowledge a Providence.

Certainly it was neither hatred against Father Fesse, nor a desire of mortifying the Jesuits that engaged him in this affair, for since the suppression of the society, he has taken a Jesuit[59] into his house, and numbers have written to him to beg he would likewise receive them. But some tempers have been found among the Ex-Jesuits, of a more unjust and uncomplying cast. Two of them, *Patouillet* and *Nonnote*, have made money by writing libels against him, and according to custom have not failed to call the Catholic religion to their assistance. One Nonnote particularly signalized himself by writing half a dozen volumes, in which he has lavished more zeal than knowledge, and more abuse than zeal. Mr. Damilaville, one of the best assistants in the Encyclopedie, has condescended to confute him, as Pasquier formerly stooped to check the absurd insolence of the Jesuit Garrasse.

But here follows the most singular and fatal adventure that has happened for a long time, and at the same time the most honourable for the King, his Council, and the Gentlemen of the Court of Requests. Who would have suspected that the first light and the first help towards clearing up the innocence of the celebrated family of *Calas*, should have originated in the ice of *Mont-Jura*, and the borders of Swisserland? *Donat Calas*, a child of fifteen years of age, and the youngest son of the unfortunate *Calas*, was apprentice to a merchant at Nismes, when he heard of the dreadful punishment by which seven, unfortunately prejudiced Judges of Toulouse, had put his virtuous father to death.

The popular outcry against this family was so violent in Languedoc, that every body expected to see all the children of Calas broke upon the wheel, and the mother burnt alive. Even the Attorney of Calas expected it. So weak, it is said, had been the defence made by this innocent family, oppressed by misfortunes, and terrified at the sight of lighted piles, wheels, and racks.

Young Donat Calas was made to dread sharing the fate of the rest of his family, and was advised to fly into Swisserland: he came and found Mr. de Voltaire, who at first could only pity and relieve him, without daring to judge his father, mother, and brothers.

Soon after, one of the brothers, who was only banished, likewise came and threw himself into the arms of Mr. de Voltaire. I can testify that for more than a month he took every possible precaution to be assured of the innocence of the family. But, when he was once convinced, he thought himself obliged in conscience to employ his friends, his purse, his pen, and his credit, to repair the fatal mistake of the seven Judges of Toulouse, and to have the proceed-

59 [Antoine Adam.]

ings revised by the King's Council. This revision lasted three years, and it is well known what honour Messrs. de Crosne and Bacquancourt acquired by conducting this memorable cause. Fifty masters of the Court of Requests unanimously declared the whole family of *Calas* innocent, and recommended them to the benevolent equity of the King. The Duke de Choiseul, who never lets slip an opportunity of signalizing the greatness of his character, not only assisted this unfortunate family with money, but obtained for them a gratuity of thirty-six thousand livres from his Majesty.

On the 9th of March, 1765, the *Arrêt* was signed which justified the family of *Calas* and changed their fate. The 9th of March was the very day on which the innocent and virtuous father of that family had been executed. All Paris ran in crowds to see them come out of prison, and clapped their hands while the tears streamed from their eyes. The whole of that family have been warmly attached to Mr. de Voltaire ever since, who thinks himself honoured by continuing their friend.

It was remarked at that time, that there was not in France a single person who did not rejoice at this decision, except the above mentioned Freron, author of an obscure periodical pamphlet, entitled *Letters to the Countess*[60], and afterwards *The Literary Year*, who in his ridiculous sheets, dated to throw out some doubts of the innocence of those whom the King, his whole Council, and the Public, had amply justified.

Several worthy men engaged Mr. de Voltaire at that time to write his treatise upon toleration, which is esteemed one of his best works in prose, and is become the catechism of all who have either good sense or moderation.

About the same time the Empress Catherine the Second, whose name will be immortal, was giving a code of laws to her empire, which contains a fifth part of the globe; and the first of her laws was to establish universal toleration.

It was the fate of our Recluse on the borders of Swisserland, to vindicate the innocence of those who were accused and condemned in France. The situation of his retreat between France, Swisserland, Geneva, and Savoy, attracted to him more than one unfortunate person. The whole family of *Sirven* condemned to death in a village near Castres, by a set of ignorant and cruel judges, fled for shelter to his estate. Though he was engaged eight years in procuring justice to be done them, he was never disheartened, and at last he succeeded.

We think it is of importance to observe, that one Trinquet, a country Judge, King's Attorney in the jurisdiction where the family of Sirven were condemned, gave his sentence in the following terms. *In the name of the King, I require that N. Sirven, and N. his wife, duly arraigned and convicted of having strangled and drowned their daughter, be banished the Parish.* Nothing can better shew the effects which the sale of judicial offices can have in a country.

Since it was the will of his kind stars, to use an expression of his own, that

60 [Or rather, *Lettres de madame la comtesse ****.]

he should be the pleader of causes already lost, it was likewise their will that he should rescue from the flames a woman of St. Omers, called Montbailly, who had been condemned to be burnt alive by the tribunal of Arras. They waited only for the woman's being delivered to carry her to the place of execution: her husband had already expired upon the wheel. What were these two victims? Two eminent examples of conjugal and parental love; two virtuous people in poverty. This innocent and respectable couple had been accused of parricide, and condemned upon proofs which would have appeared ridiculous even to those Judges who condemned the family of Calas. Mr. de Voltaire was so fortunate as to procure an order from the Chancellor Maupeou for a revival of the proceedings. The woman was declared innocent; her husband's reputation restored;—miserable restoration, unattended with either satisfaction or recompence! In what a dreadful state was criminal jurisprudence with us! What an infernal train of horrid assassinations from the time the Templars were butchered, to the death of the Chevalier de la Barre! We think we are reading the history of savage nations;—we shudder for an instant, and then set out for the Opera.

The city of Geneva was at that time immersed in troubles which had been increasing from the year 1763. These disturbances determined Mr. de Voltaire to give up his house of Delices to Messrs. Tronchin, and to reside constantly at the castle of Ferney, which he had entirely rebuilt, and ornamented with gardens laid out with agreeable simplicity.

The quarrel at Geneva, rose to such a pitch, that on the 15th of February, 1770, the one party fired upon the other; some people were killed, and a number of tradesmen with their families, came and begged an asylum with Mr. de Voltaire, which he granted. He received some of them into his castle, and in a few years had fifty houses of hewn stone built for the rest: so that the village of Ferney, which at the time of his purchase, was only a wretched hamlet tenanted by forty nine miserable peasants, devoured by poverty, scrofula and tax-gatherers, very soon became a delightful place, inhabited by twelve hundred people, comfortably situated, and successfully employed for themselves and the nation. The Duke de Choiseul protected this infant colony with all his power, so that they were soon in a situation to establish a very considerable trade.

One thing which I think worthy of attention is, that though this colony was composed of Roman Catholics and Protestants, it would have been impossible to discover that there were two different religions in Ferney. I have seen the wives of the Swiss and Genevans, with their own hands, prepare three reposoirs[61] for the host, against the procession at the festival of the holy sacrament. They assisted at the ceremony with the deepest reverence, and Mr. Hugonet, the new Clergyman of Ferney, a man of a tolerating generous spirit, took an opportunity of thanking them in his discourse. When a Catholic was sick,

61 Reposoir is an altar set up in the streets for the Corpus Christi procession. [Translator's note.]

the Protestants went to nurse him, and they met the like assistance, when they had occasion for it.

This was the effect of those principles of humanity, which Mr. de Voltaire had recommended in all his works; but more particularly in his treatise on toleration of which I have spoken. He always said that we were all brothers, and it was from facts that he reasoned. The *Guyons*, the *Nonottes*, the *Patouillets*, the *Paulians*, and other zealots, bitterly reproached him with it; but it was because they were not his brethren.

'Behold this inscription, DEO EREXIT, upon the church I have built', said he, to those travellers who came to visit him. 'It is to God, the common father of all men'. Perhaps it is indeed the only church we have, which is dedicated to God alone.

More than one sovereign Prince may be reckoned among the number of strangers, that came in crouds to visit Ferney. Several of them, whose letters are in my hands, honoured him with a constant correspondence: the most uninterrupted, was that of his majesty the King of Prussia, and his sister Madame Wilhelmina, Margravine of Bareith.

The most interesting period of this correspondence, was that which passed between the battle of Kolin (on the 18th of June, 1757), when the King of Prussia was defeated, and the affair of Rosbach, where he was victorious, on the 5th of the following November: a rare instance of a correspondence being kept up between a simple man of letters, and a royal family of heroes: of which the following memorable letter is an eminent proof.

LETTER

From her Royal Highness the Princess of Bareith, of the 12th of September, 1757.

'I was sensibly affected with your letter[62], and yours to the King[63], addressed to my care, had the same effect upon him. I hope you will be pleased with that part of his answer[64], which concerns you; but you will be as little satisfied with his resolutions, as I am. I flattered myself with the hope that your reflexions would have made some impression upon his mind, but by the inclosed note, you will see the contrary. If his fate proves unfortunate, nothing remains for me, but to follow it. I never prided myself on being a philosopher, but I have done my endeavour to become one. The little progress I have made, has taught me to despise grandeur and riches: but I have found nothing in philosophy, which can heal the wounds of the heart, except it be the getting rid of all ills, by ceasing to live. My situation is worse than death. I see the greatest man of the age, my friend and brother, in the most dreadful extremity. I see my whole family exposed to perils and dangers; my country torn to pieces by merciless enemies; the country where I am at present, perhaps threatened with similar misfortunes. I wish to Heaven that these evils which

62 [Best.D7359 (29 August 1757).]
63 [This has not survived.]

64 [Best.D7362 (9 September 1757); in this letter Frederick contemplated suicide.]

I now mention to you, were to fall upon me alone—I would suffer them with steadiness.

Pardon this detail; but the share you take in whatever regards me, engages me to open my heart to you. Alas! even hope is almost banished. Fortune when she changes, is as constant in her persecutions, as she was in her favours. History is full of these examples, but I have never seen a situation like to ours, nor so cruel or inhuman a war, carried on among civilized nations. If you knew the situation of Germany and Prussia, it would draw tears from your eyes. The cruelties which the Russians commit in Prussia, make nature shudder. How happy are you in your hermitage, resting under the shade of your laurels, where you may deliberately philosophise upon the misconduct of men! I wish you all possible happiness there.

If fortune should smile again, you may depend upon all my gratitude. I shall never forget the proofs of attachment which you have given me; my sensibility shall be my pledge: I am never a friend by halves, and I shall alway be truly one to brother Voltaire.

WILHELMINA

Present many compliments to Madame Denis. I entreat you continue to write to the King'.[65]

We may see by this affecting and well-written letter, what an amiable soul the Margravine of Bareith had, and how well she deserved the encomium bestowed upon her by Mr. de Voltaire, in an ode lamenting her death, which was printed with his other works. But what may be chiefly observed is, the dreadful misfortunes which wars, undertaken upon slight pretences by Kings, bring upon the public; they likewise may see how wretched they are in being the cause of misery to whole nations.

Then, and during the whole time of that fatal war, the Recluse of Ferney gave every possible proof of his attachment to the Margravine; of his zeal for the King, her brother, and of his love of peace. He engaged Cardinal Tencin, who had at that time retired to Lyons, to commence a correspondence with the Margravine, in order to bring about the wish'd-for peace. The letters both of the Princess and the Cardinal passed by way of Geneva, a neutral state, and through the hands of Mr. de Voltaire.

After all the misfortunes consequent on the King of Prussia's defeat at Kolin, the resolution taken by that Monarch, to march towards Saxony, near Mersbourg, and confront the combined armies of France and Austria, that were greatly superior in numbers, while Marechal de Richelieu was at no great distance with a victorious army, will be looked upon as a very singular epoch. That Monarch, in the midst of all his misfortunes, had so much presence of mind, and was sufficiently master of his ideas to make his will in verse. In it he did not conceal his misfortunes, but he spoke of them like a

65 [Best.D7380   (12   September 1757).]

philosopher, and looked upon death with a calm and steady eye. We have this piece, which is a matchless monument, written entirely by his own hand.

We have a still more heroic monument of this Royal Philosopher;—it is a letter to Mr. de Voltaire of the 9th of August, twenty-five days before his victory at Rosbach.

> Je suis homme, il suffit, & né pour la souffrance;
> Aux rigueurs du destin j'oppose ma constance.

> Enough—I'm man, and therefore born to woes,
> To rig'rous fate my firmness I oppose.

But though these be my sentiments, I am far from condemning Cato and Otho.—There was not a single glorious moment in the life of the latter, but that which concluded it.

> Voltaire dans son hermitage
> Peut s'adonner en paix à la vertu du sage
> Dont Platon nous traça la loi:
> Pour moi, menacé du naufrage,
> Je dois en affronter l'orage
> Penser, vivre & mourir en Roi.

> Voltaire in sweet retirement laid,
> Beneath his fav'rite Ferney's shade,
>   May practice Plato's sacred lore;
> For me, embark'd on stormy seas,
> No succour nigh, no fav'ring breeze,
>   My ship far distant driven from shore.

> Though fiercely tumbling wave on wave,
> My shatter'd sides the tempests lave,
>   And round my head the wild winds sing;
> Yet must I meet their fiercest hate,
> Prosp'rous, or adverse by my fate,
>   Think, live, die, as becomes a King'.[66]

Nothing can be finer or more noble than these last verses. Corneille, in his best days, could not have written any thing better: and when a battle is gained after such verses, the sublime can reach no higher.

Cardinal Tencin, as may be seen by his letters, always continued his secret negotiations for peace, though fruitlessly. It was the Duke de Choiseul who

66 [This is typical of the problems which confronted me when editing Voltaire's correspondence: he ascribes this letter to 9 August [1757], and the manuscript is in fact so dated, but it was actually written on 9 September (Best.D7373); it was the letter forwarded by Wilhelmina of Bayreuth in hers just quoted; and to complicate matters further Voltaire has merged into the letter lines which actually occur in another of 8 October (Best.D7414).]

at last began this great and necessary work which the Duke de Praslin com-
pleated; a most important service done to France, already ruined and impoverished.

France was in so deplorable a situation, that of all the Ministers of the
Finances, who rapidly succeeded one another during the twelve years of
peace, which followed this fatal war, there was not one that with the best
inclination and the most laborious assiduity, could even palliate the wounds
of the state. Such was the want of money, that a Comptroller general was
obliged, on a pressing occasion, to seize all the cash which the citizens had
deposited in the hands of Mr. Magan, the King's Banker. Two hundred
thousand livres were taken from our Recluse. It was an enormous loss, but
like a true Frenchman, he comforted himself by the following madrigal, which
he composed *ex tempore* upon receiving the news of his misfortune.

Au tems de la grandeur Romaine
Horace disait a Mécène,
Quand cesserez vous de donner?
Chez le Welche on n'est pas si tendre.
Je dois dire mais sans douleur
A Monseigneur le Contrôleur,
Quand cesserez vous de me prendre?

When Rome the world in triumph led,
Thus to Mecenas Horace said,
When will you cease to give?
But the good Welch with whom I live,
    I vow are of a different make,
I ought to say, but without choler,
An't please you my good Lord Comptroller,
    When will you cease to take?

They did not stop here. The Duke de Choiseul caused a magnificent
harbour to be built at Versoy, upon the Leman Lake, commonly called the
Lake of Geneva, and having a small frigate built there, it was seized in a port
of Savoy near the famous *Ripaille*, by some people of Savoy, who were
creditors of the undertakers. Mr. de Voltaire immediately redeemed this
royal vessel with money out of his own pocket, but has never been able to
recover it from government, for the Duke de Choiseul lost all his employments at that time, and retired to his seat at Chanteloup, not only regretted
by his friends but by all the people in France, who admired his benevolent
disposition, the nobleness of his soul, and did justice to his superior abilities.

Our Recluse was tenderly attached to that Nobleman by all the ties of
gratitude. There was no kind of favour which the Duke de Choiseul did not
readily grant on his recommendation. He made Mr. de la Houliere, nephew
of Mr. de Voltaire, a Brigadier in the king's army. Pensions, rewards, com-
missions, crosses of St. Louis, were given as soon as asked.

Nothing could be more affecting to the man who had been so much obliged by him, who had just established a colony of artists and manufacturers under his auspices. The Colony had begun to be employed very successfully for Spain, Germany, Holland, and Italy, and upon this occasion he thought they would have been ruined: but they were able to support themselves. The Empress of Russia alone, in the very heat of the war against the Turks, bought watches at Ferney to the amount of fifty thousand livres. There is no end to our astonishment, when we see this Princess at the same time laying out a million of livres in France and Holland for pictures, and some millions for jewels.

She made a present to Mr. Diderot of fifty thousand livres, and with such a pleasing delicacy as greatly heightened the value of the present. She offered to commit the principal care of her son's[67] education to Mr. d'Alembert, with a salary of sixty thousand livres; but neither the state of health, nor the philosophic turn of Mr. d'Alembert, permitted him to accept an employment at Petersburg which was equal to what the Duke de la Vaugion enjoyed at Versailles. She sent Prince *Koslousky* to present Mr. de Voltaire with some valuable furs, and a box turned with her own hands, ornamented with her picture and twenty diamonds. It sounds like the history of Aboulcassem in the Arabian Nights.

Mr. de Voltaire told her that she had certainly taken all Mustapha's treasures in one of her victories. She replied, '*That with œconomy*[68] *we are always rich, and that in this great war she would neither feel the want of men or money.*' And she has shewn it.

In the mean time Mr. Pigal, the famous Statuary, was employed at Paris in making a statue of our Recluse hidden at Ferney. This compliment was first proposed in the year 1770 by a foreign Lady, to some truly learned men, to make him amends for all the insipid libels and ridiculous calumnies which fanaticism and ignorance had heaped upon him. It was Madame Neker, the wife of the Resident from Geneva, who first conceived this project. She was a woman of a highly cultivated understanding, and if possible her worth was even superior to her genius. Her idea was eagerly catched at by all her visitants, upon condition that none but men of letters should be subscribers to the undertaking.

The King of Prussia, as a man of letters, to which title and to that of genius surely no man has a better claim, wrote to the celebrated Mr. d'Alembert, and expressed his desire to be among the first to subscribe. His letter of the 28th of July, 1770, is lodged in the archives of the Academy.

'The handsomest monument of Voltaire is that which he hath erected himself, in his works. They will last longer than the dome of St. Peter's, the Louvre, and all those buildings which vanity has consecrated to eternity. When the French language shall be no more spoken, Voltaire will be translated into the language which shall next succeed. In the mean time, while I am

67 [The future Paul i.]   68 [That is, good management.]

filled with the pleasure which his productions, so various, and each so perfect in its kind, have given me, I could not without ingratitude, reject the proposal which you have made to me, of contributing to the monument which is to be erected for him as a proof of public gratitude. You have only to let me know what is expected from me;—I will refuse nothing for a statue which does more honour to the men of letters who erect it, than it possibly can to Voltaire. It will be said, that in the eighteenth century, while so many men of letters were tearing one another in pieces through envy, there were some found so truly noble and generous, as to do justice to a man whose genius and talents were superior to every age;—that we deserved to possess Voltaire:—and our latest posterity will envy us that singular advantage. The distinguishing celebrated men, and doing justice to their merit, is the way to encourage talent and virtue. It is the only recompense of worthy minds, and is justly due to those who cultivate letters in an eminent degree. They procure the pleasures of the mind, which are more lasting than those of the body;—they soften the most savage manners;—they spread charms over the whole course of life;—they render our existence supportable, and death less terrible. Continue then, Gentlemen, to protect and celebrate all those in France who apply to, and are so happy as to succeed in, these pursuits. It will be the greatest honour you can possibly do your nation.

FREDERICK'[69]

The King of Prussia did more: he caused a Statue of his old servant to be made in his fine manufactory of porcelain, and sent it to him with the word *Immortal*, inscribed upon the pedestal. Mr. de Voltaire wrote under it,

> Vous êtes généreux. Vos bontés souveraines
> Me font de trop nobles présens.
> Vous me donnez sur mes vieux ans
> Une terre dans vos domaines.

> You're generous. Your royal bounty deigns
> To croud too noble presents on the past;
> Worn out with age, and breathing now my last,
> You grant me an estate in your domains.

Mr. Pigal undertook to execute the Statue in France with the zeal of one artist who wished to immortalise another. This adventure, which was singular at that time, will very soon become common. The erecting the statues, or at least the busts of Artists, will become the fashion, like calling out from the pit *the Author, the Author*. But he to whom this honour was done, plainly foresaw that his enemies would be only the more exasperated. He wrote what follows to Mr. Pigal, in a stile perhaps too burlesque.

> Monsieur Pigal, vôtre statue,
> Me fait mille fois trop d'honneur.

69 [Best.D16552 (28 July 1770).]

Jean Jacques a dit avec candeur
Que c'est a lui qu'elle etait due.
  Quand vôtre ciseau s'évertue
A sculpter vôtre serviteur,
Vous agacez l'esprit railleur
De certain peuple rimailleur
Qui depuis si longtems me hue.
L'ami Freron le barbouilleur
D'écrits qu'on jette dans la rue,
Sourdement de sa main crochue
Mutilera vôtre labeur.
  Attendez que le destructeur
Qui nous consume & qui nous tue
Le tems, aidé de mon pasteur,
Ait d'un bras exterminateur
Enterré ma tête chenue.
Que feriez vous d'un pauvre auteur
Dont la taille & le cou de grue,
Et la mine très-peu jouflue
Feront rire le connaisseur.
Sculptez nous quelque beauté nue
De qui la chair blanche & dodue
Séduise l'œil du spectateur,
Et qui dans nos sens insinue
Ces doux désirs & cette ardeur
Dont Pigmalion le sculpteur,
Vôtre digne prédecesseur
Brula, si la fable en est crue.
Son marbre eut un esprit, un cœur;
Il eut mieux, dit un grave auteur;
Car soudain fille devenue
Cette fille resta pourvue
Des doux appas que sa pudeur
Ne dérobait point à la vue.
Même elle fut plus dissolue
Que son père et son créateur.
C'est un example très-flatteur
Il faut bien qu'on le perpetue.[70]

A Statue! what, and wrought by you,
'Tis much, too much above my due.
Candid *Jean Jaques* with frowning stare,
Exclaims—a statue for Voltaire!
When mine's the merit—I alone

70 [*Epître à monsieur Pigalle* (1770).]

669

Ought to be grav'd in living stone.[71]
Thus hurry'd on by zeal too fervent,
When you would grace your humble servant;
You rouse again the dormant rage,
Of all the rhymers of the age,
By whom I've long been persecuted,
Pelted, defam'd, and hiss'd and hooted;
Freron, whose pamphlets you may meet,
Choaking the kennels in each street,
With crooked claw will steal upon it,
And maim your labour in a moment.
Have patience, wait a few short hours,
'Till that fell fiend which all devours,
Time, with my pious pastor's aid,
In dust my hoary head has laid.
—And after all, what can you make?
Your credit, Sir, you rashly stake;
An author—of a dwarfish stature,
By much too mean in limb and feature;
With long crane neck, and cheeks so thin,
They'll force from Connoisseurs a grin.

To please is still the sculptor's duty,
Then carve us out some naked beauty,
Whose fair plump charms may please our eyes,
And take our senses by surprize;
Shoot through our marrow lambent fires,
Kindling those raptures fierce desires,
With which as ancient stories shew,
Pygmalion felt his bosom glow;
His marble had a soul, a heart,
Still better, authors grave assert;
For soon as life inform'd the mass,
No marble now—the sprightly lass,
As she before him naked stood,
Shew'd plainly she was flesh and blood;
Boldly display'd her sweetest charms,
And hugg'd her maker in her arms.
Nay with far keener ardours glow'd
Than those to which her life she ow'd.

71 Jean Jacques Rousseau, of Geneva, in a letter to the Archbishop of Paris, entitled *Jean Jacques to Christopher*, modestly says that he is become a man of letters, by his contempt for that condition. And after begging Christopher to read his romance of his Swiss girl Eloïse, who while unmarried, brought forth an abortion; he concludes, page 127, that they ought to erect statues for him, in every well regulated state.

Your powers are as Pygmalion's ample,
Then propagate the sweet example.

It was not without reason that he said, this unexpected honour, would set all the fanatic writers of the *Pont neuf*[72] upon him. In writing to Mr. Tiriot, he said, *all these gentlemen deserve statues much better than I do; and I confess that here are some of them, whose effigies ought to be stuck up in the Greve.*[73]

The Nonottes, the Frerons, the Sabotiers, and their companions, loudly declaimed: but he who persecuted him with the greatest cruelty and absurdity, was a foreign highlander[74], who was fitter for sweeping chimnies, than directing consciences. This very familiar gentleman wrote to the King of France, in the stile of one crowned head to another, to beg the favour of him to expel a sick man, of seventy-five years of age, from the house which he built; from the lands which he had cleared, and from a hundred families, who derived their subsistence from him. The King thought the proposal was dishonest and unchristian, and gave orders that the *tatter Crape*[75] might be told so.

Our recluse of Ferney, being sick and without employment, was resolved to be revenged for this petty manœuvre, only by having extreme unction administered according to the custom at that time, by procuration. He acted as those people who are called Jansenists do at Paris: he had it signified to his Parson, who was called *Gros* (an honest drunkard, who has since killed himself by the bottle), by an usher, that the said Parson should come and anoint him in his chamber, without fail, on the first of April. The Parson accordingly came, and remonstrated to him the necessity of first taking the sacrament, and then he would give him as much oil as he pleased. The sick man accepted the proposal; the communion was brought into the chamber, and on the 1st of April, in the presence of witnesses, he declared before a notary, *that he forgave his slanderer who had endeavoured to ruin him, but had not succeeded.* The declaration was drawn up in proper form.

After the ceremony, he said, now that I have had the satisfaction of dying like Guzman in Alzira, I find myself better. The wags at Paris thought the whole an *April errand.*

His enemy, astonished at this adventure, did not value himself upon following the example; he did not forgive. He did not know what to do but to force a declaration of the sick man, quite different from the genuine one which had been made before the notary and witnesses, duly examined and authenticated. In about fifteen days after, a couple of Forgers composed a counter-profession

---

72 Answering to our Grub-street. [*Translator's note.*]

73 The Greve is the place of execution for criminals [*Translator's note,* but Voltaire had not written 'in the Greve' but merely 'in a public place'.]

74 [Jean Pierre Biord, bishop of Geneva and Annecy.]

75 [Voltaire has 'capelan', 'wretched priest'; cp. in Garth's *Dispensary*:

Avoid th' Inclemencies of Morning Air,
And leave to tatter'd Crape the Drudgery
of Pray'r.]

of faith in the dialect of Savoy, but they durst not counterfeit the signature of the man, to whom they had the stupidity to ascribe it. Mr. de Voltaire wrote the following letter upon the subject.

'I am not offended with those people, who have made me speak the words of holiness, in a stile both barbarous and impertinent; they could have expressed my true sentiments but badly; they have repeated in their jargon, what I have so frequently published in French, but they have nevertheless expressed the substance of my opinions. I agree with them; I join in their faith, my enlightened zeal seconds their ignorance, and I recommend myself to their savoyard prayers. I only beg the pious Forgers, who composed the deed of the 15th of April, to consider that they ought not to counterfeit deeds, even in favour of the truth. The more the Catholic religion is true (as all the world knows), there is the less need of telling lies for it. These little liberties which are but too common, may authorize more dangerous impositions. People may very soon think they may be allowed to fabricate false wills, false donations, and false accusations, for the glory of God. More horrid forgeries have been committed on former occasions.

Some of the pretended witnesses confess that they were suborned, but they were made to believe that they were doing good. They have declared, that they only told lies with a good intention.

All this was done no doubt with the same charitable intentions that the recantations were imputed to Messrs. de Mountesquieu, de la Chalotais, de Montclar, and so many others. These pious frauds have been in fashion about sixteen hundred years: but when these good works, go the length of falsehood, it is risking a great deal in this world, in expectation of the kingdom of Heaven'.[76]

While those people were employed in melancholy mischief, our recluse continued chearfully to do the little good in his power, and to fortify the most serious truths by sallies of humour.

He confessed that he carried his raillery too great lengths against some of his enemies. 'I was wrong', said he in one of his letters, 'but having been attacked by these gentlemen for forty years, I have lost my patience these ten years'.

The revolution which took place in all the parliaments of the kingdom, in the year 1771, could not fail to affect him, for he had two nephews[77], one of whom quitted, when the other entered the parliament of Paris. They were both men of distinguished merit and incorruptible probity, but engaged in opposite parties. He continued to love them both equally, and to preserve the same regard for them, but he loudly declared for the abolition of that venality, against which we have quoted the energetic expressions of the Marquis d'Argenson. He greatly admired the scheme of doing justice gratui-

76 [Best.D15621 (April/May 1769).]   Alexandre Marie François de Paule de
77 [Alexandre Jean Mignot and   Dompierre d'Hornoy.]

tously, like St. Louis; but chiefly he wrote in favour of unfortunate clients, who for four centuries had been obliged to come a hundred and fifty leagues from their cottages to compleat their ruin in the capital, by losing, or even by gaining their causes. He always manifested these sentiments in his writings, and was steady in his principles without paying court to any one.

Though he was at that time seventy-eight years of age, in one year he entirely new-writ the Sophonisba of Mairet, and composed the tragedy of the *Laws of Minos*. He did not look upon these productions, which he wrote in haste for the Theatre, in his own Castle, as good pieces. The connoisseurs do not find much fault with the Laws of Minos; but it must be owned, that those dramatic works which have never appeared on the stage, or that have not continued to be played for a considerable time, serve no other purpose but to swell the heap of pamphlets with which Europe is overloaded;—like those pictures and prints, which if not received into the collections of the curious, remain as if they had never existed.

In the year 1774, he had a singular opportunity of employing that same zeal which he had the good fortune to display in the fatal catastrophe of the families of Calas and Sirven.

He was informed that there was a young French gentleman of modest merit, and singular good sense, in the King of Prussia's army, at Wesel. This young gentleman was only a volunteer, and had been condemned at Abbeville, with the Chevalier de la Barre, to suffer the punishment of parricides, for not kneeling in time of rain before a procession of Capuchins, who had passed about fifty or sixty paces from them.

To this accusation was added, that of having sung a rakish song of a hundred years old, and repeating Piron's Ode to Priapus. This Ode of Piron's was a lewd flight of a young man, and looked upon as such a venial trespass, that the King of France, Louis xv, hearing that the author was very poor, gave him a pension out of his privy purse. Thus he who composed the piece was rewarded by a good King, while they who repeated it, were condemned to suffer the most dreadful punishment, by some inhuman monsters of a village.

Three Judges of Abbeville conducted the prosecution, and the sentence was as follows: That the Chevalier de la Barre, and his young friend (of whom we have been speaking), should be put to the torture ordinary and extraordinary, their hands be cut off, their tongues torn out with pincers, and their bodies thrown living into the flames.

Of the three Judges who gave this sentence, two of them were absolutely incompetent. One of them for being the declared enemy of the young people's families; the other, because having formerly got himself admitted Counsellor, he had since purchased and exercised the business of Attorney in Abbeville; that his principal employment was that of a dealer in bullocks and hogs;— he had been condemned by the Consuls of Abbeville, and the court of Aides had afterwards declared him incapable of holding any municipal employment in the kingdom.

The third Judge, intimidated by the two others, had the weakness to subscribe to their sentence, which was followed by the most poignant and fruitless remorse.

To the surprise and astonishment of all Europe, that still shudders with horror at the deed, the Chevalier de la Barre was executed: his friend was sentenced in his absence, having been in a foreign country before the beginning of the prosecution.

This sentence so execrable, and at the same time so absurd, which is an eternal disgrace to France, was much more to be condemned than that by which the innocent Calas was broke upon the wheel; for the Judges of Calas were guilty of no other fault than that of deceiving themselves, while the crime of the Abbeville Judges, was their being monsters of cruelty with their eyes open. They condemned two innocent children to suffer as cruel a death as Ravillac and Damiens, for a levity which only deserved a week's imprisonment. It may be said that since the massacre of St Bartholomew nothing so dreadful has happened. It is melancholy to relate such an instance of brutal ferocity as is not to be met with among the most savage people, but truth obliges us to it. What is chiefly to be observed is, that these horrid acts have been committed for the sake of religion, at a time when the greatest luxury, effeminacy, and unbridled dissipation, prevailed.

Mr. de Voltaire, then, having been informed that one of these youths, a victim of the most detestable fanaticism, that ever polluted the earth, was in one of the King of Prussia's regiments, he acquainted that Monarch of it, who immediately had the generosity to make him an officer. The King of Prussia enquired particularly about the young gentleman's conduct; he found that he had learnt the art of engineering and drawing without the help of a master; that he was sensible, prudent, and virtuous; and that the whole of his conduct gave the lie to his pretended Judges of Abbeville. The King called him near his person, gave him a company, appointed him engineer, and honoured him with a pension, and thus by his benevolence wiped away the crimes committed by barbarity and folly. He wrote in the most affecting terms to Mr. de Voltaire to acquaint him with what he had done for this truly valuable and unfortunate soldier. We have all been witnesses of this horrid affair, so dishonourable for France, and so glorious for a royal philosopher. This great example will inform *mankind*, but will it *correct* them?

Immediately after this the old man renewed his frozen age, in order to take advantage of the patriotic views of a new Minister[78], who was the first in France that set out with being the father of the people. The home which Mr. de Voltaire had chosen in the Pays de Gex, was a strip of land about five or six leagues in length and about two in breadth, between Mount Jura, the lake of Geneva, the Alps, and Swisserland. This country was plagued with about fourscore *Sbirri*[79] of the revenue, who disgraced their uniforms, and, un-

78 [Anne Robert Jacques Turgot.]
79 The *Sbirri* are the officers of the Inquisition, and Voltaire uses this term to express the rapacious cruelty of the Tax-gatherers in France. [*Translator's note.*]

known to their masters, tormented the poor people. The country was in the most dreadful misery, but he was so happy as to obtain a composition from his benevolent Minister, by which this solitude (we dare not say province) was delivered from all vexation; it became free and happy. 'After this', said he, 'I ought to die, for I can rise no higher.'

However he did not die at that time, but his noble rival and illustrious adversary *Freron* died; and what I find a very droll affair happened upon the occasion. Mr. de Voltaire received an invitation from Paris to be present at the funeral of this poor devil. A female, who was apparently one of the family, wrote an anonymous letter to him, which is in my hands, proposing, in the most serious manner, that he should procure a husband for the daughter of Freron, as he had done for the descendant of Corneille. She conjured him in the most pressing terms, and informed him, that he might address the Parson of the Magdalen at Paris, for that purpose. Mr. de Voltaire told me, that if Freron had written the Cid, Cinna, and Polyeuctes, he would immediately have found the girl a husband.

The letters which he received were not all anonymous. There was a Mr. Clement, a Servitor, in a college of Dijon, who set himself up for a master in the art of reasoning, and in the art of writing, that came to Paris to live by a trade which may be carried on without having served an apprenticeship;— he turned hack. The Abbé Voisenon wrote upon the occasion, *Zoilus genuit Mevium, Mevius genuit Giot des Fontaines, Giot autem genuit Freron, Freron autem genuit Clement*[80], and thus great families degenerate. This Mr. Clement had attacked the Marquis de St. Lambert, Mr. de Lille, and several other Members of the Academy, with a violence which the most irritated client could not have employed, if his whole fortune had been at stake. And for what was all this? for some verses indeed. It was like the Doctor in Moliere, who foamed at the mouth with rage, because a man had, in his hearing, said, the form of a hat, and not the figure of a hat. Here follow some lines which Mr. de Voltaire wrote to the Abbé Voisenon.

'   .   .   .   .
Il est bien vrai que l'on m'annonce
Les lettres de maitre Clement.
Il a beau m'écrire souvent,
Il n'obtiendra point de réponse.
Je ne serai pas assez sot
Pour m'embarquer dans ces querelles.
Si c'eut été Clement Marot
Il aurait eu de mes nouvelles.'

Clement, 'tis true, has often writ,
But not a line shall he receive;

80 Zoilus begot Mevius, Mevius begot Giot Des Fontaines, Giot begot Freron, Freron begot Clement. [*Translator's note.*]

I surely should have lost my wit,
To heed when stupid madmen rave.
Yet had it Clement Marot been,
My answer he had doubtless seen.

As for plain Mr. Clement, who in a volume much larger than the Henriade, proves to me that the Henriade is worth but little; alas! I have known it these sixty years as well as he. At the age of twenty-one I began with the second Canto of the Henriade. I was at that time in the same predicament that Mr. Clement seems to be in at present; I did not know what I was about. Instead of writing a large volume against me, why does not he write a better Henriade? 'Tis so easy a matter!

There are a sort of tempers, which, having once contracted a habit of writing, cannot relinquish it in their most advanced age;—such were Huet and Fontenelle. Though my author was weighed down with years and disorders, he was always chearfully employed. His Epistle to Boileau, his Epistle to Horace, the Tacticks, the Dialogue of Pegasus and the Old Man, John who Laughs and Cries, and several other pieces of that kind, were written at the age of eighty-two. In conjunction with two or three men of learning, he wrote three-fourths of *The Questions on the Encyclopédie*. As soon as each volume made its appearance, several editions of it were printed, and the whole are very incorrect.

There is a very singular fact relating to the article *Messiah*, which shews that the eyes of envy are not always clear-sighted. That article *Messiah*, already printed in the great Paris encyclopaedia, was written by Mr. Polier de Bottens, first Pastor of the church of Lausanne; a man truly respectable, both for his virtue and learning. The article is sensible, instructive, and of profound erudition;—we have the original in the author's own hand. While it was believed to be written by Mr. de Voltaire, there were a hundred faults found; but when it was known to be the work of a Clergyman, it became truly Christian.

Among the number who fell into this snare, we may reckon the Ex-Jesuit, *Nonotte*. It was the same man who thought fit to deny that there was a little town called Livron, in Dauphiny, besieged by order of *Henry the Third*; who did not know that our first race of Kings had several wives at one time;—who did not know that *Eucherius* was the first author of the fable of the Theban Legion. It was he who wrote two volumes against *the History of the Genius and Manners of Nations*, and who blundered in every page of the two volumes. His book sold, because he attacked a person who was well known.

The fanaticism of this Nonotte was so great, that in I don't know what, *philosophical, religious, or anti-philosophical Dictionary*, in the article *Miracle*, he assures us that when the *host* at Dijon was stabbed with a pen-knife, it run twenty porringers of blood:—and that another *host* being thrown into the fire at Dôle, skipped away to the altar. Frere Nonotte, to prove these two facts, quotes two Latin verses of the president Boisvin, of Franchcomté.

Impie, quid dubitas hominemque Deumque fateri?
Se probat esse hominem sanguine, et igne Deum.

These two impertinent verses, when rendered into intelligible language, say, 'Wicked wretch, wherefore dost thou hesitate to acknowledge a man-God? he proves that he is man by the blood, and God by the fire.'

Nothing could be better demonstrated; and upon this proof Nonotte exclaims in extacy: *thus ought we to proceed in regulating our belief of miracles.*

But the good Nonotte, in regulating his belief upon theological ravings, or the reasonings of Bedlam, did not know that there are more than sixty towns in Europe, where the people give out that the Jews stabbed the *host* with knives, and that blood immediately flowed;—he does not know that even in these days they commemorate a similar adventure at Brussels, and I have heard a curious song upon the subject, when I was there forty years ago.

> Gaudissons nous, bons Chrétiens, au supplice
> Du vilain Juif appellé Jonathan,
> Qui sur l'autel a, par grande malice,
> Assassiné le très saint Sacrement.[81]

He does not know the miracle of Goose-street, in Paris, where the inhabitants every year burn the figure of a Swiss or a Franc-comtois at the end of the street, for assassinating the Holy Virgin, and the Infant Jesus;—nor the miracle of the Carmalites, called *Billettes*, and a hundred others of the same kind, celebrated by the dregs of the people, and brought in evidence by the dregs of writers, who would have us give the same credit to these nonsensical tales, as to the miracle at the marriage in Cana, or that of the five loaves.

All these fathers of the church, some coming out of jail, some out of the tavern, some begging alms from him, were continually sending him either libels or anonymous letters, which he threw into the fire unopened. His reflections upon the infamous and contemptible occupation of these pitiful wretches, called *Le pauvre Diable* (*The Poor Devil*), in which he shewed clearly, that it was a thousand times better to be a footman or porter in a good family, than to drag on a life in indigence in streets, coffee-houses, and garrets, which they can scarcely support by selling libels to book-sellers, in which they judge Kings, insult women, govern states, and, without a grain of common sense, abuse their neighbours.

Of late he has shewed a perfect indifference for his own works; about which he had always been little solicitous, and which he never mentioned. They were continually reprinted without his being even acquainted with it. If an edition of the Henriade, or his tragedies, history, or fugitive pieces, was almost out of print, another was instantly produced. He frequently wrote to the Booksellers, *Do not print such a number of volumes as my works;—a man*

---

81 [The translator omitted this quatrain. 'Let us rejoice, good Christians, at the sufferings of the wretched Jew named Jonathan, who most wickedly murdered the most holy host on the altar.']

cannot reach posterity with such heavy baggage. They did not hearken to him; they reprinted in a hurry, without consulting him: and what is almost incredible, yet true, they printed a magnificent edition in Quarto at Geneva, without his ever seeing a single sheet, in which they inserted a number of pieces that were not his, and the real authors of which are well known. It was with regard to all these different editions that he said and wrote to his friends, *I look upon myself as a dead man, whose effects are upon sale.*[82]

The chief magistrate, and the principal evangelical clergyman of Lausanne, having established a printing house in that town, they published an edition, which they said was compleat, with the name of London on the title page. These editors have inserted more than a hundred little pieces in prose and verse, that could not come from him, nor from a man of any taste, nor from a gentleman; such as this which may be found among the small pieces of the Abbé Grecour.

> Belle maman soyez l'arbitre
> Si la fièvre n'est pas un titre
> Suffisant pour me disculper;
> Je suis au lit comme un bélitre
> Et c'est à force de lamper;
> Mais j'espère d'en réchaper
> Puisqu'en recevant cette épître
> L'amour me dresse mon pupitre.[83]

Such is the *apotheosis* of Mademoiselle Couvreur, made by a school master of the name of Bonneval:

> Quel contraste frappe mes yeux.
> Melpomène ici désolée
> Elève avec l'aveu des Dieux
> Un magnifique mausolée.[84]

Such as this wretched piece:

> Adieu ma pauvre tabatière,
> Adieu doux fruits de mes écus.[85]

82 This edition in quarto offends by the disorder which disfigures several volumes; by making a piece composed in 1720 follow one of 1770; by a profusion of a hundred little pieces which do not belong to the author, and are unworthy of the public; and lastly, by a number of typographical errors; yet perhaps the beauty of the paper, the type, and the engravings, may attract the attention of the curious.

83 [The translator omitted these lines. 'Dear one, judge whether a fever is not a sufficient reason to exonerate me. I am in bed like a good-for-nothing for having swigged too much; but I hope to recover since on receiving this epistle love erected my desk.']

84 [Omitted by the translator. 'What a contrast strikes my eyes. The unhappy Melpomene, with the consent of the gods, raises here a magnificent mausoleum.']

85 [Omitted by the translator. 'Farewell my poor snuff-box, farewell tender fruit of my crowns.' It is definitely by Voltaire (see pp. 43-44, above).]

Such is another called the *loup moraliste* (*moralising wolf*).[86]

Such is I don't know what sort of an ode, entitled *le vrai Dieu*[87] (*the true God*), which seems to have been the work of a coachman turned Capuchin. These pieces of dullness were carefully collected in the *compleat edition* from the new works of Madame Oudot, the Almanacks of the Muses, the Port-folio Recovered, and such other works of genius which line the *Pont-Neuf*, and the Quay of the Theatins at Paris. They may be found in plenty in the twenty-third volume of the Lausanne edition. Such trash is only fit for the pastry cooks. The booksellers have likewise been so obliging as to insert in the title page of these disgusting insipidities, *the whole revised and corrected by the author*, who assuredly had not seen a page of them. It was not thus that *Robert Etienne* printed. The former scarcity of books was greatly to be preferred to the oppressive loads of writings which now over-run Paris and London, and shower in sonnets upon Italy.

When some of his letters were counterfeited and printed in Holland, under the title of Secret Letters, he parody'd the old Epigram,

> Voilà donc mes lettres secrettes,
> Si secrettes, que pour Lecteur
> Elles n'ont que leur Imprimeur,
> Et ces Messieurs qui les ont faites.

> At last my private letters see,
> *My* letters never writ by me,
> So private, that none ever read them,
> Save they who printed and who made them.

I am unwilling to say who the worthy gentleman was, who, with a Geneva title page, printed at Amsterdam the *Letters of Mr. de Voltaire to his Friends of Parnassus, with notes critical and historical.* This bookseller reckoned the Queen of Sweden, the Elector Palatine, and the Kings of Poland and Prussia, among his friends of Parnassus. Very good friends and a charming Parnassus! Not content with this excessive impertinence, the bookseller, on purpose to make his book sell, had the knavery to follow the example first set by Baumelle. He deformed several letters which were already known, and among the rest, a letter[88] upon the French and Italian languages, written in 1761 to Mr. *Tovasi Deodati*, in which this same Forger, maltreats some of the first nobility in France with the grossest stupidity. Happily he lent his own stile to the author in whose name he wrote, on purpose to ruin him. He makes Mr. de Voltaire say, *that the Ladies of Versailles are agreeable Gossips, and that Jean Jaques Rousseau is their little puppy.* Thus it is, that in France we

---

86 [This has always been included in Voltaire's works, rightly in my opinion.]

87 [This is definitely by Voltaire;

he had simply forgotten these early writings.]

88 [To Deodati de Tovazzi; Best. D9572 (24 January 1761).]

have eminent geniuses at two-pence the sheet, who write the letters of Ninon de l'Enclos, Madame Maintenon, Cardinal Alberoni, Queen Christina, Mandrin, &c. The most honest of these *beaux-esprits* was he who said, 'I am busy composing reflexions by Rochefoucault'.

Index

681

Index

Index

Athens, 79
Atterbury, Francis, *Miscellaneous works*, ed. J. Nichols, 119n
Au régent, quoted, 67
Aucour, Jean Barbier d', 286
Audran, family of engravers, 439
Augustine, saint, 382-383
Augustus, 294
Augustus II, king of Poland, 160
Aumont, Louis Marie Auguste d'Aumont de La Rochebaron, duc d', 582, 590
Aumont, Louis Marie Victor, duc d', 582n
Austen, Jane, 545
Austria, 323, 463
autobiography, Voltaire's, 14, 623-680
Avertissement sur la nouvelle histoire de Louis XVI, 348n
Avignon, 508
Avis à l'auteur du Journal de Gottingue, 348n
Aydie, Blaise Marie, chevalier d', 63
Ayer, A. J., 218n; *The Humanist outlook*, 378n

Bababec, 429n
Babouc, 290
Bach, J. S., 380, 602
Bachaumont, François Le Coigneux de, 54, 634, 635
Bacon, sir Francis, 126
Bacquancourt, lawyer, 661
Baculard d'Arnaud, François Thomas Marie de, 200, 234, 319, 328; lover of mme Denis, 270; Frederick on, 326
Baker, Keith Michael, *Condorcet*, 46n
Bangkok, 23
Barber, Giles, 'The Financial history of the Kehl Voltaire', 611
Baretti, Giuseppe Marcantonio, *Discours sur Shakespeare*, 146n
Baron d'Otrante, 469n
Barozza, Giacoma, 238
Barr, M. M., *A Century of Voltaire study*, 613; *Voltaire in America*, 610; – and F. A. Spear, *Quarante années d'études voltairiennes*, 613

Barroux, Marius, *Soixante facsimilés de documents*, 44n
Barry, Paul de, *Le Paradis ouvert à Philagie*, 185n
Barthololemew's day, massacre of saint, 23, 181, 486, 535, 674; deeply felt by Voltaire, 103
Baskerville, John, 548
Basle, 161
Bastille, 163; Voltaire imprisoned in, 73-77, 114-116, 596, 597; the *Henriade* composed in, 97
Bastille, La, quoted, 73-74
Baudelaire, Charles Pierre, 584
Bayle, Pierre, and progress, 379; *Dictionnaire*, 110, 349, 433, 450; Voltaire on, 217, 229, 386
Beaucaire, 355
Beaumarchais, Pierre Augustin Caron de, 476, 548n, 562, 581, 611; *Mariage de Figaro*, 111
Beaumont, Christophe de, archbishop of Paris, Rousseau writes to, 470, 670n
Beauregard, related to Voltaire, 23
Beauregard, Salenne de, informs on Voltaire, 73; imprisoned, 93
Beauteville, Pierre, de Buisson, chevalier de, 514
Beauvais, 446
Beccaria, marquis Cesare Bonesana, 503, 521; Voltaire and his *Dei delitte e delle pene*, 498-499
Begon, lawyer, 240
Bégueule, La, 551
Behn, Aphra, *The Moor's revenge*, 459n
Bélébat, Voltaire at, 68, 113
Bellarmino, Roberto, his catechism, 37
Bellegarde, Voltaire at, 113
Belleisle, Charles Louis Auguste Fouquet, duc de, 308
Belloy, Pierre Laurent Buirette de, 447; *Siège de Calais*, 418
Bender, 165
Benedict XIV, pope, 51n, 583; on *Mahomet*, 261; which is dedicated to him, 260, 633-634
Benevento, earthquake of, 365

Index

Index

Index

697

Index

Index

Index

Locke, John, 125, 126, 134, 200, 371, 378, 498, 603, 630; read by mme Denis, 248; Voltaire influenced by, 198; his *Essay concerning human understanding* recommended to Voltaire, 109; his *Treatises of civil government* not known to Voltaire, 309

Lockman, John, 331n

Lodge, Oliver, 216n

Lois de Minos, Les, 553, 559, 560, 673

Lolotte *see* Constant Rebeque, F. C. de

London, Voltaire at, 118, 123

Longchamps, Sébastien, his memoirs of Voltaire, 14, 88n; involved in the theft of Voltaire manuscripts, 329-330, 336

Lorraine, bonds of, 168; Voltaire refused entry to, 349; – considers living in, 406

Lorraine, Elisabeth Charlotte d'Orléans, duchesse de, 252

Lough, J., *An Introduction to eighteenth century France*, 618

louis, the value of the, 30n

Louis IX, king of France, his anniversary celebrated, 131-132, 301, 565

Louis XI, king of France, 315

Louis XIV, king of France, 13, 41n, 44n, 53, 64, 110, 134, 257, 287, 321, 440, 512, 537, 567, 580, 593, 596, 597, 598, 623; social changes after his death, 64-65; his severity, 67; in the *Siècle*, 331-332

Louis XV, king of France, 41n, 44n, 73n, 83, 97, 100, 257, 261, 267, 283, 285, 286, 288, 312, 315, 316, 320, 321, 330, 331, 349, 400, 406, 522, 543, 559, 560, 577, 580, 596, 597, 598, 637, 646, 647, 673; at Fontenoy, 641-643; and the *parlement*, 315; Frederick's verses on, 280; his treatment of Desforges, 67; sent the *Pucelle*, 389; dies, 563

Louis XVI, king of France, 13, 44n, 132, 580; plans to seize Voltaire's papers, 563-564

Louis, dauphin, son of Louis XV, 44n; learns *Mahomet* by heart, 261

Louis, duc de Bourgogne, dauphin, 44n

Louis Eugene of Wurttemberg, 582

Louis-le-grand, Voltaire's school, 33-46, 159n, 587

Louisa Dorothea of Saxe Gotha, 344, 347, 349, 389, 401, 404, 468, 582, 650

Louisa of Hesse-Darmstadt, 565n

Louise Elisabeth, duchess of Parma, 257

Lounsbury, T. R., *Shakespeare and Voltaire*, 131n, 142

Loup moraliste, Voltaire denies his authorship, 679

Lourdes, 382

Lourdet, his *Moïsade*, 29n

Louvain, Voltaire at, 257

Louvre, 131

Lowendahl, Ulric Friedrich Waldemar, count of, 642

Lucca, 313

Luchet, Jean Pierre Louis de La Roche Du Maine, marquis de, his biography of Voltaire, 13

Lucian, 408

Luçon, 53

Lucretius, 95, 186, 377, 427; *De rerum natura*, 34n

Lunéville, 193, 252, 455; Voltaire at, 274, 293-296, 300, 645-646

Luther, Martin, 308

Luynes, Charles Philippe d'Albert, duc de, his *Mémoires*, 293n, 340n, 370n

Lyons, 63, 354, 366, 419, 514, 528, 542; Voltaire at, 351; – a member of its academy, 287

Lyttleton, George Lyttleton, first baron, 407; *Dialogues of the dead*, 408; plate 32

Mably, Gabriel Bonnot de, 308

MacCarthy, in debt to Voltaire, 629

Machiavelli, Nicolò, 314, 632; the *Prince*, 263, 308

Maffei, marchesa Francesco Scipione di, 581; his *Meropa* inspires *Mérope*, 281

Magan, banker, 666

Mahomet, 257, 265, 267, 269, 277, 278, 330, 336, 389, 628, 633, 645; and *Mérope*, 282; general remarks, 259-262

Maintenon, Françoise d'Aubigné, marquise de, 680

Index

Index

Index

Montenero, Alfonso Caraffa, duke of, 186, 637

Montesquieu, Charles Louis Secondat, baron de, 35n, 287, 308, 313, 314, 351, 482, 672; Voltaire's commentary on, 573

Montigny, Etienne Mignet de, on mme Denis, 248

Montigny, Lucas de, plate 30

Montjeu, Voltaire at, 184

Montpéroux, Etienne Jean de Guimard, baron de, 421

Montriond, Voltaire buys, 652-653; his theatre at, 358, 405

Monty, Jeanne R., *Etude sur le style polémique de Voltaire*, 487n

Moore, John, his *View of society* on Voltaire at Ferney, 555-556

Morangiés, Jean François Charles de Molette, comte de, 552, 560

Morehouse, Andrew R., 'The Voltaire collection in the rare book room', 610

Morgan, John, on Voltaire's knowledge of English, 146

Morley, John, his biography of Voltaire, 619

Mornay, Philippe de, in the *Henriade*, 101

Morris, Samuel, 146

Morris, Thelma, *L'Abbé Desfontaines et son rôle dans la littérature de son temps*, 111n

Morrison, Alfred, *The Collection of autograph letters*, 99n

Mort de César, La, 298n, 431, 648; begun, 170; published, 210; performed, 322; compared with Shakespeare, 145-154

Mort de mlle Lecouvreur, La, quoted, 169-170

Mortemart, duc de, bans *Hérode et Mariamne*, 175

Mortier, Roland, 'L'Idée de décadence littéraire au xviiie siècle', 461n

Morville, Charles Jean Baptiste Fleuriau, comte de, 118

Moses, Voltaire on, 538

Mossner, Ernest Campbell, 'The Enlightenment of David Hume', 218n

Mouhy, Charles de Fieux, chevalier de, in debt to Voltaire, 235, 239; on the success of *Mérope*, 282

Moultou, Paul Claude, 415, 468, 534

Moussinot, Bonaventure, Voltaire writes to, 234-240, 247, 249, 354, 454

Moyland, Voltaire at, 264

Müller, H. von *see* Wallich, P.

Murray, Geoffrey, *Voltaire's Candide: the Protean gardener*, 436n

Mussolini, Benito, 159, 265

Nadal, Augustin, his *Mariamne*, 108

Naigeon, Jacques André, his and Holbach's *Le Militaire philosophe*, 533n

name, Voltaire's change of, 76

Namur, 186

Nancy, 233, 293, 455

Nanine, 298, 645

Nantes, 407, 652

Nanteuil, Robert, 439

Nantua, Voltaire at, 574

Napoleon i, emperor, 159, 224, 445

Narva, battle of, 162

Nattier, Jean Marc, plate 7

Naves, Raymond, *Le Goût de Voltaire*, 445n, 452n

Necker, Jacques, 570

Necker, Suzanne, 444, 470, 545, 582; and Pigalle's statue of Voltaire, 667

Needham, John Turberville, 497, 515

Netherlands, 323, 335; Voltaire in, 55-61, 98, 107, 256, 267, 588

Neuchâtel, 401

Neuvillé, Didier Pierre Chicaneau, *Dictionnaire philosophique* and *Considérations sur les ouvrages de l'esprit*, 475n

Nevestoy, 362

Newcastle, Thomas Pelham Hollis, duke of, Voltaire recommended to, 118

Newton, sir Isaac, 124, 125, 126, 134, 216n, 291, 292, 296, 378, 385, 433, 596, 603, 630; Voltaire's opinion of, 246; – work on, 200-203, 628

Index

Index

Index

Index

Scarmentado, 429n

Sceaux, Voltaire at, 68, 259, 274, 290, 292-293, 298, 319, 588

Schelling, Friedrich Wilhelm Joseph von, on *Alzire*, 195

Scheveningen, 57

Schimberg, André, *L'Education morale dans les collèges de la compagnie de Jésus*, 43n

Schœpflin, Josef Friedrich, 651-652

school, Voltaire's *see* Louis-le-grand

Schwetzingen, Voltaire at, 347, 408

science, and Voltaire, 246-247, 267-268, 307

Scipio, 393

Scudéry, Georges, *Observations sur le Cid*, 132

Scythes, Les, 505-507

Sedaine, Michel Jean, 581

Seguier, Antoine Louis, 523

Séguin, J. A. R., *Voltaire and the Gentleman's magazine*, 614

Sélis, Nicolas Joseph, *Relation de la maladie ... de m. de Voltaire*, 414

Sémiramis, 139, 274, 289, 291, 443, 590, 645; drafted, 289; produced, 296-297

Semur, 186

Seneca, 490

Sénones, Voltaire at, 343, 350

Sentiments d'un citoyen, 500

Sermon des cinquante, 414

Sermon du rabbin Akib, 462

Sermon prêché à Bâle, 534

Servet, Michel, Voltaire on, 359-361, 370, 653-657

Servien, Abel, and Voltaire, 52; exiled and imprisoned, 64

Sesostris, 518

Seven years war, 372, 468; Voltaire attempts to end, 400-404

Sévigné, Marie de Rabutin Chantal, marquise de, 579

Sextus Empiricus, 512

Sèze, comte Raymond de, 286

Seznec, Jean *see* Diderot, D.

s'Gravesande, Willem Jacob, 245

Shackleton, Robert, *Montesquieu*, 35n

Shakespeare, William, 76, 126, 129, 163n, 202, 459, 602, 609; French ignorance of, 134-135; *Hamlet*, 31, 134, 135, 148, 158, 603; – Voltaire on, 137-142, 154; *Julius Caesar* compared with the *Mort de César*, 147-154; *Macbeth*, 137; *Othello*, 132; *Phoenix and the turtle*, 318n; *Sonnets*, 145; *The Tempest*, 132; Voltaire and, 131-158, 524, 569, 572, 603

Shaw, George Bernard, 130, 156, 265, 487, 579, 584-585, 595, 617; *Collected letters*, ed. D. H. Laurence, 144n

Shelley, Percy Bysshe, *The Revolt of Islam*, 49n

Sherburn, George *see* Pope, A.

Sherlock, Martin, his *Letters* on Voltaire at Ferney, 571-572

Shotwell, James T., *An Introduction to the history of history*, 162n

Showalter, English, *Voltaire et ses amis*, 189n, 252n

Shu Chung, 385

Shuwalov, Ivan Ivanovich, 582; sent the *Histoire de l'empire de Russie*, 362

Sidney, Algernon, Voltaire reviews his *Discourses concerning government*, 469

Siècle de Louis XIV, 28n, 42n, 111n, 173, 254, 263, 320, 348, 457n; general remarks, 330-335; and Caumartin, 64; the arts in, 439-440; Voltaire works on, 640-641, 647; plate 14

Signy, L., plates 16, 20

Silesia, Frederick invades, 268, 632

silk, made at Ferney, 542

Sirven, Elisabeth, 490

Sirven, Pierre Paul, Voltaire's work for, 490, 499, 501, 504, 521, 544, 548, 585, 661, 673

smallpox, Voltaire catches, 107

Smith, D. W., 'The First edition of the *Relation de Berthier*', 612

Smith, Logan Pearsall, 435

Socrate, 226-227

Socrates, 53, 371, 393

Solomon, 638

Solon, 393

Somerset house, 554

Sommaire des droits de s. m. le roi de Prusse sur Herstall, 265

Index

Index